Descriptive Inventories of Collections in the Social Welfare History Archives Center

Descriptive Inventories of Collections in the Social Welfare History Archives Center

UNIVERSITY LIBRARIES

UNIVERSITY OF MINNESOTA

MINNEAPOLIS, MINNESOTA

Introduction by
CLARKE A. CHAMBERS
Director

Greenwood Publishing Corporation
Westport, Connecticut

This work has been printed on long-life paper and conforms
to the standards developed under the sponsorship of the
Council on Library Resources.

Copyright © 1970 by University of Minnesota
All rights reserved. No portion of this book may be reproduced, by any process or technique, without the express
written consent of the author and publisher.

Library of Congress Catalog Card Number: 73-102265
SBN: 8371-3270-3

Greenwood Publishing Corporation
51 Riverside Avenue, Westport, Connecticut 06880
Greenwood Publishers Ltd.
42 Hanway Street, London, W.1., England

Printed in the United States of America

Contents

Introduction   vii
1 Baden Street Settlement, Rochester, New York   1
2 Big Brothers of America, Inc.   13
3 Jacob Fisher   37
4 Five Towns Community House, Lawrence, New York   41
5 Howard W. Hopkirk   85
6 International Conference of Social Work (now the International Council on Social Welfare)   91
7 Paul Underwood Kellogg   111
8 Eduard Christian Lindeman   167
9 Harry Lawrence Lurie   173
10 Mattie Cal Maxted   193
11 National Association of Social Workers, Inc.   203
12 National Association of Social Workers, Washington, D.C., Chapter   393
13 National Federation of Settlements and Neighborhood Centers   403
14 National Federation of Settlements and Neighborhood Centers, Supplement 1   465
15 National Florence Crittenton Mission   481
16 National Social Welfare Assembly (now the National Assembly for Social Policy and Development)   503
17 Survey Associates, Inc.   533
18 Louis Heiberg Towley   615
19 United Neighborhood Houses, Inc.   637
20 United States Committee of the International Conference of Social Work   745
21 United States Veterans Administration, Social Work Service   755
22 Benjamin Emanuel Youngdahl   777
23 Gertrude Folks Zimand   801
24 Savel Zimand   809
   Index   817

Introduction

The Social Welfare History Archives Center of the University of Minnesota, founded in 1964, seeks to bring together in one research center the historical records of social work, social welfare, and social reform. It concentrates particularly on collecting and preserving the records of national voluntary associations in the social service fields and the personal papers of their leaders.

Some of the central collections contain materials which bear most directly on the history of the social service profession in its many specialized divisions: casework, group work, psychiatric social work, medical social work, community organization, school social work, research and administration, and social work education. But even these highly professional collections contain materials of interest to the general historian. Other collections provide an abundance of primary documentation for twentieth-century studies of almost every subject specialty: labor, immigration, race, economics, politics, religion, civil rights and civil liberties, social insurance, city planning, conservation, health, education, and even foreign policy.

These historical documents include a great variety of kinds of material: minutes of board and committee meetings, proceedings of conventions and conferences, correspondence, annual reports, office memoranda, newsletters, photographs, press releases, newspaper clippings, special research studies, financial statements, fund-raising brochures, leaflets, pamphlets, and serial and nonserial publications. Some of the settlement house records also include program, service, and work records of their staffs. Although a few hard-covered publications have been deposited by some associations along with their other official records, the Center is not a library and does not seek to acquire books and periodicals that are available in most libraries.

Because many of the documents are unique and because many associations have chosen to use this Center as the official depository for their records, materials must be used in the Center during its regular hours. No lending service is provided.

Scholars doing research in the Center enjoy limited privileges for copying specific documents. The facilities of the Center are open to all qualified scholars, including graduate students in all disciplines of study, subject, of course, only to normal library regulations.

The Center, which is directed by Clarke A. Chambers, Professor of History, is an administrative unit of the Special Collections Department of the University of Minnesota Libraries. Training and supervision of the technical staff are the responsibilities of Maxine B. Clapp, head of the Library's Archives and Manuscripts Division, and her assistant, Clodaugh Neiderheiser. They are also ultimately responsible for the inventories, or finding aids, printed in this volume. Andrea Hinding, the Center's curator, directs daily operations.

INTRODUCTION

This volume reproduces the inventories for about a quarter of the Center's current holdings, and all of such aids completed by November 1969. As more of the collections are fully processed and described, subsequent volumes will be published in this series.

Each inventory includes a brief history of the donor association (or biographical sketch of the person's life and career), including a note on when and under what circumstances the papers were deposited at the Minnesota Center and a statement about the overall organization of the collection. Special provisions or limitations on use of a collection (some contain confidential folders that can be used only with special permission), if any, are set forth in these introductions. The inventories include a partial subject index and a folder inventory, normally consisting of a title and description of contents for each folder in the collection.

One of the principles governing organization of these collections is respect for original order of an association's or person's records; this also has meant that the terminology employed in the partial subject index and in the folder annotations reflects the terms used in the manuscripts themselves.

Potential users of the collections are advised that the subject indexes are partial, not comprehensive, and that they include reference to notable persons and important organizations and to significant and relevant concepts or topics in that particular collection. Annotations for the folders in a collection provide more information on their contents, although in no instance can they possibly detail all the data that a given folder may include.

Potential users are also advised that these inventories, which were designed for internal use, are intended to facilitate use of the records. The names of those manuscripts processors who organized and described each collection are listed with each finding aid; these persons were graduate students in history.

It is the hope and expectation of the Center's staff that this volume will help to stimulate research in the relatively new field of welfare history, that it will assist social work educators and practitioners, and that it will increase scholarly efficiency by making these descriptive inventories available to scholars in the libraries of their home universities.

CLARKE A. CHAMBERS
Director

Descriptive Inventories of Collections in the Social Welfare History Archives Center

1

An Inventory of the Papers of Baden Street Settlement

PREPARED BY
Loren W. Crabtree

BADEN STREET SETTLEMENT　　　　　　　　　　　　　　　　　　　　　　　　　2

SWD3　　　Baden Street Settlement, Rochester, New York

　　　　　Records, 1901-1966

　　　　　95 folders　　　　3 (&) folders

　　　In August, 1966, the papers of Baden Street Settlement were deposited in the Social Welfare History Archives Center of the University of Minnesota Libraries. The papers, which comprise 5 linear feet, were processed in the spring of 1967 in the Archives Center. The Center also holds the negative microfilm which was taken of the Settlement's Board of Directors' and Executive Committee's minutes. A description of the film is on file in the Center.

　　　Organized in 1901 as a non-sectarian, neighborhood center, the Baden Street Settlement traces its origins to the work of the women of the B'rith Kodesh Temple on Gibbs Street in Rochester, who felt a social responsibility to teach immigrant women the basic tasks and responsibilities of life in the United States. Their emphasis was on the practical necessities of homemaking--gardening, sewing, elementary education and child-rearing-- and this practical emphasis has remained central to the work of the settlement. These women, led by Therese R. Katz and Fannie A. Garson, decided in 1901 to expand their work into the wider community and thus formed "The Social Settlement of Rochester," which became Baden Street Settlement in 1922.

　　　Since its organization, the guiding philosophy of the settlement has been beneficent pragmatism--the adaptation of its scope of service to fit the changing needs of the community. Accordingly, its program has grown from the 1901 components of homemaking classes, Sunshine Clubs (to encourage social life), and intellectual stimulation (Shakespeare clubs, current topics courses, and German clubs) through social and athletic clubs for boys and girls, an informal kindergarten, minimal public bath facilities, and operation of a "milk station," to a well-equipped Health Center, Day Care Center and fully-elaborated programs in casework and group work. Along the way, the settlement has sponsored and/or participated in unemployment relief, community social action and reform (through such agencies as the Community Chest and urban renewal associations), promotion of literacy through adult education, and other related enterprises.

　　　Throughout its existence, the Baden Street Settlement has been acutely aware of the changing character of its neighborhood and the larger aspects of social welfare in America. Thus, the Settlement has studied the effect of the gradual influx of Negroes into the area and has adjusted its program accordingly. Correspondingly, with the growth of public welfare programs, Baden Street has recognized the necessity of cooperating with the public agencies and even the necessity of abandoning certain areas to them. In the gradual evolution of programs and policies, the settlement workers and their supporters have emphasized the importance of the family unit in healthful living and have followed the classic goals of settlement houses in America: (1) the enrichment of neighborhoods, (2) the strengthening of entire family units, (3) the promotion of legislative and social action to solve social problems, (4) the development of neighborhood leadership and the strengthening of neighborhood ties with the wider community, (5) the overcoming of prejudice and ignorance, and (6) the inculcation of democratic attitudes.

Specifically, since 1945, in an area now predominantly Negro, the settlement has attacked the problems of bad housing, inadequate education, unemployment, discrimination, cultural deprivation, hopelessness, apathy and lack of motivation with a positive program of social action including such enterprises as a speech clinic, school readiness program, music instruction, tutoring service, careers club, employment service, instruction and aid for unwed mothers, and a volunteer case-aide program in casework.

Baden Street Settlement throughout its existence has had leaders who have been able to meet the problems of the underprivileged with usually adequate funds and programs. The Presidents of the Board of Directors and the Executive Directors listed below were the key figures in this leadership:

PRESIDENTS

Fannie Adler Garson (Mrs. J.L.)	1901-1939
Ruth M. Witherspoon (Mrs. Charles R.)	1939-1942
Wilma L. Perkins (Mrs. Dexter)	1942-1951
Margaret C. Hays (Mrs. Henry W.)	1951-1954
Harry H. Suskind	1954-1956
Doris U. Pulsifier (Mrs. Libby)	1956-1958
Nancy B. Harris (Mrs. Joseph)	1958-1961
Jane A. Goldman (Mrs. Manuel D.)	1961-1964
Loma M. Allen (Mrs. De Leslie L.)	1964-1966
Dr. William J. Knox, Jr.	1966-

DIRECTORS

Mrs. Sara Vance Stewart	1901-1914
Mrs. Gertrude Montfort	1914
Gertrude M. Jerdone (Mrs. Francis, Jr.)	1915-1948
Irving M. Kriegsfeld	1948-1958
Howard C. McClary	1958-1962
Sidney J. Lindenberg	1962-

For information on these and other members of the Board of Directors, the searcher is directed toward the minutes of the Board, the Executive Committee, and other committees of the Settlement. In most cases, these individuals appear so often and so prominently in the collection that they have not been listed in the Partial Subject Inventory below.

The papers are arranged in a "hierarchical" fashion, with the materials dealing with policy-making (Board of Directors, Executive Committee, Committees, Annual Reports, etc.) coming first and those relating to the implementation of policies following. The Partial Subject Inventory, while by no means exhaustive, provides some guidelines to important persons, events and themes running throughout the collection.

BADEN STREET SETTLEMENT

PARTIAL SUBJECT INVENTORY

BADEN STREET SETTLEMENT
    Annual Reports
        Folders 36-40
    Board of Directors
        Folders 1-5, legal folder 1
    Committees
        Folders 6-35
    Finances and legal arrangements
        Folders 1-10, 13-14, 38-40, 85-87, 92-93
    Goal attainment
        Folders 10, 90
    History
        Folders 10, 36-37, 39-40
    Manual, 1963
        Folder 88
    Personnel
        Folders 6-9, 29, 31, 37-38, 88-89, 94, legal (*l*) 1
    Statistical reports
        Folders 41-84

CASEWORK
    Folders 10, 12, 31, 94

CHILD CARE - STATE REGULATION OF
    Folders 10, 91

CHILDREN
    Folders 10-11, 15-31, 34, 91

COMMUNITY FUNDS AND CHESTS
    Folders 13-14

DAY CARE
    Folders 10, 37, 91

EDUCATION OF THE UNDERPRIVILEGED
    Folder 10

EMPLOYMENT AND UNEMPLOYMENT
    Folders 39-40

FAMILY LIFE
    Folders 90, 94

GREAT DEPRESSION (of 1930's)
    Folder 38

BADEN STREET SETTLEMENT

GROUP WORK
    Folders 15-23

HEALTH (MENTAL AND PHYSICAL)
    Folders 10, 24-25, legal ( ) 2-3

HOUSING
    Folder 28

IMMIGRANTS
    Folders 10, 36-37, 39-40

KRIEGSFELD, IRVING M.
    Folder 12, 92-93

MEDICAL CARE - STATE REGULATION OF
    Folders legal ( ) 2-3

OFFICE OF ECONOMIC OPPORTUNITY
    Folder 10

PHYSICAL EDUCATION
    Folder 32

PRIMO, REVEREND QUINTIN E.
    Folder 12

PUBLIC RELATIONS
    Folders 33, 92-93

RACE PROBLEMS (THE NEGRO)
    Folders 10, 39, 90

RECREATION
    Folders 11, 15-23, 29, 32

REGIONAL AND MUNICIPAL PLANNING
    Folder 22

SETTLEMENTS AND GOVERNMENT PROGRAMS (INCLUDING LOBBYING ACTIVITIES)
    Folders 10, 26, 90-91

SOCIAL ACTION
    Folders 1-5, 26

SOCIAL WORK - RECRUITMENT
    Folders 31, 34

SOCIAL WORK - VOLUNTEERS
    Folder 94

SYRACUSE UNIVERSITY
    Folders 92-93

URBAN RENEWAL
    Folders 10, 28, 90

WORLD WAR, 1939-1945 (EFFECT ON BADEN STREET SETTLEMENT)
    Folders 38-39

BADEN STREET SETTLEMENT 7

Folder Title and Description of Contents   Folder

Board of Directors - Minutes: 1901-1964   1-5
    The Board met to consider routine operating matters, such as
    reports of the activities of the day nursery, treasurers'
    reports, membership campaigns, committees for the operation
    of the settlement, eulogies for deceased friends of the
    settlement, resolutions on financial and social-political
    problems. The minutes therefore contain reports of other
    committees, eulogies and their responses, miscellaneous reso-
    lutions and memoranda, personnel codes and regulations, occasional
    correspondence, data about the 1956-57 self-survey, By-laws
    and changes in the settlement's legal operations, budget
    statements, policy statements re: operation and use of settle-
    ment facilities. See also legal-size folder 1.

Executive Committee - Minutes: 1926-1964   6-9
    The Committee met irregularly, sometimes once a month and
    occasionally weekly. It made decisions related directly to the
    daily operation of the settlement, including such matters as
    personnel, reports of other committees and individuals, finances,
    committee lists, correspondence with other social welfare per-
    sonnel. Beginning in 1937 and carrying on until 1950, the
    Executive Committee met monthly, except for the summer months
    when it did not meet. After January, 1951, the record of the
    meetings is very incomplete.

Program Planning and Adjustment: 1960-1966   10
    The Baden-Ormond area was in a state of transition, ca.
    1960, as an urban renewal project was in progress. Consequently,
    the settlement had to rethink its programs and policies. This
    folder contains studies and recommendations on such subjects
    as health care, nursery facilities, educating the underprivileged,
    casework, urban renewal, use of public funds in settlement work,
    the 1964 Rochester riots, the Economic Opportunity Program,
    priorities in adjustment, and structural rearrangement.

COMMITTEES OF THE SETTLEMENT

Activities Committee: 1963-1964   11
    The committee met monthly to consider the various activities
    of the settlement (e.g., camping, Girl Scouts, leadership
    training) and to present recommendations to the Board of
    Directors. Minutes of these meetings.

Casework Committee: 1948-1952   12
    Minutes of the monthly meetings re: initiating, expanding
    and controlling casework at Baden Street. Committee members
    include Irving Kriegsfeld, Reverend Quintin Primo.

BADEN STREET SETTLEMENT

Folder Title and Description of Contents	Folder
Finance Committee: 1949-1965	13-14

    The committee met irregularly, often in joint session with other committees such as maintenance and personnel, whose minutes sometime overlap. Statistical analyses and budget reports. Decisions re: spending policies. Financial data and communications re: Baden Street and the Community Chest of Rochester and Monroe County.

Group Work Committee: 1949-1962   15
    Minutes of meetings. Data re: budgets, special programs, routine programs.

Group Work Committee - Beaver Subcommittee: 1953-1959   16
    Minutes of monthly meetings are relatively complete, 1953-1955, but there is only one report for 1955-1959. Concerned with the day-to-day details of the program.

Group Work Committee - Chipmunk Subcommittee: 1953   17

Group Work Committee - Gopher Subcommittee: 1953-1959   18

Group Work Committee - Gym Committee: 1952-1955   19

Group Work Committee - Lynx Subcommittee: 1953-1959   20

Group Work Committee - Percheron Subcommittee: 1952-1955   21
Group Work Committee - Raccoon Subcommittee: 1954-1959   22
Group Work Committee - Steering Committee: 1952-1955   23

Health Center Committee: 1948-1964   24-25
    Minutes of the regular monthly meetings, dealing with routine operating matters, statistical reports, etc.

Legislative Committee: 1955-1960   26
    Minutes of the Committee, which functioned as a pressure group representing the needs of the settlement in relation to proposed federal and state legislation.

Miscellaneous Committees: 1951-1960   27
    Occasional minutes of these committees: arrangements, building, survey, nominating.

Neighborhood Development Committee: 1962-1964   28
    Minutes of meetings concerned with urban renewal, housing, the settlement's role in the declining area, problems of ghettoes, city planning, etc.

Nursery Committee: 1948-1964   29
    Minutes of monthly meetings, including information re: summer day camps, enrollment, personnel, special programs, other routine operating details.

Folder Title and Description of Contents	Folder

Personal Service Committee: 1952-1964   30
    Known from 1952-1962 as the Consultation Committee, the committee assumed the responsibilities of the Casework Committee and also functioned as a general supervisory committee assisting the other committees of the settlement. Incomplete run of the minutes of the monthly meetings.

Personnel Committee: 1949-1962   31
    Minutes of meetings concerned with staff recruitment, salaries, promotions, etc.

Physical Education Committee: 1952   32
    Statement of philosophy, minutes of meetings, reports on use of gym facilities, etc.

Public Relations Committee: 1952-1964   33
    Minutes of meetings dealing with publicity of the settlement's work through such means as films, television specials, luncheons, and a 60th anniversary celebration.

Scholarship Committee: 1962-1964   34
    Minutes concerned with raising and assigning funds for scholarships for needy students.

Settlement Committee: 1948-1951   35
    Minutes of the meetings of the Committee, which exercised general supervision over the work of the settlement.

Annual Reports: 1901-1966   36-40
    Incomplete run from 1901-1925, with 1903-1904, 1906-1913 reports missing. Both typed and printed. Typical annual reports, covering the programs and problems of the settlement during each year. Information concerning the settlement's name change in 1922. Brief history of the settlement, 1901-1926. Some miscellaneous correspondence re: legal details. Insights into the fiscal and emotional problems caused by the Depression. A general annual report is provided, as well as specific reports from the various divisions of the settlement, such as the Nursery and Dispensary. Copy of a 1942 "organization and cost survey." Detailed information re: effect of the Second World War on the settlement. The intrusion of the Negro into the settlement's area is consciously being dealt with by 1944-52. Historical summary of the Dispensary (1944). Usual statistical reports are embellished by personal experiences. Historical survey of the settlement, 1901-1949. Information re: post-war "transition" period. Supplementary historical statement, covering 1951-1962.

BADEN STREET SETTLEMENT

<u>Folder</u> <u>Title</u> <u>and</u> <u>Description</u> <u>of</u> <u>Contents</u>   <u>Folder</u>

Statistical Reports: 1917-1965   41-84
    Summary statistics of the operations of the nursery, dispensary, classes and clubs. Also, general reports and annual statistical reports. The reports cover each fiscal year, April-March.

Treasurer's Reports: 1910-1938   85-87
    Monthly record of receipts and disbursements, plus occasional legal documents pertaining to the treasurer and his financial functions.

Manual of Baden Street Settlement: 1963   88
    This is a guide to Agency policies and practices, and contains a variety of forms and policies to be followed and used by Agency workers.

Newsletter: 1951-1966   89
    Incomplete run of this staff news organ. Contains information about events in the life of the settlement.

Studies of and by Baden Street Settlement: 1956-1964   90
    Copy of a M.Ed. thesis dealing with the goals of the settlement and the problems of reaching them. 1964 study prepared by the settlement on the Negro in the United States and the role of the settlement in dealing with them. Data on the self-survey of 1956-1957, including a handbook of questions, reports from the various subdivisions, resolutions on how to attack the settlement's problems.

Nursery and Day Care Center: 1934-1952   91
    Legal documents re: licensing of the Nursery. Statistical summaries, data on proposed legislation, financial statements, correspondence re: operation of the Nursery.

Film - "Neighborhood Story:" 1953-1958   92-93
    The film was produced by Baden Street Settlement to depict and interpret the work of the settlement to its supporters and the community at large. Contents include correspondence between settlement officials (especially Irving M. Kriegsfeld) and University of Syracuse audio-visual personnel (especially Donald G. Williams and Lu Snyder) re: planning, producing, promoting and distributing the film; financial and legal data re: production; request for showing the film; press clippings and reviews of the film; brochures. Copy of the script.

Volunteer Case Aide Project: 1957-1965   94
    Description of the project, which was designed to provide volunteer assistance for caseworkers who had too heavy a case load. Progress reports detailing the evolution and results of the project.

BADEN STREET SETTLEMENT 11

<u>Folder Title and Description of Contents</u>   <u>Folder</u>

LEGAL (*L*) FOLDERS

Board of Directors - Minutes: 1901-1929   1
    As described in folders 1-5.

Health Center: 1913-1952   2-3
    Incomplete run of the minutes of the Center. Reports to the
    Board of Directors. Reports of the inspection of facilities
    by New York State Department of Social Welfare. Charter by
    the State, rules and regulation, statistical reports,
    correspondence re: staff selection.

2

An Inventory of the Papers of Big Brothers of America, Inc.

PREPARED BY
Pamela J. Matson

SWD9 Big Brothers of America, Inc.

Papers, 1912-1963

104 folders 1 (*L*) folder

The Big Brother movement began in 1904 at the suggestion of Ernest K. Coulter, clerk of the Children's Court in New York City. Approximately forty members of the Men's Club of the Central Presbyterian Church of New York City each agreed to take a personal interest in one boy who had been brought into the Children's Court. The men decided to test this "One Man, One Boy" theory for a year before permitting publicity.

As the success of the theory became evident, needs became apparent for more volunteers and for a central headquarters to which boys could be systematically referred. On October 1, 1909, the New York organization incorporated and formally adopted the name, "Big Brother Movement." The Jewish Big Brothers of New York was organized in 1907, and the Catholic Big Brothers of the same city was established in 1918. The success of the Big Brother idea led to the formation of other Big Brother organizations throughout the United States and Canada; some were set up on a Catholic, Jewish, or Protestant basis, and others were non-sectarian.

By 1917, forty Big Brother groups which had sprung from the parent organization in New York were incorporated. In the same year, at the first annual conference of the Big Brother and Big Sister societies, an International Advisory Council was formed which subsequently established the Big Brother and Big Sister Federation. That organization listed as its purposes the prevention of delinquency by personal, individual, and intensive effort; extension of Big Brother and Big Sister agencies throughout the United States, Canada, and elsewhere; dispersion of information and advice to existing groups; the publication of "theses and education papers" related to the field of Big Brother and Big Sister work; and the sponsorship of conferences, training courses, and seminars. The Federation dissolved in January, 1937.

Because no formal national office for the Big Brother movement existed from 1937 through 1946, inquiries sent to the Federation were normally routed to the office of the Big Brother Movement of Greater New York, of which Joseph McCoy was the general secretary.

In 1940, a National Study and Planning Committee chaired by Kenneth Rogers of Toronto and Joseph McCoy of New York, surveyed Big Brother and Big Sister agencies to collect information about the nature of the existing organizations. The committee also planned for the structure and function of a national organization which might be set up if a need for such service seemed apparent.

In the fall of 1945, the Temporary National Big Brother Committee was formed. Joseph McCoy, Kenneth Rogers, Charles Berwind (Philadelphia) and George Casey (Philadelphia) were leaders in the promotion of a national Big Brother organization. The committee decided to conduct a study of fifteen Big Brother agencies in the United States and Canada to determine the extent, techniques, and results of efforts of Big Brother services in various cities and to learn if there was a desire for a permanent national committee or organization of Big Brother groups. In 1946, the Big Brother Association of Philadelphia hosted a conference at Camp Wyomissing at which the Robert Wynn report of the 1946 study was acted upon. Big Brothers of America was incorporated on December 24, 1946, and its office opened in Philadelphia in February, 1947. Charles Berwind was elected to the presidency, an office which he holds to the present time. Initial financing was provided through membership dues of the local Big Brother agencies and by gifts made through Charles Berwind and G. Ruhland Rebmann Jr., both active in the Philadelphia Big Brother Association.

The national organization was set up with a Council of Delegates comprising two representatives from each of the local Big Brother groups. At the annual meetings, the Council of Delegates elected the Board of Directors, which consisted of not less than thirty and not more than one hundred members who had been selected by the Nominating Committee, the President, or member agencies. In practice, the Big Brothers of America, Inc., tried to have each local group nominate one of its non-professional members or officers to the national Board of Directors. The Board of Directors also included directors-at-large or honorary directors who were men of prominence in business, finance, and social life. It was hoped that their national influence would publicize Big Brother work. A few of these honorary directors have been Thomas C. Clark, Associate Justice of the United States Supreme Court; Stuart Garson, Minister of Justice and Attorney General of Canada; Luther W. Youngdahl, Governor of Minnesota and United States District Court Judge; Thomas C. Hennings, Jr., United States Senator from Missouri; and Kenneth Johnson, Dean of the New York School of Social Work.

At the 1949 annual meeting, the Council of Delegates authorized the Board of Directors to elect an Executive Committee to meet when the Board of Directors was not in session. The Executive Committee was given all the powers of the Board of Directors except the right to amend the constitution and bylaws. In 1950, Charles Berwind appointed a Technical Planning Committee, of which Joseph McCoy was the first chairman. Membership of this committee consisted of the executives of the various member organizations as well as several lay participants. The committee was set up to develop a questionnaire to be circulated to various member organizations and to suggest improvements; to devise suitable statistical report forms for use by the Big Brothers of America, Inc. and local agencies in compiling local and national statistics; to study record forms in use by local Big Brother organizations and to try to devise a standard set of these forms which might be adopted for use by all local Big Brother groups; and to prepare a manual of procedures for guidance in the formation of new Big Brother organizations. Thomas Cairns prepared the summary of the 1950 study.

Early executive directors included Gilbert H. Gendall (February, 1947-March, 1948); Donald Jenks (March 1, 1948--ca. March, 1950); Benjamin Van Doren Hedges (September 1, 1950-1952. Hedges was hired as Executive Director but was given the title of Executive Vice President); and Felix Gentile (1952 to his death in May, 1957).

The administration of the Big Brothers of America, Inc., which was incorporated by an Act of Congress in 1958, has remained basically the same to the present day. However, the increase in the number of Big Brother agencies by the late 1950s made necessary a regional demarcation in the election of members to the Board of Directors. With one representative of each local organization on the national Board of Directors, that body would become unwieldy. The United States and Canada were divided into seven regions, and the election of the members of the Board of Directors was done proportionally by the number of member agencies (corporate members) in a region.

According to the Big Brother Bulletin, Vol. XVII, No. 2, Summer, 1967, the National Big Brother organization comprises one hundred thirteen member agencies in the United States and Canada. The Big Brothers of America, Inc., promotes Big Brother work by publicizing the work on the national level, e.g. through Big Brother Weeks; by assisting and guiding in the formation of new Big Brother groups on the local level; and by helping existing Big Brother agencies to maintain acceptable standards of service and work.

Some historical records of the Big Brothers of America, Inc., were deposited in the Social Welfare History Archives Center by Thomas O'Brien, Executive Director, in August, 1966. The three and three-fourths linear feet of papers were processed by the Archives staff in 1967 and 1968.

While the inclusive dates of the papers are 1912 to 1963, the bulk of the material covers the years 1946 through 1956. The papers contain a constitution for 1961 only; minutes and papers of the Board of Directors, the Executive Committee, and the Council of Delegates for various years between 1949 and 1963; varying amounts of materials for the annual meetings from 1949 to 1956; correspondence which deals largely with requests for information on Big Brother work, setting up Big Brother organizations, and juvenile delinquency; questionnaires and papers surrounding studies undertaken in 1940, 1946, and 1950; varying amounts of material for Big Brother Weeks in 1950 through 1953; and scattered financial materials. The Big Brothers of America, Inc., has published a quarterly since 1947 or 1948, the Big Brother Bulletin. One issue of this periodical (Vol. X, No. 1, February, 1957), which was included with the papers, has been placed in the ephemera collection. All publications have been removed from the collection.

The following publications of the national Big Brothers of America, Inc., and local Big Brother groups will be found in the ephemera collection. The publications are arranged chronologically.

Big Brothers Association of Cincinnati (Ohio). Eighteenth Annual Report, 1931.

Big Brother Association (Philadelphia, Pennsylvania). 1915-1935. Twenty Years and Twenty Little and Big Brothers, ca. 1935.

Big Brother Association (Philadelphia, Pennsylvania). Big Brother Association 1915-1935, ca. 1935.

Big Brother Association (Philadelphia, Pennsylvania). Big Brother Association, ca. 1937.

Big Brothers Association of Cincinnati, Ohio. Manual, ca. 1937.

Big Brothers, Inc. (Minneapolis, Minnesota). Eighteen Years of Service 1920-1938, ca. 1938.

Catholic Big Brothers (Toronto, Ontario). Annual Report, 1939.

Big Brother Association (Philadelphia, Pennsylvania). Annual Report, 1939-1940.

Kingsley, George. Big Brothers, Inc., Minneapolis, Minnesota. "Big Brothers," Tints and Tones of Colorcraft Press, Winter, ca. 1940.

Big Brothers, Inc. (Minneapolis, Minnesota). Optimist Club of Minneapolis. Friend of the Boy, ca. 1940.

Big Brothers, Inc. (Minneapolis, Minnesota). Do You Like Boys?, ca. 1940.

Big Brothers, Inc. (Minneapolis, Minnesota). 20th Annual Meeting. Program, February 8, 1940.

Big Brothers Association of Cincinnati (Ohio). 29th Annual Meeting. Program, April 2, 1940.

Big Brothers Association of Cincinnati (Ohio). Twenty-Eighth Annual Report, April, 1941.

Big Brothers Association of Cincinnati (Ohio). President's Report. Year 1940-1941, April, 1941.

Dallas Big Brothers, Inc. (Dallas, Texas). The Big Brother and His Boy, December, 1941.

Jewish Big Brother Association (Boston, Massachusetss). Jewish Big Brother Bulletin. Vol. XI, No. 2 (August, 1942) and Vol. XI, No. 3 (October, 1942).

Big Brother Association, Inc. (Hamilton, Ontario). Monthly Bulletin, ca. 1943.

Big Brothers (Toronto, Ontario). Thirty Years of Service to Boys. Annual Report, 1943.

Catholic Big Brothers Association (Toronto, Ontario). Annual Report, 1943.

Big Brother Association of Columbus (Ohio). Your Big Brother Association of Columbus, Ohio, May 1, 1943.

Jewish Big Brother Association (Boston, Massachusetts). Jewish Big Brother Bulletin. Vol. XII, No. 2, August, 1943.

Big Brother Association, Inc. (Hamilton, Ontario). Monthly Bulletin, September, 1943.

Big Brothers Association (Cincinnati, Ohio). Big Brother News, Autumn, 1943.

Big Brother Association of Columbus (Ohio). How Big Brothers Get Acquainted, Win the Friendship, Share the Confidence of Little Brothers, 1944.

Catholic Big Brothers Association (Toronto, Ontario). Annual Report, 1944.

Juvenile Branch of Hamilton and Wentworth Family Court. (Sent by the Big Brother Association of Hamilton, Ontario). Annual Reports for Years 1941, 1942, 1943, 1944.

Big Brother Association (Philadelphia, Pennsylvania). Annual Report, 1943-1944.

Jewish Big Brother Association (Boston, Massachusetts). Jewish Big Brother Bulletin. Vol. XIII, No. 1, June, 1944; and Vol. XIII, No. 2, August, 1944.

Big Brothers and Big Sisters of the Jewish Board of Guardians (New York, New York). The Quarterly, Vol. I, No. 1, Fall, 1944.

Big Brothers Association (Cincinnati, Ohio). Big Brother News, Winter, 1944.

Big Brothers Association of Columbus, Ohio. Boys Want to Be Men, ca. 1945.

Big Brothers Association of Columbus, Ohio. The Big Brother Camp, ca. 1945.

Big Brothers Association of Columbus, Ohio. Future Plans for the Big Brother Camp, ca. 1945.

Big Brothers Association of Columbus, Ohio. Big Brother Camp, ca. 1945.

Big Brother Organization, Inc. (St. Louis, Missouri). Big Brother Organization, 1945.

Big Brother Association of Hamilton (Ontario), Inc. Annual Report, 1945.

Rogers, Kenneth H. (General Secretary, Big Brother Movement, Toronto). Street Gangs in Toronto. A Study of the Forgotten Boy, 1945.

Dallas Big Brothers (Dallas, Texas). Annual Report, 1945.

Catholic Big Brothers Association (Toronto, Ontario). Annual Report, 1945.

Big Brother Association (Philadelphia, Pennsylvania). Annual Report, 1944-1945.

Big Brother Association, Inc. (Columbus, Ohio). Twelfth Annual Report, February 27, 1945.

Big Brothers and Big Sisters of the Jewish Board of Guardians (New York, New York). The Quarterly, Vol. I, No. 2, Spring, 1945.

Big Brother Movement of Toronto (Ontario). The Big Brother, Vol. I, No. 9, June, 1945.

Jewish Big Brother Association (Boston, Massachusetts). Jewish Big Brother Bulletin, Vol. XIV, No. 1, June, 1945.

Dallas Big Brothers, Inc. (Dallas, Texas). The Dallas Big Brothers Tom-Tom, Vol. IV, No. 6, July, 1945.

Big Brother Movement of Toronto (Ontario). The Big Brother, Vol. I, No. 10, October, 1945; Vol. I, No. 11, December, 1945.

Dallas Big Brothers, Inc. (Dallas, Texas). The Dallas Big Brothers Tom-Tom, Vol. IV, No. 8, December, 1945.

Eastern Hills Big Brother Association (Cincinnati, Ohio). Christmas Party Programs, December, 1945.

Jewish Big Brothers of the Jewish Board of Guardians (New York, New York). All He Needs from You is Time and Friendship, ca. 1946.

Big Brothers of America, Inc. (National Office, Philadelphia, Pennsylvania). Presentation, ca. 1946.

Big Brother Movement of Toronto (Ontario). The Volunteer Big Brother and His Boy, ca. 1946.

Big Brother Movement of Toronto and York Township (Ontario). Big Brother Movement, ca. 1946.

Big Brother Association (Philadelphia, Pennsylvania). Annual Report, 1945-1946.

Big Brothers, Inc. (Minneapolis, Minnesota). 27th Annual Meeting. Program, January 24, 1946.

Dallas Big Brothers, Inc. (Dallas, Texas). The Dallas Big Brothers Tom-Tom, Vol. IV, No. 9, February, 1946.

Big Brother Association, Inc. (Hamilton, Ontario). Monthly Bulletin, February 8, 1946.

Big Brother Association of Columbus, Inc. (Ohio). Thirteenth Annual Meeting. Program, February 27, 1946.

Big Brothers, Inc. (Denver, Colorado). Big Brother Shots, March, 1946.

Rogers, Kenneth H. (General Secretary of Big Brother Movement, Toronto, Ontario). "The Big Brother Idea." Radio address delivered at Ottawa in March, 1946.

Big Brother Association, Inc. (Hamilton, Ontario). Monthly Bulletin, March 14, 1946.

Big Brothers, Inc. (Denver, Colorado). Big Brother Shots, ca. April, 1946.

Big Brothers and Big Sisters of the Jewish Board of Guardians (New York, New York). The Quarterly, Vol. I, No. 3, Winter, 1946.

Big Brother Movement, Greater New York (New York). Your Adventure in Friendship, 1947.

Dallas Big Brothers (Dallas, Texas). Dallas Big Brothers, ca. 1949.

Big Brother Association (Philadelphia, Pennsylvania). Big Brother Gossip, Vol. XVIII, No. 3, April, 1947.

Big Brother Association (Philadelphia, Pennsylvania). The Big Brother. Why and How, 1949.

Big Brothers, Inc. (Denver, Colorado). The Friendship of One Man for One Boy, ca. 1950.

Big Brothers, Inc. (Denver, Colorado). A Boy's Passport to Good Citizenship, ca. 1950.

Big Brother Association (Philadelphia, Pennsylvania). Camp Wyomissing, 1950.

Jewish Big Brothers Association of Los Angeles (California). The Volunteer Big Brother, ca. 1950.

Big Brother Association of Columbus (Ohio). Little Brother Bulletin, February, ca. 1950.

Big Brothers, Inc. (Minneapolis, Minnesota). Dear Mister-When Am I Going to Get a Big Brother?, ca. 1950.

Big Brothers, Inc. (Minneapolis, Minnesota). 31st Annual Meeting. Program. January 26, 1950.

Loevinger, Gustavus, "If I Were a Big Brother." Speech given at the Thirty-first Annual Meeting of Big Brothers, Inc., Minneapolis, Minnesota, 1950.

Big Brother Movement, Inc. (New York, New York). Vocational News, Vol. VI, No. 1, Summer, 1951.

Big Brothers of America, Inc. (National Office, Philadelphia, Pennsylvania). "Crossroads," ca. 1950.

Big Brother Movement, Inc. (New York, New York). Harvest of Fifty Years. 1904-1954. Annual Report, 1954.

Big Brothers of Rhode Island, Inc. No Man Ever Stands So Straight As When He Stoops to Help a Boy, (Notebook Presented to Charles Berwind), May 17, 1954.

Big Brother Movement, Inc. (New York, New York). Annual Report, 1955-1956.

Big Brothers of Oakland County, Inc. (Pontiac, Michigan). No Man Ever Stands So Straight As When He Stoops to Help a Boy, ca. 1956.

The following publications have been placed in the ephemera file under the issuing agency.

National Information Bureau, Inc., Giver's Guide to National Philanthropies 1954-1955.

Young Mens Christian Association. Ottawa, Ontario. Shirley Bay YMCA Boys' Camp, ca. 1950.

Flint Youth Bureau. Flint, Michigan. How You Can Help to Make the Difference, ca. 1950.

Flint Youth Bureau. Flint, Michigan. The Counselor's Son, Vol. IV, No. 6, June, 1950; Vol. V, No. 1, September, 1950.

Council of Social Agencies. Cincinnati, Ohio. The Cincinnati Report, 1952.

The following materials were placed in the Jewish Board of Guardians ephemera file.

Jewish Board of Guardians. Volunteer Department (New York, New York). *Volunteer Worker*, Vol. III, February, 1940, No. 1; Vol. IV, No. 2, March, 1940; Vol. IV, No. 3, April, 1940.

Avrunin, William. "The Volunteer in Case Work Treatment," *The Family*, June, 1944.

Houtz, Fanny. "Volunteers in Treatment," *Survey Midmonthly*, October, 1944.

Alt, Herschel, and Stein, Joseph. "After Fifty Years: An Agency Looks Ahead," *The Jewish Social Service Quarterly*, December, 1944, Vol. XXI, No. 2.

The Jewish Board of Guardians. *Child and Youth Guidance Service*, New York, ca. 1946.

PARTIAL SUBJECT INVENTORY

The following inventory is not a complete index, but rather a guide to areas of the collection in which certain persons and topics are prominent. Such topics as boys, organization of local Big Brother groups, philosophy and procedures in Big Brother work, and the work of the national organization, the Big Brothers of America, Inc., are so prominent throughout the collection that they have not been included in the partial subject inventory.

ALT, HERSCHEL
    Folder 53

AYER, W. C.
    Folder 50

BENNETT, JAMES V.
    Folder 41

BERWIND, CHARLES G.
    Folders 2-3, 8-9, 12-13, 24, 30, 35-36

BIG BROTHER AND BIG SISTER FEDERATION, INC.
    Folders 10, 58

BIG BROTHER WORK
  Finance
    Folders 2-3, 5-9, 13
  Promotion and Publicity
    Folders 6-9, 13, 16, 30, 33, 39, 43, 52
  Psychiatric Services
    Folder 16
  Recruitment and Training of Volunteer Workers
    Folders 11, 16, 21, 30, 35, 41, 43, 58
  Standards
    Folder 9

BIG SISTER GROUPS
    Folder 62

BOOTH, CHARLES BRANDON
    Folder 53

CAIRNS, THOMAS
    Folders 21, 30, 80

BIG BROTHERS OF AMERICA, INC.

CAMPS, SUMMER
    Folders 41, 49

CASEY, GEORGE
    Folder 10

CHILD, LOUISE
    Folder 24

CLARK, THOMAS C.
    Folders 96-100

COMMUNITY FUNDS AND CHESTS
    Folders 2, 8, 104

DAY, A. WHITTIER
    Folder 16

DE RIEL, JUERGEN
    Folders 16, 21, 24

DEUTSCH, ALBERT
    Folder 30

ELIOT, MARTHA
    Folder 24

EPSTEIN, JOSHUA
    Folder 21

GENDALL, GILBERT
    Folders 37, 41-42, 44-45, 51, 54-56

GENTILE, FELIX
    Folders 2, 5, 7, 9, 22-24, 27-30, 35, 50

GOLDBERG, MILTON
    Folders 11, 24, 30

GROSSMAN, GEORGE
    Folders 12, 16, 50, 53-54, 57

HEDGES, BENJAMIN VAN DOREN
    Folders 5, 12-13

HINCKLEY, ROBERT
    Folder 16

HIRSCHFIELD, ERIC
    Folder 24

JENKS, DONALD
    Folders 41-46, 48, 50-56

JOHNSON, KENNETH D.
    Folder 16

JUVENILE DELINQUENCY
    Folders 30, 41

LEAF, DONALD S.
    Folder 11

LINDEMAN, EDUARD C.
    Folders 18, 21

MANGRUM, JOHN C.
    Folder 24

McCOY, JOSEPH
    Folders 8, 16, 30, 35-36, 40-44, 47-48, 51-58, 80

MENNINGER, WILLIAM C.
    Folder 35

METZ, LEONARD
    Folder 24

NEGRO YOUTH
    Folders 36, 43

PITCHER, NOAH
    Folders 16, 21

PROFESSIONAL SOCIAL WORKERS. RELATIONSHIP TO BIG BROTHER WORK.
    Folders 13, 16

RAMSEY, MAC
    Folder 24

REBMANN, G. RUHLAND
    Folder 5

RICHARDSON, W. E.
    Folders 16, 24, 30

ROGERS, KENNETH
    Folder 58

RYDER, JOSEPH
    Folder 30

SHELDON, ROWLAND
    Folder 10

STOTT, REG D.
    Folder 11

TEGER, JOHN E.
    Folder 16

VOLUNTEER WORKERS. SEE BIG BROTHER WORK. RECRUITMENT AND TRAINING OF VOLUNTEERS.

WILSON, PAUL
    Folder 30

WINNETT, NOCHEM
    Folder 11

WYNN, ROBERT
    Folder 63

BIG BROTHERS OF AMERICA, INC.

FOLDER TITLE AND DESCRIPTION OF CONTENTS	FOLDER

Big Brothers of America, Inc. Constitution, 1961.   1

Board of Directors. Papers, 1949-1953   2
    Minutes and correspondence. Financing the work of the national organization, relationships with Community Chests, establishment of an Executive Committee, hiring Felix Gentile as Executive Director, duties of the Executive Director, and notification of men of their election to Board of Directors. There is no material for 1950. Charles Berwind is prominent in the folder.

Board of Directors. Papers, 1954-1956   3
    Minutes and correspondence. Financing the national organization, notification to members of the Board of Directors of their election to the board, lists of members of the boards of directors for 1956-1957. Charles Berwind is prominent in the folder.

Board of Directors. Papers, 1962-1963   4
    Lists of national and local boards of directors of Big Brother groups. Arranged alphabetically by state and province.

Executive Committee, 1951   5
    Minutes and correspondence. Formation of national organization, financing national office, and hiring Felix Gentile as Executive Director. G. Ruhland Rebmann and Benjamin Hedges are prominent in the folder.

Executive Committee, 1952-1953   6
    Minutes and correspondence. Financing the national organization, planning for Big Brother Weeks, work of the national office, public relations, and formation of local Big Brother agencies.

Executive Committee, 1953-1954   7
    Minutes and correspondence. Financing the national organization, Big Brother Weeks, relationship of Big Brother groups to communities, and work of the national office. Felix Gentile is prominent in the folder.

Council of Delegates. Minutes, 1949-1951   8
    Formation of an Executive Committee, appointment of area directors, Technical Planning Committee and 1950 Survey of local Big Brother groups, publicity for Big Brother Week, educational scholarships for Little Brothers, financing the national organization, relationships with Community Chests, formation of local Big Brother organizations, and hiring an Executive Director. Charles Berwind and Joseph McCoy are prominent in the folder.

Council of Delegates. Minutes, 1952-1954   9
    Reports of the President and Executive Director. Arrangements by the Technical Planning Committee for regional conferences, financing the national organization, formation of local Big Brother organizations, work of the national office, standards in Big Brother work, and publicity for Big Brother work. Felix Gentile and Charles Berwind are prominent in the folder.

BIG BROTHERS OF AMERICA, INC.

FOLDER TITLE AND DESCRIPTION OF CONTENTS — FOLDER

Annual Meeting. 1932 (Big Brother and Big Sister Federation, Inc.) — 10
Correspondence, 1931-1932
    Correspondence re arrangements. Standards of membership in the Federation. Rowland Sheldon and George Casey are prominent correspondents.

Annual Meeting. 1949. Speeches and Papers — 11
    Recruitment of volunteers, qualities of successful Big Brothers. Speeches include: "Melvin's Big Brother" by Milton Goldberg; "Training the Volunteer in Casework with Boys" by Donald S. Leaf; "Training the Volunteer for Work with Boys" by Reg D. Stott; and "Big Brothers Are Not Born" by Nochem Winnett.

Annual Meeting. 1951. Correspondence, General, 1950-1951 — 12
    Correspondence re arrangements for annual meeting. George Grossman, Benjamin Hedges, and Charles Berwind are prominent correspondents.

Annual Meeting. 1951. Annual Reports — 13
    Reports of the President, Charles Berwind, and the Executive Vice President, Benjamin Hedges. Finances, work of the national office, relationship of Big Brother work to professional social work agencies, public relations, and extension of Big Brother work.

Annual Meeting. 1951. Attendance — 14
    Letters inviting local Big Brothers and other persons interested in Big Brother work to attend the annual meeting.

Annual Meeting. 1951. Nominating Committee — 15
    Nominations to the Board of Directors and designation by local agencies of their representatives to the Council of Delegates.

Annual Meeting. 1951. Speeches and Papers — 16
    Relationship of Big Brothers and Little Brothers to one another, relationship between professional and volunteer workers, recruitment of Big Brothers with the ideal characteristics of Big Brothers, relationship of Big Brother groups to social work agencies. Report of the meeting of the Technical Planning Committee. Workship Forums: "What Constitutes Good Intake Policy in a Big Brother Agency?" by John E. Teger; "Screening of Big Brothers" by W. E. Richardson; "Psychiatric Service in Big Brother Work" by Juergen de Riel; "Psychiatric Service in Big Brother Work" by Robert G. Hinckley; "Supplementary Services--Do They Help the Big Brother With the Boy?" by Noah Pitcher; and "Public Relations--Coordination of National and Local Interpretation Programs" by George Grossman. Speeches include: "Youth Conservation Through Big Brother Work" by A. Whittier Day; "Big Brothers Make Good Citizens" by Kenneth D. Johnson; and "Our National Organization" by Joseph McCoy.

Annual Meeting. 1952. Correspondence, General, 1951-1953 — 17-18
    Correspondence re arrangements for annual meeting and letter of condolence to Mrs. Eduard Lindeman after the death of her husband.

BIG BROTHERS OF AMERICA, INC.

FOLDER TITLE AND DESCRIPTION OF CONTENTS | FOLDER

Annual Meeting. 1952. Attendance   19
     Invitations to local Big Brothers and other persons interested
     in Big Brother work to attend annual meeting.

Annual Meeting. 1952. Nominating Committee   20
     Nominations to the Board of Directors and designation by local
     agencies of their representatives to the Council of Delegates.

Annual Meeting. 1952. Speeches and Papers   21
     Selection of volunteers, relationship of professional and
     volunteer workers, termination of Big Brother-Little Brother
     relationship, characteristics of good Big Brothers, and train-
     ing of Big Brothers. Speeches include: "The Urgency of Citizen
     Participation," by Eduard C. Lindeman; Groups Discussion Work-
     shops include: "Evaluation of the Use of Volunteers in Case-
     work Setting" by Thomas Cairns; "The Boy with Problems" by
     Joshua Epstein; "Selection of the Man" by Noah Pitcher; and
     "Preparation of the Man" by Juergen de Riel. Report of the
     Proceedings of the Technical Planning Committee meeting.

Annual Meeting. 1953. Correspondence, General, 1952-1953   22-23
     Correspondence re arrangements for the annual meeting. Felix
     Gentile is a prominent correspondent.

Annual Meeting. 1953. _Proceedings_   24
     Address by Charles Berwind; report of the Executive Director,
     Felix Gentile; report of the Technical Planning Committee; and
     report of the Committee on Evaluation of Minimum Standards.
     Groups Discussions include: "Camp Operations" by Mac Ramsey;
     "Maintaining Agency Records" by Juergen de Riel; "Evaluation of
     Plans for Local Agency Expansion During the Next Five Years" by
     Milton L. Goldberg; "Survey Method as a Device for Evaluating
     and Improving Programs" by Eric Hirschfeld; "Interpretation
     of Program to the Community" by W. E. Richardson; "Recruiting and
     Orientation of Big Brothers" by Leonard Metz; and "What New
     Directions are Indicated" by John E. Mangrum. Speeches include
     "Red Buttons" by Louise A. Child and "Who Cares" by Martha M.
     Eliot, M.D., Chief of the United States Children's Bureau.

Annual Meeting. 1953. Attendance   25
     Correspondence inviting local Big Brothers and other persons
     interested in Big Brother work to attend the annual meeting.

Annual Meeting. 1953. Nominating Committee   26
     Nominations to the Board of Directors and designation by local
     agencies of their representatives to the Council of Delegates.

Annual Meeting. 1954. Correspondence, General, 1953-1954   27-29
     Correspondence re arrangements for annual meeting. Felix
     Gentile is prominent in the folder.

BIG BROTHERS OF AMERICA, INC.

FOLDER TITLE AND DESCRIPTION OF CONTENTS   FOLDER

Annual Meeting. 1954. <u>Proceedings</u>   30
    Reports by Charles Berwind and Felix Gentile. Discussion
groups and leaders include: "What Distinguishes Big Brother
Work from other Community Welfare Services?" by Milton L.
Goldberg; "How Much Information Do You Require Before Accepting
a Man as a Big Brother?" by Paul Wilson; "How Active Are You in
Getting Little Brothers from Schools, Courts, Churches, Social
Agencies, Guardians, and Other Sources...How Active Are You in
Getting Big Brothers Throughout Your Community?" by W. E.
Richardson; "What Orientation Do You Give the Big Brother to
Prepare Him for his Assignment?" by Joseph McCoy; "What Specific
Activities Do You Engage in to Make Your Community Increasingly
Conscious of the Value of Big Brother Work?" by Joseph Ryder;
and "How Do You Evaluate the Effectiveness of Big Brother Work
in Your Community?" by Thomas Cairns. Speech by Albert Deutsch:
"Some New Looks at Juvenile Delinquency."

Annual Meeting. 1954. Attendance   31
    Invitations to local Big Brothers and other persons interested
in Big Brother work to attend the annual meeting.

Annual Meeting. 1954. Nominating Committee   32
    Nominations to the Board of Directors and designation by local
agencies of their representatives to the Council of Delegates.

Annual Meeting. 1954. Speeches and Papers   33
    Items for inclusion in the President's Report; frames of reference
for discussion leaders. Philosophy of Big Brother work, work of the
national Big Brother organization, and promotion of Big Brother work.

Annual Meeting. 1955. Clippings   34
    Press clippings only.

Annual Meetings. 1956. <u>Report</u>   35
    Reports by Charles Berwind and Felix Gentile. Discussion groups
and leaders include "What Do You Expect of the National and What
Are the Responsibilities of Affiliates?" by national personnel,
Felix Gentile and Margaret M. Hanley, and local personnel, Joseph
McCoy and Milton Goldberg; "Big Brother Case Clinic," and "I Am a
Big Brother" by five Big Brothers. Speech includes: "The Therapy
of Friendship" by William C. Menninger, M.D. Recruitment and
training of Big Brothers, duties of national Big Brother executives.

Correspondence. Alabama, 1939-1949   36
    Correspondence from persons wanting information on Big Brother
movement for setting up local Big Brother groups. Effect of
World War II on Big Brother work, need for a centralized Big
Brother national office, philosophy of Big Brother work, pre-
requisites for setting up local Big Brother groups, and Big
Brother work with Negro youth. Joseph McCoy is a prominent
correspondent.

BIG BROTHERS OF AMERICA, INC.

FOLDER TITLE AND DESCRIPTION OF CONTENTS	FOLDER

Correspondence. Arizona, 1936-1951   37
    Routine correspondence re requests for information on Big Brother work. Philosophy and purposes of Big Brother work. Joseph McCoy, Gilbert Gendall, and Donald Jenks are prominent correspondents.

Correspondence. Arkansas, 1945-1947   38
    Routine correspondence re requests for information on Big Brother work. Joseph McCoy is a prominent correspondent.

Correspondence. California, 1936-1950   39
    Routine correspondence re requests for information on Big Brother work. Philosophy and promotion of Big Brother movement, duties of national office, procedures in New York Big Brother organization, steps in setting up local Big Brother agencies. Joseph McCoy is a prominent correspondent.

Correspondence. Connecticut, 1939-1950   40
    Routine correspondence re requests for information on Big Brother work. Philosophy of Big Brother work, procedures in New York Big Brother organization, assigning Big and Little Brothers to one another, and steps to take in organizing local Big Brother agencies. Joseph McCoy is a prominent correspondent.

Correspondence. District of Columbia, 1938-1949   41
    Philosophy of Big Brother work, summer camps, procedures and services in Big Brother work, volunteer workers in the Bureau of Rehabilitation and National Training School for Boys (The Bureau was set up in 1930 to aid in the rehabilitation of men and women placed in correctional institutions in and around Washington, D. C.), juvenile delinquency, and speech by James V. Bennett (Director, Federal Bureau of Prisons) before the Big Brother League on the value of Big Brother work: "Big Brother Goes to Bat." Joseph McCoy, Gilbert Gendall, and Donald Jenks are prominent correspondents.

Correspondence. Florida, 1938-1951   42
    Routine correspondence. Philosophy and procedures in Big Brother and Big Sister work. Joseph McCoy, Gilbert Gendall, and Donald Jenks are prominent correspondents.

Correspondence. Georgia, 1938-1953   43
    Routine correspondence. Philosophy and procedures in Big Brother work, need for a Big Brother agency in Atlanta, juvenile delinquency, motivation for volunteer work, publicizing Big Brother work, and Big Brother work with Negro youth. Joseph McCoy and Donald Jenks are prominent correspondents.

Correspondence. Illinois, 1937-1950   44
    Routine correspondence. Work of the national office and Big Brother work in Waukegan, Illinois. Joseph McCoy, Gilbert Gendall, and Donald Jenks are prominent correspondents.

FOLDER TITLE AND DESCRIPTION OF CONTENTS	FOLDER

Correspondence. United Charities of Chicago (Illinois), 1946-1953   45
    The Chicago Big Brother Association was administered by the United Charities of Chicago. Temporary National Big Brother Committee, study of Big Brother organizations to determine need for a national office, discontinuance of Big Brother work and attempts to set it up again. Gilbert Gendall, Donald Jenks, and Mrs. Frances Higgins, administrative assistant of the United Charities of Chicago, are prominent correspondents.

Correspondence. Indiana, 1939-1950   46
    Routine correspondence. Philosophy and procedures in Big Brother work. Donald Jenks is a prominent correspondent.

Correspondence. Iowa, 1937-1949   47
    Routine correspondence and correspondence re an individual case. Joseph McCoy is a prominent correspondent.

Correspondence. Massachusetts, 1935-1951   48
    Routine correspondence and correspondence re an individual case. Philosophy of Big Brother work and need for more Big Brothers. Joseph McCoy and Donald Jenks are prominent correspondents.

Correspondence. Michigan, 1938-1949   49
    Routine correspondence. Philosophy and procedures in Big Brother work and Big Brother-sponsored summer camps for Little Brothers. Joseph McCoy and Donald Jenks are prominent correspondents.

Correspondence. St. Louis, Missouri, 1949-1958   50
    Correspondence with W. C. Ayer of the St. Louis Button Company re prevention of juvenile delinquency and promotion of Big Brother work. Donald Jenks, Felix Gentile, and George Grossman are prominent correspondents.

Correspondence. New Jersey, 1936-1950   51
    Routine correspondence. Formation of local Big Brother organizations. Joseph McCoy, Gilbert Gendall, and Donald Jenks are prominent correspondents.

Correspondence. New York, 1912, 1936-1951   52
    Routine correspondence. Philosophy and procedures in Big Brother work, publicizing Big Brother work, and formation of local Big Brother agencies. Joseph McCoy and Donald Jenks are prominent correspondents.

Correspondence. New York, New York, 1942-1951   53
    Routine correspondence and correspondence re an individual case. Establishing local Big Brother organizations. Joseph McCoy, Donald Jenks, George Grossman, Herschel Alt, and Charles Brandon Booth (Founder of the National Society of the Volunteers of America) are prominent correspondents.

FOLDER TITLE AND DESCRIPTION OF CONTENTS	FOLDER

Correspondence. Ohio, 1936-1950   54
    Routine correspondence. Philosophy and procedures of Big Brother work, history of juvenile delinquency, formation of local Big Brother agencies, and recruitment and characteristics of men who make successful Big Brothers. Joseph McCoy, Gilbert Gendall, Donald Jenks, and George Grossman are prominent correspondents.

Correspondence. Pennsylvania, 1934-1950   55
    Routine correspondence. Philosophy and procedures in Big Brother work, clubs for Little Brothers, and formation of local Big Brother agencies. Joseph McCoy, Gilbert Gendall, and Donald Jenks are prominent correspondents.

Correspondence. Texas, 1937-1950   56
    Routine correspondence. Formation of local Big Brother agencies. Joseph McCoy, Gilbert Gendall, Donald Jenks, and Charles Berwind are prominent correspondents.

Correspondence. Virginia, 1944-1950   57
    Routine correspondence and correspondence re an individual case. Formation of local Big Brother agencies and clubs for Little Brothers. Joseph McCoy, Gilbert Gendall, and George Grossman are prominent correspondents.

1940 Study. Summary, 1940   58
    The National Study and Planning Committee chaired by Kenneth Rogers and Joseph McCoy surveyed local organizations to collect information about the nature of existing organizations and to plan for the structure and function of a national office to replace the Big Brother and Big Sister Federation, Inc. if a desire for such an organization was indicated by the survey. Need for and functions of a national Big Brother organization, either with or without Big Sisters, volunteer workers, recruitment, and philosophy of Big Brother work.

1940 Study. Correspondence and Papers   59
    Correspondence and papers re purposes and methods of the study.

1940 Study. Questionnaires and Supporting Materials. Big Brother Groups   60-61
    Arranged alphabetically by state or province and city. Los Angeles, California Catholic Big Brothers, Inc.; Los Angeles, California Jewish Big Brother Association of Los Angeles; Los Angeles, California Protestant Big Brothers; Jacksonville, Florida Boys Home Association of Jacksonville, Inc.; Chicago, Illinois Big Brothers Association; Danville, Illinois Big Brother Association; Evanston, Illinois Big Brothers Association of Evanston; Peoria, Illinois Child and Family Service, Inc.; Columbus, Ohio Colored Big Brothers; Philadelphia, Pennsylvania Big Brother Association; Pittsburgh, Pennsylvania Negro Big Brother Association of Allegheny County; Scranton, Pennsylvania

BIG BROTHERS OF AMERICA, INC.

FOLDER TITLE AND DESCRIPTION OF CONTENTS   FOLDER

    Boy's Club-Big Brother Organization; Dallas, Texas Dallas Big Brothers, Inc.; Hamilton, Ontario Big Brother Program; Toronto, Ontario Big Brother Movement, Inc.; Toronto, Ontario Catholic Big Brothers, and Toronto, Ontario Big Brother Department of the Jewish Child Welfare Association.

1940 Study. Questionnaires and Supporting Materials. Big Sister Groups   62
    Chicago, Illinois Jewish Big Sisters; and Pittsburgh, Pennsylvania Interdenominational Mission Society.

1946 Study and Report of Fifteen Big Brother Organizations in the United States and Canada, June, 1946   63
    The study was undertaken by the Temporary National Big Brother Committee in the fall of 1945. Fifteen Big Brother agencies in the United States and Canada were surveyed to determine the extent, techniques, and results of Big Brother services and to learn if there was a desire for a permanent national committee or organization of Big Brother groups. Robert Wynn compiled a report of the information gained from the study.

1946 Study. Questionnaires and Supporting Papers. Denver, Colorado. Big Brothers, Inc.   64

1946 Study. Questionnaires and Supporting Papers. Boston, Massachusetts. Jewish Big Brother Association.   65

1946 Study. Questionnaires and Supporting Papers. Minneapolis, Minnesota. Big Brothers, Inc.   66

1946 Study. Questionnaires and Supporting Papers. Big Brother Organization, Inc.   67

1946 Study. Questionnaires and Supporting Papers. New York, New York. Big Brother Movement.   68-70

1946 Study. Questionnaires and Supporting Papers. New York, New York. Jewish Big Brother Movement.   71

1946 Study. Questionnaires and Supporting Papers. Cincinnati, Ohio. Big Brother Association of Cincinnati.   72

1946 Study. Questionnaires and Supporting Papers. Cincinnati, Ohio. Eastern Hills Big Brother Association.   73

1946 Study. Questionnaires and Supporting Papers. Columbus, Ohio. Big Brother Association of Columbus, Ohio, Inc.   74

1946 Study. Questionnaires and Supporting Papers. Philadelphia, Pennsylvania. Big Brother Association.   75

1946 Study. Questionnaires and Supporting Papers. Dallas, Texas. Dallas Big Brothers, Inc.   76

BIG BROTHERS OF AMERICA, INC.   34

FOLDER TITLE AND DESCRIPTION OF CONTENTS   FOLDER

1946 Study. Questionnaires and Supporting Papers. Hamilton,   77
Ontario. Big Brother Association of Hamilton.

1946 Study. Questionnaires and Supporting Papers. Toronto,   78
Ontario. Big Brother Movement.

1946 Study. Questionnaires and Supporting Papers. Toronto,   79
Ontario. Catholic Big Brother Association of Ontario.

1950 Study. Summary of 1950 Study and Surrounding Correspondence   80
    In 1950, a Technical Planning Committee chaired by Joseph
    McCoy of the New York Big Brother Movement was set up to make
    a study of member organizations of the Big Brothers of
    America. In addition to studying the practices and structures
    of the local Big Brother agencies, the committee studied forms
    in use by each organization, hoping to develop a standard set
    of forms which might be adopted for use by all local Big
    Brother groups. The summary was prepared by Thomas Cairns.
    Arranged alphabetically by state, province, city, and
    organization.

1950 Study. Questionnaires and Supporting Papers. Los Angeles,   81
California-Minneapolis, Minnesota
    Los Angeles, California Jewish Big Brothers Association of
    Los Angeles; Denver, Colorado Big Brothers, Inc.; District
    of Columbia Big Brothers of D. C. Inc.; Baltimore, Maryland
    Jewish Big Brother League; Boston, Massachusetts Jewish Big
    Brother Association; Flint, Michigan Flint Youth Bureau; and
    Minneapolis, Minnesota Big Brothers, Inc.

1950 Study. Questionnaires and Supporting Papers. St. Louis,   82
Missouri-Philadelphia, Pennsylvania
    St. Louis, Missouri Big Brother Organization, Inc.; New York,
    New York Big Brother Movement; New York, New York Jewish Big
    Brothers of the Jewish Board of Guardians; Cincinnati, Ohio
    Big Brother Association of Cincinnati; Cleveland, Ohio Jewish
    Big Brothers Association; Columbus, Ohio Big Brother Association
    of Columbus, Inc.; and Philadelphia, Pennsylvania Big Brother
    Association.

1950 Study. Questionnaires and Supporting Papers. Dallas, Texas-   83
Toronto, Ontario
    Dallas, Texas Dallas Big Brothers, Inc.; Hamilton, Ontario Big
    Brother Association of Hamilton, Inc.; Ottawa, Ontario Big
    Brothers; and Toronto, Ontario Big Brother Movement, Inc.

1950 Study. Forms Used by Local Big Brother Groups   84
    Analysis of forms sent by local organizations and forms un-
    designated by local group. General referral, school, health,
    and camp forms.

BIG BROTHERS OF AMERICA, INC.

FOLDER TITLE AND DESCRIPTION OF CONTENTS | FOLDER

1950 Study. Forms. Los Angeles, California Jewish Big Brother Association of Los Angeles. — 85

1950 Study. Forms. Denver, Colorado Big Brothers, Inc. — 86

1950 Study. Forms. Baltimore, Maryland Jewish Big Brother League, Inc. — 87

1950 Study. Forms. Minneapolis, Minnesota Big Brothers, Inc. — 88

1950 Study. Forms. St. Louis, Missouri Big Brother Organization, Inc. — 89

1950 Study. Forms. New York, New York Big Brother Movement. — 90

1950 Study. Forms. New York, New York Jewish Big Brothers of the Jewish Board of Guardians. — 91

1950 Study. Forms. Cincinnati, Ohio Big Brothers Association of Cincinnati. — 92

1950 Study. Forms. Columbus, Ohio Big Brother Association of Columbus, Inc. — 93

1950 Study. Forms. Philadelphia, Pennsylvania Big Brother Association. — 94

1950 Study. Forms. Toronto, Ontario Big Brother Movement, Inc. — 95

Big Brother Week. 1950. Correspondence and Papers, 1949-1950 — 96-100
  Materials re arrangements for Big Brother Week, 1950, which was set up to publicize Big Brother work on a national level as a prelude to a recruitment and fund-raising campaign. Correspondence, newspaper clippings, news releases, pictures, and radio scripts. Thomas C. Clark, Associate Justice of the U. S. Supreme Court, received the Big Brother of the Year award.

Big Brother Week. 1951. Correspondence and Papers, 1950-1951 — 101
  Scattered materials re publicity for 1951 Big Brother Week. Radio script and photograph of Norman Rockwell drawing for national Big Brother publicity.

Big Brother Week. 1952. Correspondence and Papers, 1951-1952 — 102
  Scattered materials. News releases and newspaper kit.

Big Brother Week. 1953. Papers, 1953 — 103
  Radio and television kit.

Financial Materials, ca. 1946, 1957 — 104
  Proposed budget for national organization; <u>Manual</u> of the National Budget Committee; Report on the Big Brothers of America, Inc., by the National Quota Committee and National Budget Committee; and approval of request for funds from the Chest and United Fund Areas for 1958.

BIG BROTHERS OF AMERICA, INC.

FOLDER TITLE AND DESCRIPTION OF CONTENTS	LEGAL FOLDER
Over-size material relating to summary of 1950 survey.	1

3

An Inventory of the Papers of Jacob Fisher

PREPARED BY
Carol E. Jenson

SWB Jacob Fisher
F534
       Papers, 1933-1939

       10 folders

This collection includes a scattering of materials donated by Jacob Fisher, a leader in the rank and file movement of social workers and one-time editor of Social Work Today. Fisher and his followers believed very strongly that only through unionization could social workers attain salaries and working conditions commensurate with the services they performed. Only after the social workers had achieved these proper working conditions could they hope to carry out the social work objectives in relation to clients.

The mainstream of the rank and file movement grew out of the Social Workers Discussion Club which began holding meetings in New York during 1932. The first National Convention of Rank and File Groups in Social Work was held in Pittsburgh, Pennsylvania, February 22-24, 1935. The convention elected Jacob Fisher as chairman and discussed the history of attempts to improve the social workers' conditions of employment. They saw a necessity for social workers achieving a better understanding of clients and their needs but felt this could not be attained until the social workers gained improved working conditions for themselves. The groups also voiced opposition to federal government cuts in relief spending and indicated that they felt the government was moving to the right in an alliance with industry. They made repeated references to the publication Social Work Today and its corresponding effort to use collective bargaining, rather than the American Association of Social Workers, as the chief method of organization. At the next conference, held in Cleveland in February, 1936, the group adopted a constitution and changed its title to National Coordinating Committee of Social Service Employee Groups.

Jacob Fisher was one of the most obvious links between the rank and file organizations and Social Work Today. The magazine was sponsored by the Social Workers Discussion Group of New York with the endorsement of similar groups in other cities and began publication with the March-April issue in 1934 and continued irregularly until May of 1942. Social Work Today observed a transition from private social work to public welfare in a class society. The magazine took as its purpose encouraging the rank and file social workers to further their professional and economic status so that in turn they might be more beneficial to their clients. Jacob Fisher was the original editor of Social Work Today; and in July-August, 1934, he was joined by two fellow editors. The number of editors varied from three to four, with Fisher among them, until Frank Bancroft became managing editor with the October, 1937, issue. The University of Minnesota Social Welfare History Archives Center holds one of the few complete runs of Social Work Today.

The papers relating to the National Coordinating Committee of Rank and File Groups in Social Work and its successor, the National Coordinating Committee of Social Service Employee Groups, are arranged chronologically.

Two folders of materials from two organizations which were related to the rank and file movement have been placed in the ephemera collection. Included are newsletters of the Emergency Home Relief Bureau Employees Association, 1934-1935; and newsletters of the Association of Federation Workers, 1932-1935.

Because of the small size of this collection, any subject inventory would be misleading.

JACOB FISHER

FOLDER TITLE AND DESCRIPTION OF CONTENTS	FOLDER
Social Work Discussion Club: 1933 Explanatory pamphlets.	1
"A Protective Organization for Jewish Social Workers": 1933 Reprint, relating to rank and file movement.	2
First National Convention of Rank and File Groups in Social Work: 1935 Proceedings, reports.	3
Constitutional Committee of National Coordinating Committee of Rank and File Groups in Social Work: 1935 Report.	4
Convention of the National Coordinating Committee of Rank and File Groups in Social Work, 1936 Proceedings, reports.	5
National Coordinating Committee of Social Service Employee Groups: 1935-1937 Relation to the National Conference of Social Work; includes "Trade Union Notes," a publication distributed at NCSW Indianapolis Conference in 1937.	6
"Rank and File Bulletins": 1935-1936 Issued by National Coordinating Committee of Rank and File Groups in Social Work.	7
Jacob Fisher: 1939 Speeches: "Professional Goals and the Trade Union," "Economics and Social Work," and "Social Work and the Democratic Tradition."	8

The remaining (2) folders have been removed from the Fisher collection and placed in the ephemera collection.

Emergency Home Relief Bureau Employees Association, New York: 1934-1935 Newsletters, pamphlet relating to rank and file movement.	9
Association of Federation Workers: 1932-1935 Newsletter, "The Bulletin," relating to rank and file movement.	10

4

An Inventory of the Papers of Five Towns Community House

PREPARED BY
John M. Herrick, Principal Processor
Douglas D. Hall
Andrea Hinding

SWD11 Five Towns Community House, Lawrence, Long Island, New York

Papers, 1907-1965

512 folders   4 (ℓ) folders

"Five Towns" is an area in the southwest corner of Nassau County, New York, which in 1955 consisted of "five contiguous localities": Hewlett, Woodmere, Cedarhurst, Lawrence, and Inwood. In 1955 Inwood, Woodmere, and Hewlett were unincorporated areas in the village of Hempstead. Lawrence and Cedarhurst were incorporated villages.

The Five Towns Community House, located in Lawrence, serves this area. House membership is racially mixed, and many residents are from low income groups.

The board of directors of Five Towns Community House deposited the organization's historical records in the Social Welfare History Archives Center in February, 1966. The collection, which contains papers from 1907 to 1965, comprised 15 linear feet after cleaning, processing, and arranging. The Center staff processed the collection during 1968-1969.

History of the agency

The Five Towns Community House began in 1907 when Mrs. Margaret Sage, wife of the noted philanthropist Russell Sage, at the suggestion of Mrs. Daniel Lord, decided to establish a small trades school at Inwood, Long Island. Mrs. Sage advanced funds to purchase the land for the school and securities to be held as a permanent endowment fund, the interest from which would be used to maintain the school. Named the Margaret Sage Industrial School, the agency's primary objective was "to develop the young people in the community into responsible citizens through helping them make normal adjustments to the complications of present-day social and economic life." The School offered recreational and cultural activities as well as vocational training for boys and girls. Its seven acres of playground were well used by the youth of the community.

By 1913, the School had developed a day nursery center for young children, strengthened its Americanization and citizenship training programs, and housed the Family Service Association (1913-1932). From 1921 to 1935 the District Nursing Association was lodged in the School. From 1926 to 1931 the School was active in establishing the Five Towns Community Chest and the Five Towns Community Council, events documented in the papers but not denoted by special sections. The School became a member of United Neighborhood Houses of New York City in 1923 and of the National Federation of Settlements and Neighborhood Centers in 1945.*

*Additional Five Towns Community House records appear in the National Federation of Settlements and Neighborhood Centers and United Neighborhood Houses of New York collections, which are also deposited at the Social Welfare History Archives Center.

During the Depression, the School operated a WPA nursery and a National Youth Administration program. The School changed its name from the Margaret Sage Industrial School to the Nassau Industrial School in 1911; and in 1942, it became the Five Towns Community House. The last name change reflected the shift in the Community House's objectives from vocational training to cultural, recreational, and educational programs for small neighborhood groups. It also coincided with an increased emphasis on group work techniques and activities on the part of the professional staff.

In November, 1910, with the primary emphasis on vocational training classes, the School's enrollment totalled 291 pupils, predominantly drawn from Inwood and North Lawrence, Long Island. The staff consisted of four teachers. Enrollment increased to 400 and the staff to six by 1913. The School suffered through the war years and the period of the Great Depression, and was forced to reduce the size of its staff, its enrollment, and budget several times. From the '30s the School continued to expand its staff and services for all ages, income groups, and nationalities. Since 1945, a professionally trained staff of social workers and graduate students from neighboring colleges has offered specialized group work services. Great emphasis has been placed on the development of a sound interracial community and the Community House has consistently worked with minority group leaders to build community-serving programs.

Organization of the collection

The collection was arranged as follows: first, papers dealing with administration and policy-making, e.g., annual meetings, board of directors, bylaws, etc. (folders 1-70); second, records of standing committees (folders 71-86); third, a subject file, arranged alphabetically, including material on House programs and activities (folders 87-171); fourth, records dealing with placement of undergraduate and graduate students in field work positions in the Community House (folders 172-180); fifth, group work records and reports of supervisory conferences, described in greater detail below (folders 181-440); sixth, papers dealing with relations with other agencies, both national and local (folders 441-502); and seventh, a study, photographs, publicity material, and newspaper clippings (folders 503-512).

Certain publications, pamphlets, etc. which were found in the collection were neither directly nor indirectly related to the programs of the Community House. These were removed and placed in the Center's ephemera collection. A list of the material removed is appended to this description.

Two scrapbooks containing newspaper clippings and photographs were removed from the collection and filed with oversize material.

Group work records

There are two sections of group work records, group work reports (folders 181-382) and reports of conferences between agency supervisors and group leaders (folders 383-436). Filed with these records are undergraduate students' reports of group work observations (folders 437-439) and papers of a Community House supervisor, Alice Suzuki (folder 440).

Group work reports are written records of leaders' work with Community House groups. These are filed in a chronological series arranged by the year and month the group began to function, and alphabetically by the name of the group ("Debs," "Boys, 8-9," "Panthers"). This arrangement generally parallels the House's program terms, that is, most groups functioned from October to May or February to May, and during the summer months. Because a new group leader was usually assigned to a group every program term, an individual group's records for a period of years will be found in several folders (e.g., "Debs," folders 184, 216, 240, 275).

Group work records generally include leader's reports of individual group meetings, evaluations of individual members of the group ("individual summaries"), and a "group summary." These reports and evaluations give the character, composition, and activities of the group and usually indicate the attitudes and policies of the worker. These records also offer insight into group work method and technique and some of its underlying assumptions, and into the nature of the community and clients involved with the agency. Some records are complete while others are fragmentary.

The supervisory reports (folders 383-436) are records of conferences between group leaders and their supervisors. These are filed chronologically by year and month, generally following the House's program terms, and alphabetically by supervisor's name. (These records are confidential and may be used only with the explicit permission of the director or the curator of the Social Welfare History Archives Center).

PARTIAL SUBJECT INVENTORY

The following is a guide, not a definitive index, to the collection.

Because the Community House functioned with a large Negro membership in a racially mixed area, much of the collection (especially the group work records, folders 181-440) pertains to the broad subject of race relations. To avoid misleading those using the records no attempt has been made to list folders containing such material.

Some entries have been made for group work, but because of the nature of the Community House as a group work agency, much of the collection contains material useful to those studying group work.

ADULT EDUCATION
Folder 71

AGED
Folders 60, 145, 378, 465, 486

AMERICAN FRIENDS SERVICE COMMITTEE
Folder 442

CASEWORK
Folders 22, 73, 94, 484

CHILD CARE CENTER
Folders 55, 96

CIVIL DEFENSE
Folder 100

COMMUNITY CHEST
Folders 33, 65-66, 475-476, 480

DAY CARE
Folders 60, 72

DRAFT DEFERMENTS FOR BOYS WORKERS (WWII)
Folder 32

FIVE TOWNS COMMUNITY CHEST
    Folders 475-476. Legal f. 4

FIVE TOWNS COMMUNITY COUNCIL
    Folders 477-483

FIVE TOWNS COMMUNITY HOUSE
    Annual Reports and Meetings
        Folders 2-9
    Board of Directors
        Folders 10-29
    Constitution
        Folder 1
    Finance
        Folders 43-53. Legal f. 2
    History of
        Folders 32, 90
    Membership
        Folders 111-123
    Personnel
        Folders 54-62, 81-82, 130-140
    Program
        Folders 35-42, 83

GROUP WORK METHODS AND TECHNIQUES
    Folders 54, 58

HOUSING
    Folders 27, 104-105, 480, 493. Legal f. 3

JUVENILE DELINQUENCY
    Folders 28, 31-34, 473

NARCOTICS
    Folder 141

NATIONAL CONFERENCE ON SOCIAL WELFARE
    Folder 446

NATIONAL COUNCIL OF JEWISH WOMEN
    Folder 447

NATIONAL FEDERATION OF SETTLEMENTS AND NEIGHBORHOOD CENTERS
    Folders 448-453

RECREATION
    Folders 480, 483, 496, 502

SOCIAL WORK. FIELD WORK
    Folders 172-180, 451-452

SUMMER CAMP
    Folder 92

SUMMER DAY CAMP
    Folders 150-164

TEEN PROGRAM   SEE ALSO GROUP WORK RECORDS
    Folders 35-42, 57-58, 60, 165-166

UNITED NEIGHBORHOOD HOUSES OF NEW YORK
    Folders 456-464

URBAN RENEWAL
    Folders 104-105, 493

VOLUNTEERS
    Folders 54-56, 65-75, 85, 168, 447

WELFARE COUNCIL OF NEW YORK CITY
    Folder 466

WPA NURSERY SCHOOL
    Folder 169

YOUTH EMPLOYMENT
    Folders 77, 86, 93

YOUTH SERVICES
    Folders 72, 77, 171, 474

FOLDER INVENTORY

Folder Title and Description of Contents	Folder
Certificate of Incorporation, Constitution, Bylaws, 1907-1965.	1

Margaret Sage Industrial School and Nassau Industrial School, Reports, 1908-1914   2
    School superintendent's reports; annual reports; manual and technical training reports; reports of the library and education committee, playground and entertainment committee, and house committee; treasurer's reports; evaluations of industrial and non-industrial classes offered.

Nassau Industrial School, Reports, 1915-1917   3
    Industrial classes attendance reports; material on boys work, relationship between school and community, house and grounds committee, recreational activities, and response to the polio epidemic (July, 1916). See legal folder 1 for supplementary papers.

Nassau Industrial School, Reports, 1930-1936   4
    Annual reports or reports of annual meetings which include class and activities reports, occasional monthly reports, and president's reports. These records reflect the shift in the school's functions from those of an industrial school to those of a settlement.

Nassau Industrial School, Five Towns Community House, Reports, 1937-1948   5
    Annual reports or reports of annual meetings which include material on activities and attendance, the National Youth Administration, group work, etc. These papers show the development and utilization of group work theory in directing activities.

Reports, Annual Meetings, 1949-1952   6
    Agendas, reports of the president and executive director, and lists of committee members and members of the board of directors.

Reports, Annual Meetings, 1953-1956   7
    Agendas, president's reports, annual reports, and committee reports. Some issues discussed are agency financing, utilization of volunteers, segments of the community served, and effectiveness of programs.

FIVE TOWNS COMMUNITY HOUSE

Folder Title and Description of Contents	Folder
Reports, Annual Meetings, 1957-1958	8

Primarily correspondence and papers dealing with the 50th anniversary of the settlement house. Includes report of president for 1957, agenda for 1958 annual meeting, and a fiftieth anniversary pamphlet detailing changing functions of the settlement house.

Reports, Annual Meetings, 1959-1965 — 9

Annual reports of the Community House, president's reports, agenda, some financial material, etc.

Margaret Sage Industrial School and Nassau Industrial School, Board of Directors, 1907, 1910, 1917-1918 — 10

Minutes and correspondence discussing the terms of Mrs. Margaret Sage's endowment of the Industrial School.

Nassau Industrial School, Board of Directors, Minutes, 1930-1941 — 11

Minutes and correspondence; includes material on activities and programs, registrants, analyses of financing, salary reductions in the Depression, regulations regarding use of the settlement building, playground, committee members, purpose of the settlement (ca. 1930), volunteers, and the community chest.

Nassau Industrial School, Five Towns Community House, Board of Directors, Minutes, 1940-1944 — 12

Minutes, agenda, and committee reports to the board of directors. Material on community chest-Community House relations, wartime programs, WPA, and NYA.

Board of Directors, Minutes, 1945-1947 — 13

Minutes, correspondence, and committee reports to the board of directors. Material on community adjustment to postwar society, volunteers, community chest-social agency interaction, child care, and financing.

Board of Directors, Minutes, 1948-1949 — 14

Material on programs, activities, problems of financing, and analyses of committee activities.

Board of Directors, Minutes, 1950-1953 — 15

Material on program, activities, casework and group work techniques, and analyses of types and numbers of persons involved in programs.

Folder Title and Description of Contents	Folder
Board of Directors, Minutes, 1954-1957 Material on special casework-group work projects and brief analyses of programs.	16
Board of Directors, Minutes, 1958-1960 Material on finance, fund-raising, and programs.	17
Board of Directors, Minutes, 1961-1963 Material on finance, programs and activities, and committee reports.	18
Board of Directors, Minutes, 1964-1965 Budget analyses, committee reports, discussion of Nassau County's approach to the problem of poverty, and material on the OEO Job Corps.	19
Board of Directors, Executive Committee, 1947-1964 Correspondence, agenda, and minutes; material on the terms of Margaret Sage's original bequest to the settlement, financial conditions in Five Towns, and committee members.	20
Board of Directors, Nominating Committee, 1946-1964 Correspondence and lists of nominations and committee members.	21
Board of Directors, Operating Committee, 1946-1948 Correspondence, minutes, and memoranda. The committee was a "small group of board members who kept informed of House programs and problems and assisted the Executive Director in determining those which should be referred to the Board of Directors." Material on policy re use of the building, casework, and interracial problems.	22
Board of Directors, Policy Committee, 1944-1946 Minutes of the special committee appointed to formulate policies for the Community House. Material on services, methods, functions of the Community House, and personnel practices.	23
Board of Directors, Proxies and Corporate Resolutions, 1938-1946 Includes proxies to be voted at annual meetings and corporate resolutions concerning finance and other business.	24
Board of Directors, Handbook, 1953-1954 The handbook provides information on the history, nature, purpose, and services of the Community House.	25

Folder Title and Description of Contents	Folder
Board of Directors, Lists of Names and Addresses, 1914-1964	26
Lists of board members and committee members.	
Board of Directors, Supplementary Material of Louis Berkowitz, 1949	27
Discussion of administrative debates over Community House programs, techniques, housing, segregation, and race relations.	
Board of Directors, Correspondence, 1934-1939	28
Material re meetings, finance, juvenile delinquency, and vocational guidance for adolescents. The correspondence is largely procedural.	
Board of Directors, Correspondence, 1953-1964	29
Primarily procedural correspondence from the Community House to board members regarding business, meetings, etc.	
Executive Director, Reports, 1940-1945	30
"Report of the Committee to Study the Survey Made by the Colored Community Service League," resolution changing the name of the Nassau Industrial School to Five Towns Community House, "The Impact of the War on the Child," and "Report of Progress of Five Towns Community House, 1931-1945." The director for this period was Miss M. Asenath Johnson.	
Executive Director and Assistant Executive Director, Correspondence, 1955-1960	31
Correspondence of Howard McClary, director, and V. Benjamin Louard, assistant director, regarding finance, racial discrimination, legislation, and juvenile delinquency.	
President, Correspondence, 1940-1961	32-34
Correspondence of Ichabod T. Williams and Horace Bowker, which is primarily routine but includes material on House finance, race relations, juvenile delinquency, social agency relationships, the community chest, day camps, history of the Community House, deferments for boys workers in World War II, etc.	
Program Evaluation, 1932-1964	35-39
Includes statistics detailing enrollment in Community House programs and evaluations of junior teen, senior teen, after-school, summer day camp, and young-adult programs.	

FIVE TOWNS COMMUNITY HOUSE

Folder Title and Description of Contents	Folder

Program Planning, 1949-1965   40-42
    Program statistics, reports, questionnaires, schedules, proposals, and memos and notices. Includes one folder (folder 40) of undated material.

Finance, 1920-1964   43-45
    Correspondence, financial statements, treasurers' reports, budgets, and auditors' reports. See also legal folder 2.

Finance, Budgets, 1935-1965   46-47
    Proposed budgets and "explanations" of these.

Finance, Camp Expenses, 1936   48
    Description and itemization of expense.

Finance, Contributions, 1954-1964   49
    Correspondence regarding contributions, cash and "in kind."

Finance, Contributions, Baird-Wingefield Foundation, 1957-1964   50
    Correspondence re the foundation's contributions.

Finance, Contributions, Norman Sarett Memorial Foundation, 1961-1964   51
    Correspondence primarily regarding donations of musical instruments to Community House music program.

Finance, Fund-raising Committee, 1958-1964   52
    Correspondence, minutes, and plans for raising funds.

Finance, Bank Passbooks, 1907-1910.   53

Staff Meetings, Minutes, 1935-1964   54-60
    Minutes and reports on House activities and programs. Material on volunteers, group work techniques, personnel practices, interracial activities, boys and girls work, etc.

Staff Meetings, After-school Staff Committee, 1957-1958   61
    Reports of meetings.

Staff Meetings, Senior Teen Staff Committee, 1960   62
    Reports of meetings.

Nassau Industrial School, Correspondence, 1908-1941   63-65
    Material on programs and activities, personnel practices, finance, industrial classes, YMCA-YWCA activities, community chest funding, impact of the Depression, use of volunteers, etc. Includes a copy of an 1884 article from the Century, "The Need of Trade Schools," and a 1941 residence map of school pupils.

Folder Title and Description of Contents	Folder
Correspondence, 1953-1964 Material re finance, recreation programs, community chest, and housekeeping and routine activities.	66-69
Correspondence, Form Letters, 1953-1964.	70
Adult Education Committee, 1946-1948 Correspondence with and papers from the American Association for Adult Education regarding House programs.	71
Agency Service Committee, 1961-1965 Correspondence, minutes, and reports. Material on day care centers, youth services, and House programs.	72
Casework Services Subcommittee, 1947-1948 This subcommittee was apparently considered a subcommittee of the Community House. Reports from psychiatric caseworkers at Henry Street Settlement, New York City, and material on casework methods.	73
Community Service Group Committee, 1962 Minutes. The committee coordinated Community House activities with the Five Towns community.	74
Education Committee, 1965 Minutes and reports on scholarships, program development, and volunteer tutoring.	75
Grounds Improvement Committee, 1962-1963 Minutes and material on the Economic Opportunity Act (OEO) of 1964, community action, and playground and recreational area development.	76
Guidance and Education Committee, 1960-1964 Correspondence, minutes, and papers. Material re vocational training, low income residents, youth employment, and youth guidance.	77
Guidance and Education Committee, Soifer Vocational Interests Study, 1947 Incomplete study of vocational interests of minority group boys served by the Community House.	78
House Committee, 1931-1964 Correspondence, minutes, reports, statements on the purposes and policies of the House, housekeeping records, and House members' handbook.	79-80
Personnel Practices Committee, 1936-1964 Minutes, recommendations to the board of directors, personnel practices guides, personnel standards and salary studies, and newspaper clippings re staff salaries.	81-82

FIVE TOWNS COMMUNITY HOUSE

Folder Title and Description of Contents	Folder
Program Committee, 1946-1960 Correspondence, minutes, agendas, and memoranda. Includes material on adolescents, interracial problems, and "Settlement House Programing in a Middle Class Suburban Community."	83
Public Relations Committee, 1938-1964 Correspondence, minutes, and press releases. Material re agency public relations, financing, and civic duties. The committee was formerly the committee on publicity and interpretation.	84
Service Volunteers Committee, 1965 Minutes. Material on the use of volunteers and Neighborhood Youth Corps.	85
Youth Employment Committee, 1961-1965 Correspondence, minutes, reports on youth employment conditions, newspaper clippings, and analyses of employment programs.	86
Adult Education Advisory Board, 1963-1964 Correspondence, minutes, and statistics relating to the income and education levels in the Inwood community.	87
Adult House Party, 1957-1963 Correspondence, reports, publicity material, and letters seeking funds to sponsor the event. Proceeds were used for scholarships for House members.	88
Adult Softball League, 1951 Material re a disagreement between members of a community softball league and members of the Community House over use of the agency's field.	89
Agency Workers' Guide, 1952-1953, 1963 Guides used to acquaint House workers with the history and purpose of the House, its functions, and their responsibilities.	90
Arts and Crafts Class, 1931-1940, 1964 Correspondence, lists of material used in classes, memoranda, and discussion of programs.	91
Camp Hurley, 1954-1965 Correspondence, reports, and brochures re this summer camp open to Community House members. Formerly Camp Juvenile.	92
Career Conference, 1961 Correspondence and program. The conference was held to acquaint House members with various careers.	93

FIVE TOWNS COMMUNITY HOUSE

Folder Title and Description of Contents	Folder

Casework Records, 1945-1949 — 94
Confidential records.

Child Care, Babysitting Course, 1963-1964 — 95
Correspondence, minutes, and attendance records.

Child Care Center, 1944-1947 — 96
Correspondence, reports, and list of center registrants. The center, which was federally funded and operated during World War II, ended its program in 1947.

Civil Defense, Emergency Rest Center, 1942-1943 — 97
The Community House was designated a "rest center" in case of attack. Includes instructions of the Five Towns Defense Council on functions of a rest center.

Club Members' Newsletters, 1953-1964 — 98
Irregular publications from various House groups which are not similar to the Community House Newsletters listed on page 41.

Clubs and Organizations of Five Towns, 1963 — 99
List of clubs and organizations functioning in the Five Towns community and a list of contributors to the Five Towns community chest.

Conference on Interracial Unity, 1944 — 100
List of those attending the conference and reports of the conference and local job discrimination in wartime industries.

Family Nights, 1950-1963 — 101
Family night program and analysis of attendance.

Hobbycraft Headquarters, 1959-1964 — 102
Papers re stamp collections and other materials to be used by hobby clubs at the Community House and in New York City settlements.

Home Visiting, 1955, 1964 — 103
Records of visits and manual, "Home Visiting in Social Group Work Agencies."

Housing Relocation, 1955-1963 — 104-105
Correspondence, reports, and papers dealing with urban renewal and specifically with relocation in Five Towns because of construction of the Nassau Expressway. Includes questionnaires completed by residents who were to be moved and analyses of housing conditions.

Folder Title and Description of Contents	Folder
Individual Contacts, 1960-1961 Records of "contacts" between staff and House members outside a group work setting.	106
John F. Kennedy Essay Contest, 1964 Announcement of contest, sample essays, and evaluations of contestants (who were House members).	107
Library Lists, ca. 1937 Lists of books used by House staff and members.	108
Members' Handbooks, n.d. Descriptions of purposes, activities, and rules and regulations of the Community House.	109
Membership Lists, 1932, 1961-1964.	110-111
Membership Records, ca. 1940-1963 Family membership records and evaluations by staff of family members. Arranged alphabetically by family name.	112-122
Membership Records, Adult Registration, 1962-1963 Forms.	123
Membership Records, Afternoon Registration, 1962-1963 Forms.	124
Merrall Memorial Fund, 1959-1960 Correspondence re the Fund. Constance Merrall, for whom the fund was named, was secretary of the Community House and a member of the board of directors.	125
Mimeograph Materials, 1948-1965 Leaflets, informational brochures, form letters, notices of House events and programs, etc.	126-127
Orientation of Graduate Students and Staff, 1954-1962 Primarily orientation schedules.	128
Peninsula Educational Nursery, 1962-1965 The nursery was co-sponsored by the Community House and the Peninsula Section of the National Council of Jewish Women. Includes minutes of steering committee, statement of purpose, records of home visits, etc.	129
Personnel, Applications, Professional Staff, 1941-1965 Correspondence, employment application forms, and personnel resumes for professional staff members.	130

Folder Title and Description of Contents	Folder
Personnel, Applications, Part-time Staff, 1941-1965 Applications from and evaluations of undergraduate student volunteers, social work graduate students in field work, and occasionally persons seeking part-time employment at the Community House. Includes letters of recommendation written for staff members.	131-139
Personnel, Staff Memoranda, 1952-1963 Material on administrative policies, discipline, house functions, program schedules, and expenditures.	140
Reports on Community House-Community Relations, 1937-1963 Material on hiring practices of the House, ideals of constitutional democracy, role of private welfare agencies in interracial relations, use of narcotics, and problems of agency-community relations.	141
Scholarships, Five Towns Democratic Club, 1955-1961 Correspondence regarding the Club's awarding of a college scholarship to a House member.	142
Scholarship Fund, 1961-1965 Correspondence re donations and applications to scholarship fund; lists of donors and applicants.	143
Scripts, 1962-1963 One play script, "The Haunted Clothesline," and one radio script re the Community House.	144
Senior Citizens Program, 1958-1964 Material on programs for the elderly.	145
Songs, 1954 Songs used in House activities.	146
Spartan Athletic Club, 1957-1960 Correspondence, memoranda, and membership lists of the club, an adult group.	147
Special Events, 1961-1964 Material re special projects: trips to New York City and Coney Island, youth activities, etc. Includes evaluation by group worker of trip to Coney Island.	148
Spring Carnival, 1954-1958 Summary report and routine planning materials.	149
Summer Day Camp, 1953-1964 Correspondence, registration forms, program schedules, financial data, analyses of attendance, staff meeting minutes, etc.	150-164

FIVE TOWNS COMMUNITY HOUSE

Folder Title and Description of Contents	Folder
Teen Program, 1960-1965 Young and senior teens. Includes correspondence, program planning and evaluation records, budgets, schedules, records of "incidents," etc.	165-166
Theatre Party Committee, 1961 Correspondence and notes re benefit performance for the Community House of <u>The Music Man</u>.	167
Volunteers, Tutorial and Homework Help Program, 1963 Correspondence and volunteer application form.	168
WPA Nursery School, 1938-1939 Correspondence concerning the activities of the WPA and its nursery school at the Nassau Industrial School.	169
Youth Employment Program, 1962-1964 Material re program to assist House members working or seeking employment.	170
Youth Service Project, 1965 Proposals from staff members for expanded programs.	171
Adelphi College, 1949-1965 Correspondence and papers re the placement of both social work graduate students and undergraduate students in field work positions in the Community House.	172
Brooklyn College, 1949-1961 Correspondence and papers re the College's community experience program which involved placing undergraduate students in volunteer positions at the Community House.	173
Columbia University, New York School of Social Work, 1946-1963 Extensive material re the School's field work program and the use of students at the Community House.	174-176
Fordham University, School of Social Service, 1949-1962 Correspondence and papers re Fordham's field work program and use of students at the Community House.	177
New York University, Graduate School of Social Work, 1951-1963 Correspondence and papers re use of students in field work positions at the Community House. Material re controversy over inclusion of the social service program within NYU's school of public administration.	178
Queens College, 1949-1965 Correspondence and papers re placement of students in field work positions at the Community House.	179

FIVE TOWNS COMMUNITY HOUSE

Folder Title and Description of Contents	Folder

Social Work Recruiting Committee of Greater New York, 1958-1963 — 180
    As a part of the Committee's recruiting work, it sponsored a "Field Experience for College Students," designed to give them a positive experience in social work. Correspondence and papers dealing with the Committee and placements at the Community House.

Group Work Records: Junior Junior Council, Jean Ober (Leader), 1951-1952 — 181
    Coed, 8-9 years. The Council was composed of representatives from afternoon groups.

Group Work Records: Jolly Rovers, Agnes Preston (Leader), 1952 — 182
    Young teen girls.

Group Work Records: Bonecrushers, V. Benjamin Louard (Leader), 1952-1953 — 183
    Teenage males. Apparently Wade Cooper took over as leader in April, 1953.

Group Work Records: Debs, Lamitsoi Bright-Davies (Leader), 1952-1953 — 184
    Young teen girls.

Group Work Records: "Game Room," George Rosenblum (Leader), 1952 — 185
    Mixed attendance.

Group Work Records: Golden Hawks, Robert Lanigan (Leader), 1952-1953 — 186
    Boys, 8-9 years.

Group Work Records: Golden Princesses, Janet Toohy (Leader), 1952-1953 — 187
    Girls, 8-9 years.

Group Work Records: Jettes, Janet Toohy (Leader), 1952-1953 — 188
    Girls, 14-18 years.

Group Work Records: Junior Junior Council, Betty Huff and George Rosenblum (Leaders), 1952-1953 — 189
    The group was composed of representatives from the House's four "youngest" clubs. Includes records of staff meetings to evaluate council work.

Group Work Records: Junior Panthers, George Rosenblum (Leader), 1952-1953 — 190
    Boys, 10-11 years.

Group Work Records: Newspaper Group, Wade Cooper (Leader), 1952 — 191
    Coed, senior (?) teens.

Folder Title and Description of Contents	Folder
Group Work Records: Panthers, V. Benjamin Louard (Leader), 1952-1953 Boys, 12-13 years.	192
Group Work Records: Playgroup, George Rosenblum (Leader), 1952-1953 Coed, pre-school children.	193
Group Work Records: Robin Hoods, Wade Cooper (Leader), 1952-1953 Boys, 7-8 years.	194
Group Work Records: Senior Lounge, George Rosenblum and Lamitsoi Bright-Davies (Leaders), 1952-1953 The workers supervised use of the senior teen lounge at the Community House.	195
Group Work Records: Silver Princesses, Lamitsoi Bright-Davies (Leader), 1952-1953 Girls, 7-8 years.	196
Group Work Records: Skulls, Robert Lanigan (Leader), 1952-1953 Teenage boys.	197
Group Work Records: Young Teen Council, Janet Toohy (Leader), 1952-1953 The council was composed of representatives of three teenage clubs.	198
Group Work Records: "Senior Play Party," Wade Cooper and Lamitsoi Bright-Davies (Leaders), 1952-1953 Coed, mixed ages.	199
Group Work Records: Senior Teen Planning Committee, V. Benjamin Louard (Leader), 1952-1953 Nina Ferrara became group leader in March, 1953.	200
Group Work Records: Newspaper Club, Nina Ferrara (Leader), 1953 Boys, 8-11 years.	201
Group Work Records: Cinderellas, Nina Ferrara (Leader), 1953 Two 8-year old girls who did "not seem to adjust to the membership in other already functioning groups."	202
Group Work Records: Dance Class, Nina Ferrara (Leader), 1953 Teenage boys.	203

FIVE TOWNS COMMUNITY HOUSE

Folder Title and Description of Contents	Folder
Group Work Records: Senior Club, Wade Cooper (Leader), 1953 Two reports re effort to organize group of teenage boys.	204
Group Work Records: Drama Group, Robert Lanigan (Leader), 1953 Young teen girls.	205
Group Work Records: Girls Friendship Group, Nina Ferrara (Leader), 1953 Girls, 10-12 years.	206
Group Work Records: Senior Lounge, Wade Cooper (Leader), 1953 Coed, senior teens.	207
Group Work Records: Boys, 8-9, Frank Abel (Leader), 1953.	208
Group Work Records: Cavalliers [sic], Stanley Ravine (Leader), 1953 Boys, 10-12 years.	209
Group Work Records: Golden Buttercups, Joan Weiss (Leader), 1953 Girls, 7-9 years.	210
Group Work Records: Lucky Girls, Nina Ferrara (Leader), 1953 Girls, 10-12 years.	211
Group Work Records: Playgroup, Mary Brown (Leader), 1953 Coed, 6-7 years.	212
Group Work Records: Afternoon Council, Roberta Chapman (Leader), 1953-1954 The council was composed of representatives of clubs which met in the afternoons. Includes memoranda from the leader to other staff members and evaluations of council work.	213
Group Work Records: Blackhawks, William Channel (Leader), 1953-1954 Boys, 17-19 years.	214
Group Work Records: Bonecrushers, William Channel (Leader), 1953-1954 Boys, 17-19 years.	215
Group Work Records: Debs, Shirley Pearse (Leader), 1953-1954 Girls, 13-17 years.	216
Group Work Records: Arts and Crafts Group, Frank Abel (Leader), 1953-1954 Coed, 10-12 years.	217

Folder Title and Description of Contents	Folder
Group Work Records: Golden Princesses, Cappy Delk (Leader), 1953-1954 Girls, 8-11 years. Cappy Delk replaced Shirley Pearse as group leader.	218
Group Work Records: Music Interest Group, Roberta Chapman (Leader), 1953-1954 The group evolved out of a coed senior-high group.	219
Group Work Records: Newspaper Club, Rita Walsh (Leader), 1953-1954 Coed, 12-14 years.	220
Group Work Records: Playgroup, Mary Brown (Leader), 1953-1954 Coed, 6-8 years.	221
Group Work Records: Silver Angels, Rita Walsh (Leader), 1953-1954 Girls, 7-9 years.	222
Group Work Records: Sub-debs, Nina Ferrara (Leader), 1953-1954 Girls, 10-12 years. The group began as a coed one.	223
Group Work Records: Young Teens Lounge and Dance Group, Rita Walsh (Leader), 1953-1954 Coed, 12-15 years.	224
Group Work Records: Tonettes, Karl Blumenkranz (Leader), 1953-1954 "Pre-instrumental" music group, coed, 8-12 years.	225
Group Work Records: Senior Teen Newspaper Club, Alice Suzuki (Leader), 1953-1954 Coed, 14-17 years.	226
Group Work Records: Dance Classes, Sol Froshnider (Leader), 1954 The leader taught dancing to three groups of teenage boys, the El Diablos, Independents, and Scorpions.	227
Group Work Records: Scorpions, Nina Ferrara and Tom Ferrara (Leaders), 1954 Boys, 15-17 years.	228
Group Work Records: Senior Boys-Workout Room, Donald Mitchell (Leader), 1954.	229
Group Work Records: Junior Panthers, Donald Mitchell (Leader), 1954 Boys, 10-12 years.	230

FIVE TOWNS COMMUNITY HOUSE

Folder Title and Description of Contents	Folder
Group Work Records: Knights, Donald Mitchell (Leader), 1954 Boys, 10-12 years.	231
Group Work Records: Vampires, Donald Mitchell (Leader), 1954 Boys, 12-15 years.	232
Group Work Records: Camp Scholarship Committee, William Channel (Leader), 1954 The committee sponsored a carnival to obtain money for summer camp "scholarships."	233
Group Work Records: Senior Teen Council, Shirley Pearse (Leader), 1954 The council was composed of representatives of teen groups.	234
Group Work Records: Young Chicks, Cappy Delk (Leader), 1954 Girls, 12-13 years.	235
Group Work Records: Senior Lounge, Donald Mitchell (Leader), 1954 Teenage, coed.	236
Group Work Records: Knights, Attilio Busillo (Leader), 1954 Boys, 10-12 years.	237
Group Work Records: Arts and Crafts, Frank Abel (Leader), 1954-1955 Mixed attendance.	238
Group Work Records: Boys, 8-9, John Garra (Leader), 1954-1955.	239
Group Work Records: Les Debutants (Debs), Marie Russo (Leader), 1954-1955 Senior teen girls.	240
Group Work Records: Golden Princesses, Marie Russo (Leader), 1954-1955 Girls, 7-8 years.	241
Group Work Records: Panthers, Donald Mitchell (Leader), 1954 Young teen boys.	242
Group Work Records: Polly Pigtails, Nina Ferrara (Leader), 1954-1955 Girls, 8-9 years.	243

FIVE TOWNS COMMUNITY HOUSE

Folder Title and Description of Contents	Folder
Group Work Records: "Y-Teen Newspaper Club," John Garra (Leader), 1954-1955 Nina Ferrara took over group leadership in February, 1955.	244
Group Work Records: Les Femmes, Mary Brown (Leader), 1954-1955 Adult women.	245
Group Work Records: Playgroup, Mary Brown (Leader), 1954-1955 Coed, children.	246
Group Work Records: Shop Group, Frank Abel (Leader), 1954-1955 Girls, 7-9 years.	247
Group Work Records: Silver Stars, Nina Ferrara (Leader), 1954-1955 Girls, 10-12 years.	248
Group Work Records: After-school Committee, Cappy Delk (Leader), 1954-1955 Coed, 7-12 years.	249
Group Work Records: Senior Newspaper Group, Cappy Delk (Leader), 1954-1955 Coed, senior teens.	250
Group Work Records: Senior Teen Planning Committee, Nina Ferrara (Leader), 1954-1955 Coed.	251
Group Work Records: Black Shields, Sol Levine (Leader), 1955 Boys, 8-9 years.	252
Group Work Records: Dancing Class, Sol Levine (Leader), 1955 Coed, 10-12 years.	253
Group Work Records: Panthers, Sol Levine (Leader), 1955 Young teen (?) boys.	254
Group Work Records: Boys, 10-12, Sol Levine (Leader), 1955.	255
Group Work Records: Diplomats, Nina Ferrara (Leader), 1955 Senior teen girls.	256
Group Work Records: Senior Council, Nina Ferrara (Leader), 1955 Coed, senior teens. The council was composed of representatives of teen clubs.	257

FIVE TOWNS COMMUNITY HOUSE

Folder Title and Description of Contents	Folder
Group Work Records: Senior Lounge and Extension Lounge, P. Wilcox (Leader), 1956-1957 Coed, senior teens.	258
Group Work Records: Be-bops, Lois Shein (Leader), 1957 Girls, 10-12 years.	259
Group Work Records: El Dorados, Norman Abzug (Leader), 1957 Boys, 10-12 years.	260
Group Work Records: Stallions, Attilio Busillo (Leader), 1957 Boys, 8-9 years.	261
Group Work Records: Summer Camp--Swimming, Robert Kaplan (Leader), 1957 Coed, mixed ages.	262
Group Work Records: Verdettes, Thelma Miller (Leader), 1957 Girls, 8-9.	263
Group Work Records: Dominoes, Nancy Ewart (Leader), 1957-1958 Teenage girls.	264
Group Work Records: Jaguars, Junious Watford (Leader), 1957-1958 Boys, 10-11 years.	265
Group Work Records: Les Morroccos, Patricia Turrini (Leader), 1957-1958 Girls, 15-17 years. Patricia Turrini replaced Ann Selter in February, 1958.	266
Group Work Records: Mouseketeers, Ann Selter (Leader), 1957-1958 Girls, 8-9 years.	267
Group Work Records: Music Groups, David Simon (Leader), 1957-1958 Records of work with "Adventures with Music" and "Fun with Music" groups.	268
Group Work Records: Senior Teen Council, Attilio Busillo (Leader), 1957-1958 The council was composed of representatives of teenage groups within the House.	269
Group Work Records: Senior Teen Lounge, Anthony DeBello (Leader), 1957-1958 Coed.	270

Folder Title and Description of Contents	Folder
Group Work Records: Wildcats, Attilio Basillo (Leader), 1957-1958 Young teen (?) boys.	271
Group Work Records: Zorros, Anthony DeBello (Leader), 1957-1958 Boys, 7-9 years.	272
Group Work Records: After-school Council, Nancy Ewart (Leader), 1957-1958 The council was composed of representatives of after-school clubs.	273
Group Work Records: Playgroup, Mary Brown (Leader), 1957-1958 Coed.	274
Group Work Records: Les Debutants (Debs), Bernice Heriot (Leader), 1958 Girls, 15-19 years.	275
Group Work Records: Arts and Crafts, Frank Abel (Leader), 1959 Coed, 6-12 years. Contains summary only.	276
Group Work Records: Playschool Group, John Canzanella (Leader), 1959 Boys, 10-12 years.	277
Group Work Records: Vikings, Daniel Gelfman (Leader), 1959 Boys, 8-9 years.	278
Group Work Records: Day Camp Group, Susan Leyner (Leader), 1959 Girls, 10-12 years.	279
Group Work Records: Day Camp Group, Mary Jane Lynch (Leader), 1959 Coed, 7 year-olds.	280
Group Work Records: Day Camp Group, Marlene Shauer (Leader), 1959 Coed, 6 year-olds.	281
Group Work Records: Day Camp Playgroup, Barbara Zenn (Leader), 1959 Girls, 8-9 years.	282
Group Work Records: Playschool and Day Camp, 1960 Reports by Martha Benson, Ted Giles, and Auma Metz.	283
Group Work Records: Beatniks, Dolores Wallace (Leader), 1960 Girls, 10-12 years.	284

Folder Title and Description of Contents	Folder
Group Work Records: Beatniks, Marilyn Ritter (Leader), 1960 Girls, 10-12 years.	285
Group Work Records: Boys, 8-9, Fred Barbara (Leader), 1960-1961.	286
Group Work Records: Boys, 10-12, Barry Rubenstein (Leader), 1960.	287
Group Work Records: Coed, 6-7, Elleves Inabinet (Leader), 1960-1961.	288
Group Work Records: Les Femmes Fatales, Elleves Inabinet (Leader), 1960-1961 Girls, 15-18 years.	289
Group Work Records: Girls, 8-9, Linda Davis (Leader), 1960-1961.	290
Group Work Records: Playgroup, Beatrice Arend (Leader), 1960-1961 Coed, 6-7 years.	291
Group Work Records: Playgroup, Elaine Forrest (Leader), 1960-1961 Coed, 6-7 years.	292
Group Work Records: Playgroup, Betty Urbanik (Leader), 1960-1961 Coed, 6-7 years.	293
Group Work Records: Senior Lounge, Fred Barbara (Leader), 1960-1961 Coed, teens.	294
Group Work Records: Top Hats, Lynne Levy (Leader), 1960-1961 Young teen girls.	295
Group Work Records: Young Teens, Fred Barbara and Elleves Inabinet (Leaders), 1960 Boys.	296
Group Work Records: Young Teens, Romi Welt (Leader), 1960-1961 Coed.	297
Group Work Records: Young Teens, Susan Shershoff (Leader), 1960-1961 A girls group was formed from the original coed one.	298
Group Work Records: Young Teens, Rudy Kemmer (Leader), 1960-1961 Boys.	299

Folder Title and Description of Contents	Folder
Group Work Records: Undergraduate Volunteer Reports, 1960-1961.	300
Group Work Records: Boys, 10-12, Hyman Pater (Leader), 1960.	301
Group Work Records: Arts and Crafts Group, Ellen Lembo (Leader), 1960-1961 Coed, young teens.	302
Group Work Records: Cavaliers, Fred Barbara (Leader), 1960-1961 Boys, 14-15 years.	303
Group Work Records: Senior Teen Council, Lawrence Shulman (Leader), 1960-1961 The council was composed of representatives of House teen groups.	304
Group Work Records: Youth Council, Lawrence Shulman (Leader), 1960-1961 The council was composed of representatives from Five Towns youth groups.	305
Group Work Records: Youth for Better Understanding, Lawrence Shulman (Leader), 1960-1961 Coed, teenagers. Includes material re the group's receipt of an award from Parent's Magazine.	306
Group Work Records: Lords, Gus Campbell (Leader), 1961 Boys, 15-18 years.	307
Group Work Records: Boys, 8-9, Gerri Cohn (Leader), 1961.	308
Group Work Records: L'Esquires, Steve Bromfield (Leader), 1961 Boys, 13-16 years.	309
Group Work Records: Girls, 7-9, Harriet Lewis (Leader), 1961.	310
Group Work Records: Girls, 10-12, Frances Miller (Leader), 1961.	311
Group Work Records: Kings, Carol Sommer and Frank Germano (Leaders), 1961 Boys, 10-12 years.	312
Group Work Records: Royal Counts, Gus Campbell (Leader), 1961 Coed.	313

Folder Title and Description of Contents	Folder
Group Work Records: Senior Teen Lounge, Steve Bromfield (Leader), 1961 Coed.	314
Group Work Records: Untouchables, Steve Bromfield (Leader), 1961 Boys, 10-12 years.	315
Group Work Records: Arts and Crafts, Evelyn Duffy (Assistant), 1961 Coed, 10-12 years.	316
Group Work Records: Boys, 8-9, Barry Rubenstein (Leader), 1961.	317
Group Work Records: Homemaking Club, Lila Gordon (Leader), 1961 Girls, 9-12 years.	318
Group Work Records: Blue Moons, Margery Henderson (Leader), 1961 Girls, 8-9 years.	319
Group Work Records: Bucaneers [sic] Paul Schwartz (Leader), 1961 Boys, 8-9 years.	320
Group Work Records: Diamonds, Jane Gilbert (Leader), 1961 Girls, 8-9 years.	321
Group Work Records: 6-7 year-olds, Carol Schneider (Leader), 1961.	322
Group Work Records: Untouchables, Hilliary Hatchett (Leader), 1961 Boys, 10-12 years.	323
Group Work Records: Bucanettes [sic], Barbara Selle Parker (Leader), 1961-1962 Girls, 12-13 years.	324
Group Work Records: Esquires, Thomas Oellerich (Leader), 1961 Young teen boys.	325
Group Work Records: G. O. Dandees, Marcia Levinson (Leader), 1961-1962 Girls, 10-12 years.	326
Group Work Records: Golden Eagles, Richard Hennessy (Leader), 1961-1962 Boys, 8-9 years.	327

Folder Title and Description of Contents	Folder
Group Work Records: After-school Playgroup, Barbara Selle Parker (Leader), 1961-1962 Coed, 6-7 years.	328
Group Work Records: Twisters, Linda Davis (Leader), 1961-1962 Girls, 9-10 years.	329
Group Work Records: Victorians, Esther Gropper (Leader), 1961-1962 Young teen girls. Esther Gropper was replaced during the year by a person whose identity cannot be determined from the records.	330
Group Work Records: Reports to Supervisor, 1961-1962 Reports of undergraduate group work assistants to Dominick Minatti.	331
Group Work Records: Conservative Counts, Richard Hennessy (Leader), 1961-1962 Boys, 13-15 years.	332
Group Work Records: Effrons, Barbara Selle Parker (Leader), 1961-1962 Girls, 13-16 years.	333
Group Work Records: Gladiators, Dominick Minotti (Leader), 1961-1962 Boys, 10-12 years.	334
Group Work Records: "Italian Group," Diana Robbins and Deborah Lewittes (Leaders), 1962 Teenage girls who were daughters of recent immigrants.	335
Group Work Records: Dominick Minotti, Evaluations of Senior Teens, 1962.	336
Group Work Records: Big Leaguers, Stephanie Talmud (Leader), 1962 Coed, 6-7 years.	337
Group Work Records: Hawaiian Watusis, Phyllis Brody (Leader), 1962 Girls, 10-12 years.	338
Group Work Records: Knights of the Round Table, Walker Brown (Leader), 1962 Boys, 10-12 years.	339
Group Work Records: Nightingales, Jane Gilbert (Leader), 1962 Girls, 8-9 years.	340

Folder Title and Description of Contents	Folder
Group Work Records: Vikings, Paul Schwartz (Leader), 1962.	341
Group Work Records: Angels from Heaven, Nancy Dorn (Leader), 1962-1963 Girls, 11-13 years.	342
Group Work Records: Bucanettes [sic], Mildred Kaufman (Leader), 1962-1963 Girls, 13 years.	343
Group Work Records: Conservative Counts, Lou Stovell (Leader), 1962-1963 Teenage boys.	344
Group Work Records: Cooking Group, Merrill Tribble (Leader), 1962-1963 Boys, 8-9 years. Tribble replaced Cecile Rosenfeld and Rae Chemers in March, 1963.	345
Group Work Records: Drama Group, Linda Boy (Leader), 1962 Girls, 10-12 years.	346
Group Work Records: Top Hats, Lynne Levy (Leader), 1960-1961 Young teen girls.	347
Group Work Records: "Immigrant Group," Mildred Kaufman (Leader), 1962-1963 The "group" consisted of one Italian-American teenage girl.	348
Group Work Records: Jetsons, Lou Stovell (Leader), 1962-1963 Boys, 9-13 years.	349
Group Work Records: Newspaper Club, Lou Stovell (Leader), 1962-1963 Coed, teenagers.	350
Group Work Records: Purple Gang, Mildred Kaufman (Leader), 1962-1963 Girls, 10-12 years.	351
Group Work Records: Imperial Gents and Debs, Lou Stovell (Leader), 1962-1963 Senior teens. The group was formed by a merger of the Effrons and the Imperial Gents.	352
Group Work Records: Water Buffaloes, Lou Stovell (Leader), 1962-1963 Boys, 8-9 years.	353

FIVE TOWNS COMMUNITY HOUSE

Folder Title and Description of Contents	Folder
Group Work Records: Arts and Crafts Group, Frank Abel (Leader), 1962-1963 Coed, 6-7, 8-9, and 10-12 years.	354
Group Work Records: Travel Club, Mildred Kaufman (Leader), 1963 Coed, young teens.	355
Group Work Records: Girls, 8-9, Evelyn Offenbacher (Leader), 1962-1963 (?).	356
Group Work Records: Angels, Mildred Jackson (Leader), 1963 Girls, 10-12 years.	357
Group Work Records: Falcons, Lou Stovell (Leader), 1963 Boys, 10-13 years.	358
Group Work Records: Jaguars, Joseph Conly (Leader), 1963 Boys, 8-9 years.	359
Group Work Records: Peppermint Pioneers, Stephanie Talmud (Leader), 1963 Coed, 6-7 years.	360
Group Work Records: Twinkle Toes, Evelyn Offenbacher (Leader), 1963 Girls, 8-9 years.	361
Group Work Records: Cassandras, Bernice Heriot (Leader), 1963-1964 Teenage girls.	362
Group Work Records: Playgroups, Bernice Heriot (Leader), 1963-1964 Coed, 6-8 years (?).	363
Group Work Records: Young Teen Photography Group, William Cosenza (Leader), 1963-1964 Boys.	364
Group Work Records: Bodybuilding Interest Group, Winston Schepps (Leader), 1963-1964 Boys, 15-18 years.	365
Group Work Records: Boys, 8-9, Donald Nelson (Leader), 1963-1964.	366
Group Work Records: Cooking Group, Donald Nelson (Leader), 1963 Boys, 8-9 years (?).	367
Group Work Records: Dr. Kildares, Judy Zipser (Leader), 1963-1964 Girls, 8-10 years.	368

Folder Title and Description of Contents	Folder
Group Work Records: Hoods, Winston Schepps (Leader), 1963-1964 Boys, 10-13 years.	369-370
Group Work Records: Imperials, Lou Stovell (Leader), 1963-1964 Senior teen boys.	371
Group Work Records: Photography Club, Merrill Tribble (Leader), 1963 Boys.	372
Group Work Records: Sloppy Gents, Donald Nelson (Leader), 1963-1964 Young teen boys.	373
Group Work Records: Superiors, Winston Schepps (Leader), 1963-1964 Senior teen boys.	374
Group Work Records: Vettes, Winston Schepps (Leader), 1963-1964 Boys, 10-13 years.	375
Group Work Records: Viennettes, Betty Adler (Leader), 1963-1964 Young teen girls.	376
Group Work Records: Falcons, Lou Stovell (Leader), 1963-1964 Boys, 10-13 years.	377
Group Work Records: Senior Citizens, Winston Schepps (Leader), 1963-1964.	378
Group Work Records: Cooking Group, Merrill Tribble (Leader), 1964 Boys, 11-12 years.	379
Group Work Records: Jaguars, Russell Gilbert (Leader), 1964 Boys, 8-10 years.	380
Group Work Records: Lollipops, Marion Collins (Leader), 1964 Girls, 8-10 years.	381
Group Work Records: Skyrockets, Bernice Heriot (Leader), 1964 Coed, 6-8 years.	382
Group Work Records: Supervisory Reports, Sally Story, 1947.	383

Folder Title and Description of Contents	Folder
Group Work Records: Supervisory Reports, Jean Ober, 1951-1952.	384
Group Work Records: Supervisory Reports, Bernice Goodman, 1951.	385
Group Work Records: Supervisory Reports, Jean Ober, 1952.	386
Group Work Records: Supervisory Reports, Bernice Goodman, 1952.	387
Group Work Records: Supervisory Reports, Lamitsoi Bright-Davies, 1952-1953.	388
Group Work Records: Supervisory Reports, Betty Huff, 1952.	389-390
Group Work Records: Supervisory Reports, V. Benjamin Louard, 1952-1953.	391
Group Work Records: Supervisory Reports, George Rosenblum, 1952-1953.	392
Group Work Records: Supervisory Reports, Lamitsoi Bright-Davies, 1952-1953.	393
Group Work Records: Supervisory Reports, Nina Ferrara, 1953.	394-397
Group Work Records: Supervisory Reports, Robert Lanigan, 1953.	398
Group Work Records: Supervisory Reports, Mary Brown, 1953-1954.	399
Group Work Records: Supervisory Reports, Roberta Chapman, 1953-1954.	400
Group Work Records: Supervisory Reports, Nina Ferrara, 1953-1954.	401-404
Group Work Records: Supervisory Reports, Shirley Pearse, 1953.	405
Group Work Records: Supervisory Reports, Roberta Chapman, 1954.	406
Group Work Records: Supervisory Reports, Nina Ferrara, 1954.	407
Group Work Records: Supervisory Reports, Roberta Chapman, 1954.	408
Group Work Records: Supervisory Reports, George Lockhart, 1954-1955.	409

FIVE TOWNS COMMUNITY HOUSE

Folder Title and Description of Contents	Folder
Group Work Records: Supervisory Reports, Shirley Pearse, 1954.	410
Group Work Records: Supervisory Reports, Nina Ferrara, 1954.	411
Group Work Records: Supervisory Reports, Cappy Delk, 1954-1955.	412
Group Work Records: Supervisory Reports, Nina Ferrara, 1954.	413-416
Group Work Records: Supervisory Reports, George Lockhart, 1954-1955.	417
Group Work Records: Supervisory Reports, Nina Ferrara, 1954-1955.	418-421
Group Work Records: Supervisory Reports, Cappy Delk, 1955.	422
Group Work Records: Supervisory Reports, Nina Ferrara, 1955.	423-424
Group Work Records: Supervisory Reports, Attilio Busillo, 1957.	425
Group Work Records: Supervisor's Records, V. Benjamin Louard, 1957.	426
Group Work Records: Supervisory Reports, Thelma Miller, 1957.	427
Group Work Records: Supervisory Reports, Lois Shein, 1957.	428
Group Work Records: Supervisory Reports, Noda Bettis, 1957-1958.	429
Group Work Records: Supervisory Reports, Attilio Busillo, 1957.	430
Group Work Records: Supervisory Reports, Nancy Ewart, 1957-1958.	431
Group Work Records: Supervisory Reports, V. Benjamin Louard, 1959.	432
Group Work Records: Supervisory Reports, V. Benjamin Louard, 1960.	433
Group Work Records: Supervisory Records, Dominick Minotti, 1960.	434
Group Work Records: Supervisory Reports, Lawrence Shulman, 1960-1961.	435
Group Work Records: Supervisory Reports, Dominick Minotti, 1961.	436

FIVE TOWNS COMMUNITY HOUSE

Folder Title and Description of Contents	Folder
Group Work Records: Observation Reports, 1961-1964 Reports of undergraduate students observing group work at the Community House.	437-439
Group Work Records: Alice Suzuki, Papers, 1948-1953 Includes supervisory reports, group work records, evaluations of House members, program outlines, etc.	440
American Field Service (AFS), 1962 AFS brochures and bylaws of the Lawrence chapter of the AFS.	441
American Friends Service Committee, 1964 Correspondence, notes, brochures, and pamphlets.	442
Boy Scouts of America, 1946-1948, 1959 Charters and brief correspondence.	443
National Association of Jewish Center Workers, 1962 Correspondence and membership lists.	444
National Conference of Christians and Jews, ca. 1953-1957 Correspondence, papers, and publications of the Conference.	445
National Conference on Social Welfare, 1948-1957 Papers concerning Community House participation in the Conference's annual forum.	446
National Council of Jewish Women, 1951-1963 Correspondence and papers reflecting use of volunteers by private welfare organizations.	447
National Federation of Settlements and Neighborhood Centers, Annual Meetings, 1955-1962 Correspondence, minutes, and bylaws.	448
National Federation of Settlements and Neighborhood Centers, Board of Directors, 1955-1963 Correspondence, minutes, memoranda, and board manual.	449
National Federation of Settlements and Neighborhood Centers, Correspondence, 1951-1964 Correspondence showing the relation of the Community House to the parent NFS.	450
National Federation of Settlements and Neighborhood Centers, Notices, Reports, and Memoranda, 1949-1964 Material on field work placement of social work graduate students, Federation finance, institutes and conferences, national legislation, personnel practices, etc.	451-452

Folder Title and Description of Contents	Folder
National Federation of Settlements and Neighborhood Centers, Publications, 1953-1960 NFS annual reports and directories of member settlement houses.	453
National Health and Welfare Retirement Association, 1962-1963 Correspondence item and "Retirement Plan Bulletin."	454
Play Schools Association, 1956-1959 Papers concerning the relation of the House to the Association.	455
United Neighborhood Houses of New York, Annual Fall Conference, 1954-1963 Programs, memoranda, and related papers.	456
United Neighborhood Houses of New York, Board of Directors, Meetings, 1957-1964 Correspondence, agenda, minutes, and memoranda.	457-458
United Neighborhood Houses of New York, Correspondence, 1956-1963.	459
United Neighborhood Houses of New York, Fund-raising, 1956-1965 Correspondence and papers.	460
United Neighborhood Houses of New York, Fund-raising Studies, 1947, 1958 Studies of potential methods of settlement fund-raising.	461
United Neighborhood Houses of New York, Notices, Reports, and Memoranda, 1936-1964 Material on settlement programs, social action, legislation, etc.	462-464
Community Council of Greater New York, 1958-1959 Correspondence; minutes; and material on intercultural and interracial programming and on the aging.	465
Welfare Council of New York City, 1936-1939 Memoranda and agenda; material on WPA workers and on boys and girls work.	466
Health and Welfare Council of Nassau County, 1949-1963 Formerly the Nassau County Council of Social Agencies. Correspondence, minutes, reports, statement of purpose, and list of member agencies. Includes a study of the need for health and welfare services, especially services to children, in Nassau County.	467-468

Folder Title and Description of Contents	Folder
Legal Aid Society of Nassau County, 1951 Notice of formation of the Society.	469
Nassau County Board of Elections, 1952-1964 Correspondence and papers concerning use of the Community House as a polling place.	470
Nassau County Department of Public Health, 1956-1957 Correspondence and notice.	471
Nassau County Department of Public Welfare, Annual Report, 1956.	472
Nassau County Police Department, 1955-1960 Correspondence re juvenile delinquency, "gang wars," and police and settlement interaction.	473
Youth Services Committee of Nassau County, 1963-1965 Correspondence and reports to the Committee from the Community House on youth guidance and employment services, description of House programs, analyses of housing and education in the Five Towns area, and suggestions for expansion of youth programs.	474
Five Towns Community Chest-United Fund, 1934-1965 While the relation of the Community Chest to the United Fund is not clear, apparently from 1960 c funds were raised for the Chest through the United Fund Campaign. Correspondence and papers re community chest work, purpose, finance, etc.	475-476
Five Towns Community Council, 1950-1958, 1964-1965 Formerly the Five Towns Council of Social Agencies. Correspondence, minutes, bylaws, and list of Five Towns clubs and organizations (1965). The Council served as a planning and coordinating body for Five Towns community health and welfare services.	477-478
Five Towns Community Council, Committee on Community-Wide Activities, 1956-1959 The committee sponsored the annual Five Towns Fair. Correspondence and clippings.	479
Five Towns Community Council, Executive Committee, 1954-1964 Correspondence; agenda; minutes; and lists of Council committees, individual and organization members, and executive committee members. Topics include recreation, housing, and community chest services.	480
Five Towns Community Council, Group Relations Committee, 1954-1963 Material re integration and religion in public schools.	481

Folder Title and Description of Contents	Folder
Five Towns Community Council, Mental Health Committee, 1958 Calendar of events sponsored by the committee and other routine materials.	482
Five Towns Community Council, Parks and Recreation Committee, 1949-1962 Correspondence, minutes of recreation leaders' training institute, and discussion of programs and purposes of the committee. Scattered material only after 1955.	483
Five Towns Family Service Association, 1946-1955 Formerly the Family Service Association of Lawrence. Correspondence and papers re joint (FSA-Community House) casework problems and services, and material on a proposed joint project involving casework and group work services.	484
Five Towns District Nursing Association, 1949-1962 Correspondence and annual reports.	485
Five Towns Golden Age Club, 1953-1963 Correspondence and material on activities for the elderly.	486
Five Towns Housing Committee, 1944 Resolution embodying aims and objectives of the committee.	487
Five Towns League of Women Voters, 1951-1958 Correspondence.	488
Five Towns Music and Art Foundation, 1957-1965 The Foundation sought "to supplement the existing creative and educational program" of the community and worked with the Community House in providing scholarships to House members. Includes correspondence with the Foundation and with scholarship recipients, Foundation reports, and programs. The House nominated the Foundation for the 1958 Lane Bryant annual award for volunteer community service.	489-490
Cedarhurst, Temple Beth El, 1950-1960 Brief correspondence which includes comments on changing nature of the Five Towns community.	491
Far Rockaway, South Shore Planned Parenthood Center, 1940-1960 Correspondence, pamphlets, and clippings.	492
Hempstead, Citizens Advisory Committee, 1962-1964 The committee was formed in response to an urban renewal project in the Inwood area of Hempstead. Primarily minutes of meetings of the committee.	493

FIVE TOWNS COMMUNITY HOUSE

Folder Title and Description of Contents	Folder
Hempstead Consultation Service, 1963-1965 The Consultation Service was a "comprehensive mental health facility." Includes "Fact Sheet of the Town of Hempstead."	494
Hewlett, Peninsula Child Guidance Center, 1957-1958 Minutes and papers of the professional advisory committee to the Center and a report, "A Clinical Demonstration of the Child Guidance Team."	495
Hewlett-Woodmere, Recreation Department, School District 14, 1952-1964 Correspondence, reports, memoranda, and clippings re recreation programs offered by the school district, and Community House participation in these.	496
Inwood Civic and Businessmen's Association, 1949-1964 Correspondence and papers re community affairs.	497
Inwood-Far Rockaway, National Association for the Advancement of Colored People (NAACP) Chapter, 1951-1962 Correspondence and papers re NAACP programs.	498
Lawrence, Peninsula Public Library, 1952-1955 Correspondence.	499
Union Free School District 15, 1946-1965 Correspondence, reports, and papers. Material dealing with relations between Community House and district, especially sharing of facilities. Includes material on racial integration.	500-501
Union Free School District 15, Central Council of Parent-Teacher Associations, 1947-1964 Correspondence, minutes, and papers. Includes material on recreation.	502
Vincent Zavatt, "Forty Years After: Experiences and Observations of an Immigrant from Southern Italy," 1955 New edition of a 1933 account.	503
Photographs, Miscellaneous, ca. 1933-1959 Photos of staff and members.	504-506
Publicity Photographs, Annual Meetings, 1954, 1956.	507
Publicity Photographs, Miscellaneous, 1951-1961.	508
Newspaper Clippings and Press Releases, 1910, 1951-1964.	509-512

LEGAL-SIZE FOLDERS

Folder Title and Description of Contents	Folder
Margaret Sage Industrial School, Program Reports, 1908-1909 Reports of sewing and industrial classes.	1
Margaret Sage Industrial School, Nassau Industrial School, Financial Statements, 1908-1917.	2
Five Towns Citizens Housing Council, 1956-1960 Minutes, agenda, and material describing committee programs.	3
Miscellaneous Studies, 1936-1963 Five Towns Community Chest study, 1936; survey and study of Negro life, 1938; guide for teachers on contributions of Negroes to American culture, 1963.	4

APPENDIX

The material listed below was removed from the Five Towns collection and placed in the Social Welfare Archives' ephemera file where it is held by publishing association or agency.

American Association of Group Workers, Chapter Development Committee. "Leadership Training Institutes," ca. 1949.

_____. Irving Miller, "A Critical Appraisal of Some Aspects of Social Group Work Theory and Practice," 1955.

AFL-CIO Community Service Activities. The Worker's Stake in Mental Health, 1959.

American Orthopsychiatric Association. Preliminary Program, 41st Annual Meeting, 1964.

Community Council of Greater New York (formerly the Welfare Council of New York City), Better Times, 1948-1964.

Five Towns Community Chest. Know Your 5 Towns, 1955.

Five Towns Community House (Nassau Industrial School), "Nassau Industrial School News," 1934-1939.

_____. "Newsletter," 1951-1962.

_____. "Playschool-Day Camp Manual," n.d.

Hamilton-Madison Settlement House, New York, New York. Mimeographed letter to the Commissioner of Internal Revenues, 1961.

Health and Welfare Council of Nassau County. "Selected General, Social and Economic Characteristics of Nassau County's Population in 1960: Part II," ca. 1961.

_____. A Survey of Research and Studies . . . Conducted by Public and Voluntary Institutions Engaged in Health and Welfare Services in Nassau County, 1956-1961, 1961.

_____. "A Follow-Up Survey of Research and Studies . . . Conducted by Institutions Engaged in Health and Welfare Services in Nassau County Newly in Process, Or Not Previously Reported, Since 1961," 1963.

Hudson Guild, New York, New York. "Newsletter," October, 1959.

Jewish Community Centers Association. JCCA Journal, 1964-1965.

Lawrence High School, Long Island, New York. Mental Pabulum, 1960.

Long Island Lighting Company. "Population Survey, 1960: Current Population Estimates for Nassau and Suffolk Counties," 1960.

Nassau County Department of Health. <u>Nassau Health</u>, 1958-1965.

Nassau County Department of Public Welfare. "Public Assistance in 1941: Fourth Annual Report of the Nassau County Department of Public Welfare," ca. 1942.

_____. "Child Welfare Services News Notes," Fall, 1964.

Nassau County Planning Commission. Maps of Nassau County, n.d.

_____. "Population Sixty: A Report on Population Based on the 1960 Federal Decennial Census," 1961.

_____. <u>Parks and Recreation</u>, 1964.

Nassau County Vocational Education and Extension Board. <u>A Plan to Improve Vocational and Special Education</u>, ca. 1964.

National Association for Mental Health. <u>Catalog of Selected Films for Mental Health Education</u>, 1959.

_____. <u>The National Association for Mental Health</u>, March, 1960.

_____. <u>List of Mental Health Publications and Audio-Visual Aids</u>, July, 1960.

_____. <u>Because You like People . . . Choose a Career in Mental Health</u>, 1960.

National Association of Social Workers. <u>NASW News</u>, 1958-1960.

_____. <u>Personnel Information</u>, 1959.

_____. Group Work Section. Questionnaire, ca. April, 1956.

_____. Group Work Section. "The Section at Work," 1956.

_____. "Goals of Public Social Policy," 1957.

National Association of Social Workers, Long Island Chapter. "Newsletter," 1956, 1959.

_____. Bylaws, Directory of Membership, and miscellaneous material, 1956-1960.

National Association of Social Workers, Nassau County Chapter. "Newsletter," 1964.

National Association of Social Workers, Nassau-Suffolk Chapter. "Newsletter," 1955-1957, and miscellaneous material, 1955-1958.

National Association of Social Workers, New York City Chapter. "Newsletter," 1955-1957, and miscellaneous material, 1955-1958.

National Association of Social Workers, New York City Chapter. Miscellaneous materials, 1955-1963.

National Committee on Employment of Youth. *Youth and Work*, 1959-1960.

National Conference on Social Welfare. *Program* for 84th Annual Forum, 1957.

National Federation of Settlements and Neighborhood Centers. *Round Table*, 1955-1965.

National Scholarship Service and Fund for Negro Students. *Annual Report, 1954-1955*, 1955.

National Social Welfare Assembly. "Residence Roundup: A Report on Recent Developments in Legal Residence Requirements for Health and Welfare Services," 1959.

National Urban League. "Year-End Report to Contributors," 1962.

New York City Youth Board. *Youth Board News*, 1956, 1962.

_____. "A Calendar of Summer Activities and Events for Young People in New York City," n.d.

New York State Education Department. *Intergroup Relations*, 1963.

New York State Welfare Conference. *Quarterly Bulletin*, 1964-1965.

Social Work Recruiting Center of Greater New York. "Careers in Social Work: 1963 Report, Summer Experience in Social Work," ca. 1963.

Soho Community House, Pittsburgh, Pennsylvania. "Annual Report," 1951, and miscellaneous materials, 1947-1949.

Travelers Aid Association of America. "Paper on Residence Laws," 1960.

United Neighborhood Houses of New York. *United Neighborhood Houses News*, 1959-1965.

World Federation for Mental Health. *World Federation for Mental Health*, 1960 (?).

_____. *World Mental Health Year: 1960*, 1960.

5

An Inventory of the Papers of Howard W. Hopkirk

PREPARED BY
Pamela J. Matson

SWB Hopkirk, Howard W. 1894-1963
H777
    Papers, 1927-1963

    8 folders

  Howard W. Hopkirk was born in Montrose, Iowa, on March 21, 1894. In 1920, he received a Bachelor of Arts from Reed College in Portland, Oregon. He also attended Union Theological Seminary from 1920 to 1923 and studied part time at the New York School of Social Work from 1922 to 1923. In 1919, Hopkirk was married to Ruth Hathaway.

  Within the profession of social work, Hopkirk concentrated on child welfare. From 1921 to 1934, he served as a consultant on child care institutions to the Child Welfare League of America, and from 1935 to 1939, he was the Superintendent of the Albany Home for Children. From 1940 to 1952, Hopkirk was on the staff of the Child Welfare League of America serving as Executive Director at intervals between 1940 and 1948 and as Senior Consultant from 1948 to 1952. From 1952 to 1959, he was Superintendent of the Louisville and Jefferson County Children's Home in Louisville, Kentucky. At the time of his death on May 16, 1963, Hopkirk was a planning consultant for children's welfare services in Corpus Christi, Texas.

  According to Who's Who in America, 1962-1963, Hopkirk was, during his lifetime, a member of the Department of Social Welfare of the National Council of Churches, the National Association of Social Workers, and the National Arts Club.

  The Social Welfare History Archives Center holds five inches of the Hopkirk Papers in eight folders arranged chronologically within each folder. The collection reveals Hopkirk's interest in the welfare of children. Prominent concerns reflected in his papers are standards in child care, church-related child welfare programs, and the relative merits of placing children in institutions with cottage mothers supervising them versus providing foster homes, where children would probably receive more individual attention. Unfortunately, there are no personal papers which might reflect Hopkirk's relationships with family and colleagues.

  A folder inventory follows the partial subject listings.

PARTIAL SUBJECT INVENTORY

The Partial Subject Inventory is a guide, not an index to prominent topics in the collection.

ALBANY HOME FOR CHILDREN, NEW YORK
    Folder 4

CARSTENS, CHRISTIAN C., EULOGY ON
    Folder 4

CHILD WELFARE
  EFFECT OF DEPRESSION
    Folder 4
  EFFECT OF WORLD WAR II
    Folder 5
  INSTITUTIONS
    Folder 2-5
  STANDARDS
    Folders 2-6

CHILD WELFARE LEAGUE OF AMERICA
    Folders 5-6

CHILDREN
    Folders 2-7

CHURCH-RELATED CHILD WELFARE
    Folders 2-6

COTTAGE MOTHERS
    Folders 3,6

FOSTER HOME CARE
    Folders 3-5

JUVENILE DELINQUENCY
    Folder 5

NEGRO CHILDREN
    Folder 5,6

PRESBYTERIAN ORPHANAGES IN THE SOUTH
    Folder 2

STEP-PARENTS
    Folder 7

FOLDER INVENTORY

Folder Title and Description of Contents	Folder
Correspondence and Papers, 1928-1962. Of particular interest are letters from various ministers to the Child Welfare League of America praising Hopkirk's work with Protestant Churches in child welfare programs. Also discussed in the folder are standards in institution personnel, although the material is very scattered.	1
Study of Southern Presbyterian Orphanages, 1927. Evaluation of Southern Presbyterian Orphanages for Henry H. Sweets, Head of the Department of Christian Education of the Presbyterian Church. Subjects include standards in child care, physical facilities of orphanages, need for professional social workers in institutions, and church involvement in child care institutions.	2
Papers, Articles, and Speeches, n.d.-1929. Standards in child care, problems of homeless children, personnel in child care institutions - recruiting, education, and standards; cooperation between the Child Welfare League of America and the Federal Council of Churches of Christ in America in subsidizing League programs, child welfare programs of churches and fraternal groups, over-specialization in institutions, discipline, and foster home care versus institutional care for children.	3
Papers, Articles, and Speeches, 1930-1939. Church-related child welfare programs, child care institutions, standards in child care, dependent children, financing child care programs, effect of the depression on child welfare programs, Albany Home for Children, foster home care, and a memorial address for Christian C. Carstens, Director of the Child Welfare League.	4
Papers, Articles, and Speeches, 1940-1948. Child Welfare League of America, overview of child welfare programs in the United States, effect of World War II on child welfare, juvenile delinquency, Negro children, child care institutions, foster home care, post-war needs of child welfare, and federal reorganization of welfare services.	5

Folder Title and Description of Contents	Folder
Papers, Articles, and Speeches, 1949-1959. Institution personnel - requirements, salaries, and standards; professionalization of church-related child care, family dynamics, Negro children, and evaluation of children's institutions.	6
Papers, Articles, and Speeches, 1960-1962. Homemaker service, psychiatric group therapy, and stepparents.	7
Hopkirk, Ruth, Correspondence, 1963. Mrs. Hopkirk circulated as a Christmas message in 1963 some thoughts taken from Hopkirk's article, "A Priceless Christmas Gift" which was published in the Child Welfare League of America Bulletin, December, 1942.	8

6

An Inventory of the Papers of the International Conference of Social Work

PREPARED BY
Nancy M. Wiggins

SWD8   International Conference of Social Work

          Papers, 1932-1964

          122 folders

The International Conference of Social Work (ICSW) is a permanent world organization for individuals and agencies concerned with meeting the social welfare needs of people. It provides an international forum for the discussion of social welfare and related issues. Nongovernmental, nonpolitical, and nonsectarian, ICSW neither takes positions on issues, nor does it have a social action function.

At the 50th National Conference of Social Work in Washington, D. C., 1923, Dr. Rene Sand, a guest from Belgium, suggested that similar conferences be organized on an international basis. His proposal was favorably received by the National Conference of Social Work (NCSW), the American Association of Social Workers, and a number of American foundations which provided financial support. In 1927 an international organization committee was organized under the chairmanship of Dr. Alice Masarykova, and national committees were formed.

The first International Conference was held in Paris in 1928, and at this Conference the organization committee was transformed into a Permanent Committee, and national committees were urged to establish themselves on a permanent basis. Succeeding Conferences were held in Frankfurt, Germany in 1932 and London, England in 1936. The fourth conference, planned for Brussels in 1940, was abandoned due to the war.

The preparatory work of the Conference was carried out by an Executive Board in conjunction with national committees, which represented the organizations and workers in the cooperating countries. The programs of each of the Conferences were the subject of careful study and preparation by these national committees, which provided both organizations and individual social workers in their respective countries with the opportunity of contributing to the forum of discussion at the quadrennial meetings.

The activities of the International Conference were of necessity suspended during the war, but after 1945 contacts were reestablished by leaders in various countries, and a Special Conference was held in Brussels in August, 1946 under the presidency of Dr. Rene Sand. Plans for reorganizing the International Conference were formulated and a provisional executive board was appointed. At an interim meeting held at the Hague in 1947, a new constitution was drafted and specific plans for the 4th International Conference were approved.

The 4th International Conference was held in conjunction with the National Conference of Social Work (USA) in Atlantic City, New Jersey, April, 1948. Successive conferences, their locations and dates were:

          5th   Paris, France   1950
          6th   Madras, India   1952
          7th   Toronto, Canada   1954

8th	Munich, Germany	1956
9th	Tokyo, Japan	1958
10th	Rome, Italy	1961
11th	Petropolis, Brazil	1962
12th	Athens, Greece	1964
13th	Washington, D. C.	1966

Since the war the Conference has attempted to fulfill a more permanent function in social work by supplying a means of consultation and study between workers in different countries. The International Conference has consultative status with the UN, UNICEF, UNESCO, WHO, International Labor Office, the Organization of American States, and the Council of Europe. Other activities of the conference include: strengthening existing national committees and establishing new ones in other countries, particularly the less developed countries; sponsoring social welfare study tours in connection with biennial meetings; publishing the proceedings of the biennial meetings and also a quarterly journal, International Social Work, in cooperation with the International Association of Schools of Social Work and the International Federation of Social Workers; and fund-raising and assisting the national committees to meet their financial commitments to the International Conference.

The ICSW papers, as received at the Social Welfare History Archives Center from the National Conference on Social Welfare in April, 1967, appear to be incomplete records when compared to the file classification schedule which was also received from the NCSW. Before shipment to the Archives Center, much of the material was sent from New York to Columbus, and in some cases, the original file folders were not retained nor were the contents of packages of documents labeled. When possible, original filing units have been retained; in other instances an attempt has been made to retrieve scattered documents and arrange them chronologically by topic.

Because of the dual functions performed by some ICSW officials within both the International Conference and the U. S. Committee of the ICSW, and due to the location of the ICSW secretariat in the United States, the papers of both organizations, as received at the Archives Center from the NCSW, were sometimes mixed. An attempt has been made to separate the correspondence of individuals which reflects their functions in the ICSW from that reflecting their responsibilities within the U. S. Committee. Material supplementing this collection may be found in the papers of the U. S. Committee of the ICSW which are also held by the University of Minnesota Social Welfare History Archives Center.

The ICSW proceedings are available on microfilm at the Minnesota Social Welfare History Archives Center. The bound proceedings are held by the NCSW.

PARTIAL SUBJECT INVENTORY

ADOPTIONS. INTER-COUNTRY
    Folder 108

ATLANTIC CITY CONFERENCE, 1948
    Folders 9, 36

CANADIAN NATIONAL COMMITTEE, REORGANIZATION OF
    Folder 43

CASEWORK
    Folder 32

CHILDREN
    Folders 80-81, 112, 115

COMMUNITY DEVELOPMENT
    Folders 55, 70, 74, 86-87

COUNCIL FOR TECHNICAL COOPERATION IN SOUTH AND SOUTH EAST ASIA
    Folder 59

CRIME PREVENTION
    Folder 87

DISCRIMINATION (RACIAL AND ETHNIC)
    Folder 72

EUROPEAN SOCIAL WORK, INTER-COUNTRY COOPERATION
    Folders 55, 61

FRANKFURT, GERMANY CONFERENCE, 1932
    Folder 4

FREEDOM FROM HUNGER CAMPAIGN
    Folder 79

GABRIEL, RALPH HENRY
    Folder 77

GENOCIDE
    Folder 93

INDUSTRIALIZATION
    Folder 45

HEALTH AGENCIES, VOLUNTARY
    Folder 24

HEALTH INSURANCE. CZECHOSLOVAKIA
    Folder 47

HOSPITALS' ROLE IN PUBLIC HEALTH PROGRAMS
    Folder 90

HOUSING
    Folders 86-87

INDIGENT FOREIGNERS (IN ALL COUNTRIES)
    Folder 68

INDUSTRIALIZATION
    Folders 10, 76

INTERNATIONAL CONFERENCES, WORK GROUP AND DISCUSSION GROUPS FOR
    Folder 119, 121

INTERNATIONAL FEDERATION OF SOCIAL WORKERS, 1950 REORGANIZATION
    Folder 104

KENDALL, KATHARINE A.
    Folders 20, 100

KOREAN WAR, UN PARTICIPATION IN
    Folder 69

LENROOT, KATHARINE F.
    Folder 112

LONDON, ENGLAND CONFERENCE, 1936
    Folder 4

MADRAS, INDIA CONFERENCE, 1952
    Folders 25, 48

MIGRANTS
    Folders 62, 95

MUNICH, GERMANY CONFERENCE, 1956
    Folders 10, 45, 54

MYRDAL, GUNNAR
    Folder 54

PERSONNEL SOCIAL WORK
    Folder 106

PREJUDICE
    Folder 72

PROSTITUTION
    Folder 68

PUBLIC HEALTH NURSES
    Folder 91

REFUGEES
    Folders 85, 95, 112

REHABILITATION OF HANDICAPPED PERSONS
    Folders 53, 97

REORGANIZATION OF ICSW, POST-WORLD WAR II
    Folders 1, 7-8, 26, 28, 33-34, 37, 56

REORGANIZATION OF ICSW, 1956
    Folder 105

ROME, ITALY CONFERENCE, 1961
    Folders 11-18

RURAL COMMUNITIES, SOCIAL WELFARE IN
    Folder 79

SOCIAL POLICY
    Folders 17, 23

SOCIAL SECURITY. CZECHOSLOVAKIA
    Folder 47

SOCIAL WORK EDUCATION
    Folders 20, 23, 49
  Admission Standards
    Folder 100

TECHNICAL ASSISTANCE PROGRAMS
    Folders 48, 78, 88

TOKYO, JAPAN CONFERENCE, 1958
    Folder 54

TORONTO, CANADA CONFERENCE, 1954
    Folders 22, 44

TRAINING OF WELFARE PERSONNEL
    Folders 86, 101

UNITED NATIONS
    Folders 5, 68-91

UNIVERSAL DECLARATION OF HUMAN RIGHTS
    Folder 72

WORLD HEALTH ORGANIZATION
    Folders 89-91

WORLD WAR II, SOCIAL WORK DURING
    Folder 100

INTERNATIONAL CONFERENCE OF SOCIAL WORK

FOLDER TITLE AND DESCRIPTION OF CONTENTS	FOLDER

Executive Committee, 1939-1954 — 1
   Correspondence, minutes, and reports. Includes documents from the December, 1937 meeting and records of the reorganization meeting, 1946.

Nominations Committee, 1948-1953 — 2
   Report and papers describing background and functions of the committee.

Permanent Committee, 1936 — 3
   Correspondence, 1936 committee membership list, and constitution.

Pre-War Conferences, 1932-1939 — 4
         Second Conference - Frankfurt, Germany, 1932
         Third Conference - London, England, 1936
   Correspondence, announcements, reports, and programs. Includes one document related to the Fourth Conference which was to have been held in Brussels, July, 1940, but was cancelled.

Subcommittee on Relationship of ICSW to United Nations, 1951 — 5
   Correspondence and minutes.

New York Office, 1952-1958 — 6
   Correspondence, budgets, wage scales, and insurance policy.

Postwar Reorganization, 1946-1948 — 7
   Includes suggested plans for reorganization of the ICSW and early drafts of the constitution approved by the Executive Committee in 1949.

Reorganization Meeting, Brussels, Belgium, 1946, 1945-1946 — 8
   Correspondence, minutes, and reports on changes in the fields of social work brought about by war and postwar conditions.

International Conference - Atlantic City, New Jersey - New York, New York, 1948, 1944-1948 — 9
   Correspondence, preparatory committee reports, delegation lists, and papers.

International Conference - Munich, 1956 — 10
   Articles on social problems and industrialization presented to the Conference.

International Conference - Rome, 1961 - Commissions, 1959-1961. — 11

International Conference - Rome, 1961 - Papers, 1956-1961 — 12
   Correspondence and programs.

International Conference - Rome, 1961 - Italian Committee, 1956-1961 — 13
   Correspondence and papers re conference arrangements made by the Italian national committee.

INTERNATIONAL CONFERENCE OF SOCIAL WORK

FOLDER TITLE AND DESCRIPTION OF CONTENTS	FOLDER

International Conference - Rome, 1961 - Pre-Conference Working Party, 1959-1961   14
    Correspondence and reports.

International Conference - Rome, 1961 - Proceedings, 1961-1964   15
    Correspondence re publication and distribution of the conference proceedings.

International Conference - Rome, 1961 - Program, 1959-1961   16
    Minutes, papers, and preliminary program.

International Conference - Rome, 1961 - Study Groups, 1959-1961   17
    Correspondence and group reports. Includes a paper on the social worker's role in social policy by Arthur Katz.

International Conference - Rome, 1961 - Study Tours, 1959-1961   18
    Correspondence, itineraries, promotional letters, and post-conference tour reports.

Correspondence - Affiliated Schools and Seminars for International Study and Training (ASSIST), 1951-1952   19
    Bylaws, correspondence, and minutes of the organizing committee of this non-profit travel cooperative.

Correspondence and Papers, General, 1944-1950   20
    Includes an article by Katharine Kendall on social work education and a paper by Hans Muthesius on "The Harmonization of Social Tasks of Industry, the State, and Voluntary Agencies."

Correspondence and Papers, General, 1951-1953.   21

Correspondence and Papers, General, 1954   22
    Bulk of the correspondence is related to Toronto Conference. An address to the Conference on self-help in modern society is included.

Correspondence and Papers, General, 1955-1956   23
    Includes a paper on social policy and social work education by Richard M. Titmuss, University of London.

Correspondence and Papers, General, 1958-1960   24
    Includes material from the National Health Council re problems faced by voluntary health agencies.

Correspondence - Bulsara, Jal F., 1949-1953   25
    Bulsara was Far Eastern Representative of the Division of Social Activities for the United Nations. A copy of his address to the Madras Conference, 1952, on the role of social service in raising the standard of living is included.

INTERNATIONAL CONFERENCE OF SOCIAL WORK

FOLDER TITLE AND DESCRIPTION OF CONTENTS | FOLDER

Correspondence - Farquharson, Alexander, 1938-1946 — 26
  Correspondence reflects increasing political tensions in prewar years and conflicting postwar proposals for re-organization of the ICSW.

Correspondence - Friedlander, Walter, 1952-1956. — 27

Correspondence - Haynes, George, 1945-1948 — 28
  Haynes served the ICSW as Treasurer-General until 1948 when he was elected President.

Correspondence - Hersey, Evelyn, 1950-1958. — 29

Correspondence - Hoehler, Fred K., 1946-1949. — 30

Correspondence - Hoey, Jane, 1947-1960. — 31

Correspondence - Kraus, Hertha, 1948-1954 — 32
  Includes her paper on the role of casework in American social work, 1948.

Correspondence - Sand, Dr. Rene, 1945-1948 — 33
  Dr. Sand served the Conference as its president from 1936 through the 1948 Conference at which he was made Honorary President.

Correspondence - Sark, Dr. H. M. L. H., 1946-1947 — 34
  Sark served the ICSW as Assistant Secretary-General for Europe during the postwar reorganization period.

Correspondence - Simons, Savilla, 1949-1951 — 35
  As Assistant Director of the Federal Security Agency's Office of International Relations, Mrs. Simons supplied the ICSW with lists of persons interested in welfare and advised the Conference regarding contacts in government.

Correspondence - United States Department of State, 1945-1947 — 36
  The State Department assisted the ICSW by transmitting invitations to foreign governments to send representatives to the Conference at Atlantic City, New Jersey, 1948.

Correspondence - Van Kleek, Mary, 1935-1948 — 37
  Miss Van Kleek, a vice-president of the prewar Conference, resigned all official responsibilities in 1947, after numerous protests re postwar reorganization plans.

Correspondence - Vergara, Laura, 1952-1960 — 38
  Miss Vergara served as U. N. Social Welfare Advisor for South America and was elected to the ICSW Executive Committee in 1954.

INTERNATIONAL CONFERENCE OF SOCIAL WORK

FOLDER TITLE AND DESCRIPTION OF CONTENTS	FOLDER

Correspondence - Woodward, Ellen S., 1949-1952   39
    As director of the Federal Security Agency's Office of
International Relations, Mrs. Woodward supplied the ICSW
with lists of persons and organizations who were potential
contributors.

Correspondence - World Study Tours, 1950-1954   40
    Includes itineraries and brochures.

Africa - Australia, 1947-1960   41
        Africa, 1956-1960
        Austria, 1957-1960
        Australia, 1947-1960
    Correspondence, minutes, and national reports.

Belgium - Burma, 1946-1960   42
        Belgium, 1958-1960
        Brazil, 1946-1960
        Burma, 1954-1957
    Correspondence and papers.

Canada, 1946-1953   43
    Correspondence, reports, and minutes of the Canadian national
committee. Papers surrounding the reorganization of the Canadian
committee in 1952 and the revised constitution are included.

Canada, 1954   44
    Correspondence, reports, and papers primarily related to the
International Conference of Social Work held in Toronto,
June, 1954.

Canada, 1955-1956   45
    Correspondence, papers, and several publications from the
Canadian Welfare Council. Includes National Report from the
Canadian Committee prepared for the 1956 Munich Conference on
social work in industrial society.

Canada, 1957-1962   46
    Correspondence and reports.

Ceylon - Czechoslovakia, 1947-1960   47
        Ceylon, 1956-1960   Congo (Belgian), 1960
        China, 1947-1959   Czechoslovakia, 1947-1948, 1955-1960
    Correspondence and papers. Much of the correspondence in the
China section concerns the problem of the participation of
the Chinese, both Communist and Nationalist, in the Madras
Conference, December, 1952. Among the Czechoslovakian papers
is a detailed report on social security and health insurance
in the Czechoslovak Republic in 1956.

INTERNATIONAL CONFERENCE OF SOCIAL WORK

FOLDER TITLE AND DESCRIPTION OF CONTENTS   FOLDER

Denmark - France, 1948-1960   48
        Denmark, 1960   Finland, 1957-1960
        Egypt, 1948-1960   France, 1951-1960
        Ethiopia, 1958-1960
    Correspondence and papers. Arab-Israeli political tensions
are reflected in the correspondence with Egypt. The French
papers include a report on technical assistance programs
which were prepared for the 1952 Madras Conference.

Germany - Hong Kong, 1950-1960   49
        Germany, 1953-1960   Ghana, 1952-1960
        Greece, 1954-1960   Hong Kong, 1950-1960
    Correspondence and reports from national committees. A report,
"Training for Social Work in Hong Kong," by Eileen L. Young-
husband, is included.

Iceland - Italy, 1947-1960   50
        Iceland, 1948-1954   Iraq, 1948-1958
        India, 1947-1960   Ireland, 1948
        Indochina, 1952-1953 Israel, 1952-1960
        Indoesia, 1951-1960   Italy, 1951-1960
        Iran, 1950-1960
    Correspondence, papers, and national reports. Among the
materials from India is a paper by Madame Vijaye L. Pandit,
"Significant Social and Economic Factors in the Far East,"
which emphasized the contrasts of modern India and pre-1947
India.

Japan - Morocco, 1941-1960   51
        Japan, 1948-1960   Liberia, 1958-1960
        Jordan, 1953-1960   Malaya, 1957-1959
        Kenya, 1956-1960   Mauritius, 1952-1960
        Latin America, 1941-1960 Morrocco, 1958-1959
        Lebanon, 1954-1960
    Correspondence and reports.

Netherlands - Philippines, 1942-1960   52
        Netherlands, 1947, 1954-1956
        New Zealand, 1947-1948, 1951-1956
        Nicuragua, 1957-1960
        Nigeria, 1960
        Northern Rhodesia, 1952-1960
        Pakistan, 1952-1960
        Philippines, 1952-1960
    Correspondence and reports.

Poland - Rumania, 1947-1960   53
        Poland, 1948, 1955-1960 Puerto Rico, 1947-1952, 1959
        Portugal, 1954-1960   Rumania, 1958-1959
    Correspondence and papers. Printed material re rehabilitation
of disabled persons is included among the papers from Poland.

FOLDER TITLE AND DESCRIPTION OF CONTENTS	FOLDER

Saudi Arabia - Syria, 1946-1960 — 54
  Saudi Arabia, 1948, 1958 Spain, 1950, 1960
  Sierra Leone, 1960 Sweden, 1948, 1952-1960
  Southern Rhodesia, 1960 Switzerland, 1949-1960
  South Africa, 1946-1960 Syria, 1952-1956
 Correspondence and reports. Included with the material from Sweden are papers re the study tour in Sweden in connection with the 1956 Munich Conference and correspondence with Gunnar Myrdal about his address to the 1958 Tokyo Conference.

Tanganyika - United Kingdom, 1948-1960 — 55
  Tanganyika, 1960 Uganda, 1960
  Tunisia, 1958-1960 Union of Soviet Socialist
  Turkey, 1951-1960 Republics, 1948-1956
          United Kingdom, 1956-1960
 Correspondence and papers. Included among papers from the United Kingdom is material from the European Regional Meeting on Cooperation in Social Work in Europe, 1959, and papers on problems of growth and change in population structure and community development.

United States, 1948-1957 — 56
 Correspondence, minutes, reports, and membership lists. Joe Hoffer, secretary-general of the ICSW, served simultaneously as executive-secretary of the NCSW and as secretary of the U. S. Committee of the ICSW until reorganization of the USC, under the auspices of the National Social Welfare Assembly, in 1952. Extensive material in the folder, prior to 1952, reflects Hoffer's multiple role in the organization and reorganization of the U. S. Committee.

West Indies - Yugoslavia, 1954-1961 — 57
  West Indies, 1958-1961
  Yemen, 1954
  Yugoslavia, 1955-1960
 Correspondence, reports, and papers. Yugoslav material includes reports on the economic and social crises following World War II and the development of social services under the Federated Peoples' Republic.

Inter-Governmental Organizations (IGOs)

IGOs - Arab League, 1956-1959 — 58
 Correspondence and papers indicating ICSW reluctance to establish affiliation with the Arab League.

IGOs - Columbo Plan, 1952-1960 — 59
 Correspondence with the Council for Technical Cooperation in South and South East Asia. Includes pamphlet describing the structure and programs of the Columbo Plan.

FOLDER TITLE AND DESCRIPTION OF CONTENTS	FOLDER

IGOs - Commission for Technical Cooperation South of the Sahara, 1955-1960   60
    Correspondence and pamphlets.

IGOs - Council on Europe, 1958   61
    Correspondence reflecting the ICSWs reluctance to establish relations with politically oriented organizations. The statute of the Council of Europe, as established at Strasbourg in 1958, and a draft of the European Social Charter are included.

IGOs - European Economic Community - Intergovernmental Committee for European Migration, 1954-1960   62
        European Economic Community, 1960
        Intergovernmental Committee for European Migration, 1954-1960
    Correspondence and pamphlets.

IGOs - Pan-American Child Congresses, 1947-1960   63
    Correspondence, agenda, and papers. Most material is related to the Ninth Congress held in Caracas, Venezuela, January, 1948, and the Tenth Congress held in Panama City, January, 1955.

IGOs - Pan-American Confederation of Social Workers, 1955-1959   64
    Correspondence and statutes of the Confederation.

IGOs - Pan-American Union, 1946-1949   65
    Correspondence and papers. The PAU performed secretarial functions for the ICSW on a regional basis in Latin America, which included translating ICSW documents and suggesting contacts and leaders in Latin America.

IGOs - Pan-American Union, 1950-1955   66
    Correspondence and papers.

IGOs - Pan-American Union, 1956-1960   67
    Correspondence and papers.

IGOs - United Nations, 1946-1949   68
    Correspondence, reports, and papers. Includes U. N. documents on prevention of prostitution and assistance to indigent foreigners.

IGOs - United Nations, 1950-1951   69
    Correspondence and documents. Includes material re assistance to the civilian population of Korea.

IGOs - United Nations, 1952-1954   70
    Correspondence, agenda, reports, and material re community organization and development.

IGOs - United Nations, 1955-1957   71
    Correspondence, reports, and documents.

INTERNATIONAL CONFERENCE OF SOCIAL WORK

FOLDER TITLE AND DESCRIPTION OF CONTENTS	FOLDER
IGOs - United Nations, 1958-1960 Correspondence, reports, and documents. Includes a copy of the Universal Declaration of Human Rights and material from the Non-Governmental Organizations' Conference on eradication of prejudice and discrimination.	72
IGOs - United Nations - Consulting Status, 1946-1964 Correspondence, meeting summaries, and documents. The Economic and Social Council granted consultative status to the ICSW on August 13, 1947.	73
IGOs - United Nations - Economic Commission for Africa, 1960 Correspondence and papers.	74
IGOs - United Nations - Economic Commission for Asia and the Far East, 1958-1960 Correspondence and papers.	75
IGOs - United Nations Educational, Scientific and Cultural Organization, (UNESCO), 1945-1955 Correspondence, papers, and pamphlets. Includes a report on the social impact of industrialization and urban conditions in Africa and formal agreements with non-governmental organizations.	76
IGOs - United Nations Educational, Scientific and Cultural Organization, (UNESCO), 1956-1962 Correspondence and pamphlets. <u>Traditional Values in American Life</u>, a booklet prepared for UNESCO by Ralph Henry Gabriel, is included.	77
IGOs - United Nations - European Office, 1958-1960 Correspondence and papers. Includes documents re housing, urban development, and technical assistance.	78
IGOs - United Nations - Food and Agriculture Organization, 1950-1960 Correspondence and papers. Includes documents related to the Freedom from Hunger Campaign and social welfare in rural communities.	79
IGOs - United Nations International Children's Emergency Fund, (UNICEF), 1949-1955 Correspondence, reports, papers, and press releases.	80
IGOs - United Nations International Children's Emergency Fund, (UNICEF), 1956-1960 Correspondence and reports. Contains U. S. Committee for UNICEF response to published attacks made in 1959 which alleged communist subversion in UNICEF.	81
IGOs - United Nations - International Labor Office, 1952-1960 Correspondence.	82

FOLDER TITLE AND DESCRIPTION OF CONTENTS   FOLDER

IGOs - United Nations - Office of the High Commissioner for   83
Refugees, 1953-1960
    Correspondence.

IGOs - United Nations Relief and Rehabilitation Administration   84
(UNRRA), 1949-1951
    Correspondence re reunions of former UNRRA personnel.

IGOs - United Nations Relief and Works Agency, 1953-1956   85
    Correspondence and papers. Includes statistics of UNRRA
    assistance to Palestine Refugees.

IGOs - United Nations Social Commission, 1953-1955   86
    Correspondence, reports, meeting summaries, and resolutions
    from the Commission. Includes material re training of welfare
    personnel and financing of housing and community improvement
    programs.

IGOs - United Nations Social Commission, 1956-1959   87
    Correspondence, reports, and statements from the Commission.
    Documents on community development, housing, levels of family
    living, and prevention of crime are included.

IGOs - United Nations - Technical Assistance Administration, 1951-1956   88
    Correspondence.

IGOs - United Nations - World Health Organization, 1950-1954   89
    Correspondence, agenda, and papers.

IGOs - United Nations - World Health Organization, 1955-1957   90
    Correspondence, agenda, and reports. Contains papers on the
    role of the hospital in public health programs and on family
    levels of living.

IGOs - United Nations - World Health Organization, 1958-1960   91
    Correspondence, agenda, and papers. Contains critical report
    of WHO executive board from ICSW representative in Geneva and
    a paper on the relationship between public health nurses and
    social workers.

Non-Governmental Organizations (NGOs)

NGOs - Associated Country Women of the World - Catholic International   92
Union for Social Service, 1948-1961
            Associated Country Women of the World, 1956-1961
            Boy Scouts International Bureau, 1950-1960
            Catholic International Union for Social Service, 1948-1961
    Correspondence, papers, and pamphlets.

NGOs - Conference of Consultative NGOs, 1947-1953   93
    Correspondence, minutes, and proceedings. Reports on the legal
    status of international non-governmental organizations and on genocide
    are included among the documents from the April, 1949 conference.

INTERNATIONAL CONFERENCE OF SOCIAL WORK

FOLDER TITLE AND DESCRIPTION OF CONTENTS	FOLDER
NGOs - Conference of Consultative NGOs, 1954-1961 Correspondence, reports, and papers. Includes papers from the 1954 special conference to consider improvements in the procedure of hearings before the Economic and Social Council Committee on NGOs.	94
NGOs - Conference of NGOs Interested in Migration, 1949-1960 Correspondence, meeting summaries, and reports. A statement of general principles for the protection of migrants and resolutions concerning problems of migrants, refugees, and repatriation under pressure are included.	95
NGOs - Conference of World Organizations Interested in the Handicapped, 1954-1957 Correspondence, minutes, and conference reports.	96
NGOs - Conference of World Organizations Interested in the Handicapped, 1958-1961 Correspondence, minutes, conference papers, and reports on rehabilitation of the handicapped.	97

NGOs - Council for International Organization of Medical Sciences - International Association of Gerontology, 1950-1959
    Council for International Organization of Medical Sciences, 1953-1959
    Friends World Committee for Consultation, 1950-1955
    International Association for Child Psychiatry, 1957-1958
    International Association for the Prevention of Blindness, 1953-1959
    International Association of Gerontology, 1954-1958
Correspondence and papers.
	98

NGOs - International Association of Schools of Social Work, 1956-1960 Correspondence, agenda, minutes, and reports. Some papers are related to the quarterly journal, International Social Work, published jointly by the IASSW and the ICSW.	99
NGOs - International Committee of Schools of Social Work, 1946-1953 Correspondence and conference materials. A summary report of schools of social work during the war years and a paper by Katharine A. Kendall on selection of students for admission to schools of social work are included.	100
NGOs - International Committee of Schools of Social Work, 1954-1956 Correspondence, minutes, and conference proceedings. Statements submitted by the ICSSW to the U. N. Social Commission concerning the training of welfare personnel are included.	101

NGOs - International Confederation of Free Trade Unions - International Council of Women, 1947-1963
    International Confederation of Free Trade Unions, 1955-1960
    International Conference of Catholic Charities, 1953-1960
	102

INTERNATIONAL CONFERENCE OF SOCIAL WORK

FOLDER TITLE AND DESCRIPTION OF CONTENTS   FOLDER

        International Congress on Home Economics, 1955-1957
        International Congress on Mental Deficiency, 1956
        International Council on Home Help Services, 1960
        International Council of Jewish Women, 1958-1960
        International Council of Nurses, 1947-1960
        International Council of Women, 1953-1963
Correspondence, minutes, papers, and news clippings.

NGOs - International Federation for Housing and Town Planning -   103
International Federation of Settlements, 1949-1960
        International Federation for Housing and Town
        Planning, 1955-1957
        International Federation for Inner Mission and
        Christian Social Work, 1959-1960
        International Federation of Business and Professional
        Women, 1955-1956
        International Federation of Settlements, 1949-1960
Correspondence and papers.

NGOs - International Federation of Social Workers, 1936-1951   104
Correspondence and papers surrounding the reorganization of
the International Permanent Secretariat of Social Workers as
the International Federation of Social Workers in July, 1950.
Reports from Czechoslovakia (location of the Permanent
Secretariat after 1934) reflect post World War II political
tensions and rivalries in that country. Statutes of the
reorganized IFSW are included.

NGOs - International Federation of Social Workers, 1952-1956   105
Correspondence, minutes, reports, and papers. The IFSW was
reorganized in 1956 at which time the ICSW offered to provide
routine administrative functions for the Federation. A paper
by Jean Nihon which traces the history and outlines the aims
and structure of the IFSW is included.

NGOs - International Federation of Social Workers, 1957-1958   106
Correspondence, minutes, and papers. The IFSW newsletter,
The Social Worker, was published and distributed by the
ICSW. Folder contains a report on Personnel Social Work.

NGOs - International Federation of Social Workers, 1959-1960   107
Correspondence and papers. Includes letter from the Cuban
Association of Social Workers in defense of "revolutionary
justice."

NGOs - International Hospital Federation - International Social   108
Service, 1949-1960
        International Hospital Federation, 1954-1960
        International Recreation Association, 1954-1960
        International Social Security Association, 1957-1959
        International Social Service, 1949-1960
Correspondence, pamphlets, and reports. International Social
Service material contains a study on inter-country adoptions.

FOLDER TITLE AND DESCRIPTION OF CONTENTS	FOLDER

NGOs - International Society for the Welfare of Cripples, 1949-1958   109
    Correspondence, annual reports, and meeting proceedings.

NGOs - International Society for the Welfare of Cripples, 1959-1960   110
    Correspondence, agenda, minutes, and bulletins.

NGOs - International Society of Criminology - International Union   111
Against the Venereal Diseases, 1947-1960
        International Society of Criminology, 1954-1960
        International Sociological Association, 1954-1957
        International Union Against Cancer, 1954-1955
        International Union Against Tuberculosis, 1954-1960
        International Union Against the Venereal Diseases,
        1947-1954
    Correspondence, reports, and pamphlets.

NGOs - International Union for Child Welfare, 1949-1960   112
    Correspondence, reports, and papers. Contains an extensive
    study by Katharine Lenroot on the needs of children throughout
    the world, existant services in different countries, and
    recommendations for future development of the IUCW.

NGOs - International Union of Family Organizations, 1948-1960   113
    Correspondence, meeting programs, and pamphlets.

NGOs - League of Red Cross Societies - The Lutheran World Federa-   114
tion, 1935-1960
        League of Red Cross Societies, 1935-1958
        The Lutheran World Federation, 1959-1960
    Correspondence and reports.

NGOs - Non-Governmental Organizations Committee on UNICEF, 1949-1955   115
    Correspondence, minutes, reports, membership lists, and
    bulletins.

NGOs - Non-Governmental Organizations Committee on UNICEF, 1956-1957   116
    Correspondence, minutes, reports, and papers.

NGOs - Non-Governmental Organizations Committee on UNICEF, 1958-1960.   117

NGOs - The Salvation Army - Union of International Associations,   118
1948-1960.
        The Salvation Army, 1948-1960
        Union of International Associations, 1948-1960
    Correspondence and papers.

NGOs - World Alliance of YMCA's, 1949-1959   119
    Correspondence, papers, and reports on services throughout the
    world. Special reports deal with the position of Christian
    organizations in Communist China, economic and social difficulties
    in South America, and suggested procedures for work group leaders
    at international conferences.

FOLDER TITLE AND DESCRIPTION OF CONTENTS	FOLDER

NGOs - World Assembly of Youth - World Council for the Welfare 120
of the Blind, 1948-1960
        World Assembly of Youth, 1951-1960
        World Association of Girl Guides and Girl Scouts,
        1948-1960
        World Confederation for Physical Therapy, 1956-1960
        World Confederation of Organizations of the Teaching
        Profession, 1956-1959
        World Council for the Welfare of the Blind, 1953-1960
    Correspondence, papers, and pamphlets.

NGOs - World Council of Churches - World Federation for Mental 121
Health, 1950-1960
        World Council of Churches, 1952-1960
        World Federation for Mental Health, 1950-1960
    Correspondence and papers. Includes a study by Alvin Zander,
University of Michigan Research Center for Group Dynamics,
describing motivations and reactions of international
conference delegates and presenting suggestions for improvements of the nature of conference discussion groups.

NGOs - World Federation of the Deaf - World YWCA, 1949-1960 122
        World Federation of the Deaf, 1955-1960
        World Federation of Occupational Therapists, 1955-1957
        World Federation of United Nations Associations, 1953-1960
        World University Service, 1953-1960
        World Veterans Federation, 1956-1958
        World YWCA, 1949-1960
    Correspondence and papers.

7

An Inventory of the Papers of Paul Underwood Kellogg

PREPARED BY
Andrea Hinding

SWB Kellogg, Paul Underwood, 1879-1958
K293
Papers, ca.1884-1958

345 folders   14 (ℓ) folders

Provenance

Paul Kellogg's papers were deposited from 1964-1968 in the Social Welfare History Archives Center by Helen Hall (Mrs. Paul Kellogg) and Richard Patrick Kellogg, Kellogg's son. Some material lent by Helen Hall, Richard Patrick, and Mercy Pearce Kellogg, Kellogg's daughter, was xeroxed and placed in the collection, and the original records returned to the family. After processing, the collection consists of 14½ linear feet of correspondence, minutes, reports, articles, speeches, clippings, pamphlets, memoranda, photographs, and financial and editorial records.

Biography

Paul Kellogg, journalist, editor, and social reformer, was born September 30, 1879, in Kalamazoo, Michigan, the son of Frank Israel and Mary Foster Underwood Kellogg. He was educated in Kalamazoo schools and took special courses at Columbia University, 1901-1906, and with the philanthropic education committee of the New York Charity Organization Society (whose summer school in philanthropy led to establishment of the New York School of Social Work), 1902. In 1911 Amherst College, Amherst, Massachusetts, awarded him an honorary master of arts degree; in 1937 Wesleyan University, Middletown, Connecticut, conferred on him an honorary doctor of letters degree.

He married Marion Pearce Sherwood, a native of Kalamazoo, in October, 1909. Their children were Richard Patrick, born in 1911, and Mercy Pearce, born in 1918. In 1934 Kellogg and his wife were divorced, and in the following year he married Helen Hall, social worker and head resident of Henry Street Settlement, New York City.

After graduation from high school (class of 1897, which elected him class historian), Kellogg became reporter for and city editor of the Kalamazoo Daily Telegraph. In 1902 he joined the staff of Charities, the house organ of the New York Charity Organization Society, as assistant editor. Charities merged with the Commons, journal of the Chicago Commons settlement, to become Charities and the Commons in 1905, and it became the Survey in 1909, taking its name from the Pittsburgh Survey, which Kellogg directed. While the magazine continued to be published formally by the Charity Organization Society, responsibility for its direction was given to a Charities Publication Committee in 1905, the year Kellogg became managing editor. In 1912, for financial reasons and for purposes of editorial independence, the Survey broke its ties with the Society, and Survey Associates, a cooperative publishing society, was formed to publish the magazine. At that time Kellogg became editor, a position he held until publication ceased in 1952. (Further information on the complicated evolution of the Survey is found in the inventory of the Survey Associates papers, also on file in the Social Welfare Archives.)

Under his editorship, the Survey, one of the foremost journals of social issues in the first half of the twentieth century, dealt with such themes as the "Negro in the Cities of the North," 1906; "Harlem, Mecca of the New Negro," 1925; and with unemployment throughout the twenties, culminating in a special graphic number, "Unemployment and Ways Out," April, 1929. Through special numbers and series, and with emphasis on graphic techniques, the Survey studied and interpreted racial and nationality groups, city and regional planning, segregation, health, education, American-Russian relations, etc. Regular coverage provided information for both practicing social workers and others directly involved in social service, and for those whom Kellogg called intelligent and concerned laymen interested in social and economic issues behind headlines.

Kellogg's career as editor paralleled a variety of related interests and activites. From 1907 to 1909 he directed the Pittsburgh Survey, the first community survey in the U.S., and edited the six-volume findings of that survey (The Pittsburgh Survey, Russell Sage Foundation, 1909-1914). He was chairman of the committee on occupational standards of the National Conference of Charities and Corrections, 1910, and secretary of the Committee to Secure a Federal Commission on Industrial Relations, 1911-1913. A member of the board of directors of the American Union Against Militarism, 1915-1917, Kellogg was also one of the founders and a board member of the Foreign Policy Association. During World War I he headed the editorial and historical bureau of the American Red Cross in Paris, and wrote with Arthur Gleason British Labor and the War (Boni and Liveright, 1919). He was a member of committees of the American Association of Social Workers and the National Federation of Settlements, and was the president of the National Conference of Social Work, 1939. In 1934 President Franklin Roosevelt named him a member of the advisory council to the Committee on Economic Security, and he chaired the state advisory council to the New York State Employment Service, 1934-1939.

In 1935 the New York *Evening Post* Alumni Association awarded him a medal for "distinguished and courageous journalism." He also received the Pugsley Award for the outstanding paper read at the 1936 National Conference of Social Work.

Arthur Piper Kellogg, 1878-1934

Arthur Kellogg, Paul Kellogg's older brother, graduated from Kalamazoo high school in 1897, where he was elected class president. He worked for the Kalamazoo *Daily Telegraph*, succeeding his brother as city editor; the Dunkley-Williams Transportation Company; and the Kalamazoo *Gazette-News*. In 1903 he joined the staff of *Charities*, and from then until his death in 1934, he served in varying capacities as assistant editor, business manager, managing editor, and secretary of Survey Associates, Inc. In 1902 he married Augusta Louise Coleman, a native of Kalamazoo; in 1925 he and his wife were divorced, and he married Florence Loeb Fleisher.

Those personal papers of his which survived were found with Kellogg's papers and have been retained as part of that collection (folders 48-54). Other material relating to him is found throughout the collection.

Organization of the collection

The papers have been separated into two sections, records dealing with Kellogg's personal life (folders 1-99) and those regarding his professional career and interests (folders 100-345).

Included in the personal papers is biographical information on Kellogg (folder 1); photographs of Kellogg, his family, his birthplace, etc. (folder 2); correspondence with his family, especially his son, and with relatives and friends (folders 3-19); notes from courses taken at Columbia University and brochures re courses given by the New York Charity Organization Society's committee on philanthropic education (folders 20-27); articles and speeches by Kellogg (folders 28-35); newspaper clippings (folders 36-40); and condolence letters to Helen Hall on Kellogg's death (folders 41-47).

Arranged with this section are personal papers of Arthur Kellogg (folders 48-54) and, finally, extensive "housekeeping" records (folders 55-99): national, state, and local tax records (folders 55-60); Kellogg's contributions to organizations (folders 61-63); and records, arranged chronologically, dealing with property, insurance, automobiles, physicians, attorneys, fuel suppliers, etc. (folders 64-99).

The bulk of professional papers (folders 100-345) document Kellogg's work as editor of the Survey. Included are records of Charities and Charities and the Commons, predecessors of the Survey (folders 100-104), and two reports of the Survey's work, issued by the editors on behalf of the Charities Publication Committee (folder 105). Records of Survey Associates (folders 106-306), which took over publication from the Committee, are arranged in so far as possible to parallel the arrangement of Survey Associates, Inc. papers: corporate, financial, editorial, and operational records.

Corporate records (folders 106-113) include a 1928 revision of Survey Associates' constitution (folder 106), annual reports or annual statements by the editor (folders 107-108), minutes of the board of directors and records of a special committee of the board of directors (folder 113).

The financial records consist of correspondence and papers, (folders 114-115), financial records (folders 116-122), material re funds and a foundation administered by Survey Associates (folders 123-126), and applications to foundations for financial assistance (folders 127-130).

Included in the editorial files are general correspondence, which contains material on staff members (folders 131-164); publishing memoranda and an inquiry to readers re content and coverage (folders 165-167); and papers re the editor's travel (folders 168-170). Two editorial subject files, one of persons (folders 171-194) and one of associations, articles, special numbers, etc. (folders 195-249), are arranged alphabetically. The editorial records also contain unpublished manuscripts from contributors (folders 254-259) and newspaper clippings re the Survey (folder 260).

The operational records consist of membership records (folder 261), advertising and circulation records (folders 262-263), field work reports (folders 264-267), and promotional material (folders 268-272). A picture-cartoon file (folders 273-304) makes up the bulk of the operational records.

The remainder of the professional papers document other activities in which Kellogg was involved (folders 307-345). The alphabet in which they are arranged includes subjects, persons, and associations.

Appended to this description is a list of ephemera removed from the collection and placed in the Social Welfare Archives ephemera file.

Extensive overlap between the Kellogg papers and the records of Survey Associates reflects the intertwining of Kellogg's personal life and professional career. Persons using this collection will also wish to consult the Survey Associates records, and personal papers of George Britt, Mary Katz Golden, Agnes Brown (Mrs. Henry Goddard) Leach, and Janet Sabloff, _Survey_ staff and board members. These papers are deposited in the Social Welfare Archives.

PARTIAL SUBJECT INVENTORY

The following guide to certain persons, subjects, and associations prominent in the collection is suggestive rather than definitive.

Staff members Beulah Amidon, Hugo Van Arx, George Britt, Bradley Buell, Helen Chamberlain, Thomas Devine, Daniel S. Gillmor, Walter F. Grueninger, Florence Loeb Kellogg, Loula D. Lasker, Victor Weybright, and Leon R. Whipple appear throughout Kellogg's <u>Survey</u> records (folders 100-306).

ADDAMS, JANE
    Folders 139, 171, 242, 252, 308-310, 331-332, 342

ADLER, FELIX
    Folder 308

ADULT EDUCATION
    Folder 139

ALLEN, ETHEL RICHARDSON
    Folder 139

AMERICAN NATIONAL RED CROSS
    Folders 196, 199, 273

AMERICAN UNION AGAINST MILITARISM, NEW YORK
    Folders 34, 308-310

AUSTIN, MARY C.
    Folders 138-139, 240

BALCH, EMILY GREENE
    Folders 308, 310

BALDWIN, ROGER NASH
    Folder 123

BIRTH CONTROL
    Folder 146

BIRTH CONTROL FEDERATION OF AMERICA
    Folder 110

BORAH, WILLIAM
    Folder 242

BRANDEIS, LOUIS DEMBITZ
    Folders 110, 123, 142-143, 150, 308-309, 311

BRENNER, ANN REED
    Folders 138-139, 149, 153, 194, 225

BRITISH LABOR PARTY
    Folders 17, 139

BRUERE, MARTHA BENSLEY (MRS. ROBERT W.)
    Folder 133

BRUERE, ROBERT WALTER
    Folders 133, 135

BURNS, ALLEN TIBBALS
    Folder 314

CABOT, CHARLES M.
    Folders 124, 131, 155

CABOT, PHILIP T.
    Folder 124

CABOT, RICHARD CLARKE, M.D.
    Folders 124, 242, 342

CALKINS, MARION "CLINCH"
    Folders 133, 135, 231-232

CAPITAL PUNISHMENT
    Folders 334-337

CHAMBERLAIN, JOSEPH PERKINS
    Folder 332

CHARITIES
    Folder 100

CHARITIES AND THE COMMONS
    Folders 101-104

CHARITIES PUBLICATION COMMITTEE
    Folders 101, 104-105

CHICAGO PEACE SOCIETY
    Folders 309-310

CHILD LABOR AND CHILD LABOR AMENDMENT
    Folders 197, 227, 277

CHILDREN
    Folder 225

CHILD WELFARE LEAGUE OF AMERICA
    Folder 322

CITY AND REGIONAL PLANNING
    Folders 184-192, 257

CIVIL SERVICE
    Folder 145

COLORADO COAL STRIKE (1914)
    Folders 203-206, 313, 316

COMMITTEE FOR EXTENSION OF LABOR EDUCATION, WASHINGTON, D.C.
    Folders 154-155

COMMITTEE ON INDUSTRIAL RELATIONS TO SECURE A FEDERAL COMMISSION
ON INDUSTRIAL RELATIONS, NEW YORK
    Folders 203-206, 313-316

COMMITTEE ON RESEARCH IN MEDICAL ECONOMICS
    Folder 162

CONSERVATION
    Folders 231-235

COOK, WALDO
    Folders 256-334

COOKE, MORRIS LLEWELLYN
    Folder 124

COOLEY, ROSSA BELLE
    Folders 162, 172

CREEL, GEORGE
    Folders 203-204

CURRENCY REFORM
    Folder 193

DAVIS, MICHAEL MARKS
    Folder 140

DAVIS, OZORA S.
    Folder 133

DE FOREST, ROBERT WEEKS
    Folders 140-141

DEMOCRACY
    Folder 28

DEVINE, EDWARD THOMAS
    Folders 100-104, 124, 131, 158, 203, 242, 308, 313-314, 316
    338, 341

DILLIARD, IRVING
    Folder 154

DISCRIMINATION
    Folders 215, 325

DOCK, LAVINIA L.
    Folder 100

EDISON, THOMAS
    Folders 308, 333

ELECTIONS (PRESIDENTIAL)
    Of 1916
        Folder 198
    Of 1924
        Folder 317

ELLIOT, JOHN LOVEJOY
    Folders 334, 338

EMERSON, HAVEN, M.D.
    Folder 146

EMPLOYMENT PLANNING
    Folders 31, 33-34

ERNST, MORRIS
    Folder 341

FELS, SAMUEL SIMEON
    Folders 173-182, 225

FITCH, JOHN ANDREWS
    Folders 124, 241-242, 313, 342

FLANNER HOUSE, INDIANAPOLIS, INDIANA
    Folders 152, 154

FORD, HENRY (INCLUDING THE HENRY FORD PEACE EXPEDITION)
    Folders 200-201, 252-253, 310

FOREIGN POLICY
    Folders 16, 35, 338

FOREIGN POLICY ASSOCIATION, NEW YORK
    Folders 29, 318

FOUNDATIONS AND PHILANTHROPY
    Folders 203-204

FRANKFURTER, FELIX
    Folders 123, 146, 334

FURUSETH, ANDREW
    Folders 183, 220

GAVIT, JOHN PALMER
    Folders 139, 144, 308, 310, 342

GEDDES, PATRICK
    Folders 184-192

GIDDINGS, FRANKLIN H.
    Folder 308

GLEASON, ARTHUR HUNTINGDON
    Folders 17-19, 183

GLEASON, HELEN HAYES (MRS. ARTHUR)
    Folders 17-19, 141-142, 169

GLENN, JOHN MARK
    Folders 131, 241, 313

GRAHAM, FRANK P.
    Folder 307

HAMILTON, ALICE, M.D.
    Folder 334

HARMON, WILLIAM E.
    Folders 170, 242

HART, JOSEPH KINMONT
    Folders 133-134, 137

HOEHLER, FRED KENNETH
    Folders 154-155

HOLMES, JOHN HAYNES
    Folders 308-310, 313, 316

HOUSE, GRACE B.
    Folder 132

HOUSING
    Folders 150, 154, 249

HOWE, FREDERICK CLEMSON
    Folders 308-310

HOWELLS, WILLIAM DEAN
    Folder 308

IMMIGRATION
    Folder 137

INDUSTRIAL CONDITIONS
    Folders 321, 324

INDUSTRIAL RELATIONS
    Folders 29, 131, 203-206, 230, 313-316

INSTITUTE OF INTERNATIONAL EDUCATION, NEW YORK
    Folder 137

INTERNATIONAL INDUSTRIAL RELATIONS INSTITUTE, THE HAGUE, HOLLAND
    Folder 142

INTERNATIONAL JOINT COMMISSION (U.S. AND CANADA)
    Folders 29, 206-207

INTERNATIONAL RELATIONS
    Folders 29-30, 206-207, 310, 312

JOHNSON, ALEXANDER
    Folder 146

KELLEY, FLORENCE
    Folders 34, 241, 308

KELLOGG, ARTHUR PIPER
    Appears throughout the collection but especially in folders 2-3, 7, 10, 48-54

KENNEDY, ALBERT J.
    Folder 224

KIRCHWEY, GEORGE W.
    Folders 309, 331

KNIGHTS OF COLUMBUS
    Folder 209

LABOR RELATIONS
    Folders 203-206, 316

LAFOLLETE'S SEAMEN'S BILL (1915)
    Folders 220-223

LASKER, BRUNO
    Folders 132, 184-185, 225, 242, 248

LEAGUE OF FREE NATIONS ASSOCIATION, NEW YORK
    Folders 319-320

LEE, JOSEPH
    Folders 100, 242

LEISERSON, WILLIAM MORRIS
    Folders 10, 241

LINDSAY, SAMUEL MCCUNE
    Folders 124, 308-309, 314

LOCHNER, LOUIS P.
    Folder 309

MACDONALD, J. RAMSAY
    Folders 17, 139

MATTHEWS, WILLIAM HENRY
    Folders 144, 148, 330

MEXICO
    Folders 210-211, 228, 312

MONTREAL, CANADA (CITY OF)
    Folders 243-247

NASMYTH, GEORGE W.
    Folders 242, 308

NATIONAL CONFERENCE OF CHARITIES AND CORRECTION
    Folder 321

NATIONAL CONFERENCE OF SOCIAL WORK
    Folders 322-323

NEUBERGER, RICHARD LEWIS
    Folder 154

NEW DEAL
    Folders 338, 341-344

NEW YORK CHARITY ORGANIZATION SOCIETY
    Folder 27

PACIFISM
    Folders 242, 250, 252

PATRIOTIC FUND OF CANADA
    Folders 243-247

PENN NORMAL INDUSTRIAL AND AGRICULTURAL SCHOOL, ST. HELENA ISLAND, SOUTH CAROLINA
    Folders 6, 162, 172, 329

PENNSYLVANIA (STATE OF)
    Folders 140, 216, 238-239

PEOPLE'S INSTITUTE, NEW YORK
    Folder 102

PERKINS, FRANCES
    Folders 307, 324

PINCHOT, AMOS RICHARDS
    Folders 317, 331, 333, 341-342

PITTSBURGH SURVEY
    Folders 155, 216, 330

PLANNING
    Folders 152, 173-182, 183-192

PLAYGROUNDS
    Folder 217

PRISONS
    Folder 225
    Prison Labor
        Folder 216

PROGRESSIVE PARTY
    Folders 171, 198, 317, 331-333
    in New York State
        Folder 333

RACE RELATIONS
    Folders 133, 135-136, 152, 213, 215

RECREATION
    Folder 135

REGIONAL PLANNING   SEE CITY AND REGIONAL PLANNING

RELIEF
    Folders 148, 200-201

ROCKEFELLER FOUNDATION
    Folders 130, 154, 203-206, 316

RUBINOW, ISAAC MAX
    Folders 225, 241

RURAL LIFE AND WELFARE
    Folder 129

RUSSIA
    Folders 132, 319

SACCO-VANZETTI
    Folders 271, 334-337

SCHWIMMER, ROSIKA
    Folders 159, 310

SEAMEN
    Folders 183, 220-223
    Unions
        Folders 183, 220-223

"SICKNESS" AND OLD AGE INSURANCE
"Sickness insurance" was a contemporary term describing what later came to be included under health insurance and social insurance.
Folder 332

SMITH, GEDDES
Folders 133, 135-138

SOCIAL GOSPEL
Folder 134

SOCIAL INSURANCE
Folders 145, 332

SOCIAL SECURITY
Folders 33, 142-143

SOCIAL SETTLEMENTS
Folders 30, 224

SOCIAL WORK
Folders 144, 154, 160
And the churches
Folder 133
Rural
Folder 219

SOCIAL WORKERS
and Unionization
Folder 33
and War
Folder 33

SPANISH CIVIL WAR
Folders 35, 148, 339-340

SPANISH REFUGEE RELIEF CAMPAIGN, NEW YORK
Folders 339-340

STEEL INDUSTRY, CONDITIONS IN
Folders 124, 131, 155, 315

STELLA, JOSEPH
    Folder 194

TAYLOR, GRAHAM R.
    Folders 132, 313-314

UNEMPLOYMENT
    Folders 29-34, 145, 173-182, 200-201, 237-239, 241

UNEMPLOYMENT COMPENSATION
    Folder 322

UNEMPLOYMENT INSURANCE
    Folders 307, 325-326

U.S. CIVILIAN CONSERVATION CORPS (CCC)
    Folders 142, 150

U.S. COMMISSION ON INDUSTRIAL RELATIONS
    Folders 203-206, 313-316

U.S. SOCIAL AND ECONOMIC CONDITIONS IN 1920'S
    Folder 240

U.S. SUPREME COURT
    Folder 230

VAN KLEECK, MARY
    Folders 142, 249, 342

VAN LOON, HENDRIK WILLEM
    Folders 7, 141, 193

VILLARD, OSWALD GARRISON
    Folders 139, 338, 341

WAGNER, ROBERT FERDINAND
    Folder 150

WALD, LILLIAN D.
    Folders 28, 139, 142-144, 308-310

WALSH, FRANK P.
    Folders 203-206, 313

WASHINGTON, D.C.
    Folders 102-103

WHITE, WILLIAM ALLEN
    Folders 10, 140

WILLIAMS, MORNAY
    Folders 308-309

WISE, RABBI STEPHEN
    Folders 308-309, 313

WITTE, EDWIN E.
    Folder 307

WOMEN'S PEACE PARTY, CHICAGO, ILLINOIS
    Folders 250, 309-310

WORKERS EDUCATION
    Folder 135

WORKMEN'S COMPENSATION
    Folders 241, 307, 332

WORLD PEACE FOUNDATION, BOSTON, MASSACHUSETTS
    Folder 250

WORLD WAR, 1914-1918
    Folders 131, 242-253

WORLD WAR, 1939-1945
    Folders 254-255

YOUNG MEN'S CHRISTIAN ASSOCIATION (YMCA)
    Folder 127

PAUL UNDERWOOD KELLOGG

FOLDER INVENTORY

"Who's Who," ca.1920-1950   1
    Biographical information on Kellogg.

Photographs, ca.1894-1955   2
    Photographs of Kellogg, Arthur Kellogg, the Kellogg family, Kellogg's birthplace and early home, etc. The material is generally not dated.

Correspondence and Papers, 1889, 1909-1916*   3
    Petition to Frank Kellogg from Paul and Arthur for an air rifle, camp supply list for Kellogg's honeymoon, and family correspondence. Includes a poem from Paul to Arthur.

Correspondence and Papers, 1917-1918   4
    Correspondence with family, relatives, and friends. Material on conditions in the Minnewaska Sanitorium, Canada.

Correspondence and Papers, 1919-1920   5
    Correspondence with family, relatives, and friends. Includes a letter to his son describing the 1919 Yale-Princeton football game and material on schooling for his children.

Correspondence and Papers, 1921-1924   6
    Correspondence with family, relatives, and friends. Includes a letter describing Penn Normal Industrial and Agricultural School and the island on which it is located, St. Helena Island, South Carolina. Material on Walden School, New York City, which the Kellogg children attended.

Correspondence and Papers, 1925   7
    Family correspondence, correspondence re and cartoons by Hendrik Willem Van Loon, and Paul and Arthur Kellogg's discussions of marriage.

Correspondence and Papers, 1926-1927   8
    Correspondence with family, relatives, and friends. Includes a letter describing "Lizzie," the family Ford.

*Many letters in folders 3-14 have been annotated by Richard Patrick Kellogg.

Correspondence and Papers, 1928   9
    Material indicating Kellogg's efforts to help relatives and friends, letters and postcards re his European trip, and a letter to his son on flying.

Correspondence and Papers, 1929-1933   10
    Correspondence with family, relatives, and friends. Includes correspondence with William M. Leiserson and William Allen White re his son, letters of recommendation to Antioch College, a letter re an alleged assault on a Negro woman by a policeman, and Kellogg "family trees."

Correspondence and Papers, 1934-1935   11
    Family correspondence and material re Kellogg's divorce and his marriage to Helen Hall.

Correspondence and Papers, 1936-1937   12
    Correspondence with family, relatives, and friends. Material re the honorary doctor of letters degree conferred on Kellogg by Wesleyan University in 1937.

Correspondence and Papers, 1938-1943   13
    Correspondence with his son and material re a boundary dispute at his Canadian summer camp at Lake Memphremagog.

Correspondence and Papers, 1944-1953   14
    Correspondence with family, relatives, and friends. Includes material re Kellogg's efforts to help Karel Mazel secure citizenship and a letter from historian Allan Nevins expressing regret that the <u>Survey</u> ceased publication in 1952.

Correspondence, European Trip, 1928   15
    Includes itinerary for his trip and correspondence from Robert Smillie, Margaret Bondfield, and other members of the British Parliament re prospective calls on them while in Europe.

Correspondence, Foreign Policy, 1938   16
    A. A. Berle, Jr., invited Kellogg as "one of our liberal friends" to comment on the direction of U.S. foreign policy. Includes Kellogg's response and comments by staff member Beulah Amidon on response.

Correspondence, Helen Hayes (Mrs. Arthur) Gleason, 1923-1924   17
    Material re the illness and death of Arthur Gleason and a memorial service held for him. Includes tributes to Gleason from J. Ramsay MacDonald, British prime minister; the British Labour Party; and Fannia M. Cohn, secretary of the International Ladies' Garment Workers' Union.

Correspondence, Helen Hayes (Mrs. Arthur) Gleason, 1924-1925   18
    Correspondence re Kellogg's effort to encourage Helen Gleason to write the "Story of Arthur Gleason," transcript of memorial service held for him, and correspondence with friends concerned about Mrs. Gleason.

Correspondence, Helen Hayes (Mrs. Arthur) Gleason, 1925-1930   19
    Material re Kellogg's assistance to Helen Gleason in writing The Book of Arthur Gleason.

Columbia University, 1901   20
    Includes Columbia brochure and introductory card for Kellogg to the president of Columbia.

Columbia University, American Literature, 1901-1902   21
    Notes for the course, taught by Professor Matthews.

Columbia University, Economics I, 1901   22
    Lecturers were Professors Day and Seligman. Includes notes for the course and Kellogg's final examination.

Columbia University, English I and II, 1901-1902   23
    Themes for the courses.

Columbia University, English II, 1902   24
    Notes for the course and Kellogg's final examination.

Columbia University, History 4, ca.1901-1902   25
    Notes from and paper written for the course, taught by Professor Dunning. Also includes test questions for History 4 for spring semester, 1902.

Columbia University, Public Law, 1902   26
    Notes for Professor Goodnow's course, spring semester.

New York Charity Organization Society, Committee on Philanthropic Education, ca.1902   27
    Kellogg took COS special courses in 1902. Preliminary program for summer course and brochure re proposed two-year training course for philanthropic work.

Articles and Speeches, 1908-1927   28
    Democracy in an industrial district, child labor legislation, Lillian D. Wald, and "Communication Among Men," a speech which includes an account of a meeting in Harlem where Kellogg spoke.

Articles and Speeches, 1928-1929   29
    Public opinion and industrial relations, social research, the Palisades in New York, the Foreign Policy Association, unemployment, and the International Joint Commission (U.S. and Canada).

Articles and Speeches, 1930   30
    Unemployment, mass credit, international relations, and social settlements.

Articles and Speeches, 1931   31
    Unemployment, employment planning, and Kellogg's statement to the U.S. Senate hearing on unemployment relief.

Articles and Speeches, 1932-1933   32
    Primarily material on the economic situation in the nation and the world. One speech commenting on woman's role in life.

Articles and Speeches, 1934-1936   33
    Economic recovery; social workers, World War I, and the current world situation; social settlements; social security; social workers and unionization; and employment planning.

Articles and Speeches, 1937-1939   34
    Federal relief, employment planning, unemployment benefits in New York State, emigres' adjustment to American life, presidential address to the National Conference of Social Work, Mary Chamberlain (former Survey staff member), Florence Kelley, and a Message from 1914 - for 1939 and After (re war).

Articles and Speeches, 1940-1947   35
    Refugees from the Spanish Civil War, foreign policy, and speeches to Survey Associates.

Newspaper Clippings, 1901-1902   36
    Clippings of stories primarily from the Kalamazoo Daily Telegraph. Probably stories written by Kellogg.

Newspaper Clippings, Kalamazoo, 1915   37
    Kellogg saved large segments of the Kalamazoo Gazette
    and the Telegraph-Press for December 30 and 31.

Newspaper Clippings, 1914-1949   38-40
    Clippings re Kellogg's personal and professional
    life, especially reporting his activities as editor
    of the Survey.

Condolence Letters, 1958   41-45
    Letters to Helen Hall on the death of Paul Kellogg.
    The correspondence is arranged alphabetically.

Condolence Letters, Partial Signatures, 1958   46
    Letters to Helen Hall from individuals whose signa-
    tures were incomplete. The letters are arranged
    chronologically.

Condolence Letters, Associations, 1958   47
    Resolutions or other expressions of sympathy from
    agencies and associations, arranged chronologically.

Arthur Kellogg, Correspondence and Papers, 1914-1931   48
    Kellogg family genealogy, notice from Arthur Kellogg
    about funeral arrangements for him, copy of his will,
    and an autograph letter signed by Franklin D.
    Roosevelt.

Arthur Kellogg, Estate, 1934-1935   49
    Correspondence and papers.

Arthur Kellogg, Scrapbook, 1893-1903   50
    Scrapbook of newspaper clippings and other materials
    relating to Arthur and Paul Kellogg's life in Kala-
    mazoo, including material on their high school grad-
    uation. Material from Michigan newspapers regarding
    both men.

Arthur Kellogg, Tributes to, 1934   51
    Tributes by Paul Kellogg, Survey staff member Leon R.
    Whipple, and others.

Arthur Kellogg, Condolence Letters, 1934   52-53
    Letters to Paul Kellogg on the death of his brother.
    Arranged alphabetically.

Arthur Kellogg, Copies of Condolence Letters, 1934.   54

U.S. Income Tax, 1913-1949   55-58
    Completed forms.

New York State Income Tax, 1919-1950   59
    Completed forms.

New York City Real Estate Tax and Water Bills, 1923-1948.   60

Contributions, 1926-1951   61-63
    Includes receipts, membership cards, and occasional
    lists of contributions by Kellogg in a given year.

Housekeeping Records, 1912-1953   64-99
    Material re insurance, property, tenants, automobiles,
    mortgages, boundary dispute at Kellogg's Canadian
    summer camp at Lake Memphremagog, physicians, dentists,
    attorneys, etc. Arranged chronologically.

Charities, 1903-1904   100
    Correspondence and material relating to publication
    plans. Includes a letter from Joseph Lee on the
    proposal to extend Charities coverage to all kinds of
    social efforts, and a letter from Lavinia L. Dock on
    district nursing and on the churches and charity work.

Charities and the Commons, 1905   101
    Scattered correspondence, memoranda, and financial
    material. Includes minutes of a meeting of the
    Charities Publication Committee and material on
    editorial plans for the magazine.

Charities and the Commons, 1906   102
    Correspondence, financial material, and plans for
    special numbers. Includes material on social prob-
    lems and conditions in Washington, D.C.; a letter
    re the merger of Jewish Charity with Charities and
    the Commons; and material re the People's Institute,
    an association which furthered contacts between
    "cultured" classes and "the people."

Charities and the Commons, 1906   103
    Correspondence, financial material, and publication
    plans. Includes a letter-report on the year's work
    which refers to Washington, D.C. as a "model city"
    and a report of work to improve social conditions
    in the District of Columbia.

Charities and the Commons, 1907-1909   104
    Correspondence and papers re editorial plans and
    programs, finance and subscriptions, and publicity.

Includes a proposed investigation of county jails (in cooperation with the National Prison Association), a report by staff member Lilian Brandt on the department of social research, a field report by Francis H. McLean, and a memorandum on the relationship of the Russell Sage Foundation to the Charities Publication Committee.

Survey, Reports, 1910 — 105
Two statements by the editors of the Survey on behalf of the Charities Publication Committee.

Survey Associates, Constitution, 1928 (revision). — 106

Survey Associates, Annual Reports, 1923-1947. — 107-108

Survey Associates, Board of Directors, Minutes, 1935-1939 — 109
Minutes, occasional memoranda to the board and the board's executive committee, and material re finance, membership, editorial policy, staff, etc.

Survey Associates, Board of Directors, Minutes, 1940-1944 — 110
Minutes, memoranda to the board, material on the handling of Louis Brandeis' bequest to Survey Associates, material on editorial and financial matters, and Paul Kellogg's citation by the National Committee for Planned Parenthood at the Birth Control Federation of America conference, 1942.

Survey Associates, Board of Directors, Minutes, 1945-1952 — 111
Minutes, memoranda, and material on editorial plans, staff, finance, membership, and the Survey's continuing financial crisis.

Survey Associates, Board of Directors, Special Committee, 1948 — 112
The committee was appointed in June, 1948, under the chairmanship of Victor Weybright, to consider the Survey's financial situation and to decide whether or not to continue publication.

Editor's Memorandum to the Special Committee of the Board of Directors, 1936 — 113
Material re the history, scope, policies, and problems of Survey Associates.

Finance, Correspondence and Papers, 1936-1951 — 114-115
Papers dealing generally with financial problems, fund-raising, contributions to Survey Associates, cost of publication, etc. Includes extensive material on the Survey's financial crisis of the 1940's and the decision to continue publication in 1948.

Finance, Records, 1924-1951   116-122
    Primarily "condensed statements" and "comparative balance sheets." Includes occasional audit reports and budget material.

Louis D. Brandeis Fund, 1941-1948   123
    Correspondence re Brandeis' bequest (of approximately $82,000) to Survey Associates and from persons seeking to use the funds. Correspondents include Josephine and Pauline Goldmark, Felix Frankfurter, Roger Baldwin, Alice Goldmark Brandeis, and other members of the Brandeis family. Includes remarks by Felix Frankfurter and Dean Acheson at the Brandeis funeral service.

Charles M. Cabot Fund, 1925-1939   124
    In his will Charles Cabot established a $50,000 trust fund for the study of industrial conditions, naming Kellogg, Philip Cabot (Cabot's brother), and Edward T. Devine as trustees. Material re Philip Cabot's request that the unspent portion of the fund be given to the Graduate School of Business Administration at Harvard. Correspondents include Richard C. Cabot, Edward T. Devine, Samuel McCune Lindsay, John A. Fitch, and Morris L. Cooke.

Paul Hagen Fund, 1941-1949   125
    Material re money raised by Survey Associates to send Karl B. Frank, a member of the anti-Nazi underground who wrote under the name Paul Hagen, to Germany as a correspondent. He was denied security clearance by the War Department.

Kyron Foundation, 1949-1950   126
    In 1949 Survey Associates formed and was the sole beneficiary of the Kyron Foundation, which acquired the stock of the Illinois Continental Pharmaceutical Corporation, producers of Kyron, a vitamin preparation used in weight reduction. Correspondence and papers re the agreement, payments, conferences, etc.

Field Foundation, 1944   127
    Application for financial assistance.

McGregor Foundation, 1937   128
    Application for financial assistance.

New York Foundation, 1948   129
    Application for financial assistance.

Rockefeller Foundation, 1944-1946   130
   Correspondence re 1944 application and copy of 1946 application.

Editorial Correspondence, 1909-1919   131
   Staff presentation to Edward T. Devine, National Council of Churches of Christ statement (1911) on industrial relations, copies of letters to Charles M. Cabot on conditions in the steel industry, statement to President Wilson on social legislation before the special session of the 63rd Congress (1913), letter from John M. Glenn, expressing his discontent on the direction of the Survey, and minutes of an informal conference of executives of national welfare agencies re helping the country in war time.

Editorial Correspondence, 1919-1923   132
   Article by Sidney D. Gamble, "The Making of the Peking Survey"; material for proposed special number on Russia; summary of 1923 legislative session in California; and Kellogg's letter re Bruno Lasker. Correspondents include Arthur Kellogg, Graham R. Taylor, and Grace House.

Editorial Correspondence, 1924   133-134
   Article and discussion of the premillenarian movement; material re social work, fundamentalism, and the churches; material re race relations courses in southern colleges; Survey staff responses to Harry Emerson Fosdick's criticisms of the social gospel; and staff correspondence. Correspondents include Marion "Clinch" Calkins, Geddes Smith, Joseph K. Hart, Ozora S. Davis, and Harry Ward.

Editorial Correspondence, 1925   135-137
   Correspondence and memoranda. Includes material on workers education; leisure; the race relations department of the Community Council of St. Louis, Missouri; social service and immigration; and an outline of a book on race relations on the Pacific Coast. Correspondents include Francis Hackett, Geddes Smith, the Foreign Language Information Service, Joseph K. Hart, Marion "Clinch" Calkins, Leon R. Whipple, and Robert W. Bruere.

Editorial Correspondence, 1926   138
   Primarily material re Survey staff, especially Ann Reed Brenner and Geddes Smith.

Editorial Correspondence, 1927-1929   139
    Material on J. Ramsay MacDonald and the British Labour Party; Kellogg's report of a conversation with Sidney Hillman, Oswald Garrison Villard, Lillian Wald, and MacDonald; clippings re Kellogg's being named to the honor roll of the Ethical Society of St. Louis. Correspondents include Arthur Kellogg, Jane Addams, Ethel Richardson Allen, Mary Austin, and John Palmer Gavit.

Editorial Correspondence, 1930-1932   140
    Material on Gandhi, the need for a Pittsburgh research organization on employment, and on Richard Patrick Kellogg. Correspondents include William M. Leiserson, William Allen White, Michael M. Davis, John D. Kenderdine, Beulah Amidon, and Robert W. De Forest.

Editorial Correspondence, 1933-1934   141
    Pierce Williams' field reports for the FERA on conditions in eastern and middlewestern cities and on employment in lumber and metal mining industries. Correspondents include Hendrik Willem Van Loon, William H. Matthews, and Robert W. De Forest.

Editorial Correspondence, 1935   142
    Includes staff memoranda on editorial plans, material on the American Farm School (Salonika, Greece), Grace Coyle's speech on group work and social change, Mary Van Kleeck's report on the International Industrial Relations Institute, report of Kellogg's being awarded the New York *Evening Post* Alumni Association medal for editorial leadership, letter of resignation from James G. McDonald (high commissioner for refugees coming from Germany), and petition to Franklin Roosevelt opposing increased militarization of the CCC. Correspondents include Mary Ross, James Forbes, Lillian D. Wald, and Helen Hayes Gleason. Includes copy of Louis Brandeis' testimony to the U.S. Industrial Relations Commission, 1914, and of John Fitch's article on Thomas Mooney.

Editorial Correspondence, 1936   143
    Includes material on staff plans, social security coverage, and Kellogg's letter to Julius Rosenwald on the needs of the *Survey*. Correspondents include Joseph K. Hart, John Palmer Gavit, and Louis Brandeis.

Editorial Correspondence, 1937   144
    Material on tenant farmers in the South and social work in Los Angeles, portion of a draft of a book by William H. Matthews re Pittsburgh and the Kingsley House Settlement, and copy of 1892 letter on strikes

from Josephine Shaw Lowell to the New York Herald Tribune. Correspondents include Lillian D. Wald, John Palmer Gavit, and Mary Ross.

Editorial Correspondence, 1938   145-147
    Material re social insurance in Great Britain, the German Civil Service Act of 1937, unemployment and relief, U.S. Civil Service, Gypsies, birth control, American Hospital Association insurance plan, medical services in Cook County, Illinois, and social security. Includes letters re Alexander Johnson, Kellogg's support of Felix Frankfurter for the Supreme Court, and Dr. Haven Emerson's resignation from the Survey staff on the grounds that the Survey was "medical baiting."

Editorial Correspondence, 1939-1940   148
    Material on William H. Matthews' defense of Harry Hopkins, the Spanish Civil War, and results of an American Association of Social Workers' survey of public relief programs.

Editorial Correspondence, 1941   149-150
    Staff memoranda and material on Louis Brandeis, housing, efforts to place control of CCC under Federal Board of Vocational Education, and labor. Includes a telegram inviting Kellogg to a private conference on war aims.

Editorial Correspondence, 1942   151
    Routine material.

Editorial Correspondence, 1943-1944   152
    Material re Flanner House (Indianapolis, Indiana), race relations, postwar planning, and hiring of staff member Bradley Buell.

Editorial Correspondence, 1945-1946   153
    Primarily routine correspondence and staff material.

Editorial Correspondence, 1947   154-157
    Material on Flanner House (Indianapolis, Indiana), housing, the Rockefeller Foundation, displaced persons, public relations and social work, hiring of staff members, workers education, India, the Pittsburgh Survey and the steel industry, physics and politics. Correspondents include Harold H. Swift, Fred K. Hoehler, Irving Dilliard, Richard Neuberger, Percy MacKaye, Albert Mayer, Thomas Devine, and Daniel S. Gillmor. Includes material on Julian Huxley's interest in primitive art and a report of the Indian Arts and Crafts Board of the U.S. Department of the Interior.

Editorial Correspondence, 1948   158
    Material re Kasturba, wife of Gandhi; Edward T.
    Devine; financial situation of Survey; and staff
    members Mollie Condon, Beulah Amidon, and Thomas
    Devine.

Editorial Correspondence, 1949   159-161
    Material re applications for positions on the Survey
    staff, Miriam Van Waters and Massachusetts penology,
    and consumers. Includes drafts of Lillie M. Peck's
    article "Beveridge Is Not Enough," (Survey, vol. 85,
    October, 1949).

Editorial Correspondence, 1950   162
    Material on Penn Normal Industrial and Agricultural
    School (St. Helena, South Carolina) and the Committee
    on Research in Medical Economics.

Editorial Correspondence, 1951-1952   163
    Primarily material re staff matters.

Editorial Correspondence, Halle Schaffner, 1930   164
    Material re the death of Halle Schaffner, staff member.

Publishing Memoranda, 1932-1933   165
    John Hanrahan, magazine consultant, analyzed the
    background and interests of readers of the Survey
    and Survey Graphic and recommended separation of
    the two magazines and increased work on Survey
    Graphic content. Includes his report, discussion
    of it by Kellogg and members of the board, pub-
    lishing and circulation figures, and a "profile"
    of the Survey reader.

Inquiry to Survey Midmonthly Readers, 1941   166
    Form letter to readers asking about content and
    coverage, and summary of replies received.

Inquiry to Survey Midmonthly Readers, Replies, 1941   167
    Replies to inquiry, arranged as the staff numbered
    them (1-50).

Editor's Intineraries, 1925-1951.   168

Editor's Pacific Coast Trip, 1925   169-170
    Correspondence and papers, including notes of
    introduction, arrangements for lectures, staff
    correspondence with Kellogg, etc.

Jane Addams, "Social Service and the Progressive Party," 1929-1930   171
    Draft of chapter for her book, The Second Twenty Years at Hull House (Macmillan, 1930).

Rossa B. Cooley, ca.1923   172
    Plans and outlines for "Day Clean," a proposed book by Miss Cooley from which the Survey drew articles, the first of which was published in vol. 51, October 1, 1923.

Samuel S. Fels, Correspondence, 1928-1933   173-177
    Correspondence and papers re Kellogg's efforts to help Fels, a manufacturer and businessman, write his book, This Changing World: As I See Its Trend and Purpose (published in 1933).

Samuel S. Fels, "This Daily Life of Ours," ca.1930   178
    Copy of early draft of manuscript by Fels, which was later published as This Changing World: As I See Its Trend and Purpose.

Samuel S. Fels, Economic Chapters, Draft, 1931-1932?   179-180

Samuel S. Fels, This Changing World: As I See Its Trend And Purpose (Partial Book Dummy), 1932?   181

Samuel S. Fels, Survey Articles, 1933   182
    Reprints of three articles, drawn from his book (This Changing World: As I See Its Trend and Purpose). The first article was published in vol. 22, February, 1933.

Andrew Furuseth, 1923-1924   183
    Correspondence and papers re a proposed series of articles on seamen Furuseth would do in collaboration with Arthur Gleason.

Patrick Geddes, Correspondence, 1919-1926   184-185
    Geddes was a professor of sociology and civics and a city and regional planner. Material re education, organization of universities, city and regional planning, etc. Correspondents include Bruno Lasker and Lewis Mumford. The Survey published a series of articles by Geddes, "Talks from My Outlook Tower," the first of which appeared in Survey, vol. 53, February, 1925.

Patrick Geddes, Lectures at the New School for Social Research, New York City, 1923.   186-187

Patrick Geddes, "Regions and Cities in Surveys and Interpretations," 1923? 188
    Early draft intended for use in series.

Patrick Geddes, "From My Outlook Tower," 1923-1924 189-190
    Revised draft from which the Survey drew its series of articles.

Patrick Geddes, "Frederic Le Play and His School of Social Science," 1924 191
    Draft of chapter for inclusion in Survey series, and material re surveys, sociology, and regional and city planning.

Patrick Geddes, Illustrative Material, 1899, n.d. 192

Henry Lowenfeld, 1924 193
    Correspondence re and draft of "Money in Fetters. Its History and Mystery Candidly Related," a proposed article on currency reform by Lowenfeld. Includes correspondence from Hendrik Willem Van Loon.

Joseph Stella, ca.1921-1925 194
    Material by and about Joseph Stella.

Academic Freedom, Freedom of Speech and Press, 1913-1916 195
    Kellogg's notes; draft of his article, "The Old Freedoms Discussed by Twentieth Century Sociologists," (Survey, vol. 33, January 9, 1915); and extensive clippings re Scott Nearing, a professor of economics who was fired by the University of Pennsylvania for his radical views.

American Red Cross, 1928 196
    Clippings and material re ARC's work during the Puerto Rico hurricane disaster.

Child Labor Amendment, 1923-1927 197
    Correspondence, clippings, press releases, and material re the child labor amendment (proposed 20th amendment) and child labor laws in Kansas, Massachusetts, and Pennsylvania. Includes copy of a letter to Florence Kelley on child labor problems in California.

Election (Presidential) of 1916 198
    Probably Kellogg's working papers for an article "Three Platforms," published in Survey, vol.36, June 24, 1916. Material on the Democratic, Republican, and Progressive party platforms.

Floods, 1936   199
> Material re floods in the eastern part of the U.S. and WPA and American Red Cross relief activities.

"Henry Ford's Hired Men," 1927-1928   200
> Material re Kellogg's two articles, published in Survey, vol. 54, February 1 and March 1, 1928. Includes draft of articles, correspondence from readers re articles, and material on relief and unemployment in Detroit.

"Henry Ford's Hired Men," Materials, 1922-1930   201
> Material re Henry Ford, profit sharing, the automobile industry, automation, etc.

Hospitals, 1915-1917   202
> Correspondence and papers re hospital social service and fire hazards in hospitals.

Industrial Relations Commission (U.S.), 1914-1917   203-204
> Statements to the Commission by Kellogg and Edward T. Devine, drafts of Survey articles, and extensive material re a controversy between Kellogg and Frank P. Walsh, Commission chairman who questioned Kellogg's relations with wealthy persons and foundations. Includes an article, "How Tainted Money Taints" (Pearson's Magazine, March, 1915), accusing the Survey of being influenced by the Rockefeller Foundation and similar interests; Kellogg's reply; and defense of Kellogg by the New Republic, Outlook, and others. Material on George Creel, the Rockefeller Foundation, history of the U.S. Industrial Relations Commission, the Colorado Coal strike (1914), and the relations of foundations to philanthropy.

Industrial Relations Commission (U.S.), Drafts of Articles, n.d.   205
> Unidentified and miscellaneous material re industrial relations, strikes, boycott, right of labor to organize, personnel of the Commission, etc.

Industrial Relations and Industrial Relations Commission, Clippings, 1911-1915   206
> Material re Theodore Roosevelt, labor relations, genesis of the Commission, the Colorado coal strike (1914), Frank P. Walsh, the Rockefeller Foundation, etc.

International Joint Commission (U.S. and Canada), 1928-1930   207
> The Commission was established to handle boundary

waters and frontier questions arising between the two countries. Correspondence with Charles A. Magrath and Lawrence J. Burpee and draft of article (or speech) by Kellogg.

International Joint Commission (U.S. and Canada), Materials, 1915-1929   208
Pamphlets and material relating to the Commission, sent to Kellogg for his information and possible use in an article or speech.

Knights of Columbus Oath, 1920-1923   209
The Ku Klux Klan evidently circulated a false version of the Knights' oath. Material re the controversy about it.

Mexico Survey (Proposed), 1915-1917   210-211
Kellogg's outline for survey, pamphlets, clippings, and material apparently used to draw up the outline. Material on Mexican-U.S. relations and social development and conditions in Mexico.

National Resources Committee, 1938   212
Report, The Problems of a Changing Population; letter of transmittal; and a memorandum by Victor Weybright re southern senators delaying publication of the report because it reflected unfavorably on the South. Includes data on population trends, internal migration, health, welfare, etc.

Negro Manuscripts, ca.1946-1948   213
Material on race relations in Gary, Indiana; segregation; and racial discrimination within the U.S. Army. Correspondence with Lester B. Granger.

Neighbors Department, 1923-1924, 1930   214
Material proposed for use in Survey's neighbors department, including material on Mary M. Bartelme (first woman circuit court judge in Illinois), James T. Shotwell, Roland Hayes, etc.

New York State Commission Against Discrimination (SCAD), 1946-1947   215
Material re proposed article by Will Maslow and Max Berking of the American Jewish Congress. Material on race relations, anti-Semitism, and possible publication of the article in Reader's Digest.

Pennsylvania Series, 1914-1915   216
Correspondence and papers re "Social Legislation in the Keystone State," a series of articles by Florence Sanville, the first of which was published in Survey,

vol. 33, February 6, 1915. Material re gubernatorial elections in Pennsylvania, prison labor and welfare, labor relations in Pittsburgh, the Pittsburgh Survey, and Kellogg's efforts to promote the series. Includes copies of AFL resolutions on prison labor, 1897-1914.

Playground Series, 1916   217
Material re "Exporting the American Playground," a series by C. M. Goethe, the first article of which was published in Survey, vol. 36, June 3, 1916. Primarily correspondence from persons in Australia, China, India, Japan, New Zealand, Brazil, and other countries, responding to notice of the series and commenting on local playground conditions.

Requests for Contributions of Articles from Britons, 1913   218
Kellogg requested certain persons to contribute articles on social and economic conditions from the British point of view. Requests and replies.

Rural Life and Welfare, 1911-1916   219
Material re rural churches, farm life conditions in the South, effects of urbanization, and ways in which the Survey might cover rural needs and rural social work.

Seamen's Bill and Safety-at-Sea, 1913-1916   220
Correspondence, memoranda, and drafts of articles. Includes material on conditions in the U.S. merchant marine, safety-at-sea legislation, Great Lakes shipping, Andrew Furuseth, cancellation of steamship advertising in the Survey, and passage of the La-Follette's seamen's bill (1915) and efforts to repeal it.

Seamen's Bill and Safety-at-Sea, 1912-1915   221-222
Material on seamen, LaFollette's seamen's bill, safety-at-sea, the United Fruit Company, International Seamen's Union of America, etc.

Seamen's Bill and Safety-at-Sea, Clippings, 1913-1915.   223

Social Settlements, 1930-1934   224
Draft of Kellogg's article on settlements for the Encyclopedia of Social Sciences, exchange between Kellogg and Alvin Johnson (Encyclopedia editor) re settlements, and correspondence with Albert J. Kennedy re his article on settlements for the Social Work Year Book, 1933 edition.

Special Numbers, 1923-ca.1932   225
    Material re proposed special numbers on crime and
    prisons, Palestine, children, the arts, the blind,
    etc. Correspondents include Samuel S. Fels, Bruno
    Lasker, Ann Reed Brenner, Isaac M. Rubinow, Julian
    Mack, Frank Tannenbaum, Alice S. Cheyney, Ethel
    Kawin, and Herman Adler.

Special Numbers, Data, 1939-1948   226
    Lists of special numbers, persons contributing to
    them, and costs of issuing them.

Special Numbers, Cotton (Proposed), 1920-1923   227
    Correspondence re child labor in the South, plan
    for the number, and clippings re the boll weevil,
    the tariff, and the industrial boom in the South.

Special Numbers, Mexico, 1930-1931   228
    Correspondence, memoranda, and list of contributors
    to the number, which was published in *Survey*, vol.
    66, May 1, 1931. Includes an undated report on
    border crossings, aliens, etc.

Special Numbers, "New Germany," 1928-1929   229
    Correspondence, memoranda, and press releases re the
    number, which was published in *Survey*, vol. 61,
    February 1, 1929. Material largely re Kellogg's
    efforts to raise funds for the issue and to promote
    circulation of it, but also includes a letter (April
    26, 1929) criticizing the issue for ignoring under-
    currents in Germany.

Special Numbers, Supreme Court and Labor (Proposed),   230
1922-1923
    Digest of Court decisions involving national regu-
    lation of industrial relations, cartoons, clippings,
    etc.

Special Numbers, Woods (Proposed), Correspondence and   231-232
Papers, 1925-1928
    Material re utilization of wood, conservation, state
    forestry and parks, U.S. Forest Products Laboratory
    at Madison (Wisconsin), Save the Redwoods League,
    American Forestry Association, etc.

Special Numbers, Woods (Proposed), Materials, 1922-1928   233-235
    Pamphlets, clippings, etc. re wood conservation,
    forestry, American Wood Preservers Association,
    U.S. Forest Products Laboratory at Madison, Wisconsin,
    etc.

Survey of National Organizations, 1914   236
    After receiving a letter from a southwestern university noting the dearth of Southerners on the board of the American Association for Labor Legislation, Kellogg sent questionnaries to "national organizations in the social field" re composition of their boards of directors and administrative staff. The returned forms are filed alphabetically by association.

Unemployment, General, 1923-1932   237
    Press releases, speech, clippings, list of Survey articles on unemployment, 1931-1932, etc.

Unemployment, 1936   238
    Material for Kellogg's article, "Not Floods But Glaciers," published in Survey Graphic, vol. 25, May, 1936. Data on wages in manufacturing industries in Allegheny County (Pennsylvania) and cases from the Family Society of Allegheny County showing the effects of unemployment.

Unemployment, Materials, 1933-1936   239
    Includes marked copies of University of Pittsburgh, Pittsburgh Business Review; Federation of Social Agencies of Pittsburgh and Allegheny County, Social Research Bulletin; and American Iron and Steel Institute, Steel Facts.

"What's Worth Fighting For in American Life?" 1926   240
    The series (the first article of which was published in Survey, vol. 57, February 1, 1927) evolved from a discussion of the 1920's as a "period of sag" in American life. Includes staff memoranda, lists of potential contributors, invitations to potential contributors, etc.

Workmen's Compensation, 1914-1915   241
    Correspondence, clippings, and draft of article. Correspondents include William M. Leiserson, John B. Andrews, John M. Glenn, Florence Kelley, Isaac M. Rubinow, Workmen's Compensation Service Bureau, National Civic Federation, and Workmen's Compensation Publicity Bureau.

World War I, Correspondence and Papers, 1914-1917   242
    Includes analysis of war coverage in the technical press, letters praising and criticizing the Survey's coverage of the war and various peace movements, and Kellogg's memorandum (February 20, 1917) defending his position. Correspondents include Jane Addams, George W. Nasmyth, Edward T. Devine, William Borah,

Joseph Lee, William E. Harmon, Frederic Almy, John A. Fitch, Bruno Lasker, and others.

World War I, "A Canadian City /Montreal/ in War Time," Correspondence, 1917-1918   243
>Correspondence re Kellogg's series, the first article of which was published in Survey, vol. 38, March 17, 1917. The series dealt with the Patriotic Fund of Canada, which gave assistance to families of armed forces men.

World War I, "A Canadian City /Montreal/ in War Time," Materials, 1915-1917   244-247
>Statements and reports of interviews, clippings, memorandum on immigration prepared for the Dominions Royal Commission at Montreal, reports of the Montreal Soldiers' Wives' League, etc. Includes reprints of Kellogg's series.

World War I, Reconstruction, 1914-1919   248
>Material, especially memoranda by Bruno Lasker, on social reconstruction after the war.

World War I, "War-Boom Towns," 1915-1916   249
>Series of articles, the first of which was published in Survey, vol. 35, December 4, 1915. Material re effect of war on a community, memoranda with suggestions for series, and correspondence with John Ihlder, Mary Van Kleeck, Margaret Dreier Robins, and Shelby M. Harrison.

World War I, Pamphlets, 1914-1917   250
>Material from World Peace Foundation, International Congress of Women, League to Enforce Peace, Women's Peace Party, etc.

World War I, Atrocity Propaganda, ca.1915   251
>Reports of a Russian Extraordinary Commission of Inquiry on atrocities committed by German and Austro-Hungarian troops.

World War I, Clippings, 1915-1917, 1924   252
>Re Karl Liebknecht, Jane Addams, preparedness, women's groups' peace efforts, Henry Ford's peace expedition, pacifism, militarism, etc.

World War I, Henry Ford Peace Ship Cartoons, 1915-1916   253
>Ford organized a peace expedition to Europe in 1915. Original cartoons and copies of them.

Unpublished Manuscripts from Contributors, 1942-1949   254-259
    Manuscripts and often surrounding correspondence.
    Material re Farm Security Administration, agricul-
    tural labor in wartime, John Collier, Weimar Repub-
    lic, impact of World War II, atomic power, Russia,
    social movements in South America, journalism,
    regional and city planning, juvenile delinquency,
    health, bureaucracy, world government, India, etc.

<u>Survey</u> Newspaper Clippings, 1914-1949   260
    Primarily re coverage given to <u>Survey</u> articles,
    features, special issues, etc.

Membership Statements, 1938-1952   261
    Members of Survey Associates contributed money be-
    yond the cost of a subscription. Records of income,
    funds, and departments to which it was allotted, and
    occasional figures on number of members.

Advertising, 1923-1943   262
    Statements of income.

Circulation Department, 1931-1937   263
    Records.

Field Work Reports, 1934-1943   264-267
    Records of subscriptions sold by field workers.

Promotion, <u>Survey Graphic</u>, 1944-1948   268
    Reports on cost of promotion, amount of returns,
    and subscriptions resulting from such efforts.

Promotion, Materials, 1924-1949   269-270
    Form letters and brochures sent to Survey Associates
    and prospective subscribers and material on promo-
    tional efforts of other magazines.

Promotion, Appeal to Signers of Sacco-Vanzetti Petition to   271
Become Members of Survey Associates, 1927
    Primarily letters replying to Kellogg's offer to send
    the signers introductory copies of the <u>Survey</u>.

Promotion, Janet Sabloff, 1950-1951   272
    Correspondence re her efforts to raise funds and
    provide publicity for <u>Survey</u>. List of funds raised
    by Miss Sabloff, Kellogg's personal secretary.

Production Department, Graphic File, American Red Cross,   273*
ca.1919.

* Folders 273-304 contain glossy prints, cartoons, clippings
from magazines and newspapers, and other material which the
<u>Survey</u> staff evidently drew on for illustrating articles.

Production Department, Graphic File, Art Education, ca.1921-1923. 274

Production Department, Graphic File, Bolshevism, ca.1921-1923. 275

Production Department, Graphic File, Books, ca.1921-1923. 276

Production Department, Graphic File, Child Labor, ca.1924. 277

Production Department, Graphic File, Child Welfare, ca.1919-1923. 278

Production Department, Graphic File, Czechoslovakia, 1906, ca.1921. 279

Production Department, Graphic File, Disarmament, 1914-1923. 280

Production Department, Graphic File, Facts on Disarmament, ca.1921. 281

Production Department, Graphic File, Foreign [sic], General, ca.1919-1923. 282

Production Department, Graphic File, Germany, ca.1919-1923. 283

Production Department, Graphic File, Charles Haag, n.d. 284
    Photographs of the work of Haag, a sculptor.

Production Department, Graphic File, Harlem, ca.1922. 285

Production Department, Graphic File, Hungary, 1920. 286

Production Department, Graphic File, India, ca.1921. 287

Production Department, Graphic File, Indian (American) Art, ca.1922. 288

Production Department, Graphic File, Indians (American), ca.1922-1926. 289

Production Department, Graphic File, Industry, ca.1922. 290

Production Department, Graphic File, Italy, ca.1922-1923. 291

Production Department, Graphic File, Maps, 1921, n.d. 292

Production Department, Graphic File, Mexico, ca.1922-1924 293
    Includes a Weinold Reiss catalog.

Production Department, Graphic File, Negro, ca.1921-1922.   294

Production Department, Graphic File, Palestine, n.d.   295

Production Department, Graphic File, Poverty, ca.1919-1921.   296

Production Department, Graphic File, Prohibition, 1914-1921.   297

Production Department, Graphic File, Public Health, ca.1920.   298

Production Department, Graphic File, Russia, 1920s   299
    Photographs probably intended for use in article by Sanford Griffith, "Russian Factory Wheels in Motion," Survey, vol. 48, July 1, 1922.

Production Department, Graphic File, Seals and Medals, n.d.   300
    Seals of countries, organizations, Women's Trade Union League, etc.

Production Department, Graphic File, Transportation, 1921.   301

Production Department, Graphic File, Vienna, n.d.   302

Production Department, Graphic File, Miscellaneous, ca.1911-1923.   303

Production Department, Graphic File, Miscellaneous, n.d.   304

Hughes Printing Company, 1949   305
    Correspondence re printing of Survey.

Type Talks (Type Book), 1928?   306

Advisory Council on Economic Security to the (President's) Committee on Economic Security, 1934-1935   307
    Material re naming of council (of which Kellogg was a member), procedure for it, Kellogg's suggestion of additional members, guaranteed employment, and extension of coverage of workmen's compensation. Kellogg drafted a minority report opposing what he considered to be inadequate unemployment insurance proposed in the council's report. Correspondents include Frances Perkins, Edwin E. Witte, William Green, and Frank P. Graham.

American Union Against Militarism, 1914-1915 308
    Primarily correspondence re publishing a statement, Towards the Peace That Shall Last. Correspondents include Jane Addams, Florence Kelley, Edward T. Devine, Lillian D. Wald, Felix Adler, Louis Brandeis, William Dean Howells, Thomas Edison, and other prominent Americans.

American Union Against Militarism, 1915 309
    After publishing the statement, several signers decided to keep the group together to make further peace efforts. Includes minutes of meeting, resolutions of the Women's Trade Union League, report of Jane Addams' peace efforts abroad, material on Chicago Peace Society and the Women's Peace Party, Louis Brandeis' speech on "True Americanism," Jane Addams' address at Carnegie Hall, etc. Correspondents include Mornay Williams, Jane Addams, Rabbi Stephen Wise, George Kirchwey, Frederic Howe, and others.

American Union Against Militarism, 1915-1917 310
    Minutes of further meetings from which evolved the AUAM, financial material, letter inquiring about conscientious objectors, Kellogg's draft of an invitation to join the Henry Ford peace expedition, etc. Correspondents and subjects include Emily Greene Balch, Rosika Schwimmer, J. Lionberger Davis, Anna Garlin Spencer, etc.

Louis D. Brandeis, Statement Supporting His Nomination to the Supreme Court, 1916 311
    Signers include Kellogg, Lillian D. Wald, Florence Kelley, John A. Fitch, Robert W. Bruere, Ernest Poole, George Alger, and others.

Committee on Cultural Relations with Mexico, 1930 312
    Kellogg participated in a seminar in Mexico sponsored by the Committee. Includes list of participants, outline of program, etc.

Committee on Industrial Relations to Secure the Appointment of a Federal Commission on Industrial Relations, 1911-1917 313
    Kellogg was the Committee's secretary. Includes lists of committee members, minutes of meetings, statements of purpose and on industrial relations, material on the bill to create a commission, and material on reaction to President Taft's nominees

for the Commission. Correspondents and subjects
include John Haynes Holmes, Rabbi Stephen Wise,
Edward T. Devine, Graham R. Taylor, Adolph
Lewisohn, John M. Glenn, George Foster Peabody,
Frank P. Walsh, John A. Fitch, and others.

Committee on Industrial Relations to Secure the Appointment of a Federal Commission on Industrial Relations, Chicago Committee, 1912-1913   314
    Graham R. Taylor was secretary of the Chicago
committee. Includes lists of members, minutes
of meetings, and material protesting the nomination of J. Mack Glenn to the commission. Correspondents include Anita McCormick (Mrs. Emmons)
Blaine, Edward T. Devine, Allen T. Burns, Samuel
McCune Lindsay, Julius Rosenwald, and others.

Committee on Industrial Relations to Secure the Appointment of a Federal Commission on Industrial Relations, Publications, ca.1912   315
    Material on hours in the steel industry, the Industrial Relations Commission, industrial relations,
etc.

Committee on Industrial Relations to Secure the Appointment of a Federal Commission on Industrial Relations, Pamphlets, 1912-1915   316
    Releases from the Committee on Coal Mine Managers,
sermon by John Haynes Holmes, report of the Industrial
Relations Commission, etc.

Election (Presidential) of 1924   317
    Kellogg campaigned for the LaFollette-Wheeler
Progressive Party ticket. Includes material on
response to attack on LaFollette by 48 "Roosevelt
progressives," and Amos Pinchot's letter to Wheeler
defending LaFollette.

Foreign Policy Association, 1921-1949   318
    Notices of meetings, minutes, clippings, 1938
letter on conditions in Germany, and material re
FPA's tenth anniversary in 1928. Kellogg was
one of the founders and a board member of FPA.

League of Free Nations Association, 1917-1920   319
    Kellogg invited a group to luncheon to discuss
problems of international adjustment which would
arise following the war. This group became the
Committee on Nothing at All, later the Committee
on Foreign Policy, and the LFNA. Includes minutes,
speeches, and material on Russian-American relations.

League of Free Nations Association, Publications, 1918-1919? 320
    Statements of principles and purpose of the LFNA.

National Conference of Charities and Correction, 1910-1912 321
    Report of the Committee on occupational standards of which Kellogg was chairman in 1910; memorandum to the committee on standards of living and labor on "Planks in a Living and Industrial Platform"; program of the 1912 National Conference; and <u>Social Standards for Industry: A Platform</u> (of the committee on standards of living and labor).

National Conference of Social Work, 1936-1950 322
    Primarily correspondence and paper re Kellogg's presidency of NCSW, 1939. Includes material re Kellogg's speech to the Child Welfare League of America at the 1938 National Conference and issues of concern to the League. Brief material re the Survey Award presented at the 1950 National Conference (the award, given annually for "imaginative and constructive contribution to social work," was established in 1949).

National Conference of Social Work, Clippings, 1939 323
    Re Kellogg's presidency of the National Conference.

National Conference on Labor Legislation, 1935-1941 324
    NCLL was an annual conference composed of delegates designated by governors; Kellogg was invited by Frances Perkins. Material re three conferences, including a report of the 1935 conference. Material on industrial "home work," report of a wage and hours committee, and material on industrial conditions.

New York State Employment Service, State Advisory Council, 1934-1940 325-326
    Kellogg chaired the advisory council. Material re the origin and development of the council, 1934 memorandum on employment of Negroes in the administrative offices of the New York State Employment Service, cost of administering unemployment insurance in New York, New York City employment service, and operating relationships with the U.S. Employment Service.

Office of Defense Mobilization, Mobilization Conference, 1951 327
    Brief correspondence and transcript of conference which was held for editors, commentators, and columnists.

Office of Defense Mobilization, Mobilization Conference, Papers, 1951   328
    Material distributed at conference and/or papers read at it.

Penn Normal Industrial and Agricultural School, St. Helena Island, South Carolina, 1938-1950   329
    Kellogg was a member of the school's advisory board. Annual report, minutes of executive and finance committees and trustees' report.

Pittsburgh Survey, 1906-1916   330
    Miscellaneous material re Pittsburgh Survey, the first community survey in the U.S., which Kellogg directed. Correspondence re editorial work on the six-volume report of the survey, material on labor conditions in Pittsburgh (1914), clippings, and draft of chapter (or portion of a chapter) by William H. Matthews. Includes a letter (June 11, 1906) from an Allegheny County, Pennsylvania, probation officer asking if it would be possible "to make a study and a report of social conditions in Pittsburgh and vicinity?"

Progressive Party, 1912-1913   331
    Memorandum re organization of an "Educational Council," George Kirchwey's memorandum on Progressive Party functions and methods, an organization blueprint for the party, incomplete stenographic notes of a meeting re party organization, and what is evidently material used in drafting the party platform.

Progressive Party, Progressive National Service, Special Committee on Sickness and Old Age Insurance, 1914   332
    Reports of the committee and digest of laws on workmen's compensation (1914). Copy of a letter from Joseph P. Chamberlain to Jane Addams on the party implementing its plank supporting the general principle of sickness insurance.

Progressive Party, Publications and Pamphlets, 1912-1913   333
    Includes Amos Pinchot's _What's the Matter with America_, Thomas Edison's decision to support the progressive party, the party platform, and publications of the Progressive National Service and the legislative committee of the National Progressive Party in New York State.

Sacco-Vanzetti, Correspondence and Papers, 1927-1929   334
    Accounts of a meeting Kellogg and others had with
    Massachusetts governor Alvan T. Fuller; Kellogg's
    account of the arrest of Powers Hapgood; who was
    addressing a group on the Boston Commons, pro-
    testing handling of the case. Correspondents
    include Dr. Alice Hamilton, Waldo Cook, John
    Lovejoy Elliot, Felix Frankfurter, John F.
    Moors, Edward S. Drown, and others.

Sacco-Vanzetti, Pamphlets, 1925-1929   335-336
    Publications of the Sacco-Vanzetti Defense Committee
    and the Independent Sacco-Vanzetti Committee, articles,
    cartoons from the Daily Worker, etc.

Sacco-Vanzetti, Clippings, 1927-1929.   337

Social Policy Committee, 1935   338
    The committee, which included Edward T. Devine, John
    Lovejoy Elliot, Helen Hall, Oswald Garrison Villard,
    Bruce Bliven, and others, organized to follow up a
    1934 statement to President Roosevelt on the direction
    of the New Deal. Material on the Wagner-Lewis Bill,
    the future of the NRA, foreign policy, etc.

Spanish Refugee Relief Campaign, 1939-1940   339-340
    Correspondence and papers re work to assist refugees
    of the Spanish Civil War. Extensive material re
    controversy over political involvement of some members
    of the board of directors and the staff, which resulted
    in members of the New York City chapter leaving the
    national organization to form a separate one. Includes
    report, "An Inside History of the Spanish Refugee Relief
    Campaign," 1940.

Statement to President Roosevelt re NRA, 1934   341
    Material re drafting of statement urging increased
    action through the NRA to aid recovery. Kellogg,
    Helen Hall, John Lovejoy Elliot, and Lucy Mason
    presented the statement to President Roosevelt in
    April, 1934. Correspondents include Amos Pinchot,
    Oswald Garrison Villard, Morris Ernst, and Edward
    T. Devine.

Statement to President Roosevelt re NRA, Second Edition, 1934   342
> Letters arranged alphabetically, from persons refusing to sign a second edition (May 23) of the statement. Among those refusing were Grace Abbott, Jane Addams, Richard C. Cabot, John A. Fitch, John Palmer Gavit, Pauline Goldmark, Amos Pinchot, Graham Taylor, Mary Van Kleeck, and T. Henry Walnut.

Statement to President Roosevelt re NRA, Replies to May 23 Form Letter, 1934   343
> With the second edition (May 23) Kellogg sent a form letter asking about steps to follow up the statement. Returned forms arranged alphabetically, from those expressing interest in further action and willing to sign later editions.

Statement to President Roosevelt re NRA, "Additional Replies," 1934   344
> Replies to May 23 edition and form letter received too late to be included in a third edition.

World Citizens Association, 1940   345
> Correspondence and material re this association which worked to secure an "effective world order."

EPHEMERA

The following is a list of material removed from the collection and placed in the Social Welfare Archives ephemera file. The material is listed below by publishing association, or by author or title where no publishing association is given.

U.S.

Algic Defense Committee. <u>The Story of the Algic Case</u>, 1938.

American Association for Labor Legislation. <u>American Labor Legislation Review</u>, 1:2 (June, 1911).

─────. <u>Three Years Under the New Jersey Workmen's Compensation Law: Report of an Investigation Under the Direction of the Social Insurance Committee of the American Association for Labor Legislation</u>, 1915.

─────. <u>Needless Coal Mine Accidents: A Program for Their Prevention</u>, 1924.

American Association of Social Workers. <u>The Compass</u>, 19:4 & 9 (January, June, 1938).

American Bar Association. Committee on Noteworthy Changes in Statute Law. <u>Report of the Committee . . . .</u>, 1916.

American Council on Race Relations. "News" (press releases), n.d.

American Friends of German Freedom. <u>Inside Germany Reports</u>, 1:6 (July, 1941).

─────. <u>In Re: Germany</u>, 1:11 (December, 1941).

American Institute of Social Service. <u>The Gospel of the Kingdom</u>, 6:6 (June, 1914).

American League Against War and Fascism. <u>Spain's Democracy Talks to America</u>, October, 1936.

American National Red Cross. <u>The Red Cross Courier</u>, June, 1942.

Antioch College, Yellow Springs, Ohio. <u>Antioch Notes</u>, 3:19, 4:3 (June 15 and October 1, 1926).

Bothin Convalescent Home, Manor, Marin County, California. *Sixteenth Annual Report of the Hill Farm: A Preventorium for Children*, 1920.

Bureau of Educational Counsel of the Lasalle-Peru Township High School and the Lasalle-Peru-Oglesby Junior College. *History and Description of a Personnel Program with Mental Hygiene Approach Attention to Individual Students Emphasis on Superior Students*, 1923-1926 report, 1927.

California Conference of Social Work. *Program* (17th annual meeting), 1925.

Committee for the Adoption of the Constitution. *Responsible Government*, 2a, 1915.

————. *Why the Constitution Should Be Adopted*, 3, 1915.

————. Henry L. Stimson. *Saving the State's Money*, 5, 1915.

————. Delancey Nicoll and Morgan J. O'Brien. *Reasons for Democratic Support*, 7, 1915.

————. Elihu Root. *Rights of Citizens Not in Danger*, 9, 1915.

Committee on the Federal Constitution. *Committee on the Federal Constitution*, ca.1915.

————. Seba Eldridge. *Need for a More Democratic Procedure of Amending the Federal Constitution*, 1915.

Common Council for American Unity. "Interpreter Releases," 24:20, 28:41 (May 2, 1947, September 14, 1951).

Common Sense, 7:7 (July, 1938).

Council for Pan American Democracy. *Starvation in Puerto Rico*, 1930s.

Czechoslovakia National Council of America. *News Flashes from Czechoslovakia Under Nazi Domination*, nos. 89-91, July, 1941.

Euthanasia Society of America, Inc. *Merciful Releases The Case for Voluntary Euthanasia*, n.d.

First United Presbyterian Church, Pittsburgh, Pennsylvania. *A Social Survey of the Twenty-Second and Twenty-Third Wards*, April-May, 1915.

Fisk University, Nashville, Tennessee. Fisk University News, 6:7, 7:9 & 10 (April, October-November, 1916).

Flanner House, Indianapolis, Indiana. 802 North West Street, 1941.

Foreign Policy Association. Foreign Policy Bulletins, 1941-1944.

_____. Foreign Policy Reports, 14:8. James F. Green, Canada in World Affairs, July 1, 1938.

_____. Headline Books No. 40. Thomas A. Bailey, America's Foreign Policies: Past and Present, May, 1943.

_____. Headline Series No. 89. Emil Langyel and Ernest O. Melby. Israel: Problems of Building, September-October, 1951.

_____. FPA, February, 1923.

_____. Foreign Policy Association Dinner in Honor of Lord Robert Cecil, 1923.

Greenwich Village Association. Bulletin, 1:1 (ca.February, 1941).

Group Health Cooperative. Directory of Participating Physicians and Surgeons, ca.1942.

Indiana State Department of Public Welfare. Public Welfare in Indiana, July, 1943.

Institute for Russian Studies of the Rand School of Social Science. Russian Affairs, 1:9 (October, 1945).

International Labor Organization. The Public and the International Labor Organization, ca.1938.

Jewish Welfare Federation of Omaha, Nebraska. Twentieth Annual Report, 1925.

K-H News-Letter, nos. 129-130, December, 1938, January, 1939.

Kingsley Association, Pittsburgh, Pennsylvania. Year Book: 1916.

Lawyers Committee on American Relations with Spain. Petition . . . . (re the Franco regime), 1939.

League for Industrial Democracy. LID News Bulletin, 14:1 (January, 1950).

League of Nations Association, Inc. League of Nations Association, January, 1939.

Medical Society of the State of New York. Frederick L. Hoffman. Compulsory Health Insurance and Disease Control, 1936.

Ministerial Union and Evangelical Churches of Pittsburgh and Allegheny County, Pennsylvania. Christian Social Service Union (an agency of the Ministerial Union), Bulletin 4 The Beast Exposed, December, 1915.

National Child Labor Committee. The American Child, 8:10 (October, 1925).

_____. It's Up to the States! 1924 or 1925.

_____. John A. Ryan. The Proposed Child Labor Amendment, 1924 or 1925.

_____. Twenty-Fifth Anniversary Conference. Program, December, 1929.

National Committee for the Defense of Political Prisoners. News You Don't Get, 1936-1938.

_____. Reports, 1937.

National Conference of Charities and Correction. Committee on Standards of Living and Labor. Social Standards for Industry: A Platform, 1912.

National Conference of Social Work. The Conference Bulletin, 41 (April and July, 1938).

_____. Daily Bulletins, 1925 Conference.

_____. Program of the Fifty-Second Annual Meeting, 1925.

_____. Conference brochure, 1925.

_____. Jane Addams: September 6, 1860-May 21, 1935, 1935.

_____. Make Your Reservations Now! (77th annual meeting), 1950.

National Consumers' League. The Door of Opportunity, 1925.

_____. "Proposed Principles for Labor Provisions of NRA Codes," December, 1933.

National Council for Prevention of War (formerly the National Peace Council). News Bulletin, 1928.

National Council of American-Soviet Friendship. Press release, November, 1949.

National Eucharistic Congress. An Address by Joseph V. Connally, 1938.

National Federation of Settlements. Miscellaneous mimeographed materials, 1949-1950.

National Lawyers Guild, New York Chapter. What Shall We do to Ensure the Servicemen's Vote? 1944.

National Urban League. This is Our Record for 1947 (annual report), 1948.

_____. "Annual Report January 1, 1946 - December 31, 1946," 1946.

_____. Press release, May 28, 1946.

_____. "Rulings," June 1, 1946.

New York State Commission Against Discrimination. Inside Facts, August, 1946.

New York State Committee on Discrimination in Housing. Forbidden Neighbors, 1950.

_____. "Toward Democracy in Housing: II," August, 1950.

Phelps-Stokes Fund. "Education for Life: Phelps-Stokes Fund and Thomas Jesse Jones. A Twenty-Fifth Anniversary, 1913-1937," 1937.

Planned Parenthood Federation of America. Information Service, no. 6, March, 1942.

Planning: A Broadsheet Issued by P E P (Political and Economic Planning, no. 138, January 10, 1939.

Public Ownership League of America. Public Ownership, 7:4 (April, 1925).

Social Workers Association of Oregon. Bulletin, 2:40 (June 17, 1925).

_____. Annual Conference of the Oregon Social Workers Association, 1925.

Social Work Publicity Council. "The Social Work Publicity Council Announces Award for 1932-1933 . . . .," 1933.

United Neighborhood Houses of New York, Inc. "50th Anniversary Dinner," 1951.

U.S. Senate. 62nd Congress, 2nd Session, Document No. 265. John R. Haynes. A Federal Mining Commission, 1912.

U.S. 82nd Congress, 1st Session. Joint Committee Print, 1951. Making Ends Meet on Less than $2,000 A Year . . . A Communication to the Joint Committee on the Economic Report from the Conference Group of Nine National Voluntary Organizations Convened by the National Social Welfare Assembly.

U.S. Federal Bureau of Prisons. "Social Service Digest. Social Treatment of the Adult Offender: Special Issue for the National Conference of Social Work," June, 1938.

U.S. "National Nutrition Conference for Defense" (called by the President), May, 1941.

U.S. National Recovery Administration. Report of the Operation of the National Industrial Recovery Act, 1935.

U.S. President's Interdepartmental Committee to Coordinate Health and Welfare Activities. National Health Conference, Material, 1938.

_____. The Need for a National Health Program: Report of the Technical Committee on Medical Care, 1938.

U.S. White House Conference on Children in a Democracy. National Citizens Committee. "Report of Activities, June, 1940 - January, 1943," December, 1942.

Washington State Conference of Social Work. Program for 1925 meeting, 1925.

Winnebago County, Illinois, Schools. Annual Report, 1913.

Woods Run Settlement Association, Pittsburgh, Pennsylvania. The Stenographer Writes (annual report), 1912-1913.

World Citizens Association. By-Laws of the World Citizens Association, December, 1939.

_____. A Platform for World Citizenship, December, 1939.

_____. Roger S. Greene. The Price of Peace, 1939.

_____. Quincy Wright. <u>World Citizens Association: A Statement of Its Purpose</u>, 1939.

_____. Eugene Staley. <u>This Shrinking World: World Technology vs. National Politics</u>, 1940.

_____. <u>The World Citizens Association . . . .</u>, 1940.

World Government News, Inc. <u>World Government News</u>, 9:94 (January, 1951).

Canadian

Legislative Assembly of Manitoba. <u>An Act Respecting the Welfare of Children</u>, 1917.

Federated Budget Board of Winnipeg, Inc. Edwart T. Devine. <u>Welfare Work in Winnipeg</u>, ca.1925.

Miscellaneous

Dowd, Matthew H. <u>The Rural Church and the Farmer</u>, 1912.

Klink, Jacob Charles. <u>Address of . . ., Grand Master of Masons in the State of New York</u>, May, 1938.

Pound, Roscoe. Jurisprudence (reprinted from <u>The History and Prospects of the Social Sciences</u>, 1925).

Weibel, Walther. <u>Russland</u> (Russia), 1916.

<u>Sam A. Lewisohn: 1884-1951</u>, 1951.

8

An Inventory
of the Papers of
Eduard Christian Lindeman

PREPARED BY
Carol E. Jenson

EDUARD CHRISTIAN LINDEMAN

SWB
L641

Eduard Christian Lindeman, 1885-1953

Papers, 1932-1945

16 notebooks

This collection comprises sixteen notebooks which are part of the papers of Eduard Christian Lindeman, philosopher, teacher, scholar, and social reformer. The journals, which contain material scattered over the years 1932 to 1945, were discovered in the library of the Delhi School of Social Work in New Delhi, India. They were secured for the Social Welfare History Archives Center in 1966 by Miss Ruby Pernell, Social Welfare Attache at the United States Embassy in New Delhi.

Lindeman was born in St. Clair, Michigan, on May 9, 1885. He was one of ten children of Danish immigrant parents, and the family usually lived under poverty-stricken conditions. Orphaned at an early age, Lindeman spent his early working years as a farm laborer. He later prepared himself to meet the admission requirements for Michigan Agricultural College (now Michigan State University) where he received a bachelor's degree in 1911. During 1911-1912, he edited The Gleaner, a Lansing, Michigan, magazine; and from 1912-1914, he was a social worker. In 1915, he joined the staff of Michigan Agricultural College as the extension director of the state's 4-H Clubs. Two years later he began a teaching career at the YMCA College in Chicago. From 1919-1921, he taught at North Carolina College for Women; and in 1924, he became Professor of Social Philosophy at the New York School of Social Work which has since become a part of Columbia University. He held the New York teaching position until his retirement in 1950. Lindeman also served on a number of university faculties as a visiting professor.

In addition to his teaching career, Lindeman was extremely active in community and professional organizations. Included among these were the American Association for Adult Education, the New York Adult Education Council, the National Urban League, the American Civil Liberties Union, the Federal Council of the Churches of Christ in America, the Federation of Protestant Welfare Agencies, and the National Child Labor Committee. He served on the American Unitarian Association Committee of Appraisal in 1934 and on the Social Planning Committee of the New Jersey Conference of Social Work. During the New Deal period, he was Director of the Division of Recreation of the Works Progress Administration in New York. In 1945, he traveled to Germany as a lecturer under the British Central Advisory Council for Adult Education in His Majesty's Forces. Lindeman was also the author of several works in the fields of sociology and social work; and he edited Emerson, the Basic Writings of America's Sage.

The Lindeman notebooks reflect his intense sensitivity to human problems, his aesthetic appreciation, and his sense of humor. The volumes contain random thoughts, often jotted down while traveling; quotes from and comments on favorite writers, especially social philosophers; magazine and newspaper clippings on current economic, social, and political problems, particularly those relating to the Depression, the New Deal, and World War II; and outlines for numerous talks and lectures.

The areas of Lindeman's most intense interests appear again and again throughout the notebooks. He was especially fond of the literary works of Ralph Waldo Emerson, and one entire volume from 1933-1939 is devoted entirely to the Concord writer. Lindeman was also a student of the social philosophies of Georg W. F. Hegel, William James, John Dewey, and Karl Mannheim.

Lindeman was particularly interested in the overall effects of planning and education, and remarks and outlines on these subjects occur frequently throughout the notebooks. He felt that systematic, long-range planning should be applied wherever possible--to the economy, the community, and to leisure-time activities. He saw education as applicable to social change, and he was concerned that social work be applied as a means for social change.

Lindeman was very interested in the relation of the New Deal to society, particularly in regard to organizations like the Ku Klux Klan, the Liberty League, and the Chamber of Commerce, all of which opposed many New Deal welfare programs. He was concerned with the course of world events during the 1930s--the rise of Hitler, the disintegration of the League of Nations, and the Spanish Civil War. When World War II came he became concerned with its effects; and as early as 1942, he began thinking of how to deal with the postwar situation. He regarded war as a social disease and feared its consequences on social progress, education, civil liberties, human welfare, and the social work profession.

PARTIAL SUBJECT INVENTORY

    Since the themes of Lindeman's notebooks are closely intertwined and at times detailed, it is very difficult to devise a subject inventory for this collection. The following inventory includes only the most prominent subjects covered in the collection. It would be nearly impossible to assess the contents of the Lindeman notebooks without reading them in their entirety.

ADULT EDUCATION
    Folders 6, 9-11, 14, 16

EMERSON, RALPH WALDO
    Folder 1-2

NEW DEAL
    Folders 6-8, 11

SOCIAL CHANGE
    Folders 1, 4, 7-11, 14, 16

SOCIAL PLANNING
    Folders 1, 5-6, 9-10, 12-13

WORLD WAR II
    Folders 10-16

EDUARD CHRISTIAN LINDEMAN

FOLDER INVENTORY   FOLDER

Lindeman Notebook: 1932-1933.	1
Lindeman Notebook, Concerned with Writings of Ralph Waldo Emerson: 1933-1939.	2
Lindeman Notebook: 1934 (?).	3
Lindeman Notebook: 1934-1935.	4
Lindeman Notebook: 1934-1935.	5
Lindeman Notebook: 1935.	6
Lindeman Notebook: 1936.	7
Lindeman Notebook: 1936.	8
Lindeman Notebook: 1936.	9
Lindeman Notebook: 1937.	10
Lindeman Notebook: 1937.	11
Lindeman Notebook: 1940.	12
Lindeman Notebook: 1941.	13
Lindeman Notebook: 1941-1942.	14
Lindeman Notebook: 1944-1945.	15
Lindeman Notebook: 1945.	16

9

An Inventory of the Papers of Harry Lawrence Lurie

PREPARED BY
Loren W. Crabtree

SWB   Lurie, Harry L. 1892-
L974
         Papers, 1927-1958

         104 folders

    The papers of Harry L. Lurie were deposited in the Social Welfare
Archives Center of the University of Minnesota Libraries on September 29,
1966. Comprising 2 linear feet, the papers were processed in July,
1967, in the Archives Center. Although the inclusive dates are 1927-
1958, the bulk of the collection deals with the years 1930-1940.

    Born in Goldingen, Latvia, on February 28, 1892, Harry L. Lurie
came to the United States in 1898 and soon entered into social work vocations.
In 1913-1914, Lurie was a staff member of the Federation of Jewish
Charities, Buffalo, New York; from 1915 to 1922 he served on the Associated
Charities Community Fund of Detroit's Department of Welfare; and from
1922 to 1924 he served on the faculty of the University of Michigan while
earning his B.A. (1922) and M.A. (1923) degrees. Lurie was superintendent
of the Chicago Jewish Social Service Bureau, 1925-1930, and concurrently
(1926-1930) was a lecturer at the University of Chicago. Moving to New
York, he served from 1930 to 1935 as the Executive Director of the Bureau
of Jewish Social Research, and then as the Executive Director of the
Council of Jewish Federations and Welfare Funds, 1935-1957. After 1962
he was editor of the Encyclopedia of Social Work, a publication of the
National Association of Social Workers.

    Throughout his career, Lurie wrote and spoke extensively on a wide
variety of social reform and social welfare topics. In the decade of the
1930's, for example, he studied the effects of local welfare programs on the
disruption caused by the Depression; prepared numerous articles and
speeches on the welfare programs of the New Deal, especially as they
affected the efforts of private agencies; served on committees of the
American Association of Social Workers which sought to define the methods
and objectives of social work; prepared reports and speeches on both public
and private relief programs of all sorts; fought strenuously for civil
liberties issues, such as the constriction of individual freedoms by the
tensions of wartime; investigated Jewish and other areas; maintained a
lively interest in foreign affairs, highlighted by a tour of the Soviet Union
and several speeches on the danger of fascism; served on government relief
committees; corresponded with state and national politicians concerning
proposed legislation; and studied the role of welfare programs in maintaining
the health and stability of the family unit, from infants to the aged.
Since he held positions throughout his life which were crucial to the
shaping of social workers' opinions on a wide variety of issues, these

papers present insights into how at least some social workers reacted to the tensions created by a great industrial democracy in peace and war.

Lurie was married to Bernice Stewart on June 20, 1922, and had 2 children, Alison Bishop and Jennifer.

The collection is basically the professional correspondence files of Lurie for the years 1927-1958, with occasional reports and other documents which support the correspondence. When received, the papers were organized in an alphabetical file by correspondent and/or subject, and this arrangement has been retained. Lurie's folder titles vary; sometimes they indicate the title of a paper or meeting, sometimes the subject, and occasionally the place or organization at or to which a paper was given. Many of the important issues and personalities can be found by referring to the partial subject inventory which follows.

PARTIAL SUBJECT INVENTORY

ABBOTT, EDITH
    Folders 26-29

ABBOTT, GRACE
    Folders 3-4, 26-29, 40

AMERICAN ASSOCIATION OF SOCIAL WORKERS (AASW)
    Folders 1-9, 83

AMERICAN LABOR PARTY
    Folder 11

ANDRESS, BART
    Folder 94

ANTI-SEMITISM
    Folder 48

ARNESON, KATHLEEN C.
    Folder 97

ASSOCIATED JEWISH PHILANTHROPIES (BOSTON)
    Folder 84

BILLIKOPF, JACOB
    Folder 17

BIRTH CONTROL
    Folder 18

BONDY, ROBERT E.
    Folder 58

BRANDT, LILIAN
    Folder 100

BRAUCHER, HOWARD S.
    Folder 94

CARE OF THE AGED
    Folders 20, 70

CASEWORK
    Folder 12-13, 20, 24, 26, 52, 72, 75

CHICAGO, UNIVERSITY OF
    Folders 26-29

CHILD LABOR
    Folder 7

CHILD WELFARE
    Folder 21

THE CHURCH AND SOCIAL WORK
    Folder 88

CIVIL RIGHTS
    Folders 22-23, 26-29, 90, 102

CIVIL WORKS ADMINISTRATION (CWA)
    Folders 26-29

COMMUNITY CHEST
    Folder 25

COMMUNITY ORGANIZATION
    Folders 14-15, 31, 39, 92

CROSBY, HELEN
    Folders 3-4

DAVIES, STANLEY P.
    Folders 3-4

DEPRESSION AND SOCIAL WELFARE
    Folders 14-15, 17, 26-29, 61, 64, 100

DISCRIMINATION
    Folders 26-29

DUNHAM, ARTHUR H.
    Folders 31, 40-41

ELDRIDGE, SEBA
    Folder 36

EMERSON, KENDALL
    Folder 94

EMPLOYMENT AND UNEMPLOYMENT
    Folders 1, 7, 9-10, 17, 26-29, 50, 52, 71, 88-89, 96, 100, 103

EPSTEIN, BENJAMIN
    Folder 49

FALK, LEON JR.
    Folder 73

FAMILY SERVICE ASSOCIATION OF AMERICA
    See FAMILY WELFARE ASSOCIATION OF AMERICA

FAMILY WELFARE AND PROBLEMS
    Folders 26, 38-39, 85

FAMILY WELFARE ASSOCIATION OF AMERICA
    Folders 40-41

FASCISM
    Folders 19, 26-29

FEDERAL CONSERVATION PROGRAM (FCP)
    Folder 42

FEDERAL EMERGENCY RELIEF ADMINISTRATION (FERA)
    Folder 43

FINANCING OF PUBLIC AND SOCIAL WELFARE
    Folders 25, 30, 64, 84

FISHER, JACOB
    Folders 26-29

FITCH, JOHN A.
    Folder 5

FORTUNE MAGAZINE
    Folders 12-13

GOLDSMITH, SAMUEL A.
    Folder 94

GOLDSTEIN, SIDNEY E.
    Folder 48

GOVERNMENT AND SOCIAL WELFARE
    Folders 2, 6, 9, 17, 26-29, 38, 40, 82

GREEN, ELIZABETH
    Folder 22

HALL, FRED S.
    Folder 88

HALL, HELEN
    Folder 10

HAMILTON, (MISS) GORDON
    Folder 8

HEALTH CARE
    Folders 14-15

HODSON, WILLIAM
    Folders 26-29

HOLSINGER, MARY B.
    Folder 65

HOPKINS, HARRY L.
    Folders 26-29, 43

JETER, HELEN R.
    Folders 39, 100

JEWISH SOCIAL WORK
    Folders 14-15, 46, 63

JUVENILE DELINQUENCY
    Folders 26-29

KAHN, DOROTHY C.
    Folder 26-29, 42

KAUFMAN, EDGAR J.
    Folder 76

KEEGAN, MONSIGNOR ROBERT F.
    Folder 65

KELLEY, FLORENCE
    Folders 26-29

KELLOGG, PAUL U.
    Folders 12-13

KLEIN, PHILIP
    Folder 73

KUOLT, OSCAR W.
    Folders 26-29

LABOR ORGANIZATION IN SOCIAL WORK
    Folders 12-13

LABOR PARTY
    Folders 11, 26-29, 51

LABOR RELATIONS
    Folders 12-13, 52, 54

LA GUARDIA, FIORELLO H.
    Folder 54

LEHMAN, HERBERT H.
    Folders 26-29

LIVERIGHT, ALICE F. (MRS. I. ALBERT)
    Folders 3-4

LUND, HARALD H.
    Folders 26-29, 95

MENTAL HYGIENE
    Folder 71

MINIMUM WAGE LAWS
    Folder 7

MINKOFF, ISAIAH
    Folder 49

MUMM, LOUISE N.
    Folder 58

NATIONAL CONFERENCE OF JEWISH SOCIAL SERVICE
    Folders 56, 84

NATIONAL RETAIL DRY GOODS ASSOCIATION
    Folder 76

NATIONAL SOCIAL WELFARE ASSEMBLY, INC.
    Folder 58

NATIONAL SOCIAL WORK COUNCIL
    Folder 94

NATIONAL YOUTH ADMINISTRATION
    Folder 59

THE NEW DEAL
    Folders 12-13, 26-29, 34, 42-43, 55, 59, 69

NEW YORK SCHOOL OF SOCIAL WORK
    Folder 61

NEW YORK STATE CONFERENCE ON SOCIAL WORK
    Folders 62-65

OFFICE OF DEFENSE HEALTH AND WELFARE SERVICES (U.S.)
    Folder 68

PERSONS, W. FRANK
    Folder 42

PRAY, KENNETH L. M.
    Folder 88

RABINOFF, GEORGE W.
    Folder 58

RELIEF
    Folders 32, 37-38, 40, 55, 66, 74, 76, 81, 99-100

RUBINOW, ISAAC M.
    Folders 3-4, 26-29, 79

RUDWIN, MAXIMILIAN
    Folder 17

RUSSIA
    Folder 80

SELEKMAN, BEN M.
    Folder 84

SHAPIRO, HARRY
    Folder 97

SLAWSON, JOHN S.
    Folder 49

SOCIAL EDUCATION AND ACTION
    Folders 12-13, 26-29, 52, 57, 74, 88, 94

SOCIAL SECURITY
    Folders 14-15, 74

SOCIAL SERVICE REVIEW
    Folder 86

SOCIAL WORK YEAR BOOK
    Folder 88

SOLLINS, I.V.
    Folder 80

SMITH, R. TEMPLETON
    Folder 73

SWIFT, LINTON B.
    Folders 3-4, 40, 97

TANDY, W. LOU
    Folder 90

TAYLOR, MAURICE
    Folder 91

TRANSIENTS
    Folder 93

ULIN, BEN
    Folder 49

VAN KLEEK, MARY
    Folder 80

WAR AND SOCIAL WORK
    Folder 97

WASHINGTON, FORRESTER B.
    Folder 98

WEBBINCK, PAUL
    Folders 26-29

WILLIAMS, FRANKWOOD
    Folder 80

WORLD WAR II
    Approach of
        Folders 12-15, 19, 26-29
    Prostitution, prevention of
        Folder 68

YWCA
    Folder 104

FOLDER INVENTORY

<u>FOLDER TITLE AND DESCRIPTION OF CONTENTS</u>   <u>**FOLDER**</u>

American Association of Social Workers - Commission on Unemployment   1
Insurance: 1931-1933
    Notes on meetings, correspondence about the continuance of
    the Commission.

American Association of Social Workers - Committee on Federal Action: 2
1933-1935
    Memoranda, reports, minutes, correspondence on government
    relief programs and their relationship to the private social
    worker.

American Association of Social Workers - Committee to Outline a   3-4
National Social Welfare Program: 1934-1935
    Minutes of the committee meetings, statements of objectives
    and proposals, correspondence among Lurie, Linton Swift, I.M.
    Rubinow, Grace Abbott, Helen Crosby, Stanley P. Davies, Walter M.
    West, Mrs. I. Albert Liveright, and other committee members
    concerning the work of the committee. Correspondence about a
    1935 controversy over a report which Lurie wrote for the committee.

American Association of Social Workers - Committee to Study   5
Organization of Social Workers in Social Agencies: 1934-1935
    Correspondence with John A. Fitch about the work of the
    committee, especially the problem of professionalism in social
    work.

American Association of Social Workers - Conference on Governmental
Objectives of Social Work: 1934   6
    Correspondence and discussion material.

American Association of Social Workers - Conference on National
Economic Objectives for Social Work: 1933   7
    Proposals on such issues as minimum wage laws, child labor,
    unemployment, public works; minutes of the meetings.

American Association of Social Workers - New York City Chapter: 8
1933
    Correspondence with Miss Gordon Hamilton about the work of
    the Chapter.

American Association of Social Workers - Steering Committee -   9
Federal Action on Unemployment: 1931-1934
    Position papers, correspondence and minutes of meetings.

American Association for Labor Legislation: 1933   10
    Lurie's comments on Helen Hall's paper on unemployment.

FOLDER TITLE AND DESCRIPTION OF CONTENTS	FOLDER
American Labor Party: 1936-1938 Correspondence and minutes dealing with the organization of this political party.	11
Articles: 1927-1955 Articles written for such journals as <u>The Family</u>, <u>The Survey</u>, <u>Social Work Today</u>, <u>The Forum</u>, <u>Better Times</u>, <u>Fortune</u>, <u>Canadian Welfare</u>. Topics include casework, marriage, New Deal Welfare programs, the Civil Works Administration, Jane Addams eulogy, social action and legislation, labor organization in social work, social security, the <u>Fortune</u> public opinion poll, the role of private philanthropy, Jews and the coming of World War II, a program for Jewish economic research, health care, united Jewish leadership, Jewish community organization, immigration, and Judaism.	12-15
Baltimore (Md.) Survey: 1933-1934 Outline, report and correspondence re: the survey conducted by Lurie of the charities receiving support from governmental funds.	16
Billikopf, Jacob: 1931-1943 Correspondence on a variety of subjects, including speeches, the problems of the Depression, employment, Billikopf's illness, government relief and welfare programs, and aiding Dr. Maximilian Rudwin in finding employment.	17
Birth Control: 1931-1934 Correspondence about Lurie's views, papers and speeches on it.	18
Buffalo, N.Y. Social Work Today Forum: 1941 Paper by Lurie on the causes of international conflict, in which he assigns blame for the war to both the fascist and democratic countries.	19
Care of the Aged: 1930 Papers on casework and the aged and the relation of the Family Service Agency to care of the aged.	20
Child Study Association: 1933-1934 Notes for a lecture on national income and family income; one copy of a <u>Child Study</u> issue devoted to the Family and its functions today.	21
Civil Liberties: 1941-1943 Correspondence concerning the trial of Elizabeth Green and others in Oklahoma on charges of "criminal syndicalism."	22
Civil Liberties Committee - New York City: 1934-1935 Correspondence about a statement of proposed police regulations.	23
Community Aspects of Research in Casework Agencies: 1950 Correspondence about a paper on this topic.	24

FOLDER TITLE AND DESCRIPTION OF CONTENTS	FOLDER
Community Chest - Welfare Fund Inquiry: 1949 Correspondence re: financial arrangements of private welfare organizations.	25
Correspondence - General: 1927-1955 Topics include caseworkers and family discord, book reviews by Lurie, discrimination, federal unemployment relief, 1932 memorial meeting for Florence Kelley, electioneering for Herbert Lehman, the Civil Works Administration, petitions to President Roosevelt on relief measure, the effect of governmental social action on individuals, Lurie's intercession in behalf of Jacob Fisher's employment, juvenile delinquency, the labor party movement, liberalism and the challenge of fascism, the coming of World War II, war and the infringement of personal liberties, "democracy" in social work, civil liberties, the "rank and file" movement, and housing legislation. Prominent individuals include Grace and Edith Abbott, William Hodson, I.M. Rubinow, Paul Webbinck, Oscar W. Kuolt, Harry Hopkins, and Dorothy C. Kahn.	26-29
Council of Social Agencies - Buffalo (N.Y.): 1950 Correspondence about and summaries of Lurie's paper on the needs and costs of welfare programs.	30
Council on Social Work Education Curriculum Study: 1957-1958 Lurie served as consultant for the Community Organization Project of the CSWE's Curriculum Study (of schools of social work). Outline of the study and correspondence re: the report Lurie prepared which was published by CSWE in 1959.	31
Dangers in Non-categorical Relief: 1938 Paper on this subject and correspondence about the paper.	32
Dayton (Ohio) Instutute for Social Work in Public and Private Agencies 1937 Correspondence concerning Lurie's 2 days of presentations on this topic to all Dayton social workers.	33
Economic Security - Roosevelt's Committee on: 1934 Correspondence regarding a report on this topic.	34
Educational Standards in the Civil Service: 1939 Correspondence with New York State legislators concerning a bill to eradicate educational qualifications within the civil service.	35
Eldridge, Seba: 1928-1936 Correspondence concerning a book by Eldridge on social work. Refusal by Lurie to participate in a 1936 study on collective enterprise.	36
Emergency Relief Bureau Supervisors Seminar - New York City: 1935-1936 Reports and minutes of meetings.	37

FOLDER TITLE AND DESCRIPTION OF CONTENTS	FOLDER
Family Relief: 1932 Minutes of the government relief committee meetings and correspondence about them.	38
Family Security Committee of the Federal Security Agency: 1941-1942 Correspondence with Helen R. Jeter, the committee secretary, concerning community organization and cooperation between government and voluntary organizations.	39
Family Welfare Association of America: 1932-1938 Correspondence and reports concerning a proposal for the establishment of a bureau of business service and research and an institute on government relief programs. Prominent correspondents include Grace Abbott, Arthur Dunham, and Linton Swift.	40
Family Welfare Association of America - Pathfinding Report: 1931-1932 Study of governmental relief methods. Arthur Dunham appears prominently.	41
Federal Conservation Program: 1933 Correspondence with W. Frank Persons and Dorothy C. Kahn concerning the "militarism" of the program.	42
Federal Emergency Relief Administration: 1933-1934 Correspondence with Harry Hopkins and other administrators about the work of the FERA.	43
Federal Income Tax Exemption: 1947-1951 Correspondence with government and welfare officials about tax exemption legislation.	44
Fourth Metropolitan New York Conference on Employment and Guidance: 1936 The Conference was sponsored by the Welfare Council of New York City. Program and a paper by Lurie.	45
Goldstein, Sidney E.: 1933-1934 Correspondence about a variety of topics, including German anti-Semitism.	46
Grand Rapids (Mich.) National Conference of Social Work: 1940 Copies of a paper on "The People's Needs in the Year 1940; How are They to be Met?"	47
Hospital Survey--New York City: 1934-1935 Correspondence re: a survey-evaluation of New York City Jewish hospitals.	48
Illusion of Authority: 1952 Copy of paper and surrounding correspondence with John Slawson, Ben Ulin, Ben Epstein and Isaiah Minkoff.	49

FOLDER TITLE AND DESCRIPTION OF CONTENTS | FOLDER

Interpretation of Unemployment Relief - Committee on: 1932   50
    Invitation to join and minutes of the meetings of this
    committee of the United Educational Program.

The Labor Club - New York City: 1939   51
    Minutes of meetings, list of members.

Los Angeles (Cal.) Institute for Social Work in Public and Private   52
Agencies: 1937
    Copies of 4 lectures, plus correspondence about Lurie's
    visit. Topics: casework, unemployment, organized labor
    and social welfare, and social action.

Maryland State Conference of Social Welfare: 1934-1935   53
    Correspondence about a paper given at the Conference.

Mayor's Board of Survey - Motion Pictures (N.Y.): 1937   54
    Correspondence about Fiorello H. La Guardia's commission to
    study labor problems in New York's theaters.

Minnesota State Conference and Institute: 1932-1934   55
    Papers on the need for a national program of public relief and the
    role of the federal government in social work.

National Conference of Jewish Social Service: 1927-1931   56
    Correspondence about programs, reports, and position papers.

National Conference of Social Work - Social Action Committee: 1941   57
    Paper on "Social Action - A Motive Force in Democracy."

National Social Welfare Assembly, Inc.: 1952-1954   58
    Minutes of the administrative committee and executive
    committee; correspondence with Robert E. Bondy about
    internal organization and social security. Other correspondents
    include George W. Rabinoff, Louise N. Mumm.

National Youth Administration: 1935   59
    Correspondence with NYA personnel concerning nominating a
    young Jew to the National Advisory Committee of the NYA.

New York City Commission Work Bureau: 1931-1933   60
    Correspondence and memoranda re: Lurie's role as executive
    director, and his resignation in disappointment at the scope
    of his position.

New York School of Social Work: 1928-1932   61
    Correspondence about papers on social work in the Depression
    and Lurie's teaching at the School.

New York State Conference on Social Work: 1932-1935   62
    Correspondence about the program, papers prepared for the
    Conference, and other articles.

FOLDER TITLE AND DESCRIPTION OF CONTENTS	FOLDER
New York State Conference on Social Work: 1939 Lecture on "Developments in Jewish Civic and Protective Activity in the United States."	63
New York State Conference on Social Work: 1948 Supporting data, correspondence and a copy of the paper which dealt with the effect of the economic situation on the administration of private health and welfare programs.	64
New York State Conference on Social Work - Executive Committee: 1932-1933 Correspondence with Mary B. Holsinger and Monsignor Robert F. Keegan concerning the lack of representation of Catholics on the Committee and the programs of the Conference.	65
New York State Department of Social Welfare - Advisory Committee of the Bureau of Home Relief: 1931-1932 Correspondence and minutes of the Committee.	66
Non-Sectarian Foundations Established by Jews: 1933 Paper by Lurie on this subject.	67
Office of Defense Health and Welfare Services - Advisory Committee on Social Welfare: 1942-1943 Correspondence and reports of this committee, which advised the government on such matters as prostitution prevention.	68
Ohio State Welfare Conference: 1934-1935 Lectures and a radio talk on the social worker and the New Deal and "What Next in Family Service?"	69
Old Age Insurance: 1949 Mimeographed proposals.	70
Pennsylvania Conference on Social Welfare: 1934 Papers on mental hygiene and unemployment, and the role of federations in American Jewish life.	71
Philosophy and Practice in Social Casework: 1938 Paper on this topic given at the New York New School of Social Research.	72
Pittsburgh (Penn.) Survey: 1933-1936 Correspondence re: Lurie's role in the survey; minutes of the committee meetings. Prominent correspondents: Leon Falk, Jr., R. Templeton Smith, Philip Klein.	73
Political Action for a Social Welfare Program: 1936 Copy of a paper given on this topic (probably to the National Conference of Social Work).	74
Providence (R.I.) Institute: 1938 Correspondence about and copy of a speech on social work and political action. Data on casework.	75

FOLDER TITLE AND DESCRIPTION OF CONTENTS	FOLDER

Relief Article: 1934 — 76
A report on relief needs and relief problems as issued by the Board of Directors of the National Retail Dry Goods Association. Lurie contributed some basic information about relief programs. Chief correspondent: Edgar J. Kaufmann.

Rochester (N.Y.) Council of Social Agencies: 1933 — 77
Correspondence about a lecture and newspaper clipping on it.

Rochester, (N.Y) Social Workers Club: 1936 — 78
Copy of a speech, with surrounding correspondence, on the role of social work in political action.

Rubinow, I. M.: 1931-1934 — 79
Correspondence about varied topics of social welfare.

Russian Tour: 1935-1936 — 80
Correspondence re: details of the trip, and the death of Frankwood Williams, who led the tour. Chief Correspondents: Mary Van Kleeck and I.V. Sollins.

St. Louis (Mo.) Survey: 1933-1936 — 81
Correspondence and reports about Lurie's role in surveying the St. Louis relief organization and practice.

Simmons School of Social Work and the Boston (Mass.) Council of Social Agencies: 1934 — 82
Lecture on the government in social work, and a paper on social casework.

Social Planning Council - St. Louis (Mo.): 1950 — 83
Lurie's paper on "How Much Social Welfare Can We Afford?" presented to the local chapter of AASW. Correspondence about it and copies of the paper.

Social Policy - National Conference of Jewish Social Service Committee: 1933 — 84
This committee was charged with preparing a report on a program on social policy for the succeeding decade. Copy of the report and correspondence with Ben M. Selekman (Executive Director of Associated Jewish Philanthropies, Boston) about it.

Social Security Board - Committee on Family Security: 1941-1942 — 85
Correspondence about the work of the committee and Lurie's role on it. Occasional remarks, memoranda and reports.

Social Service Review: 1927-1937 — 86
Correspondence about and copies of book reviews which Lurie wrote for the Journal.

FOLDER TITLE AND DESCRIPTION OF CONTENTS	FOLDER
Social Work Action Committee--New York City: 1944-1947 Material on both the New York Committee and the parent National Social Work Action Committee. Bank statements, legal data and correspondence about internal organization and work of the committees.	87
Social Work Year Book: 1932-1935 Correspondence with Fred S. Hall about publications in the Social Work Year Book, which Hall edited. Of special interest are an article by Kenneth L. M. Pray on unemployment and an article on the church and social work.	88
Staten Island (N.Y.) Council of Social Agencies: 1935 Correspondence about a paper on security of the unemployed.	89
Tandy, W. Lou: 1953 Correspondence concerning Tandy's dismissal from Kansas State Teacher's College at Emporia for reasons of national security.	90
Taylor, Maurice: 1932 Correspondence concerning Taylor's candidacy for positions in Brooklyn and Detroit.	91
Toronto University Seminar: 1955 Lecture notes and correspondence about a seminar given by Lurie on community organization.	92
Transient Study - U.S. Children's Bureau: 1930's Study of the difficult conditions of men moving to find work.	93
United Educational Program: 1932 Correspondence about the projected campaign under the auspices of the National Social Work Council to educate the public in the maintenance of established practices of social welfare and health work. Chief correspondents include Bart Andress, Samuel A. Goldsmith, Howard Braucher, Kendall Emerson.	94
United States Children's Bureau - White House Conference on Children in a Democracy: 1939-1940 Correspondence with Harald H. Lund concerning programs and publications of the Conference.	95
United States Department of Labor: 1933 Correspondence with Isador Lubin and W. Frank Persons concerning studies of re-employment.	96
War Community Services: 1943 Correspondence with government officials concerning social problems and programs resulting from the war. Prominent correspondents include Kathleen C. Arneson, Linton B. Swift, and Harry Shapiro.	97

FOLDER TITLE AND DESCRIPTION OF CONTENTS	FOLDER
Washington, Forrester B.: 1935 　　Correspondence about Lurie's speech to the Atlanta, (Ga.) School of Social Work, and a fund-raising program for the School.	98
Welfare and Relief Mobilization Conference at the White House: 1932 　　Mimeographed speeches.	99
Welfare Council of New York City: 1940 　　Correspondence with Lilian Brandt and Helen R. Jeter re: Brandt's manuscript on New York relief measures, 1929-1937. Other correspondence concerning unemployment relief and general problems of the Depression in New York City.	100
Westchester, (N.Y.) Council of Social Agencies: 1934 　　Correspondence, program and paper on social work trends and objectives.	101
Williamstown, (Mass.) Institute of Human Relations: 1935 　　Brochure, memoranda, and paper prepared for it by Lurie on problems faced by American communities.	102
Workers Unemployment Insurance Bill: 1934-1935 　　Hearings, bills, reports and correspondence about these federal bills.	103
Young Women's Christian Associations: 1933 　　Correspondence about, and a Lurie presentation on, "Trends in Social Work."	104

10

An Inventory of the Papers of Mattie Cal Maxted

PREPARED BY
Pamela J. Matson

SWB
M451   Mattie Cal Maxted, 1900-

        Papers, 1942-1957

        30 folders

    Mattie Cal Maxted deposited a portion of her papers in the Social Welfare History Archives Center in June, 1966, and the materials were processed by the Archives Center staff in 1967 and 1968. Although the papers deposited deal primarily with the National Association of Schools of Social Administration (NASSA), they also reflect Mrs. Maxted's professional associations in the Council on Social Work Education, the Department of Social Welfare at the University of Arkansas (of which she is currently chairman), and the Arkansas Conference of Social Work.

    Mattie Cal Maxted was born in Ripley, Mississippi on February 24, 1900. She attended the University of Oklahoma and received a Bachelor of Arts in 1922 and a Master of Arts in 1934. She received a diploma from the Oklahoma City Law School in 1929. Mrs. Maxted also attended the University of Chicago from 1935 to 1936 and the University of Minnesota during the years between 1939 and 1945. Mrs. Maxted was employed as a field supervisor with the Federal Emergency Relief Administration in Oklahoma from 1933-1935; as an instructor in the graduate school of social work at the University of Oklahoma from 1935-1940; and as a professor in the Department of Social Welfare at the University of Arkansas from 1940 to the present. She lectured at Oxford in 1954 and in Japan in 1957. In 1950, she was president of the Public Welfare Association.

    The impetus for the formation of NASSA came out of a meeting of the Southwestern Committee on Education for the Social Sciences of the Southwestern Social Services Association. In April, 1942, the committee was authorized to conduct a survey of persons and institutions to determine the feasibility of a new association of schools for the social sciences. As a result of this survey, NASSA was formed; Austin L. Porterfield became the first president, and Mattie Cal Maxted, the first secretary. The members of NASSA indicated a need for the formation of their new organization in response to a decision of the American Association of Schools of Social Work (AASSW) to refuse membership to a school or department which offered any part of its social service instruction on the undergraduate level. The AASSW also required that there be no connection of social welfare departments with existing social science departments, especially with sociology. Other objections by NASSA to AASSW policy centered around high membership fees, concern that national standards should not preclude the right of states to plan social work programs according to the needs of individual states, and convictions that the placement of all social work training on the graduate level was too unrealistic at a time when jobs were being filled by persons without any training in social work. Though NASSA recognized the desirability of high standards in social work training, it was felt that some concessions had to be made to the demands of a field in which there was a great shortage of trained personnel.

    Communication was maintained between NASSA and AASSW through joint annual meetings, through the establishment of a Joint Committee on Education for Social Work in 1945, and in the resulting formation of the National Council on Social Work Education in 1946, which included representatives from the American Association of Social Workers, the American Association of

Medical Social Workers, the American Association of Psychiatric Social Workers, the American Association of Group Workers, the Association of American Colleges, the Association of American Universities, American Public Welfare Association, the Joint Committee on Accrediting, and the National Association of School Social Workers as well as the Association of Schools of Social Work (AASSW) and the National Association of Schools of Social Administration (NASSA). In 1952, a new Council on Social Work Education which replaced the National Council on Social Work Education, AASSW, and NASSA, was formed. A Commission on Accrediting was set up to accredit graduate schools of social work; undergraduate departments were not accredited but had membership requirements. The Commission on Schools and Departments of Social Work had a division of undergraduate departments, of which NASSA had initial responsibility in developing, and a division of graduate schools. Mrs. Maxted was a member of the Council of Delegates of the Council on Social Work Education. After the Council went into operation in 1952, NASSA was dissolved.

The collection comprises one and one-fourth linear feet of papers and is organized to reflect Mrs. Maxted's professional activities. The bulk of the collection is related to the National Association of Schools of Social Administration. Other sections include the Council on Social Work Education; Conference on Education for Social Work, Nashville, Tennessee; Speeches; Course Notes for the Department of Social Welfare at the University of Arkansas; and the Arkansas Conference of Social Work. The need for undergraduate social work education and accreditation of social work programs on both the undergraduate and graduate level are the predominant topics in this collection.

PARTIAL SUBJECT INVENTORY

ALSTON, JOHN C.
    Folder 4

AMERICAN ASSOCIATION OF SCHOOLS OF SOCIAL WORK (AASSW)
    Folders 1, 3-16

AMERICAN PUBLIC WELFARE ASSOCIATION
    Folder 16

ANDERSON, JOSEPH P.
    Folder 16

ARONSON, ALBERT
    Folder 3

BOAN, FERN
    Folder 4

CAPE, T. WILSON
    Folders 6, 8-11

CHANDLER, JANE
    Folder 12

CLAGUE, EWAN
    Folder 3

CLARKE, HELEN I.
    Folder 4, 8

COLE, WILLIAM
    Folder 4

COUNCIL ON SOCIAL WORK EDUCATION
    Folders 4, 14-16

DE SCHWEINITZ, KARL
    Folder 3

DIMOCK, HEDLEY S.
    Folder 3

ELLIS, HELEN
    Folder 4

HARPER, ERNEST B.
    Folders 3, 6-13, 16

HOLLIS, ERNEST V. AND HOLLIS REPORT ON SOCIAL WORK EDUCATION
    Folders 9-15

INTERNATIONAL CONFERENCE OF SOCIAL WORK
    Folders 14-15

LINCOLN, ARLEIGH
    Folders 9-13

MOORE, COYLE
    Folders 9-11

NATIONAL ASSOCIATION OF SCHOOLS OF SOCIAL ADMINISTRATION (NASSA)
    Folders 1-25

NATIONAL CONFERENCE OF SOCIAL WORK
    Folders 8-15

NATIONAL COUNCIL ON SOCIAL WORK EDUCATION
    Folders 3-4, 7-15

NATIONAL SOCIAL WELFARE ASSEMBLY
    Folders 14-15

NEGROES
    Folder 4

RHYNE, J. J.
    Folders 2-3, 6-8

RURAL SOCIAL WORK
    Folders 1, 3-4, 28

SOCIAL WORK EDUCATION
    Accreditation
        Folders 3-13
    Graduate
        Folders 1, 3-4, 6, 8-11
    Undergraduate
        Folders 1, 3-4, 26

SPENCER, SUE
    Folders 7-11

TANGERMAN, MARGARETTA
    Folder 4

TASCHER, HAROLD
    Folder 4

WETZEL, H. E.
    Folders 9-13, 16, 26

FOLDER TITLE AND DESCRIPTION OF CONTENTS   FOLDER

National Association of Schools of Social Administration (NASSA)

Formation of NASSA, 1942   1
    Correspondence and minutes. Advantages and disadvantages of
    graduate and undergraduate social work training, standards
    in social work education, AASSW, Southwestern Committee on
    Education for the Social Services, need for trained social
    workers in the South, and purposes of NASSA. Austin L.
    Porterfield and J. J. Rhyne are prominent correspondents.

Constitutions and Revisions, 1942-1951.   2

Annual Meetings, Proceedings, 1944-1948   3
    Minutes, speeches, and reports. Curricula in social work
    education, graduate versus undergraduate social work training,
    training needs in public assistance work, relationship between
    NASSA and AASSW, publicity for NASSA, AASSW recommendations for
    social work education, Joint Committee on Accrediting, pro-
    posed National Council on Social Work Education, field work,
    and the need for trained social workers. Speeches include:
    "The Function of the Liberal Arts College in Preparation for
    Life and Work with Special Reference to Social Work" by Karl de
    Schweinitz, "Need for Undergraduate Trained Social Workers in
    Arkansas" by Mattie Cal Maxted, "Economic Trends and Employment
    Outlook" by Ewan Clague, "Accomplishments and Aims of the
    National Association of Schools of Social Administration" by
    Ernest B. Harper, "Resources for Field Experience in Rural
    Areas" by Mattie Cal Maxted, "Education for the Public Service:
    Social Science Orientation and the Quest for Talent" by Albert
    H. Aronson, "The Undergraduate Curriculum in Social Welfare"
    by J. J. Rhyne, and "Content of Undergraduate Curriculum in
    Group Work and Recreation" by Hedley S. Dimock.

Annual Meetings, Proceedings, 1949-1952   4
    Minutes, speeches, and reports. History and activities of
    NASSA, Council on Social Work Education, rural social work,
    undergraduate versus graduate social work training, relation-
    ships between NASSA and AASSW, and dissolution of NASSA when
    Council on Social Work Education (CSWE) went into operation.
    Speeches include: "The Use of Functional Methods in Undergraduate
    Social Work Education" by Harold Tascher; "A Comparison of Objectives,
    Content, Methods of General and Professional Education" by Helen I.
    Clarke; "The Purpose and Content of an Undergraduate Course in
    Introduction to Social Work" by Helen Ellis; "Undergraduate Field
    Work at Valparaiso University" by Margaretta Tangerman; "Train-
    ing of Social Workers for Rural Areas" by William E. Cole; "Social
    Welfare Education for Negroes" by John C. Alston; "Undergraduate
    Field Work" by Fern Boan; and "Undergraduate Social Work Education:
    Stepchild or Baby" by Mattie Cal Maxted.

FOLDER TITLE AND DESCRIPTION OF CONTENTS	FOLDER

Committee Reports, 1947, 1949   5
    Report of workshop for teachers of undergraduate social work and recreation leadership courses; accrediting committee; committee on relationships with AASSW; committee on NASSA functions; and committee on policies.

Correspondence and Papers, General, 1943-1945   6
    Arrangements for NASSA annual meetings, Children's Bureau, relationships between NASSA and AASSW, Joint Committee on Accrediting, proposed merger of NASSA and AASSW, Joint Committee on Education for Social Work, accreditation of undergraduate social work curricula, study of NASSA schools' curricula, and concept of a five-year program leading to a Master of Arts degree versus a two-year graduate program in social work. J. J. Rhyne, Ernest B. Harper, and T. Wilson Cape are prominent correspondents.

Correspondence and Papers, General, 1946   7
    AASSW, Joint Committee on Education for Social Work, Joint Committee on Accrediting, plan for a National Council on Social Work Education, and study of social work curricula of NASSA schools. Sue Spencer, Ernest B. Harper, and J. J. Rhyne are prominent correspondents.

Correspondence and Papers, General, 1947   8
    National Council on Social Work Education, relationships between AASSW and NASSA, relations between NASSA and Children's Bureau, development of graduate curricula in NASSA schools, AASSW Committee on Preprofessional Education, arrangements with National Conference of Social Work for NASSA's annual meeting, Joint Committee on Accrediting, and AASSW accreditation. Ernest B. Harper, J. J. Rhyne, T. Wilson Cape, and Sue Spencer are prominent correspondents.

Correspondence and Papers, General, 1948   9-11
    National Council on Social Work Education, National Conference of Social Work, AASSW Committee on Preprofessional Education, financing National Council on Social Work Education, relationships between NASSA and AASSW, Joint Committee on Accrediting, undergraduate social work education, arrangements for NASSA annual meeting, death of T. Wilson Cape and resulting administrative changes in NASSA, publication of the proceedings of the 1948 annual meeting, and study on social work education under the auspices of the National Council of Social Work Education by Ernest V. Hollis of the U.S. Office of Education. Ernest B. Harper, T. Wilson Cape, H. E. Wetzel, Coyle E. Moore, Arleigh Lincoln, and Sue Spencer are prominent correspondents.

Correspondence and Papers, General, 1949   12
    Hollis Report on social work education, arrangements for NASSA annual meeting, sale of proceedings of 1948 annual meeting, National Council on Social Work Education, relationships between

FOLDER TITLE AND DESCRIPTION OF CONTENTS	FOLDER

NASSA and AASSW, graduate and undergraduate social work education, salaries and working conditions in social work positions, and publication of proceedings of 1949 annual meeting. Ernest V. Hollis, Ernest B. Harper, Jane Chandler, H. E. Wetzel, and Arleigh Lincoln are prominent correspondents.

Correspondence and Papers, General, 1950   13
Arrangements for NASSA annual meeting, National Conference of Social Work, reactions to Hollis Report, financing and administering of National Council on Social Work Education, minutes of National Council on Social Work Education meetings, relationships between NASSA and AASSW, and discussion of accreditation of social work programs. Arleigh Lincoln, H. E. Wetzel, and Ernest Harper are prominent correspondents.

Correspondence and Papers, General, 1951   14-15
Arrangements for NASSA annual meeting, National Conference of Social Work, financing National Council on Social Work Education, reactions to Hollis Report, dittoed reports of the Joint Committee on Program Planning of the National Conference of Social Work and the National Social Welfare Assembly, formation of the new Council on Social Work Education (CSWE) which replaced NASSA, AASSW, and the National Council on Social Work Education, routine notices from the International Conference of Social Work, recommendations of the Hollis Report relating to public welfare programs, and American Public Welfare Association. Ernest B. Harper, H. E. Wetzel, Coyle E. Moore, and John C. Alston are prominent correspondents.

Correspondence and Papers, General, 1952   16
American Public Welfare Association, arrangements for NASSA annual meeting, election of NASSA members as delegates to the Council on Social Work Education, responses of individual schools to joining CSWE, and function of undergraduate social work programs. Ernest B. Harper, H. E. Wetzel, and Joseph P. Anderson (Secretary of CSWE) are prominent correspondents.

Formation of an Undergraduate Social Work Organization for Students in NASSA Schools, 1945-1946   17
Correspondence re formation and survey of support for such an organization.

Membership Requirements, 1945-1951   18
Lists of NASSA members and membership requirements.

Membership Applications, 1945-1952   19
Correspondence, applications for membership in NASSA, and supporting papers. (Arranged chronologically instead of alphabetically by school.)

FOLDER TITLE AND DESCRIPTION OF CONTENTS	FOLDER
Requests for Information, 1948-1952 Requests for information concerning undergraduate programs in social work sent to Mattie Cal Maxted as an executive officer of NASSA.	20
Statistical Surveys of NASSA Schools, 1945-1950 Correspondence and forms concerning number of students, courses, and faculty members in the social work programs of NASSA schools.	21-23
Studies of Social Work Curricula of NASSA Schools, 1945, 1947 Charts, correspondence, and outlines of social work programs and course content.	24
Publications, 1945-1950.	25
Council on Social Work Education, 1952, 1955-1957 Bylaws and papers issued by various commissions of the Council. Curriculum study undertaken by the Council, undergraduate education for social workers, relationship of former NASSA personnel to the Council, administration of Council, and issues in social work education. H. E. Wetzel is a prominent correspondent.	26
Nashville (Tennessee) Conference on Education for Social Work, 1948 Correspondence.	27
Speeches by Mattie Cal Maxted, 1942, 1946 "Training for Social Work in Arkansas" at State Conference W.R. 1942; and "Rural Social Work" at Fort Smith District Conference, 1946.	28
Course Notes, 1948 Miscellaneous notes and portions of lectures which were used by Mrs. Maxted as teaching materials at the University of Arkansas.	29
Arkansas Conference of Social Work, Newsletter, March, 1949 Mattie Cal Maxted served as the editor of this publication.	30

11

An Inventory of the Papers of the National Association of Social Workers, Inc.

PREPARED BY
Mary Jane Fout, Principal Processor
Andrea Hinding, Compiler and Processor
Loren W. Crabtree
Pamela J. Matson

TABLE OF CONTENTS

Introduction	1
Narratives	
American Association of Social Workers	4
American Association of Medical Social Workers	11
National Association of School Social Workers	15
American Association of Psychiatric Social Workers	18
American Association of Group Workers	21
Association for the Study of Community Organization	23
Social Work Research Group	25
Temporary Inter-Association Council	26
National Association of Social Workers	28
National Committee on Social Work in Defense Mobilization	30
Combined Partial Subject Inventory	32
File Folder Inventory	
American Association of Social Workers	58
American Association of Medical Social Workers	76
National Association of School Social Workers	112
American Association of Psychiatric Social Workers	112
American Association of Group Workers	118
Association for the Study of Community Organization	124
Social Work Research Group	128
Temporary Inter-Association Council	128
National Association of Social Workers	138
National Committee on Social Work in Defense Mobilization	165
Legal-size Folder Inventory	170
Appendix (list of ephemera removed)	173

SWC1   NATIONAL ASSOCIATION OF SOCIAL WORKERS, New York, New York

Papers, 1917-1963

1430 folders   61 (*L*) folders

INTRODUCTION

The papers of the National Association of Social Workers were deposited at the Social Welfare History Archives Center of the University of Minnesota Libraries in July, 1964. A major part of this deposit was the papers of the seven predecessor organizations—American Association of Social Workers (AASW), American Association of Medical Social Workers (AAMSW), National Association of School Social Workers (NASSW), American Association of Psychiatric Social Workers (AAPSW), American Association of Group Workers (AAGW), Association for the Study of Community Organization (ASCO), and the Social Work Research Group (SWRG). The rest of the NASW collection comprises the papers of the Temporary Inter-Association Council (TIAC), the National Committee on Social Work in Defense Mobilization (NCSWDM) and some of the working papers of the National Association of Social Workers (NASW) and its sections, c. 1955-1963. Also located at the Archives Center are the papers of the Metropolitan Washington Chapter, NASW.

Owing to the complexity and size of the collection, the papers of NASW were processed by a team of archivists, and a description of the contents for each individual section was prepared and follows this introduction. For greater accessibility to the entire collection, the partial subject inventories of each group have been combined into one alphabetical listing. For the convenience of searchers, however, a copy of the partial subject inventory prepared for each of the ten sections of the collection has been placed in the first folder of each section. Thus, the subject inventory for the American Association of Social Workers is in folder 1, the subject inventory for the American Association of Medical Social Workers is in folder 325, and so forth.

The NASW collection falls into three major sections to show the historical and professional development of the National Association of Social Workers. The first major section is devoted to the predecessor organizations and has been arranged chronologically according to the founding date of each organization, or its predecessor. Therefore, the order is as follows: AASW, 1917, folders 1-324; AAMSW, 1918, folders 325-755; NASSW, 1919, folders 756-761; AAPSW, 1926, folders 762-794; AAGW, 1936, folders 795-855; ASCO, 1946, folders 856-890; and SWRG, 1949, folders 891-895.

Following World War II, several of the professional social work organizations saw the need for a single professional social work organization. This drive toward professional unity which is reflected in the second major portion of the NASW collection, comprising the papers of the Temporary Inter-Association Council (TIAC), led to the formation of NASW, folders 896-1006. For specific information refer to the more complete description and organizational structure of TIAC that follows.

The third division deals with the National Association of Social Workers, folders 1007-1374, where the extensions of the predecessor organizations' specializations form the five sections of NASW. These papers cover the years 1955 to 1963. The holdings at this point are relatively sparse and quite selective re NASW functions. This may be amended in the future with further deposits of papers from the national organization.

Finally, the full complement of NASW papers includes as a parallel movement, rather than a separate division, the papers of the National Committee on Social Work in Defense Mobilization (folders 1375-1430). This group coincides chronologically with TIAC, but its records pertain explicitly to social work involvement in the national defense effort.

Briefly stated, the arrangement of the collection is as follows: introduction, narrative description of each individual organization, combined subject inventory, combined file folder inventory, and a listing of legal-size folders. Publications found within the NASW collection have been removed and placed in the Center's ephemera collection. A list of these publications is appended to the description.

The only restriction for use of the collection occurs in relation to 1.2 linear feet of confidential material in the AASW collection which pertains to violations of personnel standards (folders 264-324). Because of the confidentiality of the material, it has been placed at the end of the complete NASW collection and is "available to qualified scholars" only with the permission of NASW and the Archives Center director. "Specific permission" is "necessary for publication."

A listing of the initials of organizations referred to frequently in the description and the full title of each follows.

Prepared by Mary Jane Fout

ASSOCIATIONS APPEARING PROMINENTLY IN THE COLLECTION

AAGW	American Association of Group Workers
AAHSW	American Association of Hospital Social Workers
AAMSW	American Association of Medical Social Workers
AAPSW	American Association of Psychiatric Social Workers
AASSW	American Association of Schools of Social Work
AASW	American Association of Social Workers
APWA	American Public Welfare Association
ASCO	Association for the Study of Community Organization
CSWE	Council on Social Work Education
ICSW	International Conference of Social Work
NASSW	National Association of School Social Workers
NASW	National Association of Social Workers
NCSW	National Conference of Social Work (now the National Conference on Social Welfare)
NCSWDM	National Committee on Social Work in Defense Mobilization
NCSWE	National Council on Social Work Education
NSWA	National Social Welfare Assembly
SWRG	Social Work Research Group
TIAC	Temporary Inter-Association Council

NATIONAL ASSOCIATION OF SOCIAL WORKERS, INC.

American Association of Social Workers, New York, New York

Papers, 1918-1955

324 folders   26 (L) legal folders

The American Association of Social Workers was one of the seven predecessor organizations which formed the National Association of Social Workers in 1955; and its papers were included as a part of the NASW records. Correspondence (inter- and intra-national office), memoranda, reports, minutes and agendas of governing bodies and committees, and financial records constitute, in general, the type of papers contained in the collection. The organization's papers comprised thirteen linear feet with the heaviest concentration of material in the 1930's and 1940's. An invaluable aid to this collection is the Association journal, The Compass, and its successor, The Social Work Journal, which was employed to reconstruct portions of the development of the American Association of Social Workers not covered fully in the collection.

Background Data:

As the senior professional social work organization, the American Association of Social Workers traces its origin to the Intercollegiate Bureau of Occupations. The Bureau was founded in 1911 by a group of New York alumnae of various colleges to provide vocational information to young ladies seeking employment in New York City. The many questions received concerning social work positions led, in 1913, to the formation of a special department within the Bureau--the Department of Social Workers. Functioning as a clearing house for information regarding social workers and social work positions, the department also emphasized better standards in its placement and publications. The decision to become an independent organization was made in 1917, and the National Social Workers Exchange (NSWE) was established with its own board of directors. The purpose of the Exchange was "to develop a better adjustment between workers and positions in the social field, to discover new opportunities, to encourage adequate preparation and professional training, to facilitate the choice of competent candidates for positions, and to secure equitable standards of employment."

At the first annual meeting of the National Social Workers Exchange on May 18, 1918, held concurrently with the National Conference of Social Work in Kansas City, a nominating committee composed of Arthur P. Kellogg, Ida M. Cannon, Alfred Fairbank, Gertrude Vaile and Edith Abbott presented a slate of candidates for board of directors. Accepted by the membership, and elected were Richard H. Edwards, Charles A. Beard, John M. Glenn, Alexander Kohut, Mary Vida Clark, Porter R. Lee, James S. Cushman, William Breed, Margaret Byington, Philip P. Jacobs, Robert A. Woods, Eva W. White, C. C. Carstens, Joseph C. Logan, Elmer Scott,

Sophonisba P. Breckinridge, Edna Foley, William T. Crosse, Mary Van Kleeck, Karl de Schweinitz, Belle Sherwin, Gertrude Vaile, Jessica Peixotto and Frank J. Bruno. Edith Shatto King was named manager of the NSWE, while the elected officers were Richard H. Edwards, president; C. C. Carstens, vice-president; Margaret Byington, secretary; and James S. Cushman, treasurer. At the third annual meeting in New Orleans' Hotel Grunewald, a resolution for incorporation "under Article III of the Membership Corporations Laws of the State of New York, pursuant to Section 5 of said law" was authorized by the national body.

In 1920, the board of directors set up a central council, which in turn, appointed committees on placement, job analysis, training, industrial service, recruiting information, publicity and education. The official organ of the Exchange, The Compass, was first published in December, 1920. An executive committee was formed and its membership roll included C. C. Carstens, J. B. Buell, Clare M. Tousley, James S. Cushman, Harriet Anderson, Grace H. Childs, David H. Holbrook, Philip P. Jacobs, and Mary Van Kleeck. Before the annual meeting on June 27, 1921, Graham Romeyn Taylor, son of the settlement leader, Graham Taylor, was appointed national director.

The Exchange continued to function as a non-profit employment agency, but the need for a distinctly professional organization of social workers developed. In short, according to discussion in The Compass for that year, the Exchange had to become more than an employment bureau. Thus, at Kilbourn Hall in Milwaukee, Wisconsin, the NSWE became the American Association of Social Workers (AASW)--an organization formed to stimulate professional growth in social work and offering a vocational placement service. The elected officials of the newly named organization were Owen R. Lovejoy, president; Clare M. Tousley, first vice-president; Gertrude Vaile, second vice-president; Rose J. McHugh, third vice-president; Josiah B. Buell, secretary; and W. W. Norton, treasurer.

Providence, Rhode Island, was selected as the place of the annual meeting in June, 1922, and it was here that the central council became the national council. A report of a special committee, headed by Harry Hopkins, was also read. He spelled out a financial policy for the Association. Duly adopted by the assembled membership, this program, hereafter known as the "Providence Resolution," provided that all Association activities, after January 1, 1923, would be supported by dues and contributions from members only. This undertaking was ideally to be realized by January 1, 1925 and in the interim, financial assistance would come from the above mentioned sources, as well as from foundation grants. Financial difficulties forced the deadline to be extended to January, 1927. The goal was finally met when the decision was made to separate the Vocational Bureau from the Association as its operating costs were draining funds from the treasury.

Structurally the organization experimented with several types of governing bodies. Through the course of the Association's existence governmental responsibility shifted from one group to another. The original body of authority, the central council, was succeeded by the national council in 1922. An executive committee was appointed to run Association affairs between council meetings. The national council became so unwieldy and its membership so widely distributed that it caused the council to lose its directing capability. In 1926 the executive committee assumed administrative duties. The national council henceforth functioned as a delegate body acting in an intermediary, advisory capacity. To compensate for the loss of the council, an ad interim committee of the executive committee was created to act on urgent matters subject to final approval by the higher authority. The first members were Neva Deardorff, Dorothy C. Kahn, William Hodson, Linton B. Swift, John A. Fitch, and Katharine Tucker.

Since the formation of the Association, the following secretaries have held the reins of Association business in the national offices: Graham R. Taylor, 1921-1922; Edith Shatto King (acting executive secretary) 1922-1923; Philip Klein, 1923-1927, with assistance from Elizabeth de Schweinitz (Mrs. Karl de Schweinitz), prior to Walter West's nomination to the post in November, 1927.

With the advent of the "Great Depression" and social work's greater interest and involvement in government programs dealing with relief on state and federal levels, the organization was plagued by financial problems and overwork. According to Compass reports, the executive committee found itself burdened by administrative detail, and consequently lacked correlation with national committees. In 1934 action was taken to decentralize the governing committee's responsibilities by creating divisions which would be guided internally by steering committees. Certain administrative committees were left out of the divisional scheme, i.e., national membership, publications, and chapter organization. The main concerns of the Association were reflected in the division titles: government and social work, personnel standards, employment practices, and personnel practices.

A word of explanation is necessary to describe the complicated evolution of the division on government and social work. In June of 1931, the assembled membership of AASW, at its annual meeting in Minneapolis, authorized the formation of the commission on unemployment which was to gather information on local situations through AASW chapters, and, thereby, study and report on proposed programs meant to deal with unemployment, i.e., federal relief fund. A second assignment involved the study of the social and economic effects of unemployment and the possible regularization of employment by unemployment insurance. The first chairman of the commission was Mary Van Kleeck who was supported by a panel of distinguished citizens: Joseph P. Chamberlain, Stanley B. Davies, Helen Hall, David H. Holbrook, Porter R. Lee, Betsey Libbey, Harry Lurie, Linton B. Swift, Frances Taussig, and Walter West.

Coincidentally, executives of national agencies called for the Social Work Conference on Federal Action to discuss plans for action on governmental programs. The steering committee of this conference, with Linton B. Swift as its chairman, became the AASW's committee on federal relief under the auspices of the Commission on Unemployment. Not content with this label, the committee was renamed the federal action on unemployment committee with Linton Swift at the helm, and manned by an able membership: Benson Y. Landis, Frank Bane, Allen T. Burns, C. C. Carstens, Joanna C. Colcord, Helen Crosby, David H. Holbrook, Paul U. Kellogg, Harry L. Lurie, the Rev. Dr. John O'Grady, Helen Hall, Ralph G. Hurlin, Walter West, and Stanley B. Davies. Lack of funds caused the chairman of the commission to ask for the commission's discharge in April, 1933, but as many functions as possible were assumed by the division on government and social work under its first chairman, Linton B. Swift.

Dissatisfaction with this divisional structure was brought to the surface in August, 1938, by the resignation of Florence Taylor (Mrs. Graham R. Taylor), who had served as an assistant executive secretary. She pointed out that the executive committee left too much decision making to the executive secretary, the ad interim committee could not cope with the responsibilities developing because the executive committee met too infrequently, the committees were too loosely organized, there was too heavy an administrative burden for the national office, and a difference of opinion existed regarding the basic policies and program of the Association. Faced by such explicit criticism, measures were taken the following year to amend the situation by creating a new governing body, the national board of directors, from whose ranks an executive committee would be selected to exercise the powers of the national board between meetings of the latter group. Due to the reorganizational shuffle, the divisional apparatus gradually faded out to be replaced by regionalized national committees. By March, 1941, the outstanding committees were executive, national membership, government and social work, personnel practices, chapter, personnel practices for national staff, and nominating. This basic pattern, changed only by addition or deletion of national committees, remained true of the Association's structure till dissolution in 1955.

The problem of administrative structure was thus amended. However, matters of procedures continued to plague personnel and employment practices' investigations, *i.e.*, employment practices inquiry, 1940. The division of opinion regarding basic doctrine of the Association remained unresolved. One member commented that the struggle to solve these issues caused a loss of momentum in the Association's forward progress and resulted in the resignations of president, executive secretary, and members of the executive committee and board of directors. This period, 1941-1943, was one of internal dissension within all sections of the organization. After Walter West's resignation in the early part of 1942, Elisabeth Mills served as acting executive secretary until the appointment of Joseph P. Anderson as executive secretary on May 15, 1942. Anderson continued in that capacity until the dissolution of AASW in 1955 at which time he assumed the executive secretaryship of the National Association of Social Workers.

Beset with financial difficulties and a scattered membership involved in defense concerns during the Second World War, national conferences were cancelled in 1943 and 1945. However, during the postwar period, the Association grew steadily. Reflecting the growth of professionalism in social work, The Compass became The Social Work Journal in 1948. Simultaneously preliminary discussions were initiated with other professional social work organizations to examine the possibility of merging operations to best further the social work profession as a whole. This inquiry led to the formation of the Temporary Inter-Association Council in which the AASW took a leading role. (The records of AASW's participation on the Council have been placed with others to form a more unified TIAC Section.)

Organization of the Collection:

AASW's records have been divided into two major sections, the first of which shows chronologically the organizational development of the Association, i.e., constitution, bylaws, policy statements, board and committee minutes, conference proceedings, registration of members, personnel practices, finances, and chapter information (folders 1-154). The second division also includes papers of the organization; however, because of their degree of specialization, they are arranged in an alphabetical, topical order, i.e., armed forces, ethics, government and social work, Donald S. Howard correspondence (AASW president, 1947-1949), migrants, National Recovery Administration, political parties, the practitioners movement, Social Security Act, war activities and the Wartime Committee on Personnel (folders 155-263). A list of publications removed from the AASW section and placed in the Minnesota Center's ephemera collection is included in the appendix. A chronological statement of organizational highlights follows:

SUMMARY OF AASW ORGANIZATIONAL HIGHLIGHTS

DATE	EVENT
1918	National Social Workers Exchange formed. Board of directors, NSWE, elected.
1920	Created central council. First publication of The Compass, official organ. Formed first executive committee.
1921	Graham Romeyn Taylor appointed national director, NSWE.
1922	American Association of Social Workers created. "Providence Resolution" at annual meeting established a financial policy for AASW. Central council became the national council. Edith Shatto King served as acting executive secretary.
1923	Philip Klein appointed to the position of executive secretary.

1926	Executive committee assumed administrative duties of national council which became a delegate body with advisory capacities only. Ad interim committee of executive committee appointed. Vocational Bureau separated from AASW.
1927	Walter West nominated and selected for post of executive secretary.
1934	Structural change to divisions rather than national committees, exceptions being administrative committees such as national membership, publications and chapter organization. First delegate conference--"Governmental Objectives for Social Work."
1939	National board of directors created to take over duties of executive committee. Executive committee henceforth to be selected from the ranks of the national board.
1940	Employment Practices Inquiry.
1941	Structural changes made within the organization from divisions to national committees.
1942	Walter West resigned; Elisabeth Mills served as acting executive secretary. Special study of program, policies and operation of AASW by the executive committee.
1943	Joseph P. Anderson became the last executive secretary for AASW.
1948	The Compass became The Social Work Journal.
1948-1949	Preliminary talks led to the formation of the Temporary Inter-Association Council.
1953	"Procedures for Considering Complaints of Unethical Conduct of Members." Delegate Conference became Delegate Assembly.
1955	AASW dissolved and NASW formed.

LIST OF AASW PRESIDENTS, 1921-1955

C. C. Carstens	1921-1923
Owen R. Lovejoy	1922-1923
Harry Hopkins	1922-1924
William Hodson	1924-1926
Neva R. Deardorff	1926-1928
Frank J. Bruno	1928-1930
Frances Taussig	1930-1932
Stanley P. Davies	1932-1934
Dorothy C. Kahn	1934-1936
Linton B. Swift	1936-1938
Harry Greenstein	1938-1940
Wayne McMillen	1940-February, 1942
Frank J. Bruno	February-October, 1942
Grace L. Coyle	1942-1944
Irene Franham Conrad	1944-1946
Paul L. Benjamin	1946-1947
Donald S. Howard	1947-1949
Ernest Witte	1949-1951
Benjamin E. Youngdahl	1951-1953
Arthur H. Kruse	1953-1955

Prepared by Mary Jane Fout

American Association of Medical Social Workers, Inc., Washington, D.C.

Papers, 1917-1956

431 folders   17 (*L*) folders

History of the Association

The American Association of Hospital Social Workers (AAHSW) was formed with the adoption of a constitution and bylaws on May 20, 1918. In 1926 AAHSW was incorporated under the laws of the Commonwealth of Massachusetts, and in 1934 it became the American Association of Medical Social Workers, a name it retained until its merger, in 1955, with six other social work membership organizations to become the National Association of Social Workers.

The formal origin of medical social work in America came in 1905 when Dr. Richard Clarke Cabot, staff member of Boston's Massachusetts General Hospital, arranged for the employment of a "person of experience in health and social work" to assist in the out-patient department in solving problems of sickness and ill health related to social factors. Though volunteers and hospital auxiliaries had been engaged for many years in friendly visiting, sewing, and other services to hospitals and patients, this marked the beginning of an effort to provide adequate, consistent professional service to clients.

Organization of hospital social workers on a national scale came in May, 1917, when approximately thirty workers met in Pittsburgh in connection with the National Conference of Social Work to discuss the question of a national organization. Because of the war, further efforts were delayed until the 1918 National Conference in Kansas City when a series of meetings were held culminating in the organization of AAHSW.

According to its original constitution, the purpose of AAHSW was "to serve as an organ of intercommunication among hospital social workers, to maintain and improve standards of social work in hospitals and dispensaries, and to stimulate its intensive and extensive development." (The purpose was amended in 1944, reflecting changed emphases within the profession, to read: "to promote the quality and effectiveness of social work in relation to health and medical care.") The constitution provided for the offices of president, first and second vice-president, secretary, and treasurer, and opened membership to institutions and individuals in the United States and Canada. The bylaws adopted (folders 326-327) set forth duties of the officers and an executive committee, listed qualifications for membership, and provided for an advisory council, annual meetings, and procedures for amendment of bylaws.

Original membership qualifications established active, associate, and honorary classes. Active members were paid hospital social workers or executives of social service departments. Associate members included individuals who had been active in hospital social work or allied fields but were not eligible at the time, or those who had only recently begun this work, and social service departments or organizations and institutions in fields allied with medical social work. Honorary members were individuals deemed by the Association to have made a significant contribution to medical social work. Subsequent changes in the constitution (which was repealed in 1944), bylaws, membership qualifications, etc., can be found in the bylaws themselves and the records of the bylaws and membership committees (folders 326-327, 352-353, 507-509).

An executive secretary (titled executive director after 1953) was employed part-time from 1918 and full-time from 1922. From 1936 to 1955 a business manager, Mrs. Ellen Michaels, directed the national office. Other part-time or full-time professional staff members were the consultant on education, Kate McMahon, 1925-1955; consultant on practice, Addie Thomas, 1953-1955 (this position was established in 1953); and consultant on recruitment (a position also established in 1953), Elma Phillipson and, later, Opal Gooden.

In 1920, in an effort to make a national organization less remote and more relevant to individual members scattered across the country, a plan for organization of the Association on a district basis was proposed. At the semi-annual meeting, held in conjunction with the American Hospital Association, the district plan was accepted by the membership with the provision that district limits be approved by the executive committee and that district constitutions conform to the national constitution. In 1945 specific criteria for districting were adopted. These included, among others, a minimum of 25 potential members, leadership, financial stability, and proposed district limits. During reorganization of the Association, 1940-1942, a plan for establishing five regions for members living in undistricted areas was adopted.

At the 1921 annual meeting, a group of psychiatric social workers who were members of AAHSW, petitioned to form a psychiatric section within AAHSW. In 1922 the Section was formed with its own bylaws, officers, etc. In 1926 the Section dissolved its ties with AAHSW and formed the American Association of Psychiatric Social Workers.

One of the major study projects of the Association rose from an education committee subcommittee on medical social workers' participation in teaching medical students (folders 393-412). In 1943 this subcommittee formed a joint committee with a subcommittee of the Association of American Medical Colleges. With a grant from the Milbank Foundation the joint committee on teaching of social and environmental factors in medicine studied and evaluated the teaching of information, attitudes, and skills in selected medical colleges and schools (folders 401-404). After publication of the study, Widening Horizons in Medical Education: A Study of the Teaching of Social and Environmental Factors in Medicine, in 1947, a small

Association subcommittee carried on related projects. In 1953 this subcommittee began cooperation with the American Association of Psychiatric Social Workers; this resulted in a joint committee of the two associations which carried on under the National Association of Social Workers as the joint committee on participation in medical education.

Mary A. Stites' detailed History of the American Association of Medical Social Workers (1955) gives a complete picture of the Association's structure and program, its committees and projects, and its development from 1918 to 1955. The Association's executive committee minutes, 1918-1941, (folders 339-345) are also useful in understanding the evolution of the Association and of the medical social work profession.

Organization of the Collection

The collection comprises 16.5 linear feet of records covering the years 1917 to 1956. The papers, which have been arranged in so far as possible to reflect the working structure of the Association, are divided in sections.

The first section (folders 325-350) consists of papers tracing the formation and incorporation of AAMSW, its constitution and bylaws, papers of the officers and staff, and records of its policy-making committees and councils. The second section (folders 351-593) constitutes Association committee records, including regular, advisory, joint, and special committees (as far as these can be identified). Because the Association carried on projects largely through its committees and because these records are extensive, many major interests and accomplishments of the Association are reflected here. The third section is papers of the Psychiatric Section (folder 594). Records of the Association consultants on education, practice, and recruitment comprise the fourth section (folders 595-643). The fifth section (folders 644-678) includes papers of Association districts and regions, arranged by date of admission to the Association. These records reflect the implementation of Association policies on a local level and provide information on activities and concerns of groups of members. The sixth section (folders 679-755) consists of the correspondence and papers of the Association in a subject arrangement. Included among these are financial records (folders 679-690), material pertaining to the transition from AAMSW to the National Association of Social Workers (folder 691), and records of the Association's relations with other voluntary associations and governmental agencies (folders 714-747).

It should be noted that certain themes recur in the AAMSW records so frequently that it is misleading to attempt to single out sections of the collection where they are contained. The records trace the problems of an emerging profession with its concern for definition of function, professional education, standards in practice, and relations with other professions. Maintenance of an adequate supply of trained medical social workers was a central concern of the Association long before the establishment of a recruitment committee in 1953. Also reflected in these records is the impact of war and the Depression on the profession and the interest of medical social workers and persons in related health field agencies in rehabilitation of persons handicapped by disease or injury. The collection, of course, documents trends in medical social work, casework method and skills, the generic-specific debate in social work, etc.

It should also be noted that the following individuals appear prominently in these papers: Edith M. Baker, Harriett Bartlett, Helen Beckley, Zdenka Buben, Ida M. Cannon, M. Antoinette Cannon, Eleanor Cockerill, Ruth Cooper, Ruth Emerson, Dora Goldstine, Eckka Gordon, Mary L. Hemmy, Ruth E. Lewis, Mary Maxwell, Kate McMahon, Mary Blanche Moss, Mary L. Poole, Elizabeth P. Rice, Marian E. Russell, Pauline Ryman, Agnes H. Schroeder, Addie Thomas, Lenore Gottfried Van Vliet, Ruth Wadman, Margaret Wagner, Lena R. Waters, and Grace White.

A list of publications removed from the AAMSW section and placed in the Center's ephemera collection is included in the appendix.

Prepared by Andrea Hinding

National Association of School Social Workers, New York, New York

Papers, 1922-1955

6 folders   2 (l) folders

In 1916, fifteen visiting teachers met to consider the formation of a national organization of visiting teachers. The First World War effected a temporary postponement of their plans, but in 1919, the National Association of Visiting Teachers and Home Visitors was established, with Jane Culbert elected the first president. Because the field was closely allied to both education and social work, the Association held its annual meetings alternately with the National Education Association or the American Association of School Administrators and the National Conference of Social Work. The organization's name was changed several times.

1919	Group met at National Conference of Social Work to form National Association of Visiting Teachers and Home Visitors.
1929	Name changed to American Association of Visiting Teachers (AAVT).
1942	Name changed to American Association of School Social Workers (AASSW).
1945	Name changed to National Association of School Social Workers (NASSW).
1955	Became School Social Work Section of NASW.

Through the years the major objectives of the Association involved defining the role of school social workers, organizing the development of social work programs in schools, and improving standards of training. Several surveys were undertaken to meet these objectives. One survey, done in 1921, The Visiting Teacher in the United States, published by the New York City Public Education Association, considered the organizational structure and methods of the work, the preparation and training of visiting teachers, and the possibilities for future developments of visiting teacher services. In 1940, the standards committee of the AAVT, under the chairmanship of Margaret Sager, published Visiting Teacher Service Today: A Study of Its Philosophy and Practice in the United States. The NASSW and the American Association of Social Workers co-sponsored and published Report of a Study of School Social Work Practice in Twelve Communities, a project undertaken by Mildred Sikkema in 1950.

The National Committee on Visiting Teachers was made up of many members of the National Association of Visiting Teachers, but apparently an independent committee seems to have advised the Association from 1921 to 1930. It worked to extend the establishment of social workers in more and more schools, set up demonstration centers, and issued reports which were published by the Commonwealth Fund.

The Association was administered by the executive officers, consisting of a president, vice-president, secretary, and treasurer who were elected annually at first and biennially after 1931. Standing committees on membership, education, standards, program, ways and means, nominating, publicity, as well as regional committees, did much of the work of the Association. Other administrative and study committees such as resolutions and amendments, were formed when the need for them arose. By 1947, the Association was able to establish a permanent office with a full-time executive secretary, Mildred Sikkema. Inadequate funds forced the closing of the office and the elimination of the position in 1951, but they were re-established in 1954, with financial help from the Grant Foundation and with individual contributions. The office employed Marjorie Case as a professional consultant. Interest in forming a comprehensive national organization of social workers, which had been building since the late 1940's, culminated in the NASSW joining six other professional organizations to form the National Association of Social Workers in October, 1955.

This collection, containing material from 1922 to 1955, comprises six regular and two legal-size folders. The papers are scattered and most of the material covers the years from 1928 to 1934. The Membership News-Letter, of which there is a complete run in the Center's ephemera collection, is indispensible for 1947 through 1955, where there is no correspondence or substantive material. A list of publications removed from the NASSW section is included in the appendix.

LIST OF AASSW PRESIDENTS, 1919-1955

Jane Culbert	1919-1921
Emma Case	1921-1922
Sara Holbrook	1922-1924
Edith Everett	1924-1926
Rhea Boardman	1926-1928
Helen Smith	1928-1929
Julia Drew	1929-1931
Wilma Walker	1931-1933
Shirley Leonard	1933-1935
Gladys Hall	1935-1937
Marion Echols	1937-1941
Alma Laabs	1941-1945
Florence Poole	1945-1947
Ethel Batschelet	1947-1949
Emilie Rannells	1949-1951
Opal Boston	1951-1955

Prepared by Pamela J. Matson

American Association of Psychiatric Social Workers, New York, New York

Papers, 1921-1958

33 folders   1 (*l*) folder

In 1920, the American Association of Psychiatric Social Workers began in Boston as an informal discussion group of seventeen members, headed by Mary C. Jarrett, who called themselves the National Psychiatric Social Workers Club. In 1922, the group was organized on a national basis as the Section on Psychiatric Social Work of the American Association of Hospital Social Workers. In May of 1926, the members of the Section voted to withdraw from the Association (which later became the American Association of Medical Social Workers) and form an independent national organization, the American Association of Psychiatric Social Workers.

In these early years, the purposes of the Association were:

1. to promote association among members.
2. to establish standards of training.
3. to improve practice.
4. to engage in continuous study of function in order to define the relationship of social work to psychiatry.[1]

The growing membership, employed in a variety of agencies, represented an expanding field. By 1929, it was evident that a single basis of definition of field work was causing confusion as to which of two areas of activity the Association was pledged to foster and promote, whether it was to be ". . . social work practiced in connection with psychiatry . . .," or ". . . social work in whatever setting a worker took adequate working knowledge of mental hygiene . . . ."[2]

The bases for membership in the AAPSW, dependent upon the individual's vocational position as well as his educational background, were broadened throughout the first decade of its existence, but discussion of membership qualifications continued. An analysis of trends in the AAPSW was undertaken by a study committee under the leadership of Mrs. Lois Meredith French in the 1930's, and the report was formally published in 1941. At the annual business meeting, the AAPSW membership voted to clarify the responsibility of the Association in ". . . fostering social work in relation to the practice of psychiatry and contributing to the study, treatment, and prevention of mental disease. Relationship with other professional social work organizations . . . [would] be strengthened." In addition, the Association hoped

---

[1] "Reflections from the Trend Study, Memorandum I," Executive Committee, Correspondence and Papers, February 3, 1938, p. 2.

[2] Ibid., p. 3.

to achieve a closer relationship with the field of psychiatry.[3]

The Second World War indicated a need for additional training of personnel and integration with other professional groups. The war service office, with Elizabeth Healy Ross as secretary, was set up by the AAPSW in 1942 in response to the greatly increased demand for psychiatric workers during World War II and was financed through a grant from the Rockefeller Foundation. In 1944, the National Committee for Mental Hygiene joined the AAPSW in sponsoring the office, and the name was changed to the war office of psychiatric social work. The work of the office included recruiting psychiatric social workers, evaluating military social work and standards, undertaking studies of personnel, and coordinating the placement of psychiatric social workers in the most urgent positions. The office was also concerned with the Veterans Administration, the American National Red Cross, standards in psychiatric social work, and the Wartime Committee on Personnel. Members of the joint committee to the war office included Mrs. Ethel Ginsburg, Dr. Marion Kenworthy, Dr. David Levy, Marion McBee, Madeleine Moore, Mildred Scoville, Dr. Frank Fremont Smith, and Dr. George S. Stevenson.

During the war years, two other war-oriented committees were established: the committee on relations with the Red Cross, and a committee which worked with the American Psychiatric Association and later with the American Association of Medical Social Workers in stressing the importance of keeping up standards of psychiatric and medical social service in military installations. The AAPSW was also represented on the Wartime Committee on Personnel, along with the American Association of Social Workers, the American Association of Medical Social Workers, the American Association of School Social Workers, and the American Association of Group Workers.

After the war, the AAPSW continued to increase in size. In the tradition of the Trend Study, a study of AAPSW personnel was undertaken from 1947 to 1949. The AAPSW also sponsored the Dartmouth Conference on Education for Psychiatric Social Work in September, 1949, at which there were ". . . representatives from all schools of social work offering a psychiatric social work sequence who met to review, consider, and revise current educational programs in relation to the practice of psychiatric social work." An educational secretary, Madeleine Lay, was employed through grants from the Commonwealth Fund from 1947 to 1950 to assist schools in the development of their educational programs. In the 1950's, a research project was undertaken to study the work experience of the membership.

---

[3] Lois Meredith French, The AAPSW. Its History, Purposes, and Activities, 1941, pp. 26-27.

Discussion of forming a national social work organization began in the late 1940's and AAPSW worked through the Temporary Inter-Association Council to study the situation. Over the years, AAPSW representatives to TIAC were Ethel Ginsburg, Christine Robb Thompson, George E. Levinrew, Luther Woodward, Leon Lucas, Anna Aldridge, Maida Solomon, and Ruth I. Knee. The merger was a major topic of consideration until the AAPSW and other social work groups combined to form the National Association of Social Workers in October, 1955.

The collection comprises three and one-half linear feet, and includes thirty-three regular folders and one legal-size folder. The papers cover the years from 1921 to 1958, but the bulk of the material is found between 1926 and 1955. The collection is arranged in three basic sections. Annual material includes minutes of the annual meetings, secretary's reports, and presidential addresses. The committees are divided by function, whether administrative or study. Not all the committees are covered for all the years of AAPSW's existence. AAPSW publications include the serial publications, which are the News-Letter, the Journal of Psychiatric Social Work, and the Bulletin; pamphlets and reprints. The Social Welfare History Archives Center holdings of the News-Letter, the Journal, and the Bulletin are nearly complete, and these publications, which are held in the Center's ephemera collection, contain much important information on the work of the Association. A list of the publications removed from the AAPSW section is included in the appendix.

Prepared by Pamela J. Matson

American Association of Group Workers, Chicago, Illinois

Papers, 1936-1955

61 folders

The American Association of Group Workers (AAGW), a national professional organization, evolved out of the National Association for the Study of Group Work (NASGW). The NASGW was organized in May, 1936, to develop and refine the aims, methods, and practice of group work. This purpose was accomplished through local study groups, an annual conference, and by publication and distribution of material of interest to the practitioner. Membership was open to any person interested in the study of group work, regardless of their prior affiliation in other social welfare organizations. As an organization of professional group workers, the NASGW cut across all agency, religious, racial, and occupational lines. In 1939 the organization became the American Association for the Study of Group Work, and in April, 1946, the AAGW was formed, replacing the AASGW as the professional organization of group workers. By 1948, membership in the AAGW had grown to 1,811, with members from such organizations as the settlements, YMCA's, YWCA's, Jewish Community Centers, Girl Scouts, Boy Scouts, Camp Fire Girls, Schools of Social Work, recreation organizations, etc. For most members, the AAGW was not the primary professional organization. The AAGW tried to professionalize group work wherever it existed, rather than to initiate new programs independent of already existing social welfare enterprises.

The AAGW sought constantly to professionalize its work, and by 1948 it had defined quite clearly what it conceived group work to be. A 1947 description of the AAGW's nature and functions (folder 806) states:

> Group work is a method of group leadership used in organizing and conducting various types of group activities. While group work developed first in connection with recreation and voluntary informal education...its use is not confined to those fields. It is increasingly being used in various types of institutions, in hospitals and clinics, in the extra-curricular activities of schools and in similar situations. The guiding purpose behind such leadership rests upon the common assumptions of a democratic society; namely, the opportunity for each individual to fulfill his capacities in freedom, to respect and appreciate others and to assume his social responsibility in maintaining and constantly improving our democratic society.

The inter-agency character of the AAGW is demonstrated by the fact that the executive personnel were already heavily involved in other professional occupations. For example, Arthur L. Swift, Jr., a professor at Union Theological Seminary, New York City, was actively involved in the formation and early operation of the Association. Similarly, other people prominent in the organization, such as Louis Kraft (of the National Jewish Welfare Board and chairman of many important AAGW committees), Ann Elizabeth Neely (on the national board of the YWCA, chairman of the AASGW, 1940-1942, and active on numerous AAGW committees), and Edna d'Issertelle (of Girl Scouts, Inc. and secretary of the AASGW), were prominent in the work of their own agencies. Until 1946, there was no full-time, paid executive secretary for the organization, indicating the voluntary nature of the AAGW. For a more complete description of internal organization, see folders 795-796 and 811-813.

Other individuals who appear prominently in the collection are Theodore T. Tarail, executive secretary of the AAGW from 1946 to 1948; Agnes Leahy of the Girl Scouts of America, who was secretary of the AASGW from 1938 to 1941; Charles Hendry, first chairman of the Association; Joe R. Hoffer, who succeeded Neely as chairman of the AASGW and is currently (1969) executive secretary of the National Conference on Social Welfare; Helen Rowe, president, 1946-1948; Saul Bernstein, president, 1948-1950, and prominent in the merger with the NASW; John McDowell, treasurer from 1946 to 1948 and president, 1950-1952; Harleigh Trecker, president from 1952 to 1955 and active in the area of publications; and Janet W. Korpela, who served as administrative secretary, 1953-1955.

Prominent issues include cooperation with similar groups, recruitment of social workers in general and group workers in particular, accreditation of schools of social work, problems of recreation and leisure, professionalization of group work, discussion groups at the local level, cooperation with government agencies and programs, social welfare in wartime, psychiatric casework, juvenile delinquency, labor disputes in welfare organizations, standards in group work, and the 1955 merger with the NASW. The papers dealing with the merger have been removed and placed with the "TIAC" section of the NASW collection.

The papers, which comprise 1.5 linear feet and cover the years 1936-1955, were arranged in alphabetical order and this order has been retained in the final organization.

Prepared by Loren W. Crabtree

Association for the Study of Community Organization,
New York, New York

Papers, 1944-1955

35 folders   1 (∅) folder

The Association for the Study of Community Organization (ASCO), a national non-professional organization, was a temporary organization from August, 1946, to August, 1947, when it was incorporated and bylaws were adopted. The primary purpose of the Association was to study community organization, and consequently membership was open to anyone interested in that subject. As Arthur Dunham, first president of ASCO, said in January, 1947: "We are of course interested in improving standards of professional practice in community organization, and in this our aims are similar to the established professional associations." However, "We are not strictly a 'professional organization' in the sense that we limit membership to persons with certain qualifications of professional education and experience." (letter of January 6, 1947, folder 857) Thus ASCO attempted to improve the study of community organization without professionalizing it to the extent that many interested practitioners were excluded. The membership, which peaked at around 500, included professional social workers, educators, professors, and practitioners from diverse occupations and positions in life. ASCO merged with the NASW in October, 1955, and thereafter the NASW assumed all ASCO functions. Information concerning this merger was contained in a folder labeled "TIAC," which has been removed and placed with other NASW-TIAC materials.

The Association provided many services during its brief existence, including publication of a Newsletter and a quarterly Checklist of Current Publications on Community Organization; investigation of cooperation with other national welfare organizations; preparation of a book of readings on community organization; sponsorship of local discussion groups; definition and elaboration of the principles of community organization; and participation in the Temporary Inter-Association Council (TIAC) as the representative of students of community organization. Prominent individuals who appear in the collection include Arthur Dunham, a professor of community organization at the University of Michigan, who was active in the origins of ASCO and was its first president, 1946-1948; John B. Dawson, president of ASCO, 1948-1949; C. F. McNeil, of Ohio State University's School of Social Administration and president of ASCO, 1949-1951; Ernest B. Harper, a professor in the Department of Social Service at Michigan State University and president of ASCO, 1951-1952; Merrill F. Krughoff, president from 1952-1954; Philip E. Ryan, executive director of the National Health Council and president of ASCO, 1954-1955; and Joseph P. Anderson, then executive secretary of the American Association of Social Workers (AASW) and a leading participant in both ASCO and TIAC.

The collection comprises 1¼ linear feet and covers the years 1944-1955. When received, the folders were arranged in alphabetical order, and this order has been retained in the final organization. The Partial Subject Inventory provides finding aids for scattered materials pertaining to the subjects listed.

Prepared by Loren W. Crabtree

NATIONAL ASSOCIATION OF SOCIAL WORKERS, INC.

Social Work Research Group, New York, New York

Papers, 1949-1956

5 folders

    The Social Work Research Group (SWRG) was formally established at the National Conference of Social Work in June, 1949, ". . . to provide a medium of communication for social work practitioners . . . [and to establish] a permanent organizational structure to further the development of research in social work." Communication, standards of practice including ethics and personnel practices, public relations, and research were the major objectives of the group.

    The governing body of SWRG consisted of three elected officials--president, secretary, and treasurer--and a steering committee. Three committees were set up to fulfill the objectives of the organization: the committee on research function and practice, the committee to study structure of advisory committees, and a committee on education. The group published SWRG Periodical Abstracts which included articles on research in social work, or on research in a field other than social work where the method had application to social work, and a Newsletter. No issues of the Newsletter were found in the collection.

    In October, 1955, SWRG joined NASW and became the research section of that organization. Prominent members of SWRG included Ann Shyne, David French, and Tessie Berkman.

    Folder 895 labeled "SWRG Research, 1952-1955," contains extensive material relating to the American Association of Social Workers.

                                      Prepared by Pamela J. Matson

NATIONAL ASSOCIATION OF SOCIAL WORKERS, INC.

Temporary Inter-Association Council of Social Work Membership Organizations, New York, New York

Papers, 1946-1955

111 folders   8 (*l*) folders

    The Temporary Inter-Association Council of Social Work Membership Organizations, hereafter referred to as TIAC, grew out of a meeting called by the American Association of Social Workers and the American Association of Schools of Social Work in the fall of 1947. The meeting itself was entitled "Conference on Proposals for Inter-Association Activities" and the American Association of Social Workers (AASW), the American Association of Medical Social Workers (AAMSW), the American Association of Psychiatric Social Workers (AAPSW), the American Association of Group Workers (AAGW), and the National Association of School Social Workers (NASSW) were all represented. This preliminary session created the Committee on Inter-Association Structure of Professional Organizations in Social Work which met in December, 1948, and began functioning actively in January, 1949. The purpose of the Committee was to exchange information about the participating associations' objectives, membership requirements, programs and administrations, finances, etc., and in this way work toward a plan for one unified professional social work organization.

    As the talks progressed, the need for a more permanent organization arose. The Committee, after due discussion, dissolved on June 10, 1950, and became TIAC. The discussions of TIAC centered on two major problems--the type of organization needed for a new association and the actual deliberations necessary in constructing a functioning social work association. During the years of negotiation and discussion, the Association for the Study of Community Organization (ASCO) and the Social Work Research Group (SWRG) were invited to and accepted membership on the Council, in 1952 and 1954 respectively. The Council itself was guided by two chairmen, Dora Goldstine, 1950-1953, and Sanford Solender, 1953-1955, who appears prominently in these records.

    The member associations rejected the idea of an organization for social workers that was merely an inter-professional committee, and the same fate lay in store for the projected plan of a federated professional organization. The need for a single unified organization was found most appealing to the TIAC delegates and their home organizations. It met the needs of an entire profession by having a broad membership base, creating division of members grouped according to specialized interest, and establishing committees to deal with projects related to broad interests. Therefore, following the structural lines of a single membership organization, the governing body was composed of a delegate assembly which elected the top officials and a board of directors. To reflect the evolution of specialization within social work, five sections were developed; group work, medical social work, psychiatric social work, school social work, and social work research. (It was determined by the Council that ASCO would be represented by a committee on community organization and could petition for section status once NASW began functioning.)

In October, 1955, the plans for a single professional organization for social workers reached fruition and the National Association of Social Workers (NASW) began operating. Its first president was Nathan Cohen, and Joseph P. Anderson was selected to serve as executive secretary.

The collection has two major divisions. The first pertains strictly to the activities and functioning of TIAC (folders 896-965), and the second reflects the reaction of the participating associations to the aforementioned activities (folders 966-1006).

Within the first division the papers have been arranged in such a manner as to trace the three chronological phases of TIAC's development: the initial stage of inter-association cooperation under the Committee on Inter-Association Structure (1948-1950), the formation of TIAC and its deliberations in negotiating for a single professional social work organization (ca. 1950-1953), and finally, the actual process of planning for the operations of NASW (1954-1955). The second major division contains the papers of four of the constituent organizations, and they are arranged alphabetically: AAGW, AAMSW, AASW, and ASCO. Within each of the subdivisions the organization's papers have generally been arranged chronologically.

On receipt of the NASW collection, there were specific records of Dora Goldstine, chairman of TIAC and member of AAMSW; and Joseph P. Anderson, secretary and treasurer of TIAC and executive secretary to TIAC. For greater cohesiveness these papers have been placed in those sections to which they best pertain: Dora Goldstine, folders 896, 905-906, 924, and 970; Joseph P. Anderson, folders 908, 938-941, 983-987, 991 and 998-999; and, Melvin Glasser, folders 982, 988-990, 992-997 and 1000-1003. The TIAC section of the NASW collection comprises approximately four linear feet.

Prepared by Mary Jane Fout

NATIONAL ASSOCIATION OF SOCIAL WORKERS, INC.

National Association of Social Workers, New York, New York

Papers, 1955-1963

368 folders   1 (ℓ) folder

    In October, 1955, the National Association of Social Workers (NASW) was established following five years of careful planning by the Temporary Inter-Association Council (TIAC) in which seven organizations were represented: American Association of Social Workers (AASW), American Association of Medical Social Workers (AAMSW), National Association of School Social Workers (NASSW), American Association of Psychiatric Social Workers (AAPSW), American Association of Group Workers (AAGW), Association for the Study of Community Organization (ASCO), and Social Work Research Group (SWRG). The papers of NASW deal approximately with the first five years of the organization and the process of transition to the present professional organization of social workers. Records of the actual formation and organization of NASW can be found in the papers of the Temporary Inter-Association Council.

    At the time the predecessor organizations united, provision was made for an analysis of NASW after the first five-year period of operation. A committee for the purpose of review of NASW's structure was formed and its final report and recommendations were adopted by the delegate assembly in 1963; the changes went into effect on July 1, 1963. The papers of this review of structure give the best description of the format of the current organization (folders 1067-1078).[1]

    There are two divisions of the NASW papers. The first represents the broad scope of the national organization's activities during its initial phase of operation and includes papers of the delegate assemblies, plans for certification of social workers, and material on personnel standards and practices, social work practice, and review of NASW structure (folders 1007-1079). The specializations of the predecessor organizations were maintained in NASW by the creation of five sections (group work, medical social work, psychiatric social work, social work research, and school social work), and the second division comprises the papers of these sections (folders 1080-1374). The papers are arranged alphabetically by section, except that those of the social work research section precede the school social work section in accordance with its position on the organization charts of the Temporary Inter-Association Council. Although each section is represented nominally in the present holdings, the medical social work section is more nearly complete.

---

[1] See the organization chart for the present structure of NASW in David G. French's "Professional Organization," *Encyclopedia of Social Work*, 15th issue (New York: National Association of Social Workers, 1965), p. 577.

The medical social work section (folders 1081-1355) has been arranged to show continuity between the section and its predecessor, the American Association of Medical Social Workers. Therefore, papers illustrating the relationship between the national organization and the medical social work section have been placed first (folders 1081-1087), followed by those of the section itself. Within the latter part are represented the activities of section chairmen (folders 1091-1093), committees (folders 1094-1152), joint committees (folders 1153-1218), consultants on education, practice, and recruitment (folders 1220-1324), relations with other organizations related to social work (folders 1325-1345), regional and chapter organization (folders 1346-1354), and finances (folder 1355). The arrangement of each division can best be seen by use of the folder inventory.

Because the formal operation of NASW began on October 1, 1955, this date was used as a guideline in separating those papers of the predecessor organizations which overlapped the period of transition. However, in the NASW papers, one will discover instances where some of the papers may predate the formation of NASW; in most cases, by necessity, this has been done to preserve continuity.

Prepared by Mary Jane Fout

National Committee on Social Work in Defense Mobilization,
New York, New York

Papers, 1950-1955

56 folders   5 (∅) folders

In 1950, five national social work organizations, the American Association of Group Workers, the American Association of Medical Social Workers, the American Association of Psychiatric Social Workers, the American Association of Social Workers and the National Association of School Social Workers with liaison representatives from the National Social Welfare Assembly and the Council on Social Work Education (at first, the American Association of Schools of Social Work) created the National Committee on Social Work in Defense Mobilization. The police action of Korea was seen by the social work profession as an occasion which called for a maximum concentration of social work services. The Committee on Inter-Association Structure, which had been recently formed to investigate ways to coordinate activities of national social work organizations, could not undertake the additional task of dealing with governmental and non-governmental agencies in a national defense emergency. Capitalizing on the prior experience of these constituent members as participants in the Wartime Committee on Personnel which functioned during the Second World War, the primary concerns of the Committee were: the role of social work in national defense on both civil and military levels, the development of needed social welfare services in military and in defense-affected communities, the utilization of manpower, and recruitment for the social work profession.

The National Committee on Social Work in Defense Mobilization (NCSWDM) was financed by the United Defense Fund from 1951-1955 and was one of fourteen organizations comprising the United Community Defense Services. The American Association of Social Workers served as the Committee's fiscal agent. The various chairmen of the Committee were William Kirk, Ethel Ginsburg, Frank J. Hertel, and Harold Roberts, while Evelyn F. Cooper served as vice-chairman and Joseph P. Anderson succeeded Ethel Ginsburg as treasurer-secretary. Mrs. Cathryn S. Guyler was appointed executive secretary in January, 1952, and remained in that position until termination of the Committee in September, 1955, when the activities of NCSWDM were assumed by the National Association of Social Workers.

There are four sections to this collection, the first being organizational papers (folders 1375-1405), followed by one dealing with liaison activities between the social welfare profession and various public and private agencies and organizations related to the national defense effort (folders 1406-1419). The third part is devoted to the Committee's services to individuals

NATIONAL ASSOCIATION OF SOCIAL WORKERS, INC.

(folders 1420-1426), and the last, to the relationship of NCSWDM with the United Community Defense Services (folders 1427-1430). The arrangement of the first section reflects the organization and activities of the Committee; the last three are alphabetical. A list of publications removed from the NCSWDM section and placed in the Center's ephemera collection is included in the appendix.

Prepared by Mary Jane Fout

PARTIAL SUBJECT INVENTORY

The following inventory is not an index but rather a guide to persons, associations, and themes appearing in the collection. Narratives for individual sections may suggest persons or topics which appear frequently, e.g., as noted in the narrative, a substantial portion of the American Association of Medical Social Workers records contain material dealing directly or indirectly with casework method and skills. Use of the file folder inventory may also facilitate certain approaches to the papers.

ABBOTT, GRACE
    Folders 66-67, 202

ACADEMY OF CERTIFIED SOCIAL WORKERS
    Folders 1019, 1024-1025, 1035

ACCREDITATION OF SCHOOLS OF SOCIAL WORK
    Folders 799-800

ADAMS, MARGARET E.
    Folders 837-839

ADDAMS, JANE
    Folder 1007

ADMINISTRATION OF SOCIAL WORK ORGANIZATIONS, PHILOSOPHY OF
    Folders 892-893

ALLEN, KATHLEEN
    Folder 1090

ALT, HERSCHEL
    Folder 64

AMERICAN ASSOCIATION FOR HEALTH, PHYSICAL EDUCATION AND RECREATION
    Folder 797

AMERICAN ASSOCIATION FOR ORGANIZING FAMILY SOCIAL WORK
    Folder 714

AMERICAN ASSOCIATION OF GROUP WORKERS
    Folders 795-855, 898, 918-920, 944-945, 966-967, 990, 1375-1378
    Business Affairs
        Folders 804, 836
    Commissions:
        Intercultural Problems
            Folder 823
        Interpersonal Aspects of Group Work
            Folder 824
    Committees:
        Administrative
            Folders 795-796
        Central (Executive)
            Folders 806, 811-812
        Clarification of Terminology
            Folder 855
        Editorial
            Folder 809
        Government Relations
            Folder 815
        Group Work in Medical and Psychiatric Settings
            Folders 818-819
        Local Study Groups
            Folders 810, 825-827
        Membership
            Folder 828
        Professional Education
            Folders 837-840
        Publications
            Folders 816, 842
        Research and Study
            Folder 847
        Study Outlines
            Folder 853
    History
        Folders 806, 811, 814
    Publications
        Folders 816-817, 837, 850

AMERICAN ASSOCIATION OF HOSPITAL SOCIAL WORKERS
    Folder 765

AMERICAN ASSOCIATION OF LEISURE TIME EDUCATORS
    Folder 798

AMERICAN ASSOCIATION OF MEDICAL SOCIAL WORKERS
    Folders 325-755, 894, 898, 918-920, 943-944, 968-981, 993, 995,
        1375-1378. Legal f. 27-43, 50
    Annual Meetings
        Folder 328
    Constitution and Bylaws
        Folders 326-327, 338, 352-353. Legal f. 28

Dissolution
    Folders 330, 700
Executive Committee
    Folders 338-347, 593
Executive Director
    Folders 331-333
Finance
    Folders 435-438, 564-565, 679-690. **Legal f. 33-34**
History
    Folder 697
Officers
    Folders 334-336
Publications
    Folders 363-368. **Legal f. 29**
Relations with Other Organizations
    Folders 346, 714-747
Relations with Other Professions
    Folders 393-412, 414, 417-421, 503
Reorganization
    Folders 533-535
Taxes
    Folders 338, 683-686
Transition to NASW
    Folders 348, 691

AMERICAN ASSOCIATION OF PSYCHIATRIC SOCIAL WORKERS
Folders 502, 573, 594, 715, 762-794, 898, 918-920, 944-945,
    947, 949, 978, 990, 1375-1378. **Legal f. 46**
Constitution and Bylaws
    Folders 765, 767-768, 770, 772-773, 776, 779-784. **Legal f. 46**
Finance
    Folders 766, 768, 770, 776-777, 781, 786
Local Organization
    Folders 767-771, 773, 775, 784, 788
Membership:
    Classification
        Folders 766-769, 772, 775, 777-787
    Requirements
        Folders 765-768, 771-772, 775, 779-784, 786, 791
Personnel Policies
    Folders 768, 778, 790
Psychiatric Social Work Standards
    Folders 765-767, 769, 773, 785-786, 789, 791-792
Recruitment
    Folders 766-767, 770, 785-786, 792
Section on Psychiatric Social Work of AAHSW
    Folder 765
Trend Study
    Folders 767-769, 773-774, 782
War Services Office
    Folder 170

AMERICAN ASSOCIATION OF SCHOOLS OF SOCIAL WORK
    Folders 260, 262, 422-423, 559, 694, 716, 799-800, 856,
        896, 970, 982, 1375

AMERICAN ASSOCIATION OF SOCIAL WORKERS
    Folders 1-324, 559, 705, 717, 857, 895, 898, 906, 918-920,
        944-945, 948, 978, 982-1003, 1375-1378. Legal f.
        1-26, 51-54
    Annual Meetings and Conferences
        Folders 2, 66-94. Legal f. 1
    Association Program
        Folders 4-10
    Chapter Information
        Folders 147-154
    Committees
        Folders 13-65. Legal f. 2-5, 12, 14
    Constitution and Bylaws
        Folders 1, 3
    Finance
        Folders 114-146
    Government and Social Work Division
        Folders 195-232. Legal f. 12-18
    Grievance Procedure
        Folders 31-40
    Merger with AAMSW
        Folders 651-654, 667
    Personnel Practices
        Folders 31-40, 99-110. Legal f. 4-5
    War Activities (1940-1945)
        Folders 256-258. Legal f. 10-18
    Wartime Committee on Personnel
        Folders 259-263

AMERICAN COMMITTEE ON MATERNAL WELFARE
    Folder 1326

AMERICAN DIETETIC ASSOCIATION
    Folder 574

AMERICAN HOSPITAL ASSOCIATION
    Folders 482, 575-579, 693, 720, 1153-1160, 1224

AMERICAN NATIONAL RED CROSS
    Folders 165, 171, 559, 569, 770, 778, 785, 802, 1408

AMERICAN OCCUPATIONAL THERAPY ASSOCIATION
    Folder 1327

AMERICAN ORTHOPSYCHIATRIC ASSOCIATION
    Folders 767, 769

AMERICAN PSYCHIATRIC ASSOCIATION
    Folders 767-769, 1328

AMERICAN PUBLIC HEALTH ASSOCIATION
    Folders 425, 580, 721, 1329

AMERICAN PUBLIC WELFARE ASSOCIATION
    Folders 473-475, 944, 993, 1041

ANDERSON, JOSEPH P.
    Folders 14-18, 96, 111-113, 155-160, 174, 248, 812, 857, 895-896, 938-941, 966, 985-987, 991, 1004-1006, 1011, 1074, 1076, 1078, 1375, 1379, 1384. **Legal f. 6**

ARMED FORCES
    Folders 156-191, 1382, 1386-1389, 1415, 1420-1426.
        Legal f. 7-11, 58

ASSOCIATION FOR THE STUDY OF COMMUNITY ORGANIZATION
    Folders 856-890, 984-985, 995, 1004-1006. Legal f. 47, 55
    Annual Meetings
        Folder 859
    Board of Directors
        Folders 860-863
    Committees:
        Book of Readings
            Folder 864
        Education for Community Organization
            Folder 871
        Local Discussion Groups
            Folder 869, 876
        Nominating
            Folder 885
        Program
            Folder 886
        Publications
            Folder 887
        Recording
            Folder 888
    Financial Affairs
        Folders 872-874. Legal f. 47
    History
        Folders 859, 868-869, 875, 887, 890
    Membership
        Folders 879-880
    Newsletter
        Folders 865-867
    Scrapbook
        Folders 889-890

ASSOCIATION OF AMERICAN MEDICAL COLLEGES
    Folders 393-407, 1325

ASSOCIATION OF PSYCHIATRIC SOCIAL WORKERS
    Folder 794

ASSOCIATION OF TEACHERS OF PREVENTIVE MEDICINE
    Folder 1162

ASSOCIATION OF TRAINING SCHOOLS
    Folder 2

BARTLETT, HARRIETT M.
    Folders 1039-1040, 1047, 1050, 1073, 1125, 1137

BECH, ELIZABETH BROCKETT
    Folder 773

BECK, BERTRAM
    Folders 1012-1014, 1018, 1020, 1024-1025, 1029-1031, 1035,
        1038, 1040, 1042-1043, 1047, 1051-1052, 1056-1057,
        1061, 1067, 1073

BECK, FRANCIS
    Folder 790

BELLSMITH, ETHEL
    Folder 771

BENNER, PAUL V.
    Folders 1055-1056

BERKMAN, TESSIE
    Folders 771, 893

BERNSTEIN, SAUL
    Folders 818-821

BLENKNER, MARGARET
    Folders 1009, 1047, 1214-1216, 1358, 1360

BOARDMAN, RHEA
    Folders 757, 760

BONUS ARMY
    Folder 196

BRUNO, FRANK J.
    Folders 2, 19-20

CABOT, RICHARD CLARKE, M.D.
    Folder 354

CANADIAN ASSOCIATION OF SOCIAL WORKERS
    Folders 961, 995

CANNON, M. ANTOINETTE
    Folder 202

CARPENTER, NILES
    Folders 207, 252

CARTER, GENEVIEVE W.
    Folders 1047-1048

CASEWORK
    Folders 817, 823, 831

CATHOLIC HOSPITAL ASSOCIATION
    Folder 1330

CERTIFICATION OF SOCIAL WORKERS
    Folders 1018-1025

CHECKLIST (PERIODICAL)
    Folders 865-867

CHILD LABOR AMENDMENT
    Folder 13

CHILD WELFARE
    Folder 993

CHILDREN
    Folders 476, 758, 761

CIVIL DEFENSE
    Folders 517, 551-552, 663-664, 692, 1381, 1414

CIVIL RIGHTS
    Folder 1031

CIVIL SERVICE
    Folders 424-425

COCKERILL, ELEANOR
    Folders 1092, 1137

COHEN, NATHAN
    Folders 807-808, 966

COLCORD, JOANNA C.
    Folders 233, 295

COMMITTEE ON INTER-ASSOCIATION STRUCTURE
    Folders 896-901, 968-970

COMMON HUMAN NEEDS (CHARLOTTE TOWLE)
    Folder 336

COMMUNITY CHESTS AND COUNCILS OF AMERICA
    Folders 1375, 1416

COMMUNITY ORGANIZATION
    Folders 868-869, 871, 876, 884

CONRAD, IRENE
    Folders 1004-1006

CONSCIENTIOUS OBJECTORS
    Folder 164

COSTIGAN, EDWARD P.
    Folders 195-196

COUNCIL FOR PHEUMATIC FEVER
    Folders 719, 1331

COUNCIL ON SOCIAL WORK EDUCATION
    Folders 428, 725-726, 807-808, 963, 989, 995, 1039, 1086,
        1107-1109, 1316-1317, 1362, 1378, 1412

CRIPPLED CHILDREN
    Folders 476, 708

DARTMOUTH CONFERENCE ON EDUCATION FOR PSYCHIATRIC SOCIAL WORK
    Folder 771

DAVIES, STANLEY P.
    Folder 13

DAVIS, MICHAEL M.
    Folder 202

DAWLEY, ALMENA
    Folder 764, 770

DAWSON, JOHN B.
    Folders 860-863

DEARDORFF, NEVA R.
    Folder 2

DEPRESSION
    Psychiatric Social Work
        Folder 767
    School Social Work
        Folder 758

DE SCHWEINITZ, ELIZABETH
    Folders 769-770

DE SCHWEINITZ, KARL
    Folders 2, 19

DISPLACED PERSONS
    Folder 233

D'ISSERTELLE, EDNA
    Folder 843

DOCTORS DRAFT BILL, PUBLIC LAW
    Folders 779, 1390

DREW, JULIA K.
    Folder 760

DUNHAM, ARTHUR
    Folders 856, 860-863, 866, 874-875, 887

EDUCATION AND PLACEMENT OF SOCIAL WORKERS
    Folders 797-798, 802-803, 806-808, 818-819, 834, 837-839, 840

ELLIOTT, LULA JEAN
    Folder 192

FAMILY WELFARE ASSOCIATION OF AMERICA
    Folder 175

FEDERAL CIVIL DEFENSE ADMINISTRATION
    Folders 1381, 1414

FIERMAN, FRANK
    Folder 809

FINCH, NORMAN B.
    Folders 860-863

FITCH, JOHN A.
    Folders 31, 43-44

FOSTER HOMES. CHILDREN
    Folder 439

FRENCH, DAVID
    Folder 96, 891

FRENCH, LOIS MEREDITH
    Folder 767

GIBBS, HOWARD
    Folder 812

GINSBURG, ETHEL
    Folders 771, 790, 1375, 1402-1403

GLASSER, MELVIN
    Folders 984-985, 988, 991, 994, 1000-1003

GOLDSTINE, DORA
    Folders 896, 905-906, 924, 962, 968, 971-972, 1004, 1088-1089

GORDON, WILLIAM E.
    Folders 1012, 1050, 1053, 1132

GOVERNMENT AND SOCIAL WORK
    Folders 195-232, 815. Legal f. 12-18

GRANGER, LESTER
    Folder 29

GRANT, IRENE
    Folders 459, 770, 775, 1090

THE GROUP (PERIODICAL)
    Folders 809, 816

GROUP WORK
    Folders 807-808, 817, 827, 844, 849, 852, 854, 1080

GUYLER, CATHRYN
    Folders 1379, 1384, 1394, 1405

HAGAN, MARGARET
    Folder 771

HAMBRECHT, LEONA
    Folders 764-770, 775

HAMILTON, GORDON
    Folder 182

HARPER, ERNEST B.
    Folders 860-863, 866, 871, 886, 1004-1006

HAYNES, GEORGE
    Folders 242-243

HEALTH INSURANCE
    Folder 202

HEMMY, MARY
    Folders 1088-1089, 1110, 1125, 1153-1154, 1328, 1330,
        1332, 1339-1340, 1343, 1345

HENDRY, CHARLES E.
    Folders 795-796, 806

HODGES, BARBARA
    Folder 1410

HODSON, WILLIAM W.
    Folder 200

HOEHLER, FRED K.
    Folders 66-67, 200, 242-243

HOEY, JANE
    Folders 162, 179

HOFFER, JOE R.
    Folders 96-97, 837, 840, 882

HOLBROOK, DAVID H.
    Folders 159-160, 195, 251

HOPKINS, HARRY L.
    Folders 1-2, 19-20, 196

HOUSING
    Folders 203-207. Legal f. 14

HOWARD, DONALD S.
    Folders 182, 200, 233-248. Legal f. 19-23

INTERNATIONAL ASSOCIATION OF PUPIL PERSONNEL WORKERS
    Folder 1368

INTERNATIONAL CONFERENCE OF SOCIAL WORK
    Folders 41-42, 236-248. Legal f. 20-23

INTERNATIONAL SERVICES AND PROGRAMS
    Folders 41-42, 236

JACOBS, ELIZABETH R.
    Folders 1143, 1295-1296

JARRETT, MARY C.
    Folders 765-766

JOINT COMMISSION ON ACCREDITATION OF HOSPITALS
    Folders 622, 727

JOINT VOCATIONAL SERVICE.   SEE ALSO SOCIAL WORK VOCATIONAL BUREAU
    Folders 468, 768-769, 787

JUVENILE DELINQUENCY
    Folders 833, 854

KAHN, DOROTHY C.
    Folders 159-162, 182, 212-230, 249

KELLEY, JERRY L.
    Folders 1052, 1368

KELLOGG, ARTHUR P.
    Folders 2, 19

KELLOGG, PAUL U.
    Folder 251

KENDERDINE, JOHN D.
    Folder 192

KIDNEIGH, JOHN
    Folders 807-808

KONOPKA, GISELA
    Folders 818-821, 1051

KORPELA, JANET
    Folders 807-809, 812, 818-821, 839, 966

KRAFT, LOUIS
    Folders 795-796, 825-827

KRUGHOFF, MERRILL F.
    Folders 860-863

KURTZ, RUSSELL
    Folders 156-160

LABOR RELATIONS IN SOCIAL WELFARE ORGANIZATIONS
    Folder 850

LANSDALE, ROBERT T.
    Folder 194

LAY, MADELEINE
    Folders 771, 790

LEAHY, AGNES
    Folders 795-796, 806

LEE, PORTER R.
    Folders 2, 19, 66-67

LENROOT, KATHARINE F.
    Folders 161-162, 195, 993

LEVINREW, GEORGE
    Folder 771

LOVEJOY, OWEN R.
    Folders 2, 19

LURIE, HARRY L.
    Folders 195, 199-200

McCLOY, JOHN J.
    Folders 160, 185

McDOWELL, JOHN
    Folder 1375

McMILLEN, WAYNE
    Folders 15-18, 27-28, 66-67

McNEIL, C. F.
    Folders 860-863

MAETZGOLD, AUDREY J.
    Folder 42

MALLACH, AUBREY
    Folders 871, 877-878

MARCUS, GRACE
    Folders 63-64, 182, 207

MAYO, LEONARD
    Folders 207, 243

MEDICAL SOCIAL WORK
    Folders 1081-1355. Legal f. 27-43
    Administration
        Folders 351, 493
    Casework
        Folders 355-359, 377, 408, 440-444, 463, 491
    Curriculum
        Folders 379-381, 389-391, 414, 422-423, 426, 694
    Group Work
        Folders 818-821
    Public Medical Care Programs
        Folders 431, 488-490, 667, 721. Legal f. 36
    Public Programs
        Folders 470-475, 477-478, 514, 516

MENTAL HYGIENE
    Folders 172, 766-767

MIGRANTS
    Folder 249. Legal f. 24

MILFORD CONFERENCE
    Folder 766

MILITARY SOCIAL WORK
    Folders 771, 775, 778, 785

MILLS, ELISABETH
    Folders 159-160

MOORE, JOHN
    Folders 1402-1403

MOSS, CELIA R.
    Folders 1132, 1134

MOSS, MARY BLANCHE
    Folders 968, 971-972

MUDGETT, MARGARET
    Folders 812, 847

MUNICIPAL PLANNING
    Folders 203-207

MURRAY, CLYDE
    Folders 896-897

MYRICK, HELEN
    Folders 764, 766

NATIONAL ASSOCIATION FOR THE STUDY OF GROUP WORK
SEE
AMERICAN ASSOCIATION OF GROUP WORKERS

NATIONAL ASSOCIATION OF SCHOOL SOCIAL WORKERS
    Folders 756-761, 898, 906, 918-920, 948, 978, 1375-1378.
        Legal f. 44-45
    Bylaws
        Folder 760
    Finance
        Folders 757-759
    Membership Requirements and Classification
        Folders 757-759
    Standards
        Folders 757-759. Legal f. 44

NATIONAL ASSOCIATION OF SOCIAL WORKERS
    Folders 1007-1374, 1379. Legal f. 49-53, 56
    AAGW
        Folders 809, 812-813, 830
    Commission on Personnel Standards and Practices
        Folders 1026-1038
    Commission on Social Work Practice
        Folders 1039-1066
    Committee on Review of NASW Structure
        Folders 1067-1078
    Delegate Assemblies
        Folders 1007-1017
    Group Work Section
        Folder 1080
    Medical Social Work Section
        Folders 1081-1355. Legal f. 56
    Psychiatric Social Work Section
        Folder 1356
    School Social Work Section
        Folders 1364-1374
    Social Work Research Section
        Folders 1357-1363

NATIONAL COMMITTEE ON MENTAL HYGIENE
    Folders 766, 785, 790

NATIONAL COMMITTEE ON PERSONNEL IN THE SOCIAL SERVICES
    Folder 728-729

NATIONAL COMMITTEE ON SOCIAL WORK IN DEFENSE MOBILIZATION
    Folders 963, 995, 1375-1430. Legal f. 57-61
    Committees
        Folders 1376-1385
    Finance
        Folders 1401-1404. Legal f. 61
    History
        Folder 1375. Legal f. 57
    Personnel
        Folder 1394

NATIONAL COMMITTEE ON VISITING TEACHERS
    Folders 757, 761

NATIONAL CONFERENCE OF CATHOLIC CHARITIES
    Folder 1332

NATIONAL CONFERENCE OF SOCIAL WORK
    Folders 243, 882, 945

NATIONAL ASSOCIATION OF SOCIAL WORKERS, INC.

NATIONAL CONFERENCE ON SOCIAL WELFARE
    Folders 1114-1115, 1173

NATIONAL COUNCIL ON REHABILITATION
    Folders 559, 731

NATIONAL COUNCIL ON SOCIAL WORK EDUCATION
    Folders 771-772, 883

NATIONAL FOUNDATION FOR INFANTILE PARALYSIS
    Folders 348, 537, 732-736, 747, 1231-1237, 1319-1324, 1333

NATIONAL HEALTH COUNCIL
    Folders 737, 1334

NATIONAL HEALTH PROGRAM AND PLANNING
    Folders 585, 591, 699

NATIONAL ORGANIZATION FOR PUBLIC HEALTH NURSING
    Folder 582

NATIONAL REHABILITATION ASSOCIATION
    Folder 1335

NATIONAL SOCIAL WELFARE ASSEMBLY
    Folders 41, 739-741, 950, 1266, 1318, 1336. Legal f. 2

NATIONAL SOCIAL WORK COUNCIL
    Folder 251

NATIONAL SOCIAL WORKERS EXCHANGE
    Folders 1-2, 19, 46, 59

NEELY, ANN ELIZABETH
    Folders 837-839

NEGROES IN MEDICAL SOCIAL WORK
    Folder 382

NORDLY, CARL L.
    Folders 797, 834

ODENCRANTZ, LOUISE
    Folders 43-44

O'GRADY, JOHN
    Folder 195

OLD AGE
    Folders 13, 114-116

PEARL HARBOR
    Folders 547-550

PERSONNEL PRACTICES
SEE
SOCIAL WORK. PERSONNEL

PLAY AND RECREATION
    Folders 797-798, 802-803, 806, 835, 845

POOLE, MARY
    Folders 1089-1090, 1329, 1331

PRACTICE
SEE
SOCIAL WORK PRACTICE

PRACTITIONERS MOVEMENT
    Folder 253

PRAY, KENNETH
    Folders 66-67

PROFESSIONALISM (OF GROUP WORK)
    Folder 806

PSYCHIATRIC SOCIAL WORK
    Folders 181, 185, 765, 1173, 1356
    Group Work
        Folders 818-821

PUBLIC ASSISTANCE
    Folders 208-230. Legal f. 15-18

PUBLIC SOCIAL POLICIES
    Folder 238

RACE RELATIONS
    Folders 823, 854

RAY, FLORENCE
    Folders 839, 1042-1043, 1045, 1052

RECRUITMENT (SOCIAL WORK)
    Folders 528-531, 1143-1149, 1294-1324, 1383, 1391-1393, 1412.
        Legal f. 59

RICE, ELIZABETH
    Folders 968, 971-972, 1042-1043

ROSS, ELIZABETH HEALY
    Folders 156-160, 181, 183-184, 770, 778, 785

RUSSELL SAGE FOUNDATION
    Folders 688-690, 848, 887

RYAN, PHILLIP E.
    Folders 860-863, 875, 1004-1006

RYMAN, PAULINE
    Folders 971-972, 980

SAND, RENÉ
    Folders 242-243, 247

SCHOOL RECORDS RE SOCIAL SERVICE TO STUDENTS
    Folders 757-758, 760

SCHOOL SOCIAL WORK
    Folders 1364-1374

SCHWARTZ, EDWARD E.
    Folder 1358

SCOVILLE, MILDRED
    Folders 756-767, 773, 782

SHIMP, EVERETT
    Folder 866

SHYNE, ANN
    Folders 891, 894

SILVER, HAROLD
    Folders 1015, 1020, 1024-1025, 1031

SOCIAL POLICY AND ACTION
    Folders 951, 980, 993, 1150

SOCIAL SECURITY
    Folders 114-116, 231, 254

SOCIAL WORK. CANADA
    Folders 805, 961, 995

SOCIAL WORK EDUCATION
    Folders 53-54, 63-65, 255, 369-433, 716, 725-726, 767-768,
        771-773, 775-776, 791-792, 797-798, 802-803, 806-808,
        818-819, 834, 837-839, 840, 856, 883, 952
    Medical Students
        Folders 393-412, 1105
    Nurses
        Folders 417-419, 1241

SOCIAL WORK ETHICS
    Folders 106, 192-194, 331, 1025-1036

SOCIAL WORK. PERSONNEL
    Folders 31-40, 99-110, 511-516, 703-704, 790-791, 945-946,
        1026-1038. Legal f. 4-5

SOCIAL WORK. PRACTICE
    Folders 1039-1066, 1080, 1101, 1117-1137, 1223-1293, 1364-1368

SOCIAL WORK RESEARCH GROUP
    Folders 472, 742, 891-895, 944, 1357-1362
    Membership Requirements
        Folders 891-892

SOCIAL WORK VOCATIONAL BUREAU
    Folders 96-97, 743, 770, 851, 1029

SOLENDER, SANFORD
SEE
TIAC PAPERS   ESPECIALLY PERIOD FROM 1953-1955

SOULE, THEODATE
    Folders 13, 1110

SPRINGER, GERTRUDE
    Folders 66-67

STANDARDS IN SOCIAL WORK ORGANIZATIONS
    Folder 892

STEVENSON, GEORGE S.
    Folder 1415

STEWART, JANE
    Folder 886

SWEAT, LILI G.
    Folders 1358, 1360-1361, 1363

SWIFT, ARTHUR L., JR.
    Folder 814

SWIFT, LINTON B.
    Folders 175-176, 195

TARAIL, THEODORE T.
    Folders 797, 803, 835, 839

TAYLOR, GRAHAM ROMEYN
    Folders 2, 19, 194

TEMPORARY INTER-ASSOCIATION COUNCIL
    Folders 26, 95, 329, 338, 771-772, 809, 812-813, 830, 857,
        859, 895-1006, 1039, 1385, 1405. Legal f. 48-55

TEMPORARY INTER-ASSOCIATION COUNCIL
    Bylaws
        Folder 901
    Bylaws, Memorandum of Understandings, Certificate of Incorporation
    for NASW, Proposed Legislation
        Folders 934, 977, 989-990. Legal f. 51
    Committees
        Folders 907-908. Legal f. 49
    Correspondence
        Folders 904-906, 971-972, 992, 1004-1006
    Finance
        Folders 909-917. Legal f. 48
    Minutes
        Folders 903-904, 973-975
    Planning for NASW Committees
        Folders 932, 934-943, 947-952, 954-960, 978-979, 994-997.
            Legal f. 49-50, 52-54
    Reports
        Folders 921-928, 976, 986

THOMAS, ADDIE
    Folders 1090-1091, 1135, 1224-1293, 1337

THOMPSON, CHRISTINE ROBB
    Folders 766-767, 773-774

TRECKER, HARLEIGH
    Folders 809, 811, 847

TUBERCULOSIS
    Folders 1226, 1341-1342

UNEMPLOYMENT INSURANCE
    Folders 197-198

UNITED COMMUNITY DEFENSE SERVICES
    Folders 1375, 1402-1403, 1405, 1421, 1427-1430

UNITED DEFENSE FUND
    Folder 1428

UNITED NATIONS
    Folder 42

UNITED NATIONS RELIEF AND REHABILITATION ADMINISTRATION
    Folders 233, 563

NATIONAL ASSOCIATION OF SOCIAL WORKERS, INC.

U.S. AIR FORCE
Folders 1406-1407

U.S. ARMY
Folders 430, 744, 1409-1411

U.S. BUREAU OF STATISTICS
Folder 1343

U.S. CHILDREN'S BUREAU
Folders 199-200, 1339

U.S. CIVIL SERVICE COMMISSION
Folder 1337

U.S. CIVIL WORKS ADMINISTRATION
Folders 197-198

U.S. DEPARTMENT OF DEFENSE
Folder 1413

U.S. DEPARTMENT OF HEALTH, EDUCATION AND WELFARE
Folders 1228, 1328-1342

U.S. DEPARTMENT OF LABOR
Folders 1343-1344

U.S. FEDERAL EMERGENCY RELIEF ADMINISTRATION
Folders 196-198

U.S. FEDERAL SECURITY AGENCY
Folder 251

U.S. NATIONAL HOUSING AGENCY
Folder 206

U.S. NATIONAL RECOVERY ADMINISTRATION
Folders 250-251. Legal f. 25

U.S. NATIONAL RESOURCES PLANNING BOARD
Folder 209

U.S. NAVY
    Folder 1417

U.S. OFFICE OF VOCATIONAL REHABILITATION
    Folders 432, 748, 1340

U.S. PUBLIC HEALTH SERVICE
    Folders 560-562, 571-572, 747, 1157-1158, 1341-1342

U.S. SELECTIVE SERVICE
    Folders 30, 163, 175-182, 1418-1419. Legal f. 9-10

U.S. VETERANS ADMINISTRATION
    Folders 184, 459-461, 766, 770-771, 785, 790, 1228, 1345

U.S. VETERANS ADMINISTRATION CORPS BILL
    Folder 184

U.S. WOMEN'S BUREAU
    Folder 1344

VAN HYNING, CONRAD
    Folder 182

VAN KLEECK, MARY
    Folders 2, 194, 239

VASEY, WAYNE
    Folders 1074, 1076

VENEREAL DISEASE
    Folders 505, 557

VOCATIONAL REHABILITATION
    Folders 62, 359, 748

VOLUNTEERS
    Folders 469, 545-546, 558, 651-652

WAGNER, ROBERT F.
    Folders 203-205

WAR OFFICE OF PSYCHIATRIC SOCIAL WORK
    Folders 770, 776, 785

WARTIME COMMITTEE ON PERSONNEL
    Folders 181, 259-263, 831, 1375
SEE ALSO
NATIONAL COMMITTEE ON PERSONNEL IN THE SOCIAL SERVICES

WEST, WALTER M.
    Folders 4-5, 7-8, 15-18, 21-25, 27, 63, 252

WHITE, GRACE
    Folders 1161, 1171, 1220-1222

WICKENDEN, ELIZABETH
    Folders 951, 993, 1386-1399, 1428

WICKMAN, KATHERINE MOORE
    Folders 764-765, 769, 774, 782

WITTE, ERNEST F.
    Folders 85-86, 243, 1375, 1412

WOODWARD, LUTHER E.
    Folders 176, 179, 181, 770

WOODS, HELEN
    Folder 1092

WORLD WAR II
    Japanese Resettlement
        Folders 554, 740-741
    Psychiatric Social Work
        Folders 769-770, 775-776, 778, 786
    Social Welfare
        Folders 256-263, 822, 831, 854

YOUNG, HELEN
    Folder 765

YOUNGDAHL, BENJAMIN E.
    Folders 896, 985-987

YOUTH
    Folder 841

ZUCKER, HENRY L.
    Folder 874

NATIONAL ASSOCIATION OF SOCIAL WORKERS, INC.

FOLDER INVENTORY

Folder Title and Description of Contents	Folder
AASW: Constitution, 1918, 1920 Copy of first approved constitution of National Social Workers' Exchange and a proposed constitution for a new professional organization of social workers.	1
AASW: Annual Meetings, 1918-1929 Historical data on formation of NSWE and transition to AASW in 1921. Minutes of meetings of NSWE and AASW, joint meeting with Association of Training Schools re training problems, round table discussions on terminology, "Providence Resolution," separation of Vocational Bureau from AASW.	2
AASW: Bylaws, 1946, 1951.	3
AASW: Association Program, 1938-1942 Statements on Association program for the years 1938-1940 and excerpts by Walter West, executive secretary, and Wayne McMillen, president, from a special study of the Association, 1941-1942.	4-5
AASW: Structure and Organization Hearing, Chicago, 1939 Proceedings of hearing on Association program by national office, questions for discussion, and miscellaneous correspondence.	6
AASW: Employment Practices Inquiry, 1940 Inquiry report by Walter West, executive secretary, re employment practices of the Family Service Society of St. Louis County, Missouri.	7-8
AASW: Special Study of Program, Policies, and Operation, 1942 Study by executive committee.	9-10
AASW: National Board Meetings, 1942-1945 Minutes cover investigation of Association, 1941-1942, problems of qualification for membership, and over-view of organizational affairs.	11-12
AASW: Annuities and Retirement Plans Committee, 1932-1936 Minutes and correspondence re group insurance and retirement benefits. Correspondents include Theodate Soule (American Association of Hospital Social Workers), Walter West, and Sophonisba P. Breckinridge, who requested support for the Child Labor Amendment and suggested an insurance plan.	13

NATIONAL ASSOCIATION OF SOCIAL WORKERS, INC.

Folder Title and Description of Contents	Folder
AASW: Evaluate Executive Secretary Committee, 1947-1948 Correspondence re evaluating executive secretary.	14
AASW: Executive Committee Correspondence, 1941-1947 Correspondence re Association difficulties, 1941-1942; search for a new executive secretary; appointment of Joseph P. Anderson as secretary; and membership qualifications of group workers within AASW.	15-18
AASW: Executive Committee, Minutes, 1920-1949 Historical data on Association progress from NSWE to AASW; minutes of central council; financial difficulties of AASW; Association disagreements, 1942-1943; wartime activities; and formation of Temporary Inter-Association Council.	19-26
AASW: Executive Committee, Appendices to Report to National Board, 1942 Report stating grievances against Walter West, executive secretary, and Wayne McMillen, president.	27
AASW: Executive Committee, Conduct of President Study, 1941-1942 Statements by Wayne McMillen re Association program; accumulation of data for charges re president's conduct by the executive committee; tentative statement, "The Conduct of the President as a Factor in the Association Problem."	28
AASW: Executive Committee, Management Study Subcommittee, 1941-1942 Report of subcommittee, headed by Lester Granger, NAACP executive secretary, re personnel study of AASW, including budget statement, change of address procedures, membership applications' processing, job descriptions, dues collection, and accounting systems.	29
AASW: Government and Social Work Committee, Selective Service Subcommittee, 1941-1942 Minutes, memoranda, reports, and correspondence re local draft boards and AASW aid; public social services; report, "Recreation, Education and Welfare of the American Soldier"; summary of activities; and dissolution material of committee reflecting Association financial difficulties.	30

Folder Title and Description of Contents	Folder
AASW: Grievance Procedures Committee, 1926-1939 Correspondence re grievance procedures from John A. Fitch and the National Association of Legal Aid Organizations re disciplinary action in grievance proceedings; reports from Chicago chapter re development of statement of principles.	31
AASW: Grievance Procedure Committee, Correspondence re Grievance Cases, 1927-1934 Brief correspondence covering a series of cases showing the interest of politicians in relief programs.	32
AASW: Grievance Procedure Committee, Cases, 1923-1934 Correspondence and newspaper clippings[1] re grievances in Columbus, Ohio, and Denver, Colorado, as well as six individual cases.	33-40
AASW: International Cooperation for Social Welfare Committee: National Social Welfare Assembly, International Welfare Organization, 1941-1947 Reports, bulletins, memoranda, and minutes re formation of an international social welfare organization, continuation of services during the war, social welfare activities of the League of Nations, and cooperation services in Gary, Indiana.	41
AASW: International Cooperation for Social Welfare Committee: Maetzgold Committee Material, 1947-1948 Audrey J. Maetzgold, student at New York School of Social Work and former Red Cross worker, compiled a report for AASW committee on the United Nations involvement with international cooperation for social welfare. Contains progress report and summary minutes re the United Nations' activities in social welfare.	42
AASW: Job Analysis Committee, Minutes and Correspondence, 1926-1934 Consists largely of process whereby committee gathered information to be published in a job analysis series, e.g., Louise Odencrantz, The Social Worker in Family, Medical and Psychiatric Social Work.	43
AASW: Job Analysis Committee, Salary Data, 1931-1934 Memoranda, reports, and correspondence to gather information from other organizations on salaries.	44

---

[1] Newspaper clippings have been placed in the backs of folders for better preservation of manuscripts, unless they are an integral part of the material.

NATIONAL ASSOCIATION OF SOCIAL WORKERS, INC.

Folder Title and Description of Contents	Folder
AASW: Membership Committee, Annual Membership Count, 1953.	45
AASW: Membership Committee, Application Forms, Membership Cards, Bills, and Sample Stencils, 1919-1945.	46
AASW: Membership Committee, Minutes, 1927-1936 Minutes of applications and national membership committee wherein discussions evolve around clarification of classification of elected members, membership qualifications, standards, and members elected under provision of Section 6 qualification.	47-52
AASW: Membership Committee, Training Courses Subcommittee Minutes, 1933-1939 Study of application of standards to technical courses at colleges and universities offering courses in social work.	53-54
AASW: Membership Committee, Directory of Members, 1923-1936.	55-56
AASW: Membership Committee, Regulations and Requirements, 1930-1953 Data on readmission of former members, definition and purpose of membership policy, and membership requirements.	57
AASW: Membership Committee, Requirements--Handbook for Membership Chairman, 1935-1938.	58
AASW: Membership Committee, Publicity Leaflets and Pamphlets, 1919-1955 Brochures from NSWE and AASW.	59
AASW: Membership Committee, Special Study of Membership Standards, 1943.	60
AASW: Organization and Planning Committee, 1942-1946 Memoranda and minutes "outlining the general content and plan for study of the problems related to the organization and planning of social services" in wartime and reconstruction.	61
AASW: Organization and Planning Committee, Vocational Rehabilitation Subcommittee, 1943-1944 Correspondence with Michael J. Shortly, director of vocational rehabilitation, Federal Security Agency; Compass article, "Rehabilitation of Handicapped Persons."	62

Folder Title and Description of Contents	Folder
AASW: Professional Education Committee, 1925, 1933-1941 Reports and memoranda re approved technical courses, professional membership, skills of relief workers, and standards in social work stated by Grace Marcus and Walter West.	63
AASW: Professional Education Committee: Special Committee on Professional Education, 1939 Correspondence between Herschel Alt, chairman of national committee on education, and Grace Marcus, chairman of division on personnel standards, re developing and supporting professional education in cooperation with American Association of Schools of Social Work.	64
AASW: Recruitment: Advisory Committee on Professional Education, 1942-1943 Correspondence, agendas, and memoranda re recruiting personnel for professional education.	65
AASW: Conferences, 1934-1953 Proceedings and manuals for AASW conferences; first delegate conference: "Governmental Objectives for Social Work," 1934, with Grace Abbott, Fred Hoehler, Porter R. Lee, Wayne McMillen, Gertrude Springer, Kenneth Pray, Harry Hopkins, and Arthur Dunham re tasks of those in social work involved with governmental policies and agencies. Other proceedings included: 1935-1937, 1939-1941, 1947, 1949, and 1953. Delegates manuals for the years 1941, 1948, and 1950 are also included, plus a list of nominating districts for the 1953 delegate assembly.	66-92
AASW: Regional Workshop Proceedings, 1951-1955 Proceedings of regional workshops: Southeast States, February, 1952; Chicago, May, 1952; Los Angeles, November, 1952; New England Regional, November, 1952; Fort Worth, Texas, February, 1953; North Mid-Western, October, 1953; St. Louis, February, 1954; District 5 (Ann Arbor, Michigan), April, 1954; North West, April, 1954; Mountain States, May, 1954; District 6, October, 1954; AASW Workshop on Legal Regulation of Social Work Practice, February, 1955.	93-94
AASW: Nominations and Elections, 1953-1955 Office manual on nomination and election procedure including a time schedule for July 1, 1953	95

Folder Title and Description of Contents   Folder

    to June 30, 1954; personnel of nominating
    committee; 1954 ballot; "Proposed Bylaws
    and Memorandum of Understanding," of TIAC;
    list of officers and members of the board
    of directors of NASW, September, 1955.

AASW: Central Registry, 1945-1958   96
    Materials on use of punch card tabulating
    equipment to handle membership records for
    a central registry of social workers under-
    taken by David French, Joe R. Hoffer, and
    Joseph P. Anderson; classification of social
    work studies; Joe R. Hoffer, "Basic Schedule--
    Social Workers."

AASW: "Classification of Social Welfare Positions,"   97
1948
    Progress report by Joe R. Hoffer, (then director
    of Social Work Vocational Bureau) re need of
    classifying workers and positions to aid in
    placement service for social welfare workers.

AASW: Progress Report of Committee on Mid-Century   98
Appraisal of Association Objectives and Programs, 1950
    Report sent out to members to stimulate dis-
    cussion of Association objectives and program
    at the 1951 delegate conference.

AASW: Personnel Practices: Personnel Practices in   99
Social Work Agencies, 1928
    Unofficial report.

AASW: Personnel Practices: Facts about Personnel   100
Standards, 1937
    Booklet prepared for fourth annual AASW con-
    ference.

AASW: Personnel Practices: National Board Pro-   101
cedures for Handling Complaints against Members
under Article V, Section 3 of the Bylaws, 1941.

AASW: Personnel Practices: Policy Statement on   102
Regulation of Social Work Practices, 1947
    Statement adopted at 1947 delegate conference.

AASW: Personnel Practices: Licensing of Social   103
Workers, 1950
    Statement prepared by committee on licensing to
    encourage discussion among members re licensing
    social workers.

Folder Title and Description of Contents	Folder
AASW: Personnel Practices: Personnel Handbook, Draft, 1950 Draft of handbook prepared for Personnel Practices Institute by personnel practices committee.	104
AASW: Personnel Practices: Ohio Welfare Conference, et al., Personnel Practices Institute Proceedings, 1950 Proceedings of institute sponsored by the Ohio Welfare Conference, National Conference of Social Work, National Social Welfare Assembly, and Ohio Citizens Council.	105
AASW: Personnel Practices: Standards for the Professional Practice of Social Work, Draft and Revision, 1951 Statement re standards for social work personnel, code of ethics, civil rights in social work, and personnel practices in social work adopted by 1961 delegate assembly.	106
AASW: Personnel Practices: Policies and Procedures for the Consideration of Personnel Practices in Social Work, 1951 Mimeographed statement approved by 1951 delegate assembly.	107
AASW: Personnel Practices: Procedures for Considering Complaints of Unethical Conduct of Members, 1953.	108
AASW: Personnel Practices: National Committee on Standards for Professional Practices in Social Work, 1955 Correspondence and reports of procedure in grievance cases using specific cases as examples.	109
AASW: Personnel Practices: "How to Handle a Grievance," Handbook, 1955 Handbook for AASW chapter committees on violation of personnel practices.	110
AASW: Mimeographed Materials, 1951-1952 Sample of mimeographed materials circulated by the national office; agendas, memoranda, handbooks, committee reports, chapter communiques, etc. (Folders 111-112 arranged numerically, folder 113 arranged chronologically.)	111-113
AASW: Financial Records: Insurance, Social Security, Old Age Benefits--Staff Negotiations with State of New York, 1935-1945 Chiefly correspondence re inclusion of national staff of AASW, a non-profit organization, for social insurance benefits; chronological history of negotiations compiled by Dorothy C. Kahn.	114-115

Folder Title and Description of Contents	Folder
AASW: Financial Records: Insurance, Social Security, Unemployment Compensation--Staff, Records, 1935-1941 Memoranda, pamphlets, and printed statements re staff records on social security, etc. Historical data on beginnings of social security and processes involved in securing enrollment under plan, especially in New York State; suggested social workers' platform on social security.	116
AASW: Financial Records: National and Chapter Dues, 1953.	117
AASW: Financial Records: Sample records 1954-1955 Alphabetical arrangement of financial records of AASW from late 1954 till dissolution in September, 1955.	118-146
AASW: Chapter Information: Chapter Activity, General 1929-1945 Reports from chapters: Cleveland, Toledo, New York City; position papers of AASW; 1945 handbook for chapter officers.	147
AASW: Chapter Information: Chapter Handbook, 1937-1945 Reference manual on chapter administration.	148
AASW: Chapter Information: Chapter Officers Handbook, 1952.	149
AASW: Chapter Information: Final Reports of Chapters, 1955-1956 Alphabetical listing, by state, of chapters' final report preceding dissolution, October, 1955.	150-152
AASW: Chapter Information: Handbook for Chapter Officer, Twin City Chapter, 1952-1954.	153
AASW: Chapter Information: Folder of Membership Chairman, Twin City Chapter, 1946-1954.	154
AASW: Anderson, Joseph P. (Executive Secretary, 1943-1955): Letters of Recommendation, 1943-1947.	155
AASW: Armed Forces: Executive Correspondence, 1940-1945 Correspondence, newspaper clippings, reports, handbooks, pamphlets, and memoranda from national office. Prominent in the folders are David H. Holbrook, Katharine F. Lenroot, Russell H. Kurtz, Helen R. Jeter (secretary, Family Security Committee), Walter McGuinn (dean, Boston College School of Social Work),	156-160

Folder Title and Description of Contents	Folder

Robert Lane (executive director, Welfare Council of New York City), Elizabeth Ross (director, AAPSW War Service Office), and John J. McCloy. Material re selective service, Canadian social workers in Royal Canadian Army, morale of servicemen, placement of social work graduates, cooperation with AAPSW in War Service Office, formation of Wartime Committee on Personnel, military classification of social workers, WACs as psychiatric social workers, and social work standards in the U.S. Army.

AASW: Armed Forces: Allowances and Allotments, 1940-1945   161-162
   Correspondence, press releases, newspaper clippings, pamphlets, and report re family allowances and allotments of servicement. Correspondents include William Hodson, Dorothy C. Kahn, Jane Hoey, Paul Webbink, and various chapter members.

AASW: Armed Forces: Chapter Activity; Selective Service, 1940-1945   163
   Correspondence, newsletters, statements, and memoranda re chapter activities and selective service, and position of public welfare departments or agencies re conscription, local public welfare activities, and consultation centers.

AASW: Armed Forces: Conscientious Objectors, 1941-1944   164
   Correspondence, newspaper clippings, pamphlets, and bulletins re protection and rights of conscientious objectors; Louisiana laws re objectors.

AASW: Armed Forces: Consultation Centers, 1943   165
   Correspondence re need for psychiatric social workers in centers and classification needed for Army social workers.

AASW: Armed Forces: Deferment--Class III, 1940-1943   166
   Correspondence, reports, bulletins, press releases, and newspaper clippings re Class III deferment (deferred because of dependents); drafting social workers; New York chapter statement, "Suggested Position of AASW on Deferment of Social Workers."

AASW: Armed Forces: Deferment--Students, 1939-1941   167
   Correspondence, press releases, and newspaper clippings re student deferment and deferment of medical students.

Folder Title and Description of Contents	Folder

AASW: Armed Forces: Detention Units, 1942-1943 168
    Correspondence with social worker in Armed Forces re detention unit at Camp Pickett, Virginia.

AASW: Armed Forces: "Guide to Evaluation of Educational Experiences in the Armed Services," 1944-1945 169
    Information guide published by American Council on Education.

AASW: Armed Forces: List of Social Workers in Armed Forces Exchanged with AAPSW, 1943-1944 170
    Survey of social caseworkers in Army and number of graduates of schools of social work or with partial training in Armed Forces; military classification; listing of men in service and degree of social work education.

AASW: Armed Forces: List of AASW Members in Armed Forces, 1944. 171

AASW: Armed Forces: Mental Hygiene Units, 1941-1945 172
    Correspondence and memoranda. Correspondence between AASW and a member, 1941-1943, re organization of Fort Monmouth, New Jersey, mental hygiene units; Mental Hygiene reprint, "Mental Hygiene Unit"; Transportation Corps school, New Orleans Army Base, Mental Hygiene Aids for the Line Officer (August, 1945).

AASW: Armed Forces: Military Government, 1943 173
    Correspondence with social worker in service connected to the War Department and national office re pool of specialists available for service; commissions for social workers; Lehman committee; and program of division of military government.

AASW: Armed Forces: Office of War Information, Newsletter, 1944 174
    Correspondence of Joseph P. Anderson re social work material for newsletter.

AASW: Armed Forces: Selective Service, 1940-1941 175
    Bulletins, memoranda, and pamphlets re information on selective service; selective service regulations; explanation of Class III deferments

AASW: Armed Forces: Selective Service, Classification, 1940-1944 176
    Correspondence, pamphlets, memoranda, and statements re classification problems in Army, particularly securing classification for social workers;

Folder Title and Description of Contents	Folder

    an address, "Classification Problems"; Luther E. Woodward, National Committee for Mental Hygiene, "The Value of Social History in Selection for the Armed Forces"; New Jersey chapter, AASW, "Handbook for Guidance of Social and Health Counsellor"; draft of a platform for wartime welfare services in relation to manpower problems, and chapter activity for induction centers.

AASW: Armed Forces: Selective Service, Counseling, 1942-1943   177
    Correspondence, news release, interview report re screening process of selective service, data collected for use of Medical Advisory Board, military classification of social workers.

AASW: Armed Forces: Selective Service, Local Boards, 1940-1943   178
    Materials re medical survey registrants.

AASW: Armed Forces: Selective Service, Medical Survey, 1943-1944   179
    Correspondence, releases, reports, radio script re medical survey. Reports and memoranda from Luther E. Woodward re survey, financial assistance from Social Security Board for survey (Jane Hoey), instructions to medical field agents, and sample information cards used in the medical survey.

AASW: Armed Forces: Selective Service, Medical Survey--Chapter Activity, 1943-1944   180
    Correspondence and memoranda re chapter volunteers for gathering material for medical survey in Chicago, New York City, Washington, D.C.; question of violating civil rights raised by membership.

AASW: Armed Forces: Selective Service, Social Service Advisory Committee, 1943-1944   181
    Reports of advisory committee re medical survey, evaluation of Negro social workers, WACs used as psychiatric social workers, standards for Red Cross social workers; designation of Elizabeth Ross (AAPSW) to represent Wartime Committee on Personnel on social service advisory committee to selective service headquarters; Luther E. Woodward's reports re medical survey, summation of meeting with Army, Navy, psychiatric advisory committee and selective service re medical field agent program.

Folder Title and Description of Contents	Folder
AASW: Armed Forces: Selective Service, Social Work Service to, 1939-1940 Correspondence, memoranda, and statements re social work contributions to selective service, i.e., volunteering aid of social workers to selective service (Donald S. Howard, Grace Marcus, and D. C. Kahn); suggestions by Conrad van Hyning, principal assistant, director of public welfare, Washington, D.C., re activity in national defense; Gordon Hamilton, "Suggested Principles for Social Workers on Selective Service Administration"; and reports from chapters on relations with selective service boards.	182
AASW: Armed Forces: War Service Office, 1942-1945 Correspondence with E. H. Ross of AAPSW's war service office concerning problems of social workers in armed forces; Army hygiene units; classification of social workers; formation of Wartime Committee on Personnel by AASW; standards for military psychiatric social work; statement on Veterans Administration social work personnel and practice, and the Veterans Administration Corps Bill.	183-184
AASW: Armed Forces: Women, 1944-1945 Correspondence re enlistment of WACs as psychiatric social workers, American Nurses Association, John J. McCloy, Elizabeth de Schweinitz; definition of military psychiatric social workers; WAC recruiting standards.	185
AASW: Armed Forces: Correspondence with Members in the Armed Forces, 1941-1946 National organization correspondence collecting information on members' activities, on use made of social work skills and experience in armed services, and, in turn, keeping members informed of Association activities as well as maintaining membership records and continuing dues collection. Arranged chronologically.	186-191
AASW: Ethics: Correspondence, 1922-1934 Material re need for code of ethics, copies of chapter and private organization codes, correspondence with John D. Kenderdine (associate editor of The Survey) re ethics, publication of Lula Jean Elliott's pamphlet, Social Work Ethics.	192
AASW: Ethics: Codes from Other Organizations, 1920-1931.	193

Folder Title and Description of Contents	Folder
AASW: Ethics: Suggested Codes for Social Workers, 1922-1933 Suggested codes of ethics from chapters.	194
AASW: Government and Social Work Division: Social Work Conference on Federal Action on Unemployment, Steering Committee, Committee on Methods of Administration, 1931-1932 Correspondence, reports, minutes, and conference notes. Correspondents include Joanna C. Colcord, David H. Holbrook (National Social Work Council), Harry L. Lurie, Linton B. Swift, Rt. Rev. John O'Grady, Edward P. Costigan (U.S. Senator, Colorado); conferences with Katharine Lenroot (U.S. Children's Bureau) and Senator Costigan. Concerns the part social work should have in formulating a program of federal aid for unemployment relief.	195
AASW: Government and Social Work Division, Committee on Federal Action on Unemployment, 1932-1933 (Successor to Steering Committee, Social Work Conference on Federal Action on Unemployment) Minutes, correspondence, and memoranda re Costigan-LaFollette hearing and bill, Federal Relief Administration, Emergency Relief Construction Act (1932), and the Bonus Army (1932); conference with Harry Hopkins, Temporary Emergency Relief Administration (1933).	196
AASW: Government and Social Work Division, Committee on Federal Action in Social Welfare, Steering Committee, 1932-1934 (Successor to AASW Committee on Federal Action on Unemployment) Correspondence, minutes, questionnaire, and reports re Federal Emergency Relief Administration, Conference on Governmental Objectives for Social Work, unemployment relief funds, subsistence homesteads, and Civil Works Administration.	197-198
AASW: Government and Social Work Division, Department of Welfare (proposed) Subcommittee, 1932-1943 Reports, statements, bulletins, and minutes. Resume of materials includes federal reorganization plans affecting the Children's Bureau; federal government in field of social service, Harry L. Lurie's statement, "Administrative Basis for Social Welfare Programs in the Federal, State, and Local Governments"; program to continue relief after dissolution of FERA; charts of proposed Bureau of Welfare; and formation of subcommittee on federal Department of Welfare.	199-200

NATIONAL ASSOCIATION OF SOCIAL WORKERS, INC.

Folder Title and Description of Contents	Folder
AASW: Government and Social Work Division, National Social Work Program Outline Subcommittee, 1934 Memoranda and statements of subcommittee assigned to "develop general social principles basic in planning a national social welfare program . . . ."	201
AASW: Government and Social Work Division, "Invalidity," and Health Insurance Committee, 1937-1938 Correspondence and minutes re unemployment compensation due to sickness. Correspondents include Grace Abbott, Antoinette Cannon, and Michael M. Davis (Committee on Research in Medical Economics).	202
AASW: Government and Social Work Division, Housing Committee, Bulletins, 1934-1940 Includes scrapbook of committee, information on Wagner-Ellenbogen Bill (1936), and bulletins.	203
AASW: Government and Social Work Division, Housing Committee, National Activities, 1934-1942 Minutes and correspondence involve discussion of Wagner Bill, rent policies, and summation of housing activity in United States, 1942.	204-205
AASW: Government and Social Work Division, Housing Committee, National Housing Agency, 1942-1943 Information re formation of NHA and its functions. Series of case reports on solutions of housing management problems.	206
AASW: Government and Social Work Division, Housing Committee, Training for Housing Subcommittee, 1943-1944 Minutes, correspondence, and comments on training social workers for housing by Leonard Mayo (Western Reserve) and others.	207
AASW: Government and Social Work Division: Public Assistance, Bibliographies on Relief, 1934-1946.	208
AASW: Government and Social Work Division: Public Assistance, National Resources Planning Board Studies, 1939-1940 Memoranda, minutes, and correspondence re formation of a technical advisory committee on national relief policy.	209
AASW: Government and Social Work Division: Public Assistance, National Activities, 1934-1942 Memoranda, reports, questionnaires, bulletins, and reprints re relief problems and the Emergency Relief Appropriation Act of 1935.	210-211

Folder Title and Description of Contents	Folder
AASW: Government and Social Work Division: Public Assistance, Chapter Activities, 1932-1945	212-230

Contains information from chapters re relief programs and attempts to solve problems as seen through the chapters. Situations included are in California, Colorado, Connecticut, Georgia, Illinois, Indiana, Michigan, Ohio, Puerto Rico, Washington, D.C., and Washington State.

AASW: Government and Social Work Division: Social Security Act, 1935-1937 — 231

Bulletins; clippings re provisions of Economic Security Bill (S. 1130); and material on administering relief and security program, child welfare services under Social Security Act, and unemployment insurance proposals and reports.

AASW: Government and Social Work Division, Steering Committee, Report for Delegate Conference, 1939-1940 — 232

Report stating objectives of division on government and social work.

AASW: Howard, Donald S., AASW National Correspondence, 1930-1948 — 233

Correspondence with charity organization society division of Russell Sage Foundation, particularly Joanna C. Colcord and Donald S. Howard (AASW President, 1947-1949). Subjects covered are Joanna C. Colcord's participation in AASW (until 1940), surplus commodities, AASW statement on foreign relief programs, UNRRA and the AASW draft statement on long range provision for displaced persons.

AASW: Howard, Donald S., AASW Chapter Correspondence, 1947 — 234

Brief correspondence re National Vocational Service, committee structure, and Southern participation in Association.

AASW: Howard, Donald S., AASW Delegate Conference Folder, 1948 — 235

Preparatory material.

AASW: Howard, Donald S., AASW International Cooperation for Social Welfare Committee, 1947-1948 — 236

Brief folder including agendas, AASW public welfare platform (1947), and minutes.

Folder Title and Description of Contents	Folder
AASW: Howard, Donald S., AASW Organization and Planning of the Social Services in the War and Post War Periods Committee, 1942-1945 Correspondence, memoranda, and minutes. Statements on "New Frontiers in Social Work," AASW public social services, effect of war on social work in local communities, and foreign relief.	237
AASW: Howard, Donald S., AASW Public Social Policies Committee, 1946-1947 Minutes, correspondence, agendas, statement of committee assignment, and drafts for proposed statement by the Association.	238
AASW: Howard, Donald S., International Conference of Social Work, Constitution, 1947-1948 Several drafts of constitution with suggestions from Mary Van Kleeck.	239
AASW: Howard, Donald S., International Conference of Social Work, Correspondence, 1938-1944 Historical data on plans for the fourth international convention.	240
AASW: Howard, Donald S., International Conference of Social Work, Hospitality Committee, 1947-1948 Notes on committee meeting and request for funds to support conference.	241
AASW: Howard, Donald S., International Conference of Social Work, Program Committee, General Correspondence, 1947-1948 Notice of Howard Knight's death (executive secretary of the National Conference of Social Work), correspondence from Dr. René Sand (president, ICSW), Fred Hoehler, George Haynes (treasurer-general, ICSW), Leonard Mayo (then president of NCSW), Ernest F. Witte, and Melvin Glasser, plus a membership list of the program committee.	242-243
AASW: Howard, Donald S., International Conference of Social Work, Program Committee, Invitations and Thank-Yous to Speakers, 1947-1948.	244
AASW: Howard, Donald S., International Conference of Social Work, Program Committee, Speakers' Refusals, 1948.	245
AASW: Howard, Donald S., International Conference of Social Work, Program Committee, Suggestions re Speakers and Meetings, 1944-1948 Correspondence, memoranda, and listing of topics.	246

Folder Title and Description of Contents	Folder
AASW: Howard, Donald S., International Conference of Social Work, Program Committee, Speeches, 1948 Copies of three of the speeches.	247
AASW: Howard, Donald S., International Conference of Social Work, United States National Committee, 1947-1948 Correspondence, minutes, memoranda, agendas, reports on reorganization of ICSW, tentative ICSW program schedules, material on appointment of Joseph P. Anderson as ICSW acting secretary general, United States Department of State "briefs" for foreign visitors, and committee membership list.	248
AASW: Migrants, 1936-1945 Correspondence and bibliographies concerned with transient and homeless in South Carolina and Illinois; material on migratory labor in California, Dorothy C. Kahn's participation in Tolan committee hearings (House of Representatives' committee to investigate interstate migration of destitute citizens), and the platform on interstate migration.	249
AASW: National Recovery Administration: Codes for Professions and Industries, 1933 Largely correspondence re information on NRA.	250
AASW: National Recovery Administration: Codes for Social Work, 1933-1934 Correspondence with National Social Work Council, Linton B. Swift, David H. Holbrook, and Paul U. Kellogg re codes; proposed "Code for Social Service Workers" by Chicago's Social Workers Discussion Group.	251
AASW: Political Parties, 1936-1944 Correspondence with Niles Carpenter of the 1936 Republican National Committee; Walter West's statement of social work planks to Robert F. Wagner; Walter West's support of Franklin D. Roosevelt.	252
AASW: Practitioners Movement, 1933 Brief folder.	253
AASW: Social Security Act: Inclusion of Non-Profit Organizations, National Committee on, 1934-1941 Correspondence re meetings with national organizations and opposition to the Social Security Act.	254
AASW: Social Work Scholarship and Fellowship Information, 1935-1953 Compilation of listings of social work scholarships and fellowship information.	255

Folder Title and Description of Contents	Folder
AASW: War Activities: Chapter, 1940-1944 Correspondence and reports on chapter activities in communities near war installations. Material from the North Carolina chapter and the "Eastern Groups." Effects of national defense on rural and farm problems, work relief and social conditions near defense operations in North Carolina, and survey of chapter members' role in defense activities.	256-257
AASW: War Activities: National Defense, New York City, 1940-1941 Minutes and memoranda re community problems of national defense, selective service, and confidentiality of records.	258
AASW: Wartime Committee on Personnel, Civil Service Subcommittee, 1944-1946 Correspondence and memoranda re securing well-qualified social work personnel for civil service administration, job descriptions from Office of Vocational Rehabilitation, and material on the merit system for civil administration.	259
AASW: Wartime Committee on Personnel, Questionnaire, "Post War Educational and Employment Plans," 1944 Correspondence, memoranda, questionnaire, and reports on questionnaire sent to members of professional organizations re their educational plans, employment, training, employment records, and experience in Armed Forces.	260
AASW: Wartime Committee on Personnel: Newsletters from Other Organizations, 1942-1944 Contains newsletters from New York School of Social Work and Louisiana State Department of Public Welfare.	261
AASW: Wartime Committee on Personnel: Newsletter to Social Workers in Armed Forces, 1944-1945 Correspondence and newsletter re activities of Wartime Committee on Personnel, membership list of AASSW, and newsletters to answer questions about social work from those leaving the armed forces.	262
AASW: Wartime Committee on Personnel: Newsletters to Social Workers in Armed Forces, Orders, 1944-1945.	263
AASW: Confidential Records Pertaining to Violations of Personnel Standards. See introduction for instructions on use of these records.	264-324

Folder Title and Description of Contents	Folder
AAMSW: Formation and Incorporation, 1917-1927 Notes of the May, 1917, meeting to consider formation of a national organization of hospital social workers. Correspondence and papers regarding the incorporation of the American Association of Hospital Social Workers in 1926.	325
AAMSW: Constitution and Bylaws, 1918-1954 Correspondence; papers; and copies of constitutions, bylaws, and amendments to these. Includes lists of early members of the Association.	326-327
AAMSW: Annual Meetings, 1918-1955 Reports of annual meetings held each year in conjunction with the National Conference of Social Work.	328
AAMSW: Cleveland Referendum, 1954 Association members voted on the question of whether or not AAMSW should continue to participate in the Temporary Inter-Association Council (TIAC), which resulted in formation of the National Association of Social Workers.	329
AAMSW: Special Membership Meeting, 1955 Correspondence, minutes, and legal documents. This meeting to formally dissolve the Association was held at Massachusetts General Hospital, Boston (where Richard C. Cabot established the first hospital social service department in 1905).	330
AAMSW: Executive Director, Correspondence, 1948-1955 Primarily requests for information addressed to the director (formerly the executive secretary) regarding tuberculosis, blinded veterans, ratio of medical social workers, rehabilitation of handicapped persons, a code of ethics for social workers, etc.	331
AAMSW: Executive Director, Reports, 1921-1955 Annual and semi-annual reports to the executive committee or to the Association.	332
AAMSW: Executive Director, Reports on Field Trips, 1923-1947 Reports of visits to hospitals, Association districts and regions, attendance at conferences, etc.	333

Folder Title and Description of Contents	Folder
AAMSW: President's Papers, 1922-1954 Addresses to annual or business meetings of the Association and reports (1948-1949) to the executive committee.	334
AAMSW: Treasurer's Reports, 1938-1949.	335
AAMSW: Association Officers, 1950-1955 Correspondence of Association officers. Copy of the Association's resolution criticizing the destruction of Charlotte Towle's <u>Common Human Needs</u> by Federal Security Administrator, Oscar R. Ewing.	336
AAMSW: Advisory Council, 1920-1947 Brief correspondence. Primarily lists of members of the council, appointed annually by the President to serve as advisors to officers, staff, and members of the Association.	337
AAMSW: Executive Committee, Correspondence and Papers, 1921-1955 Chiefly memoranda to the committee from the executive director. Material on repeal of the Association constitution, conference on problems of Mexican war workers, hiring of a recruitment consultant, Temporary Inter-Association Council (TIAC), Association tax exempt status, etc. Includes a 1934 Association committee organization chart.	338
AAMSW: Executive Committee, Minutes, 1918-1940.	339-345
AAMSW: Executive Committee, Relationships with Other Organizations, 1929-1942 Excerpts from executive committee meetings regarding policy toward relationships with other organizations.	346
AAMSW: Executive Committee, Subcommittee to Recommend an Executive Secretary, 1934 The subcommittee, appointed in July, 1934, recommended the retention of the current secretary, Helen Beckley.	347
AAMSW: Administrative Committee, 1944-1956 Correspondence, reports, and memoranda. Includes material on the Association's application to the National Foundation for Infantile Paralysis for funds, organization of the National Association of Social Workers, hiring of personnel, etc.	348

Folder Title and Description of Contents	Folder
AAMSW: Study Council, 1934-1942 Correspondence and reports re the work of the council, whose purpose was to integrate Association study committees and to build a sound program.	349-350
AAMSW: Administration Committee, 1941-1944 The committee was established to study the administration of medical social work.	351
AAMSW: Bylaws Committee, 1918-1953 Correspondence, reports, and copies of proposed amendments to the constitution and the bylaws.	352-353
AAMSW: Cabot (Richard C.) Memorial Committee, 1938-1942 Correspondence, memorial speeches, and articles about Cabot, who founded the first social service department at Massachusetts General Hospital, Boston.	354
AAMSW: Case Evaluation Committee, 1924-1938 Formerly the case competition committee, which sponsored an annual contest to encourage casework skills. As the case evaluation committee, it evaluated treatment processes in medical social work.	355-356
AAMSW: Case Evaluation Committee, Case Records, 1928-1937 Individual case records submitted to the committee's annual contest or submitted for evaluation by the committee.	357-359
AAMSW: Committee on Committees, 1930 One report. The committee sought to study the functions and activities of the Association's standing committees.	360
AAMSW: Committee to Study (Association) Regions, 1950-1952 Reports.	361
AAMSW: Community Relations Committee, 1923-1933 Correspondence and reports of the committee, which dealt with relations of hospitals and social service departments to the community, especially to community chests.	362

Folder Title and Description of Contents	Folder
AAMSW: Editorial Committee, 1921-1955 Formerly the publications committee. Correspondence, reports, and memoranda. Material on advertising, editorial policy, editorial consultants, evolution of a professional journal, public relations, and publication of the Association journal, <u>Medical Social Work</u>.	363-364
AAMSW: Editorial Committee, Evaluation and Disposition of Manuscripts, 1951-1955 Correspondence, reports, and manuscripts submitted for use by the Association or for publication in <u>Medical Social Work</u>.	365-368
AAMSW: Education Committee, 1918-1955 Correspondence, minutes, and reports.	369-376
AAMSW: Education Committee, Casework in Illness Subcommittee, 1945-1947 Scattered correspondence of the committee, which was concerned with "psychosomatic thinking" in the casework training of the medical social worker.	377
AAMSW: Education Committee, Concepts Subcommittee, 1952-1955 The subcommittee sought to identify and define medical social work concepts.	378
AAMSW: Education Committee, Curriculum Content Subcommittee, 1930-1955 Correspondence, reports, bibliographies, and course outlines.	379-381
AAMSW: Education Committee, Educational and Employment Opportunities in Medical Social Work for Negroes Subcommittee, 1945-1949 Correspondence and papers.	382
AAMSW: Education Committee, Eye Course Subcommittee, 1934-1936 Correspondence and reports re special training for eye clinic staff. Includes a 1936 "Report Regarding Special Courses in Eye Work."	383
AAMSW: Education Committee, Field Work Content Subcommittee, 1930-1947 Correspondence, reports, and memoranda. Includes material on the study of field work, definition of terms, problems of field work supervisors, supervision of students in medical social work placements, and contents of field work instruction.	384-385

Folder Title and Description of Contents	Folder

AAMSW: Education Committee, Field Work Teaching 386-387
Subcommittee, 1951-1956
    Correspondence and reports re the study of practice in field work training. Includes a final report, <u>Field Work Teaching in Medical Social Work: A Descriptive Study</u>.

AAMSW: Education Committee, Growth and Develop- 388
ment Subcommittee, 1950-1956
    Primarily correspondence re establishing the subcommittee and defining the area of study.

AAMSW: Education Committee, Medical Information 389-391
Courses Subcommittee, 1928-1950
    Correspondence and reports. Material on medical courses for social workers, public health content in the curriculum, medical social work subject matter, and health problems in casework.

AAMSW: Education Committee, Orientation of the 392
Worker on Her First Job Subcommittee, 1938-1945
    Correspondence and reports re the "induction" period.

AAMSW: Education Committee, Participation in 393-397
Teaching Medical Students Subcommittee, 1933-1955
    Formerly the committee on participation in teaching social and environmental factors in medicine. Correspondence, minutes, and reports.

AAMSW: Education Committee, Participation in 398-400
Teaching Medical Students Subcommittee, 1943 Social Service Departments Survey, 1943-1945
    Questionnaires regarding hospital social service departments' participation in teaching medical students. Includes questionnaire forms, replies from 24 departments, and evaluations by Eleanor Cockerill, chairman of the committee.

AAMSW: Education Committee, Participation in 401-404
Teaching Medical Students Subcommittee, Medical School Surveys, 1945-1946
    Surveys done of medical school teaching of social and environmental factors in illness.

AAMSW: Education Committee, Participation in 405-406
Teaching Medical Students Subcommittee, "Widening Horizons in Medical Education," 1946
    First draft of the committee's report.

Folder Title and Description of Contents	Folder
AAMSW: Education Committee, Participation in Teaching Medical Students Subcommittee, <u>Widening Horizons in Medical Education: A Study of the Teaching of Social and Environmental Factors in Medicine</u>, 1947 Final report.	407
AAMSW: Education Committee, Participation in Teaching Medical Students Subcommittee, 1950 Medical School Questionnaire Questionnaires re use of current casework methods in teaching medical students and re inter-department relationships.	408
AAMSW: Education Committee, Participation in Teaching Medical Students Subcommittee, Medical Social Workers Participate in Medical Education, 1954 A casebook of illustrative material demonstrating specific contributions by medical social workers in teaching medical students.	409
AAMSW: Education Committee, Participation in Teaching Medical Students Subcommittee, Casebook Material, 1950-1952 Material used in compiling <u>Medical Social Workers Participate in Medical Education</u>.	410-412
AAMSW: Education Committee, Principles of Medical Social Work Subcommittee, 1940-1942 This project to secure information regarding concepts covered in medical social work courses was abandoned in 1942. Correspondence and papers.	413
AAMSW: Education Committee, Psychiatric Content for Medical Social Workers Subcommittee, 1929-1937 Correspondence, reports, and scattered course outlines. The material reflects problems of relationships between medical social work and psychiatric social work. The subcommittee studied psychiatric course content in the medical social work curriculum.	414
AAMSW: Education Committee, Recruiting Subcommittee, 1940-1941 The subcommittee did a preliminary survey of recruiting practices and needs in 1940 but declined to undertake an extensive project. It prepared a tentative report in 1941.	415
AAMSW: Education Committee, Registration Subcommittee, 1934-1939 The subcommittee attempted to secure and interpret data on medical social workers and to formulate a simplified method for reporting all students completing the medical social work sequence.	416

Folder Title and Description of Contents	Folder
AAMSW: Education Committee, Teaching of Nurses Subcommittee, 1925-1954	417-419

Correspondence and reports re teaching aspects of medical social work to nurses. Includes material on medical social work in the nursing curriculum, and nursing in the medical social work curriculum.

AAMSW: Education Committee, Teaching of the Social Component in Hospital Administration, 1941-1956 — 420-421

Formerly the subcommittee on teaching of students in hospital administration. Correspondence, minutes, and reports re social work content of the hospital administration curriculum. Includes pilot study of the University of California School of Public Health's hospital administration curriculum.

AAMSW: Education Committee: American Association of Schools of Social Work, 1941-1952 — 422-423

Correspondence and reports regarding matters of common interest to the education committee and AASSW, especially to its curriculum committee: curriculum content, recruitment, professional education, and accrediting of schools of social work. Contains material re the transferring of the accrediting function from the Association to AASSW.

AAMSW: Education Committee: Civil Service Commission, 1941-1943 — 424

Correspondence re medical social work positions in civil service and the Association's role in determining standards for such positions.

AAMSW: Education Committee: American Public Health Association Merit System Unit, 1946-1947 — 425

APHA asked the Association to assist in developing material for civil service merit system examinations in medical social work.

AAMSW: Education Committee: Approval of Medical Social Work Curricula, 1941-1956 — 426

Material re procedure for Association approval of medical social work courses initiated by schools of social work.

AAMSW: Education Committee: Ida M. Cannon, 1939 — 427

Correspondence re a proposed history of medical social work to be done by Ida Cannon.

Folder Title and Description of Contents	Folder

AAMSW: Education Committee: Council on Social Work Education, Teaching Cases, 1945-1955 — 428
Correspondence and reports re appointment of Association representatives to CSWE's subcommittee on teaching materials and the importance of the use of medical social work case records for teaching.

AAMSW: Education Committee: Definition of "Full Course" in Medical Social Work, 1940-1946 — 429
Material re formulating a definition of "full course" which determined eligibility for active membership in AAMSW. The education committee decided in 1946 to allow individual medical social work faculty to define the term.

AAMSW: Education Committee: Medical Social Consultation with the U.S. Army, 1951-1953 — 430
Medical social work consultants were members of the education committee. Chiefly correspondence re concern for adopting the best of medical social work practice to Army needs.

AAMSW: Education Committee: Public Programs Teaching Materials, 1937-1947 — 431
The committee compiled materials illustrative of medical social work activities in public programs. Includes sample case records and samples of consultation services to state and county health departments.

AAMSW: Education Committee: Office of Vocational Rehabilitation, 1944-1950 — 432
In 1944 and 1945 the education committee contacted schools of social work in an attempt to assist OVR in finding medical social workers for state rehabilitation programs. Material re the education committee's advisory committee to OVR.

AAMSW: Education Committee: Use of Films in Medical Social Sequences in Schools of Social Work, 1949 — 433
One report of a survey of sixteen instructors.

AAMSW: Exhibits Committee, 1924-1935 — 434
Chiefly reports and memoranda re committee planning for Association exhibits at annual meetings of the American Hospital Association and other organizations.

AAMSW: Finance Committee, 1933-1955 — 435-438
Formerly the plans and estimates committee and later the planning and finance committee. Minutes and correspondence of the committee, which had responsibility for long-range financial planning, year-by-year budgeting, and staff administration.

Folder Title and Description of Contents	Folder
AAMSW: Foster Home Care Facilities Committee, 1935 Report of a study of eight clinics' placement of convalescing children in foster homes.	439
AAMSW: Functions Committee, 1920-1942 Correspondence and reports. Includes material on the inter-relationship of disease and social maladjustment, the contribution of the social casework method to institutional practice of medicine, the persisting concern of AAMSW for casework method and skills, and early attempts to define the functions of medical social work. Following the reorganization of the Association, 1940-1942, the functions committee was disbanded and its work carried on by the medical social practice committee.	440-444
AAMSW: Functions Committee, "Exhibit of Steps in the Study and Definition of the Hospital Social Worker's Function," 1930 Exhibit manual which traces the history of the committee on functions, 1920-1930.	445
AAMSW: Functions Committee, Three Long Cases, 1934 Case material for use of instructors which was also used as source material for the publication, Medical Social Work: A Study of Current Aims and Methods in Medical Social Case Work.	446
AAMSW: Functions Committee, Functions Study, 1930-1934, "Selected Statistics and Study Outlines" Includes list of participating social service departments, instructions to participants, plan of publication and plan of presentation of the study, etc.	447
AAMSW: Functions Committee, Functions Study, 1936-1940, "Selected Statistics and Study Outlines" Material on study projects, 1936-1940, including sample forms, memoranda, etc.	448
AAMSW: Functions Committee: Case Material, Colorado General Hospital, Denver, Colorado, 1936-1939 Material regarding the cardiac, pediatrics, and eye and ear clinics.	449
AAMSW: Functions Committee: Case Material, University of Chicago Clinics, Chicago, Illinois, 1933-1939 Material illustrating individual referral cases, orthopedic ward cases, pediatrics cases, and a "full demonstration of a brief case."	450

Folder Title and Description of Contents	Folder
AAMSW: Functions Committee: Case Material, State University of Iowa Hospitals, Iowa City, Iowa, 1937-1938 Six cases from the diabetes ward.	451
AAMSW: Functions Committee: Case Material, Massachusetts General Hospital, Boston, Massachusetts, 1933-1939 Material illustrating individual referral and "full demonstration of brief cases."	452
AAMSW: Functions Committee: Case Material, University of Minnesota Hospitals, Minneapolis, Minnesota 1930-1939 Mixed (medical) services cases illustrating individual referral and 100 percent contact.	453
AAMSW: Functions Committee: Case Material, Mayo Clinic, Rochester, Minnesota, 1936-1939 Mixed (medical) services cases.	454
AAMSW: Functions Committee: Case Material, Presbyterian Hospital, New York City, 1938-1939 Eighteen cases, "fully recorded," showing the method of 100 percent social review. Cases from dermatology, eye, surgical, and medical services.	455
AAMSW: Functions Committee: Case Material, University Hospitals of Cleveland, Ohio, 1936-1939 Material regarding ear, nose, and throat cases; medical clinic cases; medical ward cases; pediatrics ward cases; and "full demonstration of brief cases."	456
AAMSW: Functions Committee: Case Material, University of Pennsylvania Hospitals, Philadelphia, Pennsylvania, 1937-1938 Six cases.	457
AAMSW: Functions Committee: Case Material, Children's Hospital, Washington, D.C., 1936-1939 Mixed (medical) services cases.	458
AAMSW: Functions Committee: Case Material, Correspondence with the Veterans Administration, 1937-1938 Correspondence re cases sent to AAMSW. Includes evaluation, by Irene Grant, of all cases submitted.	459

Folder Title and Description of Contents	Folder
AAMSW: Functions Committee: Case Material, Veterans Administration Hospitals, 1937-1939 　　Forty-one "brief cases" from VA hospitals in Hines, Illinois; Pittsburgh, Pennsylvania; Indianapolis, Indiana; Cheyenne, Wyoming; and Hot Springs, South Dakota.	460-461
AAMSW: Functions Committee: Case Material, AAMSW Gulf District, 1938 　　Cases submitted by the District for functions committee projects.	462
AAMSW: Functions Committee: Case Material, Middle Atlantic District, 1938 　　The District appointed a study committee to analyze case records illustrating trends in casework practice. Includes five cases submitted to the Association and a report of the study committee's analysis.	463
AAMSW: Functions Committee: Case Material, Minnesota District, 1938 　　Cases submitted from the University of Minnesota Hospitals, the Wilder Clinic, Mayo Clinic, and Minneapolis General Hospital.	464
AAMSW: Functions Committee: Case Material, New England District, ca. 1929-1930 　　Case of a diabetic child, illustrating the relationship of disease and social maladjustment.	465
AAMSW: Functions Committee: Case Material, Miscellaneous Hospitals, 1937-1938 　　Cases submitted for Functions Project C, "full demonstration of a brief case."	466
AAMSW: Future Program Committee, 1951 　　The committee considered the expanding need for professional personnel and the Association's inability to provide it, and the problem of increasing use of non-medical social workers in medical settings.	467
AAMSW: Joint Vocational Service Committee, 1930-1939 　　The Joint Vocational Service was an organization offering "vocational" and placement service to nurses, public health nurses, and social workers.	468
AAMSW: Lay Participation Committee, 1935-1942 　　Correspondence and reports re volunteers.	469

Folder Title and Description of Contents	Folder
AAMSW: Medical Care in Community Health Committee, 1933-1942 Correspondence and reports. Includes material on the Federal Emergency Relief Administration (FERA), public relief clients, venereal disease programs, social aspects of expanding medical care programs, and medical social work in tax-supported health and welfare services.	470-472
AAMSW: Medical Care in Community Health Committee, Subcommittee on the "Study of Medical Social Work in Public Programs," 1938-1940 The Study was conducted as a joint project of APWA and AAMSW with APWA providing most of the financial support. Includes preliminary report which was never released for circulation.	473-474
AAMSW: Medical Care in Community Health Committee, Report of the Joint Committee of the American Public Welfare Association and the American Hospital Association, 1938-1939 Contains material re AAMSW's response to the joint committee's report, "Hospital Care for the Needy."	475
AAMSW: Medical Care in Community Health Committee, Crippled Children's Program, 1936 Material re formulating a statement submitted by AAMSW to the U.S. Children's Bureau suggesting qualifications and appropriate activities for medical social workers in state programs for crippled children.	476
AAMSW: Medical Care in Community Health Committee, Studies, 1935 The committee did "Two Studies of the Social Aspects of Health Problems of Public Relief Clients." The studies focused on Cook County, Illinois; and Philadelphia, Pennsylvania.	477-478
AAMSW: Medical Social Practice Committee, 1942-1955 Correspondence, minutes, and reports. The report of the reorganization committee resulted in placing various Association study committees involved in practice under the practice committee. The committee was concerned with continuous study of medical social work needs, definition of function, and correlation of education to practice.	479-481

NATIONAL ASSOCIATION OF SOCIAL WORKERS, INC.

Folder Title and Description of Contents | Folder

AAMSW: Medical Social Practice Committee, Subcommittee on Administration, 1944-1947 — 482
The subcommittee functioned also as a joint committee with the American Hospital Association's committee on the administration of social service departments in hospitals. Correspondence; reports; and a statement describing the structure and organization, standards and procedure, and intramural and extra-mural relationships of a social service department.

AAMSW: Medical Social Practice Committee, Case Records Subcommittee, 1945-1955 — 483
Correspondence and reports re the use of case material in classroom teaching.

AAMSW: Medical Social Practice Committee, Chronic Illness Subcommittee, 1947-1954 — 484
Correspondence and reports re social and emotional implications of chronic illness for patients, families, and society.

AAMSW: Medical Social Practice Committee, Criteria for Evaluating Social Service Departments in Hospitals and Clinics Subcommittee, 1949-1954 — 485
Correspondence and reports re determining of methods of evaluating social service departments.

AAMSW: Medical Social Practice Committee, Definition of a Medical Social Work Position Subcommittee, 1953-1955 — 486
Correspondence. Concern for definition arose out of the study of the use of non-medical social workers in medical social work positions.

AAMSW: Medical Social Practice Committee, Function of the Medical Social Worker in Rehabilitation Programs Subcommittee, 1945-1950 — 487
Correspondence and reports re clarification of the role of the medical social worker in rehabilitation programs.

AAMSW: Medical Social Practice Committee, Medical Social Activities in Public Medical Care Programs Subcommittee, 1946-1952 — 488-490
Correspondence, minutes, reports, and interviews with state health department staff members.

AAMSW: Medical Social Practice Committee, Medical Social Casework Study Subcommittee, 1946-1953 — 491
Correspondence and reports.

Folder Title and Description of Contents	Folder
AAMSW: Medical Social Practice Committee, Medical Social Work with Private Patients Subcommittee, 1945-1947 Reports.	492
AAMSW: Medical Social Practice Committee, Processes of Administration in a Hospital Social Service Department Subcommittee, 1949-1956 Correspondence and reports. Final report: <u>Administering a Hospital Social Service Department</u>.	493
AAMSW: Medical Social Practice Committee, Ratios Subcommittee, 1930-1953 Correspondence, minutes, and reports re ratios (defined as the number of medical social workers needed per patient per year).	494
AAMSW: Medical Social Practice Committee, Recording Social Data on Medical Records Subcommittee, 1944-1945 Reports.	495
AAMSW: Medical Social Practice Committee, Revision of the Statement of Standards Subcommittee, 1946-1950 Correspondence and reports. The statement was intended to be a guide in organizing and improving social service departments in hospitals and clinics.	496-497
AAMSW: Medical Social Practice Committee, Selection and Focus of Cases Subcommittee, 1942-1945 Correspondence and reports. The subcommittee considered the effects of World War II on practice.	498
AAMSW: Medical Social Practice Committee, Social Service Participation in a Community Rheumatic Fever Program Subcommittee, 1946-1949 Correspondence, reports, and final statement.	499
AAMSW: Medical Social Practice Committee, Statistical Recording Subcommittee, 1950-1953 Correspondence, reports, and material re methods of recording in hospital social service departments.	500
AAMSW: Medical Social Practice Committee, Subcommittee on the Use of Psychosomatic Understanding in Medical Social Casework Services, 1943-1945 Correspondence and reports. This subcommittee attempted to define elements in medical social work which might be changing or developing as psychosomatic factors were given increasing recognition in medical practice.	501

Folder Title and Description of Contents	Folder

AAMSW: Medical Social Practice Committee, Subcommittee to Develop a Single Statement of Standards with the American Association of Psychiatric Social Workers, 1954-1955 502
    Scattered correspondence.

AAMSW: Medical Social Practice Committee, Subcommittee to Develop the Study of Working with Other Professional Persons Within the Medical Setting, 1953-1955 503
    Correspondence and report, "Working with Other Professional Personnel in the Medical Setting."

AAMSW: Medical Social Practice Committee, Use of the Non-Medical Social Worker Subcommittee, 1949-1953 504
    The subcommittee was formed out of concern for the trend away from specialization in social work education and its effect on social service departments.

AAMSW: Medical Social Practice Committee, Venereal Disease Subcommittee, 1944-1947 505
    Correspondence re medical social work practice in venereal disease settings. Study to determine the effect, if any, that new medical treatment and new public health organization were having on medical social workers. Includes final reports, "Medical Social Work in Relation to Venereal Disease."

AAMSW: Medical Social Practice Committee, 1948 Graduate Questionnaire, 1951-1952 506
    The practice and education committees cooperated in sending questionnaires to 1948 graduates of medical social work sequences in schools of social work to determine how effectively their education had prepared them for practice. Includes a copy of the questionnaire and tabulation of data obtained.

AAMSW: Membership Committee, 1920-1955 507-509
    Correspondence and reports re eligibility for membership, problems of standards in hospital social service departments, analysis of Association membership groups, recruiting, student membership, and establishing and altering membership requirements.

AAMSW: Nominations Committee, 1921-1955 510
    Correspondence and reports.

Folder Title and Description of Contents	Folder
AAMSW: Personnel Committee, 1937-1953 The committee was concerned with sound personnel practices both in the field of medical social work and with AAMSW's national staff. Includes material on hiring, contracts, tenure, hours, physical conditions, and minimum standards. Includes <u>A Statement of Personnel Practices in Medical Social Work</u>.	511-512
AAMSW: Personnel Committee, Subcommittee on Evaluation of National Staff, 1949-1953 Correspondence and reports.	513
AAMSW: Personnel Committee, Subcommittee on Qualifications of Medical Social Workers in Public Health Agencies, 1949-1951 Correspondence and reports.	514
AAMSW: Personnel Committee, Special Committee to Review the Statement of Personnel Practices in Medical Social Work, 1951-1952 The committee's report recommended similar minimum standards for medical social workers in both hospitals and public health programs. Reflects flux within the profession because of the debate of generic vs. specific social work, the use of non-medical social workers in a medical setting, and the future of professional social work organizations.	515
AAMSW: Personnel in Public Service Committee, 1935-1942 Correspondence and reports re the Association's concern for establishment of satisfactory qualifications and examinations for medical social work positions under public auspices, and its relations with the Civil Service Assembly.	516
AAMSW: Place of the Medical Social Worker in Civil Defense Committee, 1950-1952 (?) Correspondence; drafts of the "Place of the Medical Social Work in Civil Defense."	517
AAMSW: Program Committee, 1920-1955 Correspondence, reports, and programs. The committee had responsibility for planning Association participation in the Annual Forum of the National Conference of Social Work, and planning the Association's annual meeting, which was held in conjunction with the National Conference.	518-519

Folder Title and Description of Contents	Folder

AAMSW: Proportionate Representation Committee, 1930-1932 — 520
   Correspondence, minutes, and reports. Material on the numbers of members in Association districts and the amount of dues paid by members. The committee was formed in response to criticism of the basis of representation on the Association executive committee.

AAMSW: Public Relations Committee, 1949-1953 — 521
   Correspondence, minutes, and reports. Includes material on exhibits and interpretation of medical social work to related professions and to the public.

AAMSW: Public Relations Committee, Contest, 1952-1953 — 522
   A prize was awarded for the article submitted which best interpreted the medical social work function to non-social workers. Includes correspondence and contest articles.

AAMSW: Public Relations Committee, Exhibit Materials, 1949-1953 — 523-524
   Pamphlets, radio scripts, and lists of films with medical social work implications.

AAMSW: Records Committee, 1922-1940 — 525-527
   Correspondence and reports. The committee was concerned with recording of "social information" by the hospital social service department and making this information available to other hospital departments.

AAMSW: Recruitment Committee, 1953-1955 — 528-529
   Correspondence, minutes, and reports. The committee was responsible for long-range development of recruitment policies and served as advisor to the recruitment consultant.

AAMSW: Recruitment Committee: Advisory Committee on Recruitment, 1953-1955 — 530
   The committee was composed of representatives from health, social work, education, and vocational guidance fields.

AAMSW: Recruitment Committee, Recruitment Materials, 1951-1955 — 531
   Pamphlets, leaflets, and brochures.

AAMSW: Relationship Between Social Service Committees and Professional Workers Committee, 1930-1933 — 532
   Reports. Social service committees, composed of representatives from hospital administration, the medical staff, the community, etc., served in an advisory capacity to social service departments.

Folder Title and Description of Contents	Folder
AAMSW: Reorganization Committee, 1934-1942 The committee was appointed by the president in June, 1940, to make recommendations regarding reorganization of the Association. Includes preliminary and final reports, and material on functions of standing committees and duties of national staff members.	533-535
AAMSW: Reprints Committee, 1952-1955 The committee was established in 1953 as a subcommittee of both the public relations committee and the publications committee (which later became the editorial committee). Later in 1953 the subcommittee became the reprints committee, whose function was to review literature from periodicals and to arrange for reprinting of articles of interest to Association members.	536
AAMSW: Scholarships Committee, 1924, 1944-1954 Correspondence and reports. The committee, which apparently was reactivated after 1944 following a series of scholarship grants from the National Foundation for Infantile Paralysis, had responsibility for developing a continuous scholarship program.	537
AAMSW: Standards (Minimum) Committee, 1925-1942 Correspondence, minutes, and reports re standards to be met by hospital social service departments.	538-540
AAMSW: Statistics Committee, 1929-1940 Correspondence, minutes, and reports re statistical reporting of services to patients by social service departments.	541-543
AAMSW: Tellers Committee, 1942-1955 Reports of votes cast for the election of Association officers.	544
AAMSW: Volunteers Committee, 1938-1944 Material re the use of volunteers in medical social work.	545-546
AAMSW: Wartime and Reconstruction Services Committee, 1940-1945 Correspondence, minutes, reports, and memoranda. Includes a letter (February 14, 1942) describing conditions in Hawaii after the bombing of Pearl Harbor.	547-550

Folder Title and Description of Contents	Folder

AAMSW: Wartime and Reconstruction Services Committee: 551-552
Emergency Medical Services, 1941-1944
    Material re efforts of the Association to involve
    its districts and regions in the Office of Civilian
    Defense's emergency medical services programs.

AAMSW: Wartime and Reconstruction Services Committee: 553
Industry, 1943-1944
    Material reflects the concern with problems of the
    relation of medical social work and war industry.

AAMSW: Wartime and Reconstruction Services Committee: 554
Japanese Resettlement, 1942-1944
    Material re medical social work participation in
    resettlement and in programs for Japanese in re-
    location centers.

AAMSW: Wartime and Reconstruction Services Committee: 555
Rehabilitation Project, 1942-1944
    Material re concern for new emergency rehabilitation
    needs, new groups of people seeking services, and
    the importance of rehabilitation of those not normally
    "usable" during wartime.

AAMSW: Wartime and Reconstruction Services Committee: 556
Selective Service, 1941-1943
    Material re medical needs of rejected draftees.

AAMSW: Wartime and Reconstruction Services Committee: 557
Venereal Disease, 1942-1945
    Material re medical social work in venereal disease
    programs, clinics, and treatment centers.

AAMSW: Wartime and Reconstruction Services Committee: 558
Volunteers, 1942-1943
    Correspondence re collection of material on
    volunteers.

AAMSW: Wartime and Reconstruction Services Committee,   559
Relations with Voluntary Associations, 1940-1945
    Correspondence, minutes, and reports dealing
    generally with the involvement of these associa-
    tions in various defense or war-related programs:
    American Association of Schools of Social Work,
    American Association of Social Workers, American
    National Red Cross, CIO's White Collar Conference,
    National Council on Rehabilitation, and the
    National Roster of Scientific and Specialized
    Personnel.

Folder Title and Description of Contents	Folder
AAMSW: Wartime and Reconstruction Services Committee, Relations with U.S. Governmental Agencies, 1941-1942 Correspondence, minutes, and reports dealing generally with Association involvement in and services to the following agencies: Office for Emergency Management, War Manpower Commission; Office of Civilian Defense; Office of Defense, Health and Welfare Services, Family Security Committee and its subcommittee on personnel; Office of Defense, Health and Welfare Services, Social Protection Division; Office of Education; Office of Foreign Relief and Rehabilitation Operations; Office of War Information; U.S. Public Health Service.	560-562
AAMSW: Wartime and Reconstruction Services Committee: United Nations Relief and Rehabilitation Administration (UNRRA), 1943-1944 Role of medical social workers in UNRRA.	563
AAMSW: Ways and Means Committee, 1918-1941 Material on Association budgets and financing. The committee had responsibility for seeking contributions from Association districts and individual members.	564-565
AAMSW: Advisory Committee on the History of the Association, 1950-1955 The committee was appointed in 1949 to assist Mary Stites in writing her history of medical social work.	566
AAMSW: Advisory Committee on Rehabilitation Project, 1943-1948 The advisory committee, formerly a subcommittee of the medical social practice committee, advised Caroline H. Elledge in her study, Rehabilitation and the Patient.	567
AAMSW: Advisory Committee on U.S. Children's Bureau's Maternal and Child Welfare Services, 1942-1946 Material re child welfare services under the Social Security Act.	568
AAMSW: Advisory Committee to the American National Red Cross Hospital, 1943-1946 Material on the need for hospital social workers overseas.	569
AAMSW: Advisory Committee to the Association President, 1942-1943 Minutes and memoranda.	570

NATIONAL ASSOCIATION OF SOCIAL WORKERS, INC.

Folder Title and Description of Contents	Folder
AAMSW: Advisory Committee to U.S. Public Health Service Hospital Division, 1920, 1949 　　The Association committee advised the Public Health Service in 1920 to establish a social service section in its Hospital Division.	571
AAMSW: Advisory Committee to U.S. Public Health Service Tuberculosis Control Division, 1945-1949 　　Correspondence and reports re medical social work in tuberculosis control programs.	572
AAMSW: Joint Committee with American Association of Psychiatric Social Workers, 1930-1935 　　Correspondence and reports reflecting concerns for differences between medical and psychiatric social work and the work of psychiatric social workers in hospital settings.	573
AAMSW: Joint Committee with American Dietetic Association, 1923-1934 　　Correspondence and reports. Material re use of diet as therapy.	574
AAMSW: Joint Committee with American Hospital Association, 1952-1955 　　Correspondence, minutes, and reports. The committee, which was established to promote understanding and cooperation between the two associations, surveyed hospital social service departments to provide information on relationships within the hospital.	575-577
AAMSW: Joint Committee with American Hospital Association, 1954 "Study of Social Work in Hospital Facilities," 1954-1955 　　Correspondence with hospital social service departments participating in the committee study.	578-579
AAMSW: Joint Committee with the American Public Health Association, 1932-1936 　　Material re function of medical social workers in public health organizations.	580
AAMSW: Joint Committee with the American Society for Control of Cancer, 1932-1934 　　Correspondence and handbook for medical social workers in cancer clinics.	581
AAMSW: Joint Committee with the National Organization for Public Health Nursing, 1941-1943 　　Correspondence and reports reflecting concern with the function of medical social workers and the relations of public health nurses to medical social workers.	582

Folder Title and Description of Contents	Folder

AAMSW: Special Committee on Association Policy Relating to Legislation, 1949-1950 — 583
Reports. The committee recommended that the Association ask its members to respond to proposed legislation as individuals rather than have it take a position as an association.

AAMSW: Special Committee on Association Program, 1945-1946 — 584
The committee's study recommended that the administrative committee take greater responsibility for planning the Association program.

AAMSW: Special Committee on Medical Care, 1943-1946 — 585
The committee prepared a "Statement of Principles Relating to Medical Social Aspects of a National Health Program."

AAMSW: Special Committee on Organization of Districts and Regions, 1944-1946 — 586
Material on criteria for organizing Association districts.

AAMSW: Special Committee on Publications and Public Relations, 1949 — 587
The committee was established to clarify policies of communication between districts and national office and to examine the need for more effective publications.

AAMSW: Special Committee on Responsibilities of Association Officers and Staff, 1953 — 588
The committee prepared a series of statements of responsibilities of the executive director, president, first vice-president, business manager, and consultants on education and practice.

AAMSW: Special Committee to Consider Creation of the Office of President-Elect, 1951 — 589
Report. The committee voted against substituting the office of president-elect for that of first vice-president.

AAMSW: Special Committee to Recommend an Executive Director and Practice Consultant, 1952-1954 — 590
Correspondence and report.

AAMSW: Special Committee to Review Association Statement on Medical Care, 1952 — 591
The committee considered whether or not the Association should issue a new statement on national health planning to replace the 1948 statement.

Folder Title and Description of Conents	Folder

AAMSW: Special Committee to Secure an Executive Secretary, 1947
    Reports.
Folder: 592

AAMSW: Special Committee to Study Relationships of Executive Committee to Membership, 1934-1935
    Reports and memorandum.
Folder: 593

AAMSW: Psychiatric Section, 1922-1927 (1944)
    Correspondence, minutes, and reports of the Section, which was established within the Association in 1922 and separated from it in 1926 to become the American Association of Psychiatric Social Workers. Includes a 1944 letter from an Australian social worker re the relation of psychiatric and medical social workers.
Folder: 594

AAMSW: Education Consultant, 1927-1956
    Correspondence, reports, and papers of Kate McMahon, consultant from 1927-1956. Material on the shortage of trained workers, the impact of the Depression, and the quality of medical social work education.
Folder: 595-596

AAMSW: Practice Consultant, 1951-1955
    Correspondence, reports, and papers of Addie Thomas, who was appointed consultant in 1953.
Folder: 597-598

AAMSW: Practice Consultant, Consultation Reports, 1953-1955
    Formal reports of consultation visits to hospitals, medical schools, and Association districts and regions.
Folder: 599

AAMSW: Practice Consultant Visit, Orthopaedic Hospital, Los Angeles, California, 1955
    Material re social service departments.
Folder: 600

AAMSW: Practice Consultant Visit, National Jewish Hospital at Denver, Colorado, 1955
    Material re the physical lay-out of the social service department.
Folder: 601

AAMSW: Practice Consultant Visit, Grace-New Haven Community Hospital, Grace-New Haven, Connecticut, 1954-1955
    Material re the organization and general problems of social service departments.
Folder: 602

NATIONAL ASSOCIATION OF SOCIAL WORKERS, INC.

Folder Title and Description of Contents	Folder
AAMSW: Practice Consultant Visit, Indiana University Medical Center at Indianapolis, 1954-1955 Material re supervision, "recording," and participation in medical education.	603
AAMSW: Practice Consultant Visit, University of Kansas Medical Center at Kansas City, Kansas, 1953-1955 Material re statistics and "recording."	604
AAMSW: Practice Consultant Visit, Veterans Administration Center, Wadsworth, Kansas, 1954 Material re "recording."	605
AAMSW: Practice Consultant Visit, Charity Hospital of Louisiana at New Orleans, 1954 Correspondence re concern for standards of social service departments.	606
AAMSW: Practice Consultant Visit, Council of Social Agencies, New Orleans, Louisiana, 1955.	607
AAMSW: Practice Consultant Visit, Tulane University of Louisiana, Hutchinson Memorial Clinic, New Orleans, Louisiana, 1954-1955.	608
AAMSW: Practice Consultant Visit, Touro Infirmary, New Orleans, Louisiana, 1954.	609
AAMSW: Practice Consultant Visit, Confederate Memorial Medical Center, Shreveport, Louisiana, 1954 Correspondence chiefly re arrangements for visit.	610
AAMSW: Practice Consultant Visit, University of Michigan, University Hospital, Ann Arbor, Michigan, 1955.	611
AAMSW: Practice Consultant Visit, United Community Services of Metropolitan Detroit, Michigan, 1954-1955 Community Services sought to develop a concept of normal practice in a social service department.	612
AAMSW: Practice Consultant Visit, Alfred Benjamin Clinic, Kansas City, Missouri, 1954.	613
AAMSW: Practice Consultant Visit, Kansas City General Hospitals nos. 1 and 2, Kansas City, Missouri, 1954 Material re social service departments in these hospitals, which were designated for Negro patients.	614
AAMSW: Practice Consultant Visit, Children's Hospital, Buffalo, New York, 1954-1955.	615

Folder Title and Description of Contents	Folder
AAMSW: Practice Consultant Visit, Roswell Park Memorial Institute, Buffalo, New York, 1954-1955 The Institute was the cancer research center for the New York State Health Department.	616
AAMSW: Practice Consultant Visit, Syracuse Memorial Hospital, Syracuse, New York, 1954.	617
AAMSW: Practice Consultant Visit, Hospital of the Good Shepherd (Syracuse University Hospital) and Syracuse Dispensary, Syracuse, New York, 1953-1955.	618
AAMSW: Practice Consultant Visit, Albert Einstein Medical Center, Philadelphia, Pennsylvania, 1954.	619
AAMSW: Practice Consultant Visit, Jefferson Hospital, Philadelphia, Pennsylvania, 1954-1955.	620
AAMSW: Practice Consultant Visit, Greenville General Hospital, Greenville, South Carolina, 1953-1955.	621
AAMSW: Practice Consultant Visit, Salt Lake County General Hospital, Salt Lake City, Utah, 1953-1955 The hospital was, in effect, removed from the list of accredited hospitals by the Joint Commission on Accreditation of Hospitals. Material re the controversy about alleged political control of the hospital.	622
AAMSW: Practice Consultant Visit, Children's Memorial Hospital, Montreal, Quebec, 1951-1954 Material re fee-charging in social service departments.	623
AAMSW: Practice Consultant Visit, Jewish General Hospital, Montreal, Quebec, 1953-1955 Routine correspondence re proposed trip.	624
AAMSW: Practice Consultant Visit, Montreal General Hospital, Montreal, Quebec, 1954-1955 Material re fee-charging, "recording," working with groups of glaucoma patients, and social service departments.	625
AAMSW: Practice Consultant Visit, Montreal Neurological Institute, Montreal, Quebec, 1955.	626
AAMSW: Practice Consultant Visit, Royal Victoria Hospital, Montreal, Quebec, 1952-1955 Correspondence and "Social Service Department Anthology," a collection of articles re activities of a social service department in a general hospital.	627-628

Folder Title and Description of Contents	Folder
AAMSW: Practice Consultant, Meetings with Association Districts, Sections, and Regions, 1953-1955 Correspondence re visits to Region II and to the Gulf and Eastern Canada districts.	629
AAMSW: Practice Consultant, New England Consultation Trip, 1953-1954 Correspondence re planning of the orientation trip.	630
AAMSW: Practice Consultant, Southern Consultation Trip, 1953 Correspondence and reports of visits to Louisville, Kentucky; Oklahoma City, Oklahoma; and Texas.	631
AAMSW: Practice Consultant, Teaching Materials, 1947-1953 Reports of student-supervisor evaluation conferences, case records, medical social work students' self-evaluations, and case conferences of social work teams.	632
AAMSW: Practice Consultant, Chicago University Workshop, 1953 Correspondence and proceedings of the School of Social Service Administration's Summer Workshop on Consultation in which Addie Thomas participated.	633
AAMSW: Practice Consultant, Harvard Institute, 1954 Correspondence and Addie Thomas' shorthand notes on the Institute on Growth and Development of Children, which was sponsored by the Harvard University School of Public Health and the Massachusetts Department of Public Health.	634
AAMSW: Practice Consultant, National Rehabilitation Association's Second Atlantic City Rehabilitation Conference, 1954 Correspondence, lists of topics to be discussed and of participants, and Addie Thomas' shorthand notes.	635
AAMSW: Practice Consultant, North Atlantic District Workshop on Recording, 1955 Addie Thomas led the workshop. Correspondence, minutes, and resource materials.	636-637
AAMSW: Practice Consultant, Pennsylvania College for Women Training Course for Leaders of Medical Social Institutes, 1955 Correspondence, outlines of program, preliminary materials, study materials, and speeches given at	638-641

Folder Title and Description of Contents	Folder

the Institute, which was titled "Social Work Practice in Medical Care and Rehabilitation Settings: Goals, Principles, Techniques and Problems in the Comprehensive Study, Treatment and Restoration of Ill and Disabled Individuals: A Training Course for Leaders of Regional Medical Social Work Institutes."

AAMSW: Recruitment Consultant, 1953-1955   642-643
    Correspondence and reports. The Association recruitment program was supported by a National Foundation for Infantile Paralysis grant.

AAMSW: Association District Constitutions, 1917-1953   644-645
    Correspondence and copies of district constitutions and bylaws. Each district drew up its own constitution.

AAMSW: Council of Districts and Regions, 1940-1955   646
    Minutes and reports of the council, which was composed of district chairmen.

AAMSW: Memoranda to all Districts and Regions, 1936-1956   647
    Material re Association financing, medical social work personnel, social legislation, membership, procedure for terminating Association business in 1955, and recruiting.

AAMSW: Middle Atlantic District, 1918-1956   648-649
    Correspondence, minutes, reports, and financial and membership data.

AAMSW: Missouri-Kansas District, 1920-1956   650
    Correspondence and reports.

AAMSW: Illinois District, 1921-1956   651-652
    Correspondence and reports. Material re training of medical social workers, volunteers, and recruitment. In 1938 the district urged consideration of a merger with the American Association of Social Workers.

AAMSW: New England District, 1918-1956   653-654
    Correspondence, minutes, and reports. Includes material on the effect of World War II, recruitment, and consideration of a merger of district medical social workers with the local chapter of the American Association of Social Workers.

Folder Title and Description of Contents	Folder
AAMSW: North Atlantic District, 1923-1956 Correspondence and reports. Material on membership problems and recruitment.	655-657
AAMSW: Minnesota District, 1921-1956 Correspondence and reports.	658
AAMSW: Indiana District, 1920-1932 Correspondence and reports. The district was dissolved about 1932.	659
AAMSW: Michigan District, 1925-1956 Correspondence and reports.	660
AAMSW: Eastern Canada District, 1923-1956 Correspondence and reports. Historical material and material on recruitment.	661-662
AAMSW: Eastern Central District, 1920-1956 Correspondence and reports. Material on hospital social service in Cleveland (Ohio), civil defense and medical social work, and the Depression.	663-664
AAMSW: Potomac District, 1926-1956 Correspondence and reports. Material on the history of the district and World War II.	665
AAMSW: California District, 1930-1934 Correspondence and reports. The district petitioned the Association in 1934 to be permitted to dissolve and form two California districts.	666
AAMSW: Northern California District, 1935-1956 Correspondence and reports. Includes material regarding cooperation with the American Association of Social Workers, standards for patient eligibility for county medical care in California, and personnel standards.	667
AAMSW: Southern California District, 1934-1956 Correspondence and reports. Includes material on cooperation with the local American Association of Social Workers.	668
AAMSW: Gulf District, 1933-1956 Correspondence and reports. Includes material on community health, recruitment, and the development of the district.	669
AAMSW: Pacific Northwest District, 1944-1956 Correspondence and reports.	670

Folder Title and Description of Contents	Folder
AAMSW: Wisconsin District, 1941-1956 Correspondence and reports. The material reflects the problems and procedures of formation of a district.	671
AAMSW: Colorado District, 1949-1956 Correspondence and reports. Material re the formation of a district.	672
AAMSW: Western Pennsylvania District, 1952-1956 Correspondence and reports.	673
AAMSW: Region I, 1932-1953 The region comprised the Hawaiian Islands. Correspondence and reports reflecting problems of organizing and maintaining a functioning region.	674
AAMSW: Region II, 1945-1955 The region included all or parts of Arkansas, Oklahoma, Texas, and New Mexico. Correspondence.	675
AAMSW: Region III, 1941-1956 The region included all or parts of Indiana, Kentucky, Tennessee, and West Virginia. Correspondence and reports.	676
AAMSW: Region IV, 1941-1956 The region included all or parts of Iowa, Nebraska, and North and South Dakota. Correspondence and reports.	677
AAMSW: Region V, 1944-1956 The region included all or parts of Virginia, Georgia, Florida, and North and South Carolina. Correspondence and reports.	678
AAMSW: Finance: General, 1948-1955 Correspondence re Association financial matters.	679
AAMSW: Finance: Audit Reports, 1919-1953.	680-681
AAMSW: Finance: Reports to the Commonwealth of Massachusetts, 1927-1955 Brief financial statements submitted annually to the state of Massachusetts.	682
AAMSW: Finance: Taxes, 1933-1956 Tax forms and correspondence re tax-exempt status of the Association and its status in regard to social security, old age insurance, and Washington, D.C., unemployment compensation.	683-686

NATIONAL ASSOCIATION OF SOCIAL WORKERS, INC.

Folder Title and Description of Contents	Folder
AAMSW: Finance: Group Insurance, 1953-1956 Correspondence re group sickness and accident plans.	687
AAMSW: Finance: Appeals to Foundations, 1922-1955 Correspondence, reports, and applications which frequently include discussion of the Association's program and financial needs. Early financial support came principally from the Russell Sage Foundation.	688-690
AAMSW: National Association of Social Workers, Medical Social Work Section Organization, 1955 Material re hiring of secretaries for the section, referral of membership applications to NASW, and memoranda re section organization.	691
AAMSW: Civil Defense, 1950-1955 Correspondence and reports re the role of medical social workers in civil defense.	692
AAMSW: Education: American Hospital Association, 1919-1922 Report of the AHA survey committee and discussion of it by medical social workers; copy of the "Report of the Committee on the Training of Hospital Social Workers of the American Hospital Association," 1922.	693
AAMSW: Education: Certification, 1937-1955 Material re approval of medical social work curricula in schools of social work. The accreditation function was transferred in 1950 to the American Association of Schools of Social Work. Includes lists of schools of social work with approved medical social work curricula.	694
AAMSW: Education: School Registration Reports, 1950-1955 Correspondence and forms. Material re enrollment of medical social work students in schools of social work.	695-696
AAMSW: Historical Material, 1930-1938 Includes chart showing the distribution of social service departments in the U.S. and miscellaneous historical statements.	697
AAMSW: Legal Opinions, 1949-1956 The Association sought legal opinions on the confidentiality of social worker-client relationships, membership dues, procedures for mailing of ballots, and liquidation of the Association.	698

NATIONAL ASSOCIATION OF SOCIAL WORKERS, INC.   310

Folder Title and Description of Contents	Folder
AAMSW: Legislation, 1944-1954 Correspondence re congressional and state hearings and legislation of interest to the Association. Includes material on hearings on the 1946 National Health Bill.	699
AAMSW: Members, 1954-1956 Correspondence sent to associate members informing them of dissolution of the Association; to emeritus members elected at the June, 1955 meeting; and to honorary members elected at the June, 1955 meeting.	700
AAMSW: Members: Honors and Obituaries, 1934-1955 Obituaries of Association members or material on honors awarded them. Includes material on Edna G. Henry, Ruth Lewis, Mary E. Wadley, Elizabeth E. Payne, Agnes H. Schroeder, Edith M. Baker, Ida M. Cannon, and Garnet I. Pelton.	701
AAMSW: Members: Dora Goldstine Memorial Lecture, 1955 After Miss Goldstine's death, a fund was set up to commemorate her work through a series of University of Chicago lectures. Correspondence re contributions.	702
AAMSW: Personnel: Job Descriptions, 1941-1953 Job descriptions for the following positions: executive director; president; first vice-president; business manager; consultants on education, practice, and recruitment; and secretary to the recruitment consultant. Includes forms for clerical positions.	703
AAMSW: Personnel: Personnel Practices Policy Book, 1939-1949 Association policies regarding personnel, business practice, and travel.	704
AAMSW: Policy re Association Special Representatives at Non-Association Meetings, 1947-1953 Correspondence and statement of policy. Includes report of the Association representative to the 1949 American Association of Social Workers' delegate conference.	705
AAMSW: Program, 1921-1955 Includes statements of the function, objectives, and program of the Association; material on the relation of AAMSW to other associations; and a "Summary of Program of the American Association of Medical Social Workers, 1952-1954, and Projected Program to October, 1955."	706

Folder Title and Description of Contents	Folder
AAMSW: Salary Studies, 1922-1945 Correspondence and reports of salary studies of medical and other social workers.	707
AAMSW: Social Service: Cerebral Palsy, 1947-1953 Correspondence and reports. Material on Association participation in revision of <u>The Cerebral Palsied Child and His Care in the Home</u>, a book published by the Association for Aid to Crippled Children.	708
AAMSW: Social Service: Fee-charging, 1951-1955 Chiefly inquiries addressed to the Association re policy of hospital social service departments charging fees.	709
AAMSW: Social Service: Ratios, 1946, 1954 Correspondence and report, "A Method of Determining the Number of Medical Social Workers Needed for Case Work in a General Hospital."	710
AAMSW: Social Service: Statistical Recording, 1942-1950 Material on case loads and reporting of statistics.	711
AAMSW: Social Service: Surveys of Social Service Departments, 1928-1931 In 1928 the Association sought the advice of nine organizations re the advisibility of making surveys of social service departments to determine how to improve standards, conditions, etc.	712
AAMSW: Social Service: "Techniques of Hospital Social Service," 1925 Report of an unidentified committee.	713
AAMSW: American Association for Organizing Family Social Work, 1922 Minutes of an informal committee meeting on the relationship of national organizations interested in social casework. Ida M. Cannon represented the Association.	714
AAMSW: American Association of Psychiatric Social Workers, 1952-1955 Correspondence, minutes, and reports.	715

NATIONAL ASSOCIATION OF SOCIAL WORKERS, INC.

Folder Title and Description of Contents	Folder
AAMSW: American Association of Schools of Social Work, Advisory Committee on Study of Training Needs in Public Social Service, 1938 The committee was composed of members of national agencies, including AAMSW, and functioned under the auspices of AASSW.	716
AAMSW: American Association of Social Workers, Social Policy Committee, 1954 Minutes of a meeting of "concerned" professional social work organizations with AASSW's committee to discuss implications of federal legislation affecting civil service classification.	717
AAMSW: American College of Surgeons, 1946-1949 Material re revision of manual used by ACS to rate hospitals. The Association revised the section on social service departments.	718
AAMSW: American Heart Association, Council for Rheumatic Fever, 1952-1955 Correspondence re Association representation on the Council.	719
AAMSW: American Hospital Association, 1943-1952 Correspondence re relations between the two associations. Includes material about a study of hospital care of chronic alcoholics conducted by AHA in 1943.	720
AAMSW: American Public Health Association, 1947-1955 Correspondence and reports. Includes material on the function of medical social workers in public health and public medical care programs.	721
AAMSW: California Association of Collectors, 1955 Correspondence re the California Association's offer of money for medical social work scholarships. AAMSW was concerned about the implications of accepting money from this collecting agency.	722
AAMSW: Commission on Hospital Care, 1945 The Commission was a private "public service committee" studying hospital service in the U.S. Includes report of the Association president to the executive committee re the work of the Commission.	723
AAMSW: Committee on the Cost of Medical Care, 1932 Report on the development and status of medical social work prepared for the committee by AAMSW.	724

Folder Title and Description of Contents	Folder

AAMSW: Council on Social Work Education, 1946-1955   725-726
   Correspondence, minutes, and reports. Material
   on the Ernest Hollis-Alice Taylor study of
   social work education (the Hollis-Taylor Study);
   the formation of CSWE from the National Council
   on Social Work Education and the American Association of Schools of Social Work; and accreditation
   of schools of social work.

AAMSW: Joint Commission on Accreditation of Hospitals,   727
1953?-1956
   Material issued by the Commission, which based
   its accreditation on hospital structure, organization, and facilities.

AAMSW: National Committee on Personnel in the Social   728-729
Services, 1942-1947
   Correspondence, minutes, and reports. Formerly
   the Wartime Committee on Personnel. The committee,
   which was affiliated with the American Association
   of Social Workers, began as an inter-association
   committee to increase the supply of trained social
   work personnel. Includes material on recruitment
   and training.

AAMSW: National Committee on Social Work in Defense   730
Mobilization, 1950-1955
   This inter-association committee, of which AAMSW
   was a member, represented the social work profession to the national defense program. Correspondence and reports.

AAMSW: National Council on Rehabilitation, 1945-1949   731
   Correspondence and reports re rehabilitation of
   the handicapped. AAMSW withdrew from representation
   on the Council in 1949.

AAMSW: National Foundation for Infantile Paralysis,   732
Educational Grants to AAMSW, 1951-1956
   Correspondence, applications, and reports. The
   grants, which were intended to "support the
   educational program" of the Association, were
   used to provide consultation services to schools
   of social work and medicine and services to the
   field of practice in medical social work.

AAMSW: National Foundation for Infantile Paralysis,   733
File Reorganization Grant, 1948-1950
   NFIP granted $3,000 to the Association to reor-
   ganize its office files.

AAMSW: National Foundation for Infantile Paralysis,   734-735
Scholarship Grants, 1941-1955
   Correspondence and material re grants.

NATIONAL ASSOCIATION OF SOCIAL WORKERS, INC.

Folder Title and Description of Contents	Folder
AAMSW: National Foundation for Infantile Paralysis, Advisory Committee on Medical Social Scholarships, 1949-1952 Brief routine correspondence.	736
AAMSW: National Health Council, 1951-1955 Correspondence re Association participation in NHC, especially in a Health Careers Project.	737
AAMSW: National Rehabilitation Association, 1955 Report of an NRA conference by an Association representative.	738
AAMSW: National Social Welfare Assembly, 1948-1955 Correspondence and reports re the function and program of NSWA.	739
AAMSW: National Social Welfare Assembly, Conference on Individualized Services, 1940-1946 The Conference was established in 1940 as the Social Case Work Council of National Agencies to consider problems and opportunities of national agencies in regard to industries, refugee travel, alien registration, and military concentration. Includes material on Japanese resettlement during World War II.	740-741
AAMSW: Social Work Research Group, 1955 Requests for information on research studies related to casework practice.	742
AAMSW: Social Work Vocational Bureau, 1947-1948 Material re the Bureau's review of its function of counselling and placement.	743
AAMSW: U.S. Army, 1950-1954 Correspondence and reports. When the American National Red Cross transferred its casework program to the Army, the Association provided consultants to assist in incorporating these services into the Army program.	744
AAMSW: U.S. National Institute of Neurological Diseases and Blindness, Traineeships in Rehabilitation, 1952-1953 Correspondence about these traineeships established for medical social workers by the National Institute.	745
AAMSW: U.S. President's Commission on the Nation's Health, 1951-1952 The Association provided information on medical social work for the Commission.	746

NATIONAL ASSOCIATION OF SOCIAL WORKERS, INC.

Folder Title and Description of Contents | Folder

AAMSW: U.S. Public Health Service - National Foundation for Infantile Paralysis Personnel Shortages Study, 1952-1953   747
    Correspondence, reports, and memoranda re the personnel situation in social work. Includes a preliminary draft of the Public Health Service Health Manpower Source Book.

AAMSW: U.S. Office of Vocational Rehabilitation, 1943-1955   748
    Correspondence re the Association's efforts to cooperate with OVR, which expanded its programs following the Vocational Rehabilitation Act Amendments of 1943. Includes material re the availability of rehabilitation training grants under the Vocational Rehabilitation Act of 1954.

AAMSW: Institutes and Conferences, 1931-1955   749
    Reports of institutes and conferences re development of social work in medical institutions, administration of hospitals, community health needs, community organization, etc.

AAMSW: University of Chicago School of Social Service Administration, Collaboration Workshop, 1953-1954   750
    Proceedings of the workshop on social workers' collaboration in multi-discipline programs.

AAMSW: Medical Social Work, 1955-1956   751
    Correspondence re termination of publication after 1955.

AAMSW: Exhibits, Photographs, and Films, 1918-1955   752
    Scattered correspondence, clippings, and exhibit material. Includes photographs of Edna G. Henry, Mary L. Hemmy, Opal Gooden, Agnes H. Schroeder, and participants in the 1931 annual meeting of the Association.

AAMSW: Studies, Correspondence and Papers, 1933-1955   753-755
    Correspondence, requests for information, and other material re studies conducted by individuals and organizations. Includes material on clinic admissions; study of dues, income, and expenses of various national associations; private nursing homes in Monroe County, New York; Association membership; rehabilitation of the handicapped worker over 40; and establishing social service departments in Saskatchewan.

Folder Title and Description of Contents	Folder
NASSW: Constitutions of NAVT and AAVT, 1922-1932	756

NASSW: Constitutions of NAVT and AAVT, 1922-1932 — 756
Shows various constitutional changes throughout these years.

NASSW: Annual Business Meetings, Minutes, 1926-1931 — 757
This folder contains agendas and reports of standing committees re keeping records, financing the Bulletin, voting by mail, and the National Committee on Visiting Teachers.

NASSW: Annual Business Meetings, Minutes, 1932-1935 — 758
Committee reports and some speeches re the effects of the Depression, keeping records, publicizing the Association, and standards in the field and the Association.

NASSW: Executive Committee, Minutes, 1928-1931 — 759
Membership standards and classification, publicity for the Association, financing the Association, and proposed employment of an executive secretary. The papers are scattered.

NASSW: Correspondence and Papers, 1928-1934 — 760
Membership requirements and classification, committee personnel, correspondence with the National Education Association re formation of a department of school attendance in NEA, active members in the Association, and procedures in keeping records.

NASSW: National Committee on Visiting Teachers, Minutes of Annual Conference, 1926 — 761
Discussions and papers were presented re the visiting teacher's relations with parents and school officials, clerical service for the Association, teacher training courses, keeping records, attendance officers, status of the visiting teacher, cooperation with state and national agencies, casework, psychiatric clinics, advisory services, and supervision of visiting teachers.

AAPSW: Annual Reports of the Secretary, 1924-1942 — 762
A summary of the year's work read at the annual business meeting. Arranged chronologically. Not all reports are available.

AAPSW: Annual Business Meetings, Minutes, 1928-1951 — 763
Arranged chronologically. The minutes for some years are missing.

NATIONAL ASSOCIATION OF SOCIAL WORKERS, INC.

Folder Title and Description of Contents | Folder

AAPSW: Annual Presidential Addresses, 1927-1942   764
Summaries of each year's work in the Association, which usually reflect trends. These addresses were given at the annual business meeting. Not all the speeches for these years are available.

AAPSW: Section on Psychiatric Social Work of AAHSW,   765
1921-1926
Correspondence and papers re the separation of the Section from the AAHSW and the formation of AAPSW. These papers are possibly part of a manual on AAPSW early history which was passed down to the various chairmen of the bylaws committee. Maida Solomon and Katharine Moore Wickman are prominent in the folder.

AAPSW: Executive Committee, Minutes, 1926-1943,   (766-772)
1948-1952
The executive committee, comprised of the president, vice-president, secretary, treasurer, and from four to six elected members, met formally about once a month from September to the annual meeting usually held in May or June. The main body of the minutes contains reports from the various committees such as nominating, publications, standards, bylaws, membership, ways and means, child guidance, professional education, conference, and mental hospitals.

Committee personnel through 1940-1941 is found in Executive Committee Correspondence and Papers, 1941.

The file of minutes is not complete.

AAPSW: Executive Committee, Minutes, 1926-1929   766
Setting up the new Association, members delinquent in paying dues, standards, Veterans Bureau social work, membership requirements and classifications, local groups, quorum, the relationship of psychiatric social workers to public and private agencies, National Committee on Mental Hygiene, Milford Conference, recruiting, and International Congress of Mental Hygiene.

AAPSW: Executive Committee, Minutes, 1930-1933   767
Committee reports, Trend Study, standards, bylaws, membership requirements and classification, International Congress on Mental Hygiene, recruitment, National Organization of Public Health Nurses, American Orthopsychiatric Association, educational standards, local groups, effect of the Depression on standards and salaries, and American Psychiatric Association. Prominent people include Maida Solomon, Mildred Scoville, Christine Robb Thompson, and Lois Meredith French.

Folder Title and Description of Contents	Folder
AAPSW: Executive Committee, Minutes, 1935-1938 Ways and means committee, local groups, Trend Study, membership classification and requirements, considered merger with AASW, evaluation of committee structure, bylaws, social security, American Psychiatric Association, educational standards, Joint Vocational Service, and specific grievances on personnel standards and practices.	768
AAPSW: Executive Committee, Minutes, 1939-1941 Membership classifications, mental hospitals, Joint Vocational Service, civil service standards, relations with American Psychiatric Association, American Orthopsychiatric Association, Trend Study, membership classification, district branches, effects of World War II, and the government and psychiatric social work. Important correspondents include Katharine Wickman, Leona Hambrecht, and Elizabeth de Schweinitz.	769
AAPSW: Executive Committee, Minutes, 1942-1943 Defense committee, Red Cross, local groups, membership committee, dues, civil service, effect of World War II, Veterans Administration, "encompassable jobs," social work vocational bureau, recruiting, Inter-professional Advisory Committee (AAPSW, AASSW, AAMSW, AASGW), war service office, development of a constitution, and financing the News-Letter.	770
AAPSW: Executive Committee, Minutes, 1948-1950 Personnel survey, National Council on Social Work Education, military psychiatric social work, district branches, Veterans Administration, membership qualifications, professional education, research project, Study of Training and Practice in Psychiatric Social Work, Dartmouth Conference on Education for Psychiatric Social Work, and merger of professional social work organizations. Noteworthy correspondents include Ethel Ginsburg, Margaret Hagan, George Levinrew, Madeleine Lay, Ethel Bellsmith, and Tessie Berkman.	771
AAPSW: Executive Committee, Minutes, 1951-1952 Professional education, membership requirements and classification, TIAC, bylaws, National Council on Social Work Education, teaching social work in medical schools, research project on work experience of membership and curriculum study.	772

NATIONAL ASSOCIATION OF SOCIAL WORKERS, INC.

Folder Title and Description of Contents	Folder
AAPSW: Executive Committee, Correspondence and Papers, 1927-1937 Membership requirements, AAPSW executive procedures, local groups, Trend Study, American Psychiatric Association, training, standards, bylaws, suggested affiliation with AASW, standards in national organizations, and attempts to define "approved social work agencies." Names prominent in the folder are Maida Solomon, Christine Robb Thompson, Mildred Scoville, and Elizabeth Brockett Bech.	773
AAPSW: Executive Committee, Correspondence and Papers, 1938-1939 Memoranda on the Trend Study, membership qualifications, administrative procedures, and compilations of committee personnel. Katharine Moore Wickman, Christine Robb Thompson, and Maida Solomon are prominent.	774
AAPSW: Executive Committee, Correspondence and Papers, 1940-1941 Membership standards and procedures, quorum, educational requirements, district branches, military psychiatric social work, effect of World Warr II, cooperation between psychiatry and psychiatric social work, statements of "encompassable jobs," and lists of committee personnel to 1941. Leona Hambrecht and Irene Grant are prominent in the folder.	775
AAPSW: Executive Committee, Correspondence and Papers, 1942-1943 "Encompassable jobs," child guidance study committee, effects of World War II, development of a constitution, facilities for training psychiatric social workers, refresher courses, financing the war office of psychiatric social work through a grant from the Rockefeller Foundation, civil service, and Social Work Vocational Bureau.	776
AAPSW: Executive Committee, Correspondence and Papers, 1946-1953 Psychiatric nursing, basic issues in psychiatric social work, payment of dues, membership classifications, and Council on Social Work Education. The papers for these years are scattered.	777
AAPSW: Advisory Committee to the American National Red Cross, 1942-1946 This committee, chaired by Elizabeth Healy Ross, was established in 1942 as a response to the increased need for psychiatric social workers in military and naval hospitals and for the purpose	778

Folder Title and Description of Contents	Folder
of advising the Red Cross on employment practices and personnel policies. Subjects covered include military social work, military classification of social workers, in-service training, scholarship program for psychiatric social workers, job supervision, and generally the effect of World War II on professions.	
AAPSW: Bylaws Committee, 1927-1954 Arranged chronologically. Minutes, papers, and correspondence re membership requirements and standards in AAPSW, membership classification, suspension of members, quorum, and changes in specific bylaws.	(779-784)
AAPSW: Bylaws Committee, 1927-1929 Minutes and correspondence re checking with other national professional organizations for the form and content of their bylaws.	779
AAPSW: Bylaws Committee, 1930-1931 Minutes and correspondence.	780
AAPSW: Bylaws Committee, 1932-1935 Voting by mail, local and regional organization, election of the membership committee, dues, and change in the dates of the fiscal year.	781
AAPSW: Bylaws Committee, 1937-1938 Parliamentary procedure and the Trend Study. Mildred C. Scoville and Katharine Moore Wickman are prominent in the folder.	782
AAPSW: Bylaws Committee, 1939 Minutes and correspondence.	783
AAPSW: Bylaws Committee, 1940-1954 District branches, functions of the bylaws committee, and the development of a constitution. The material is only scattered after 1941.	784
AAPSW: Joint Committee to the War Office of Psychiatric Social Work, 1942-1946 Correspondence, articles, reports, and speeches. Joint committee members include Mrs. Ethel Ginsburg, Dr. Marion Kenworthy, Dr. David Levy, Marion McBee, Madeleine Moore, Mildred Scoville, Dr. Frank Fremont Smith, and Dr. George S. Stevenson.	785

Folder Title and Description of Contents	Folder

AAPSW: Membership Committee, 1928-1953   786
Policies and procedures re processing AAPSW membership applications according to the bylaws and the constitution, which set up standards of membership based on educational background and professional experience. Membership requirements and classification, standards in psychiatric social work, American Association of Schools of Social Work, dues, bylaws, membership statistics, recruiting, and effect of World War II on membership.

AAPSW: Ways and Means Committee, 1926-1943   787
A standing committee chaired by the treasurer of the Association whose duties centered around financing the organization. Included are summaries of meetings, treasurers' reports, and budgets. Changing the fiscal year, the relationship of membership classification to dues, traveling expenses, financing administrative positions, dropping members for non-payment of dues, and Joint Vocational Service.

AAPSW: District Branches Committee, c. 1954   788
A resource book prepared by the committee to explain procedures through which a group of AAPSW members could establish a district branch.

AAPSW: Mental Hospitals Committee, 1934-1942   789
Pamphlets, reports, and statements put out by the committee. "Essentials of Psychiatric Social Service Techniques in Mental Hospitals and Mental Hygiene Clinics Attached to Mental Hospitals," 1934, 1939-1940. Statements regarding practices and standards for social service in mental hospitals, 1939-1940, 1942.

AAPSW: Personnel Survey Committee, 1948-1949   790
The survey was undertaken by the AAPSW and the National Committee for Mental Hygiene to determine the state of the field. Correspondence and papers re setting up the survey and reporting the findings. Prominent individuals include Madeleine Lay, Ethel Ginsburg, and Francis Bech, the chairman of the committee.

AAPSW: Practice Committee, 1953-1955   791
The committee examined psychiatric social workers' jobs in specific settings with the ultimate goal of relating this to an evaluation of training, experience, job responsibilities and the special problems in the field. Subcommittees were established on standards in hospitals, clinics, and private agencies. Minutes, papers, and correspondence.

Folder Title and Description of Contents	Folder
AAPSW: Professional Education Committee, 1931-1943 Minutes and papers re the study of curricula and training programs in various schools offering degrees in social work, standards in the field, recruitment, and relations with other professional associations.	792
AAPSW: Legal Dissolution of the Association, 1957-1958.	793
AAPSW: Association of Psychiatric Social Workers (British Counterpart of AAPSW), 1929-1943 Memorandum, articles of association, and reports.	794
AAGW: Administrative Committee, 1939-1942 Minutes of meetings; statement on the function of the committee, AASGW officers, and the central committee; description of the roles of the Association's committees.	795-796
AAGW: American Association for Health, Physical Education and Recreation, 1946-1948 Primarily correspondence re affiliation of AAGW with AAHPER. Minutes of one AAHPER executive committee meeting.	797
AAGW: American Association of Leisure Time Educators, 1938-1940 Constitution, statement of origins and purpose of AALTE, and report of regional meeting (1938). Correspondence and studies re cooperation of AALTE and AASGW, including a comparison of nature and functions.	798
AAGW: American Association of Schools of Social Work, 1942-1952 Notices of meetings, information and correspondence re shortage of social workers, copies of AASGW bylaws, minutes of the accrediting committee meetings, newsletters to directors of schools, reports of the accrediting committee, reports on students in schools of social work, and statements on various aspects of social work education.	799-800
AAGW: American Association of Social Workers, Committee on Group Work, 1944-1946 Information on AASW's position on group work.	801
AAGW: American National Red Cross, 1943-1947 Statements on Red Cross hospital recreation, especially in military hospitals. Correspondence re a Conference on Training Resources for Hospital Recreation and scholarships for hospital recreation workers.	802

NATIONAL ASSOCIATION OF SOCIAL WORKERS, INC.

Folder Title and Description of Contents	Folder
AAGW: American Recreation Society, 1945-1948 Report of a conference for hospital recreation workers, reports and minutes of joint committee on recreation, and general correspondence re problems of recreation.	803
AAGW: Annual Business Meetings, 1937-1946 Conference transcripts and notes of the sessions.	804
AAGW: Canadian Group Work, 1946-1947 Correspondence re group work in Canada and its affiliation with AAGW.	805
AAGW: Central Committee, 1938-1946 Memoranda on play, recreation, and leisure; minutes and agendas of meetings; and correspondence and committee reports re the professionalization of AAGW.	806
AAGW: Council on Social Work Education, 1946-1955 Bulletins, minutes of meetings, bylaws, notices of meetings, information of the Commission on Accreditation, lists of committees and their members, and correspondence re programs of CSWE and their relationship to AAGW. Prominent individuals include John Kidneigh, Nathan E. Cohen, and Janet W. Korpela.	807-808
AAGW: Editorial Committee, The Group, 1954-1955 Correspondence among contributors, editorial staff, and committee members re publication and review of articles submitted for publication. Information re relationship of The Group to the new NASW journal, Social Work. Prominent correspondents are Frank Fierman, Harleigh Trecker, and Janet W. Korpela.	809
AAGW: Evaluation of Local Study Groups, 1940-1942 Study, questionnaire, and report of the committee.	810
AAGW: Executive Committee, Minutes, 1948-1949 This committee is a continuation of the old central committee (folder 806).	811
AAGW: Executive Committee, Terminal Activities, 1955 Correspondence, minutes, and reports re termination of AAGW and creation of NASW group work section. Summary reports (August, 1955) of the activities of all AAGW committees since their inception. General summary of AAGW work, 1946-1955. Prominent correspondents are Janet W. Korpela, Howard Gibbs, Margaret Mudgett, Joseph P. Anderson, and Harleigh Trecker.	812

NATIONAL ASSOCIATION OF SOCIAL WORKERS, INC.

Folder Title and Description of Contents	Folder
AAGW: Final Chapter Reports, 1955 Summary of AAGW activities before merger with NASW.	813
AAGW: Formation of NASGW, 1936-1944 Minutes of organizational conferences, descriptive brochures, list of nominees for coordinating committees, bylaws, and membership requirements and information.	814
AAGW: Governmental Relationships Committee, 1944-1945 List of members and correspondence re nature and functions of the committee, which was to represent the needs of AAGW to various federal agencies.	815
AAGW: The Group, 1938-1955 Correspondence re the organization and editorship of this official AAGW publication and minutes of the editorial committee and the publications committee meetings. An incomplete run of the publication, 1945-1955, is filed in the Center's ephemera collection.	816
AAGW: Group Work, 1939 Three papers on the correlation of group work and casework services.	817
AAGW: Group Work in Medical and Psychiatric Settings, Committee on, 1948-1955 Correspondence, reports, and minutes of the committee, which sought to define precisely the role of group workers and group therapy in relation to group psychiatric therapy. Prominent correspondents include Gisela Konopka, Saul Bernstein, Etta Saloshin, John McDowell, Grace Weyker, and Janet W. Korpela. Materials re education for group work in these settings.	818-819
AAGW: Group Work in Medical and Psychiatric Settings, Institute on, 1953-1956 Correspondence among Gisela Konopka, Janet W. Korpela, Raymond Fisher, and others, and the Department of Health, Education and Welfare re institute of June 27-July 2, 1955; papers re applying for NIMH grant, inviting participants, and planning the program; and financial statements and material re publication of the results of the institute.	820-821

NATIONAL ASSOCIATION OF SOCIAL WORKERS, INC.

Folder Title and Description of Contents	Folder
AAGW: Group Work in Wartime, 1940-1945 Primarily papers relating to the committee on an emergency program and the committee on group work in wartime. Minutes of meetings, statements on the war's impact on group work and vice versa, and correspondence re these statements and the general problems of war and group work.	822
AAGW: Intercultural Problems, Commission on, 1944 Correspondence re racism and list of the commission members.	823
AAGW: Interpersonal Aspects of Group Work, Commission on, 1939-1943 Correspondence re membership of the Commission, list of members, minutes, and reports. The material deals primarily with local study groups.	824
AAGW: Local Study Groups, Committee on, 1936-1955 Correspondence and memoranda re committee organization and meetings, manual and study guides for local groups, minutes of the committee, studies and correspondence re narrative group records, and list of AASGW members. Also includes evaluation of local study groups and a list of these groups, minutes and other material re the activities of local chapter development committee, copies of study outlines on group work with surrounding documents, and papers on group work topics. Louis Kraft is a prominent correspondent.	825-827
AAGW: Membership Committee, 1937-1946 Descriptive brochure of AASGW, statement of membership qualifications, list of members, and minutes of committee meetings.	828
AAGW: Membership Directory, 1953.	829
AAGW: Membership: Transfer to NASW, 1955 Correspondence between AAGW administrative officials and members who were ineligible to become NASW members until they paid full dues.	830
AAGW: National Committee on Wartime Personnel, 1942-1946 All the studies and correspondence deal with problems of war and social welfare. Includes a study of group work in wartime and critiques of the study, reports on activities of the Committee, minutes of the meetings, material re psychiatric casework, communications with Veterans Administration and various war offices, and correspondence re formation of a National Committee on Personnel in the Social Services.	831

Folder Title and Description of Contents	Folder
AAGW: National Conference of Social Work, 1937-1944 Programs of conference on social group work, analysis of the social group work section of NCSW, proposed programs of the various conferences, and minutes of the annual meetings.	832
AAGW: National Conference of Prevention and Control of Juvenile Delinquency, 1948 Mimeographed communications and handbook on prevention of juvenile delinquency.	833
AAGW: National Conference on Professional Preparation in Health Education, Physical Education and Recreation, 1947-1948 Minutes of the steering committee (headed by Carl L. Nordly) which met to organize the conference.	834
AAGW: National Recreation Policies Committee, 1948 Correspondence re cooperation of private and public recreation groups, minutes of the committee, report on committee objectives and operations, and material on the relationship of AAGW and the National Recreation Association.	835
AAGW: Proceedings of AAGW, April 22, 1948 Transcript of the annual meeting.	836
AAGW: Professional Education, Committee on, 1938-1955 Minutes and reports of the committee, correspondence and studies re professional education for group work, surveys of schools and colleges offering courses in group work, lists of personnel and papers of faculty conferences, statements on the content of professional education for group work, reprints on such education, and pamphlets on group work. Prominent correspondents include Ann Neely, Joe R. Hoffer, Margaret E. Adams, Theodore T. Tarail, Florence Ray, and Janet W. Korpela.	837-839
AAGW: Professional Standards, 1945-1946 A booklet published by AAGW and entitled <u>Toward Professional Standards</u> is a selection of articles on group work and education for it.	840
AAGW: Program for Youth, 1945-1947 Correspondence and reports re legislation for services to youth. Minutes of a joint committee of AASW, AASGW, and Associated Youth-Serving Organizations (AYSO).	841

Folder Title and Description of Contents	Folder

AAGW: Publications Committee, 1939-1948   842
Minutes of meetings and correspondence re meetings.

AAGW: Radio Workshop Planning Committee, 1940-1942   843
Edna d'Issertelle, secretary of AASGW, is prominent in the correspondence, which deals with the script and details of the broadcast. Includes minutes of meetings and plans of the committee.

AAGW: Rampart Material, 1941   844
Material re Margaret Svendsen's report on group work, including critiques of it and a copy of her study, "An Attempt to Discover What Happens to People in Groups."

AAGW: Recreation Platform, 1946   845
The National Conference on Facilities for Athletics, Recreation, Physical and Health Education was formed in 1946 to sponsor workshops on physical education and athletic and recreation facilities. Includes minutes of steering committee and a copy of a platform on recreation.

AAGW: Relationships to State, Regional and National Conferences, Committee on, 1942   846
Report of the committee and report on conference planning and group work.

AAGW: Research and Study Committee, 1949-1954   847
Correspondence and mimeographed forms re the compilation of Selected Studies and Research Projects in Group Work, 1948-1953. As chairmen of the committee, Harleigh Trecker and Margaret Mudgett headed the study.

AAGW: Russell Sage Foundation, 1941   848
Correspondence re loan to AASGW for publications; budget for AASGW publications.

AAGW: Social Group Work Manual Project, 1941-1942   849
Summary of 1941 meeting; 1942 summary of entire project.

AAGW: Social Service Employees' Union, Local 19, United Office and Professional Workers of America, CIO, 1947-1948   850
Correspondence and papers re the dispute of employees of the Federation of Jewish Philanthropies, the strike of Brooklyn YWCA workers, and problems of collective bargaining.

Folder Title and Description of Contents	Folder
AAGW: Social Work Vocational Bureau, 1947-1948 Data on the nature and work of the Bureau, minutes of Bureau meetings, occupational study questionnaires, and material on classification of social welfare positions.	851
AAGW: Standards of Group Work, 1936 Reprint of an article and tentative report on criteria and standards for group work agencies.	852
AAGW: Study Outlines, 1939-1942 Suggested studies of camping, juvenile delinquency, role of volunteers in social agencies, board and staff relations, group workers in wartime, record-keeping in group work, public relations, needs of racial and nationality groups, and "democracy" in the operation of an agency.	853-854
AAGW: Terminology, Committee on Clarification of, 1939-1940 Memoranda re clarification of the term "group work."	855
ASCO: American Association of Schools of Social Work, 1946-1948 Correspondence re the organization and operation of a joint committee on teaching materials on community organization. Prominent correspondents are Arthur Dunham, president of ASCO, and Sue Spencer, executive secretary of AASW.	856
ASCO: American Association of Social Workers, 1947-1951 Correspondence re TIAC. Prominent correspondents include Arthur Dunham and Joseph P. Anderson, executive secretary of AASW.	857
ASCO: American Association of Social Workers, Employment Practices Inquiry, 1940 Report of the investigation into the methods of the Family Service Society of St. Louis, Missouri, in recognizing the supervisory responsibility in the agency.	858
ASCO: Annual Meetings, Minutes, 1948-1954 Historical statements, reports of the various committees, and extensive information re TIAC.	859
ASCO: Board of Directors, 1946-1955 Minutes of meetings, list of members, bylaws, notices and agendas of meetings, and correspondence re the business of the board. Prominent correspondents are Merrill F. Krughoff, Amy Wells, Arthur Dunham, Philip E. Ryan, C. F. McNeil, John B. Dawson, Ernest B. Harper, Norman B. Finch, and Paul L. Benjamin. Includes	860-863

Folder Title and Description of Contents	Folder
ASCO: Book of Readings Committee, 1947 Report of the chairman, outline of readings, and list of participants.	864
ASCO: Checklist and Newsletter, Annual Reports, 1948-1951 The Checklist, which began publication in October, 1948, focused on bibliographies of community organization. The Newsletter was a more general publication providing news of ASCO. The annual reports contain information re publication policies and costs, editorial staff, and the nature and scope of these publications.	865
ASCO: Checklist and Newsletter, Correspondence, 1950-1955 Deals primarily with operating details, including such matters as printing and editorial personnel. Editors and contributors to the publications include Ernest B. Harper, Everett Shimp, Virginia S. Ferguson, Arthur Dunham, and Evelyn Butler. Copies of the two publications are found in the Center's ephemera collection.	866
ASCO: Checklist and Newsletter, Editorial Manual, 1948-1952 Historical statement, list of staff, policies on content, manual of style, classification plan, printing and mailing procedure, and distribution-of-copies policy.	867
ASCO: Community Organization, 1947 A copy of Community Organization, a newsletter of ASCO which included a summary of the development of ASCO to February, 1947. Definition of "community organization." A bibliography of community organization for health and welfare services.	868
ASCO: Community Organization Discussion Group, Southern Michigan, 1945-1947 Minutes of meetings, history of ASCO, and correspondence re meetings.	869
ASCO: Council of National Organizations of the Adult Education Association of the United States, 1953-1954 Correspondence inviting ASCO to meet with the Council.	870
ASCO: Education for Community Organization, Committee on, 1952 Correspondence among Aubrey Mallach (chairman of the committee), Ernest B. Harper, and prospective members of the committee.	871

Folder Title and Description of Contents	Folder
ASCO: Financial Accounts, 1946-1951 Invoices, communications with banks, bills, receipts, budgetary statements, reports of treasurer and chairman, and expense statements and accounts. See also material which was removed and placed in legal folder 47.	872-873
ASCO: Financial: Treasurer, 1946-1948 Correspondence between the treasurer of ASCO, Henry L. Zucker, and the chairman of ASCO, Arthur Dunham, concerning requests for funds, payment of bills, etc. Includes financial statements.	874
ASCO: History, 1946-1948 Minutes of early formative meetings, correspondence with Arthur Dunham and Philip E. Ryan concerning early organization problems, progress reports from Dunham to the executive committee of ASCO, and summaries of the historical development of ASCO.	875
ASCO: Local Discussion Groups, Committee on, 1946-1951 Communications with local groups re nature and extent of the discussions and organizations, reports of the committee, and minutes of local discussion groups.	876
ASCO: Mallach, Aubrey, 1951-1953 Mallach was a member of the board of directors and head of the committee on education for community organization. Includes notices of meetings of the board, minutes of the meetings, and correspondence between ASCO officials and Mallach re operating matters of the organization.	877-878
ASCO: Membership, 1947-1953 Membership lists, letters, application blanks, and correspondence re membership problems.	879-880
ASCO: NASW, Committee on Community Organization, 1956-1957 Material relating to NASW's takeover of ASCO functions and publications.	881
ASCO: National Conference of Social Work, 1947-1952 Correspondence between ASCO officials and Joe Hoffer regarding cooperation of ASCO and NASW. Certificate of ASCO's membership in NCSW.	882

Folder Title and Description of Contents	Folder
ASCO: National Council on Social Work Education, 1948-1951 Certificate of incorporation (copy) of NCSWE. Correspondence re cooperation of ASCO and NCSWE and article on social work education.	883
ASCO: National Planning Association, 1947 Notes taken at "inter-group meetings" on community organization held at Princeton University in January and April, 1947.	884
ASCO: Nominating Committee, 1948-1954 Invitations to serve on the committee, reports of the committee, evaluations of candidates and suggestions for candidacy, and correspondence re the work of the committee.	885
ASCO: Program Committee, 1946-1953 Program suggestions from various sources; description of the work of ASCO; and correspondence among committee members, especially Ernest B. Harper and Jane Stewart, chairman of the committee.	886
ASCO: Publications Committee, 1944-1953 Correspondence re the various ASCO publications, minutes of the committee, and reports to the board of directors. Arthur Dunham's suggestion (1944) for a journal of community organization. Correspondence between Dunham and the Russell Sage Foundation re publications and financing of them.	887
ASCO: Recording Committee, 1946-1952 Correspondence concerning keeping records in community organization and on the composition of the committee.	888
ASCO: Scrapbook, Volumes I and II, 1946-1948 Progress reports, minutes of the board of directors, etc. The scrapbook contains a sample of every piece of printed or mimeographed material issued by ASCO. A few pieces of typed material--reports, notices, etc.--are also included. Materials are arranged in chronological order. Volume II contains a description of the history, nature, and scope of the work of ASCO. Indexed.	889-890

Folder Title and Description of Contents	Folder

SWRG: Correspondence and Papers, General, 1949-1956 891
The papers include minutes and reports re TIAC,
legislation on research in various aspects of
child life (Douglas and Battle bills, 1950),
membership requirements, standards in social
work research, and statements on the organization and role of SWRG. The material is
scattered.

SWRG: Committee on Research Function and Practice, 892
1951-1952
This committee had the dual responsibility of
defining both theoretical and actual standards
and practices in social work research. It also
considered whether SWRG should be an informal
group of interested persons or a professional
organization with standards that would be eligible
to join NASW. Prominent persons in the folder
include Isaac Hoffman, William Gordon, and Werner
Boehm.

SWRG: Committee to Study Structure of Advisory 893
Committees, 1951-1953
Reports.

SWRG: Committee on Education, 1955 894
Reports from other associations: AAMSW, AAGW,
AAPSW, and AASW re studies of research practices
and topics undertaken by these groups. Minutes
of one meeting. Ann Shyne, as chairman of the
committee, is a prominent correspondent.

SWRG: Research, 1952-1953 895
Papers and correspondence re a social work research seminar conducted by the University of
Michigan Department of Sociology on the research
basis of welfare practice and material on a project by the Welfare Federation of Cleveland on
leisure-time services. Prominent correspondents
are Joseph Anderson, Virginia K. White, and Wilber
Newstetter.

TIAC: Committee on Inter-Association Structure, Corre- 896
spondence, 1948-1950
Invitations to set up joint committee on inter-
association structure; correspondence of temporary
chairmen Helen Rowe, Clyde Murray, and Ruth Smalley,
and of Dora Goldstine, permanent chairman of TIAC
(1950-1953). Other correspondents include Benjamin
Youngdahl and Joseph P. Anderson.

TIAC: Committee on Inter-Association Structure, Local 897
Joint Executive Committee Meetings, 1949
Local chapters of associations met to discuss
formation of one single social work membership

Folder Title and Description of Contents   Folder

    organization in St. Louis, Washington, D.C., Maryland, etc.

TIAC: Committee on Inter-Association Structure, Structure   898
and Program, 1949
    Reports re purpose, membership, and summary of Committee's work (January to May, 1949); summary of materials on administration and program of AAGW, AAMSW, AAPSW, AASW, NASSW; and report on structure and program of same organizations.

TIAC: Committee on Inter-Association Structure, Minutes,   899
1949-1950
    Minutes re discussions over types of cooperation to develop between organizations and material on setting up formal organization for discussion--Council of Social Work Membership Associations.

TIAC: Committee on Inter-Association Structure, Sub-   900
committee Reports, 1949-1950
    Correspondence, minutes, and reports of subcommittees on one organization and structure and program on and financing.

TIAC: Bylaws, 1950   901
    Correspondence, draft and revision of bylaws for TIAC, policy statements, and material on suggested areas of responsibility for social work profession.

TIAC: Joint Meeting of Associations' Boards, 1950   902
    Correspondence, minutes, report, and recommendations of Committee on Inter-Association Structure.

TIAC: Minutes, 1950-1953   903-904
    Correspondence, memoranda, minutes, and reports re TIAC; resolutions of NASSW and AASW re establishment of TIAC; and draft of "Plan for a Single New Organization of Social Workers."

TIAC: General Correspondence, 1949-1953   905-906
    Chiefly correspondence of Dora Goldstine as chairman of TIAC: regular business of Council, relationship of SWRG and ASCO to TIAC, defense mobilization, AASW national board resolution re TIAC; reports on principles, proposals, and issues in inter-association cooperation; and Dora Goldstine's letter of resignation.

TIAC: Membership of Council and Council Committees,   907
Correspondence, 1950-1955.

Folder Title and Description of Contents	Folder
TIAC: Membership of Council and Council Committees, Listings, 1950-1955.	908
TIAC: Finances, Budget, 1950.	909
TIAC: Finances, Bank Resolution, 1954.	910
TIAC: Finances, Requests to Foundations for Grants, 1954-1955.	911
TIAC: Finances, Financial Statements, 1950-1955.	912
TIAC: Finances, Income, 1950-1955.	913
TIAC: Finances, Paid Vouchers, 1950-1955.	914-916
TIAC: Finances, Bank Statements, 1955.	917
TIAC: Associations' Bylaws, 1951 Bylaws of AAGW, AAMSW, AAPSW, AASW, and NASSW.	918
TIAC: Associations' Objectives and Functions, 1951 Reports from AAGW, AAMSW, AAPSW, AASW, and NASSW re respective associations' objectives and functions.	919
TIAC: Associations' Committees and Functions, 1951 Listings from AAGW, AAMSW, AAPSW, AASW, and NASSW on their respective committees and committees' functions.	920
TIAC: Report, "Principles, Proposals and Issues in Inter-Association Cooperation," 1951 Contains material available in national office of each constituent member of TIAC re basic materials used in implementing report, distribution of report, and recorded reactions to it.	921
TIAC: Report, "Principles, Proposals and Issues in Inter-Association Cooperation," Subcommittee Reports, 1950-1951 Chiefly correspondence and memoranda re subcommittee activities, drafts of reports, and listing of membership of subcommittees.	922
TIAC: Report, "Principles, Proposals and Issues in Inter-Association Cooperation," Correspondence, 1951 Reaction of membership organizations to the report and dispersal of report.	923

Folder Title and Description of Contents	Folder
TIAC: Report, Papers on "Plan for a Single New Organization," 1950-1952 Preparatory folder compiled by Dora Goldstine containing reports to presidents of participating associations; drafts of materials to be used in the report; and information on subcommittees.	924
TIAC: Report, "Plan for a Single New Organization of Social Workers," 1952 Copy of report and revisions.	925
TIAC: Report, "Plan for a Single New Organization," Subcommittee Reports, 1952 Correspondence and reports of subcommittees; membership; program and structure; sections, officers, board of directors, and executive committee; delegate body; commissions and committees; chapter organization; and statement of purpose and finances.	926-927
TIAC: Report, "Plan for a Single New Organization," Action of Member Organizations, 1953 Correspondence of member associations indicating reactions to report, and compilation of reactions sent to all participating associations.	928
TIAC: Reports to Presidents, 1950-1955 Correspondence and reports on TIAC activities and replies from presidents of participating associations.	929-930
TIAC: Memoranda to Members of TIAC, 1950-1954 Dissemination of material re TIAC activities to members of TIAC.	931
TIAC: Special Planning Committee for NASW, 1950-1954 Minutes.	932
TIAC: Meeting with Attorneys, 1954 Discussion of questions dealing with incorporation procedures, dissolution, and disposition of assets and liabilities of membership organizations.	933
TIAC: Bylaws, Memorandum of Understanding, Certification of Incorporation for NASW, 1954 Proposed TIAC legislation.	934
TIAC: Local Chapter Organization for NASW Committee, 1953-1955 Correspondence, minutes, and reports re local organization; formulation of petition for chapter status in NASW; and report and recommendations of the committee.	935

Folder Title and Description of Contents	Folder
TIAC: Planning Committee for NASW, 1954-1955 Minutes and correspondence re planning for NASW.	936-937
TIAC: Planning Committee for NASW (Anderson), 1954-1955 Papers collected by Joseph P. Anderson re planning committee and its activities.	938-941
TIAC: Planning Committee for NASW, Subcommittee to Review Program, 1955 Formulation of questionnaires sent out to seven associations re individual associations' program; one general, the second re specific committees of the associations; and report of questionnaire results.	942
TIAC: Planning Committee for NASW, AAMSW Mail Referendum, 1954 Results of AAMSW mail referendum re AAMSW negotiations with TIAC reported to planning committee and, in turn, reported to membership.	943
TIAC: Associations' Policy Statements, 1954-1955 Policy statements for AAGW, AAMSW, AAPSW, American Public Welfare Association (APWA), AASW, and SWRG.	944
TIAC: Personnel Practices of Member Organizations, 1955 Statements on personnel policies and practices of several social work organizations: AAPSW, AAGW, AASW, and National Conference of Social Work (NCSW).	945-946
TIAC: Program Committee for NASW, 1954-1956 Reports, memoranda, and correspondence re recruiting members for committee; questionnaires for personnel practices and chapter development; summary of data re program committee activities; report on AASW and AAMSW program; and material on consultation services of AAMSW and NASSW.	947-948
TIAC: Publications Committee for NASW, 1954-1955 Memoranda and minutes re publication of unified journal and goals of publications program.	949
TIAC: Relationship with Other Organizations Committee for NASW, 1954-1955 Minutes and reports re membership in other social work organizations, annual report of National Social Welfare Assembly, and statement of principles and recommended criteria governing AASW affiliation with other organizations.	950

Folder Title and Description of Contents	Folder
TIAC: Social Policy and Action Committee for NASW, 1955 Minutes. Policy statements dealing with legislation in fields of health and welfare and material on proposed areas on which positions and actions should be taken prior to formal organization of NASW. Draft statement on public welfare prepared by Elizabeth Wickenden.	951
TIAC: Social Work Education Committee for NASW, 1955 Reports and recommendations from committee and material on the relationship of NASW with the Council on Social Work Education.	952
TIAC: Membership Referendum on Formation of NASW, 1955 Correspondence and final report re dissolution of constituent bodies and formation of NASW.	953
TIAC: Nominations and Elections Committee for NASW, 1954-1955 Selection of two nominees for each office on the slate.	954
TIAC: Nominations and Elections Committee for NASW, Candidates' Telegrams, 1954-1955.	955
TIAC: Nominations and Election Committee for NASW, Biographical Data on Candidates, 1954-1955 Information arranged alphabetically.	956-957
TIAC: Nominations and Election Committee for NASW, Conduct of Election, 1955 Contains memoranda and minutes for committee of tellers, procedure for counting ballots, sample ballot, time schedule for election, and final report of nominations and elections committee re conduct of election.	958
TIAC: Inventory, Records and Office Procedures Committee for NASW, 1955 Minutes, reports, and recommendations.	959
TIAC: Personnel Practices for National Office Staff, Committee on, 1955 Minutes, report, and recommendations re national office policy and procedures for closing national offices of membership organizations.	960

NATIONAL ASSOCIATION OF SOCIAL WORKERS, INC.

Folder Title and Description of Contents	Folder
TIAC: Canadian Association of Social Workers, 1953-1954 Correspondence re TIAC and reaction of Canadian Association to reorganization and possibility of joining the organization in the United States.	961
TIAC: Goldstine, Dora, Resolution on, 1955 Correspondence and TIAC resolution on former chairman's death.	962
TIAC: Social Work and Defense Mobilization, 1950-1955 Correspondence and report of TIAC re effective use of social work personnel in defense mobilization, and report of NASW and CSWE assuming functions of NCSWDM.	963
TIAC: Press Releases on NASW, 1955 Reports on election of NASW officers and formation of a new social work association.	964
TIAC: Final Report of TIAC Activities, 1955 Accumulated reports of the TIAC committees.	965
TIAC: AAGW, Correspondence, 1955 Materials dealing with the transition of national and local AAGW organization into the group work section of NASW. Prominent correspondents include Janet Korpela, Nathan Cohen, Joseph P. Anderson, and officials of TIAC and AAGW. Data on nominations for the new section's committee.	966
TIAC: AAGW, Reports, 1955 Listing of NASW personnel on the committee for organizing group work section, statement on content of group work practice, and notices of meetings.	967
TIAC: AAMSW, Committee on Inter-Association Structure, Correspondence, 1948-1949 Communications re formation of committee, appointment of AAMSW representatives on committee, and ideas AAMSW should press for in committee meetings. Correspondents include Dora Goldstine, Mary Blanche Moss, and Elizabeth Rice.	968
TIAC: AAMSW, Committee on Inter-Association Structure, Minutes and Materials, 1949 Minutes and summary of AAMSW program and objectives for committee.	969

NATIONAL ASSOCIATION OF SOCIAL WORKERS, INC.

Folder Title and Description of Contents	Folder
TIAC: AAMSW, Committee on Inter-Association Structure, Reports, 1947-1950 Minutes of Conference on Proposals of Inter-Association Activities, report of relationship of associations' relationship with AASSW, and review of scope and character of inter-association activities.	970
TIAC: AAMSW, Correspondence, 1949-1954 Correspondence and memoranda re Association participation in TIAC.	971-972
TIAC: AAMSW, TIAC Minutes and Materials, 1950-1955 Communications from TIAC and committees and AAMSW reaction to TIAC activities.	973-975
TIAC: AAMSW, Special Committee on TIAC, 1952-1953 Report of committee to study results on questionnaire/opinion poll sent to local AAMSW chapters re TIAC, analysis of poll on TIAC report, and supplementary poll on TIAC future activities.	976
TIAC: AAMSW, Bylaws, Memorandum of Understanding, Certificate of Incorporation for NASW, 1954-1955 Copies of proposed NASW legislation and comments by AAMSW officials.	977
TIAC: AAMSW, TIAC Planning Committee for NASW, 1954-1955 Minutes, statements, and correspondence re planning for NASW and reaction of AAMSW; statements on job descriptions from AAPSW and NASSW employment practices of AASW; and information on AAMSW office personnel.	978-979
TIAC: AAMSW, TIAC Social Policy and Action Committee for NASW, 1955 Correspondence re AAMSW membership on committee and draft of general principles on health.	980
TIAC: AAMSW, Vote on Approval of NASW, 1955 Material re elections for NASW.	981
TIAC: AASW, Unification Attempts, 1946-1955 Documents illustrating attempts to discuss merger with other social work groups dating from 1946 AASW delegate conference, negotiations with AASSW re subject, national board recommendations re TIAC report, etc.	982
TIAC: AASW, Executive Committee Resolution re Single Professional Organization, 1951 Correspondence and resolution of AASW executive committee re TIAC activities and discussion of continuing participation of AASW in TIAC.	983

Folder Title and Description of Contents	Folder
TIAC: AASW, National Board Decisions re TIAC, 1950-1953 Correspondence and reports re AASW relationship with TIAC, resolutions of 1951 AASW delegate assembly delegating authority to national board to negotiate with TIAC, questionnaires to chapters re AASW participation in TIAC, AASW resolution favoring invitation to ASCO to participate in TIAC, and appointment of Melvin Glasser as chairman of AASW delegation to TIAC.	984-985
TIAC: AASW, Membership Comments on TIAC Report, "Plan for a Single New Organization," 1953 Correspondence asked for clarification of national board resolutions re TIAC Report.	986-987
TIAC: AASW, Delegate Assembly, 1953 Materials on actions taken by assembly on national board resolution re TIAC, national board recommendations re sections in NASW, action on inviting SWRG to TIAC, highlights of delegate assembly, and Melvin Glasser's notes on presentation to delegate assembly on TIAC.	988
TIAC: AASW, Bylaws, Memorandum of Understanding, Constitution and Constitutional Convention for NASW, 1952-1955 Statements on purpose, program, and structure of TIAC; suggested plans for constitutional convention; drafts of proposed legislation for NASW; and letter re legality of Council on Social Work Education bylaws.	989
TIAC: AASW, Certificate of Incorporation for NASW, 1953-1954 Copy of certificate. Correspondence re AASW national board decision re TIAC legislation, as well as communications from AAPSW and AAGW.	990
TIAC: AASW, Reports to National Board re TIAC, 1954 Reports re time schedule for establishing new association, progress report of TIAC.	991
TIAC: AASW, General Correspondence, 1953-1955 Invitation extended to Melvin Glasser to represent AASW on TIAC, correspondence re national board decision on TIAC Report, reactions of other organizations to TIAC, and evaluation of Joseph P. Anderson as executive secretary of AASW.	992

Folder Title and Description of Contents	Folder
TIAC: AASW, TIAC Social Policy and Action Committee for NASW, 1948-1955 Correspondence, statements, reports, and minutes re formulation of policy statements for NASW; testimony of Katharine Lenroot on child welfare; statement by APWA re social policy and action; and list of social issues and legislation.	993
TIAC: AASW, TIAC Local Chapter Organization Committee for NASW, 1952-1955 Statements, minutes, reports, and correspondence dealing with preparation for local organization of NASW; Glasser speech notes re AASW local chapter organization; compilation of chapter information from all member organizations.	994
TIAC: AASW, TIAC Relationship with Other Organizations Committee for NASW, 1952-1953 Reports and minutes re ASCO participation in TIAC, statement of principles and recommended criteria governing AASW affiliation with other organizations, and relationship with AAMSW, Canadian Association of Social Workers, NCSWDM, and CSWE.	995
TIAC: AASW, TIAC Planning Committee for NASW, 1953-1955 Consists largely of minutes, but includes some correspondence and reports to presidents, AASW instructions re plans for single organization and timetable for action, and summary of inter-association activity leading to NASW.	996
TIAC: AASW, TIAC Publications Committee for NASW, 1954-1955 Minutes, report, and recommendations of committee, and summary of information re publication committees of constituent members of TIAC.	997
TIAC: AASW Organization and Transition Committee, 1953-1955 Correspondence, reports, and minutes re procedure for transition from AASW to NASW; material re membership corporations law in New York State; referendum and work schedule of new organization; and policy and procedure certifying AASW members in NASW.	998-999
TIAC: AASW, Papers on Planning for a Single Organization (Glasser), 1950-1955 Compilation by Melvin Glasser of important materials tracing formation of NASW through committee on inter-association structure and TIAC.	1000-1001

NATIONAL ASSOCIATION OF SOCIAL WORKERS, INC.

<u>Folder Title and Description of Contents</u>   <u>Folder</u>

TIAC: AASW, Speech Notes for "A Single Professional   1002
Organization" (Glasser), 1954-1955
    Speech notes of Melvin Glasser for meetings of
    local chapters of AASW re TIAC and NASW.

TIAC: AASW, Journal Article, "Development of the   1003
Movement for a Single Professional Association,"
(Glasser), 1955
    Correspondence and rough draft of article by
    Melvin Glasser for the last issue of <u>Social
    Work Journal</u>.

TIAC: ASCO, Correspondence, 1951-1955   1004-1006
    Correspondence between ASCO officials and TIAC
    officials re ASCO's participation in TIAC and
    problems in the dissolution of ASCO. Chief
    correspondents are Ernest B. Harper, Irene
    Conrad, and Philip E. Ryan.

NASW: 1956 Delegate Assembly, Delegate Mailings, 1956   1007
    Material sent to delegates.

NASW: 1956 Delegate Assembly Handbook, 1956   1008
    Material handed out to delegates.

NASW: 1956 Delegate Assembly, Report and Evaluation of   1009
Delegate Assembly, 1956.

NASW: 1958 Delegate Assembly, Workbooks, 1957-1958   1010
    Correspondence re distribution of delegate
    assembly workbooks I and II to chapters.

NASW: 1958 Delegate Assembly, Report on, 1958   1011
    Report by executive director and copy of resolutions
    approved by assembly.

NASW: 1960 Delegate Assembly, 1958-1960   1012
    Memoranda and correspondence re discussion material
    for assembly, i.e., voluntary certification; list
    of official delegates.

NASW: 1960 Delegate Assembly, Requests for Delegate   1013
Assembly Material, 1959-1960
    Correspondence.

NASW: 1960 Delegate Assembly, <u>NASW News</u>--Special Delegate   1014
Assembly Issue, 1959-1960
    Correspondence re special edition.

NASW: 1960 Delegate Assembly, Chapter Statements re   1015
Topics for Discussion at Delegate Assembly, 1960
    Correspondence re national voluntary certification
    between chapters and national organization.

Folder Title and Description of Contents	Folder
NASW: 1960 Delegate Assembly, Publicity, 1960 Press releases and correspondence re publicity.	1016
NASW: 1960 Delegate Assembly, Jane Addams Centennial, 1960 Official folder for delegates.	1017
NASW: National Voluntary Certification Plan, Southern Minnesota Projects, 1957-1959 Correspondence and reports re drafting of policy statements on regulation of social work by the Southern Minnesota Chapter.	1018
NASW: National Voluntary Certification Plan, 1958-1960 Reports and memoranda re steps toward certification; announcement of Academy of Certified Social Workers.	1019
NASW: National Voluntary Certification Plan, Correspondence re NASW Implementation, 1958-1961 Correspondence re proposed regulation of practice for NASW members and schedule for implementation of certification.	1020
NASW: National Voluntary Certification Plan, Chapter Reports, 1959 Chapter reaction to certification.	1021-1023
NASW: National Voluntary Certification Plan, Correspondence re Operation, 1961-1962 Correspondence re Academy of Certified Social Workers.	1024-1025
NASW: Commission on Personnel Standards and Practices, Meetings, 1955-1963 Minutes.	1026-1027
NASW: Commission on Personnel Standards and Practices, Correspondence re Meetings, 1961-1963 Routine correspondence.	1028
NASW: Commission on Personnel Standards and Practices, NASW Personnel Information--Preliminary Study, 1956-1957 Correspondence and memoranda of joint committee of NASW and Social Work Vocational Bureau re job information service.	1029
NASW: Commission on Personnel Standards and Practices, NASW Personnel Information--Advisory Committee, 1956-1959 Correspondence and memoranda appointing committee to oversee job information service.	1030
NASW: Commission on Personnel Standards and Practices, Development of Civil Rights Statement, 1955-1957 Correspondence, memoranda, and reports re rewriting civil rights statement.	1031

Folder Title and Description of Contents	Folder
NASW: Commission on Personnel Standards and Practices, Development of Code of Ethics, 1956-1961 Minutes of NASW Chicago area chapter committee project proposing code of ethics; report to delegate assembly.	1032
NASW: Commission on Personnel Standards and Practices, Basic Documents, 1957-1961 Statements on legal regulation, retirements, and code of ethics.	1033
NASW: Commission on Personnel Standards and Practices, "Policies and Procedures in Membership Administration," 1959 Manual in draft form.	1034
NASW: Commission on Personnel Standards and Practices, Revised Procedures, Unethical Conduct, 1960-1961 Correspondence and reports re ACSW and procedure re unethical behavior of members.	1035
NASW: Commission on Personnel Standards and Practices, Procedural Documents re Social Work Ethics, ca. 1961 Documents re standards of personnel practices, complaints involving violations of social work personnel practices, etc.	1036
NASW: Commission on Personnel Standards and Practices, Handbook for Chapter Chairmen, 1961.	1037
NASW: Commission on Personnel Standards and Practices, Selection and Preparation of Certain Teaching Materials, Subcommittee, 1957-1962 Minutes, correspondence re subcommittee study of social work ethics and violations for use in teaching.	1038
NASW: Commission on Social Work Practice, 1955-1963 Final reports of TIAC on NASW program; assignments of personnel to commission on practice.	1039
NASW: Commission on Social Work Practice, General, 1956-1961 Minutes and reports of sections and subcommittees re social work practice.	1040
NASW: Commission on Social Work Practice, Memoranda from Chairman, 1956-1962 Harriett Bartlett's memoranda re commission and its projects.	1041

Folder Title and Description of Contents	Folder
NASW: Commission on Social Work Practice, Policy and Planning Committee, General, 1955-1963 Correspondence, memoranda, agendas, minutes, and position statements re development of research proposal to study social work practice.	1042-1043
NASW: Commission on Social Work Practice, Policy and Planning Committee, Correspondence, 1958-1959 Correspondence re appointment of members, committee structure and composition, and meeting attendance of the committee.	1044
NASW: Commission on Social Work Practice, Policy and Planning Committee, Comments, 1959-1962 Correspondence and memoranda re proposal for social work practice research and conceptual framework for study.	1045
NASW: Commission on Social Work Practice, Development of a Conceptual Framework for the Study of Social Work Practice (Blenkner-Carter Project), 1959-1960 Minutes, reports, draft of proposal for study, and memorandum of understandings re project.	1046
NASW: Commission on Social Work Practice, Blenkner-Carter Project, 1957-1958 Correspondence and proposed statements re research for development of methodology and instruments to study social work practice; comments on research proposal by members of commission. Main correspondents include Margaret Blenkner, Genevieve W. Carter, Bertram Beck, and Harriett Bartlett.	1047
NASW: Commission on Social Work Practice, Blenkner-Carter Project, Fund Raising, 1958 Correspondence requesting funds for project.	1048
NASW: Commission on Social Work Practice, Working Definition, Golden Gate Chapter Project, 1958-1960 Exploratory study by chapter on social work practice and its report on final results.	1049
NASW: Commission on Social Work Practice, Working Definition, Original Statements, 1956-1959 Minutes and statements on definition by Harriett Bartlett, William E. Gordon, and committee members.	1050
NASW: Commission on Social Work Practice, Working Definition, Chapters' Reactions, 1958-1960 Correspondence illustrating reactions to draft of working definition.	1051

Folder Title and Description of Contents	Folder
NASW: Commission on Social Work Practice, Working Definition, Subcommittee Correspondence, 1959-1962 Correspondence re committee membership, minutes, and revision of definition.	1052
NASW: Commission on Social Work Practice, Working Definition, Subcommittee Reports, 1959-1962.	1053
NASW: Commission on Social Work Practice, Working Definition, Memoranda, 1960-1962 Pre-meeting memoranda, progress reports re working definition, and report to commission.	1054
NASW: Commission on Social Work Practice, Trends, Issues, and Priorities Committee, Minutes, Reports, and Position Statements, 1956-1961 Minutes; reports; memoranda; correspondence; preliminary statements on delinquency and crime, supervision, and various aspects of social work practice; and comments by chapters on statements.	1055-1056
NASW: Commission on Social Work Practice, Trends, Issues, and Priorities Committee, Statement on Prevention and Treatment, 1959-1961 Routine correspondence and reports.	1057
NASW: Commission on Social Work Practice, Trends, Issues, and Priorities Committee, Consensus Statements, 1962-1963 Correspondence and chapter responses to consensus statements.	1058
NASW: Commission on Social Work Practice, Ad Hoc Committee on Nomenclature, 1956-1959 Correspondence re formation and assignment of committee.	1059
NASW: Commission on Social Work Practice, Private Practice, Commission Report, 1959-1961 Correspondence, reports, and statements.	1060
NASW: Commission on Social Work Practice, Private Practice Special Committee, 1963 Memoranda and correspondence re establishment of communications between private practice and NASW to explore ways to administer private practice procedure.	1061
NASW: Commission on Social Work Practice, Value-Goals Project, 1958-1959 Background report prior to study of inconsistencies between social work activities and social work values.	1062

Folder Title and Description of Contents	Folder
NASW: Commission on Social Work Practice, Chapter Program Reports, 1956-1960 Minutes of NASW Southern Minnesota chapter re social work practice committees of chapter and comments on national activities in the field of practice; routine correspondence.	1063
NASW: Commission on Social Work Practice, Chapter Program Inquiries, 1956-1963 Correspondence re development of social work practice committees and/or activities by local chapters.	1064
NASW: Commission on Social Work Practice, Chapter Program, Loan Folder, 1958-1960 Depository central file containing reports, minutes, and correspondence of local NASW chapters' activity in the field of social work practice.	1065
NASW: Commission on Social Work Practice, Chapter Program, Requests for Loan Folder, 1956-1961 Correspondence.	1066
NASW: Committee on Review of NASW Structure, Operational Memoranda, 1956-1960 Memoranda re plan for structure review, committee membership, formation of task forces, and setting up priorities for program review.	1067
NASW: Committee on Review of NASW Structure, Agendas and Materials, 1958-1961.	1068-1069
NASW: Committee on Review of NASW Structure, Minutes, 1958-1960.	1070-1071
NASW: Committee on Review of NASW Structure, Task Forces' Minutes and Reports, 1958-1960 Reports and recommendations of steering committee, plan for structure review, and membership listing of task forces.	1072
NASW: Committee on Review of NASW Structure, Interim Report, 1961-1962 Correspondence with members of central review committee and material on distribution of report and chapter reactions to it.	1073
NASW: Committee on Review of NASW Structure, Material from NASW Sections, Chapters, Commissions, and Individuals, 1956-1962 Correspondence re structure review, procedure manual of psychiatric social work section, statement on	1074

Folder Title and Description of Contents   Folder

   interim report, and material on relations with
   the Council on Social Work Education.

NASW; Committee on Review of NASW Structure, Section   1075
Comments, 1961
   Correspondence and reports from sections re interim
   report.

NASW: Committee on Review of NASW Structure, Excerpts   1076
Folder, 1961-1962
   Excerpted comments re structure review from indi-
   viduals and chapters for committee and staff use.

NASW: Committee on Review of NASW Structure, Final   1077
Reports, 1962

NASW: Committee on Review of NASW Structure, Letters   1078
of Appreciation, 1962
   Correspondence with central review committee and
   task forces.

NASW: Committee on Review of NASW Structure, Revision   1079
of Bylaws, 1962-1963
   Correspondence re chapter reaction.

NASW: Group Work Section, Reports, 1956   1080
   Lists of NASW personnel, statement on content of
   group work practice, and notices of meetings.

NASW: Medical Social Work Section, NASW Board of   1081
Directors Correspondence, 1955-1956
   Correspondence re transition from American
   Association of Medical Social Workers to
   National Association of Social Workers'
   medical social work section.

NASW: Medical Social Work Section, Correspondence with   1082
NASW, 1955-1956.

NASW: Medical Social Work Section, Correspondence with   1083
NASW Sections, 1955-1956.

NASW: Medical Social Work Section, Communication from   1084
NASW Commissions, 1955-1956
   Communiques from the commissions on social work
   education, social action and policy, and personnel
   standards, practices, and interpretation.

NASW: Medical Social Work Section, Correspondence with   1085
NASW Committees, 1955-1956
   Memoranda and correspondence on publications, public
   relations, nominations, membership, finance, and
   chapter organization and administration.

Folder Title and Description of Contents	Folder
NASW: Medical Social Work Section, NASW Chapter Services, 1955-1956 "Chapter Service Packet for Chapter Chairmen," recruitment material available from Council on Social Work Education.	1086
NASW: Medical Social Work Section, Information on NASW--Reference, 1956-1958 Information on formation and functions of NASW for use by section staff.	1087
NASW: Medical Social Work Section, Correspondence, General, 1955-1957 Correspondence re operation of section, Dora Goldstine memorial lectures, and tributes to Irene Grant and Kathleen Allen. Main correspondents include Mary Hemmy, Edith Alt, Addie Thomas, and Catherine Purcell.	1088-1090
NASW: Medical Social Work Section, Correspondence re Personnel Recruiting for Hospitals, 1955-1956 Correspondence re recommendations by section executives for placement of medical social work personnel.	1091
NASW: Medical Social Work Section, Reports of Chairman, 1958-1962 Reports of section chairmen: Eleanor Cockerill, Helen E. Woods, and Eleanor Barnett.	1092
NASW: Medical Social Work Section, Chairman's Conference, 1958 Proceedings of conference held in Chicago (February, 1958) to discuss the philosophy, purpose, and program of the section.	1093
NASW: Medical Social Work Section, Administrative Committee, 1955-1956 Minutes of the committee and budgets of the section.	1094
NASW: Medical Social Work Section, Executive Committee, Chairman's Notes, 1955-1956 Mary Poole's correspondence, memoranda, and notes re executive committee meetings.	1095-1096
NASW: Medical Social Work Section, Education Committee, Correspondence, General, 1955-1956 Correspondence re use of grant funds and study of medical social work education; policy statement on approval of committee reports.	1097

Folder Title and Description of Contents	Folder
NASW: Medical Social Work Section, Education Committee, Minutes and Reports, 1955-1963.	1098-1099
NASW: Medical Social Work Section, Education Committee, Special Committee Meetings, 1958-1960 Proceedings of meetings evolving from chairman's conference to discuss the professional education program of schools of social work.	1100
NASW: Medical Social Work Section, Education Committee, Description of Practice Subcommittee, 1955-1958 Memoranda and reports re "Description of Medical Social Work Practice."	1101
NASW: Medical Social Work Section, Education Committee, Field Work Subcommittee, 1958-1959 Report of "Pilot Study of Second Year Medical Social Fieldwork."	1102
NASW: Medical Social Work Section, Education Committee, Scholarship Subcommittee, 1962-1963 Minutes and reports on activities of subcommittee.	1103
NASW: Medical Social Work Section, Education Committee, Study Committee on Concepts, 1954-1960.	1104
NASW: Medical Social Work Section, Education Committee, Teaching Medical Students, 1955-1956 Correspondence re participation of social workers in training medical students.	1105
NASW: Medical Social Work Section, Education Committee, Teaching of Social Component in Hospital Administration Subcommittee, 1956 Final Report.	1106
NASW: Medical Social Work Section, Education Committee: Council on Social Work Education, Correspondence, 1955-1956 Correspondence and data re relationship with CSWE and study of medical social work curriculum.	1107
NASW: Medical Social Work Section, Education Committee: Council on Social Work Education, Accreditation Commission, 1955-1956 Reports and correspondence re review of medical social work curriculum.	1108

NATIONAL ASSOCIATION OF SOCIAL WORKERS, INC.

Folder Title and Description of Contents	Folder
NASW: Medical Social Work Section, Education Committee: Council on Social Work Education, Consultation Services, 1955-1958 Reports and correspondence re council of delegates (CSWE) and educational consultants' services.	1109
NASW: Medical Social Work Section, International Exchange of Social Workers Committee, 1955-1959 Reports and correspondence re placement and international exchange of social workers. Main correspondents are Mary Hemmy and Theodate Soule.	1110
NASW: Medical Social Work Section, Interpretation Committee, 1956-1960 Reports.	1111
NASW: Medical Social Work Section, Local Section Program Committee, 1955-1963 Reports, memoranda, and correspondence re the study of local medical social work sections' programs.	1112
NASW: Medical Social Work Section, Membership Committee, 1955-1959 Reports, membership statistics, and material on revision of membership requirements.	1113
NASW: Medical Social Work Section, National Conference on Social Welfare Program, Committee on, 1955-1962 Correspondence and memoranda re arrangments for medical section meetings at the National Conference.	1114-1115
NASW: Medical Social Work Section, Nominating Committee 1955-1956 Correspondence and memoranda re nominations for medical social work section and NASW.	1116
NASW: Medical Social Work Section, Practice Committee, Correspondence, General, 1955-1956 Correspondence re Army social services and committee budget, report on studies in medical social work section, and draft revision of statement on policies and procedures of committee.	1117
NASW: Medical Social Work Section, Practice Committee, Minutes and Reports, 1955-1963 Minutes of committee and reports from chairmen of committees and subcommittees.	1118-1120
NASW: Medical Social Work Section, Practice Committee, Case Records Subcommittee, 1955-1956 Correspondence re notice of meetings.	1121

Folder Title and Description of Contents	Folder
NASW: Medical Social Work Section, Practice Committee, Contribution of Other Professions in Care of Patient Subcommittee, 1956 Correspondence.	1122
NASW: Medical Social Work Section, Practice Committee, Contribution of Medical Social Workers to Professional Team, 1956 Correspondence.	1123
NASW: Medical Social Work Section, Practice Committee, Medical Social Work Participation in Program Planning, 1959 Report: "Some Considerations Regarding Studies of Medical Social Work Participation in Policy Making and Program Planning in the Agency and Participation in Community Planning."	1124
NASW: Medical Social Work Section, Practice Committee, Outline for Study of Practice Subcommittee, ca. 1960 Questionnaire for study of medical social practice, outline for study of practice (Harriett Bartlett, Mary Hemmy, and Margaret Shutz), and results of 1960 questionnaire.	1125
NASW: Medical Social Work Section, Practice Committee, Professional and Non-Professional Aspects Subcommittee, 1955 Correspondence re use of aides for social workers.	1126
NASW: Medical Social Work Section, Practice Committee, Rehabilitation Subcommittee, 1955-1957 Correspondence re development of a statement on medical social worker in rehabilitation, minutes reports, and questionnaire.	1127
NASW: Medical Social Work Section, Practice Committee, "Social Worker's Responsibility to Select" [sic] Subcommittee, 1959-1960 Reports re preparation of a statement establishing professional controls and guidelines over social work services and decisions.	1128
NASW: Medical Social Work Section, Practice Committee, Statement of Standards Subcommittee, 1955-1960 Correspondence and reports re development of a statement on standards for social service departments in hospitals issued by the medical and psychiatric social work sections.	1129

NATIONAL ASSOCIATION OF SOCIAL WORKERS, INC.

Folder Title and Description of Contents	Folder
NASW: Medical Social Work Section, Practice Committee, Statistics Subcommittee, 1956-1963 Correspondence and reports re statistical system to record medical social work services, including "Social Work in Medical Settings."	1130
NASW: Medical Social Work Section, Practice Committee, Working with Others Subcommittee, 1955-1956 Correspondence and pilot study re inter-disciplinary conferences ("Medical Social Contributions, Objectives, Principles, Techniques and Factors in the One to One Patient-Centered Conference with Another Professional Person").	1131
NASW: Medical Social Work Section, Practice Committee, Plan Extension of Pilot Study, Ad Hoc Committee, 1957 Memoranda and reports re extension of study into inter-professional conferences.	1132
NASW: Medical Social Work Section, Practice Committee, Key Questions in Medical Social Work Practice, Ad Hoc Committee, 1958 Minutes.	1133
NASW: Medical Social Work Section, Practice Committee, Criteria for Evaluating Social Service Departments in Hospitals, 1958 Memoranda.	1134
NASW: Medical Social Work Section, Practice Committee, Definition of Medical Social Work Position, 1956 Correspondence and report. Principal correspondent is Celia R. Moss.	1135
NASW: Medical Social Work Section, Practice Committee, Staffing Patterns, 1958-1959 Correspondence.	1136
NASW: Medical Social Work Section, Practice Committee, Reports, 1958 Eleanor E. Cockerill, "The Life Process Continuum as a Frame of Reference for the Further Delineation and Analysis of Social Work Practice in Health, Medical Care and Rehabilitation Settings"; Harriett Bartlett, "Characteristics of Medical Social Work: Tentative Discussion" and "Essentials of Medical Social Work as a Field of Social Work Practice: Comprehensive Description and Analysis" (preliminary outline).	1137

Folder Title and Description of Contents	Folder
NASW: Medical Social Work Section, Program Development Committee, 1955-1956 Correspondence.	1138
NASW: Medical Social Work Section, Publications Committee, Correspondence, General, 1955-1956 Correspondence re expenses, organization of the committee, responsibilities of the section editor, and other routine matters.	1139
NASW: Medical Social Work Section, Publications Committee, Minutes and Memoranda, 1956-1959.	1140
NASW: Medical Social Work Section, Publications Committee, Newsletter, 1955-1956 Correspondence re format of newsletter and copy for it.	1141
NASW: Medical Social Work Section, Publications Committee, Reprints, 1957-1958, 1962 Correspondence re search for reprintable material and request for dismissal of committee.	1142
NASW: Medical Social Work Section, Recruitment Committee, Correspondence, 1956-1960 Correspondence re recruitment on state and local level, plans for recruitment, foreign exchange programs, and scholarships for social workers.	1143
NASW: Medical Social Work Section, Recruitment Committee, Minutes, 1955-1960.	1144
NASW: Medical Social Work Section, Recruitment Committee, Advisory Committee, 1956 Minutes.	1145
NASW: Medical Social Work Section, Recruitment Committee, Reports, 1955-1956.	1146
NASW: Medical Social Work Section, Recruitment Committee, National Recruitment Workshop, 1955-1957 Agenda and proceedings of workshops sponsored by the section's recruitment committee.	1147
NASW: Medical Social Work Section, Recruitment Committee, Regional Workshops, 1958-1959 Agendas and list of participants for workshops.	1148
NASW: Medical Social Work Section, Recruitment Committee, "Follow-up of Referrals of College Students to Medical Social Workers," 1959 Manuscript written by Anne Shyne.	1149

Folder Title and Description of Contents	Folder
NASW: Medical Social Work Section, Social Policy and Action Committee, 1955-1956 Correspondence.	1150
NASW: Medical Social Work Section, Relationships of Medical Workers with Agencies and Associations in the Fields of Health, Medical Care and Rehabilitation, Ad Hoc Committee, 1958-1959 Minutes, correspondence, and memoranda.	1151
NASW: Medical Social Work Section, Section Committees Rotation and Tenure, Ad Hoc Committee, 1960 Recommendations of committee.	1152
NASW: Medical Social Work Section: Joint Committee with American Hospital Association, Correspondence and Minutes, 1955-1963 Agendas, reports, minutes, and correspondence re joint study and AHA institute. Main correspondents include Sarah Hardwicke and Mary Hemmy.	1153-1154
NASW: Medical Social Work Section: Joint Committee with American Hospital Association, AHA Institute, 1955-1963 Correspondence and materials re institutes and medical social work section participation.	1155
NASW: Medical Social Work Section: Joint Committee with American Hospital Association, Definition of Medical Social Work, 1957 Statements and suggestions on definition of medical social work.	1156
NASW: Medical Social Work Section: Joint Committee with American Hospital Association, "Social Workers in General and Tuberculosis Hospitals," 1955-1956 Correspondence re study and draft of study.	1157-1158
NASW: Medical Social Work Section: Joint Committee with American Hospital Association, "Social Work in Hospitals," 1956 Draft and revisions of study undertaken by AHA and medical social work section; the study was financed by the U.S. Public Health Service.	1159-1160
NASW: Medical Social Work Section: Joint Committee on Participation in Medical Education, Correspondence, 1955-1958 Routine correspondence re continuation of study of joint committee with psychiatric section. Principal correspondent is Grace White.	1161

NATIONAL ASSOCIATION OF SOCIAL WORKERS, INC.

Folder Title and Description of Contents	Folder
NASW: Medical Social Work Section: Joint Committee on Participation in Medical Education, Correspondence-Committee Members, 1956-1958 Correspondence with members re meetings and appointment to committee and resource material from the Association of Teachers of Preventive Medicine.	1162
NASW: Medical Social Work Section: Joint Committee on Participation in Medical Education, Minutes, 1954-1959 Minutes and correspondence re formulation of study questionnaire, list of participants, and reports of the committee.	1163-1164
NASW: Medical Social Work Section: Joint Committee on Participation in Medical Education, Survey Questionnaire Analysis, 1955 Card file made from 1955 questionnaire.	1165
NASW: Medical Social Work Section: Joint Committee on Participation in Medical Education, Survey Questionnaire Bibliography, 1955-1957 Bibliographies on social workers' participation in medical education.	1166
NASW: Medical Social Work Section: Joint Committee on Participation in Medical Education, Survey Questionnaire Correspondence, 1955-1956 Correspondence and results of questionnaire from preliminary survey.	1167
NASW: Medical Social Work Section: Joint Committee on Participation in Medical Education, Survey Questionnaire Responses re Meetings, 1955-1957 List of social workers involved in medical school teaching and summary of replies to questions on topics for regional meetings re medical education and social worker participation.	1168
NASW: Medical Social Work Section: Joint Committee on Participation in Medical Education, Region Responses to Participation in Study, 1955 List of regions for the 1955 survey and responses to regional meetings on social workers' participation in medical education.	1169
NASW: Medical Social Work Section: Joint Committee on Participation in Medical Education, Outline of Study, 1955-1958 Schedule for reporting social workers' participation in first and second year undergraduate medical curriculum and drafts and final copy of study questionnaire.	1170

NATIONAL ASSOCIATION OF SOCIAL WORKERS, INC.

Folder Title and Description of Contents	Folder
NASW: Medical Social Work Section: Joint Committee on Participation in Medical Education, Organization, 1956-1957 Correspondence re follow-up of 1955 preliminary study on the regional level and plans for the future course of the study.	1171
NASW: Medical Social Work Section: Joint Committee on Participation in Medical Education, Residency Training, 1955-1956 Replies to questionnaires re medical social workers' participation in residency training. Arranged alphabetically by state.	1172
NASW: Medical Social Work Section: Joint Committee on Participation in Medical Education, National Conference on Social Welfare Meetings, 1956-1958 Correspondence re joint meeting with psychiatric social workers at NCSW to study participation in medical education.	1173
NASW: Medical Social Work Section: Joint Committee on Participation in Medical Education, Finances, 1956-1957 Correspondence about the committee's budget.	1174
NASW: Medical Social Work Section: Joint Committee on Participation in Medical Education, Questionnaire, Subcommittee on Contents, Correspondence, 1955-1959 Routine correspondence.	1175-1176
NASW: Medical Social Work Section: Joint Committee on Participation in Medical Education, Questionnaire, Subcommittee on Content, 1955-1958 Drafts and revisions of questionnaires for survey.	1177
NASW: Medical Social Work Section: Joint Committee on Participation in Medical Education, Questionnaire, Trial-run Replies, 1957 Preliminary sampling for survey questionnaire.	1178
NASW: Medical Social Work Section: Joint Committee on Participation in Medical Education, Regional Committee of Social Workers Participating in Medical Education, 1957-1959 Minutes and correspondence re questionnaire.	1179
NASW: Medical Social Work Section: Joint Committee on Participation in Medical Education, Correspondence with Deans of Medical Schools and NASW Chapters, 1958-1959 Correspondence re developing roster of social workers participating in medical education.	1180-1181

Folder Title and Description of Contents	Folder
NASW: Medical Social Work Section: Joint Committee on Participation in Medical Education, Correspondence with Deans of Medical Schools with No Social Work Teaching, 1958-1959.	1182
NASW: Medical Social Work Section: Joint Committee on Participation in Medical Education, Correspondence with Social Workers re Non-participation by Individuals or Staffs, 1958-1959 Correspondence with persons or staffs not participating in medical education.	1183
NASW: Medical Social Work Section: Joint Committee on Participation in Medical Education, Responses of Deans to Questionnaire, ca. 1959 Replies from medical schools. Material arranged by regions with key indicating distribution of medical colleges within regions.	1184-1185
NASW: Medical Social Work Section: Joint Committee on Participation in Medical Education, Social Workers' Responses to Questionnaire, ca. 1959 Tabulations on forms with responses of social workers. Arranged alphabetically by state.	1186-1188
NASW: Medical Social Work Section: Joint Committee on Participation in Medical Education, States' Reports on Personnel Participating and Teaching, 1959 Completed questionnaire forms from social work personnel participating in medical education. Arranged alphabetically by state.	1189-1211
NASW: Medical Social Work Section: Joint Committee on Participation in Medical Education, States Reports on Personnel Participating and Not Teaching, 1959 Completed forms from personnel participating in medical education but not teaching. Arranged alphabetically by state.	1212-1213
NASW: Medical Social Work Section: Joint Committee on Participation in Medical Education, Study--Descriptive Material re Course Work, 1960 Reports from medical schools re social work curriculum in school. Arranged alphabetically by state.	1214-1215
NASW: Medical Social Work Section: Joint Committee on Participation in Medical Education, Study, 1960 Evaluation of study made by Margaret Blenkner which includes tables and charts for study of content area in social work courses offered in medical schools.	1216-1217

Folder Title and Description of Contents	Folder
NASW: Medical Social Work Section: Joint Committee on Participation in Medical Education, Study, 1960 Final tables, statistics, and notes and correspondence re questionnaire returns.	1218
NASW: Medical Social Work Section: Joint Social Science Project, 1959 Memorandum of decisions and proposal for planning grant by the steering committee of the joint project with the psychiatric social work section.	1219
NASW: Medical Social Work Section, Education Consultant, Reports, 1955-1958 Reports to the executive committee on relationship to other organizations and activities in social work education, material on appointment of technical advisory committee, and miscellaneous correspondence.	1220
NASW: Medical Social Work Section, Education Consultant, Technical Advisory Committee for Consultation on Practice and Education, 1957-1959 Minutes, study of practice consultation, and analysis of education consultant's activities.	1221
NASW: Medical Social Work Section, Education Consultant, Professional Education of Medical Social Workers, 1955-1956 Correspondence.	1222
NASW: Medical Social Work Section, Practice Consultant, Correspondence, General, 1955-1957 Routine correspondence, job descriptions, reports to executive committee, agendas and memoranda, information on consultation services, statements on financing consultation visits, and "The Practice of Social Group Work" (report).	1223
NASW: Medical Social Work Section, Practice Consultant, Correspondence re Joint Survey with American Hospital Association, 1956.	1224
NASW: Medical Social Work Section, Practice Consultant, Correspondence, Personal, 1956-1957 Correspondence re recommendations, congratulatory notes, and Addie Thomas' resignation.	1225
NASW: Medical Social Work Section, Practice Consultant, Bibliographies on Tuberculosis, 1956.	1226
NASW: Medical Social Work Section, Practice Consultant, District-Region-Section Meetings, 1956-1957 Correspondence re attendance at meetings and requests for consultant to speak at meetings.	1227

Folder Title and Description of Contents	Folder
NASW: Medical Social Work Section, Practice Consultant, Federal Consultants, 1955 Listings of federal consultants in U.S. Department of Health, Education and Welfare and the Veterans Administration.	1228
NASW: Medical Social Work Section, Practice Consultant, Fees for Social Service, 1955-1956 Statements re social service departments charging fees.	1229
NASW: Medical Social Work Section, Practice Consultant, Field of Practice, 1955-1958 Reading material on medical social work field of practice and a statement, "Description of the Field of Medical Social Work Practice," prepared by the committee on description-of-practice.	1230-1231
NASW: Medical Social Work Section, Practice Consultant: Films, 1955-1956 Information sheet on available films related to medical social work.	1232
NASW: Medical Social Work Section, Practice Consultant, National Foundation for Infantile Paralysis, Case Material, 1957 Material collected for Arden House meeting (March, 1957).	1233
NASW: Medical Social Work Section, Practice Consultant: National Foundation for Infantile Paralysis, Conference on Preparation and Practice in Medical Social Service--Staff Development, 1956-1957 Correspondence re preparations for conference, material for use at conference, job descriptions, material on staff committees and functions, reports on hospital services, summary of a staff development situation, and workshop proceedings and list of attendants.	1234-1235
NASW: Medical Social Work Section, Practice Consultant: National Foundation for Infantile Paralysis, Conference on Preparation and Practice in Medical Social Service--Proceedings, 1956-1957 Correspondence, list of persons attending, agenda, and proceedings of workshops.	1236-1237
NASW: Medical Social Work Section, Practice Consultant: National Foundation for Infantile Paralysis, Conference on Preparation and Practice in Medical Social Work--Workshops, 1957-1958 Draft statements from workshops V and VI on professional development for experienced workers in preparation for publication.	1238

NATIONAL ASSOCIATION OF SOCIAL WORKERS, INC.

<u>Folder Title and Description of Contents</u>   <u>Folder</u>

NASW: Medical Social Work Section, Practice Consultant,   1239
Teaching Hospital Administration Students, 1955
     Correspondence re bibliography.

NASW: Medical Social Work Section, Practice Consultant,   1240
Case Records for Teaching Purposes, 1956
     Correspondence and case records.

NASW: Medical Social Work Section, Practice Consultant,   1241
Teaching Nurses, 1956-1958
     Correspondence re sample curricula for nursing
     education.

NASW: Medical Social Work Section, Practice Consultant,   1242-1256
Resource Files, 1944-1958
     Addie Thomas' resource files containing pamphlets,
     studies, Beth Israel Hospital's publications, <u>Chronic
     Illness Newsletter</u>, and medical social work job
     descriptions. Includes information on Los Angeles
     County Health Department, Conference on Individualized
     Services (National Social Welfare Assembly), private
     patients, recording, statistics, tuberculosis, and
     chapter talks.

NASW: Medical Social Work Section, Practice Consultant,   1257
Social Service Standards--Provisions Criteria, 1956-1958
     Revisions of criteria for evaluating social service
     departments in hospitals; Joint Commission on
     Accreditation of Hospitals report, "Standards for
     Hospital Accreditation"; joint committee of NASW
     medical social work section, American Hospital
     Association, and U.S. Public Health Service report,
     "Social Work in Hospitals."

NASW: Medical Social Work Section, Practice Consultant,   1258-1291
Consultation Services, 1955-1958
     Survey of practice consultant's visits, correspondence
     and reports re consultation services, and information
     and pamphlets collected during consultation visitations.
     Arranged alphabetically by state and within state.

NASW: Medical Social Work Section, Practice Consultant,   1292
Consultation Services, Itinerary Worksheets, 1955-1958
     Expense sheets, bills, travel vouchers, report of
     educational consultant, and schedule of practice
     consultant's visits.

NASW: Medical Social Work Section, Practice Consultant,   1293
"A Study of Practice Consultation Provided by the Medical
Social Section, NASW," 1958
     Study of practice consultation by Ethel Cohen.

NASW: Medical Social Work Section, Recruitment Consultant, 1294
Correspondence, 1955-1959

NATIONAL ASSOCIATION OF SOCIAL WORKERS, INC.

Folder Title and Description of Contents	Folder

Correspondence re approved medical social work curricula, complimentary letters on recruitment publications, material for picture story on National Foundation for Infantile Paralysis scholarship program, and summary of recruitment program for medical social work.

NASW: Medical Social Work Section, Recruitment Consultant, Reports, 1956-1960.   1295

NASW: Medical Social Work Section, Recruitment Consultant: New England Regional Consultant on Recruitment, 1958-1959   1296
    Statement on policies and principles in medical social work section recruitment program, job description for regional consultant on recruitment, and routine correspondence re appointment of New England regional consultant.

NASW: Medical Social Work Section, Recruitment: Films, 1957-1958   1297
    Correspondence re production and showing of one-minute film on medical social work, correspondence re use of recruitment filmstrip, and special orders for films, slides, and brochures.

NASW: Medical Social Work Section, Recruitment: Newspaper Clippings, 1951-1960   1298-1299
    Clippings re stories on medical social work and/or medical social workers used for recruitment purposes in pamphlets, brochures, etc.

NASW: Medical Social Work Section, Recruitment: Scrapbook, 1958-1959   1300
    Scrapbook containing newspaper clippings on medical social work.

NASW: Medical Social Work Section, Recruitment: Photograph Releases, 1957-1960   1301
    Releases permitting the section to use photographs in all phases of publications and communications media.

NASW: Medical Social Work Section, Recruitment: Recruitment Material, 1957-1962   1302-1310
    Data on requested recruitment material; revision and stock of recruitment pamphlets; routine correspondence re production of pamphlets: "Ten Questions and Answers," "A Man-Sized Job," "A Message from Dr. Paul Dudley White," and "Decision"; and recruitment kits and posters.

Folder Title and Description of Contents	Folder
NASW: Medical Social Work Section, Recruitment: Out-of-Print Material, Correspondence, 1955-1961.	1311
NASW: Medical Social Work Section, Recruitment: Out-of-Print Material, n.d. Out-of-print recruitment pamphlets, brochures, etc.	1312
NASW: Medical Social Work Section, Recruitment: Incompleted Plate Order, 1956 Correspondence.	1313
NASW: Medical Social Work Section, Recruitment: NASW Recruitment Material, 1961 Material on distribution of information on medical social work recruitment literature and samples of other NASW sections' recruitment literature.	1314
NASW: Medical Social Work Section, Recruitment: MSW Recruitment News, 1960-1961 Two issues of newsletter.	1315
NASW: Medical Social Work Section, Recruitment: Literature from Other Organizations, 1957-1960 Literature for social workers issued by American Medical Association Women's Auxiliary, American Sociological Society, American Psychological Society, and the Council on Social Work Education; information on summer work experience.	1316
NASW: Medical Social Work Section, Recruitment: Council on Social Work Education, 1962 CSWE recruitment kit, "Organizing for Social Work Recruitment."	1317
NASW: Medical Social Work Section, Recruitment: AFL-CIO Social Work Scholarships, 1956-1957 Correspondence.	1318
NASW: Medical Social Work Section, Recruitment: National Foundation for Infantile Paralysis Scholarships--Information, 1958-1960 Memoranda and brochures re health scholarship program of NFIP, sample application forms, and routine correspondence.	1319
NASW: Medical Social Work Section, Recruitment: National Foundation for Infantile Paralysis Scholarships--Correspondence, 1959-1960 Lists of 1959 NFIP health scholarship winners in medical social work, data on NFIP health scholarships for mailings, and letters to chapters urging selection of a college student candidate for medical social work scholarship.	1320

NATIONAL ASSOCIATION OF SOCIAL WORKERS, INC.

Folder Title and Description of Contents	Folder
NASW: Medical Social Work Section, Recruitment: National Foundation for Infantile Paralysis Scholarships--Letters to Chapters and Sections re Involvement, 1960.	1321-1322
NASW: Medical Social Work Section, Recruitment: National Foundation for Infantile Paralysis Scholarships--Requests for Scholarship Information, 1960 Requests for application forms and information on the NFIP scholarships.	1323-1324
NASW: Medical Social Work Section: Association of American Medical Colleges, 1956-1957 Correspondence re participation of social workers in medical education, 1956 report of AAMC's committee on educational research and services, and summary of activities at the AAMC annual meeting.	1325
NASW: Medical Social Work Section: American Committee on Maternal Welfare, 1955 Correspondence re formation of a joint committee on standards.	1326
NASW: Medical Social Work Section: American Psychiatric Association, 1956 Correspondence re participation in the APA annual meeting.	1327
NASW: Medical Social Work Section: American Occupational Therapy Association, 1956 Correspondence re Mary Hemmy's resignation.	1328
NASW: Medical Social Work Section: American Public Health Association, 1955, 1961 Minutes of the committee on public health and the behavioral sciences (October, 1955), program of annual meeting, and revised statement on educational qualifications for social workers in public health programs.	1329
NASW: Medical Social Work Section: Catholic Hospital Association, 1956 Correspondence re annual convention and medical social work section's participation.	1330
NASW: Medical Social Work Section: Council for Rheumatic Fever, 1955 Correspondence re appointment of a representative to the Council.	1331

Folder Title and Description of Contents	Folder
NASW: Medical Social Work Section: National Conference of Catholic Charities, 1956 Correspondence re workshop on medical social work at the Conference.	1332
NASW: Medical Social Work Section: National Foundation for Infantile Paralysis, 1956-1958 Correspondence re requests to NFIP for grants for practice, education, and recruitment programs of the section; report to NFIP on use of grants.	1333
NASW: Medical Social Work Section: National Health Council, 1955-1956 Minutes of meeting of executive committee on health education, board of directors, and committee on research administration of NHC; correspondence re medical social work section's participation in NHC.	1334
NASW: Medical Social Work Section: National Rehabilitation Association, 1956 Summary of first meeting of National Advisory Committee on Rehabilitation Counselor Education.	1335
NASW: Medical Social Work Section: National Social Welfare Assembly, 1955-1956 Correspondence re medical social work section representation, program of tenth anniversary meeting, and report on tax exemption and national agency salaries.	1336
NASW: Medical Social Work Section: U.S. Civil Service Commission, 1956-1957 Correspondence re revision of classification standards for clinical social workers, draft of statement, and comments by practice consultant (Addie Thomas) on tentative draft.	1337
NASW: Medical Social Work Section: U.S. Department of Health, Education and Welfare--Conference with Secretary Flemming, 1958-1959 Correspondence, agenda, and list of participants in joint conference of national organizations related to work of HEW.	1338
NASW: Medical Social Work Section: U.S. Children's Bureau, 1956 Letter re Mary Hemmy's resignation.	1339
NASW: Medical Social Work Section: U.S. Office of Vocational Rehabilitation, 1956 Correspondence re OVR teaching and traineeship grants and Mary Hemmy's resignation.	1340

Folder Title and Description of Contents	Folder
NASW: Medical Social Work Section: U.S. Public Health Service, 1955-1956 Correspondence re conference with schools of social work, notes on conference on social work research in tuberculosis, and list of social workers involved in medical school teaching.	1341
NASW: Medical Social Work Section: U.S. Public Health Service, 1948-1956 Reprints, near-print material, and articles on tuberculosis; list of tuberculosis reprints.	1342
NASW: Medical Social Work Section: U.S. Bureau of Labor Statistics, 1956 Draft of proposed survey of salaries and working conditions in hospitals in large communities.	1343
NASW: Medical Social Work Section: U.S. Women's Bureau, 1955-1956 Correspondence re national conference on "The Effective Use of Womanpower" and revision of <u>Handbook on Women Workers</u>.	1344
NASW: Medical Social Work Section: U.S. Veterans Administration, 1956 Correspondence re Mary Hemmy's resignation.	1345
NASW: Medical Social Work Section, "Guide Book on the Regional Institute Program," 1958 Job description of field director for regional institute program and guidebook to facilitate the establishment and maintainance of the program.	1346
NASW: Medical Social Work Section, "Guide Book: Regional Institute Program," 1962 Revised edition (chapter one missing).	1347
NASW: Medical Social Work Section, Medical Social Work Sections in NASW Chapters, Correspondence, 1956 Correspondence re organization of sections within the local chapters and membership status of former members, copies of newsletters and bylaws, and petitions for formation of sections.	1348
NASW: Medical Social Work Section, Medical Social Work Sections in NASW Chapters, Chairmen, 1955-1958 List of chairmen, notification to section of National Health Council's health forum, and requests for lists of members affiliated with medical schools.	1349

Folder Title and Description of Contents	Folder
NASW: Medical Social Work Section, Medical Social Work Sections in NASW Chapters, Membership, 1955-1956 Requests for information on members joining medical social work sections, lists of new members in these sections, and membership figures.	1350
NASW: Medical Social Work Section, Medical Social Work Sections in NASW Chapters, Reports, 1956 Tentative recommendations re purposes, functions, and suggested structure for medical social work sections; proposed bylaws for sections.	1351
NASW: Medical Social Work Sections, Medical Social Work Sections in NASW Chapters, Approved, 1955-1956 Routine correspondence re establishment and organization of sections in newly-formed NASW chapters, lists of sections, petitions, and list of chapter chairmen.	1352
NASW: Medical Social Work Section, Medical Social Work Sections in NASW Chapters, Approved, 1955-1956 Routine correspondence notifying of formal approval of medical social work sections. Arranged alphabetically by state and chapter.	1353
NASW: Medical Social Work Section, Medical Social Work Sections in NASW Chapters, Affiliates, 1955 Routine correspondence notifying approval of affiliation with medical social work sections.	1354
NASW: Medical Social Work Section, Medical Social Work Sections in NASW Chapters, Finance, 1955-1956 Correspondence re payments for consultation services, travel expenses, publication costs, budgets, payroll payments, and expense account forms.	1355
NASW: Psychiatric Social Work Section, Practice, 1955 Minutes, report of national private practice committee, statement on purpose and scope of study of job responsibilities of social workers in psychiatric hospitals and clinics, and memoranda on preparatory material for the commission on social work practice.	1356
NASW: Social Work Research Section, Executive Committee, 1955-1957 Minutes; reports of section committees, NCSW meetings, and of the subcommittee on social research: "Social Security Cooperative Research and Demonstration Grant Program: Role of Voluntary Agencies in Cooperative Social Research Program"; budget.	1357

Folder Title and Description of Contents	Folder
NASW: Social Work Research Section, Program Committee, 1955-1956 Correspondence re establishment and membership of committee, minutes, and draft report of program planning committee. Main correspondents are Margaret Blenkner, Edward E. Schwartz, and Lili G. Sweat.	1358-1359
NASW: Social Work Research Section, Methodology Committee, 1956-1958 Correspondence and memoranda re establishment and membership of committee, report on developing monograph on methodology in social work research, suggestions for developmental workshop, and reports of subcommittees.	1360
NASW: Social Work Research Section, Other Committees, 1955-1958 Minutes of education, publications, and workshop committees; progress report of committee on research component of social work curriculum; and final report and recommendations of communications committee.	1361
NASW: Social Work Research Section, NASW Program, Ad Hoc Committee, 1956 Report of conference on NASW program and meeting with representatives of the Council on Social Work Education.	1362
NASW: Social Work Research Section, Needs and Problems of Research Workers, Ad Hoc Committee, 1956-1957 Correspondence re assignment, membership, and establishment of committee.	1363
NASW: School Social Work Section, Practice--Reports and Surveys, 1956-1961 Report on "School Social Work Practice in Twelve Communities"; survey of public school trends in Texas and educational preparation for Michigan visiting teacher program; survey of pre-social work program at Southern University, Baton Rouge, Louisiana; workshops on practice; paper on special services in schools; questionnaire on role of school social workers in consultation service; correspondence and reports illustrating development of school social work program.	1364-1367
NASW: School Social Work Section, Practice--International Association of Pupil Personnel Workers, 1960-1961 Definition of consultation, correspondence re International Association of Pupil Personnel Workers and school social work participation in convention, and copies of papers presented at the convention.	1368

NATIONAL ASSOCIATION OF SOCIAL WORKERS, INC.

Folder Title and Description of Contents	Folder
NASW: School Social Work Section: Institute on School Social Work, 1959-1960 Proceedings of the Institute on School Social Work sponsored by Fordham University School of Social Service.	1369
NASW: School Social Work Section, "School Social Work with Delinquents," ca. 1959 Manuscript by Joseph Rosner.	1370-1371
NASW: School Social Work Section: Masters' Thesis re School Adjustment Counsellor Program, 1960 "A . . . Study of the School Adjustment Counsellor Program in . . . Massachusetts . . . ," by Doria Amelia Berggren, Phyllis Marie Borah, Beverly Elizabeth Ringer, Albert Scofield, and Mary Kate Siedle, Boston University School of Social Work.	1372-1373
NASW: School Social Work Section: Unpublished Doctoral Dissertation on the School Social Worker, 1960 "The School Social Worker: An Analysis of Present Teaching Programs in Relationship to Job Functions," by Robert Bernard Rowen, University of Arizona.	1374
NCSWDM: Historical Data, 1944-1955 Correspondence, memoranda, pamphlets, and financial statements re origins of NCSWDM.	1375
NCSWDM: Full Committee Reports, 1950-1955 Minutes of meetings of representatives from the participating associations: AAGW, AAMSW, AAPSW, AASW, and NASSW.	1376-1377
NCSWDM: Committee Meetings with Presidents of the Member Associations, 1952-1955 Minutes.	1378
NCSWDM: Executive Committee, Minutes, 1952-1955 Minutes and draft of letter to Nathan Cohen, president-elect of the National Association of Social Workers, requesting that NASW assume NCSWDM activities.	1379
NCSWDM: Steering Committee, Minutes, 1952-1955.	1380
NCSWDM: Civil Defense Subcommittee, 1953-1954 Material on role of social workers in civil defense, setting up local organizations of health and welfare services in time of emergency, and need for civil defense (folder incomplete).	1381

Folder Title and Description of Contents	Folder
NCSWDM: Planning Subcommittee, 1954 Minutes and material on the possibility of study of social work in relation to the armed forces.	1382
NCSWDM: Recruitment Subcommittee, 1955 Brief folder re funds.	1383
NCSWDM: Rules and Procedures Subcommittee, 1952 Includes a statement covering purposes and goals of NCSWDM.	1384
NCSWDM: Termination Subcommittee, 1955 Minutes re meeting of representatives of TIAC and NCSWDM discussing continuance of NCSWDM activities under NASW.	1385
NCSWDM: "Military Defense and Social Welfare," 1955 First draft of a report by Elizabeth Wickenden. Includes comments and criticisms of the report.	1386
NCSWDM: "Military Program and Social Work," 1952-1955 Correspondence, reports, and comments on and criticisms of Elizabeth Wickenden's report by social work leaders as well as by military men involved in social work.	1387-1389
NCSWDM: Doctors Draft Bill, 1950-1953 Correspondence and clippings re Public Law 779 ("Doctors and Dentists Draft Bill") as applicable to social workers in the armed forces.	1390
NCSWDM: Recruitment: Activities, 1953-1955 Correspondence re advice on recruitment methods for social work.	1391
NCSWDM: Recruitment: Display, 1955.	1392
NCSWDM: Recruitment: Publications and Reports, 1950-1955 Memoranda, recruitment literature, and some correspondence re recruitment activities of social work profession as well as of NCSWDM.	1393
NCSWDM: Personnel, 1952-1955 Confirmation of Cathryn S. Guyler as executive secretary of NCSWDM; statements on job qualifications and responsibilities and personnel policies and practices.	1394
NCSWDM: Reports, Releases, and Memoranda, 1951-1955.	1395-1400

NATIONAL ASSOCIATION OF SOCIAL WORKERS, INC.

Folder Title and Description of Contents	Folder
NCSWDM: Finance: Contributions, 1951 Correspondence re request to member organizations for contributions of funds to support NCSWDM.	1401
NCSWDM: Finance: Correspondence, 1951-1955 Correspondence and memoranda re financial budgeting and planning of NCSWDM. Principal correspondents are Ethel Ginsburg, Joseph P. Anderson, and John Moore, executive director of United Community Defense Services.	1402-1403
NCSWDM: Finance: Monthly Financial Reports, 1952-1955 Detailed information on financial budgeting and planning.	1404
NCSWDM: Termination, 1953-1955 Minutes, memoranda, and correspondence re termination of NCSWDM and negotiations with TIAC and NASW to preserve the functions of NCSWDM.	1405
NCSWDM: Air Force, Department of, 1951-1955 Minutes, official reports, memoranda, and correspondence related to Committee activities in connection with Air Force headquarters, specific installations, and personnel practices.	1406
NCSWDM: Air Force: Lackland Air Force Base Project, 1953-1954 Correspondence re personnel practices at Lackland Air Force Base Separation Center.	1407
NCSWDM: American National Red Cross, 1951-1954 Memoranda and correspondence re withdrawal of American Red Cross social casework services in Army hospitals, replacement of Red Cross medical and psychiatric social workers, and developments within the Red Cross in relation to the military social work program.	1408
NCSWDM: Army, Department of, 1950-1955 Reports, symposium proceedings, memoranda, and correspondence related to Committee activities in connection with Army headquarters, specific installations, and personnel practices.	1409-1410
NCSWDM: Army Legislation: HR 509, Colonels in Medical Services Corps, 1954 Correspondence re legislation for additional colonels in MSC and positions then available to social workers, as well as medical benefits for dependents (known as medicare in the armed services).	1411

Folder Title and Description of Contents	Folder
NCSWDM: Council on Social Work Education, 1954-1955 Correspondence re recruitment for social work profession.	1412
NCSWDM: Defense Department, 1950-1955 Correspondence re utilization and training of social workers in Army, and Military Adoption Boards in Germany.	1413
NCSWDM: Federal Civil Defense Administration, 1953-1955 Correspondence showing Committee relationship to federal civil defense program, and matters of mutual concern between FCDA and NCSWDM; material on preparation of a pamphlet discussing the role of social workers in civil defense.	1414
NCSWDM: National Social Welfare Assembly, Committee on Services to Armed Forces and Veterans, 1953-1955 Minutes, correspondence, report on the military situation, and a list of activities and problems of organizations involved in defense program.	1415
NCSWDM: National Social Welfare Assembly, Conference on Emergency Community Needs, 1951-1954 Agendas and minutes of special meeting of NSWA to discuss cooperation of social welfare agencies and the military, and an inventory of national emergency needs and services.	1416
NCSWDM: Navy, Department of, 1951-1955 Correspondence related to activities in connection with Naval headquarters, specific installations, and personnel practices.	1417
NCSWDM: Schools of Social Work, 1954-1955 Correspondence re NCSWDM questionnaire sent to schools of social work re students' draft eligibility and reserve status.	1418
NCSWDM: Selective Service, 1951-1954 Statements, memoranda, and correspondence chiefly concerned with requests for deferment of social work students and officer classification of social work graduates.	1419
NCSWDM: Assignment and Aid Information on Social Work in the Armed Forces, 1950-1953 Chiefly correspondence gathering information about armed forces and social work and dispensing said information to interested people and agencies.	1420-1421

Folder Title and Description of Contents	Folder
NCSWDM: Correspondence with Social Workers Serving in the Armed Forces, 1951-1955 Summary of information services to social workers re military social work, programs, policies, and procedures. Includes a partial list of correspondents.	1422
NCSWDM: Social Workers and Military Service, 1951-1955 Correspondence re problems of social workers in military service.	1423-1426
NCSWDM: United Community Defense Services, Agreements, 1951-1952 Correspondence re initiation of NCSWDM as a participating organization in UCDS.	1427
NCSWDM: United Community Defense Services, Program, 1952-1955 Correspondence, memoranda, and service reports showing relationship with United Defense Fund and reports of NCSWDM activities as a member of UCDS.	1428
NCSWDM: United Community Defense Services, Selected Reports, 1952-1955.	1429-1430

LEGAL FOLDER INVENTORY

Folder Title	Legal Folder
AASW: Conferences.	1
AASW: International Cooperation for Social Welfare Committee, National Social Welfare Assembly.	2
AASW: International Cooperation for Social Welfare Committee, Maetzgold Committee Material.	3
AASW: Job Analysis Committee.	4
AASW: Job Analysis Committee: Salary Data.	5
AASW: Anderson, Joseph P., Letters of Recommendation.	6
AASW: Armed Forces, Allowances and Allotments.	7
AASW: Armed Forces, Deferment.	8
AASW: Armed Forces, Selective Service, Medical Survey.	9
AASW: Armed Forces, Selective Service, Social Work Service to.	10
AASW: Armed Forces, Correspondence with Members in the Armed Forces.	11
AASW: Division on Government and Social Work, Committee on Federal Action on Unemployment.	12
AASW: Division on Government and Social Work, Proposed Federal Department of Welfare.	13
AASW: Division on Government and Social Work, Housing Committee, National Activities.	14
AASW: Division on Government and Social Work, Public Assistance.	15
AASW: Division on Government and Social Work, Public Assistance, Colorado.	16
AASW: Division on Government and Social Work, Public Assistance, Indiana.	17
AASW: Division on Government and Social Work, Public Assistance, Ohio.	18
AASW: Howard, Donald S., AASW National Correspondence.	19

Folder Title	Legal Folder
AASW: Howard, Donald S., International Conference of Social Work, Correspondence.	20
AASW: Howard, Donald S., International Conference of Social Work, Program Committee, General Correspondence.	21
AASW: Howard, Donald S., International Conference of Social Work, Program Committee, Speakers' Refusals.	22
AASW: Howard, Donald S., International Conference of Social Work, Program Committee, Suggestions re Speakers and Meetings.	23
AASW: Migrants.	24
AASW: National Recovery Administration, Codes for Professions and Industries.	25
AASW: Political Parties.	26
AAMSW: Administrative Committee.	27
AAMSW: Bylaws Committee.	28
AAMSW: Editorial Committee.	29
AAMSW: Education Committee, Teaching of Student Nurses Subcommittee.	30
AAMSW: Education Committee, Public Programs Teaching Material.	31
AAMSW: Exhibits Committee.	32
AAMSW: Finance Committee, Correspondence.	33
AAMSW: Finance Committee, Minutes and Reports.	34
AAMSW: Functions Committee.	35
AAMSW: Medical Social Practice Committee, Medical Social Activities in Public Medical Care Programs Subcommittee, Outlines and Data.	36
AAMSW: Medical Social Practice Committee, Statistical Recording Subcommittee.	37
AAMSW: Nominations Committee.	38
AAMSW: Program Committee.	39

Folder Title	Legal Folder
AAMSW: Public Relations Committee.	40
AAMSW: Records Committee.	41
AAMSW: Standards (Minimum) Committee.	42
AAMSW: Salary Studies.	43
NASSW: Annual Reports of the Standards Committee, 1930-1931.	44
NASSW: Miscellaneous Newsletters of AAVT, 1932-1935.	45
AAPSW: Proposed Changes in Bylaws, 1939.	46
ASCO: Financial Accounts.	47
TIAC: Finances, Bank Resolution.	48
TIAC: Local Chapter Organization Committee for NASW.	49
TIAC: AAMSW, TIAC Planning Committee for NASW.	50
TIAC: AASW Certificate of Incorporation for NASW.	51
TIAC: AASW, TIAC Social Policy and Action Committee for NASW.	52
TIAC: AASW, TIAC Local Chapter Organization Committee for NASW.	53
TIAC: AASW, Papers on Planning for a Single Organization (Glasser).	54
TIAC: ASCO, Correspondence.	55
NASW: Medical Social Work Section, Joint Committee on Participation in Medical Education.	56
NCSWDM: Historical Data.	57
NCSWDM: Military Program and Social Work--Outline for Statement, Comments and Criticism.	58
NCSWDM: Recruitment, Publications and Reports.	59
NCSWDM: Reports, Releases, and Memoranda.	60
NCSWDM: Finance, Correspondence.	61

APPENDIX

The following is a list of ephemera removed from the collection and placed in the Center's ephemera file. The material is listed below by section of the collection from which it was removed (AASW, AAMSW, etc.). Within these sections, the material is listed alphabetically by publishing association. An association's serial publications are listed first; non-serial publications are listed chronologically with undated material first. Pamphlets and reprints with no publishing association are listed chronologically with undated material first. No ephemera was removed from the Social Work Research Group, TIAC, and the National Association of Social Workers (post-1955) sections.

No attempt has been made to secure exact bibliographic information.

The material is held in the Social Welfare Archives ephemera collection by publishing association.

American Association of Social Workers

American Association of Social Workers. AASW Bulletin (formerly the Membership Bulletin), 1947-1955.

_____. Committee on International Cooperation for Social Welfare. International Social Welfare News Bulletin, 1947-1951.

_____. Public Social Policy Bulletin, 1953-1954.

_____. Social Work Journal (formerly the Compass) reprints, 1935-1955.

_____. Notes to Chapters from the Executive Secretary, 1943-1951.

_____. Studies in the Practice of Social Work, no. 1. Interviews: A Study of the Methods of Analysing and Recording Social Case Work Interviews, 1931.

_____. Studies in the Practice of Social Work, no. 2. Social Case Work: Generic and Specific. A Report of the Milford Conference, 1935.

_____. Studies in the Practice of Social Work, no. 3. Lula Jean Elliott. Social Work Ethics, 1931.

_____. Vocational Studies Series, no. 1. Vocational Aspects of Psychiatric Social Work, 1929.

_____. Vocational Studies Series, no. 2. Vocational Aspects of Family Social Work, 1926.

_____. Vocational Studies Series, no. 3. Vocational Aspects of Medical Social Work, 1927.

_____. Alice S. Cheyney. The Nature and Scope of Social Work, 1926.

_____. Frances N. Harrison. The Growth of a Professional Association, 1935.

_____. Some Points on Professional Standards: A Report on Group Discussion (summarized by Martha Maltman and Grace Marcus), 1936.

_____. Four Papers on Professional Function, 1937.

_____. Dorothy C. Kahn. Unemployment and Its Treatment in the United States, 1937.

_____. Joe Hoffer. Outline for Agency Self-Evaluation of Personnel Practices Based on Personnel Practices in Social Work, AASW, 1947.

_____. "Information on S. 866, Taft-Ellender-Wagner National Housing Commission Bill," 1947.

_____. Donald S. Howard (ed.). Community Organization: Its Nature and Setting, 1947.

_____. Social Work as a Profession, ca. 1947.

_____. Research in Social Work: A Report of the Workshop on Research in Social Work, 1948.

_____. Myron Falk. Settlement Laws: A Major Problem in Social Welfare, 1948.

_____. Philip Klein and Ida C. Merriam. The Contribution of Research to Social Work, ca. 1948.

_____. Harriett M. Bartlett. "Objectives and Methods of Social Work Practice: A Tentative Bibliography," 1949.

_____. "A Social Policy for Today: AASW Policy Statements on Social Assistance and Social Insurance, Health and Medical Care, National Housing Program, International Cooperation for Social Welfare," 1949.

_____. Felix M. Gentile and Donald S. Howard. General Assistance With Special Reference to Practice in 47 Localities of the United States, 1949.

_____. Elizabeth de Schweinitz and Karl de Schweinitz. The Content of the Public Assistance Job, ca. 1949.

_____ and the American Psychological Association. "Proceedings of Conference on Cooperation Between Psychology and Social Work," 1951.

_____. Confidentiality of Assistance Records, 1952.

_____. "Selected Bibliography on Issues in Public Assistance, 1952," 1952.

_____. "Preliminary Directory of Agencies with International Social Welfare Programs," 1952.

_____. Ernest V. Hollis and Alice L. Taylor. Abridgment of Social Work Education in the United States, 1952.

_____. "The Role of Social Service in Raising the Standard of Living," 1952.

_____. Harleigh B. Trecker et al. Education for Social Work Administration, 1952.

_____. Social Workers in 1950: A Report on the Study of Salaries and Working Conditions in Social Work, Made by the Bureau of Labor Statistics, 1952.

NATIONAL ASSOCIATION OF SOCIAL WORKERS, INC.

_____. Charlotte Towle. Common Human Needs, 1952.

_____. Mildred Sikkema. Report of a Study of School Social Work Practice in Twelve Communities, 1953.

_____. "Preliminary Directory of Organizations Affording Foreign Opportunities for Social Welfare Personnel," 1954.

_____. Elizabeth Wickenden. How to Influence Public Policy: A Short Manual on Social Action, 1954.

_____. New York City Chapter. "United Nations--How It Works and What It Does in the Field of Social Welfare," 1952.

_____. Toledo (Ohio) Chapter. "Toledo Social Workers: A Study Made by the Toledo Consumers League," 1929.

_____. District of Columbia Chapter. Principles of Confidentiality in Social Work, 1946.

American Library Association. Economic Status of Library Personnel: 1949, 1950.

American Public Welfare Association and National Association of Housing Officials. Joint Committee on Housing and Welfare. Where Housing and Welfare Meet: A Statement of Joint Administrative Responsibility, 1940.

_____. "Relations Between Public Housing and Community Services: A Report by the Joint Committee on Housing and Welfare," 1946.

Association for the Study of Community Organization. ASCO Checklist and Newsletter (formerly the ASCO Newsletter), 1947-1955.

_____. Current Publications on Community Organization: A Bibliographical Checklist, 1955.

_____. "Toward a Bibliography on Community Organization for Social Welfare," 1950.

International Union, United Automobile, Aircraft and Agricultural Implement Workers of America (UAW-CIO). Homes for Workers in Planned Communities Thru /sic/ Collective Action, 1943.

_____. Memorandum on Post War Urban Housing, 1944.

National Association of Housing Officials. Journal of Housing, v. 5, June, 1948.

_____. Administrative Personnel for Local Housing Authorities, 1937.

_____. 4,000,000 Tenants: A Study of English Public Housing Management, 1940.

_____. Housing for the United States after the War, 1944.

_____. The Rent Certificate Plan, 1944.

_____. Community Services and Public Housing, 1947.

National Association of Real Estate Boards. Post-War Cities, 1944.

National Association of School Social Workers. Membership Newsletter, 1950-1955.

National Committee on Housing. Your Stake in Community Planning, 1944.

National Committee on Service to Veterans (under the auspices of the National Social Work Council). Community Services for Veterans: A Guide for Planning and Coordination, 1944.

National Conference of Catholic Charities. Msgr. John O'Grady. Housing for Middle Income Families, ca. 1947.

National Education Association. Report of the First National Conference on Citizenship, 1946.

_____. Report of the Second National Conference on Citizenship, 1947.

National Planning Association. Hans Christian Sonne. Democratic Planning in Action, 1946.

National Public Housing Conference. *A Housing Program . . . for Now and Later*, 1948.

National Recreation Association. *Recreation Leadership Standards*, 1949.

Pittsburgh (Pennsylvania) Housing Association. "Standard for Dwellings of Client Families," 1931.

Pittsburgh Housing Authority. *The First Seven Years*, 1944.

Public Administration Service. *Housing and Welfare Officials Confer: A Summary of Discussion at the Joint Conference of Housing and Welfare Officials*, 1939.

Temporary Inter-Association Council of Social Work Membership Organizations (TIAC). *Plan for a Single New Organization of Social Workers*, 1952.

U.S. Department of the Interior. United States Housing Authority. Edith Elmer Wood. *Slums and Blighted Areas in the United States*, 1938.

U.S. Federal Works Agency. United States Housing Authority. *Planning for Recreation in Housing*, 1939.

_____. *Housing and Welfare: Report of Survey*, 1940.

U.S. National Housing Agency. Federal Public Housing Authority. "Handbook on Project Services of the Federal Public Housing Authority for the Use of Cooperating Agencies," 1944.

_____. *Report of the National Conference of FPHA Project Services Advisers on Community Services and Tenant Activities*, 1946.

_____. *Reference and Source Material*, 1947.

U.S. 80th Congress 1st Session. Senate Report no. 140. Committee on Banking and Currency. *National Housing Commission Act*, 1947.

U.S. National Resources Planning Board. *Housing: The Continuing Problem*, 1940.

Welfare Council of New York City. Housing Handbook for Social Workers, 1942.

Woman's Foundation. Improved Family Living Through Improved Housing, 1945.

World Federation for Mental Health. Annual Report: 1954, 1954.

Wickenden, Elizabeth. "The Situation in Public Welfare," 1955.

American Association of Medical Social Workers

American Academy of Pediatrics. Committee on School Health and School Health Education. "The Improvement of School Medical Service," 1940.

American Association of Medical Social Workers. Bulletin, 1929-1945.

_____. Newsletter, 1950-1955.

_____. Medical Social Work, 1954-1955.

_____. "Report of the Reorganization Committee," 1941.

_____. "Second Report of the Reorganization Committee," 1942.

_____. "Study of Medical Social Curricula Approved by the American Association of Medical Social Workers in 1944," 1944.

_____ and the Association of American Medical Colleges. Joint Committee on the Teaching of Social and Environmental Factors in Medicine. Widening Horizons in Medical Education: Teaching of Social and Environmental Factors in Medicine, 1947.

_____. Education for Medical Social Work: The Curriculum Content, 1951.

_____. A Statement of Standards to be Met by Social Service Departments in Hospitals, Clinics, and Sanatoria, 1954.

_____. *A Statement of Personnel Practices in Medical Social Work*, 1954, 1955.

_____. North Atlantic District. "A Report on Staff Education," ca. 1950.

_____. North Atlantic District. "Criteria for Staff Education Programs in Hospital Social Service Departments," ca. 1951.

American Association of Schools of Social Work. "Recommendations and Report of the Curriculum Committee," 1944.

_____. *Accredited Graduate Professional Schools of Social Work*, 1952.

American Association of Social Workers. "A Survey of the Current Relief Situation in Twenty-Eight Selected Areas of the United States," 1937.

_____. Press release re preceding survey, 1937.

_____. 1946 Delegate Conference. "Statement of Principles Governing a Program of Comprehensive Health and Medical Services," 1946.

_____. *Report from Washington, 1955*.

American Public Health Association. "Medical Care Bibliographies," 1953.

American Social Health Association. Celia S. Deschin. *Teenagers and Venereal Disease: A Sociological Study*, 1961.

Colorado State Department of Public Welfare. Denver Bureau of Public Welfare. *The Denver Relief Study: A Study of 304 General Relief Cases Known to the Denver Bureau of Public Welfare on January 15, 1940*, ca. 1940.

Commission on Chronic Illness. *Chronic Illness News Letter*, 1953-1956.

Council on Social Work Education. "Focus and Direction for Social Work Education," two undated editions.

Family Service Association of America. "'Freedom from Want' Goal Slipping" (press release), 1948.

National Committee for Mental Hygiene. Medicine and the Neuroses: Report of the Hershey Conference on Psychiatric Rehabilitation, 1945.

National Conference of Social Work. Edith G. Seltzer. "Some Experiments in Studying Case Loads in Medical Social Service Departments," 1941.

National League of Nursing Education. List of Accredited Schools of Nursing, 1944.

_____. Statement of Policy for the Accreditation of Schools of Nursing, 1944.

National Rehabilitation Association. "Problems in Developing Understanding Among the Professions Concerned with Rehabilitation," 1955.

National Social Welfare Assembly. "What the Social Agency Needs and Could Use in Consultant Service," 1954.

Pittsburgh University. School of Social Work. Eleanor E. Cockerill. "A Conceptual Framework for Social Casework (A Suggestive Outline)," 1952.

Russell Sage Foundation. "Statistics of Medical Social Casework Service in 1943 in 52 Hospitals in New York City," 1944.

_____. Statistics of Medical Social Casework in New York City: 1944, 1945.

_____. Statistics of Medical Social Casework in New York City: 1945, 1946.

U.S. Office of Defense, Health and Welfare Services. Office for Emergency Management. Family Security Committee. "Medical Social Work Personnel," 1942.

Welfare Council of Metropolitan Chicago. "Cooperation Between Family or Children's Agencies and Social Service Departments of Medical Agencies," 1949.

Farmer, Gertrude L. *A Form of Record for Hospital Social Work*, 1921.

National Association of School Social Workers

American Association of Schools of Social Work. *Member Schools of the American Association of Schools of Social Work*, 1949.

*American Association of Visiting Teachers. "Social Case Work in Public Schools," 1941.

National Association of School Social Workers. *Membership Newsletter*, 1947-1955.

_____. "National Association of School Social Workers," n.d.

_____. "Would You Like to Do School Social Work?" n.d.

_____. "Selected Readings of School Social Workers," 1949.

_____. "Formation of Local Chapters," 1954.

_____. "Selected Readings for School Social Workers," 1954.

_____. "The Swing Is to NASSW," 1954.

_____. "National Association of School Social Workers," ca. 1955.

*National Association of Visiting Teachers. *Bulletin*, 1928-1929.

Pamphlets

John J. Alderson. "The Specific Content of School Social Work," n.d.

W. Mason Matthews. "Practical Approaches in Understanding a Child's Intelligence and School Achievement," n.d.

*Predecessor of National Association of School Social Workers (NASSW).

Grace W. Mitchell. "The Process of Interprofessional Relationship Between Teacher and School Social Worker," n.d.

Joseph C. Noethen. "The Parent, the Citizen, and the School," n.d.

Helen L. Palmeter. "The Child-In-School and the Helping Team," n.d.

Emilie Rannells. "Teachers and the School Counselling Service," n.d.

Ruth Smalley. "The School Social Worker and the Social Development of the Child," n.d.

Jane Wille. "School Social Work in Relation to the Use of Community Agencies," n.d.

Carmelite Janview. "Essentials of a Training Program for School Social Workers," 1948.

Dorothy Hankins. "Cooperative Working Relationships Between School Social Workers and Agency Social Workers," 1949.

Florence Poole. "Relating Case Working Agencies to School Programs," 1949.

Mary N. Taylor. "Contributions of Professional Social Work Training to the Development of Essential School Social Work Skills," 1949.

Oakland (California) Public Schools. "Handbook for Teachers," 1955.

Reprints

Edith M. Everett. "Information Needed in a Case Study," Elementary School Principals Fifteenth Yearbook, n.d.

Jane F. Culbert. "The Visiting Teacher," College Women and the Social Sciences, 1934.

Alma Laabs. "Development of Social Work in Education," Compass, March, 1945.

Jane Wille. "The Relation of the School to Protective Services for Children," NASSW Bulletin, June, 1949.

Mildred Sikkema. "An Analysis of the Structure and Practice of School Social Work Today," Social Service Review, December, 1949.

Florence Poole. "The Social Worker's Contribution to the Classroom Teacher," Journal of Exceptional Children, December, 1950.

Ruth Smalley. "Some Elements of Supervision in School Social Work," NASSW Bulletin, June, 1951.

Jules V. Coleman. "Meeting the Mental Health Needs of Children in School Today: Psychiatric Implications for the Practice of School Social Work," NASSW Bulletin, September, 1951.

Mildred Sikkema. "School Social Services," Social Work Year Book, 1951.

Ruth Smalley. "The Significance of Believing--for School Counsellors," NASSW Bulletin, September, 1952.

Hyman S. Lippman. "Emotional Problems Presented by the Child in the School Setting," NASSW Bulletin, December, 1952.

Lois Meredith French. "Where We Went Wrong in Mental Hygiene," NASSW Bulletin, March, 1953.

Hyman S. Lippman. "The Role of Parents in Emotional Problems Presented by Children in the School Setting," NASSW Bulletin, June, 1953.

Philippa Eggleston. "The Role of the Clinic Social Worker in Relation to the School Child," Journal of Psychiatric Social Work, January, 1954.

Mary-Alice Sarvis. "Unique Functions of Public School Guidance Programs," Mental Hygiene, April, 1954.

Mildred Sikkema. "Removing the Causes of Non-Attendance at School," NASSW Bulletin, June, 1954.

Robert C. Taber. "Children Caught in Cross-Currents," NASSW Bulletin, June, 1954.

Helen E. Weston. "School Social Work: 1953," NASSW Bulletin, December, 1954.

John C. Nebo. "Interpretation of School Social Welfare Services to Educators and Other Professionals Who Serve the Schools," NASSW Bulletin, March, 1955.

Paul Simon. "Social Group Work in the Schools," NASSW Bulletin, September, 1955.

Jane Wille. "The School Social Worker Helps the Child Through Collaboration with Other School Personnel," NASSW Bulletin, September, 1955.

John R. Altmeyer. "Public School Services for the Child with Emotional Problems," Social Work, April, 1956.

Morton M. Hunt. "The Truant Officer Learns to Smile," Saturday Evening Post, December 15, 1956.

American Association of Psychiatric Social Workers

American Association of Psychiatric Social Workers. Journal of Psychiatric Social Work (formerly the News-Letter of AAPSW), 1926-1955. Includes index for 1931-1941.

_____. News Bulletin, 1950-1955.

_____. Membership Directories:
"Members of the American Association of Psychiatric Social Workers," 1930.
Membership List, 1936-1937.
"Geographic Distribution of Members of the A.A.P.S.W.," 1938.
Membership List, 1938, 1940-1942.
"Additions and Corrections to the A.A.P.S.W. Membership List Since 1942," 1943.
Membership List, 1948.
Members, 1951, 1954.

_____. Psychiatric Social Work, 1926.

_____. American Association of Psychiatric Social Workers, 1926.

_____ and the American Association of Social Workers. Vocational Aspects of Psychiatric Social Work: The First of a Series of Vocational Studies, 1926.

_____. Psychiatric Social Work and the State Hospitals, 1928.

_____. American Association of Psychiatric Social Workers, 1928.

_____. American Association of Psychiatric Social Workers, ca. 1930.

_____. A Case in Attitude Therapy, 1935.

_____. Lois Meredith French. The American Association of Psychiatric Social Workers: Its History, Purpose, and Activities, 1941.

_____. Mary-Ellen Woodcock. All in the Day's Work of Miss Morton, Psychiatric Social Worker, 1943.

_____. Minna Field. Bibliography of the Development and Practice of Military Psychiatric Social Work, 1945.

_____. "American Association of Psychiatric Social Workers," 1950.

Reprints

Mary C. Jarrett. "The Development of Social Work," American Review, n.d.

Kathleen Ormsby. "Round Table--A Study of the Education of Psychiatric Social Workers," American Association of Hospital Social Workers Bulletin (?), n.d.

"The Psychiatric Social Worker," American Review, 1923.

"Suggestions for a Course of Training for Psychiatric Social Work," Mental Hygiene, ca. 1925.

Mary C. Jarrett. "Present Conditions in Education for Psychiatric Social Work," Hospital Social Service, v. 27, 1928.

Katharine Moore, "Psychiatric Social Service in a General Hospital Clinic," Hospital Social Service, v. 31, 1930.

Mildred C. Scoville, "An Inquiry into the Status of Psychiatric Social Work," American Journal of Orthopsychiatry, v. 1, 1931.

Ethel B. Bellsmith. "Some Industrial Placements of Women Patients Paroled from a State Hospital," Mental Hygiene, v. 24, 1940.

Tessie D. Berkman. "Research in Psychiatric Social Work," Journal of Psychiatric Social Work, v. 21, 1951.

Elizabeth B. Bech. "Implications from the Viewpoint of Social Work Practice in Mental Hospitals," Journal of Psychiatric Social Work, v. 21, 1951.

American Association of Group Workers

American Association of Group Workers. The Group, 1945-1952.

_____ AAGW Newsletter, 1950-1955.

Association for the Study of Community Organization

Association for the Study of Community Organization. Current Publications on Community Organization. A Bibliographical Checklist, 1947-1956.

_____ ASCO Checklist and Newsletter (formerly the ASCO Newsletter), 1948-1955.

National Committee on Social Work in Defense Mobilization

U.S. Defense Department. The Armed Forces Officer, 1950.

U.S. Department of Health, Education and Welfare. Public Health Service. Mental Health Implications in Civilian Emergencies, 1953.

U.S. Selective Service. Annual Report of the Director of Selective Service for the Fiscal Year 1953, 1954.

U.S. War Department. Officer Classification, Commissioned and Warrant, 1946.

An Inventory of the Papers of the National Association of Social Workers Metropolitan Washington Chapter, Washington, D.C.

PREPARED BY
Loren W. Crabtree

SWC1 National Association of Social Workers, Metropolitan Washington
W276 Chapter, Washington, D.C.

Papers, 1924-1965

30 folders

A portion of the papers of the Metropolitan Washington, D.C., Chapter of the National Association of Social Workers (NASW) was deposited in the Social Welfare History Archives Center of the University of Minnesota Libraries on January 20, 1966. The papers, which are closely related to those of the National organization, include materials for the years 1924-1965, but center on 1958-1964. The collection, which was processed in July, 1966, is comprised primarily of published (printed or mimeographed) materials, although there is some correspondence which relates directly to the local activities of the Chapter. Approximately one-half of the 2.5 lineal-foot collection contained pamphlets, government publications, bulletins and reports from other social welfare agencies, and incomplete runs of journals and news bulletins. These materials, which are listed at the end of this description, were removed and placed in the Center's pamphlet collection. Generally, four kinds of materials remain in the collection:

(1) mimeographed minutes of the Chapter's committee meetings, along with agendas and notices of meetings;
(2) article reprints from "trade" journals and opinion journals such as the Nation;
(3) speeches, reports, and papers on various social welfare issues; and
(4) statements on certain items of national legislation.

These materials provide information on a wide variety of topics of which some of the most prominent are:

(1) health care for the aged,
(2) "corruption" in public welfare,
(3) civil rights generally and segregation in particular,
(4) the "professionalization" of social work,
(5) the confidentiality of the agency-client relationship,
(6) curricula for schools of social work,
(7) care of children and the problems of juvenile delinquency,
(8) legal regulation of social work,
(9) standards in social work, including the problem of private practice,
(10) mental health and psychiatric casework,
(11) social action, especially lobbying for welfare legislation, and
(12) education for social workers.

The collection contains quite extensive material on all these topics, especially if the pamphlets are consulted, but subjects 2, 5, 9, 10 and 11 are covered most thoroughly.

For the most part, the collection appears to be the "research files" of the Chapter; i.e., those materials and studies which the Chapter office prepared on certain important problems in social welfare and then communicated to the membership. Except, then, for copies of the By-laws, occasional reports of the various committees and the rather extensive materials relating to the Private Practice Committee, these papers do not contain the actual operating data of the Chapter. Consequently, very little about the Chapter itself can be learned from the collection, and no historical sketch or work summary can be prepared for it. The Partial Subject Inventory which follows, however, provides leads to some of the important problems which engaged the interest of the Chapter.

PARTIAL SUBJECT INVENTORY

CASEWORK - PSYCHIATRIC
    Folder 4

EDUCATION FOR SOCIAL WORK
    Folders 9, 28

GROUP WORK
    Folder 11

HEALTH CARE FOR THE AGED
    Folders 1-2

LEGAL REGULATION OF WELFARE ENTERPRISES
    Folders 13, 23-24

LOBBYING ACTIVITIES
    Folder 29

METROPOLITAN WASHINGTON CHAPTER OF THE NASW
    Committees
        Changing Policies in Public Welfare: folder 3
        Ethics: folder 4
        Executive: folder 10
        Practice: folder 15
        Private Practice: folders 16-17
        Social Policy and Action: folder 29
    Internal Organization: folder 12
    Member Communication Service: folder 14
    Private Practice Directory: folders 18-22

OLD AGE - PROBLEMS OF
    Folders 1-2

PERSONNEL RECRUITMENT AND PLACEMENT
    Folders 25-26, 30

PRIVATE PRACTICE (OF CASEWORK)
    Folders 15-22

RACE RELATIONS
    Folders 5-6

SOCIAL WORK ETHICS ("CONFIDENTIALITY")
    Folder 7

NASW, WASHINGTON, D.C., CHAPTER

FOLDER INVENTORY

Folder Title and Description of Contents	Folder

Aging: 1957-1964. 1-2
    Mimeographed and printed materials re: how government and private social agencies may better serve the aged, especially in the realm of health care. Materials re: White House Conference on Aging (January 9-12, 1961). Government and NASW publications re: health care for the aged through social security.

Committee on Changing Policies in Public Welfare: 1964-1965. 3
    Summaries of discussions and proposals for action.

Committee on Ethics: 1950. 4
    Report of committee and a copy of the code of ethics.

Community Organization: 1956-1962. 5-6
    Copies of materials re: types of local organization, racial tensions in cities, the Action Reporter; mimeographed papers of the NASW Metropolitan Washington Chapter Community Organization Practice Committee. Bibliography for community organization courses. Study entitled "Voluntary Health and Welfare Agencies in the United States."

Confidentiality: 1924-1953. 7
    Extensive correspondence, studies and digests of articles re: the confidentiality of social agency-client relationships.

Consumer Affairs - Urban League Committee on: 1964. 8
    Letter and agenda for a meeting of the committee.

Curriculum Study: 1959-1962. 9
    Mimeographed communications and a speech by Alice Taylor Davis on the NASW's attempts to prepare a standard curriculum for professional schools of social work.

Executive Committee: 1961-1964. 10
    Action of the committee re: financial policies, structure and programs, overall chapter planning, and budgetary matters.

NASW, WASHINGTON, D.C., CHAPTER

Folder Title and Description of Contents	Folder
Group Work: 1955-1961. Definitions of group work and the professional qualifications for it, studies of group work in Washington, D.C., minutes of recreation conference, study of the effects of population shifts on group work.	11
Internal Chapter Organization: 1960-1964. Copies of the Chapter's By-laws, with proposed revisions and then the revised By-laws. Reports and memoranda of the Structure Committee.	12
Legal Regulation of Social Work: 1942-1964. Copy of M.A. thesis by Katherine A. Stanton on registration of social workers in California. Reports to California Governor by the Board of Examiners (1947, 1949, 1953). Various American Association of Social Workers policy statements on legal regulation. Report of a New York state committee.	13
Member Communication Service: 1964-1965. This committee functioned to coordinate the activities of the Washington Chapter. Communications re: that function.	14
Practice Committee: 1957-1964. Committee minutes, annual reports, list of members.	15
Private Practice Committee: 1956-1964. Various NASW policy statements on private practice, paper clippings on fraudulent counseling operations, addresses on the standards and practices of private casework, bibliography on private practice, list of Los Angeles private caseworkers. Minutes of the committee.	16-17
Private Practice Directory (Interim): 1960-1964. NASW Code of Ethics (1960). Forms re: listing in the Directory. Reports on the Directory to the Chapter Board of Directors. Extensive material re: applications for listing in the Directory.	18
Private Practice Directory, Budget: 1964.	19

Folder Title and Description of Contents	Folder
Private Practice Directory, Financial Planning Report: 1964.	20
Private Practice Directory, Impact on Chapter Office: 1963.	21
Private Practice Directory, Subcommittee Memoranda: 1962-1964. Minutes of meetings, copy of questionnaire and lists of respondents, reports.	22
Public Welfare: 1956-1964. Extensive booklets, pamphlets, brochures and reports on the state of Aid to Dependent Children in Washington, D.C., and across the country. Much published material re: the debate over "chiselers" in public welfare, especially concerning the Newburgh, N. Y., case, in which the city manager sought to eliminate "corruption" in public welfare.	23-24
Recruitment: 1952-1964. Extensive brochures, posters, pamphlets, lists of publications, news clippings, NASW publications, bibliography of recruiting materials; all related to the problems of recruiting sufficient personnel for social work.	25-26
Research, Social Work: 1963-1965. Mimeographed materials re: research section of the NASW.	27
Scholarships in Social Work: 1960-1962. Brochures, application forms and reports re: the National Health Foundation Scholarship Program.	28
Social Policy and Action Committee: 1960-1965. Brief reports of the committee, copies of statements made before Congressional committees, general pronouncements on social welfare issues, communications to members in behalf of certain legislation.	29
United States Employment Service: 1957-1965. Minutes of the social welfare advisory committee, and brochures re: social work placement.	30

NASW, WASHINGTON, D.C., CHAPTER

REMOVED PAMPHLETS - FOLDER TITLES

(Listed below are the folders containing the pamphlets which were removed from this collection and placed in the Center's pamphlet collection.)

(1) Administration, Social Work: 1961
Communication guide for research in social welfare administration.

(2) Children and Youth: 1960-1963
Brochures on Project Head Start (OEO), final reports and recommendations for the 1960 White House Conference on children and youth.

(3) Chronic Illness: 1960
Charts demonstrating the various aspects of chronic illness in America.

(4) Church and Social Work: 1962
Text of an address by Episcopalian Biship Rt. Reverend Arthur Lichtenberger.

(5) Citizens Committee on the Public Welfare Crisis: 1963-1965
Publications of the Committee, which sought to define the needs of the District of Columbia.

(6) Civil Defense Emergency Welfare Service: 1961
Memorandum of understanding between the NASW and the Social Security Administration.

(7) Civil Rights: 1956-1964
Magazine reprints, mimeographed speeches, brochures. Several different civil rights organizations, such as CORE, are represented.

(8) Community Health: 1962-1964
Brochures and newsletters of the National Commission on Community Health Services, Inc.

(9) Consultation in Social Work
Paper by Dr. Reuben S. Horlick on "Combined Individual and Group Psychotherapy with the Reluctant Patient."

(10) Corrections: 1961
NASW brochures.

(11) Curriculum Policy in Graduate Schools
Excerpts from the official statement of policy.

(12) Day Care: 1961
Report on D.C. day care prepared by the Health and Welfare Council of the National Capital Area.

(13) Domestic Peace Corps: 1963
Text of President Kennedy's speech, report to the President by his Study Group on the subject.

(14) Education for Social Work: 1957-1964
NASW statements on continuing education; notices of courses at George Washington, the University of Maryland, and Catholic University; brochures on adult education.

(15) Employment in Metropolitan Washington: 1963
Pamphlet prepared by the U.S. Employment Service for the District of Columbia.

(16) Family and Child Welfare: 1959-1965
United States Department of Health, Education and Welfare study of why workers leave this field; NASW and other United States Department of Health, Education and Welfare studies on various aspects of this subject.

(17) Girard Street Project: 1964
The story of a block project organized by all Souls Unitarian Church in Washington, D.C.

(18) How to Influence Public Policy:
A short manual on social action prepared by Elizabeth Wickendon of the AASW.

(19) Journal of Social Work Process: 1959-1960
Issues of this publication of the University of Pennsylvania School of Social Work.

(20) Juvenile Delinquency: 1962-1964
Pamphlets and speeches issued by the National Conference on Social Welfare and the President's committee on the employment of youth; and one copy of Children.

(21) League of Women Voters: 1964
Descriptive brochure and copies of League News.

(22) Medical Social Work: 1954-1964
Brochures and pamphlets produced by the AAMSW and the Medical Social Work Section of the NASW.

(23) Mental Deficiency: 1962-1964
Publications of the American Association on Mental Deficiency and the U.S. Department of Public Health re: mental retardation.

(24) Mental Health: 1961-1964
Reprints of magazine articles, NASW publications.

(25) NASW News: 1955-1960
Incomplete run of this official newsletter.

(26) Peace Corps and Social Workers
U.S. government brochure.

(27) Personnel Information: 1958-1965
Incomplete run of this NASW publication - 2 folders.

(28) "Plays for Living:" 1961-1964
NASW Group Work Section brochures and communications on plays dealing with social, health and family problems.

(29) Professionalism: 1962
Paper by Joseph Fletcher before the National Conference on Social Welfare on professionalism and democracy.

(30) Psychiatric Social Work: 1958-1964
Publications of NASW and U.S. Government on this subject; magazine articles.

(31) Public Health Service Grants: 1959-1961
Forms for applying for grants through the public health service.

(32) Publication Lists: 1960-1964
From several welfare organizations, such as National Association of Rehabilitation Officials (NAHRO) and National Social Welfare Assembly.

(33) Social Work Education: 1959-1961
Broken run of this bimonthly news publication of Council on Social Work Education.

(34) The Social Worker: 1959-1964
Complete run from January 1959 to March 1964 of this quarterly bulletin of the International Federation of Social Workers.

(35) Social Work Opportunities Abroad: 1958-1960
NASW pamphlets.

(36) Washington Center for Metropolitan Studies: 1960-1963
Annual reports.

13

An Inventory of the Papers of the National Federation of Settlements and Neighborhood Centers

PREPARED BY
Loren W. Crabtree

NATIONAL FEDERATION OF SETTLEMENTS AND NEIGHBORHOOD CENTERS

SWD. 1   National Federation of Settlements and Neighborhood Centers, New York, New York.

Papers, 1891-1961.

604 folders

Introduction

The papers of the National Federation of Settlements and Neighborhood Centers were deposited in the Social Welfare History Archives Center of the University of Minnesota Libraries in August, 1964, after they were released to the University by order of the Federation's Board of Directors. The papers are quite complete for the years 1911-1955, and in some instances are complete to 1962. They comprise 25 linear feet and at present are stored in 20 Paige boxes. Also included in the collection are numerous miscellaneous pamphlets (see Appendix no. 2), 55 books, 4 volumes of Neighborhood, and 2 volumes of NFS annual reports and papers, 1911-1930 (see Appendix no. 3). The papers were processed from December, 1964, to June, 1965, in the Archives Center, and form an integral part of the social welfare history collection.

NFS History

The National Federation of Settlements and Neighborhood Centers (NFS), organized in 1911 and still in operation, is a social welfare organization devoted to the betterment of settlement work throughout the United States. The NFS grew out of informal conferences to which the early pioneers in neighborhood work came to share their experiences, hopes, and enthusiasm, and to work together on national issues of concern to them and their "neighbors." The initial steps toward the NFS were taken in 1908 by seventeen settlement leaders who met in New York City to consult about fuller settlement cooperation. Instrumental at this meeting and in later years were Jane Addams, Gaylord S. White, Robert A. Woods, Albert J. Kennedy, Graham Taylor, and Lillian D. Wald. After two years of planning and fund raising, the NFS was launched in 1911. Robert A. Woods became the first secretary and Jane Addams the first president (for a list of officers since then, see Appendix no. 1).

The first major project of the NFS was to work in 1912 for legislation in behalf of a United States Children's Bureau. Since that time it has engaged in kindred projects and has greatly expanded its services. The Federation's general policy as stated in its 1929 articles of incorporation was:

> ... to federate the social settlements, neighborhood houses and similar institutions for the purpose of promoting the welfare of the settlements and the neighborhoods in which they are located; to encourage the development and maintenance of settlements in conjunction with the people of the various neighborhoods; to organize conferences, groups and studies;

to cooperate with private and governmental agencies; to consider and act upon public matters of interest to settlements and their neighbors and to act in an advisory capacity to settlements and neighborhood houses.

More specific programs of the Federation since 1929 have proved to be elaborations of these basic policies.

NFS Services

Generally, the NFS programs, past and present, fall into 12 categories. The first is field service, which provides for experienced professional personnel to visit periodically communities which already have or wish to establish community centers. On these visits, the NFS personnel meet with the local workers to exchange information about current programs, appraise the local programs, and to suggest plans of action. They also meet with other local persons, such as the heads of community chests and city planning councils, to inform them of the nature and purposes of settlement work. The field visits also are employed to screen prospective members in the NFS, and to help meet local emergencies.

The second area of work is personnel training, which includes brief workshops conducted by Federation staff for settlement executives, program directors, and departmental supervisors, and institutes conducted by schools of social work with the cooperation of national agencies. In addition, the NFS conducts miscellaneous seminars on topics of interest to settlement workers.

The NFS publishes the Round Table, a periodical issued eight times a year, as well as various bulletins, articles and messages devoted to the results of experience with programs, methods and standards, and other material of interest to settlements.

A fourth area of service, international work, has long engaged the interest of the Federation. It arranges for reciprocal visits of social workers, for cooperation with the United Nations, especially UNESCO, and for participation in the International Federation of Settlements and its various programs. The NFS also carries on fairly extensive contacts with various European national federations.

A major function of the NFS is its efforts in social education and action. This involves providing information on public issues and legislation of special concern to settlements, coordinating local settlement studies of social conditions and publishing the results.

The NFS employs a research consultant who prepares maps, population data, city planning reports, housing data and reports of existing social welfare studies for many of the Federation's member communities. These are employed in self-studies and field reports.

The seventh area is closely related to the first, as it involves preparing special studies of individual houses or cities. These studies are used to determine locations for new buildings, to appraise services, or to resolve administrative or program difficulties. The NFS prepares a few such studies each year, usually on request of the local agencies.

An eighth function of the NFS is its representation of its members in work with other national groups, such as the advisory committees of Community Chests, the National Conference of Social Work, and the Consumers National Federation.

One of the key functions of the Federation is to conduct annual national and regional conferences. These are attended by staff, board members, and representatives of the more than 255 member houses and city federations. The NFS holds its annual business meeting in conjunction with the national conference.

The tenth area of work involves consultation by correspondence with local welfare and governmental agencies. The consultation covers such matters as plans for buildings, agency programs, and extension or relocation of the work of the settlements.

The NFS also conducts a program of personnel recruitment and referral. Agencies list their vacancies and job-seekers file their papers at the national office, and then the NFS refers candidates to an appropriate opening. The Federation also conducts a yearly recruiting campaign in colleges and graduate schools of social work.

The final area of NFS service applies only in war-time, or in war-economy areas, and involves services to temporary residents or to military personnel. During World War II and the Korean emergency, this was an area of vital concern to the Federation.

These many areas of service are provided by a small staff (of about 7 full-time professional workers) for a membership of some 255 member houses and city federations. A board of directors, headed by an elected cabinet, meets twice yearly to establish general policies and programs. The actual administration is left in the hands of an executive secretary, of which there have been four in the Federation's history: Albert J. Kennedy, 1911-1934; Lillie M. Peck, 1934-1948; John McDowell, 1948-1958; and Margaret Berry, 1959 to the present (1965). The NFS depends on dues from the member agencies ($3 per $1,000 of expenditures) and the contributions of interested persons and foundations to finance its work.

Organization of the Collection

The papers cover the years 1911-1961 and are organized alphabetically in a subject file. Generally, two kinds of materials comprise the collection: personal papers and the papers of various member organizations and subdivisions of the NFS itself. In addition, the papers themselves are divided into certain obvious sections.

The first such division is composed of folders labeled "Chronological Mimeographed Materials," and contains information on routine operating matters arranged chronologically from 1945 to 1961.

Folders labeled "Committees" comprise a second division. These are miscellaneous committees established by the Federation at various times to deal with certain crucial issues, such as prohibition and peace.

Conferences of various types, including "Annual NFS Conferences," compose a third logical division. These contain quite complete reports of all the conventions.

A large section contains the papers of the city federations which are members of the National Federation, and approximately one-half of the entire collection is composed of papers of the member houses. These two sections are perhaps the richest part of the papers, for they contain detailed information about the activities of the NFS in relation to local agencies, and also about the activities of the settlement movement throughout the twentieth century. Of special interest are the houses' annual reports which, while far from complete, are nevertheless surprisingly informative.

A highly significant portion of the collection is on microfilm and is on deposit in the Archives Center. This is what the National Federation refers to as its "Bible", and contains all the important financial and year by year operating data of the Federation. The possession of this important section ensures that virtually the complete story of the NFS can be told from this collection alone.

Significant issues and personalities march across this collection with detailed clarity. Individuals of great interest include Jane Addams, Paul Kellogg, Robert A. Woods, Albert J. Kennedy, Canon Barnett, Ellen W. Coolidge, Charles Cooper, John L. Elliot, Helen Hall, Frances Ingram, Frances McFarland, Clyde Murray, Lillie M. Peck, Dr. Jane Robbins, Graham and Lea D. Taylor, Julia Lathrop, and many others. Some of the significant issues are the "Americanization" of immigrants in the settlements; the peace movement, especially between 1914 and 1941; the establishment and direction of youth work programs; the role of settlements in their national defense efforts; the establishment of such federal welfare schemes as unemployment relief and social security; music in the settlements; the relationship of the settlements to the New Deal welfare programs; the settlements and the Great Depression; prohibition; the trade union movement; various White House conferences; and enemployment generally. The detailed information about these issues and individuals makes this a key collection for the study of social welfare in twentieth century America.

PART I. SUBJECT INVENTORY

This list is intended to be a guide to some of the scattered materials on prominent topics and personalities in the collection. Most of the topics and persons have folders of their own because of the bulk of the materials, and thus can be found quite easily in the folder inventory. This list is provided as a guide only to the location of more scattered materials, and does not preclude the distribution of other such materials throughout the rest of the papers. This list, moreover, does not pretend to contain all the important people and themes found in the collection. In addition to the list below, the collection contains folders on these individuals: George L. Cohen, Amelia Earhart, Mary E. McDowell, Frances McFarland, Eleanor McMain, Dr. Jane Robbins, and Gaylord S. White.

ADDAMS, JANE
    Folders 1-3, 19-25, 118-119, 193, 292-294, 597.

THE ARTS (music, drama, poetry)
    Folders 17, 42, 73, 147, 151-170, 216-226, 245, 328, 388, 419-420, 425-428, 432, 464, 458.

BARNETT, CANON SAMUEL and DAME HENRIETTA
    Folders 18-25.

BELLAMY, GEORGE
    Folders 35-36, 549.

BOWEN, LOUISE DE KOVEN
    Folders 184-185, 292-294.

CASE WORK
    Folders 40, 241.

CHILD WELFARE
    Folders 101, 435, 583-587, 596.

CIVIL LIBERTIES ISSUE (including immigrants, minority groups and refugees)
    Folders 6, 67, 198, 216-226, 240, 252.

COOLIDGE, ELLEN
    Folders 19-25, 118-119.

COOPER, CHARLES
    Folders 120, 184-185.

DEFENSE
    Folders 116, 122-125, 301, 541, 561-582, 588, 591-592, 602.

EDUCATION IN AND FOR THE SETTLEMENTS
    Folders 4, 5, 7, 66, 76, 164-167, 173-174, 333, 338, 365, 600.

ELLIOT, JOHN L.
    Folders 35-36, 131.

GROUP WORK
    FOLDERS 69, 75, 121, 450-451.

HALL, HELEN
    Folders 126, 132, 136. References to her and to her work with the
    NFS appear in the papers of the member houses after about 1935.

HEALTH (mental and physical)
    Folders 133-136, 216-226, 230-232, 405, 409, 425-428, 441-442.

HOUSING
    Folders 43-61, 137-138, 320-321, 350-351, 398, 425-428, 512.

IMMIGRANTS
    See Civil Liberties Issues.

INGRAM, FRANCES
    Folders 139, 320-321.

INTERNATIONAL SETTLEMENT WORK
    Folders 19-25, 141, 152, 159, 175-178, 601.

KELLY, FLORENCE
    Folders 1-3, 133-134, 143, 207, 548.

KENNEDY, A. J.
    Folders 19-25, 35-36, 68, 107, 118-120, 131, 138, 394, 425.

LABOR AND UNIONISM
    Folders 144, 512, 560, 590.

THE LIQUOR PROBLEM
    Folders 68, 193.

MINORITY GROUPS
    See Civil Liberties Issues and Racial Problems.

MCDOWELL, JOHN
    Folder 124 and the later papers of the city federations and member
     houses.

THE NATIONAL FEDERATION OF SETTLEMENTS
        Anniversaries: folders 10, 272.
        Annual reports: folder 16.
        Board of directors: folders 26-33.
        Business arrangements: folders 16, 26-33, 78-99, 102-103, 140, 594.
        Conferences, Annual: folders 78-99.
        Conferences, Regional: folders 102-103.
        Directories and addresses: folder 127.
        Field visits: see the individual folders of the member houses and
                federations.

International work: folders 19-25, 141, 152, 159, 175-178, 601.
Personnel practices: 43-61, 65, 72.
Publications: folders 194, 202-205, 560.
In addition, the individual folders of the member houses and federations should be consulted to determine what the relationship of the NFS to them was, and to determine the actual work of the National Federation.

THE PEACE MOVEMENT
Folders 8, 71, 116. See also the folders on YOUTH for references to programs among young people for the promotion of peace. The folders on DEFENSE also have some interesting material on the attitudes of settlement workers toward war and peace, especially in relation to the coming of World War II.

PECK, LILLIE M.
Folders 19-25, 118-119, 128, 183, 190-191, 207, 236, 544. See also the papers of the individual houses and the city federations for miscellaneous correspondence from her during her term as executive secretary and international secretary of the NFS.

POVERTY
Folders 145, 278, 425-428, 518.

RACIAL PROBLEMS
Folders 186, 307-308, 310-311, 314, 448. See also the folders on CIVIL LIBERTIES ISSUES.

REFUGEES RESETTLEMENT AND ADJUSTMENT
See CIVIL LIBERTIES ISSUES.

RELIGION AND THE SETTLEMENTS
Folders 199-200, 595.

THE SETTLEMENT MOVEMENT
Anniversaries: folders 11-15.
History:
    general: folders 43-61, 206-207.
    individual houses: folders 242-243, 276, 279, 289, 334, 343, 354, 360, 362, 394, 401, 419, 422, 425, 444, 447, 469, 481, 487, 495, 502, 505-507, 534.
Miscellaneous programs: folders 4, 40, 74.

THE SETTLEMENTS AND GOVERNMENT PROGRAMS (including lobbying activities)
Folders 116-117, 42-61, 137, 183, 216-226, 323-324, 543-545, 559, 583-587, 589-590, 599.

THE SETTLEMENTS AND THE GREAT DEPRESSION
Folders 539-540. See also the folders under SETTLEMENTS AND GOVERNMENT PROGRAMS AND YOUTH.

SIMKHOVITCH, MARY K.
    Folders 419-420, 542.

TAYLOR, GRAHAM
    Folders 19-25, 131, 549.

TAYLOR, LEA
    Folders 19-25, 550-554.

UNEMPLOYMENT
    Folders 42, 173-174, 547, 555-559, 590, 598-600. See also the
    folders under SETTLEMENTS AND GOVERNMENT PROGRAMS AND YOUTH.

WALD, LILLIAN
    Folders 68, 593.

WOODS, ROBERT A. and ELEANOR
    Folders 18, 120, 131, 425, 597.

YOUTH WORK
    Folders 8-9, 35-39, 41, 70, 110-115, 175-177, 179-183, 208,
    216-226, 269, 384, 432, 435, 590, 601-604.

FOLDER INVENTORY

Folder Title and Description of Contents	Folder
Addams, Jane: 1910-1935 Miscellaneous correspondence with Mary Simkhovitch, Paul Kellogg, A. J. Kennedy, and NFS officers, about routine conventions, conferences, etc., 1910-1935. Letters both to and from Miss Addams. Press clippings and testimonial statements upon her death. Correspondence about the testimonials. Miscellaneous public statements by Miss Addams.	1-3
Adult Education in Settlements: 1933-1945 Historical statements about this phase of settlement work. Descriptions of a few adult education programs in selected settlements.	4
Affiliated Schools for Workers: 1936-1939 Announcements and bulletins about vocational schools for office workers. A 1939 report of the director of one such school	5

Folder Title and Description of Contents	Folder
Alien Legislation Committee: 1939-1942 This folder details the role the settlements played in encouraging aliens to register, and contains detailed correspondence between NFS personnel and interested persons regarding the civil liberties issue. Also contains U. S. Government pamphlets regarding alien registration, and correspondence with appropriate officials.	6
American Council on Education: 1937-1943 A 1937 bibliography on youth problems. Pamphlets and bulletins on the American Youth Committee.	7
American Educational Labor Service See folder number 5.	
American Youth Congress: 1937-1940 Extensive correspondence between the Congress and the NFS about cooperation in interest and support. Public statements and publications of the Congress. Minutes of the meetings of the Congress and its Board of Directors. Activities in relation to the coming of World War II. Press clippings.	8
American Youth for World Youth: 1946-1948 Budget statements, 2 news bulletins, minutes of the executive committee meetings, correspondence with the NFS.	9
Anniversary, NFS--50th: 1961 Correspondence about the plans for the celebration. Information packet on the anniversary.	10
Anniversary, Settlement Movement in England--50th: 1934 Correspondence and other materials relating to the establishment of an exhibit about the anniversary at the Chicago World's Fair, 1933-1934. Correspondence, scripts and reactions to the international radio broadcast of December 24, 1934.	11
Anniversary, Settlement Movement in United States--50th: 1936 Correspondence and surveys relating to the composition of a report on the spread of the settlement movement in U. S. A. Copy of an address given at the celebration.	12

Folder Title and Description of Contents	Folder
Anniversary, Settlement Movement in United States--60th: 1946 Correspondence between the NFS and concerned persons, including Eleanor Roosevelt, about the planning of the celebration. Speeches, press accounts, and personal reactions by letter and telegram.	13
Anniversary, Settlement Movement in United States--60th: 1947 Programs, press clippings, historical statement.	14
Anniversary, Settlement Movement in United States --60th: Research Reports Studies on local community planning and organization.	15
Annual Reports of the NFS, 1946-1957 For the years 1946-1947, 1950, 1952-1953, 1956-1957. See also the bound volume for the years 1911-1930.	16
Arts-NFS National Exhibition of Arts and Crafts: 1925 Press clippings about the exhibit and photographs of it. It traveled to various settlements across the country.	17
Barnett, Canon: 1913-1920 Press clippings about his death in 1913. Correspondence between Dame Henrietta Barnett and the NFS (especially R. A. Woods) about Canon Barnett, 1913-1920.	18
Barnett Fellowship, 1923-1936 Extensive correspondence about the formulation of the idea of the Fellowship, collection of finances, selection of the Fellows, and the actual operation of the program. Prominent correspondents include Jane Addams, J. J. Mallon (warden of London's Toynbee Hall), Ellen Coolidge, Albert Kennedy, Lillie Peck, Lea Taylor, and Erlund Field. Brochures about the Fellowship; lists of subscribers to the fund; copies of Mr. Field's study of Old Age Pensions in England.	19-25

Folder Title and Description of Contents	Folder

Board Members Division, NFS: 1931-1943   26
    Reciprocal correspondence between the NFS office
    and members of the board of directors. Deals
    with routine matters such as the time and place
    of meetings, and with procedural matters, such
    as liaison with local settlements.

Board of Directors, NFS--Minutes of Meetings: 1932-1961   27-33
    The minutes are very incomplete, with many gaps,
    especially from 1932-1946. In most cases, the
    minutes are digests of action, and are mimeographed.
    They are quite complete for 1952-1961.

Boyd, Neva L.: 1935-1946   34
    She was an instructor in the Sociology Department
    of Northwestern University. Correspondence about
    her and articles and speeches by her.

Boys and Girls Work Division--Boys Division: 1921-1935   35
    Extensive correspondence about the initiation,
    operation and details of the Division. Correspondents
    include George Bellamy, John L. Elliot, A. J. Kennedy.

Boys and Girls Work Division--Girls Division: 1921-1935   36
    Correspondence dealing with all aspects of girls
    work in many different cities and regions. Same
    correspondents as folder 35.

Boys and Girls Work Division: 1936-1944   37-38
    Conference reports and reports on special projects.
    Correspondence about the business of the Division.
    Minutes of the meetings. By-laws of the Division.

Boys Work Bulletins: 1932-1936   39

Case Work: 1922-1932   40
    Reports from various Houses about case work.
    General statement re the settlements' position
    on case work.

Character Building: 1932-1936   41
    Pamphlets dealing with youth work and aspects of
    moulding character.

Child Welfare Information Service
    See Social Legislation Information Service, folder 544.

Chronological File: 1929   42
    Correspondence and reports about group work,
    unemployment, the NFS music division, organization

Folder	Title and Description of Contents	Folder

plan for the NFS, girls work, work accounting, the poetry division, and miscellaneous matters.

Chronological Mimeographed Material: 1945-1961   43-61
    Miscellaneous publicity releases, memoranda, and address lists. Reports on housing, field visits, legislative issues and seminars, neighborhood goals, membership procedures, miscellaneous committees, and 1960 self study. Statements before Congressional hearings, and miscellaneous pamphlets, resolutions, and historical statements.

"City or Community," by Elizabeth Handasyde: 1948-1949   62
    Correspondence about the publication of this book.

Cohen, George L.: 1930-1946   63
    Correspondence between Cohen and the NFS about his position as a board member and legal counsel.

Coit, Dr. Stanton: 1944.   64
    Memorial tribute to Dr. Coit, 1944.

Committee on Annuities and Retirement Policies: 1939-1940   65

Committee on Consumer's Education: 1936-1942   66
    List of committee members. Materials on functions of the committee, especially in the legislative realm.

Committee--Good Neighbor: 1938-1943   67
    Deals with the ways this committee helped the refugees to adjust to American life. Correspondence, addresses, programs, by-laws.

Committee on Liquor Control and Lotteries: 1926-1939   68
    Much correspondence and reports on the problem of prohibition as the settlements saw it. A copy of A. J. Kennedy's article on "Saloons" and correspondence about it. Lillian Wald is an important correspondent.

Committee on Needs in Group Work--Joint Vocational Service: 1934-1938   69
    Minutes of meetings and reports of studies.

Committee on Participation of Young People: 1938-1940   70
    Correspondence and miscellaneous reports about the work of the committee.

Folder Title and Description of Contents	Folder

Committee on Peace Education: 1934-1940   71
   Extensive correspondence and publicity material
   about the issues of peace, war, and pacifism
   as related to the interests of the NFS. The
   committee was active in the peace movement, with
   Rebecca Krupp as its chairman and chief correspondent.

Committee on Personnel Practices: 1935-1936 and 1949-
1960   72
   Correspondence about personnel matters. Studies of
   settlement practices. Minutes of the committee's
   meetings, 1949-1960. Statements of NFS standards
   and practices.

Committee on Poetry: 1923-1938   73
   New Republic article (1923) on American poetry.
   Miscellaneous correspondence, reports of the
   Chairman, list of books, bulletins.

Committee on Recreation: 1933-1937   74
   Correspondence and reports about the concern of
   settlements with the proper use of increasing
   leisure time.

Committee on the Study of the Records of Groups: 1929-
1936   75
   Correspondence and reports dealing with studies
   of group work in settlements.

Committee on Worker's Education: 1934-1943   76
   Correspondence, bulletins, papers, scrapbooks,
   about the work of the committee and its relationship to the settlements. Minutes of the committee
   meetings.

The Commons   77
   Index to Volume 1-10, excluding no. 9.

Conferences, Annual, NFS: 1932-1961   78-99
   These folders include reports of various committees
   and chairmen to the NFS, publicity handouts and press
   clippings, notebooks, papers presented to the conferences,
   resolutions passed, and public addresses. The folders
   are complete and comprehensive for the years indicated.

Folder Title and Description of Contents   Folder

    Conference-Miscellaneous-Citizens on Community
    Responsibility for Human Welfare: 1928   100
        Reports and correspondence.

    Conference-Miscellaneous-White House Conference on
    Children: 1930-1933   101
        Correspondence between NFS officials and
        conference officials about the conference.
        Miscellaneous conference reports.

    Conference - NFS Regional - 1955   102
        Reports from the several conferences held in this
        year relative to the work of each region's settle-
        ment houses.

    Conference - NFS Regional: 1959-1961   103
        Reports and addresses presented to the several
        conferences, dealing essentially with aims, goals
        and prospects of the settlements.

    Conference - National, of Social Work: 1947-1953   104-109
        These folders contain printed programs revealing
        all the pertinent information about the meetings,
        including a detailed schedule. Folder 107 has an
        interesting address by Albert J. Kennedy.

    Conference - Regional of Settlement Boys Workers: 1933-
    1939   110-112
        Complete copies of the programs and reports made to
        the conferences in each of these years. Also, some
        miscellaneous publicity material .

    Conference - Regional of Settlement Boys and Girls, Work
    Division: 1939-1942   113-115
        Programs, reports, resolutions dealing with the
        growth and development of youth and programs for
        youth.

    Conscientious Objectors - Service in Settlements: 1941-
    1945   116
        Correspondence between the NFS, its member houses,
        and the appropriate government officials regarding
        the use of conscientious objectors in settlement
        programs during war time.

    Consumer Program - NFS: 1934-1945   117
        Studies, publicity and correspondence on the price
        control of various commodities, especially dairy
        products. Statements of the purpose of the various
        NFS programs and proposals.

Folder Title and Description of Contents	Folder
Coolidge, Ellen W.: 1903-1954 Materials written by her, for publication and otherwise. Extensive correspondence between Miss Coolidge and such figures as Jane Addams, Florence Kelley, Lillie Peck, and A. J. Kennedy, about various aspects of the international settlement movement. Several biographical sketches of her life and work.	118-119
Cooper, Charles: 1913-1931 Cooper was a long-time member of the NFS executive committee and was president of the board of directors from 1926-1930. His extensive correspondence with such leaders as R. A. Woods, A. J. Kennedy and others clearly reveals his relationship to the NFS and the activities of the NFS in its early days.	120
Council on Social Work Education: 1943-1946 Questionnaire on group work curricula. Minutes of the meetings of the executive committee.	121
Defense - Activities and Participation in: 1940-1943 Reports from the settlements, 1941-1942. Correspondence and reports about the role of the settlements. Miscellaneous publicity handouts.	122-123
Defense Mobilization: 1950-1952 Reports from the cities on mobilization during the Korean War and its impact on the settlement communities. Memoranda from the NFA to its member houses about defense mobilization issues. John McDowell is the chief correspondent.	124
Defense - National Council on: 1940-1941 Correspondence and reports dealing with the role the settlements played in aiding the defense effort on the local level in these years.	125
Dies Committee: 1939-1940 Statements by Helen Hall and others protesting the violation of civil liberties by the committee. Press clippings about the Committee and these statements.	126
Directories and Addresses - NFS: 1953-1959	127

Folder Title and Description of Contents   Folder

    Dramatics Division: 1930-1940   128
        Extensive correspondence between Lillie Peck
        and Fonrose Wainwright about the activities of
        the Division. Some copies of the Dramatics
        Bulletin. Lists of plays available through the
        NFS which would be suitable for use in settle-
        ments. Other correspondents include Ruth Harker
        and Gertrude Dobkins.

    Eastmen, Joseph B.: 1945   129
        Memorial statement by Carl B. Swisher in the
        Public Administration Review, Winter, 1945.

    Earhart, Amelia: 1928   130
        Clippings about her flight across the Atlantic.
        She was a former social worker.

    Elliot, John Lovejoy: 1915-1953   131
        He lived 1868-1942. Correspondence with A. J.
        Kennedy, R. A. Woods, Graham Taylor, and others.
        Articles and speeches by Elliot. Eulogies,
        biographical statements, and press clippings upon
        his death.

    Golden Age Clubs
        See folder 188.

    Hall, Helen: 1931-1958   132
        This folder contains some of her published and
        mimeographed articles and speeches, her statements
        before Senate committees, and some articles about
        her. She was, and is, an influential person in the
        work of the National Federation.

    Health Insurance with Medical Care: 1937-1940   133-134
        Correspondence with authors Mr. and Mrs. Douglass
        W. Orr about sales, reviews, etc., of their book.
        Other correspondence with the publishers, and some
        significant correspondence with Paul Kellogg.

    Health - NFS Study of Medical Care in Settlement Neigh-
    borhoods: 1939-1952   135
        Mimeographed reports about the general situation,
        and reports from the settlements.

Folder Title and Description of contents	Folder
Health - Testimony on the National Health Bill: 1938-1940 Statement by Helen Hall. Publicity about the 1940 bill.	136
Housing, Committee on: 1930-1942 Extensive correspondence. Some studies of the housing problem in settlement neighborhoods. Interesting information about NFS reaction to the New Deal housing programs.	137
Housing - General: 1920-1953 Statements about housing. Chief correspondent is Albert J. Kennedy.	138
Ingram, Frances: 1928-1954 Correspondence about aspects of the settlement movements in southern United States. Clippings about her and articles by her.	139
Insurance - Savings: 1932 Correspondence between settlements, the NFS, and banking officials about financial matters.	140
International Conference of Social Work: 1948-1954 Bulletins, programs of several conferences, correspondence about the revival of the Conference and its functions.	141
Kelley, Florence: 1932 Testimonial statement about her.	142
Kellogg, Paul: 1931-1958 Correspondence with him about donations and publications. Speeches by him and memorial statements about him, including a brief biographical sketch.	143
Labor - Connections with: 1938-1948 Correspondence and mimeographed reports which reveal the attitude of the NFS toward the labor union movement, and the cooperation between the two in social welfare enterprises.	144
Low Income Case Studies: 1948-1952 Reports from the settlement houses, correspondence about the reports.	145

Folder Title and Description of Contents	Folder

McDowell, Mary E.: 1931-1936 — 146
   She lived 1854-1936, and was a long-time settlement worker. The correspondence is miscellaneous. Bibliography of works by and about her. Clippings about her.

McFarland, Frances: 1940 — 147
   She was active in settlement music programs. Most of this folder deals with a 1940 testimonial dinner in her honor.

McMain, Eleanor: 1924-1954 — 148
   She was on the NFS executive committee intermittently from 1911 to 1930. There is some correspondence with her, and some seeking information on her life. Correspondence and clippings about her death on May 12, 1934.

Morton, Helen: 1952 — 149
   A "farewell" letter.

Murray, Clyde: 1945-1951 — 150
   Copies of 3 of his addresses.

Music: Relation to NFS Music Clubs: 1928 — 151
   Material concerning cooperation of the National Federation of Music Clubs with the NFS Music Division.

Music Conference: Anglo-American at Lausanne, July-August, 1931 — 152
   Correspondence about planning the settlement sessions at Lausanne; programs; Mrs. McFarland's address to the conference and her report to the NFS.

Music Division - NFS: 1912-1943 — 153-157
   Pamphlets about music in America. Minutes of the Music Division's meetings; reports and budgets. Reports to the Carnegie Foundation on the use of grants. Miscellaneous correspondence about the aims and activities of the Division.

Music Division: Conferences: 1924-1936 — 158
   Reports presented to the NFS conferences, and correspondence about their preparation. Programs and press clippings.

Folder Title and Description of Contents	Folder
Music Division: International Toy Festival of: 1932 General report of the Festival; minutes of the Festival committee and of the New York Association of Music Schools; Clippings and photographs.	159
Music Division: Johan Grolle, Chairman, 1931-1936 Much substantive correspondence between Grolle and NFS executives about the nature and scope of the work of the Division. Reports and studies of local situations.	160
Music Division - Library and Program Service: 1931-1941 Minutes of the committee meetings. Lists of songs and suggested music programs. Song books which were used at the NFS annual conferences, 1931-1941.	161
Music Division - Newsletters: November 1932-July, 1934	162
Music Division - Publicity and Speeches: 1927-1932	163
Music Division - Survey of College Credits; 1930 Surveys made of individual schools in the effort to ascertain how much credit they gave for settlement music school training.	164
Music Division - Training Courses at New York School: 1930 Announcements and bulletins of general offerings. Detailed syllabi of a special one-year course offered to teachers of settlement music courses, and analysis of those who attended the courses. Correspondence concerning these matters.	165-167
Music Division: United Neighborhood Houses Questionnaires: 1939-1940	168
Music Division: Work with New York City Welfare Council: 1928-1930 Correspondence, reports and publicity about a cooperative survey conducted in 1928 of the settlement's music programs.	169
Music Schools - New York Association of: 1924-1933 Minutes of the Directors' meetings; publicity information and miscellaneous reports.	170
NFS Midwestern Regional Office, 1922-1924 Minutes of meetings and annual reports.	171

Folder Title and Description of Contents	Folder
National Commission on Children and Youth See U. S. Children's Bureau	
National Information Bureau: 1923-1927 Announcements and minutes of meetings.	172
National Social Welfare Assembly (NSWA) - Education Recreation Council of: 1933-1948 Correspondence and reports about recreation for the unemployed. Statements regarding the work of federal agencies in these areas. Correspondence about routine matters such as attendance at conferences. Minutes of the Council meetings, 1947-1948.	173-174
NSWA - German Youth Leadership, 1947-1951 Correspondence about the German youths who were brought to the International Youth Congress. Minutes of the committee in charge of the project, which was sponsored by the Youth Division of the NSWA. Extensive report made after the project was completed.	175-177
NSWA - International Organization of Social Work, 1945-1948 Report on social welfare and the League of Nations. Mimeographed materials and correspondence concerning the formation of UNESCO. Minutes of the National Committee on International Organization for Social Welfare.	178
NSWA - Young Adult Council: 1947-1951 Statements of the organization, by-laws, and purpose of this committee. Reports concerning the formation of the council. Correspondence about various conferences, and copies of the reports made to them. Minutes of the meetings of the executive committee, and summaries of action.	179-182
National Youth Administration, 1935-1941 Correspondence and other information about the relation of the NYA to the NFS and other related organizations. Correspondents include Lillie Peck, Howard Braucher, and Aubrey Williams. Minutes and summaries of meetings about NYA, and clippings and photographs.	183

Folder Title and Description of Contents	Folder
Necrology: 1930-1953 Clippings, memorials, published addresses, etc., about such notables as Charles Cooper, and Louise de Koven Bowen.	184-185
Negro in American Life Exhibit, 1944-1945 Charts and publicity releases about the exhibit.	186
Neighborhood, 1925-1929 Correspondence about initiating the periodical, and suggestions for financing it and designing the format, 1925-1927. Extensive correspondence about the actual business arrangements, 1927-1929. Several volumes of Neighborhood are shelved with the book collection.	187
Neighborhood House Golden Age Clubs - History of: 1952 Historical statement.	188
Nelson, Max: 1930 A letter of recommendation of him.	189
Peck, Lillie M.: 1930-1957 Miscellaneous correspondence with her. Eulogies, clippings, photographs and correspondence about her death. Biographical statements.	190-191
Pierce, Willett: 1949-1950 Thesis (1950) on student residents in settlement programs. Correspondence about it, and a preliminary outline of it.	192
Professional Schools of Recreation and Group Work See folder 121.	
Prohibition Committee See folder 68.	
Prohibition Study, 1924-1928 Sample questionaire and general conclusions of the study. Some of the prominent correspondents include Jane Addams, Bruno Lasker, and Mark McCloskey.	193
Publications - Miscellaneous Articles and Manuscripts Lists of publications and copies of a few.	194

Folder Title and Description of Contents	Folder
Radio - Here's to Youth: 1943-1945 Correspondence about financing the program and determining its contents. Minutes of the committee; script for the programs; letters to NBC; an "idea kit" for the program.	195-197
Refugees Committee - Work for: 1938-1940 Memoranda and reports of the committee.	198
Religion - Church Sponsored Houses Memorandum on problems created by these houses.	199
Religion - Conference on Urban Work: 1947 Correspondence about it and reports on it.	200
Robbins, Dr. Jane: 1930-1947 Dr. Robbins was a long-time settlement worker, and an honorary president of the NFS. This extensive correspondence deals with her many activities in all phases of the work. Clippings and a photograph of her.	201
The Round Table, 1936-1961 An incomplete run of this NFS mimeographed publication. See also folder 560.	202-205
Settlement Leaders: 1915-1949 Miscellaneous correspondence and statements about settlement work by various leaders and friends of the movement.	206
Settlement Movement - Statements of its Nature and Purposes: 1923-1950 A 1931 bibliography of writings by settlement leaders about the settlements. Statements of the movement's nature by Paul Kellogg, Lillie Peck, Bruno Lasker, various NFS executives, et al.	207

SETTLEMENTS - CITY FEDERATIONS OF

Boston - United Settlements of Greater Boston: 1933-1950 Incomplete run of the publications of the boys work groups.	208

Folder Title and Description of Contents	Folder
Chicago – Chicago Federation of Settlements: 1928-1960 Membership lists; miscellaneous correspondence; minutes of the executive committee; addresses to the staff; annual reports; admission policies; studies of community problems and statements about them. Material on the city federation's self-study 1949-1950. Memoranda to the NFS and member houses.	209-213
Cleveland – Federation of Settlement Houses: 1946-1949 Statements of the social action committee.	214
Detroit – The Detroit Federation of Settlements: 1938-1949 Constitution and by-laws; lists of member houses; correspondence with NFS about dues and regular operating matters; bulletins and miscellaneous reports.	215
New York City – United Neighborhood Houses, 1932-1963 Pamphlets on arts and crafts. Copies of <u>The Neighbor</u>. Survey on freedom of speech and other civil liberties issues. Bulletins of the youth work. Minutes of the Board of Directors; financial correspondence; historical statement (1950); annual reports and studies on varied issues. Materials on mental health, price controls and lobbying activities.	216-226
Philadelphia – The Association of Philadelphia Settlements; 1924-1956 Correspondence with the NFS about membership, dues, conferences, and visits of NFS personnel to Philadelphia; committee minutes and reports; directories of the Association's members; publicity releases and statements on matters of social welfare.	227-229
Pittsburg – Health and welfare Federation of Allegheny County: 1942-1956 Minutes of the committees helping to organize the Federation. Correspondence about lobbying activities; minutes of various committees, including the social action committee. A record of 1947 contacts with the NFS; annual and miscellaneous reports.	230-232

Folder Title and Description of Contents	Folder
Twin Cities Federation of Settlements: 1924-1951 Correspondence about the organization of the Federation and its developing relationship with the NFS, and about its operating procedures. Minutes of the annual meetings.	233

SETTLEMENTS - NFS MEMBER HOUSES

Alabama

Birmingham - Bethlehem Center: 1943 Correspondence about membership in the NFS.	234
Ensley - Community House: 1935-1944 Correspondence about dues, expansion plans, conferences, visits of NFS staff members.	235

California

Los Angeles - The All Nations Community House: 1929-1954 Correspondence about membership in the NFS; field report by Lillie Peck; programs of the settlement.	236
Los Angeles - Avalon Community Center 1946-1954 Field visits and reports; annual report; correspondence about NFS membership.	237
Los Angeles - Cleland House: 1944-1946 Correspondence about membership in the NFS.	238
Los Angeles - Miscellaneous: 1946-1951 Correspondence between the NFS and the Henderson Community Center and the Soto-Michigan Jewish Center about NFS membership and miscellaneous conferences. NFS field report.	239
Los Angeles - Neighborhood Settlement: 1929-1941 Correspondence about such matters as Mexican migrant laborers and books written by the head resident. Later correspondence deals with routine matters such as dues and conferences.	240
Pasadena - Settlement Association: 1946-1954 Substantive correspondence about case work techniques in settlements. Correspondence about membership in NFS; by-laws of the Association; miscellaneous and annual reports.	241

Folder Title and Description of Contents	Folder
Riverside - Community Settlement Association: 1926-1954 Correspondence about NFS membership, dues, and personnel. Historical sketches; annual and miscellaneous reports.	242-243
San Diego - Neighborhood House: 1926-1949 Correspondence about NFS membership and dues; the future of the House and the work appropriate to it. Schedules of activities and programs.	244
San Francisco - The Community Music School: 1929-1942 Correspondence about NFS membership and dues; settlement personnel and activities. Annual reports for 1934-1935.	245
San Francisco - Good Samaritan Community Center; 1945-1957 Brief description of the Center; correspondence about NFS membership; field survey by NFS, 1953. Annual reports, 1945-1946, 1952-1953, 1955-1956.	246-247
San Francisco - Mission Community Center; 1945-1956 By-laws; brief description of the Center; correspondence about membership in the NFS. Annual report.	248
San Francisco - Precita Valley Community Club, Inc.: 1941-1957 Fact sheets and financial statements; brief description of the Center; miscellaneous reports; correspondence about NFS membership and Center personnel.	249
San Francisco - Telegraph Hill Neighborhood Association: 1932-1947 Substantive correspondence about the activities of the Association; mimeographed reports about defense activities; correspondence and reports about field visits.	250
San Francisco - Visitacion Valley: 1922-1950 Correspondence about NFS membership; Center activities and personnel; brief description of the Center and its work.	251

Folder Title and Description of Contents   Folder

   San Gabriel - La Casa de San Gabriel: 1948-1953   252
       Correspondence about NFS membership, the Mexican-
       American problem, and a 1953 CBS broadcast on
       teenagers. Annual report, 1953.

   San Pedro - Home Toberman Settlement House: 1940-1953   253
       Constitution, miscellaneous pamphlets, and reports.
       Correspondence about NFS membership and dues, House
       personnel, and a 1946 field visit.

   Wilmington - Community Center: 1947-1951   254
       By-laws; correspondence re membership NFS. Annual
       report, 1947.

Canada

   British Columbia - Vancouver - Alexandra Neighborhood
   House: 1940-1950   255
       Historical statement, 1892-1940. Field visit,
       1947; miscellaneous correspondence with NFS, 1948-
       1949. Annual reports, 1941, 1944, 1949, 1950.

Colorado

   Denver - Auraria Community Center: 1945-1952   256
       Fact sheets; personnel policies; by-laws,
       miscellaneous reports; correspondence re NFS
       membership and field visits, housing problems, and
       activities of the Center, especially in relation
       to the Community Chest and financial problems.

   Denver - Grace Community Center: 1946-1951   257
       Brochures. Letter of 1949 describing the Center
       and correspondence about the activities of the
       Center.

   Denver - The North Side Community Center, Inc.: 1950   258
       Correspondence re NFS membership and building plans.

   Denver - Steele Community Center: 1947-1952   259
       Correspondence about NFS membership; budget
       estimate; miscellaneous pamphlets and clippings.

Connecticut

   Bridgeport - Hall Settlement: 1934-1954   260
       Annual reports and minutes of the Board of Directors.
       Correspondence and studies dealing with raising the
       standards of the settlement.

Folder Title and Description of Contents	Folder
Hartford - North End Community Center; 1952-1954 Material re NFS membership; constitution and personnel practices; Center activities. Financial statement, 1954.	261
Hartford - Union Settlement: 1934-1952 Correspondence from NFS on the upgrading of the settlement's standards. Descriptive brochures and statements of philosophy behind the settlement. Annual reports, 1933, 1945, 1951.	262
New Haven - Farnam Community House, 1933-1951 Descriptive brochures. Correspondence re NFS membership, which was a sore point with Farnam, and personnel. Annual reports, 1943, 1945, 1947, 1951.	263
New Haven - Neighborhood House, 1933-1936 Personal correspondence about the activities of the House.	264
New London - B. P. Learned House: 1944-1948 Correspondence re personnel. Annual and quarterly reports.	265
Stamford - The Italian Center: 1934-1949 Financial statements, reports, clippings. Correspondence re dues and Center personnel.	266
Stratford - Sterling House: 1936-1954 Annual reports.	267
Waterbury - Pearl Street Neighborhood House: 1936 Annual report, clippings, miscellaneous correspondence.	268
West Haven - Community House Association: 1941-1951 Reports; correspondence re youth work and NFS membership.	269
Wilmington - People's Settlement: 1951-1952 Self-study committee report; field visit report.	270

District of Columbia

Barney Neighborhood House: 1940-1943 Miscellaneous reports and clippings.	271

Folder Title and Description of Contents   Folder

    Friendship House: 1936-1955   272
        Correspondence re building plans, 50th anniversary
        of NFS. Historical statement; self-study report,
        1951; annual and miscellaneous reports.

    Southeast House: 1936-1953   273
        Brochures, photographs, historical statement,
        descriptive studies, self-studies and annual
        reports.

    Miscellaneous, 1934-1951   274
        Field trip reports, studies of the areas served
        by the settlements.

    Northwest Settlement House: 1944-1951   275
        Annual and self-study reports.

Florida

    Miami - James E. Scott Community Association: 1949-   276
    1953
        Historical statement and enrollment statistics.

Georgia

    Augusta - Bethlehem Center: 1950-1954   277
        Brochure and annual reports.

Hawaii

    Honolulu - Palama Settlement: 1930-1948   278
        Correspondence re dues, wage studies; annual and
        statistical reports.

Illinois

    Chicago - Abraham Lincoln Center: 1937-1946   279
        Correspondence re NFS membership and dues; his-
        torical statement.

    Chicago - Association House: 1944-1951   280
        Correspondence re NFS membership; annual reports.

Folder Title and Description of Contents	Folder
Chicago – Benton House: 1930-1951 Correspondence re membership in NFS and House problems; annual reports and self-study appraisals.	281
Chicago – Christopher House: 1948-1954 Correspondence re membership and dues in NFS.	282
Chicago – Chicago Commons Association: 1899-1951 Published stories, miscellaneous publications about important people and events. Financial reports, press clippings about the 1947 Chicago fire, descriptive brochures, routine correspondence with NFS. Annual reports for 1899, 1904, 1911, 1918, 1919, 1925, 1927, 1930, 1934-1945.	283-286
Chicago – Emerson House Association: 1934-1949 Annual reports; field reports; correspondence re membership and dues in NFS, conferences, miscellaneous operating matters.	287
Chicago – Fellowship House: 1935-1952 Annual reports.	288
Chicago – Gads Hill Center: 1928-1955 Descriptive brochures; historical pageant; miscellaneous reports about the activities of the Center. Annual reports: 1928, 1930-1931, 1934-1938, 1940-1944, 1946-1947, 1951.	289
Chicago – Henry Booth House: 1935-1955 Constitution; 1953 fact sheet; miscellaneous reports. Press clippings about House activities. Correspondence re dues and personnel. Annual reports: 1946-1947, 1949.	290
Chicago – Howell Neighborhood House: 1945-1950 Statement of House aims, 1945; correspondence re dues to NFS and the Chicago self-study.	291
Chicago – Hull House: 1900-1950 Annual reports: 1901, 1925, 1929, 1931, 1940-1941, 1947-1950, 1952, 1954. Miscellaneous and financial reports; press clippings about House activities; correspondence from Charlotte Carr and Louise de Koven Bowen revealing the controversy with the Board of Directors in the early 1940's.	292-294

Folder Title and Description of Contents	Folder

Chicago – Hyde Park Neighborhood Club: 1935-1955
    Correspondence re membership in NFS; Annual
    reports: 1939, 1944-1945, 1954.
	295

Chicago – Madonna Center: 1944 Correspondence re NFS membership.	296

Chicago – Newberry Avenue Center: 1938-1958
    Correspondence re NFS membership; Annual
    reports: 1947, 1950, 1952, 1954.
	297

Chicago – Northwestern University Settlements: 1932-1954 Correspondence re NFS membership. Annual reports: 1950-1951, 1953, 1956.	298
Chicago – Olivet Institute: 1946 Report to the Board of Trustees.	299
Chicago – Parkway Community House: 1943-1954 Annual reports 1943, 1953; study of the House.	300
Chicago – South Chicago Community Center: 1934-1954 Correspondence re NFS membership, defense mobilization, adult work; annual reports: 1945, 1947, 1951, 1953.	301
Chicago – University of Chicago Settlement: 1931-1944 Miscellaneous correspondence.	302
Miscellaneous Houses: 1935-1946	303
Peoria – Neighborhood House: 1944-1953 Annual reports, miscellaneous correspondence.	304

Indiana

Evansville – Neighborhood House: 1944-1953
    Annual reports 1947-1950; correspondence re
    NFS membership, miscellaneous matters. Survey
    of the area served by the House.
	305

Fort Wayne – Westside Center: 1952 Self-studies.	306

Gary – Campbell Friendship House: 1943-1952
    Annual reports; correspondence re NFS membership;
    statements on racial policies.
	307

Folder Title and Description of Contents	Folder

Gary - Neighborhood House: 1944-1953
    A 1944 study of the Gary Negro population.
    Field report, 1944; descriptive brochures;
    annual reports 1949-1955.
	308

Indianapolis - Communal Center Association: 1935-1953
    Correspondence re NFS membership, relationship to
    NFS, and the financing of settlements. A manual
    of the Center (1953), salary schedule, membership
    analyses.
	309

Indianapolis - Flanner House: 1939-1947
    Correspondence re building plans, personnel, NFS
    dues. Much information on racial problems. 1939
    program institute.
	310-311

Indianapolis - Hawthorne Social Service Association: 1944-1946 Correspondence re membership; 1946 field report.	312

Indianapolis - Southwest Social Center: 1944-1953
    Correspondence re membership in NFS, building
    plans; field report.
	313

Iowa

Cedar Rapids - Jane Boyd Community House: 1933-1945 Correspondence re NFS membership, training for settlement work, field reports. Negro survey.	314

Davenport - Friendly House: 1950-1951
    Correspondence re NFS membership and dues.
    Field visit.
	315

Des Moines - Roadside Settlement: 1937-1954
    Annual reports 1937, 1944, 1949-1951, 1954.
    Statements of objectives; correspondence re
    NFS membership and dues.
	316

Des Moines - South Side Community House: 1947-1951 Annual reports 1947 and 1951. Field survey	317
Des Moines - Wilkie House	318

Sioux City - Community House: 1945-1951
    Notes on 1940 and 1948 field trips. Annual report
    1944; correspondence re NFS membership, building
    plans.
	319

Folder Title and Description of Contents	Folder

Kentucky

Louisville - Neighborhood House: 1898-1950   320-321
    Photographs of early 20th century scenes. Annual reports 1898, 1906, 1910, 1913, 1921-1923, 1925-1926, 1928, 1938. Report of the 1909 Tenement House Commission and other "muckraking" commissions. Clippings, brochures and statements about the work of the House. Chief correspondent: Frances Ingram.

Louisville - Wesley House: 1942-1953   322
    Annual reports 1942-1943, 1948, 1950-1951, 1953. Descriptive brochures.

Louisiana

New Orleans - Kingsley House: 1920-1954   323-324
    Annual reports 1927, 1944, 1948-1953. 1942 Charter. Correspondence re NFS membership. Materials on relationship to federal government.

Massachusetts

Boston - Denison House: 1900-1953   325
    Annual reports 1900, 1933, 1935, 1937, 1952-1954. Correspondence re House personnel; descriptive brochures. Minutes of Board of Directors.

Boston - Dorchester House: 1933-1953   326
    Correspondence re membership in NFS, activities of the House. Annual reports 1937, 1948, 1950-1951.

Boston - East Boston Social Centers Council: 1932-1950   327
    1932 description of the Center; correspondence re NFS membership; clippings.

Boston - Elizabeth Peabody House: 1936-1950   328
    Radio script, 1937; Science Fair brochures; descriptive statement. Information on community music schools.

Boston - Ellis Memorial: 1928-1953   329
    Annual reports 1928, 1930-1933, 1935, 1939, 1940, 1942-1945. Miscellaneous correspondence.

Folder Title and Description of Contents	Folder
Boston - Good Will Neighborhood House: 1944-1952 Annual report 1944; by-laws. Material re selection of workers, NFS membership.	330
Boston - Gray Houses, Inc.: 1940-1948 Miscellaneous correspondence.	331
Boston - Hale House Association: 1943-1944 Correspondence re dues to NFS.	332
Boston - Hecht Neighborhood House: 1934-1950 Correspondence re NFS membership and dues. Resume of vocational guidance program.	333
Boston - Jamaica Plain Neighborhood House: 1943-1953 Annual report 1943. Obituaries and historical statement (1952).	334
Boston - Lincoln House Association: 1948 Correspondence re field visit, House organization.	335
Boston - The Little House: 1929-1958 Annual reports 1929, 1932, 1941, 1943, 1945-1948, 1951-1954, 1958. 1953 field visit. Descriptive statement; correspondence re NFS membership.	336
Boston - Norfolk House Center: 1915-1951 Annual reports 1915, 1917, 1924, 1930-1931, 1933-1937, 1939-1949. Correspondence re NFS membership and dues; descriptive statements.	337
Boston - North Bennett Street Industrial School: 1950 Brochures; letters about the relationship of NFS to the school.	338
Boston - North End Union: 1934-1954 Annual reports 1936-1937, 1941, 1943; brochures and description. Correspondence re NFS membership, financial and other difficulties.	339
Boston - Olivia James House: 1939-1954 Annual reports 1939-1941, 1943, 1949, 1952, 1954. Correspondence re NFS membership.	340
Boston - Robert Gould Shaw House, Inc.: 1930-1958 Annual reports 1931-1932, 1938, 1942-1943, 1948, 1958. Correspondence re selection of a head worker. 1953 confidential report on the work of the House.	341

Folder Title and Description of Contents   Folder

    Boston - Roxbury Neighborhood House: 1921-1953   342
        Annual reports 1944, 1953. Correspondence re a
        study of the House; descriptive brochures and
        statement.

    Boston - South End House Association: 1929-1951   343
        Annual reports 1929-1936, 1950. Miscellaneous
        studies; historical statement; clippings;
        correspondence re work of Association.

    Boston - Trinity Neighborhood House: 1932-1953   344
        Correspondence re NFS membership and dues. Annual
        reports 1945, 1951-1953.

    Cambridge - Cambridge Community Center: 1944-1953   345
        Miscellaneous pamphlets; survey of the Center's
        work; descriptive brochures. Annual report 1945.

    Cambridge - Cambridge Neighborhood House: 1932-1933   346
        Correspondence re NFS dues.

    Cambridge - East End Union: 1941   347
        Descriptive statement.

    Cambridge - Margaret Fuller House: 1940-1953   348
        Correspondence re NFS membership and dues; field
        report and descriptive statement.

    Cambridge - The House of Seven Gables: 1923-1952   349
        Annual reports 1923, 1942-1943, 1951-1952.
        Correspondence re NFS membership; descriptive
        brochures.

Michigan

    Detroit - Brightmoor Community Center: 1926-1954   350-351
        Annual reports 1949-1954. Correspondence re NFS
        membership, housing study, self-study; descriptive
        statement, 1940; miscellaneous reports and
        committee minutes. Minutes of Board of Directors,
        1948-1949.

Folder Title and Description of Contents	Folder
Detroit - Del Ray Christian Neighborhood House: 1946-1952 Correspondence re NFS membership; information on personnel practices.	352
Detroit - Dodge House: 1925-1954 Annual reports 1930, 1937. Correspondence re NFS dues, operating matters.	353
Detroit - Franklin Settlement: 1937-1953 Press clippings; photographs; historical statement; correspondence re self-studies and various NFS surveys.	354
Detroit - Gleiss Memorial Center: 1947 Minutes of the self-study group and its recommendation.	355
Detroit - Highland Park Community Center: 1941-1944 Annual report 1943. Study of the Center. Correspondence re conferences.	356
Detroit - Industrial School Association: 1947-1950	357
Detroit - Lutheran Settlement House: 1943-1945 Correspondence re NFS membership, building plans; descriptions.	358
Detroit - Neighborhood House Settlement: 1947-1954 Annual reports 1947 and 1954.	359
Detroit - Polish Activities League: 1947-1954 Historical statement; miscellaneous reports; annual report 1951.	360
Detroit - Sophie Wright Settlement: 1930-1953 Correspondence re NFS membership and dues. Annual reports 1944, 1951-1952; miscellaneous reports.	361
Detroit - Tau Beta Community House: 1926-1954 Historical brochure. Correspondence re NFS dues, conferences, field visit, miscellaneous matters.	362
Ferndale - Pleasant Ridge Community Center: 1944-1954 By-laws; annual reports 1944-1945, 1948, 1952-1954. Correspondence re decentralization of the Center. Photographs of the work.	363

Folder Title and Description of Contents	Folder
Grosse Pointe - Mutual Aid and Neighborhood Club: 1936 Correspondence re membership in the NFS.	364
Hamtramck - Tau Beta Community House: 1928-1953 Annual report 1928; field report. Photographs and brochures on camping program, summer play school.	365
Highland Park - Community Center: 1950 Annual report.	366
Rouge-Ecorse - United Centers: 1951-1954 Descriptive statement of facilities and program. Membership visit, 1953; correspondence re membership and dues, building plans.	367

Minnesota

Minneapolis - Eliot Park Neighborhood House: 1941-1950 Annual reports 1942-1945, 1948, 1950. Summary of the facilities and program. Correspondence re personnel and organizational problems.	368
Minneapolis - Margaret Barry House: 1944-1949 Correspondence re dues, membership, Twin City Federation plan.	369
Minneapolis - North East Neighborhood House, Inc.: 1938-1956 Annual reports 1941-1944, 1948, 1951, 1954-1955. An analysis of personnel practices by Robbins Gilman.	370-372
Minneapolis - Phyllis Wheatley Settlement House: 1926-1949 Correspondence re NFS membership, dues, personnel. Annual reports 1945-1949.	373
Minneapolis - Pillsbury Settlement House: 1933-1955 Annual report 1944; correspondence re miscellaneous matters.	374
Minneapolis - Unity Settlement House: 1940-1953 Correspondence re community survey; annual reports 1941, 1947, 1953.	375

Folder Title and Description of Contents	Folder
Minneapolis - Wells Memorial, Inc.: 1929-1953 Annual reports 1929, 1944; field study, 1947. Studies and photos of the work. Correspondence re 1929 conference in Minneapolis.	376
St. Paul - Capitol Community Center: 1949-1952 Correspondence re NFS membership, personnel. 1952 dedication program.	377
St. Paul - Christ Child Community Center: 1938-1950 Correspondence re NFS membership; annual report 1948.	378
St. Paul - Hallie Q. Brown Community House: 1944-1951 Annual report 1951; personnel information; correspondence re NFS membership. Anniversary celebration.	379
St. Paul - Merriam Park Community Center: 1953 Annual report.	380
St. Paul - Neighborhood House: 1933-1953 Annual reports 1933, 1938, 1941. Correspondence re NFS membership; brochures and miscellaneous reports, and clippings about House Work.	381

Missouri

Kansas City - George Washington Carver Neighborhood Center: 1944-1949 Correspondence re NFS dues and membership; descriptive statement.	382
Kansas City - Guadalupe Center: 1932-1948 Correspondence re NFS dues and membership; clippings; annual report 1948.	383
Kansas City - Mattie Rhodes Memorial Society: 1929-1951 Correspondence re NFS membership and dues, miscellaneous agency concerns; brochures; clippings on boys and girls work.	384
Kansas City - Minute Circle Friendly House: 1932-1954 Correspondence re NFS membership and dues; brochures; annual report 1951.	385

Folder Title and Description of Contents	Folder
Kansas City - Whatsoever Circle Community House: 1937-1951 Correspondence re NFS membership. Testimonial to the House.	386
St. Louis - Caroline Mission: 1951-1952 Annual report 1952; handbook for workers; field visits.	387
St. Louis - Community Music Schools Foundation: 1930-1950 Correspondence re NFS dues, musical repertoire; annual report 1940.	388
St. Louis - Fellowship Center; 1949-1953 Annual reports 1951-1952; correspondence re NFS membership and dues; brochures. 1951 field visit.	389
St. Louis - George Washington Carver House: 1948-1952 Field reports; miscellaneous correspondence.	390
St. Louis - Grace Hill House: 1931-1952 Annual reports 1947-1949. Miscellaneous reports; correspondence re NFS membership and miscellaneous operating matters.	391
St. Louis - Kingdom House : 1952-1954 Annual report 1953; Studies on housing and administration; program schedule. 50th anniversary report.	392
St. Louis - Monsignor Butler Neighborhood Center: 1954 Description of programs and facilities.	393
St. Louis - Neighborhood Association: 1931-1955 Personal correspondence J. A. Wolf and A. J. Kennedy. Historical sketches, descriptive brochures, miscellaneous correspondence.	394
St. Louis - Wesley House : 1935-1953 Annual reports 1935, 1946, 1953. Correspondence re NFS dues and membership, speaking engagements, miscellaneous matters.	395

Nebraska

Lincoln - Urban League: 1944 Annual report.	396

Folder Title and Description of Contents	Folder
Omaha - Neighborhood House: 1939-1953 Annual report 1939; descriptive statements of programs and facilities.	397
Omaha - Omaha Social Settlement: 1930-1945 Annual reports 1930-1933, 1935, 1938, 1940, 1945. Press clippings; studies of housing problems; correspondence re NFS membership and dues.	398
Omaha - Woodson Center: 1933-1950 Annual report 1933; correspondence re NFS membership and dues, agency relocation, financing, agency self-study, building plans.	399

New Jersey

Bayway - Bayway Community Center: 1950-1953 Annual reports 1950-1952; photographs and brochures.	400
Morristown - Neighborhood House: 1937-1955 Annual reports 1943-1945, 1947-1948, 1951, 1955; field report; historical statement. Correspondence re NFS membership, dues, and NFS assistance.	401
Newark - Fuld Neighborhood House: 1931-1957 Annual reports 1943, 1945, 1951-1954. Miscellaneous reports and clippings; correspondence re NFS membership, personnel, field visit, 1940.	402
Plainfield - Neighborhood House: 1938-1954 Field visit, 1938; correspondence re membership, consultations with NFS.	403
South Orange - Community House: 1934-1946 Correspondence re NFS dues; annual report, 1944.	404
West Orange - Community League: 1934-1955 Annual report 1944; correspondence re NFS membership, health surveys; descriptive statements. Lists of Board of Directors.	405
West Orange - The Orange Valley Social Settlement: 1943-1954 Correspondence re personnel, conferences; statement of program.	406

Folder Title and Description of Contents	Folder
New York	
Buffalo - Neighborhood House Association: 1938-1954 Annual reports 1940, 1944-1945, 1949-1950, 1953; correspondence re NFS membership, personnel, conferences.	407
Elmira - Neighborhood House, Inc.: 1931-1948 Correspondence re membership, dues, and agency operating matters.	408
Long Island - Lawrence Five Towns Community House: 1936-1954 Annual reports 1936, 1943, 1950-1954; by-laws; correspondence re personnel. Lists and minutes of Board of Directors. A study of emotionally disturbed children and adolescents.	409
[New York City] Bronx House: 1940-1947 Annual report 1942; clippings, miscellaneous pamphlets and brochures.	410
Christodera House: 1926-1948 Annual reports 1926-1933; brochures and miscellaneous reports.	411
College Settlements Association: 1891-1928 Annual reports 1891, 1893, 1903-1905, 1907, 1911-1913, 1915, 1920, 1924-1928.	412-413
Colony House : 1945-1954 Annual reports 1945-1946, 1954; correspondence re NFS dues.	414
East Side Settlement House: 1892-1950 Correspondence re NFS membership, personnel matters. Annual reports: 1892-1893, 1898-1902, 1904-1923, 1925-1927, 1929, 1937, 1939, 1941-1945.	415-417
Goddard Neighborhood Center: 1934-1949 Annual reports 1935-1937, 1941; minutes of meetings; descriptive brochures. Correspondence re NFS membership and dues.	418

Folder Title and Description of Contents	Folder
Greenwich House: 1921-1954 Correspondence re NFS dues; constitution; extensive information on the music school. Annual reports 1940-1944, 1920, 1925, 1928, 1930-1933, 1938-1939.	419-420
Haarlem House: 1913-1955 By-laws; annual reports 1929-1940; correspondence re membership.	421
Hamilton-Madison House: 1931-1954 Annual reports 1936, 1938, 1940-1941, 1944, 1954. Historical statement; correspondence re NFS membership and dues, personnel.	422
Hartley House: 1947-1953 Miscellaneous brochures; correspondence re membership.	423
Grosvenor Neighborhood House: 1926-1944 Correspondence re NFS membership; annual reports 1926, 1936, 1941, 1943-1952.	424
Henry Street Settlement: 1903-1958 Historical statement, 1893-1910, by Kennedy and Woods; various and miscellaneous reports. Extensive information on music and medical-psychiatric work at Henry Street. List of community studies, 1933-1958.	425-428
Hudson Guild: 1920-1956 Anniversary and descriptive brochures; photographs, clippings, and correspondence about Guild activities. Reports on the New Neighbor Project, 1953-1956.	429-430
James Weldon Johnson Community Center, Inc.: 1948-1953 Information about NFS membership; 1952 field report.	431
Lenox Hill Neighborhood Association: 1928-1947 Annual report 1928; correspondence re NFS membership, personnel. Information on music and youth work, history of the Association.	432
Manhattanville Community Centers, Inc.: 1946-1955 Annual reports 1946, 1948, 1950-1955; reports of plans, progress, finances and self-study. Newsletters, 1952-1953.	433-434

Folder Title and Description of Contents	Folder
Recreation Rooms and Settlements: 1935-1954 Correspondence re membership in NFS. Delinquency report.	435
Riis House: 1926-1943 Annual report 1926, 1943; correspondence re NFS membership.	436
School Settlement Association: 1930-1941 Annual reports 1930, 1932, 1936; correspondence re NFS dues and membership.	437
Stuyvesant Community Center: 1946 Annual report.	438
Union Settlement: 1895-1952 1895 circular about the establishment of the settlement. Annual reports 1909-1910, 1915, 1920, 1923, 1931, 1943, 1945-1947; miscellaneous publications. Description of the area, program and facilities of the settlement.	439-440
University Settlement Society: 1911-1958 Annual reports 1911, 1936-1938, 1940, 1943-1944; guides and brochures. Information on psychiatric work in settlements, anniversary celebrations. Correspondence re personnel and miscellaneous publications.	441-442
Willoughby House Settlement: 1937-1944 Annual reports 1937, 1944.	443
Rochester - Baden Street Settlement: 1935-1956 Correspondence re NFS dues, personnel, conferences, finances; annual reports 1932, 1951-1953; historical statement; brochures.	444
Rochester - Charles Settlement House: 1928-1946 Correspondence re membership, dues; field report.	445
Rochester - Genesee Settlement House: 1945-1953 Correspondence re NFS membership; statement of principles and practices; annual report, 1953.	446
Rochester - Lewis Street Center: 1933-1958 Annual report 1933; historical statement, 1937; correspondence re miscellaneous settlement matters. 50th anniversary brochure.	447

Folder Title and Description of Contents	Folder
Rochester – Montgomery Neighborhood Center: 1952-1956 Annual reports 1953-1956; 1953 field visit. Information on inter-racial day camping. Handbook of the settlement.	448
Syracuse – Dunbar Association: 1944-1955 Annual reports 1944-1945, 1951, 1954. Correspondence re NFS membership; conferences; programs of the Association.	449
Syracuse – Huntington Club: 1943-1955 Correspondence re conferences, field visits, personnel, agency programs, NFS membership. 1944 field visit report. Materials on camping, family and group work. Anniversary brochures.	450-451
Utica – Cosmopolitan Center: 1948-1956 Annual reports 1948-1949, 1952-1955; correspondence re NFS membership, agency programs, building programs, conferences.	452
Utica – Neighborhood Center: 1949-1955 Annual report 1954; field report, 1954; description of program and facilities. Correspondence re speaking engagements, NFS membership.	453

Ohio

Cincinnati – Emanuel Community Center: 1946-1954 Annual reports 1946, 1949, 1951, 1954; correspondence re NFS membership.	454
Cincinnati – Findlay Street Neighborhood House: 1950-1954 Field visit, 1950; information about NFS membership.	455
Cincinnati – Riverview Neighbors House: 1950-1954 Annual report, 1954; agency appraisal report; 1952 field report.	456
Cleveland – Alta Social Settlement: 1931-1953 Correspondence re Cleveland Federation. Press clippings and brochures.	457

Folder Title and Description of Contents	Folder

Cleveland - Music School Settlement: 1931-1954
    Annual reports 1937-1938, 1940, 1949, 1954.
    Correspondence re NFS dues, miscellaneous matters;
    reports on other school activities.
	458

Cleveland - East End Neighborhood House: 1932-1951
    Summaries of programs, 1932, 1934, 1944-1945.
    Studies of the work of the House and the Cleveland
    Federation. Correspondence re social actions.
	459

Cleveland - The Friendly Inn: 1932-1947
    Annual reports, 1935, 1938; correspondence re NFS
    dues, miscellany.
	460

Cleveland - Goodrich House: 1934-1952
    Annual reports, 1934-1943, 1951-1952. Photos and
    radio script.
	461

Cleveland - Hiram House: 1932-1944
    Annual reports, 1932-1942. See also bound volumes,
    1899-1926. House Organization, 1906-1933, also
    bound.
	462-463

Cleveland - Karamu House: 1935-1957
    Correspondence re NFS membership and dues, miscellany.
    Brochures and other information on Karamu Theater.
    Application for a grant from the Rockefeller Founda-
    tion.
	464

Cleveland - League Park Center, Inc.: 1952-1955 Annual reports, 1952, 1954; descriptive statement.	465

Cleveland - Merrick House: 1929-1952
    Annual reports, 1945, 1950; Anniversary brochures;
    workers manual, 1952.
	466

Cleveland - Neighborhood Settlement Association: 1946-1955
    Annual reports, 1946, 1949, 1953, 1955; 1946
    field report. Information about the origins of the
    Cleveland Federation.
	467

Cleveland - University Settlement: 1931-1947
    Miscellaneous correspondence. Settlement manual,
    1941.
	468

Cleveland - West Side Community House: 1931-1954
    Year books: 1935, 1938, 1941, 1944, 1945, 1947,
    1952, 1954. Historical statements, 1931 and 1945;
    miscellaneous correspondence and statements.
	469

Folder Title and Description of Contents	Folder
Columbus – Central Community House: 1940-1955 Annual reports, 1940-1941, 1944, 1953-1954; 1955 fact sheet; correspondence re NFS membership.	470
Columbus – Friendship House: 1952 Report of a membership visit.	471
Columbus – Gladden Community House: 1930-1949 Annual reports 1930, 1932-1934, 1936-1941, 1943; correspondence re conferences, operating matters, NFS membership.	472
Columbus – Godman Guild Association: 1923-1947 Annual report, 1928; field report, constitution, anniversary material.	473
Columbus – Neighborhood House, Inc.: 1944-1954 Annual reports, 1944, 1951, 1954; press clippings.	474
Columbus – South Side Settlement House: 1936-1954 Annual report, 1936; correspondence re NFS membership.	475
East Akron – Community House: 1953-1955 Correspondence re relocating the settlement because of new highway.	476
Lorain – Neighborhood House Association: 1929-1955 Annual reports, 1929, 1933, 1935, 1941, 1943-1945, 1947; correspondence re NFS dues, NFS membership, housing study, building plans, conferences, population studies, agency programs. 1950 field report; 1947 housing study.	477-478
Mansfield – Friendly House: 1933-1952 Annual report, 1933; miscellaneous correspondence.	479
Springfield – Union Settlement House: 1930-1953 Annual reports, 1930-1931, 1951; correspondence re NFS membership.	480
Toledo – North Toledo Community House: 1935-1941 Correspondence re financial matters, NFS dues; historical statement; survey of facilities and program, 1941.	481
Toledo – Reports (field): 1944-1946	482

Folder Title and Description of Contents	Folder
Warren - Rebecca Williams Community House: 1952 Survey of the area and of the work of the House.	483
Youngstown - Miscellaneous: 1938-1958 Anniversary brochure, 1938; field report, 1951.	484

Oklahoma

Oklahoma City - Neighborhood Clubs: 1949-1959 By-laws; request for help, 1949; field report, 1953; annual report 1955. Application for membership, 1957.	485

Oregon

Portland - Field Reports: 1945-1952	486
Portland - Friendly House Community Center: 1952-1955 History; field reports; annual report, 1955.	487
Portland - Linnton Community Center: 1945-1952 Annual reports, 1949-1951; field report; descriptive statement.	488
Portland - Neighborhood House: 1933-1955 Correspondence re personnel, NFS visit, conferences; annual reports, 1951-1953.	489

Pennsylvania

Munhall - Neighborhood House: 1935-1945 Policy pamphlet; annual reports: 1935, 1938; correspondence re membership, conferences. Descriptive statement.	490
Philadelphia - College Settlement: 1942-1950 Miscellaneous brochures, pamphlets, and reports.	491
Philadelphia - Eighth Ward Street House: 1942-1950 Miscellaneous reports and correspondence.	492
Philadelphia - Field reports: 1933	493

Folder Title and Description of Contents	Folder

Philadelphia - Friends Neighborhood Guild: 1935-1955
    Annual reports, 1938-1939; field reports,
    descriptive statements.
	494

Philadelphia - Germantown Settlement: 1945-1954
    Annual reports, 1951-1954; correspondence re
    history, miscellany.
	495

Philadelphia - The Lighthouse: 1925-1955
    Annual reports, 1925, 1954-1955; statements of
    policies and programs. Copies of the Lantern.
	496

Philadelphia - Lutheran Settlement: 1945-1955
    Annual reports, 1945-1946, 1955; field report;
    descriptive statement.
	497

Philadelphia - Neighborhood Centre: 1929-1949
    Annual reports, 1943-1944, 1946, 1948-1949;
    correspondence re NFS membership.
	498

Philadelphia - North Light Boys Club: 1952-1953 Statements of the programs and facilities.	499
Philadelphia - Reed Street Neighborhood House: 1933-1950 Correspondence re membership and dues to NFS.	500

Philadelphia - St. Martha's House: 1927-1948
    Annual reports, 1927-1928, 1945; field report,
    1945; correspondence re NFS dues, personnel,
    conferences.
	501

Philadelphia - United Neighbors Association: 1928-1955
    Annual reports, 1933, 1936, 1942, 1944-1945;
    field report; history and description. Information
    re membership and dues.
	502

Philadelphia - University Settlement: 1931-1952 Annual report, 1931. Study of the area. Correspondence re personnel and dues.	503

Philadelphia - Wharton Centre: 1927-1955
    Annual reports, 1927, 1931, 1942, 1944, 1949,
    1951; field reports, miscellany.
	504

Pittsburgh - Anna B. Heldman Community Center: 1926-1953
    Annual reports, 1939-1942, 1950-1953; historical
    statement, 1937; miscellaneous correspondence and
    photos. Originally the Irene Kaufmann Settlement.
	505-507

Folder Title and Description of Contents	Folder
Pittsburg - The Brashear Association: 1936-1955 Annual reports, 1936-1938, 1942. Description of the work of the agency.	508
Pittsburg - Kingsley House: 1911-1954 Descriptive brochures and publications; yearbook, 1933; copies of the Kingsley Record, 1936, 1939, 1946, 1948. Annual reports, 1911-1925, 1927, 1929, 1933, 1935-1937.	509-511
Pittsburg - Sono Community House: 1940-1953 Annual reports 1939-1942, 1948-1950; correspondence re personnel, legislative issues. Information re housing, 1952 employees strike, policy meetings.	512
Pittsburg - Woods Run Settlement: 1923-1955 Annual reports 1923, 1938, 1952; miscellaneous reports, studies, clippings and brochures.	513-514
Wilkes Barre - Georgetown Community House: 1929-1944 Correspondence re NFS dues, internal surveys, conferences; annual report 1930.	515

Rhode Island

Providence - Federal Hill House: 1928-1951 Statements of the programs and facilities of the House.	516
Providence - John Hope Settlement House: 1944-1955 Annual reports 1948, 1950-1951, 1955; 1950 field report; correspondence re NFS membership.	517
Providence - Lyra Brown Nickerson Settlement House: 1947-1955 Annual reports 1945, 1955. Statement on the cost of living, 1947.	518
Providence - Nickerson Neighborhood House: 1930-1953 Annual reports 1939, 1943-1945, 1949, 1951-1952; correspondence re NFS membership and miscellaneous matters.	519

Folder Title and Description of Contents   Folder

South Carolina

Spartanburg - Bethlehem Center: 1951-1955   520
    Annual reports 1951-1954; field report; membership report.

Tennessee

Knoxville - Dale Avenue Settlement House: 1945-1954   521
    Miscellaneous reports and correspondence; field report, 1948; report on the work of the settlement, 1945.

Nashville - Bethlehem Center: 1933-1952   522
    Annual report 1950; miscellaneous reports; correspondence re NFS membership; personnel.

Texas

Corpus Christi - Community Settlement House: 1942-1953   523
    Annual report, 1947; field reports; correspondence re NFS membership, personnel conflicts.

Houston - Neighborhood Centers Association: 1930-1954   524-525
    Miscellaneous annual reports; correspondence re NFS membership, miscellaneous matters, conflicts among the staff members. Statements of aims, programs, and facilities.

San Antonio - Mexican Christian Institute: 1947-1948   526
    Field report, 1947; correspondence re NFS membership, personnel, agency improvements.

San Antonio - Wesley House: 1949-1953   527
    Field report, 1949, 1953; correspondence re NFS membership, miscellaneous brochures, and statements of policies.

Virginia

Richmond - William Byrd Community House: 1931-1954   528
    Annual reports 1943-1944, 1947, 1951-1952, 1954; field study, including maps and census.

Folder Title and Description of Contents	Folder

Washington

Seattle - Atlantic Street Center: 1947-1954   529
    Field reports 1947, 1952; annual reports 1952-1954.

Seattle - Jackson Street Community Council: 1946-1953   530
    Annual reports 1946-1951; correspondence re NFS
    membership; field report, 1952.

Seattle - Neighborhood House: 1947-1954   531-532
    Annual report 1954; field reports, 1947, 1952;
    correspondence re NFS membership; personnel,
    conferences; by-laws. Miscellaneous manuals,
    brochures and reports. 1952 survey of Seattle
    settlements.

Seattle - Social Center for the Blind: 1949-1955   533
    Annual reports, 1949-1950; correspondence re
    NFS membership.

Wisconsin

Madison - Neighborhood Centers: 1931-1953   534
    Annual report 1946; correspondence re NFS member-
    ship, health study. Historical statement, workers
    manual, anniversary material.

Milwaukee - Christian Center: 1951-1952   535
    Annual reports 1951-1952.

Milwaukee - Neighborhood House: 1948-1953   536
    Annual reports, 1948-1952; field report, 1953;
    correspondence re NFS membership and dues.

Settlements - New York City - Organization and Adminis-   537
tration of: 1931
    A study made in 1931.

Settlements, Organization of: 1921-1922   538
    A study made in 1921-1922.

Settlements in the Great Depression: 1932   539-540
    Reports from various settlements on attempts to
    remain effective in the crisis.

Folder Title and Description of Contents	Folder
Settlements in War Time: 1936-1943 Correspondence re programs and policies of settlements in time of war. Minutes of committees dealing with the new problems.	541
Simkhovitch, Mary K.: 1915-1950 Miscellaneous correspondence; testimonial statements and publications.	542
Smith, Hilda W.: 1938-1951 Correspondence re use of "Vineyard Shore" as a camp, the WPA and its relations with settlements, miscellaneous settlement matters.	543
Social Legislation Information Service: 1944-1946 Correspondence re Lillie Peck's service on the Board; by-laws; 1945 minutes of the Board of Directors.	544
Social Security Committee: 1931-1943 Press clippings, publicity releases, and correspondence re aid for older people.	545
Social Work Yearbook, Articles for by the NFS: 1930-1947 Correspondence about the reports, and copies of them.	546
Social Workers Committee on Ful Employment: 1945 Correspondence and reports re the 1945 bill on this subject.	547
Survey Associates, Inc.: 1939-1952 Correspondence and reports re notices and articles by the NFS to be published in the Survey; termination of the Survey, 1948-1952. Minutes of the meetings of the Survey editorial advisory committee.	548
Taylor, Graham: 1915-1942 Mr. Taylor's dates: 1841-1938. Miscellaneous publications, testimonials, and press clippings. Miscellaneous correspondence, including a 1915 letter from George Bellamy, about the nature and purpose of settlements.	549
Taylor, Lea D.: 1929-1953 Extensive correspondence re NFS membership, meetings and leadership; conferences, operating matters. Miscellaneous press clippings and addresses made to various meetings.	550-554

NATIONAL FEDERATION OF SETTLEMENTS AND NEIGHBORHOOD CENTERS

Folder Title and Description of Contents	Folder
Unemployment: 1929-1943 Symposia, committee reports, case studies, published articles, and correspondence about them. Summary evaluation, 1931, of the effects of unemployment.	555-557
Unemployment and Recreation, Conference on: 1929-1932 Correspondence re the conference and NFS participation in it. Reports.	558
Unemployment and Social Security Study: 1935-1936 Material dealing with the NRA, including clippings, correspondence, and miscellaneous reports.	559
Unions - Relations with Settlements: 1938-1939 Articles in the Round Table.	560
United Community Defense Services, Inc.: 1950-1956 This organization was related to the National Social Welfare Assembly and Community Chest. It raised funds to meet the needs of social welfare agencies in war time. Correspondence and bulletins re its establishment; minutes of the various committees; by-laws; extensive budgetary data; annual reports. Studies of special programs in local areas. Data on legislative matters, regional work, publicity, and organizational aspects of the work.	561-581
The United Defense Fund: 1950-1955 Summary of budget needs, descriptive reports and history, 1950-1955.	582
United States Children's Bureau: 1945-1952 Correspondence re federal aid to day-care center, the establishment and work of a National Commission on Children and Youth. Historical statement of the contribution of settlement workers to the Federal Children's Bureau. Programs, annual reports, minutes of the National Commission. Correspondence and reports re the Midcentury White House Conference on Children and Youth. Material on the 1964 "committee to save the U. S. Children's Bureau." Reports of the committee concerned with defense planning, 1951.	583-587
United States Civilian Defense: 1941-1944 Extensive correspondence and reports re cooperation of the NFS and its member settlements in organizing and administering the civilian war effort.	588

Folder Title and Description of Contents	Folder
United States Emergency Committee for Food Production: 1942-1945 Correspondence dealing with the establishment and work of the Farm Security Administration.	589
United States Employment Service - Department of Labor: 1947-1948 Charts, reports, and correspondence dealing with the problems of youth unemployment.	590
United States War Manpower Commission: 1943 Decisions re social workers and the war. Children's summer camps.	591
United States War Production Board: 1941 Material dealing with settlement properties and their employment.	592
Wald, Lillian D.: 1928-1956 Articles by and correspondence with Miss Wald. Obituaries and memorial and biographical statements.	593
Ways and Means Committee of the NFS: 1939-1950 Correspondence re the activities of the committee in fund-raising.	594
White, Gaylord S.: 1924-1932 Article by White on "Religion and the Settlement." Obituaries and memorial statements.	595
White House Conference on Children and Youth: 1950 List of available reports. Fact-finding reports, platforms, findings of the work groups.	596
Woods, Robert A. and Eleanor: 1899-1942 Two pamphlets on University settlements and democracy. Correspondents include Jane Addams and Julia Lathrop. Correspondence and material about R. A. Woods' death. Miscellaneous correspondence with Eleanor Woods.	597
Work Camps for America: 1938-1944 Extensive correspondence and reports dealing with the camps.	598
WPA - Program in Settlements: 1932-1941 Extensive correspondence and reports re the work of the WPA and the relationship of the settlements to this work.	599

Folder Title and Description of Contents	Folder
World Assembly of Youth - World Youth Conference: 1945 Charter of the Assembly, and the report of the U. S. delegation to the conference.	601
World War II: 1941-1945 Material re the settlement strategy in the war and plans for post-war reconstruction. Reports and correspondence re the "High School Victory Corps." Information on war-time community services, and on youth in war time agricultural production programs.	602
Young Adult Group Members: 1949 Correspondence re young adult councils in local settlement.	603
Youth Food Committee: 1946 Correspondence and memoranda about the committee.	604

APPENDIX I: NFS OFFICERS

```
1911:       President    Jane Addams
            V. P.        Gaylord S. White
            Sec-Treas    Robert A. Woods
            Ass't Sec    A. J. Kennedy

1912:       President    Lillian D. Wald
            V. P.        Graham Taylor
            Sec-Treas    Robert A. Woods
            Ass't Sec    Albert J. Kennedy

1913-1914:  President    Mary E. McDowell
            V. P.        Mrs. V. G. Simkhovitch
            Sec-Treas    Robert A. Woods
            Ass't Sec    Albert J. Kennedy

1915-1916:  President    Mrs. V. G. Simkhovitch
            V. P.        George A. Bellamy
            Sec-Treas    Robert A. Woods
            Ass't Sec    Albert J. Kennedy

1917-1918:  President    Graham Taylor
            V. P.        Francis Ingram
            Sec-Treas    William E. McLennan
            Ass't Sec    Albert J. Kennedy

1919-1921:  President    John L. Elliot
            V. P.        Cornelia Bradford
            Secy         Robert A. Woods
            Treas        William E. McLennan
            Ass't Sec    Albert J. Kennedy
```

APPENDIX I: NFS OFFICERS

1922-1925:
- President   John L. Elliot
- V. P.   Cornelia Bradford
- Secy   Robert A. Woods
- Treas   Louis J. Affelder
- Ass't Sec   Albert J. Kennedy

1926-1930:
- President   Charles C. Cooper
- V. P.   Lillian D. Wald
- Secy   Albert J. Kennedy
- Treas   Louis J. Affelder

1931-1934:
- President   Lea D. Taylor
- V. P.   Mrs. V. G. Simkhovitch
- Secy   Albert J. Kennedy
- Treas   Walbridge S. Taft

1935-1938:
- President   Helen Hall
- V. P.   Wilber I. Newstetter
- Treas   W. S. Taft
- Secy   Lillie M. Peck

1939:
- President   Helen Hall
- V. P.   Alice P. Gannett
- Treas   Albert J. Kennedy
- Secy   Lillie M. Peck

1940-1943:
- President   Alice P. Gannett
- V. P.   Clyde E. Murray
- Treas   Albert J. Kennedy
- Secy   Lillie M. Peck

1944-1945:
- President   Clyde E. Murray
- V. P.   Franklin I. Harbach
- Treas   Albert J. Kennedy
- Secy   Lillie M. Peck

1946-1947:
- President   Franklin I. Harbach
- V. P.   Cleo W. Blackburn, Sanford Solender, Paul Simon
- Treas   David Rosenstein
- Secy   Lillie M. Peck

1948:
- President   Franklin I. Harbach
- V. P.   Cleo W. Blackburn, W.H. Brueckner, Helen M. Harris
- Treas   David Rosenstein
- Secy   Lillie M. Peck

1949:
- President   Franklin I. Harbach
- V. P.   Cleo W. Blackburn, H. Daniel Carpenter, W.H. Brueckner
- Treas   Amory H. Bradford
- Secy   John McDowell

APPENDIX I: NFS OFFICERS

1950-1951:	President	David Rosenstein
	V. P.	H. Daniel Carpenter
		Mary Blake
		Mrs. Harry Kerr
	Treas	Stephen B. Sweeney
	Sec	Mrs. Carl Goldmark, Jr.
	Exec Dir	John McDowell
1952:	President	Lea D. Taylor
	V. P.	Margaret Berry
		H. Daniel Carpenter
		Stephen B. Sweeney
	Treas	Albert J. Kennedy
	Exec Dir	John McDowell
1953:	President	David Rosenstein
	V. P.	Mary E. Blake
		Mrs. Dexter Perkins
		Mrs. Harry W. Kerr
	Treas	Stephen B. Sweeney
	Exec Dir	John McDowell
1954-1955:	President	H. Daniel Carpenter
	V. P.	Mrs. Dexter Perkins
		Mrs. J. H. Stephenson
		Mrs. C. S. Whitney
	Treas	Mrs. Carl Goldmark
	Secy	Richard D. Peters
	Exec Dir	John McDowell
1956-1957:	President	Mrs. J. Howard Stephenson
	V. P.	Stephen B. Sweeney
		Mrs. R. A. Tsanoff
		Ralph MacGilvra
	Treas	Mrs. Carl Goldmark, Jr.
	Secy	Richard D. Peters
	Exec Dir	John McDowell
1958-1959:	President	Mrs. R. A. Tsanoff
	V. P.	Carl Lauterbach
		Robert L. Bond
		P. L. Prattis
	Treas	Mrs. Carl Goldmark, Jr.
	Secy	Mrs. Burdette E. Ford
	Exec Dir	John McDowell
1960-1961:	President	Carl Lauterbach
	V. P.	Winslow Carlton
		Frederick Taylor
		Mrs. Addison Parker
	Treas	Robert Rosenbaum
	Secy	Mrs. Ethel Mathiason
	Exec Dir	Margaret Berry

APPENDIX II – PAMPHLETS

1. Addams, Jane. *The Pioneer Settlement.* (n.d.)
2. Addition, Henrietta. *City Planning for Girls.* Chicago, 1928.
3. Ashe, Elizabeth. *Intimate Letters from France.* San Francisco, 1931.
4. Campbell, Elise H. *National Youth Administration of Michigan.* Detroit, 1938.
5. Chicago Theological Seminary. *Register.* November, 1928.
6. Clark, B. Preston, et al. *Tribute to Robert A. Woods*
7. *Clubs in Action.* Boston, 1934.
8. Committee on the Economic Report. *Making Ends Meet.* Washington, 1951.
9. Davis, Allen F. *Raymond Robins.* Chicago, 1959.
10. Davis, R. E. G. *A Primer of Guidance Through Group Work.* New York, 1940.
11. Ephraim, M. R. *Toward Professional Standards.* New York, 1947.
12. *First National Training Laboratory in Group Development.* 1948.
13. Fisher, Winifred. *The People are Ready to Discuss the Post-War World.* New York, 1943.
14. *Group Work in a Year of Crisis.* New York, 1941.
15. Handasyde, Elizabeth. *City or Community.* New York, 1949.
16. Harrison, Shelby M. *The Social Survey.* New York, 1931.
17. Hendry, Charles E. and Johns, Ray. *Group Work.* New York, 1940.
18. Hynd, J. Hutton. *The Creative Task of Rational Religion.* St. Louis, 1944.

APPENDIX II - PAMPHLETS

19. International Conference of Settlements. *Settlements and Their Outlook.* London, 1922.

20. Kingman, John M. and Sidman, Edward. *A Manual of Settlement Boys Work.* New York, 1935.

21. Lawrence, Rev. William. *Address at the Noonday Lenten Services.* Boston, 1926.

22. McDowell, John. *Settlements and Neighborhood Houses.* New York, 1949.

23. McDowell, John and Maxwell, Jean M. *We Believe.* New York, (n.d.)

24. *Midcentury White House Conference on Children and Youth: Program.* Washington, 1950.

25. *Midcentury White House Conference on Children and Youth: Reports.* Washington, 1950.

26. *Midcentury White House Conference on Children and Youth: Fact Finding Report.* Washington, 1950.

27. Montgomery, Mrs. Frank H. *Bibliography of Settlements.* Chicago, 1905.

28. Murray, Clyde E. *New Horizons for the Settlement Movement.* New York, 1944.

29. NFS: *Report and Forecast.* Boston, 1920.

30. NFS: *The Administration and Activities of Chicago Settlements.* Boston, 1921.

31. NFS: *Letter from Robert A. Wood.* Boston, 1920.

32. Newstetter, Wilbur I. *Wawokiye Camp.* Cleveland, 1930.

33. Ogg, Elizabeth. *Longshoremen and Their Homes.* New York, 1939.

34. *Settlement Goals for the Next Third of a Century.* Boston, 1926.

35. Simkhovitch, Mary K. *The Settlement Primer.* Boston, 1926.

36. Soule, Frederick J. *Settlements and Neighborhood Houses,* New York, 1947.

APPENDIX II - PAMPHLETS

37. Taylor, Graham. *Social Action*. New York, 1939.
38. Todd, T. Wingate. *Pioneering on Social Frontiers*. Cleveland, 1937.
39. *Toynbee Hall Annual Report, 1912-1913*. London, 1913.
40. Valentine, G. Robert. *The Human Element in Production*. New York, 1917.
41. Woods, Robert A. *Alcohol and Prostitution in America*. Shanghai, 1919.
42. Woods, Robert A. *Democracy-A New Unfolding of Human Power*. Boston, 1906.
43. Woods, Robert A. *University Settlements, Their Point and Drift*. New York, 1899.
44. Zachry, Caroline B. *The Adolescent's Challenge to Education*. New York, 1939.

APPENDIX III - BOOKS

1. Addams, Jane. *Democracy and Social Ethics*. New York, 1902.
2. Addams, Jane. *The Long Road of Woman's Memory*. New York, 1916.
3. Addams, Jane. *A New Conscience and An Ancient Evil*. New York, 1912.
4. Addams, Jane. *The Second Twenty Years at Hull House*. New York, 1930.
5. Barnett, Dame Henrietta. *Matters that Matter*. London, 1930.
6. Barnett, Dame Henrietta. *Canon Barnett*. 2 volumes, New York, 1919.
7. Barnett, Samuel and Henrietta. *Practicable Socialism*. London, 1895.
8. Barrows, Ester G. *Neighbors All*. Boston, 1929.
9. Bosanquet, Bernard. *Essays and Addresses*. London, 1891.
10. Calkins, Clinch. *Some Folks Won't Work*. New York, 1930.
11. *The True History of Joshua Davidson, Communist*. Philadelphia, 1873.
12. Duffus, R. L. *Lillian Wald*. New York, 1938.
13. Dreier, Mary E. *Margaret Dreir Robins*. New York, 1950.

APPENDIX III - BOOKS

14. Dugdale, R. L. The Jukes. New York, 1900.
15. Ginx's Baby. London, 1870.
16. Goldmark, Josephine. Impatient Crusader. Urbana, 1953.
17. Hapgood, Norman and Moskowitz, Henry. Up from the City Streets: Alfred E. Smith. New York, 1927.
18. Hiram House. Annual Reports, 1899-1926.
19. Hiram House. Organ, 1906-1933.
20. Hoffman, William. Those Were the Days. Minneapolis, 1957.
21. International Association of Settlements. Reports, 1922-1930.
22. Jephcott, Pearl. Rising Twenty. London, 1948.
23. Johnson, Charles S. Growing up in the Black Belt. Washington, 1941.
24. Kennedy, Albert J., and Farra, Kathryn. Social Settlements in New York City. Philadelphia, 1935.
25. Mary McDowell and Municipal Housekeeping. New York, 1929.
26. Matthews, William H. Adventures in Giving. New York, 1939.
27. Mogey, J. M. Family and Neighborhood. London, 1956.
28. Morris, William. A Dream of John Ball. Portland, Maine, 1904.
29. Morrison, Arthur. Tales of Mean Streets. Cambridge, 1895.
30. National Federation of Settlements. Conference Announcements and Programs, 1911-1930.
31. National Federation of Settlements. Bulletins, Conference Reports, Reprints. 1911-1930.
32. Neighborhood, v. 1-4, 1928-1932.
33. Orr, Douglass W. and Jean. Health Insurance with Medical Care. New York, 1938.

APPENDIX III - BOOKS

34. Pimlott, J. A. R. *Toynbee Hall*. London, 1935.
35. Presland, John. *Deedes Bey*. London, 1942.
36. *James Bronson Reynolds; a Memorial*. New York, 1927.
37. Robinson, Lilian V. *Children's House*. Boston, 1937.
38. Shaw, G. Bernard. *Fabian Essays in Socialism*. London, 1889
39. Simkhovitch, Mary K. *Here is God's Plenty*. New York, 1949.
40. Simkhovitch, Mary K. *Neighborhood*. New York, 1938.
41. Sumner, William Graham. *What Social Classes Owe to Each Other*. New York, 1903.
42. Taylor, Graham. *Chicago Commons Through Forty Years*. Chicago, 1936.
43. Taylor, Graham. *Pioneering on Social Frontiers*. Chicago, 1930.
44. Taylor, Graham. *Religion in Social Action*. New York, 1913.
45. Towne, Florence H. *Neighbors*. Chicago, 1940.
46. Webb, Sidney and Beatrice. *Industrial Democracy*, v. 1-2. London, 1897.
47. Wilson, Howard E. *Mary McDowell, Neighbor*. Chicago, 1928.
48. Woods, Eleanor H. *Robert A. Woods: Champion of Democracy*. Boston, 1929.
49. Woods, Robert A. *The Neighborhood in Nation-Building*. Boston, 1923.
50. Woods, Robert A. *The Preparation of Calvin Coolidge*. Boston, 1924.
51. Woods, Robert A. and Kennedy, A. J. *Handbook of Settlements*. New York, 1911.
52. Woods, Robert A. and Kennedy, A. J. *Young Working Girls*. Boston, 1913.
53. Worrell, Dorothy. *History Of the Women's Municipal League of Boston*. Boston, 1943.

14

An Inventory of the Papers of the National Federation of Settlements and Neighborhood Centers, Supplement 1

PREPARED BY
Loren W. Crabtree

SWD. 1   National Federation of Settlements and Neighborhood Centers,
          New York, New York

          Supplement No. 1, 1911-1965

          88 Folders

A supplement to the papers of the National Federation of Settlements and Neighborhood Centers was deposited in the Social Welfare History Archives Center of the University of Minnesota Libraries on August 16 and October 17, 1965, after the documents were released to the University by order of the Federation's Board of Directors. The papers comprise 4.5 linear feet. Also included in the supplement are numerous pamphlets, one book, and 30 congressional documents (see appendix). The papers were processed from June 20 to July 12, 1966, and then were appended to the original NFS holdings.

The inclusive dates of the supplemental papers are 1911-1965, but the material focuses on the years 1960-1965. Most of the documents are related in some manner to the activities of the Social Education and Action Committee of the NFS. As in the original holdings, the materials are organized in an alphabetical subject file, with, however, two innovations in the arrangement. First, there is a section entitled "Committees of the NFS" which does not appear in the original inventory. This subsection was added because the committee materials are more extensive in the supplement than in the original holdings. Second, a subdivision entitled "Settlements - Community Studies" was added to differentiate between documents related directly to the work of local settlement houses and those dealing with studies of the community in which the house operates.

Because the Social Education and Action Committee (SEA) dominates the papers, Fern M. Colborn, who chaired the Committee for most of its existence, and other committee personnel are the most prominent individuals in the supplement. Consequently, persons who were important in the original holdings, such as Helen Hall, appear only peripherally in the supplement. Since the work of the SEA emphasizes pressure group action for legislation, much of the correspondence in the supplement is with important legislative leaders on such issues as urban renewal, public housing, and juvenile delinquency. The SEA usually avoids partisan politics, and consequently there is no material dealing with Presidential elections and the like.

Also contained in this supplement is a copy of the NFS "Bible" (Folders 609-611), which is a chronological index to the activities of the NFS in the years 1911-1965. The Social Welfare History Archives

Center also has on deposit a microfilm of the "Bible", along with microfilms of most of the documents to which the "Bible" is an indispensable guide (Social Welfare Archives Film no. 2). This, and the materials mentioned above, significantly enrich the already extensive NFS collection.

PARTIAL SUBJECT INVENTORY

AMERICAN COUNCIL TO IMPROVE OUR NEIGHBORHOODS "ACTION"
    Folders 642, 655

CARPENTER, H. DANIEL
    Folders 637, 650

BARNETT FELLOWSHIP
    Folder 624

CHILD WELFARE
    Folder 634

CIVIL RIGHTS AND LIBERTIES
    Folders 613-616, 636-637, 642, 644

COLBORN, FERN M.
    Most of the material in this supplement is related to the Committee
    on Social Education and Action, of which Miss Colborn was Chairman.
    Consequently, most of the folders contain correspondence from her.
    The heaviest concentration, however, appears in Folders 632-646,
    651-658, and 660-666.

CONSUMERS
    Folders 635, 644, 649

COST OF LIVING (INCLUDING RENT AND PRICE CONTROL)
    Folders 632, 634-635, 637

EDUCATION IN AND FOR THE SETTLEMENTS
    Folder 690

HEALTH (INCLUDING CARE FOR THE AGED)
    Folders 634, 636, 640

HOUSING
    Folders 613-616, 625-626, 632-642, 650-659, 691

IMMIGRATION
    Folders 634, 636

INTERNATIONAL WORK
    Folder 624

JUVENILE DELINQUENCY
    Folders 637, 639-640, 660-666

KENNEDY, ALBERT J.
    Folders 672-673, 679

KRIEGSFELD, IRVING M.
    Folder 636

LABOR (largely AFL-CIO)
    Folder 644

LOBBYING ACTIVITIES
    Folders 632-646, 651-658, 660-666

MEDICAL CARE AND INSURANCE
    Folders 634, 640, 642   see also the folders under HEALTH

NATIONAL ASSOCIATION OF HOUSING AND REDEVELOPMENT OFFICIALS ("NAHRO")
    Folders 651-658

NATIONAL SOCIAL WELFARE ASSEMBLY, INC.
    Folders 637, 644, 651-658

OLD AGE LEGISLATION
    Folders 632-633, 637, 642

PERSONNEL IN SETTLEMENT WORK
    Folders 629-630

POVERTY
    Folders 612-616, 625-626, 634, 641-642

RACE RELATIONS
    Folder 642

SETTLEMENTS AND GOVERNMENT PROGRAMS
    Folders 612-616, 651-658, 691

UNEMPLOYMENT
    Folders 632, 637, 640

URBAN RENEWAL
    Folders 619, 637, 641-642, 651-658

WAR AND PEACE
    Folders 635, 637

WASHINGTON CONFERENCES ON SOCIAL WELFARE
    Folders 640-641

YOUTH WORK
    Folders 612-616, 675-676

FOLDER INVENTORY

Folder Title and Description of Contents	Folder
Board of Directors, NFS: 1962-1965 Minutes of Board meetings, list of the members, brief biographical descriptions of the members, etc.	605-607
Business Affairs, NFS: 1962-1965 Minutes of business meetings, agendas, By-Laws of the Federation, work plans, budgets, financial statements, descriptions of the NFS, annual reports, ballots.	608-609
Chronological Index (the "Bible") to the Activities of the NFS: 1911-1965 These folders contain a skeleton summary of the NFS's annual meetings, officers and staff members, finances, studies, publications, resolutions, mailings, announcements, notices, positions on legislation, affiliated organizations, summary of field visits, additions and subtractions to membership, Round Table topics, and important activities for every year of its existence. The "Bible" thus provides a capsule view of NFS activity year by year.	610-612
Chronological Mimeographed Materials: 1962-1965 Information bulletins contain communications re: government grants and welfare programs (e.g., VISTA), eulogies, honorary statements, suggested outline for self-study, NFS film, war on poverty, etc. Also included are papers presented at various national and regional conferences, memoranda from NFS Personnel Standards and Practices Committee, NFS Youth Employment Kit (1962), and a suggested outline for agency self-studies. The topics of the papers vary widely and include civil rights, housing, youth, cooperation of government and private welfare agencies, family problems, rediscovery of poverty, etc.	613-617

Folder Title and Description of Contents	Folder
Chronological Printed Materials: 1962-1965 Lists of books, pamphlets and papers published by the NFS. The printed materials include paperbound books, pamphlets, brochures, article reprints, NFS annual reports, etc. Topics include summer jobs in settlements, settlements' place in cities today, adolescent problems, and a Board Orientation Kit (1965). Note especially a study by Fern M. Colborn, The Neighborhood and Urban Renewal (1963).	618-622

COMMITTEES OF THE NFS

Executive Committee: 1962-1964 Minutes of meetings and materials about the meetings.	623
Financial Development Committee: 1962-1965 Reports of the Dues Compliance Committee, correspondence about payment of dues, and minutes of the Financial Development Committee.	624
International Committee: 1962-1963 Minutes, correspondence re: international work, Barnett Memorial Fellowship.	625
Low Income Families Committee: 1952-1955 Materials re: housing study of 1954 (questionnaires, summary of the study and a copy of it, correspondence), and other materials concerning low income families.	626-627
Membership Standards and Admissions Committee: 1962-1964 List of members, minutes, agendas, memoranda.	628
Nominating Committee: 1962-1964 Statement of policies and pleas for nominations.	629

Folder Title and Description of Contents	Folder
Personnel Committee of the Board of Directors: 1962-1964 Deals with the NFS's own personnel. "Code of Personnel Policies" and materials relevant thereto. Valuable for determining the internal functioning of the Federation.	630
Personnel Standards and Practices Committee: 1962-1965 This is a committee for all settlement workers. Lists of committee members, correspondence re: placement, Peace Corps returnees; minutes of meetings, questionnaires, salary standards, etc.	631
Public Relations Committee: 1962-1965 Minutes of meetings, miscellaneous correspondence, awards, and speeches.	632
Social Education and Action Committee: 1911-1965 Most of the material deals with the post-1945 years. This committee deals with legislation about social reform, broadly conceived. The folders include information re: various Washington conferences on social welfare issues, housing problems, cost of living, child welfare, rent control, McCarthyism, activities in behalf of legislation, studies of various social issues, local institutions, platforms of social reform adopted by other agencies (e.g., YWCA, AASW), resolutions, with questionnaires and correspondence about them; old age medical insurance, civil rights, statements before Congressional hearings, minutes of meetings of the Committee, etc. Also included are digests of resolutions on social action, 1911-1961. These folders clearly define the NFS's positions on social reform. Fern M. Colborn and Irving M. Kriefsfeld figure prominently. See the Partial Subject Inventory for exact locations of important materials.	633-647

- -

Conferences, NFS National and Regional: 1962-1965 Conference manuals, minutes of planning committees, press releases, miscellaneous conference materials, correspondence about arrangements and conference details.	648-649

Folder Title and Description of Contents	Folder
Consumers, Food Stamp Program: 1962 Reports on food stamp operations.	650
Housing, General: 1942-1950 Correspondence and materials re: public housing, housing for the underprivileged, etc. H. Daniel Carpenter figures prominently. Bulk of the material is for 1942-1945.	651
Housing, Joint Committee on Housing and Welfare of the National Association of Housing and Redevelopment Officials and the National Social Welfare Assembly: 1952-1958 This committee formed to coordinate public housing and welfare efforts and for mutual information. Fern Colborn was chairman. Materials include policy statements and correspondence re: public housing, urban renewal and legislation; extensive data re: American Council to Improve Our Neighborhoods (ACTION), including copies of the Action Reporter and reports on impediments in the housing marked; routine operating correspondence; minutes of meetings; studies on housing; surveys and comments on the relationship of social workers and local public housing project managers. Excellent, detailed materials.	652-659
Housing, Study: 1956-1958 Reports, correspondence, policy statements and studies obtained from the NFS central staff and its member houses. Note especially the detailed studies prepared by the Philadelphia and Chicago Federations of Settlements.	660
Juvenile Delinquency: 1955-1958 Statement by John McDowell before the Senate (1955); lobbying activities, including copies and analyses of proposed legislation, and suggested legislation; correspondence between Fern Colborn and such groups as the Child Welfare League of America and the American Parents Committee, as well as other national agencies and many local leaders; correspondence and materials re: March, 1957, seminar.	661-667

Folder Title and Description of Contents	Folder
Maternal and Child Welfare Hearings: 1946 Transcript of Russell W. Ballard's (of Hull House) testimony before the Congressional hearing.	668
Neighborhood Goals in a Rapidly Changing World: 1957-1958 Workshop held by the NFS, February 13-15, 1958. Programs, press clippings, miscellaneous correspondence.	669
Settlements, City and Regional Federations of: 1962-1965 List of representatives from these Federations on the NFS Board of Directors; studies on a few Federations.	670

SETTLEMENTS - COMMUNITY STUDIES

California, Los Angeles: 1951 Two mimeographed studies by the Welfare Council of Los Angeles: (1) Social Welfare Standards and (2) Forecast for Planning. They deal with the entire scope of settlement work in the city.	671
Connecticut, New Haven: 1948 A study by Winnifred A. Frazier on the location for a group work center in New Haven. Miscellaneous clippings and memoranda.	672
Massachusetts, Worcester: 1936-1937 A population study by A. J. Kennedy of the southeastern district of Worcester.	673
New Jersey, Morristown: 1940 A study by A. J. Kennedy of the city of Morristown and of the role Neighborhood House played in it. Interesting, sophisticated analysis.	674
New York, Elmira: 1954 A report with detailed recommendations on a county-wide area by the Community Activities Committee. Comprehensive study of local welfare efforts as aided by the governmental agencies.	675

| Folder Title and Description of Contents | Folder |

New York, New York City: 1928-1930   676-677
    Three studies of the services afforded by the settlements in New York City: (1) <u>Personal Service in 42 Settlements in the City of New York</u> (May, 1928), (2) <u>Day Nurseries, Nursery Schools and Kindergartens in Six Settlements in the City of New York</u> (May, 1929), (3) <u>A Survey of the Work with Little Children in 11 Settlements in New York City</u> (April, 1930).

Ohio, Cincinnati: 1950-1952   678-679
    Reports, citywide in scope, of governmental and volunteer social services, 1950-1952; and of recreation, informal education and group work in the same years.

Pennsylvania, Pittsburgh: 1948   680
    Two copies of a field study of the Shadyside Area by Albert J. Kennedy. Purpose of the study: to determine if there were social needs which should be met by the churches, especially the Presbyterian.

SETTLEMENTS - NFS MEMBER HOUSES

Directories to Member Houses: 1962-1965   681
    Directories, 1962-1963, 1963-1964, 1964-1965. Also, eulogies and miscellaneous correspondence.

Connecticut - New Haven, Dixwell Community House: 1936, 1959   682
    Annual Report, 1936. General report for 1959.

District of Columbia - Barney Neighborhood House   683
    Reports and descriptions of the work in Washington, focusing on Barney.

Kentucky - Louisville, Wesley Community House: 1947   684
    Copy of a self-study conducted in that year.

Minnesota - Minneapolis, Wells Memorial Settlement: 1947, 1951   685
    Detailed self-studies carried out in these two years.

Folder Title and Description of Contents	Folder
New Jersey - Montclair, Neighborhood Center, 1943-1947 Financial data, evaluations of the program, miscellaneous reports.	686
New York - Brooklyn, Neighborhood Houses: 1945-1949 Correspondence and reports on the nature and work of the Brooklyn settlements.	687
New York - New York City, Union Settlement: 1943 A typewritten copy of Ellen S. Marvin's *As I Remember Union Settlement* (1943), which is a historical and personal reminiscence by a long-time staff worker. It is a good summary, though it is not intended to be coldly impartial.	688
Pennsylvania - Pittsburgh, Kingsley House: 1948 A June, 1948 report of the programs, activities and services of the House.	689

- -

Settlements - NFS Non-Member Houses: 1962-1964 Form letters concerning membership matters and a questionnaire. Also, a 1964 directory of non-member organizations.	690
Training Center of the NFS: 1960-1965 The center is located in Chicago. Lists of courses, illustrative brochures, description of faculty, services and financing; newsletters. See also additional NFS Training Center records held by the Social Welfare History Archives Center.	691
United States Government - Relations with Settlements: 1930's Papers on such problems as centralization, work relief, unemployment, propaganda, housing and the Federal Art Project. Such prominent people as Helen Hall authored these papers.	692

APPENDIX: PAMPHLETS, BOOKS AND CONGRESSIONAL DOCUMENTS

List of Printed Pamphlets Contained in Folders 14-18

1. The Board of Directors of a Neighborhood Center. New York, 1960.
2. Colborn, Fern M. The Neighborhood and Urban Renewal. New York, 1963.
3. Conference on Girls in Crisis, Serving the Teenage Girl. New York, 1964.
4. Neighborhood Centers Serve the Troubled Family. New York, 1964.
5. 100,000 Hours a Week. New York, 1965.
6. Standards for Neighborhood Centers. New York, 1960.
7. Structure and By-laws for a Neighborhood Center. New York, 1965.
8. Young People and the World of Work. New York, 1965.

Books

1. Sussman, Marvin B. and White, R. Clyde, Hough, Cleveland, Ohio: A Study of Social Life and Change. Cleveland, Ohio, 1959.

Congressional Documents (arranged in chronological order)

1. U. S. Congress, Senate Special Committee to Investigate Unemployment and Relief, Amending Social Security Act, 76th Congress, 1st Session, 1939.
2. U. S. Congress, Senate Committee on Education and Labor, National Health Programs, 79th Congress, 2nd Session, 1946.
3. U. S. Congress, Senate Committee on Rules and Administration, Poll Tax, 80th Congress, 2nd Session, 1948.
4. U. S. Congress, Joint Committee on the Economic Report, Low-Income Families, 81st Congress, 1st Session, 1949.
5. U. S. Congress, House Committee on Banking and Currency, Cooperative Housing, 81st Congress, 2nd Session, 1950.

6. U. S. Congress, Senate Committee on Finance, Social Security Revision, 81st Congress, 2nd Session, 1950.

7. U. S. Congress, Senate Committee on Banking and Currency, Defense Housing Act, 82nd Congress, 1st Session, 1951.

8. U. S. Congress, Joint Committee on the Economic Report, Making Ends Meet on Less than $2,000 a Year, 82nd Congress, 2nd Session, 1952.

9. U. S. Congress, Senate Committee on Labor and Public Welfare, Health Care for Dependents of Servicemen, 82nd Congress, 2nd Session, 1952.

10. U. S. Congress, House Committee on the Judiciary, Hearings Before the President's Commission on Immigration and Naturalization, 82nd Congress, 2nd Session, 1952.

11. U. S. Congress, Senate Committee on Banking and Currency, Housing Act of 1954, 83rd Congress, 2nd Session, 1954.

12. U. S. Congress, House Committee on Banking and Currency, Housing Amendments of 1955, 84th Congress 1st Session, 1955.

13. U. S. Congress, Senate Committee on Labor and Public Welfare, Juvenile Delinquency, 84th Congress, 1st Session, 1955. (2 copies)

14. U. S. Congress, Senate Committee on Appropriations, Second Supplemental Appropriation Bill, 84th Congress, 1st Session, 1955.

15. U. S. Congress, House Committee on Banking and Currency, Housing Act of 1956, 84th Congress, 2nd Session, 1956.

16. U. S. Congress, Senate Committee on Appropriations, Departments of State, and Justice, the Judiciary, and Related Agencies Appropriation, 84th Congress, 1st Session, 1956.

17. U. S. Congress, House Committee on Education and Labor, To Combat and Control Juvenile Delinquency, 85th Congress, 1st Session, 1957.

18. U. S. Congress, House Committee on Government Operations, Donation of Surplus Government Property to Volunteer Fire-Fighting Organizations, and for Other Purposes, 85th Congress, 2nd Session, 1958.

19. U. S. Congress, Senate Committee on Labor and Public Welfare, A Survey of Major Problems and Solutions in the Field of the Aged and the Aging, 86th Congress, 1st Session, 1959.

20. U. S. Congress, House Committee on Ways and Means, Unemployment Compensation, 86th Congress, 1st Session, 1959.

21. U. S. Congress, Senate Committee on Banking and Currency, Housing Act of 1959, 86th Congress, 1st Session, 1959.

22. U. S. Congress, Senate Committee on Labor and Public Welfare, Juvenile Delinquency Prevention and Control, 86th Congress, 1st Session, 1959.

23. U. S. Congress, Senate Committee on the Judiciary, Juvenile Delinquency, 86th Congress, 2nd Session, 1960.

24. U. S. Congress, Senate Committee on Labor and Public Welfare, Youth Employment Act, Youth Conservation Corps, 87th Congress, 1st Session, 1961.

25. U. S. Congress, House Committee on Education and Labor, Youth Employment Opportunities Act of 1961, 87th Congress, 1st Session, 1961.

26. U. S. Congress, House Committee on Ways and Means, Temporary Unemployment Compensation and Aid to Dependent Children of Unemployed Parents, 87th Congress, 1st Session, 1961.

27. U. S. Congress, House Committee on Ways and Means, Health Services for the Aged under the Social Security Insurance System, 87th Congress, 1st Session, vols. 1,2,3,4, 1961.

28. U. S. Congress, House Committee on Banking and Currency, Urban Mass Transportation Act of 1962, 87th Congress, 2nd Session, 1962.

29. U. S. Congress, House Committee on Ways and Means, Public Welfare Amendments of 1962, 87th Congress, 2nd Session, 1962.

30. U. S. Congress, House Committee on Banking and Currency, Housing and Community Development Legislation, 88th Congress, 2nd Session, 1964.

15

An Inventory of the Papers of the National Florence Crittenton Mission

PREPARED BY
Pamela J. Matson

SWD6   National Florence Crittenton Mission, Alexandria, Virginia

Papers, 1895-1959

149 folders   5 ( ) folders

The first Florence Crittenton Mission was opened on New York City's Bleeker Street by Charles Nelson Crittenton, a wealthy New York merchant, in memory of his daughter, Florence, who had died at the age of four. The purposes of this home were to preach salvation and hope and to provide shelter to homeless and pregnant women and girls. With the success of the Bleeker Street Mission, Crittenton became a traveling evangelist preaching the Christian Gospel to all men and women, but especially to the prostitute and the unwed mother. As a result of his effort, Crittenton rescue stations or homes permeated by an atmosphere of Christian evangelism were established throughout the United States.

In 1893 at a Christian Workers Convention in Atlantic City, New Jersey, Crittenton met Dr. Kate Waller Barrett, a physician, who had long been interested in such rescue work. After the death of her husband in 1896, Dr. Barrett assisted Crittenton in organizing homes and in forming a national association which would provide a link between the various individual homes. Florence Crittenton Circles were also established in many cities to give financial support to the Crittenton homes. In 1896, Dr. Barrett became the superintendent of the newly formed National Florence Crittenton Mission (NFCM), of which Charles Crittenton was the President. The NFCM was granted a national charter by a special act of Congress in 1898.

Dr. Barrett and Crittenton traveled across the United States to bring to the attention of the public the problems of prostitution and sexual offences They hoped to dispense information to change society's attitude toward motherhood outside of marriage so that unwed mothers would not fall into despair and an illicit life because of society's condemnation. If the ostracism of society could be removed, the problem would become mainly one of morals and religion, with no societal implications at all aside from the support of the child involved. The early battles against white slavery and hard core prostitution became focused on concern for the unwed mother, her need for adequate medical care, and her right to raise her child free from the scorn of society. Except in extreme circumstances, the Crittenton policy opposed the separation of mother and child for adoption.

After Crittenton's death in 1909, Dr. Barrett succeeded him in the presidency of the NFCM. Until her death in 1925, she worked to increase the influence of the National Mission and to raise standards in the individual homes. She did much to call public attention to society's responsibility for the problems of unwed motherhood and worked to overcome frequent community opposition toward the mere mention of a subject which had long been prohibited by strict social taboos.

Robert South Barrett succeeded his mother as the President of the National Mission after her death in 1925 and her daughter, Reba Barrett Smith, became the General Superintendent. Issues faced in the succeeding years were professional training of social workers, changing attitudes toward adoption, and meeting standards set by state welfare agencies. Meanwhile, the chain of Florence Crittenton homes continued to grow until it reached a peak of sixty-five homes throughout the United States.

The bylaws of the NFCM provdied for the establishment of a Central Extension Committee, a group of fifteen members elected by the homes to serve as an advisory body to the National Mission. The bylaws of the Central Extension Committee stated the purpose as follows: "To further the work of the NFCM in accordance with the policies of its founders regarding the spiritual, physical, social, and economic well-being of those whose rehabilitation is the goal of the organization." The executive officer was designated the National Extension Director, and her work involved visiting the homes and working with community people to solve problems. The Central Extension Committee had complete responsibility for planning the annual national conferences and organizing the work of the Extension Director. Elizabeth Collier served as National Extension Director in the 1930's, and Hester Brown succeeded her in this position in 1940.

In the mid-1940's, Robert Barrett and Reba Smith announced their intention to retire by 1950 or 1951. Barrett then worked through a joint committee from the Trustees and the Central Extension Committee toward the organization of an association which would be legally constituted to assume the responsibility for work with the individual homes at the time of the retirement of the President and the General Superintendent. Hester Brown, National Extension Director, was also anticipating retirement. The Florence Crittenton Homes Association (FCHA), an autonomous federation of Crittenton homes, was founded in 1950, and it was financed partly by the National Mission and also through dues paid by the member homes. Chicago was designated as the headquarters of the FCHA because of a desire for a more central location than Alexandria, Virginia, where the National Mission was located. Gladys Revelle, onetime chairman of the Central Extension Committee, worked very closely with Robert Barrett in the formation of the new association, and she became its first president. Early executive directors included Roxana Jackson (1950), Virgil Payne (1951-1958), and Mary Louise Allen (1958-present). In 1960, the Delegate Assembly voted to change the name of the Florence Crittenton Association of America. Robert Barrett retired as the President of the National Mission in 1950, but he retained his position as Chairman of the Board of Trustees until his death in 1959. His son, Rear Admiral John P. B. Barrett, U.S.N., ret., succeeded him as President of the National Mission, a position he still retains.

The papers of the National Florence Crittenton Mission were deposited in the Social Welfare History Archives Center by Admiral Barrett in September, 1966. The collection comprises 6¼ linear feet and includes administrative and policy-making papers; annual reports; correspondence re individual homes; a study of unwed mothers undertaken by the San Francisco home and data collected for the study; papers which reveal the relationships the NFCM had with the Child Welfare League of America and the National Conference of Social Work; and publications. The administrative and policy-making papers are in a basically chronological organization, and the correspondence with the individual homes is arranged alphabetically by state. The section on annual national conferences includes correspondence re arrangements and a few speeches. Accounts of the national conferences are found in Fourteen Years Work Among "Erring Girls," 1897, (folder 136) and in the Florence Crittenton Bulletins, 1925-1945, (folders 132-135). The section on publications of the NFCM includes incomplete runs of the Florence Crittenton Magazine (1899-1900) and the Florence Crittenton Bulletin (1925-1945); books; and pamphlets. These publications are especially helpful for the early years of Crittenton work for which few or no papers are available.

PARTIAL SUBJECT INVENTORY

The following inventory is not a complete index, but rather a guide to areas of the collection in which certain topics are prominent. The collection chronicles the development of societal concern for the care of unwed mothers and their children. Robert South Barrett and Reba Barrett Smith as NFCM President and General Superintendent, respectively, are so prominent throughout the entire collection that their names have not been included in the partial subject inventory.

ADMISSION POLICIES
    Juvenile Delinquents
        Folders 31-33, 40-43, 55-56, 59, 70, 72-73, 112
    Non-Caucasians
        Folders 4, 10, 20, 25-26, 54, 66, 68, 74, 88, 108

ADOPTION POLICIES
    Folders 1, 13, 23-24, 35, 40-43, 59, 78, 83, 88, 91, 109-110, 113, 124

BARRETT, REAR ADMIRAL JOHN P. B.
    Folder 28

BARRETT, KATE WALLER, M.D.
    Folders 40, 54-57, 61, 67, 75, 95, 107-108, 129-130, 136-139, 146

BROWN, HESTER (MRS. JOSEPH)
    Folders 11, 13-18, 51, 70, 84

CHILD WELFARE LEAGUE OF AMERICA
    Folders 123-124

COMMUNITY CHESTS AND FUNDS
    Folders 11, 14, 17, 26, 30, 35, 37, 51, 56-58, 65, 78-79, 84

COMMUNITY RELATIONSHIPS
    Folders 15, 26, 51, 55-56, 59, 72-73, 78, 82-84, 92-94

CRITTENTON, CHARLES NELSON
    Folders 38, 78, 95, 129-130, 136, 140, 146

DEPRESSION, EFFECTS ON CRITTENTON WORK
    Folders 51, 65, 96-102

EISENHOWER, DWIGHT D.   (Telegram greeting Crittenton workers at
    Folder 26   national conference)

EMPLOYMENT POLICIES
    Folders 11, 14, 16, 19, 23-24, 30-33, 51, 83, 87, 95-106

EXTENSION WORK
    Folders 10-19, 51, 70, 84, 88

FINANCE
    Folders 1-5, 17, 19, 21-30, 36-37, 40-47, 50, 52-59, 61-62, 65-67,
            71-74, 79, 81-82, 85-86, 89, 91-92

FLORENCE CRITTENTON HOMES ASSOCIATION
    Folders 3, 4, 19-29, 31-33, 70, 78

FOSTER HOME CARE OF UNWED MOTHERS AND THEIR CHILDREN
    Folders 11, 37, 83, 124, 126

JUVENILE DELINQUENTS   SEE ADMISSION POLICIES, JUVENILE DELINQUENTS

MORLOCK, MAUD
    Folders 127-128

NATIONAL CONFERENCE OF SOCIAL WORK
    Folder 125

NEGROES   SEE ADMISSION POLICIES, NON-CAUCASIANS

NICHOLSON, CHARLES T.
    Folders 3, 23-24

NOTTINGHAM, RUTH D.
    Folders 127-128

PAYNE, VIRGIL
    Folders 25-27

POST-PARTUM RETENTION OF UNWED MOTHERS IN CRITTENTON HOMES
    Folders 40-43, 54, 65

PRESTON, CLARENCE R.
    Folders 1, 3, 59

PROFESSIONALLY TRAINED WORKERS IN CRITTENTON HOMES
    Folders 11, 16, 19, 25, 51, 59, 83, 88

PUBLICITY FOR CRITTENTON WORK
    Folders 40-43, 49, 51

RELIGIOUS EMPHASIS AND TRAINING
    Folders 11, 38, 61, 65-66, 70, 112

RETIREMENT PENSION FOR CRITTENTON WORKERS
    Folders 1-2, 40-43, 71, 86

REVELLE, GLADYS (MRS. EUGENE)
    Folders 10-12, 19-25, 28, 78

ROOSEVELT, FRANKLIN DELANO   (Letter greeting Crittenton workers at national conference)

SALVATION ARMY MATERNITY HOMES
    Folders 13-14, 17, 92, 112

SEGREGATION   SEE ADMISSION POLICIES, NON-CAUCASIANS

SIBLEY, ELOISE PEARCE
    Folders 127-128

SPELLMAN, D. D.
    Folders 1-2, 63

STANDARDS FOR CRITTENTON HOMES
    Folders 11-18, 26, 30-33, 44, 50-53, 66, 70, 72-74, 78, 84, 88-89, 94

STATE WELFARE AGENCIES
    Folders 14-15, 17, 53, 70, 72-73, 81, 83, 93

THOMAS, MAJOR JULIA   (SALVATION ARMY)
    Folder 112

VENEREAL DISEASE
    Folder 53

VOCATIONAL TRAINING OF UNWED MOTHERS
    Folders 1, 23-24, 65, 87, 91, 109-110

WOMEN'S CHRISTIAN TEMPERANCE UNION
    Folder 94

WORLD WAR II, EFFECTS ON CRITTENTON WORK
    Folder 11, 35, 68, 70, 72-73, 92, 103-106, 124

NATIONAL FLORENCE CRITTENTON MISSION

FOLDER INVENTORY

FOLDER TITLE AND DESCRIPTION OF CONTENTS	FOLDER

Board of Trustees, Correspondence and Papers, 1934-1939 — 1
Constitution and bylaws of National Florence Crittenton Mission, finances of Mission and local homes, Kate Waller Barrett Scholarship Fund, report of conditions in local homes, Crittenton policy re adoption. D. D. Spellman and Clarence R. Preston are prominent correspondents.

Board of Trustees, Correspondence and Papers, 1940-1945 — 2
Minutes of trustees' annual meetings, finances, proposed retirement pension for Crittenton workers, reorganization of Chicago Crittenton home. D. D. Spellman is a prominent correspondent.

Board of Trustees, Correspondence and Papers, 1946-1949 — 3
Minutes of trustees' annual meetings, finances, reorganization of NFCM. Clarence R. Preston and Charles T. Nicholson are prominent correspondents.

Board of Trustees, Correspondence and Papers, 1950-1955 — 4
Minutes of trustees' annual meetings, finances, formation of Florence Crittenton Homes Association and hiring Roxana Jackson as executive director, publicizing Crittenton work, statement on segregation in Crittenton homes (June 22, 1954). Gladys Revelle is a prominent correspondent.

Board of Trustees, Correspondence and Papers, 1955-1957 — 5
Finances, plans for celebration of the 75th Anniversary of Crittenton work.

Charter Form, ca. 1920's — 6
The form provides certification of an individual home as an authorized branch of the National Florence Crittenton Mission.

Annual Reports, 1918-1928 — 7-9
The folder contains annual and biennial reports of the president and officers of the National Mission and individual Crittenton homes, and minutes of annual national conferences. The Florence Crittenton <u>Bulletins</u>, 1925-1945 (folders 132-135) also contain annual reports.

Central Extension Committee, Correspondence and Papers, 1940-1941 — 10
Setting up the committee, philosophy and issues in Crittenton homes and work, selection of Hester Brown as extension director, preparations for annual national conference, duties of the extension director, homes for Negro unwed mothers. Gladys Revelle and Elizabeth Collier are prominent correspondents.

NATIONAL FLORENCE CRITTENTON MISSION

FOLDER TITLE AND DESCRIPTION OF CONTENTS   FOLDER

Central Extension Committee, Correspondence and Papers, 1941-1943   11
    Relations with Community Chests, employment of professionally
    trained workers, emphasis on religious training for unwed
    mothers, placement of workers in homes, standards in social
    work and Crittenton homes, foster home care of the unwed
    mother and her child, issues in individual Crittenton homes:
    Phoenix, Arizona; South Bend, Indiana; Terre Haute, Indiana;
    and Spokane, Washington. Gladys Revelle and Hester Brown
    are prominent correspondents.

Central Extension Committee, Correspondence and Papers, 1944-1946   12
    Plans for annual national conference, problems of individual
    homes, financing the work of the extension director and local
    homes, relationship of the Committee to the National Mission,
    report of the Committee for 1945-1946. Gladys Revelle is a
    prominent correspondent.

Extension Director, Correspondence and Papers, 1940   13
    Policy re adoption, work of local boards, Salvation Army
    maternity homes, raising standards of Crittenton homes,
    duties of extension director, general philosophy of Crittenton
    work, issues in individual homes: Charlotte, North Carolina;
    Norfolk, Virginia; and Spokane, Washington. Hester Brown
    is a prominent correspondent.

Extension Director, Correspondence and Papers, 1941   14
    Relations with welfare agencies of various states and
    their standards, relations with local Community Chests,
    Crittenton policy re hiring Catholic workers in homes
    (August 11, 1941), relationship of National Mission to local
    homes, raising standards in Crittenton homes, Salvation
    Army maternity homes, issues in individual homes: South
    Bend, Indiana; Detroit, Michigan; Jackson, Michigan; Charlotte,
    North Dakota; Erie, Pennsylvania; and Spokane, Washington.
    Hester Brown is a prominent correspondent.

Extension Director, Correspondence and Papers, 1942   15
    Policies in local homes, work of local boards, relationship
    of local homes to National Mission, raising standards in
    Crittenton homes, relations between local homes and state
    welfare agencies, retirement of aged Crittenton workers,
    needs of communities for maternity homes, issues in individual
    Crittenton homes: Chicago, Illinois; Erie, Pennsylvania;
    Scranton, Pennsylvania; and Charleston, South Carolina.
    Hester Brown is a prominent correspondent.

Extension Director, Correspondence and Papers, 1943   16
    Personnel problems, work and responsibilities of local boards,
    standards in Crittenton homes and in hiring Crittenton workers,
    relations with local Community Chests, employment of

FOLDER TITLE AND DESCRIPTION OF CONTENTS	FOLDER

    professionally trained workers, issues in individual Crittenton homes: Phoenix, Arizona; Sioux City, Iowa; and Youngstown, Ohio. Hester Brown is a prominent correspondent.

Extension Director, Correspondence and Papers, 1944   17
    Salvation Army maternity homes, relations with local Community Chests, fund-raising activities in local homes, relations with state welfare agencies, issues in local homes: Baltimore, Maryland; Patterson, New Jersey; Norfolk, Virginia. Hester Brown is a prominent correspondent.

Extension Director, Correspondence and Papers, 1945   18
    Raising standards in Crittenton homes, personnel problems in local homes, issues in individual Crittenton homes: Phoenix, Arizona; and Atlanta, Georgia. Hester Brown is a prominent correspondent.

Florence Crittenton Homes Association, 1948   19
    Need for reorganization of NFCM (upon retirement of Robert Barrett and Reba Smith), study of Crittenton homes, hiring professionally trained workers in Crittenton homes, Central Extension Committee, organization of FCHA: constitution, bylaws, and financing. Gladys Revelle and Mayme Swanson are prominent correspondents.

Florence Crittenton Homes Association, 1949   20
    Survey of Crittenton homes, presentation of plans for FCHA to Crittenton homes, finances, local autonomy over the admission of Negro girls to Crittenton homes, articles of incorporation and bylaws of FCHA, responses of individual Crittenton homes to joining FCHA. Gladys Revelle and Mayme Swanson are prominent correspondents.

Florence Crittenton Homes Association, 1950   21-22
    Responses of individual homes to joining FCHA, administration of FCHA and search for an executive director, legal aspects of formation of FCHA, finances, establishment of office procedures and services to member homes, routine correspondence re work of FCHA. Gladys Revelle is a prominent correspondent.

Florence Crittenton Homes Association, 1951   23-24
    Staff qualifications and duties, hiring an executive director, finances, FCHA policy re adoption, history of Kate Waller Barrett Training School in Akron, Ohio (December 31, 1951), minutes of Executive Committee meeting, annual report, relationship of Patterson, New Jersey Crittenton home to National Mission and FCHA, retirement of Robert Barrett, Reba Smith, and Charles Nicholson from National Mission. Gladys Revelle is a prominent correspondent.

NATIONAL FLORENCE CRITTENTON MISSION

FOLDER TITLE AND DESCRIPTION OF CONTENTS | FOLDER

Florence Crittenton Homes Association, 1952 — 25
    Routine correspondence, finances, relationship between FCHA executive director and National Mission Board of Trustees, employment of professionally trained workers in Crittenton homes (June 6, 1952), policies re admission of non-Caucasian girls to Crittenton homes (December 16, 1952), reports of the executive director and summaries of visits of field worker to individual Crittenton homes: Phoenix, Arizona; Los Angeles, California; Jackson, Michigan; Cleveland, Ohio; Columbus, Ohio; Toledo, Ohio; Pittsburgh, Pennsylvania; Williamsport, Pennsylvania; and Seattle, Washington.

Florence Crittenton Homes Association, 1953 — 26
    Relationship between Columbus, Ohio Crittenton board and Council of Social Agencies, finances, publicizing Crittenton work, facilities for Negro unwed mothers, summaries of field visits to individual homes, standards for Crittenton homes in Columbus, Ohio and Boston, Massachusetts, reports of the executive director, minutes of Executive Committee meeting, copy of telegram from President Dwight D. Eisenhower greeting NFCM at annual national conference, annual report of FCHA, and resignation of Mobile, Alabama Crittenton home from FCHA. Virgil Payne and Ruth Thorpe (president of FCHA) are prominent correspondents.

Florence Crittenton Homes Association, 1954 — 27
    Relationship of Columbus, Ohio Crittenton home to National Mission and FCHA, finances, summaries of visits to individual homes, reports of the executive director, minutes of Executive Committee meeting, plans for the celebration of the 75th Anniversary of Crittenton work. Virgil Payne, Ruth Thorpe, and Josephine Wright (president of FCHA succeeding Ruth Thorpe) are prominent correspondents.

Florence Crittenton Homes Association, 1955 — 28
    Fund-raising campaign, summaries of visits to individual homes, reports of the executive director, revision of bylaws, relationship between National Mission and FCHA, and financial aid of FCHA by the National Mission. Josephine Wright, Gladys Revelle and Rear Admiral John P. B. Barrett (President of National Mission after retirement of Robert Barrett in 1951) are prominent correspondents.

Florence Crittenton Homes Association, 1956-1959 — 29
    Scattered correspondence. Preparations for annual national conference, finances, plans for the celebration of the 75th Anniversary of Crittenton work, and revision of bylaws.

FOLDER TITLE AND DESCRIPTION OF CONTENTS	FOLDER

Florence Crittenton Homes Folders 30-92

Mobile, Alabama, 1935-1943 — 30
Correspondence between National Mission and local Crittenton officials, finances, administrative problems, standards of Crittenton workers, physical standards in Crittenton homes, general philosophy of Crittenton work, and relationship of local board to Mobile Community Chest.

Phoenix, Arizona, 1933-1954 — 31-33
Correspondence between National Mission and local officials. Finances, statistical monthly reports, keeping delinquent girls from juvenile court with unwed mothers, physical standards of home, employment of Catholic workers in home (February 28, 1941), and Florence Crittenton Homes Association.

Hot Springs, Arkansas, ca. 1930-1931 — 34
One report, two letters.

Little Rock, Arkansas, 1926-1943 — 35
Policy re adoption, relationship of home to Little Rock Community Chest, administrative policies, standards of home, relationship of National Mission to local home, standards in licensing maternity homes, and effects of World War II.

Los Angeles, California, 1951-1954 — 36
Financing building program, financial aid from National Mission to local home. Correspondence is very scattered.

San Francisco, California, 1941-1950 — 37
Foster home program, financing new Crittenton homes, and relationship of home to San Francisco Community Chest.

San Jose, California, 1908 — 38
Single letter describing visit of Charles N. Crittenton to city and his participation in a revival meeting.

Wilmington, Delaware, 1932-1944 — 39
Correspondence between Reba Smith and Mrs. Charles Evans (member of the Wilmington Board of Directors of Crittenton home and personal friend of the Barretts and Smiths). Policy re accepting married women and children in home, policy re accepting unwed mothers with second offenses, and correspondences re individual cases.

District of Columbia, 1914-1956 — 40-43
Letter to Kate Waller Barrett protesting the promotion of Crittenton work by holding baby shows in local store windows and her reply (1914). After 1935, there is routine correspondence between National Mission and officials of local home.

NATIONAL FLORENCE CRITTENTON MISSION

FOLDER TITLE AND DESCRIPTION OF CONTENTS | FOLDER

Monthly reports of caseworker and superintendent, need for retirement plans for Crittenton workers, history of the home and its policies, policy re keeping girl in home for a specified length of time after birth of baby (October 2, 1937), policy re keeping mother and child together rather than adoption, Ivanoka Farm, work of Florence Crittenton Circles. The material is very scattered after 1942. Jean Cole, Superintendent of the Washington, D.C. Home, is a prominent correspondent.

St. Petersburg, Florida, 1936-1943   44
Financing purchase of property for new home, physical standards in home, and problems in staffing home.

Atlanta, Georgia, 1904, 1950-1956   45
Petition of incorporation (1904), fund-raising activities, relationship between National Mission and local home.

Columbus, Georgia, 1931-1935   46
Legal complications following the closing of the home due to financial difficulties.

Savannah, Georgia, 1935   47
A form letter requesting financial support and a Christmas poem are the only papers in the folder.

Chicago, Illinois, 1955   48
Two letters concerning the establishment of the Florence Crittenton Anchorage in Chicago.

Peoria, Illinois, 1936   49
Brochure publicizing the Peoria home.

Indianapolis, Indiana, 1931-1934   50
Financial difficulties, aid from the National Mission to raise physical standards in the home, Reba Smith's views on sterilization of feeble-minded and highly-sexed girls.

South Bend, Indiana, 1926-1951   51
Publicity for Florence Crittenton Circles, developing community support for Crittenton work, effects of depression, problems with Crittenton personnel and repercussions, follow-up work with unwed mothers, extension work, attitudes toward hiring professionally trained workers in Crittenton homes, relations between the National Mission and South Bend Community Chest, and standards in Crittenton work.

Terre Haute, Indiana, 1907, 1930-1955   52
Receipt for purchase of property (1907), articles of incorporation and bylaws, policies and standards in home, fund-raising plans for new building. The papers are scattered after 1935.

FOLDER TITLE AND DESCRIPTION OF CONTENTS	FOLDER

Sioux City, Iowa, 1926-1937, 1951-1953   53
    Policies and activities of home, correspondence between National Mission and local board, fund-raising, relationship between local board and superintendent of home, personnel problems in Seattle, Washington home, Crittenton policies re treatment of venereal disease, state standards for fire and health protection.

Topeka, Kansas, 1919-1930, ca. 1946-1956   54
    Scattered, routine correspondence. Letter of recommendation from Kate Waller Barrett to Sarah Malone re collection of funds to start homes for Negro unwed mothers; constitution and bylaws, Negro unwed mothers, finances and plans for construction of new home, length of time required for girls to stay in home after birth of baby.

Ashland, Kentucky, 1920-1921   55
    Scattered letters to Kate Waller Barrett.

Lexington, Kentucky, 1894-1957   56
    Letters to Kate Waller Barrett, Articles of Incorporation, establishment of home with local financial support. The papers are widely scattered.

Louisville, Kentucky, 1912   57
    Letters to Kate Waller Barrett re establishing and financing the home.

Baltimore, Maryland, 1941-1944   58
    Study of local home by Baltimore Council of Social Agencies; outline and evaluation of policies, programs, and finances of the home; bylaws and amended Charter (1944).

Boston, Massachusetts, 1926-1951   59
    Need of the community for maternity home, history and policies of the Welcome House which transfered its assets to the Florence Crittenton League of Compassion (the local Crittenton organization), shelter for care of delinquent and pregnant women, amended constitution and bylaws, relations with Community Fund, finances, response of Crittenton workers to changing theories of social work practice re adoption and professional training of staff members. Clarence Preston is a prominent correspondent.

Lowell, Massachusetts, n.d., 1953   60
    Miscellaneous papers and correspondence re situations faced by local Crittenton League.

Lynn, Massachusetts, 1907-1908   61
    Letters to Kate Waller Barrett showing the development of the local Crittenton branch, finances, and plans for revival meetings.

NATIONAL FLORENCE CRITTENTON MISSION

FOLDER TITLE AND DESCRIPTION OF CONTENTS | FOLDER

Swampscott, Massachusetts, 1927-1940   62
     Scattered correspondence re mortgage on Crittenton property.

Detroit, Michigan, 1944-1954   63
     Response to death of D. D. Spellman. Scattered correspondence re proposed monograph on Crittenton work.

Minneapolis, Minnesota, 1958   64
     Correspondence re location of a birth record after the Minneapolis Crittenton home had closed.

Kansas City, Missouri (Caucasian), 1927-1934   65
     Finances, policy re length of time a girl must remain in home after birth of baby, local management of home by Women's Inter-denominational Missionary Council, vocational training, religious services in home, effects of depression on community funds, annual statistical reports.

Kansas City, Missouri (Negro), 1926-1934   66
     Facilities for Negro unwed mothers, finances, construction of a new home, scattered monthly reports, effects of depression, concern over conditions in Topeka Home for Colored Girls, promotion of religion in the home, concern over holding annual national conference in the South when Negro Crittenton workers attend.

Helena, Montana, 1906-1956   67
     Very scattered and miscellaneous papers. Letter from Kate Waller Barrett re property of home in Portland, Oregon; fund-raising.

Atlantic City, New Jersey, 1931, 1941-1946   68
     Care of Negro as well as Caucasian unwed mothers in New Jersey, threat of need to close home, effects of World War II. The correspondence is very scattered.

Newark, New Jersey, 1955   69
     Correspondence re death of Dr. William Ward, a member of the local Crittenton board.

Patterson, New Jersey, 1940-1952   70
     Concern over standards in the home by National Mission and New Jersey Department of Institutions and Agencies, relationship of National Mission and Patterson Crittenton officials, relations between National Mission and officials of New Jersey Department of Institutions and Agencies, promotion of religious evangelism in the home, record-keeping practices, extension work, effects of World War II, attitudes of Patterson Crittenton officials toward Newark Crittenton home and policies, attitudes of local and National Mission officials re "sinfulness" of the state of unwed motherhood, refusal of Patterson home to join Florence Crittenton Homes Association, withdrawal of home from

FOLDER TITLE AND DESCRIPTION OF CONTENTS   FOLDER

      the National Florence Crittenton Mission to become the
      Florence Christian Home, policy re sheltering older child-
      ren, delinquent girls, and whole families as well as unwed
      mothers in the home. Jacob Stamm (President of the local
      board) is a prominent correspondent.

Trenton, New Jersey, 1940-1953   71
      Routine financial matters, need for retirement pension
      for Crittenton workers, building addition to home. The
      correspondence is very scattered.

New York City, New York, 1926-1959   72-73
      Relationship between National Mission and local officials,
      physical standards of home, inspection of home by New York
      State Department of Welfare, analysis of population of home,
      finances, policy re keeping delinquent girls from the juvenile
      courts, change from a locked shelter to an open home, analysis
      of needs and facilities of New York City for unwed mothers,
      fund-raising projects. From 1957-1959, there are minutes of
      some meetings of the Board of Directors of the Florence
      Crittenton League of New York. Judge William Bayes (President
      of the League) is a prominent correspondent.

Charlotte, North Carolina, 1929-1953   74
      Scattered, routine correspondence. Standards of medical
      care in the home, need for facilities for Negro unwed
      mothers, financial assistance from the National Mission.

Fargo, North Dakota, 1924-1929   75
      Scattered, routine correspondence. Letter from Kate
      Waller Barrett re deed to home; 1930 annual report,
      sale of property.

Akron, Ohio, 1935-1938   76
      Scattered, routine correspondence between National Mission
      and local officials. General policies and operation of the
      home, formation of junior boards, recreation in the home.

Cleveland, Ohio, 1953-1956   77
      Scattered, routine correspondence.

Columbus, Ohio, 1906, 1953-1954   78
      Letter from Charles Crittenton re purposes of Crittenton
      work, public relations, practice of girls boarding their
      children while they work, and attitudes of girls' families
      toward their pregnant daughters (1906); there is also
      material re the relationship of the home to FCHA, reaction
      to criticism of standards in home, junior boards, policy
      re adoption, relationship of local home to Community Chest,
      relationship of local officials to National Mission and FCHA.
      Gladys Revelle is a prominent correspondent.

NATIONAL FLORENCE CRITTENTON MISSION

FOLDER TITLE AND DESCRIPTION OF CONTENTS   FOLDER

Toledo, Ohio, 1948-1954   79
    Correspondence between National Mission and Toledo Council
    of Social Agencies, decrease in number of Crittenton homes,
    fund-raising drive to finance construction of a new home,
    statistical breakdown of Crittenton facilities into maternity
    homes, circles, protective homes, and training schools.

Portland, Oregon, 1903   80
    Clipping re founding the home.

Erie, Pennsylvania, 1937-1941   81
    Very scattered correspondence. Relations between National
    Mission and Pennsylvania Department of Public Welfare, finances.

Harrisburg, Pennsylvania, 1927-1941   82
    Very scattered correspondence. Closing of Crittenton
    home, financial arrangements, concern of Reba Smith for an
    individual case.

Philadelphia, Pennsylvania, 1941-1948   83
    Scattered, routine correspondence. Panel discussion re
    policies of home and social agencies on planning for
    adoption; employment of professionally trained workers,
    foster home care, purchase of new building for home.

Scranton, Pennsylvania, 1938-1944   84
    Evaluation of home and its policies, extension work, relations
    with Council of Social Agencies re need for institutional care
    for unwed mothers in Scranton, closing of home.

Charleston, South Carolina, 1942-1954   85
    Very scattered correspondence. Financial aid from National
    Mission to local home, re-organization of home.

Chattanooga, Tennessee, 1936-1954   86
    Very scattered correspondence. Financial aid from National
    Mission to local home, soliciting funds from community,
    need for retirement pensions for Crittenton workers.

Nashville, Tennessee, ca. 1930's   87
    Notes on care of children used in training course, standards
    for hiring Crittenton workers, vocational training of unwed
    mothers for nursing and child care positions.

Houston, Texas, ca. 1936, 1947   88
    Hiring professionally trained workers in Crittenton homes,
    Crittenton policy re adoption, welfare services for Negro
    unwed mothers in Houston, standards in Crittenton homes.

NATIONAL FLORENCE CRITTENTON MISSION

FOLDER TITLE AND DESCRIPTION OF CONTENTS	FOLDER
Ogden, Utah, 1926-1942 Very scattered correspondence. Relationship between National Mission and local officials, standards and philosophy of Crittenton work, finances, sale of Crittenton property.	89
Lynchburg, Virginia, 1944-1955 Very scattered correspondence. Basic policies of Crittenton work, effect of location of a home for unwed mothers on surrounding property, correspondence re an individual case.	90
Norfolk, Virginia, 1944-1955 Description of home and its policies and practices, activities of junior board, policies re adoption, history of home, financial aid from National Mission to local home, vocational training for unwed mothers.	91
Seattle, Washington, 1943-1953 Consideration of closing home because of declining population, evaluation of community need for home, effect of World War II, Salvation Army maternity homes, construction of new home, financial aid from National Mission to local home.	92
Spokane, Washington, 1935-1943 Scattered, routine correspondence. Relations with state social welfare agencies, decision to close home.	93
Correspondence re Formation of New Homes, 1927-1946 Correspondence from individuals and organizations re needs and possibilities of establishing homes for unwed mothers. Letters from an official of the Women's Christian Temperance Union on prostitution, white slave trade, and unwed mothers in the Philippine Islands. Costs and standards in Florence Crittenton homes.	94
Applications for Positions in Florence Crittenton Homes, 1920's Arranged alphabetically. Requests to Kate Waller Barrett, Charles N. Crittenton, and National Mission for employment.	95
Applications for Positions in Florence Crittenton Homes, 1930's Arranged alphabetically. Application blanks, surrounding correspondence, and scattered photographs. Papers show the effects of the depression in employment, qualifications for Crittenton workers, training programs for Crittenton workers and personnel problems in local homes.	96-102
Applications for Positions in Florence Crittenton Homes, 1940's Arranged alphabetically. Application blanks, surrounding correspondence, and scattered photographs. Papers show the effects of World War II, qualifications for Crittenton workers, training programs for Crittenton workers, and personnel problems in local homes.	103-106

FOLDER TITLE AND DESCRIPTION OF CONTENTS	FOLDER
State Registration of Illegitimate Births, 1920, 1941 Letter to Kate Waller Barrett re birth record which revealed the illegitimacy of a child (1920). In 1941, Reba Barrett Smith wrote to individual state health departments asking for samples of birth registration forms. Arranged alphabetically by state.	107
Individual Requests, 1920-1942 Letter received by the National Mission from girls requesting assistance.	108
Kate Waller Barrett Scholarships, 1940-1945 The fund was established by Robert Barrett in memory of his mother to give financial aid to girls who kept their babies and who wished to continue their education as a means of supporting the child. Arranged chronologically by applicant and local home. The folder contains correspondence between Reba Smith, individual applicants, and local Crittenton officials.	109-110
Annual National Conferences, 1927-1928, 1932 Programs are available for 1927 and 1928. For 1932, correspondence re arrangements, speakers, etcetera. Policy re exchanging cases between Crittenton homes.	111
Annual National Conferences, 1932-1934 Correspondence re arrangements. Copies of speeches at 1933 conference: "Salvation Army Work With Unmarried Mothers" by Major Julia Thomas, "Handling of Illegitimacy" by the Illinois Children's Home and Aid Society, "The Illegitimate Child in the Juvenile Court," and "Religious Aspects of Florence Crittenton Work."	112
Annual National Conferences, 1935 Correspondence re arrangements. Views of a speaker re keeping mother and child together whenever possible.	113
Annual National Conferences, 1935-1936 Correspondence re arrangements. Letter of greeting from President Franklin D. Roosevelt. There is no material on the 1937 conference.	114
Annual National Conferences, 1938-1939 Correspondence re arrangements. Concern re food costs in Crittenton homes, environmental influences on the intelligence of children, arrangements for Florence Crittenton Day at the New York World's Fair.	115
Annual National Conferences, 1939-1941 Correspondence re arrangements.	116
Annual National Conferences, 1941-1944 Correspondence re arrangements.	117

NATIONAL FLORENCE CRITTENTON MISSION   500

FOLDER TITLE AND DESCRIPTION OF CONTENTS   FOLDER

Florence Crittenton Bulletin Subscriptions, 1931-1942.   118-122

Child Welfare League of America, Correspondence, 1940-1943   123
    Correspondence re National Florence Crittenton Mission
    associate membership in CWLA.

Child Welfare League of America, Publications, 1939-1945   124
    As an associate member of CWLA, the National Mission
    received pamphlets and dittos which the League distri-
    buted and published.

National Conference of Social Work, 1938-1944   125
    Correspondence and papers re National Mission membership
    and participation in the National Conference of Social
    Work.

Studies of Unmarried Mothers, 1942-1943   126
    A study undertaken by the Florence Crittenton home of
    San Francisco, California, The Foster Home Program
    Demonstration, January, 1942-January, 1943.

Studies of Unmarried Mothers, 1935-1943   127-128
    These studies were probably collected by the San Francisco
    Crittenton home to make use of earlier studies by others
    of unwed mothers.

    Nottingham, Ruth D. Abstract of Psychological Study of
        Forty Unmarried Mothers. PhD Dissertation. Ohio
        State University, 1935.
    Nottingham, Ruth D. "A Psychological Study of Forty Unwed
        Mothers." Genetic Psychology Monographs. Vol. 19,
        No. 2, May, 1937.
    Child Welfare League of America. General Report of the Study
        of Children's Program of the District of Columbia with
        Recommendations, 1937.
    Morlock, Maud. "Foster Home Care for Unmarried Mothers."
        The Child. Vol. 3, No. 3, September, 1938.
    Sibley, Eloise Pearce. A Study of the Vocational Success
        of Fifty Unmarried Mothers. M.A. Thesis. Ohio State
        University, 1938.
    Morlock, Maud. U.S. Department of Labor, Children's Bureau.
        The Fathers of Children Born Out of Wedlock. March 1,
        1939.
    Sub-committee of the Unmarried Parenthood Committee of the
        Welfare Council of Toronto and District. A Study of the
        Adjustment of Teen Age Children Born out of Wedlock Who
        Remained in the Custody of Their Mothers or Relatives, 1943.

NATIONAL FLORENCE CRITTENTON MISSION

FOLDER TITLE AND DESCRIPTION OF CONTENTS | FOLDER

Florence Crittenton Magazine, March, 1899-December, 1900 — 129-130
Volumes I and II. Contains reports from the National Mission officers, individual Crittenton homes, and circles. Writings describe the work and philosophy of the Mission and its homes. Published monthly by the National Mission from 1899 to 1917. While they are not included in this collection, Volumes XIII to XX were titled Girls.

Florence Crittenton Magazine, n.d. — 131
"A Modern Heroine" reprint from April, n.d. issue of the magazine.

Florence Crittenton Bulletin, 1925-1945 — 132-135
The Bulletin was published quarterly, beginning in 1925, by the National Mission. The run of Bulletins is not complete. There is some duplication in the two volumes covering 1941-1945, but the contents of the volumes are incomplete and sometimes supplement one another. The Bulletins contain annual reports of the National Mission, articles re the philosophy of Crittenton work, minutes of the annual national conferences, and reports of individual homes and circles.

Books, 1897-1933 (folders 136-145)
National Florence Crittenton Mission, Fourteen Years Work Among "Erring Girls" As Conducted by the NFCM with Practical Suggestions for the Same. Washington D.C.: 1897. — 136
Barrett, Kate Waller, M.D. Some Practical Suggestions on the Conduct of a Rescue Home. Washington D.C.: National Florence Crittenton Mission, 1900. — 137-139
Crittenton, Charles Nelson. The Brother of Girls. The Life Story of Charles N. Crittenton. Chicago: World's Events Company, 1910. — 140
Barrett, Robert South. The Care of the Unmarried Mother. Alexandria, Virginia: 1929. — 141-143
Wilson, Otto, in collaboration with Robert South Barrett. Fifty Years Work With Girls, 1883-1933. Alexandria, Virginia: 1933. — 144-145

Pamphlets, ca. 1897-1945 — 146
Barrett, Kate Waller, M.D. Motherhood: A Means of Regeneration. Washington D.C.: ca. 1897.
Life Sketch and Work of Evangelist Charles N. Crittenton. Washington D.C.: ca. 1912.
What Presidents of the United States Think of Florence Crittenton Homes. ca. 1936.
Barrett, Robert South. Twenty Years as President of the National Florence Crittenton Mission. 1945.

NATIONAL FLORENCE CRITTENTON MISSION   502

FOLDER TITLE AND DESCRIPTION OF CONTENTS   FOLDER

Government Documents, 1942-1946   147
    U.S. Department of Labor, Children's Bureau. <u>Maternity Homes for Unmarried Mothers</u>. Washington D.C.: Government Printing Office, 1946.
    State of Virginia. <u>Child Welfare</u> (Report to the Governor of Virginia by Virginia Advisory Legislative Council), 1942.
    State of Virginia. <u>Bill Regulating Child Welfare Agencies</u>. January, 1942.

Poetry and Memorabilia, n.d.   148
    The materials reveal the emphasis the National Mission and local Crittenton homes placed on religion.

Photographs   149
    Undated photographs.

Legal Folder #1
    Legal-size materials from individual homes. Bylaws and articles of incorporation from Wilmington, Delaware; legal material re property from Ogden, Utah; legal material re property from Fargo, North Dakota.

Legal Folder #2
    Legal-size material re Florence Crittenton Homes Association. Constitution, bylaws, articles of incorporation, and minutes of meetings of Board of Directors.

Legal Folder #3
    Application blanks for Florence Crittenton positions in the 1930's.

Legal Folder #4
    Legal-size material concerning training course in Nashville, Tennessee Crittenton home.

Legal Folder #5
    Florence Crittenton <u>Bulletins</u>, 1925-1928.

16

An Inventory of the Papers of the National Social Welfare Assembly

PREPARED BY
Nancy M. Wiggins

SWD4   National Social Welfare Assembly

          Papers, 1911-1956

          197 folders

Recognizing the similarity of their problems and desiring closer coordination of their work, executives representing twelve leading national social work organizations began regular monthly meetings in 1920 for conference. Formally organized in 1923, the National Social Work Council (NSWC) retained the same spirit and method until 1945 when, upon revision of its by-laws, the Council expanded its functions and became the National Social Welfare Assembly.

The National Social Work Council did not undertake any new activities of its own, but sought, rather, to help existing agencies better fulfill their functions by mutual informational exchanges and open discussion of common problems. Until 1925, administrative work incidental to arranging meetings and the printing and distribution of materials was undertaken on a volunteer basis by two executives of national organizations, Howard S. Braucher and David H. Holbrook. After that date, David Holbrook served as full-time secretary to the Council through 1945.

Representatives of government, philanthropic foundations and agencies outside the NSWC were frequently invited to speak at the Council's monthly meetings and examine with its members topics of mutual concern. Other meetings revolved around reports from member agencies of programs and projects undertaken, and topics of current importance for social work which were discussed at the Council's "Round-Table Meetings."

Meeting topics and studies originated by committees of the Council reflect the changing attitudes and objectives of voluntary social work organizations and developments in the larger society in which they evolved. Early NSWC meetings were largely concerned with bases of financial support, budgets, and endorsement. Subsequent topics of discussion included: attempts to achieve better understanding and closer cooperation between agencies functioning in related areas or the same communities; relationships between national organizations and their local agencies; problems arising from the Depression, including the financial pressures toward retrenchment in a period of increasing welfare and relief requests; defense mobilization and its social repercussions; and, a few years later, demobilization and the social needs and problems created by massive relocation.

At an all-day meeting January 18, 1945, Council members concluded that some structural and functional alterations were necessary in order to create an organization capable of meeting more effectively the diverse social welfare problems in the post-war community. A Special Committee on Reorganization was appointed and worked through 1945 to design a more functional framework for the Council. The Special Committee's Proposed Constitution was approved by the membership, and at its December 1945 meeting, the National Social Work Council became the National Social Welfare Assembly.

Prior to assuming executive responsibilities for the Council in 1925, David H. Holbrook had served as Executive Director of the American Association for Organizing Family Social Work. This Association, originally the American Association of Societies for Organizing Charities, was formed in 1911 and was the forerunner of the present Family Service Association of America. Francis Herbert McLean, a pioneer in social welfare and charity organization, was largely responsible for bringing together the participating charity agencies in the AASOC and remained an important and active force in the Association through its subsequent reorganizations. David Holbrook retained a special interest in family social work and close ties with McLean through the years he served the Council.

In 1923, a number of social agency executives in the casework field came together on the invitation of David Holbrook to discuss informally and unofficially their various specialities of work with the hope of achieving clearer understandings and cooperation in over-lapping areas. Taking its name from the town of Milford, Pennsylvania where the first meeting was held in 1923, the Milford Conference continued to meet annually until 1929. In 1928 the American Association of Social Workers published a report of the Milford Conference, Social Case Work, Generic and Specific, which emphasized the common base of practice among all social caseworkers regardless of areas of specialization.

Exigencies of the depression period prevented meetings of the Milford Conference for several years until 1932, when the "mass methods" being called into use in relief work and other problems arising out of the national situation indicated the desirability of calling another conference for discussion. The Milford Conference met again in 1933 and issued a report on social casework in 1934. As the initiator of the Conference in which he remained an active participant, David Holbrook retained correspondence, papers and reports of the Milford Conference among the NSWC files.

The two broad functions of the National Social Welfare Assembly, according to the 1965 edition of the Encyclopedia of Social Work, were to define and study problems of broad social policy affecting the needs of people and to plan action to meet these needs and, also, to serve national organizations and local communities in developing effective programs, operations, and administration in the field of social welfare.

In 1942, six national agencies, five of which were members of the National Social Work Council, combined to promote joint financing and joint planning of their war service projects in local communities. Established as the American War Community Services (AWCS) and certified by the War Relief Control Board, the agencies undertook cooperative projects of health and welfare services in local communities where the war effort had created serious problems. The functional group of the AWCS, the Service Cooperation Committee, made field studies and coordinated services in those communities selected as projects. On May 1, 1946 the minutes of the Service Cooperation Committee and the files of the AWCS were deposited with the NSWA. After June 1, 1946 the Service Cooperation Committee of the AWCS also served as the Service Cooperation Committee of the NSWA and continued its functions under the Assembly after the dissolution of the AWCS in 1947.

The social health and welfare problems accompaning the relocation of Japanese-Americans during the war were studied by the National Social Work Council and again became a topic of concern for the Assembly when the difficult post-war resettlement began. The Assembly's Committee on Japanese-Americans prepared a series of bulletins covering problems related to discrimination in housing and employment, legislation under consideration and prejudices against Japanese-Americans.

Social welfare agencies serving the interest of youth combined in several bodies of the Assembly to coordinate their work and undertake special projects. One such association, the Young Adult Council (YAC), was founded in 1948 as the coordinating organization for 28 national student and young worker organizations. Particularly concerned with youth in the 18-30 year age group, YAC sponsored a United States Assembly of Youth in 1953 at Ann Arbor, Michigan and also represented young adult organizations in the United States to the World Assembly of Youth (WAY).

The collection is divided into three sections which have been arranged chronologically. Some exceptions occur in the cases of organizations functioning simultaneously and projects begun under the Council and continued by the Assembly.

Section I. Papers which appear to be included in the collection because of David Holbrook's associations and work prior to his appointment as Executive Secretary of the NSWC in 1925 and which indicate his social welfare activities outside the Council after that date. Papers included within this section are: Annual Reports of the American Association for Organizing Family Social Work (folder 1); David H. Holbrook-F.H. McLean Correspondence (folder 2); Milford Conference papers (folders 3-8). <u>Social Case Work, Generic and Specific</u>, the product of the first six years of work by the Conference, is contained in folder 4.

Section II. Papers of the National Social Work Council which have been arranged as follows: Monthly meetings (folders 9-101). Most of the meetings before 1933 include stenotyped records of all proceedings which are infrequently included for later meetings. A card index to meeting speakers and topics was included with the collection and is available at the Minnesota Welfare Archives Center; Service Records of the Council (folders 102-104); Mimeographed and printed material distributed by the Council (folders 105-125); Publications of the NSWC (folder 126).

Section III. The following projects of the National Social Welfare Assembly: Papers of the American War-Community Services (folders 127-157); Problems of Relocation and Resettlement of Japanese Americans (folders 158-161); Reports from the Associated Youth Serving Organizations, Inc. (folder 162); Projects of the Young Adult Council (folders 163-197). Material related to the United States Assembly of Youth at Ann Arbor, Michigan in 1953 is contained in folders 163-168. Information sheets not used in the 1954 Youth Directory are in folders 169-170. Papers of the YAC, as United States representative to the World Assembly of Youth, are in folders 171-197.

NATIONAL SOCIAL WELFARE ASSEMBLY

At the time of its reorganization in December 1945, the National Social Work Council membership included the following organizations:

AMERICAN PUBLIC WELFARE ASSOCIATION
AMERICAN RED CROSS
AMERICAN SOCIAL HYGIENE ASSOCIATION
BOY SCOUTS OF AMERICA
BOYS' CLUBS OF AMERICA
CAMP FIRE GIRLS
CHILD WELFARE LEAGUE OF AMERICA
COMMUNITY CHESTS AND COUNCILS, INC.
COUNCIL OF JEWISH FEDERATIONS AND WELFARE FUNDS
FAMILY WELFARE ASSOCIATION OF AMERICA
GIRL SCOUTS
NATIONAL ASSOCIATION OF LEGAL AID ORGANIZATIONS
NATIONAL BOARD Y.W.C.A.
NATIONAL CHILD LABOR COMMITTEE
NATIONAL COMMITTEE FOR MENTAL HYGIENE
NATIONAL CONFERENCE OF CATHOLIC CHARITIES
NATIONAL CONSUMERS LEAGUE
NATIONAL COUNCIL Y.M.C.A.
NATIONAL FEDERATION OF SETTLEMENTS
NATIONAL JEWISH WELFARE BOARD
NATIONAL ORGANIZATION FOR PUBLIC HEALTH NURSING
NATIONAL PROBATION ASSOCIATION
NATIONAL PUBLICITY COUNCIL
NATIONAL RECREATION ASSOCIATION
NATIONAL SOCIETY FOR THE PREVENTION OF BLINDNESS
NATIONAL TRAVELERS AID ASSOCIATION
NATIONAL TUBERCULOSIS ASSOCIATION
NATIONAL URBAN LEAGUE
THE SALVATION ARMY

NATIONAL SOCIAL WELFARE ASSEMBLY

PARTIAL SUBJECT INVENTORY

The following inventory is not a complete index, but, rather a guide to areas of the collection in which certain topics are prominent. Information relevant to each of the member agencies of the National Social Work Council is contained in the NSWC minutes. The Council's mimeographed and printed material is largely related to meeting topics of the same time period and contemporary trends and events from the national scene. No attempt has been made to index those topics of continuing concern for the Council, which include: cooperation between national agencies, relationships between national associations and their local agencies, problems of supporting social work, and the proper role of voluntary organizations as government assumed a wider responsibility in the fields of social health and welfare.

ACADEMIC FREEDOM
    Folder 168

AMERICAN ASSOCIATION FOR ORGANIZING FAMILY SOCIAL WORK
    Folders 1-2

AMERICAN WAR COMMUNITY SERVICES
    Folders 97, 127-157

ASSOCIATED YOUTH SERVING ORGANIZATIONS
    Folders 97, 162

BOY SCOUTS OF AMERICA
    Folder 89

BRAUCHER, HOWARD S.
    Folders 45, 93

BUDGETS
    Folders 18, 32, 42-43, 88, 96-98, 137, 141

BYINGTON, MARGARET F.
    Folder 27

CARNEGIE CORPORATION
    Folder 26

CASEWORK
    Folders 3-8

NATIONAL SOCIAL WELFARE ASSEMBLY

CHILD WELFARE
    Folders 58, 62, 87, 91, 100

COMMONWEALTH FUND
    Folder 21

COMMUNITY CHESTS AND COUNCILS
    Folders 31, 33, 37, 40-41, 43-44, 65, 72, 77, 88-90, 96-97, 137-138

COMMUNITY ORGANIZATION (PARTICULARLY COORDINATION OF SOCIAL WELFARE ACTIVITIES)
    Folders 30, 77, 80, 82, 85, 87-88, 96

CONFERENCE METHODS
    Folders 9, 38

CONSOLIDATION IN SOCIAL WORK (COMBINING ACTIVITIES OF AGENCIES)
    Folder 5

CONSUMERS
    Folder 87

COOPERATION AMONG AGENCIES
    Folders 51, 83, 85, 91, 93, 96-97, 117, 113, 142

COOPERATION WITH GOVERNMENT
    Folders 58, 82-83, 93

DEFENSE HEALTH AND WELFARE
    Folders 92-97, 127-157

DEMOBILIZATION, INDUSTRIAL
    Folders 98, 122

DEMOBILIZATION, MILITARY
    Folders 97-98, 122

DEPRESSION
    Folders 6-7, 51, 54, 67-69, 74-76, 81-82, 87

ENGLAND, SOCIAL WORK
    Folders 94, 98-99

FAMILY SERVICE ASSOCIATION OF AMERICA
    Folders 1-2

FIELD WORK
    Folders 3-4, 28, 57, 59, 83, 90, 145-149

FINANCING SOCIAL WORK
    Folders 12, 18-20, 25, 69, 96-97, 127, 139

FOUNDATIONS
    Folders 17, 21, 23-24, 26-27, 64, 84

GARY, INDIANA, FIELD REPORT
    Folder 148

GERMANY, SOCIAL WORK
    Folders 70, 82

HEALTH
    Folders 71, 83, 91, 99

INTERNATIONAL CONFERENCE OF SOCIAL WORK, JULY 1928
    Folder 35

INTERNATIONAL MIGRATION SERVICE
    Folder 90

INTERNATIONAL YOUTH MOVEMENTS
    Folders 171-197

JAPANESE-AMERICANS, WORLD WAR II
    Folders 96, 98, 158-161, 168

LABOR
    Folder 97

MCLEAN, FRANCIS HERBERT
    Folder 2

MIGRATION IN THE U.S.
    Folders 92, 96, 99

NATIONAL SOCIAL WELFARE ASSEMBLY

MILBANK MEMORIAL FUND
    Folder 24

MILFORD CONFERENCE
    Folders 3-8

MINORITY GROUPS
    Folders 90-98

NATIONAL CONFERENCE OF CATHOLIC CHARITIES
    Folder 136

NATIONAL CONFERENCE OF SOCIAL WORK
    Folders 14, 38, 66, 84

NATIONAL INFORMATION BUREAU
    Folders 10, 12

NATIONAL RECOVERY ADMINISTRATION
    Folder 82

NATIONAL SOCIAL WORK COUNCIL, REORGANIZATION 1945
    Folders 99-101

NEGROES
    Folders 98, 145, 148

PERKINS, FRANCES
    Folder 82

PERSONNEL (SOCIAL WORK)
    Folders 82, 89, 112

PRESIDENT'S WAR RELIEF CONTROL BOARD
    Folder 134

RELIEF
    Folders 7, 54, 67-68, 75, 84-85, 87, 89, 110

RELIGIOUS SOCIAL WORK
    Folder 62

NATIONAL SOCIAL WELFARE ASSEMBLY

RESEARCH ON SOCIAL PROBLEMS AND TRENDS
Folders 56, 58, 77-78

ROCKEFELLER FOUNDATION
Folder 23

RURAL PROBLEMS
Folders 5, 47, 52, 67

RUSSELL SAGE FOUNDATION
Folders 17, 19, 84

SOCIAL SECURITY
Folders 83, 88, 91, 93, 114

SURVEYS
Folders 9, 83, 87, 90

TAX-SUPPORT OF WELFARE ACTIVITIES
Folders 9, 49, 53

TAXATION
Folders 79, 83-84

TENNESSEE VALLEY AUTHORITY
Folder 80

TOLAN COMMITTEE
Folder 96

TRANSIENTS (SEE MIGRATION)

UNITED SERVICE ORGANIZATIONS (USO)
Folders 96-97

UNITED STATES ASSEMBLY OF YOUTH 1953
Folders 163-168

UNITED STATES CHILDREN'S BUREAU
Folder 84

NATIONAL SOCIAL WELFARE ASSEMBLY

UNITED STATES DEPARTMENT OF LABOR
　　Folder 82

VETERANS
　　Folders 98, 126

VOLUNTEERS
　　Folders 39, 85, 88, 107

WORLD ASSEMBLY OF YOUTH
　　Folders 171-194

WORLD WAR II (SEE DEFENSE HEALTH AND WELFARE)

YOUNG ADULT COUNCIL
　　Folders 163-197

YOUTH
　　Folders 85, 97-98, 162-197

NATIONAL SOCIAL WELFARE ASSEMBLY

FOLDER INVENTORY

FOLDER TITLE AND DESCRIPTION OF CONTENTS — FOLDER

American Association for Organizing Family Social Work - Annual — 1
Reports, 1911-1923
    (The American Association of Societies for Organizing Charity
    until 1919.) Reports re service, finance and membership included.

Francis H. McLean - David H. Holbrook - Correspondence, 1911-1945 — 2
    Correspondence, newsclippings and articles indicating Holbrook's
    continuing interest in the American Association for Organizing
    Family Social Work and personal friendship with McLean, one of
    the founders of the Association and a member of its staff until
    his retirement in 1935.

Milford Conference, 1923-1927 — 3
    Minutes and correspondence re annual conferences. Included
    with material from the 1925 conference is a study of card
    exchanges between agencies making field reports.

Milford Conference, 1928-1929 — 4
    Minutes and correspondence re annual conferences. Included is the
    Final Report of the Committee of Five, <u>Social Case Work, Generic
    and Specific</u>.

Milford Conference - Committee on Undifferentiated Case Work, 1925- — 5
1927
    Proceedings of meetings, a study undertaken in North
    Carolina, and the 1927 report to the Conference.

Milford Conference, 1932 — 6
    Meeting proceedings.

Milford Conference, 1933 — 7
    Correspondence, meeting proceedings and reports.

Milford Conference - Report, 1934 — 8
    Report on Social Case Work.

NSWC - Monthly Meetings, October - December 1925 — 9
    Correspondence and notes on proceedings. Meeting topics:
    October - "The Renewed Interest in Community Services," Shelby M.
      Harrison (Russell Sage Foundation).
    November - "The Purposes, Methods and Results of Annual Conferences
      or Conventions of National Agencies."
    December 4 - "Under What Conditions Should Local, State, and
      National Social Work Be Given Over to Governmental Agencies?"
      Dr. William F. Snow (American Social Hygiene Association).
    December 31 - "The Relation Between Scientific Research and the
      Development and Administration of Social Work," Rowland C.
      Haynes (Cleveland Welfare Federation).

NATIONAL SOCIAL WELFARE ASSEMBLY

FOLDER TITLE AND DESCRIPTION OF CONTENTS	FOLDER

NSWC - Monthly Meetings, February 1926   10
    Correspondence, minutes and stenotyped report of meeting.
    Topic: The National Information Bureau.

NSWC - Monthly Meetings, March 1926   11
    Correspondence, minutes and stenotyped report of meeting.
    Topic: "The Endorsement of Local and National Civic, Educational and Social Undertakings," Henry Stewart (Subscriptions Investigating Committee, Chicago Association of Commerce).

NSWC - Monthly Meetings, April 1926   12
    Correspondence, minutes and stenotyped report of meeting.
    Topic: "The Study of Financial Support of National Organizations," Pierce Williams (National Information Bureau).

NSWC - Monthly Meetings, May 1926 (Annual Meeting)   13
    Correspondence and stenotyped report of meeting. Topic: "What Services Does Bridgeport Feel the Need of Having from the National Social Work Organizations?"

NSWC - Monthly Meetings, June 1926   14
    Stenotyped report of meeting. Topics for discussion: "The National Conference of Social Work Meeting" and "Unfinished Matters in NSWC."

NSWC - Monthly Meetings, October 1926   15
    Minutes and stenotyped report of meeting. Topic: "What Has Been the Most Significant Achievement in Each Field of Work During the Last Twelve Months, the Greatest Failure and the Greatest Present Need?"

NSWC - Monthly Meetings, November 1926   16
    Minutes and stenotyped record of meeting. Topic: "Social Work as an Art," Joseph Lee.

NSWC - Monthly Meetings, December 1926   17
    Correspondence, minutes and stenotyped record of meeting.
    Topic: The Russell Sage Foundation, John M. Glenn.

NSWC - Monthly Meetings, January 1927   18
    Minutes. Topic: "Budgets and Budget Making in National Social Work Organizations."

NSWC - Monthly Meetings, January 21 - February 1927   19
    Minutes and stenotyped records of meetings.
    January 21 - Special meeting re money raising methods of member organizations.
    February - "The Financing of National Social Work Movements," John M. Glenn (Russell Sage Foundation).

FOLDER TITLE AND DESCRIPTION OF CONTENTS	FOLDER
NSWC - Monthly Meetings, March 1927 Minutes and stenotyped record of meeting. Topic: Summary of discussions of past three meetings on financial problems.	20
NSWC - Monthly Meetings, April 1927 Minutes and stenotyped record of meeting. Topic: The Commonwealth Fund, Barry C. Smith.	21
NSWC - Monthly Meetings, April 14, 1927 (Special Meeting) Stenotyped record of meeting. Topic: "Classification of Income and Expenditures."	22
NSWC - Monthly Meetings, May 1927 (Annual Meeting) Minutes and stenotyped record of meeting. Topic: The Rockefeller Foundation, George E. Vincent.	23
NSWC - Monthly Meetings, June 1927 Correspondence, minutes and stenotyped record of meeting. Topic: The Milbank Memorial Fund, John A. Kingsbury.	24
NSWC - Monthly Meetings, October 1927 Minutes and notes on meeting. Topic: "Cooperation in Financial and Fiduciary Matters," A.W. Anthony (Committee on Financial and Fiduciary Matters of the Federal Council of Churches of Christ in America).	25
NSWC - Monthly Meetings, November 1927 Minutes and stenotyped record of meeting. Topic: The Carnegie Corporation, Frederic P. Keppel.	26
NSWC - Monthly Meetings, December 1927 Minutes and stenotyped record of meeting. Topic: "What Are the Strengths and Weaknesses of Foundations as Observed and Felt Through Our Experiences with Them?" The folder includes a summary of Council meetings with foundations prepared by Margaret F. Byington.	27
NSWC - Monthly Meetings, January 1928 Correspondence, minutes and stenotyped record of meeting. Topic: "Field Work Problems."	28
NSWC - Monthly Meetings, January 23, 1928 (Special Meeting) Stenotyped minutes of meeting to consider the tables sent to Council members, entitled "Some Financial Information Regarding Twenty National Social Work Organizations."	29
NSWC - Monthly Meetings, February 1928 Minutes and summary of discussion. Topic: "Radburn, New Jersey, the New Town" (a project of the City Housing Corporation).	30

NATIONAL SOCIAL WELFARE ASSEMBLY

FOLDER TITLE AND DESCRIPTION OF CONTENTS	FOLDER
NSWC - Monthly Meetings, March 1928 Minutes and stenotyped record of meeting. Topic: Questions raised at the Community Chest Conference of Laymen at Washington, February, 1928.	31
NSWC - Monthly Meetings, April 1928 Correspondence and minutes. Topic: Agency Budgets.	32
NSWC - Monthly Meetings, May 1928 (Annual Meeting) Correspondence, minutes and stenotyped record of meeting. Topic: "Cooperation Between National Welfare Organizations and Local Communities," Henry G. Stevens.	33
NSWC - Monthly Meetings, June 1928 Correspondence, minutes and stenotyped record of meeting. Topic: The Welfare Council of New York City, William Hodson.	34
NSWC - Monthly Meetings, September 1928 Minutes and stenotyped record of meeting. Topic: "Work of the Council from the Secretary's Point of View," David H. Holbrook. Stenotyped record includes a report by Mrs. Glenn on the International Conference of Social Work held in July 1928.	35
NSWC - Monthly Meetings, November 1928 Minutes and stenotyped record of meeting. Topic: Discussion of work of the Council by its members.	36
NSWC - Monthly Meetings, December 1928 Report on meeting with A.W. McMillan re Registration of Social Statistics (project of the University of Chicago and Association of Community Chests and Councils).	37
NSWC - Monthly Meetings, January 1929 Minutes and stenotyped record of meeting. Topic: "Conferences and Convention Methods," Howard R. Knight (National Conference of Social Work).	38
NSWC - Monthly Meetings, January 18, 1929 (Special Meeting) Minutes and stenotyped record of meeting re Lay Participation.	39
NSWC - Monthly Meetings, February 1929 Minutes and stenotyped record of meeting. Topic: "Interpretation of National Social Work Movements to Community Chests."	40
NSWC - Monthly Meetings, February 15, 1929 (Special Meeting) Minutes and stenotyped record of meeting. Revision of by-laws re delegates was considered and steps to form a Joint Committee with the Association of Community Chests and Councils were discussed.	41

NATIONAL SOCIAL WELFARE ASSEMBLY

FOLDER TITLE AND DESCRIPTION OF CONTENTS	FOLDER
NSWC - Monthly Meetings, April 1929 (Special Conference of Board Members) Minutes and stenotyped record of meeting. Topic: "What America Is Spending for National Social Work - Budgets of National Social Work Organizations."	42
NSWC - Monthly Meetings, May 1929 Minutes and stenotyped record of meeting. Topic: Local councils of social agencies.	43
NSWC - Monthly Meetings, June 1929 (Annual Meeting) Report of Special Committee to meet with the Association of Community Chests and Councils.	44
NSWC - Monthly Meetings, November 1929 Correspondence, minutes and stenotyped record of meeting. Topic: "Important Things in the National Social Work Field and the Place That the National Social Work Council Should Have," H.S. Braucher, Chairman of NSWC.	45
NSWC - Monthly Meetings, November 15, 1929 (Extra Meeting) Minutes and stenotyped record of meeting. Topic: Braucher's Report given at the last meeting.	46
NSWC - Monthly Meetings, December 1929 Minutes and stenotyped record of meeting. Topic: "The Alleged Neglect of Rural Communities and Problems by National Social Work Organizations."	47
NSWC - Monthly Meetings, December 20, 1929 (Special Meeting) Correspondence and minutes. Topic: Financing the NSWC.	48
NSWC - Monthly Meetings, January 1930 Correspondence, minutes and stenotyped record of meeting. Topic: "Tax Supported Social Work," Sherrard Ewing (National Association of Travelers Aid Societies).	49
NSWC - Monthly Meetings, January 13, 1930 (Special Meeting) Notes on meeting. Sadie Orr Dunbar, Portland, Oregon, spoke informally on social work.	50
NSWC - Monthly Meetings, February 1930 Minutes and stenotyped record of meeting. Topic: "What Consolidation, If Any, Should Be Considered in the National Social Work Field?"	51
NSWC - Monthly Meetings, March 1930 Minutes and correspondence. Topic: "The Social Needs of Village and Farm People." Representatives of fourteen organizations made brief reports on their experiences regarding the White House Conference on Child Health and Protection.	52

NATIONAL SOCIAL WELFARE ASSEMBLY

FOLDER TITLE AND DESCRIPTION OF CONTENTS	FOLDER

NSWC - Monthly Meetings, April 1930 — 53
    Minutes and stenotyped record of meeting. Topic: "Is Public Tax Support an Ultimate Goal for All Social Work?" Mrs. John M. Glenn (Family Welfare Association of America).

NSWC - Monthly Meetings, May 1930 (Annual Meeting) — 54
    Minutes and stenotyped record of meeting. Topic: Joint and related services of national social work organizations. The record contains a report by Linton Swift on his impressions gained on a recent trip West re unemployment and relief problems.

NSWC - Monthly Meetings, June 1930 — 55
    Stenotyped record of meeting. Topic: Consideration of special problems raised by members of the Council.

NSWC - Monthly Meetings, October 1930 — 56
    Minutes and stenotyped record of meeting. Topic: Research work being carried on by organizations in the Council.

NSWC - Monthly Meetings, November 1930 — 57
    Minutes and stenotyped record of meeting. Topic: "Field Work of National Social Work Organizations in Some of Its More Practical Aspects."

NSWC - Monthly Meetings, November 13 - December 1930 — 58
    November 13 - (Special Meeting on Research) Notes from meeting.
    December - Notes and Minutes. Topic: White House Conference on Child Health and Protection.
    December 19 - (Special Meeting) Minutes and stenotyped record of meeting. Topic: D. H. Holbrook speaking on the work the NSWC has been doing through its secretary.

NSWC - Monthly Meetings, January 1931 — 59
    Correspondence, minutes and stenotyped record of meeting. Topic: "Interpretation to the General Public of What Is Being Done by the National Social Work Organizations."

NSWC - Monthly Meetings, January 26-27, 1931 — 60
    Correspondence and agenda for meeting with Ohio State University class in Social Administration.

NSWC - Monthly Meetings, February 1931 — 61
    Minutes and stenotyped record of meeting. Topic: "Training Methods in National Social Work," Emma P. Hirth (YWCA).

NSWC - Monthly Meetings, March 1931 — 62
    Correspondence, minutes and stenotyped record of meeting. Topic: "Social Work Under Religious Auspices," B.Y. Landis (Federal Council of Churches of Christ in America). The record contains a talk by Courtney Dinwiddie, "Is the Work of the National Child Labor Committee Done?"

NATIONAL SOCIAL WELFARE ASSEMBLY

FOLDER TITLE AND DESCRIPTION OF CONTENTS	FOLDER

NSWC - Monthly Meetings, April 1931 — 63
  Minutes and stenotyped record of meeting. Topic: "What Is at Stake for National Agencies in the Present Industrial Emergency?" Harlow S. Person (Taylor Society).

NSWC - Monthly Meetings, May 1931 (Annual Meeting) — 64
  Minutes and stenotyped report of meeting. Topic: "What New Projects Have Been Undertaken by the Foundations During the Last Two Years?" Dr. William Snow.

NSWC - Monthly Meetings, June 1931 — 65
  Stenotyped record of meeting. Topic: "National Cooperation in Helping Communities Plan Their Local Social Work, with Particular Reference to Portland, Oregon," Homer W. Borst (Association of Community Chests and Councils).

NSWC - Monthly Meetings, June 26, 1931 (Special Meeting) — 66
  Notes on meeting of NSWC to discuss National Conference of Social Work.

NSWC - Monthly Meetings, September 1931 — 67
  Minutes and stenotyped record of meeting. Topic: "Local, State and National Planning for Meeting the Relief Situation This Winter."

NSWC - Monthly Meetings, October 1931 — 68
  Stenotyped report of meeting. Topic: "The Place of Federal Aid in Unemployment Relief and the Implications for Social Work." The folder includes papers written by Henry C. Taylor and Harry L. Lurie on federal aid.

NSWC - Monthly Meetings, November 1931 — 69
  Minutes and stenotyped record of meeting. Topic: "The Present Problems of National Social Work Organizations in Financing Their Work."

NSWC - Monthly Meetings, December 1931 — 70
  Correspondence, minutes and stenotyped record of meeting. Topic: "Social Aspects of National Planning - The Kind of National Planning in Which National Social Work Organizations Should Be Interested," Mary Van Kleeck (Russell Sage Foundation).

NSWC - Monthly Meetings, January 1932 — 71
  Minutes and stenotyped record of the meeting. Topic: "The Future of National Public Health Organization Work," Dr. Kindall Emerson (National Tuberculosis Association and American Public Health Association).

NATIONAL SOCIAL WELFARE ASSEMBLY

FOLDER TITLE AND DESCRIPTION OF CONTENTS   FOLDER

NSWC - Monthly Meetings, January 1932   72
    Minutes and stenographic record of meeting. Topic: "The
    Local Community and National Agencies," C.M. Bookman (Executive
    Director, Cincinnati Community Chest).

NSWC - Monthly Meetings, February 29, 1932 (March Meeting)   73
    Minutes of the General Meeting of the Representatives of
    National Social Work Agencies, held immediately preceding the
    Council meeting to consider the proposal for a United Educational
    Campaign. Correspondence, minutes and notes from the Council
    meeting at which action was taken on the proposal of the General
    Meeting are also included.

NSWC - Monthly Meetings, April 1932   74
    Minutes and stenotyped record of meeting. Topic: "Guiding
    Principles in the Allocation of Funds--Local and National--In
    This Emergency Period."

NSWC - Monthly Meetings, May 1932 (Annual Meeting)   75
    Minutes and stenotyped record of meeting. Topic: "Some High
    Spots in a Reconnaissance Trip to the Far West," Miss J.C. Colcord
    (Russell Sage Foundation). Miss Colcord, in reporting on relief
    and welfare programs in the West, described the unique plan of the
    Seattle "Unemployed Citizens League" which ran twenty-two commissaries
    and provided for its members a wide range of goods and services.

NSWC - Monthly Meetings, June 1932   76
    Minutes and stenotyped record of meeting. Topic: "The
    Educational-Recreational Movements in Social Work."

NSWC - Monthly Meetings, September 1932 - January 6, 1933   77
    September - (Special Meeting). Minutes and notes. Topic: Reports
      of the United Educational Program.
    November - Correspondence and minutes. Topic: "Social Work
      Education, Not Propaganda -- How Shall We Do It and Why?"
      Clare M. Tousley (New York Charity Organization Society).
    December - Minutes and proceedings. Discussion with local Community
      Chest executives re securing national support for local
      communities.
    December 21 - (Special Meeting). Minutes and notes on meeting.
      Recommendations for the Program Committee and Education Com-
      mittee were presented to and accepted by the Council. Julius
      Amberg and Howard O. Hunter discussed some of the problems
      of Grand Rapids, Michigan with the national social work
      organizations in New York City.
    January 6 - Minutes. Topic: "What Share Should and Can National
      Social Work Agencies Have in the Reorganization Plan Now
      Taking Shape in Many Localities?"

NATIONAL SOCIAL WELFARE ASSEMBLY

FOLDER TITLE AND DESCRIPTION OF CONTENTS   FOLDER

NSWC - Monthly Meetings, January 23, 1933 (Extra Meeting)   78
    Stenotyped record of meeting. Discussion of the report of the
    President's Research Committee on Social Trends with Dr. William
    F. Ogburn of the University of Chicago.

NSWC - Monthly Meetings, March - May 1933   79
    March - Minutes and stenotyped record of meeting. Topic: "The
        Type of Planning and Study Incumbent Upon Social Agencies,
        Suggested or Implied by the Report of the President's Com-
        mittee on Social Trends," Dr. Sydnor Walker (Rockefeller
        Foundation).
    April - Minutes. Topic: "Fundamental Economic Problems Which
        Social Workers Need to Be Thinking About in the Present
        Emergency," David Cushman Coyle.
    May - (Annual Meeting). Minutes and notes on meeting. Topic:
        "What a Social Worker Needs to Know About Taxation in the
        Present Emergency," Frank A. Fetter and Denzel Cline
        (Princeton University).

NSWC - Monthly Meetings, June 1933   80
    Correspondence, minutes and stenotyped record of meeting.
    Topic: "Planning to Meet Local Community Needs," Arch Mandel,
    (Council of Social Agencies in Dayton, Ohio).

NSWC - Monthly Meetings, June 23, 1933 (Extra Meeting)   81
    Correspondence, minutes and summaries. Topic: "What the
    Service of National Social Work Organizations to the Whole
    Field Should and Can Be at This Critical Time."

NSWC - Monthly Meetings, September 1933 - April 1934   82
    Correspondence, proceedings and minutes.
    September - Meeting with Charles F. Horner (National Recovery
        Administration).
    October - Material re Proposed Employment Code for Social Health
        and Welfare Organizations in Support of President's Re-employment
        Agreement. Frances Perkins, Secretary of Labor, spoke about
        the National Administration program.
    November - "What Is Social Work's Part in the Whole National Effort
        for Recovery and Reconstruction?"
    December - "Minimum Employment Provisions for Non-Professional
        Employees in Social Work and Health Agencies."
    January - "Social Work Mirrors of Washington," Linton B. Swift, and
        "Program of Social Legislation and Public Welfare Activities,"
        Dr. Hertha M. Kraus.
    February - "What Kind of a Community Does Social Work Want?"
        Karl De Schweinitz.
    March - "Are Citizens' Boards Essential?" Louis Brownlow,
        (Public Administration Clearing House in Chicago).
    April - "How the Challenge of New Opportunities Is Being Met by
        National Social Work Organizations."

NATIONAL SOCIAL WELFARE ASSEMBLY

FOLDER TITLE AND DESCRIPTION OF CONTENTS	FOLDER

NSWC - Monthly Meetings, May 1934 - April 1935 83
Correspondence, proceedings and minutes.
   May - (Annual Meeting)."National Organizations as a Group in the Field of Social Work," James L. Fieser (Vice Chairman in Charge of Domestic Operations of the American Red Cross).
   November - "The Present Status of the Efforts Being Made for a Greater Social Security," Barbara N. Armstrong (President's Committee on Economic Security).
   December - "Taxation Problems," Franklin Spencer Edmonds.
   January - "The Necessity for Year-Round Publicity for the Welfare Needs Being Met by Social Work."
   January 25 - (Special Meeting). Discussion with government officials on the social security legislation under consideration by Congress.
   February - Leroy A. Ramsdell (Hartford Community Chest and Council of Social Agencies) discussed implications of the Hartford Survey (a study to appraise the work of individual chest-financed agencies).
   March - "Partnership of Governmental and Voluntary Organizations in the Fields of Health, Education-Recreation, Social Case Work and Social Legislation."
   April - "An Experiment in Delegating Power to One Person in Working on a Special Problem in a Locality," Eugene T. Lies (National Recreation Association).

NSWC - Monthly Meetings, May - December 1935 84
Correspondence, proceedings and minutes.
   May - (Annual Meeting). "Taxation for Social Services."
   May 24 - (Special Meeting). "Work of the National Resources Board," Charles W. Eliot.
   June - Discussion of National Conference of Social Work at Montreal.
   September - Katharine Lenroot and Josephine C. Brown spoke on the activities of the federal government in certain branches of social work.
   October - "Questions Confronting National Social Work Organizations Today."
   November - Discussion of questions underlying adequate interpretation of social work.
   December - "Some Material Interests with the Russell Sage Foundation," Shelby M. Harrison.

NSWC - Monthly Meetings, December 13, 1935 - February 1936 85
Correspondence, proceedings and minutes.
   December 13 - (Special Meeting). Stenotyped record included. "Questions Growing Out of the Cessation of Federal Appropriations to the States for Unemployment Relief," Dorothy Kahn and Ellen C. Potter.
   January - "Problems of Youth," Dr. James S. Plant.

NATIONAL SOCIAL WELFARE ASSEMBLY

FOLDER TITLE AND DESCRIPTION OF CONTENTS	FOLDER
February - "The Best Way for Doing What Has To Be Done Cooperatively in a Community by All the Organized Forces in the Community." Discussion with volunteers active in social agencies from eight cities.	
NSWC - Monthly Meetings, March 1936 Correspondence, minutes and stenotyped record of meeting. Topic: "The Raising of Standards in Public Service," Professor George A. Graham (Princeton University).	86
NSWC - Monthly Meetings, April - November 1936 Correspondence, proceedings and minutes. April - "Problems of National Organizations as Illustrated in the Children's Field," C.C. Carstens. May - (Annual Meeting). Discussion of the responsibilities of national agencies as consumers and of their relation to labor conditions, R.L. Mason (National Consumers League). June - Report of Committee on Community Problems and Relationships. October - "Effects of the Depression on Social Work Other Than Relief," F. Stuart Chapin (University of Minnesota). November - "Questions Confronting the National Organizations Today."	87
NSWC - Monthly Meetings, December 1936 - May 1937 December - Ewan Clague explained the organization and functions of the Social Security Board, Washington, D.C. January - "Standards and Criteria for the Evaluation of Local Agencies." Stenotyped record of meeting included. February - Harry A. Wann spoke on the Social Planning Council at Madison, New Jersey and experiments in community organization. March - "Attracting, Selecting, and Training Volunteers in a Social Work Movement," Margaret Murray (Girl Scouts). April - "Problems Involved in Board Service," Homer Folks (State Charities Aid Association). May - "Budgets of National Social Work and Health Organizations."	88
NSWC - Monthly Meetings, October 1937 - May 1938 Correspondence, proceedings and minutes. October - Discussion of immediate problems for the Council. November - "Securing and Maintaining Professional Personnel in a Social Work Field," H. F. Pote (Boy Scouts). December - Continuation of discussion at November meeting re personnel methods and problems. January - Program on Relief and Public Welfare being urged upon the U.S. Senate Committee on Unemployment and Relief was discussed by Charles P. Taft. February - "Federal and Local Responsibilities in a National Public Relief and Welfare Program." February 17 - (Special Meeting). Consideration of the statement to the Council of the work of the Committee on Contributions to National Agencies from Community Chest Cities.	89

NATIONAL SOCIAL WELFARE ASSEMBLY

FOLDER TITLE AND DESCRIPTION OF CONTENTS   FOLDER

    April - "To What Lengths Should National Agencies Go in Pro-
      moting Their Work in Local Communities?" Sanford Bates
      (Boys' Clubs of America).
    May - (Annual Meeting). "The Program of the Welfare Council of
      New York City," Leonard Mayo and Robert P. Lane.

NSWC - Monthly Meetings, June 1938 - May 1939   90
    Correspondence, proceedings and minutes.
    June - "The Field Work of National Social Work Organizations."
    September - Report of items of current interest by David Holbrook.
    November - Open discussion with Program Committee on problems of
      immediate concern.
    December - "Cooperation Within the Localities as Seen by Each
      National Agency."
    December 12 - (Special Meeting). Discussion of Vocational Service
      for Social Workers with Arthur Dunham.
    January - "What Secretaries of Social Agencies See as Their
      Responsibilities and Problems in Relation to National
      Social Work Organizations."
    February - "What Councils of Social Agencies Do," Bradley Buell
      (Community Chests and Councils, Inc.).
    March - "Cooperation with Social Agencies in the Social Work
      Planning in the Localities from the Viewpoint of Outside
      Organizations."
    April - "Responsibilities of National Social Work Organizations
      in the Face of Increasing Racial and Religious Prejudice,"
      and "Problems of European Refugees in the U.S."
    May - (Annual Meeting). "Community Chests and Councils' Exper-
      ience with Community Surveys," Bradley Buell.
    May 12 - (Special Meeting). Report from the Committee on
      Contributions to National Agencies from Community Chest
      Cities.

NSWC - Monthly Meetings, June 1939 - February 1940   91
    June - Report of "Rittenhouse Committee on Cooperation of
      Social Agencies, Locally, Nationally, with Each Other and
      with Councils of Social Agencies."
    October - "Problems Related to Children That the Council Should
      Face Together,"Paul T. Beisser.
    October 20 - (Special Meeting). Discussion of effects of present
      taxation laws regarding charitable organizations.
    November - "Social Work Strategy in World War Times."
    December - "National Understanding and Cooperative Projects
      Between National Social Work Agencies."
    January - "Toward a National Health Program," Professor Ira V. Hiscock.
    February - "The Present Social Security Program," Alice Webber (Social
      Security Board).

NSWC - Monthly Meetings, March - November 1940   92
    Correspondence, proceedings and minutes.
    March - "The Place of Private Social Work in Our American
      Democracy," Robert E. Bondy.

NATIONAL SOCIAL WELFARE ASSEMBLY

FOLDER TITLE AND DESCRIPTION OF CONTENTS   FOLDER

    March 27 - (Special Meeting). Consideration of "What Should
       Be the Primary Function of the Council at This Time?"
    April - "The Program of the National Social Work Council."
    May - (Annual Meeting). "Social Work's Concern for People in Motion,"
       Bertha McCall (National Travelers Aid Association).
    June - (Adjourned session of the Annual Meeting). "Should There
       Be Changes in the Council's Policy of Refraining from Expression
       of Opinion as a Council?"
    October - "Effect of Present Emergency on National Social Work."
    October 15 - (Special Meeting). Consideration of the problems of
       organizations of community services for military and industrial
       workers.
    November - Consideration of alternative formulations of statements
       of welfare standards and activities created by defense conditions.

NSWC - Monthly Meetings, January - November 1941   93
    Correspondence, proceedings and minutes.
    January - Dinner meeting to honor Howard Braucher. Topic: "Cooper-
       ative Efforts of Citizens Agencies with Governmental Organ-
       izations in the Field of Education and Recreation in the
       Field of Social Work."
    February - General discussion of social work problems and national
       defense emergency.
    February 17 - (Special Meeting). Wayne Coy, Assistant Federal Security
       Administrator, discussed health and welfare problems as related
       to defense.
    March - "Participation of National Social Work Organizations in
       Total Defense."
    April - "What Is Happening in Communities Re Military and
       Industrial National Defense?" Dorothy De la Pole (National
       Travelers Aid Association).
    May - (Annual Meeting). "How Can the Larger City Gain Momentum
       in Planning to Meet Its Health and Welfare Needs That Are
       Created or Revealed by National Defense Activities?" Anna D.
       Ward, Baltimore.
    June - Reports from National Conference of Social Work at Atlantic
       City.
    October - Report of Committee on Relations of National Agencies to
       Community Chests and Community Councils (Rittenhouse Committee).
    November - "Governmental Organization for Defense Health and Welfare,"
       Philip Schafer (Director of Public Assistance in Regional
       Office of Social Security Board).

NSWC - Monthly Meetings, December 1941   94
    Correspondence, proceedings and papers. All-Day Conference on
    Health, Welfare and Defense.

NSWC - Monthly Meetings, December 1941   95
    Stenotyped record of All-Day Conference on Health, Welfare
    and Defense.

NATIONAL SOCIAL WELFARE ASSEMBLY

FOLDER TITLE AND DESCRIPTION OF CONTENTS	FOLDER

NSWC - Monthly Meetings, January - December 1942   96
    January - "What the War Is Going To Mean."
    February - The work of the Tolan Committee (re national defense migration), Robert K. Lamb.
    March - "The USO as an Experiment in Cooperative Planning and Action Among National Agencies," Louis Kraft (Jewish Welfare Board).
    April - Proposal to create a commission of human needs in wartime as a planning and advisory body.
    May 1 - (Annual Meeting). Report of special group considering proposal on wartime commission.
    May 28 - "Community Organization in Wartime," Ralph Blanchard (Community Chests and Councils, Inc.).
    October - Financing war relief projects.
    November - Reports of the three functional Councils (National Education-Recreation Council, Social Case Work Council, and National Health Council).
    November 13 - (Special Meeting). Discussion with representatives of War Relocation Authority re Japanese-Americans.
    December - "The Role of Social Work in Public Education."

NSWC - Monthly Meetings, January 1943 - January 1944   97
    Correspondence, proceedings and minutes.
    January - Cooperation in field of welfare services, Chester I. Barnard (U.S.O.)
    February - "Labor's Point of View on Social Work," Abe Bluestein, Charles Livermore.
    March - "What Is the Wartime Situation Doing to the Financing of National Social Work?" Robert O. Loosley (National War Fund).
    April - "Program Making," Mrs. Paul Rittenhouse (Girl Scouts).
    April 23 - Special conference on wage stabilization.
    May - (Annual Meeting). "Functions and Programs of Voluntary and Governmental Agencies," Charles P. Taft (Office of Community War Services).
    June - Cooperative efforts among national agencies: American War-Community Services and Associated Youth Serving Organizations.
    October - "Is Something New in Accrediting Needed?'
    November - Discussion of statement from Program Committee re self-analysis by the NSWC of "The Contribution of National Agency Programs Toward Winning the War and the Peace That Follows."
    December - "Listing Basic Human Needs and Problems Toward Which Programs Are Being Directed by Members of the Council."
    January - "Men and Women Discharged from the Armed Forces."

NSWC - Monthly Meetings, February - November 1944   98
    February - "Men and Women Leaving War Industry," Margaret Creech (National Travelers Aid Association).
    March - "Government's Part in Serving Demobilized People," Howard L. Russell (American Public Welfare Association).
    April - "Problems of Young People in Wartime and During the Post-War Period," J. Edward Sproul (YMCA).

NATIONAL SOCIAL WELFARE ASSEMBLY   528

FOLDER TITLE AND DESCRIPTION OF CONTENTS   FOLDER

    May - (Annual Meeting). Budget presentations by the National
      Child Labor Committee and the National Tuberculosis
      Association.
    June - British National Council of Social Service, Erwin
      Schuller.
    October - "Integration of Minority Groups into the Total Life
      of the Country - The Concern and Activities of the YWCA,"
      Myra A. Smith.
    November - "Service to Veterans in Boston, Mass.," Roland R. Darling.

NSWC - Monthly Meetings, December 1944 - June 1945   99
    Correspondence, minutes and proceedings.
    December - "The Economic Setting in Which We Must Plan Our
      Programs," W.S. Woytinsky (Bureau of Employment Security,
      Social Security Board).
    January - "The Tasks Ahead for Social Work" (continued discussion
      of Woytinsky's paper presented at December meeting).
    January 18 - Special all-day meeting in executive session
      re future of the Council and enlargement of its functions.
    February - "Form and Organization of Federal Council of Churches,"
      Samuel McCrea Cavert.
    March - Report of Special Planning Committee on Reorganization.
    April 6 - "Emerging Social Policies and Programs for Social
      Work," Louis Worth.
    April 24 - Tea for George Haynes, British National Council of
      Social Service.
    May - (Annual Meeting). "Implications of the Current International
      Scene for Social Work Programs in the United States,"
      Joseph Chamberlain.
    June - "A Progress Report of Replies from National Agencies and
      Functional Groupings of Agencies to Proposals for Reorganization
      of the National Social Work Council."

NSWC - Monthly Meetings, September - November 1945   100
    Correspondence, minutes and proceedings.
    September - Meeting with Katharine F. Lenroot re relation of
      U.S. Children's Bureau to current proposals for a new
      Federal Department of Education, Health, and Welfare.
    October - Progress report from Special Planning Committee on
      Reorganization. Proposed Constitution for a National
      Social Welfare Assembly included.
    November - Suggestions for program of activities of proposed
      National Social Welfare Assembly.

NSWC - Monthly Meetings, December 1945 (Reorganization Meeting)   101
    Correspondence, proceedings and ballots. Major item of
    business was vote on The Proposed Constitution for a National
    Social Welfare Assembly in Amendment of the Constitution of
    the National Social Work Council.

NSWC - Service Record, November 1925 - August 1930   102
    Daily log of conferences attended, correspondence received
    and sent, advice and information given, etc. by Council's
    Executive Secretary, David Holbrook.

NATIONAL SOCIAL WELFARE ASSEMBLY

FOLDER TITLE AND DESCRIPTION OF CONTENTS	FOLDER

NSWC - Service Record for Member Organizations, September 1930 - January 1933. 103

NSWC - Service Record for Non-Members, September 1930 - April 1933. 104

NSWC - Mimeographed and Printed Materials, October 1925 - January 1946 105-125
   Arranged chronologically. Materials generally included are: minutes and discussion summaries from meetings, financial statements, special studies and reports, and reprints of journal articles. Most of the folders contain an index of the materials included.

NSWC - Publications of the National Social Work Council, 1939 - 1945 126
   The folder contains an index to included materials. Reoccurring topics are demobilization and problems of veterans.

AWCS - War Service Appeals of Six Agencies, September 1942 - August 1943 127
   Correspondence and papers re the application of six agencies to the War Appeals Budget Committee for approval of their special war service projects.

AWCS - Organizing Committee, Minutes of Meetings, May - September 1943. 128

AWCS - Correspondence, National War Fund, 1943. 129

AWCS - Legal Materials, 1943 - 1949 130
   By-Laws, Certificate of Incorporation, Tax Exemption Affidavit, Certificate of Dissolution, cancelled checks, etc.

AWCS - Board of Directors, October 1943 - March 1947 131
   By-laws, minutes of meetings, and financial reports presented to Directors.

AWCS - Executive Committee, November 1943 - April 1947 132
   Minutes of meetings.

AWCS - Correspondence and Papers, August 1943 - March 1947 133
   Material in this folder is primarily related to the organization, program, and services of AWCS member agencies.

AWCS - Correspondence - President's War Relief Control Board, May 1943-July 1944 134
   The War Relief Control Board certified the AWCS to the National War Fund in May 1943 and made periodic reviewals and approvals of budgets of the AWCS and its member agencies.

AWCS - Correspondence - Federal Office of Community War Services, October 1943 - January 1946 135
   The correspondence is related to cooperation between this federal office and the AWCS in selecting war-affected communities and coordinating relief operations and services in those areas.

NATIONAL SOCIAL WELFARE ASSEMBLY

FOLDER TITLE AND DESCRIPTION OF CONTENTS	FOLDER
AWCS - Correspondence - Requests for Admission to AWCS, July 1943 - December 1944 Predominantly correspondence with Msgr. John O'Grady regarding his application for inclusion of the National Conference of Catholic Charities within the AWCS.	136
AWCS - National War Service Budget Committee, January 1944 - June 1945 This Committee was appointed jointly by the Community Chests and Councils, Inc. and the AWCS. The folder contains minutes of meetings and reports re budget reviewal.	137
AWCS - Record of Chest Commitments to AWCS, 1943-1946.	138
AWCS - Fund Raising Campaign Committee, 1944 Minutes and publicity releases.	139
AWCS - John Price Jones Corporation Report, September 1944 The corporation was retained to assist AWCS in gaining admission to local community war chest budgets.	140
AWCS - Central Office Budgets and Expenses, 1945-1946.	141
AWCS - Service Cooperation Committee, February 1944 - March 1946 Correspondence and papers. As the functional body of the AWCS, the Service Cooperation Committee undertook field studies of local communities under consideration by the AWCS for war-community services, formulated plans of action for the areas, and coordinated the field operations of member agencies.	142
AWCS - Service Cooperation Committee - Minutes, August 1943 - April 1946.	143-144
AWCS - Material to be Gathered by Field Staffs, 1943-1944 The type of information requested by member agencies when considering service to war communities.	145
AWCS - Field Reports - Atlanta, Georgia, 1944.	146
AWCS - Field Reports - Bay Area of California, 1946.	147
AWCS - Field Reports - Gary, Indiana, 1946 Contains an extensive study of social and economic conditions of the Negro population prepared by the National Urban League.	148
AWCS - Field Reports - Wilmington, North Carolina 1944.	149
AWCS - Service Record of Agencies, 1944-1945 Report of cities serviced by the AWCS and the member agencies participating in each community.	150

NATIONAL SOCIAL WELFARE ASSEMBLY

FOLDER TITLE AND DESCRIPTION OF CONTENTS	FOLDER
AWCS – Special Committee on the Future of AWCS, 1944-1945 Notes from meetings, statements from member agencies on functions in the reconversion period and the Final Report of the committee.	151
AWCS – Report of Committee on the Relationship of AWCS to NSWA, 1946 Material relating to the dissolution of AWCS and the transference of the Service Cooperation Committee minutes and files to the NSWA.	152
AWCS – Institute, January 4-5, 1945.	153
AWCS – Papers Read at National Conference of Social Work Cleveland, May 25, 1944 Papers describing the function and operations of the AWCS by Harry Carey and Perry Hall.	154
AWCS – Reports, 1943-1947 Information re operations, finances and history of the AWCS.	155
AWCS – Publications, 1943-1946.	156
NSWA – Associate Groups – AWCS Service Cooperation Committee, 1946 - 1947 Correspondence and notes on meetings.	157
NSWA – Relocation and Resettlement of Japanese-Americans, 1942 - 1947 The material includes correspondence, papers, and a stenotyped record of the Working Conference on Problems Relating to Resettlement of Japanese-Americans, January 17, 1946.	158-160
NSWA – Bulletins on Problems of Japanese-Americans These bulletins, prepared under the sponsorship of the NSWA Committee on Japanese-Americans, include material related to housing, employment, recreation, proposed legislation and attitudes toward Japanese-Americans.	161
NSWA – Associated Youth Serving Organizations, Consultation on Post-War Needs of Youth, November 1945 Reports on economic, personal and social adjustments of youth prepared by sub-committees of AYSO.	162
NSWA – Young Adult Council – U.S. Assembly of Youth, 1953 - Correspondence With University of Michigan re Facilities for Assembly.	163
NSWA – Young Adult Council – U.S. Assembly of Youth, 1953 – Working Committees.	164
NSWA – Young Adult Council – U.S. Assembly of Youth, 1953 – Sub-Commissions.	165
NSWA – Young Adult Council – U.S. Assembly of Youth, 1953 – Rejected Applications Includes correspondence surrounding investigation of political associations of some applicants.	166

NATIONAL SOCIAL WELFARE ASSEMBLY

<u>FOLDER TITLE AND DESCRIPTION OF CONTENTS</u>   <u>FOLDER</u>

NSWA - Young Adult Council-U.S. Assembly of Youth, 1953   167-168
Correspondence re Assembly Arrangements, 1952-1953
     Invitations to speakers, resource people, discussion leaders,
     etc., and requests for "Working Papers" to be used at the
     Assembly.

NSWA - Young Adult Council-Youth Directory 1954 - Information Not   169-170
Used
     Information sheets from youth-related organizations.

NSWA - Young Adult Council-World Assembly of Youth-Correspondence   171-192
with Individuals and Youth Organizations in Other Countries
(1950-1956)
     The bulk of the material is composed of application forms
     from youth of foreign countries to WAY meetings held in the
     U.S. A few pamphlets and brochures describing foreign youth
     organizations are included. Materials have been arranged
     Alphabetically by country.

NSWA - Young Adult Council-World Assembly of Youth-Way Contacts re   193
Delegates from Hawaii, Alaska, Puerto Rico and Virgin Islands, 1951
     Question of treating these four areas as part of the United
     States or independent countries with separately organized
     National Committees.

NSWA - Young Adult Council-World Assembly of Youth - Correspondence   194
With Eastern European Exiles, 1952.

NSWA - Young Adult Council - World Assembly of Youth - Studies of   195
Problems in the Near and Middle East.

NSWA - Young Adult Council - World Assembly of Youth - 1954 Meeting,   196
Orientation Material
     Includes bibliographies of Eastern countries.

NSWA - Young Adult Council - World Assembly of Youth - West European   197
Publications, October 1953 - May 1954.

17

An Inventory of the Papers of Survey Associates, Inc.

PREPARED BY
Andrea Hinding

SURVEY ASSOCIATES, INC.

TABLE OF CONTENTS

INTRODUCTION. 1

PARTIAL SUBJECT INVENTORY 5

DESCRIPTION OF THE COLLECTION 14
    1. Corporate Records (Folders 1-23). 14
    2. Financial Records (Folders 24-45) 14
    3. Membership Records (Folders 46-325) 15
    4. Editorial Files (Folders 326-1614). 17
    5. Operational Records (Folders 1615-1721) 22

"FORGET-ME-NOT" FOLDER INVENTORY. 24

SUPPLEMENTS 67

SURVEY ASSOCIATES, INC.

SWA1   Survey Associates, New York

Papers, 1891-1952

1721 folders   59 (*L*) folders   31 Paige boxes

Survey Associates, Inc., was a cooperative publishing society which sought to "advance the cause of constructive philanthropy by the publication and circulation of books, pamphlets, and periodicals, and by conducting any investigations useful or necessary for the preparation thereof." The certificate of incorporation, signed on October 31, 1912, by Robert W. de Forest, Edward T. Devine, John M. Glenn, Alfred T. White, and Paul U. Kellogg, named twelve original directors: Jane Addams, Robert S. Brewster, Robert W. de Forest, Edward T. Devine, John M. Glenn, V. Everit Macy, Julian W. Mack, Charles D. Norton, Simon N. Patten, Frank Tucker, Paul M. Warburg, and Alfred T. White.

Survey Associates was a non-partisan, non-profit organization whose primary work was the publication of the Survey magazines. It was incorporated without capital endowment; contributions from members made up deficits which ordinary publishing receipts could not cover. The organization was managed by a board of directors and advised by the National Council of Survey Associates. Officers of the organization were a president, a chairman of the board of directors, vice-presidents, a secretary, a treasurer, and an editor. Presidents of Survey Associates, which was disbanded by order of the board of directors in 1952, were Robert W. de Forest, 1912-1931; Lucius Eastman, 1931-1938; and Richard B. Scandrett (the last president), 1938-1948. Chairmen of the board of directors were Julian W. Mack (the first chairman), 1938-1943; and Joseph P. Chamberlain, 1943-1952. Officers were elected at the annual meetings of Survey Associates, held by constitutional provision on the last Monday of October and open to all members. (One became a member by contributing not less than ten dollars to Survey Associates.)

The Survey had roots in several other magazines which were concerned with philanthropy. It developed from the Charities Review, a monthly organ of the New York Charity Organization Society (COS).* First issued in 1891 as a monthly journal of sociology, the Charities Review was financed by Robert W. de Forest and edited by Paul Leicester Ford and Frederick Howard Wines. In March, 1897, the Charities Review merged with Lend-A-Hand, founded and edited by Edward Everett Hale. In December, 1897, the COS began publishing a second house organ, the Charities (published with various subtitles), edited by Edward T. Devine. It was

*The Charity Organization Society is now the Community Service Society of New York City.

intended to be a weekly review of philanthropy which would serve COS members. In 1905, at the time that the Charities Publication Committee of the COS assumed responsibility for publishing the Charities, it was merged with the Commons, a magazine edited first by John Palmer Gavit and later by Graham Taylor, founder of the Chicago Commons Settlement. As Charities and the Commons it absorbed in 1906 Jewish Charity, edited by Lee K. Frankel. In April, 1909, the magazine took the name the Survey because, as the editors stated, "letters and messages continually re ceived have strengthened the conviction that not by the name of charity do most men call the movements we have stood for." The source of the name was the Pittsburgh Survey, an investigation of the "life and labor" of the Pittsburgh steel district made under the direction of Paul Kellogg, 1907-1909. In 1912, for financial reasons and for purposes of editorial independence, the magazine broke its ties with the COS and formed an independent publishing organization, Survey Associates, Inc.

From 1912 the Survey was published weekly, but because weekly publication was prohibitively expensive and because of a constant clash between readers seeking technical material and readers seeking an overall view of philanthropic fields, the Survey split into two publications, the Survey Midmonthly and the Survey Graphic. The Midmonthly was formally founded in June, 1922, as a "modern service periodical" which was a digest of social work and experience. It was directed at social workers and board members, and it dealt with all fields of social work, health, recreation, and human welfare. The Survey Graphic, formally founded in October, 1921, dated from a series of reconstruction numbers published during and after World War I. It was a magazine of "social interpretation" directed at intelligent laymen who were concerned with social and economic problems which underlay headlines. It focused on areas of industrial relations, health, education, international relations, housing, race relations, consumer education, and related fields. Financial problems caused the two magazines to merge in 1949. Publication of the Survey was suspended in 1952.

Paul Underwood Kellogg (1879-1958), editor of the Survey from 1912 to 1952, is the crucial figure in this collection. Born in Kalamazoo, Michigan, he served as an editor of the Kalamazoo Daily Telegraph before coming to New York to study at Columbia University. He joined the staff of the Charities and, after directing the Pittsburgh Survey and editing the six volume report of that investigation, became editor of the Survey in 1912. Kellogg was one of the founders of the Foreign Policy Association, a member of the Committee on Research in Medical Economics, and vice-chairman of the Advisory Committee to President Roosevelt's Committee on Economic Security. His brother, Arthur P. Kellogg (1878-1934), served as treasurer of Survey Associates and managing editor of the Survey and Survey Graphic until his death in 1934.

Paul Kellogg conceived of the Survey as a broadly educational enterprise operating "along the borders of research, journalism, and the general welfare"; it was to be an open forum limited only by the facts. The emphasis of the Survey was on first-hand inquiry and investigation, and regular procedure involved submitting controversial articles in draft form to concerned parties, considering suggested revisions, rechecking disputed sections, and offering opportunity for rebuttal. The Survey featured articles by staff members and by paid and volunteer contributors. In the January, 1949, issue Paul Kellogg named those factors which had characterized the Survey's working scheme since 1912: swift research, visualization, human interest, things of the spirit, public concern, and free discussion.

ORGANIZATION OF THE COLLECTION

The collection was deposited in the Social Welfare History Archives Center by Helen Hall (Mrs. Paul Kellogg) in August, 1964. It was shipped to the Center from Columbia University where it had been held. With the 27 four-drawer file cabinets came the editor's volumes of the Survey. The collection consists primarily of correspondence, both personal and professional, but also includes drafts of articles, minutes of meetings, financial records, reports, pamphlets, newspaper clippings, photographs, and office memoranda. While the inclusive dates of the collection are 1891-1952, the correspondence centers on the period 1917-1952.

An effort was made to preserve the arrangement of the collection, but parts of it had obviously been jumbled and convenience of searchers and staff dictated certain changes. The collection, then, was organized into five sections:

Section one:	Corporate records (Folders 1-23)
Section two:	Financial records (Folders 24-45)
Section three:	Membership records (Folders 46-325)
Section four:	Editorial files (Folders 326-1614)
Section five:	Operational records (Folders 1615-1721)

A detailed description of these sections follows; the description includes a folder-by-folder inventory of the richest section of the collection, the editorial "Forget-Me-Not"* file (Folders 326-902). Unprocessed membership records contained in 31 Paige boxes (P1-P31) are appended to the collection.

The arrangement of the collection reflected the day-to-day work of the Survey staff and board and thus the collection is most easily used with this approach. Searchers seeking information about a specific individual or subject area will wish to use the Partial Subject Inventory

---

*The editor (or perhaps a member of the staff) designated this inactive, permanent file the "Forget-Me-Not" file.

SURVEY ASSOCIATES, INC.

and other finding aids which have been prepared. Because of Paul Kellogg's relation to the Survey, the searcher will also wish to use the Paul Kellogg collection.

This collection, which reveals the Survey's central role in 20th century social work and social welfare, contains correspondence with nearly every major figure in American welfare work and in related fields. Included in these are Jane Addams, Louis D. Brandeis, Richard C. Cabot, Helen Hall, Karl de Schweinitz, Edward T. Devine, Homer Folks, Felix Frankfurter, John Haynes Holmes, Alexander Johnson, Mary Van Kleeck, Hendrik Van Loon, Lillian D. Wald, William Allen White, and Rabbi Stephen Wise. Besides providing information on the routine and the problems of publishing a magazine, the collection contains substantial amounts of material on unemployment, the Great Depression, industrial and labor relations, race relations, civil liberties, health, housing, social insurance, World War I, social work and social welfare.

SURVEY ASSOCIATES, INC.

PARTIAL SUBJECT INVENTORY

This list is intended to be a guide to some of the scattered materials on prominent topics and personalities in this collection. But because the Survey papers are extensive, this list cannot be comprehensive and does not preclude the existence of other such materials in the collection. Because other sections of the collection are somewhat self-descriptive, this guide focuses on the "Forget-Me-Not" file more thoroughly, though far from completely. The searcher will also wish to use finding aids which have been appended as supplements.

Certain individuals (particularly staff members) and subjects appear so frequently in the Survey papers that little effort was made to list them. Material pertaining to Paul Kellogg and to the policy, scope, and function of the Survey magazines is contained in nearly every folder. Extensive material re unemployment, depression-related matters, and social welfare broadly conceived can be found throughout the collection.

Academic Freedom
    Folders 410, 424, 507

Airplane Safety
    Folder 459

Americanization   see Immigrants

American Legion
    Folder 502

American Red Cross
    Folders 377, 387, 488, 523-524, 539, 562-563, 580, 640, 654-655, 769, 793

American Union Against Militarism
    Folders 329, 499, 692, 719

Brandeis, Louis D.
    Folders 41, 395-396, 657

British Labor Party and Movements
    Folders 389, 395, 499, 501, 558, 575, 582, 674, 718, 772, 792, 814

Cabot Fund
    Folders 40, 332, 416-419, 465

Child Labor see Child Welfare

Child Welfare (including child labor)
    Folders 494, 540, 558, 585, 603, 619, 701-702, 785, 855, 899

Children's Bureau
    Folders 326-327, 510-511, 701, 714, 748, 791, 855, 871

Civil Liberties
    Folders 365-366, 376, 411, 507, 515, 587-588, 593, 598, 620, 642, 880, 1480-1498
  In Wartime: Folders 366, 417, 425, 598, 642
    See also related topics: Academic Freedom, Editorial Freedom and Responsibility, etc.

Community Chests and Councils
    Folders 412-414, 453, 455, 748, 837-840

Conservation
    Folders 348, 444, 673, 750, 752, 769-770, 688, 826

Consumers
    Folders 521, 526-528, 588, 594, 625, 661, 686

Coolidge, Calvin
    Folders 452, 896

Depression
    Folders 334, 396, 408, 410, 500, 581, 694, 698, 748
  See also Relief
            Unemployment

Economic Affairs (including planning)
    Folders 372, 427, 442, 500, 526-528, 627, 657, 844, 858-860

Editorial Freedom and Responsibility
    Folders 5, 20, 327, 392, 397, 417, 481-482, 641

Education (including visual education)
    Folders 341, 446-451, 507, 605, 637, 754-756, 834, 896, 1395-1397,
        1525-1545

Elections, Presidential
  of 1924: Folder 466
  of 1928: Folders 332, 363, 491, 625, 870
  of 1932: Folders 405, 629, 761
  of 1936: Folders 327, 388, 768, 890

Fascism
    Folders 1558-1559

Forbes, James
    Folders 541, 579, 616, 730, 765, 771

Foreign Affairs
    Folders 375, 411, 685

Foreign Policy Association
    Folders 410, 497, 542-556, 662, 692, 695, 719, 733, 795

Gandhi, Mohandas
    Folders 772-774

Harmon Foundation
    Folders 341, 393-394, 595-596

Health (including public health)
    Folders 414, 512, 665-667, 717, 752, 759-760, 778-779, 856, 901
        1410-1411, 1553, 1555, 1566-1568

Health Insurance
    Folders 351, 353, 423, 471-478, 667, 763, 794, 1593-1594

Hine, Lewis
    Folders 614-615, 1697-1699

Housing
    Folders 384-385, 432, 557, 627, 629-631, 689, 731-732, 832-833,
        865, 1398-1400

Immigrants (including Americanization)
    Folders 335, 341, 412, 509, 565, 598-599, 674, 685

Income Tax (including rulings on deductibility of contributions)
    Folders 44, 424, 494, 606, 839

Indian Affairs
    Folders 357, 436-438, 629, 643, 809

Industrial Relations
    Folders 407, 439, 518, 530-537, 747, 857-859, 1406-1409, 1549

Industrial Workers of the World (IWW)
    Folders 358, 407, 675

International Conference on Social Welfare
    Folders 409, 580, 668-672, 858

Isolation   see Neutrality and Isolation

Juvenile Courts and Corrections
    Folders 369, 419, 503, 707, 864

Juvenile Delinquency
    Folders 369, 392, 498, 702, 885

Labor Relations
    Folders 363, 501, 530-537, 562-564, 576, 613, 649, 652, 698-700,
        747, 802, 804, 819-821, 844, 874, 892, 1569-1578

Liquor Problem   see Prohibition and the Liquor Problem

MacDonald, J. Ramsey
    Folders 389, 718, 726, 870-873

Medical Economics
    Folders 431-433, 469-478, 526, 794

Mental Health and Mental Illness
    Folders 498, 604, 640-641, 780, 834-835

Mexico
    Folders 357, 423-424, 463, 745, 847, 851, 1550-1552

Mooney-Billings cases
    Folders 365, 434, 531, 881

Municipal Planning   see Regional and Municipal Planning

National Conference on Social Welfare
    Folders 327, 343-344, 361, 453, 531, 536, 539, 578, 580, 601
        668-672, 690, 790, 829, 851-859

Neurath, Otto
    Folders 754-756, 859, 1704

Neutrality and Isolation
    Folders 410, 571, 692, 805-806, 887, 890

Opium Problem
    Folders 424, 565-567

Pacifism and Militarism
    Folders 329, 392, 499, 620-621, 626, 661, 692, 887

Penn Normal, Agricultural, and Industrial School, St. Helena Island,
South Carolina
    Folders 446-451, 461, 624, 761

Planning   see Economic Affairs

Prisons and Prison Reform
    Folders 434, 603, 680, 682-683, 703, 779

Progressivism, Progressive movements
    Folders 333, 558, 677, 718, 787, 881

Prohibition and the Liquor Problem
    Folders 370, 395, 454-455, 510-511, 579, 642, 684, 870-872, 879-880,
        893

Public Employment Services
    Folders 664-647, 699, 705, 766, 801

Public Health   see Health

Public Utilities
    Folders 441-443, 607, 728, 769, 788

Race Relations and Problems
    Folders 361, 507, 601-602, 684, 687, 708, 710-713, 761, 850, 866,
        1412-1415, 1499-1524

Reader's Digest
    Folders 594, 776-784, 876-878

Refugees
    Folders 514, 580, 597, 767
  Nazi-World War II: Folders 382, 424-425, 505, 719, 846, 895

Regional and Municipal Planning
    Folders 688, 731, 738, 828, 868, 871, 1554, 1560

Relief
    Folders 390-391, 413, 487, 492, 500, 532, 601, 616-617, 623, 641,
        667, 730, 800, 826

Roosevelt, Mrs. Franklin D.
    Folders 430-792

Rural Life and Welfare
    Folders 628, 717, 728, 779

Russia
    Folders 398, 622, 841, 1420-1449

Sacco-Vanzetti Case
    Folders 379, 515, 538, 558, 642, 659, 793

Salvation Army
    Folder 349

Settlements
    Folders 332, 336, 346, 396, 453, 491, 586-587, 684, 706, 823, 858

Social Insurance
    Folders 353, 382, 799-800

Social Reform
    Folders 344, 350, 391, 435, 694, 749, 837-838

Social Security
    Folders 424, 763-764, 800, 868

Social Work
    Folders 339, 359, 361, 414, 435, 479, 536, 578, 694, 749, 796-797,
        837-838, 852, 857, 886, 1563-1565, 1579-1588

Social Work
    Nature and development of: Folders 378, 418-419, 435, 486, 492,
                                        640-641
    Social Work ethics and the law: Folders 418-419, 748, 771, 799, 839

Spanish Civil War
    Folders 463, 597, 758, 841

Steel Industry
    Folders 332, 417-419, 465, 493, 530, 535, 607, 662, 761, 802,
        819-820, 854, 892

Steel Strike of 1919
    Folders 453, 482, 578, 819-820, 894

Survey Associates
    Financial matters: Folders 3-19, 368, 378, 397, 592, 632-636, 652,
                                663, 732, 737, 876-878
    Editorial matters
        Scope and policy: Folders 417, 481-483, 569-570, 584, 652,
                                   705, 889

        Survey Graphic: Folders 378, 560, 592, 814-815, 830, 843,
                                 846, 883, 894, 1598, 1600

        Survey Midmonthly: Folders 356, 830, 1589-1592, 1599

Tennessee Valley Authority (TVA)
    Folders 521, 559, 736-738

Unemployment
    Folders 352-353, 359, 379-381, 395-396, 458, 487, 495, 512, 531-532,
        586-587, 627, 644-647, 677, 694, 696, 698-699, 705, 712,
        722, 727, 754, 766, 771, 858-859, 883, 892, 1416-1419

Unemployment Insurance
    Folders 424-425, 479, 495, 531, 623, 647, 696, 698, 794, 800, 868

Van Kleeck, Mary
    Folders 360, 857-860

SURVEY ASSOCIATES, INC.

Visual Education   see Education

Wald, Lillian D.
    Folders 404, 499, 869-873, 882

War Production Board
    Folders 29-30, 1652

Welfare, Public and Private
    Folders 339, 379, 390-391, 412, 414, 617, 641, 799-800, 1595-1598

World War I
    Folders 5, 20, 329-330, 344, 351, 363, 392, 417, 488, 562, 575,
        626, 630, 654, 661, 676, 678, 792

Youth Work
    Folder 739

SECTION ONE: CORPORATE RECORDS (Folders 1-23)

This section contains a copy of the certificate of incorporation (Folder 1) and copies of the constitution of Survey Associates and amendments to it (Folder 2). Folders 3-19 comprise the minutes of the meetings of the board of directors and of the annual meetings of Survey Associates. The minutes are nearly complete for the years 1914-1936, 1938-1944, and 1946-1950; they include memoranda to the board from the editor, discussion of plans and policies, and material on Survey personnel and finances.

The editor's "board meeting" folder (Folder 20) contains material on items brought before board meetings, 1913-1919. Especially significant is Paul Kellogg's memorandum on questions of editorial freedom and responsibility (February 20, 1917). It was written after several board members and contributors objected to Kellogg's article in the February 17 Survey urging Americans to move in the "opposite direction from war."

This section also includes Kellogg's memorandum to the board (Folder 21) on the occasion of the Survey's 25th anniversary; this detailed the Survey's history, policies, scope, and financial situation. The incomplete papers of a Special Committee of the board of directors (Folder 22) which met in 1948 to consider suspension of publication and a folder containing Kellogg's correspondence with board members, 1950-1952 (Folder 23), complete this section.

SECTION TWO: FINANCIAL RECORDS (Folders 24-45)

The financial records of Survey Associates are fragmentary and furnish more detail for the years after 1930 than before. The minutes of the meetings of the board of directors (Folders 3-19) will provide the searcher with additional information.

Annual statements by the editor (Folder 24), published as annual reports to Survey Associates for the years 1926-1927 through 1930, and material used in compiling Survey budgets, 1925-1948 (Folders 25-28) are included in this section. Folders 29-32, those of the business manager, Walter F. Grueninger, give added information on the Survey's financial situation, 1938-1948. They include material on the World War

II War Production Board and paper limitations, circulation, promotional campaigns, budgets, investments, Survey retirement plans, and staff matters. Records of payments to authors, 1925-1952 (Folders 33-37), and correspondence with the Survey's banks, 1917-1951 (Folders 38-39), are included in this section.

Charles M. Cabot, Boston financier, established in his will a $50,000 trust fund for "charitable uses," particularly the study of industrial conditions and the publication of such studies, and named as trustees Philip T. Cabot, Edward T. Devine, and Paul Kellogg. Of this sum, $10,000 was given to Survey Associates for the investigation of conditions in industry. Material re this fund, the Cabot Fund, is found in Folder 40. Correspondence re the $100,000 (approximately) willed to Survey Associates by Louis D. Brandeis for the "maintenance of civil liberty and the promotion of Workers' Education in the United States" is contained in Folder 41.

This section also includes material on investments made by Survey Associates, 1944-1947 (Folder 42), and on their appeals to foundations for financial support, 1946-1948 (Folder 43). Folder 44 contains material re city, state, and federal taxes and re the ruling that contributions to Survey Associates were deductible because it was an educational and charitable enterprise. Folder 45, a list of contributors to Survey Associates, 1912-1917, completes this section.

SECTION THREE: MEMBERSHIP RECORDS (Folders 46-325)*

This section contains records of members of Survey Associates (distinct from subscribers to the Survey magazines), those who donated a sum of money greater than the price of a subscription; the inclusive years are 1908-1952 (included are some records from the years before 1912 when the magazine was published by the COS), though the material is concentrated in the years 1930-1952. Contributors were classified as cooperating members, those who gave not less than $10 per year; as sustaining members, those who gave not less that $25 per year; and as contributing members, those who gave not less that $50 or not less than $100 per year (there were

*Section Three was processed by Clarence T. Griep, graduate research assistant.

two classes of contributing members). The membership records are incomplete: notations on folders indicated that correspondence prior to given dates was "in the stockroom." These records were not recovered, and, in addition, the folders "Mc-Po" from the main body of contributors were not among those shipped to the Center.

The membership files contain the folders of nearly 3,000 individuals and organizations which were arranged in three alphabets:

1) An alphabet of individuals who were substantial contributors

2) The longer main body of contributors

3) An alphabet of subscribers to the Survey after the merger of the Midmonthly and the Survey Graphic in 1949.

The entire alphabet (1) of substantial contributors was processed, and from the main alphabet (2) were pulled and processed folders of board members, prominent individuals, foundations, and all the folders included in three sampling letters (A, B, and I). All these were integrated into one alphabet (Folders 46-325). A list of individuals in this alphabet is Supplement One.

The unprocessed section of the main body of contributors (2) is held in Paige boxes numbering P1-P27, and the alphabet of subscribers (3) is held as P28-P31. A list of those individuals and organizations in P1-P27 is filed at the beginning of the unprocessed section (P1).

From these unprocessed papers were selected representative form letters used to solicit contributions; these are filed chronologically in Folders 46-49. In addition, certain substantive letters were removed from the unprocessed folders; these are filed alphabetically in Folders 50-51. The searcher will undoubtedly find these six folders valuable.

The membership correspondence is primarily solicitation of contributions (not subscriptions), especially by Paul Kellogg and Ann Reed Brenner, financial and membership secretary of Survey Associates for many years. Prominent contributors include Jane Addams, Frank Bruno, Benjamin Cardozo, Stuart Chase, Samuel S. Fels, Edward A. Filene, Homer Folks, Arthur Garfield Hays, Sidney Hillman, Charles Evans Hughes, Harold Ickes, Howard Knight, Julia Lathrop, David Lawrence, Mary E. McDowell, Gifford Pinchot, Roscoe Pound, Eleanor Roosevelt, Mary Simkhovitch, and Mary Van Kleeck.

Among agencies and organizations contributing to Survey Associates were the American Friends Service Committee, local chapters of the American Association of Social Workers and the American Red Cross, and numerous family service societies, community chests, school and public libraries, departments of public welfare, Catholic and Jewish social welfare organizations, and USO groups.

SURVEY ASSOCIATES, INC.

The membership files contain material dealing with appeals to foundations for financial support. Among applications were those made to the Field Foundation, the Haynes Foundation, the Hofheimer Foundation, the Rockefeller Foundation, the Julius Rosenwald Foundation, the Russell Sage Foundation, and the Twentieth Century Fund.

SECTION FOUR: EDITORIAL FILES (Folders 326-1614)

These folders comprise the current and inactive working editorial files of the Survey magazines. The inclusive dates are 1891-1952, but the correspondence is concentrated between 1917-1952. The editorial files have been divided into six sections:

1. "Forget-Me-Not" file (Folders 326-902)
2. Working editorial file (Folders 903-1333)
3. General editorial file (Folders 1334-1386)
4. "Calling America" series (Folders 1387-1548)
5. Special issues (Folders 1549-1565)
6. Miscellaneous editorial files (Folders 1566-1614)

These segments are described in detail below.

1. "FORGET-ME-NOT" FILE (Folders 326-902)

The "Forget-Me-Not" file, the single richest section of the collection, consists of correspondence arranged alphabetically by correspondent. The inclusive dates are 1891-1952, but the correspondence is concentrated between 1917-1952. When the working files were weeded by the Survey staff, correspondence marked for preservation was transferred to a permanent file (the "Forget-Me-Not" file). As the collection was organized, folders in the working editorial files labelled "do not destroy" (indicating that these would eventually have been transferred to the permanent file) and folders of individuals whose previous correspondence appeared in the "Forget-Me-Not" file were integrated with that file.

Because the "Forget-Me-Not" file contains substantive correspondence with many significant individuals and because the editor and staff selected these folders for preservation, a folder-by-folder inventory of this file was made. This appears on pages 24-66. The correspondence in the file usually involved the correspondent's work or an article he wrote for the Survey; it is almost exclusively between that person and members of the staff. Most folders contain routine editorial correspondence, and many contain pamphlets, newspaper clippings, and obituary material which are not mentioned in the folder-by-folder inventory. (The dates following the names indicate inclusive dates of correspondence.) The folder description is not, of course, definitive.

2. WORKING EDITORIAL FILE (Folders 903-1333)

The correspondence in this file, arranged alphabetically by correspondent, is almost exclusively for the years 1935-1952. While much of it is routine, prominent individuals--Pearl Buck, Eveline Burns, Loula Dunn, Fiorello LaFuardia, Leonard W. Mayo, Lea D. Taylor, Henry A. Wallace--are included. Material pertaining to juvenile delinquency, labor relations, penal reform, the profession of social work, community chests and fund-raising, and other topics may be found in this file.

3. GENERAL EDITORIAL FILE (Folders 1334-1386)

These folders comprise what the staff labelled the "general" file. The material contained in this alphabet, again arranged alphabetically by correspondent, is more current (ca. 1945-1952) and less significant than that in the other two files.

4. ."CALLING AMERICA" SERIES (Folders 1387-1548)

The "Calling America" series (Folders 1387-1548) was a series of special issues of the Survey Graphic conceived of as "variants of books, reports, and periodical" and built around a single theme. They were edited by staff members or by guest editors and made use of "graphic arts in interpreting facts and situations." The "Calling America" series had a wide circulation: the first number went into three editions, selling more than 90,000 copies. The second sold over 40,000 and was published by Farrar and Rinehart for school and college use.

"Calling America: The challenge to Democracy Reaches Over Here," issued in February, 1939, was the first of the series. It was edited by Raymond Gram Swing, and contributors included Archibald MacLeish, Thomas Mann, John Masefield, Bertrand Russell, Dorothy Thompson, Hendrik Willem

Van Loon, and William Allen White. Felix Frankfurter and Julian W. Mack were among those who helped plan the issue.

Thirteen succeeding numbers were published:

Folders	
1395-1397	"Schools: The Challenge of Democracy to Education," October, 1939; edited by Beulah Amidon
1398-1400	"Homes: Front Line of Defense for American Life," February, 1940; edited by Albert Mayer and Loula D. Lasker
1401-1405	"The Americas: South and North," March, 1941; edited by Victor Weybright
1406-1409	"Manning the Arsenal for Democracy: Industrial Relations and Defense," November, 1941; edited by Victor Weybright
1410-1411	"Fitness for Freedom: Health and Fitness in Wartime," March, 1942; edited by Victor Weybright
1412-1415	"Color: Unfinished Business of Democracy," November, 1942; edited by Alain Locke
1416-1419	"From War to Work: How to Get Full Employment and Keep It Going," May, 1943; edited by Stuart Chase
1420-1449	"American Russian Frontiers," February, 1944; edited by Richard B. Scandrett and Albert Rhys Williams
1450-1479	"The British and Ourselves," June, 1945; edited with the cooperation of Victor Weybright, Lewis Gannett, and Ferdinand Kuhn
1480-1498	"The Right of All People to Know," December, 1946; edited by Henry Christman
1499-1524	"Segregation: Color Pattern from the Past--Our Struggle to Wipe It out," January, 1947; edited by Thomas Sancton
1525-1545	"Education for Our Time," November, 1947; edited by Beulah Amidon
1546-1548	"Food for a Hungry World," March, 1948; edited by George Britt

5. SPECIAL ISSUES (Folders 1549-1565)

Special issues, built around a single theme, were published throughout the Survey's existence. This editorial section contains folders on some of these issues (Folders 1549-1565), but the following list is not all-inclusive. Special numbers on Ireland, Harlem, woman's place, mental health, and other subjects were also published.

Folders	
1549	"Coal: Mines, Miners, and the Public," April, 1922
1550-1552	"Mexico: A Promise," May, 1924
1553	"Hearts" (heart disease), November, 1924
1554	Regional planning number, May, 1925
1555	"City Health: Where Does Your City Stand?" November, 1925
1556	"The Great Crime Wave," March, 1926
1557	"East by West: Our Windows on the Pacific," May, 1926
1558-1559	"An American Look at Fascism," March, 1927
1560	Proposed regional number, 1934
1561-1562	"Juvenile Delinquency: A Challange to Concerted Action Now and After the War," March, 1944
1563	"Family Life Today" series, beginning December, 1949
1564-1565	"Social Work in the Far East" series, beginning 1951

6. MISCELLANEOUS EDITORIAL FILES (Folders 1566-1614)

Folders 1566-1568 contain material re attempts to secure foundation support to expand the Survey's work in the health field in 1924-1925 and in 1944.

The U.S. Office of Inter-American Affairs gave $67,900 to Survey Associates to provide for "conducting a program for the study of employer-employee relations in the United States by representatives of union labor from the other American republics." Survey Associates appointed Samuel Guy Inman to direct the project, but it was vetoed by the State Department before it was seriously underway. Folders 1569-1578 contain discussions of policies and plans, reports, and correspondence re this project.

In 1948 Survey Associates established an annual award for "imaginative and constructive contribution to social work." The Survey Award, conferred at the National Conference on Social Welfare, was established in memory of Edward T. Devine. Any person, lay or professional, who made such a contribution, could be nominated (on the assumption that social work embraced all "human services"). Nominations were made by the public, and the winner was chosen by a special committee from those nominated. The recipients were Dr. Howard A. Rusk, 1948; Arthur J. Altmeyer, 1949; Katharine F. Lenroot, 1950; Edith Abbott, 1951; and Jerome Kaplan, 1952. Folders 1579-1588 contain nominations and material on selection of the winner. Folder 1585 contains material on Survey Award procedure.

The editorial files include correspondence re articles written for the Survey Midmonthly, 1944-1948 (Folders 1589-1592) and material re the 1938 National Health Conference (Folders 1593-1594). Correspondence re the Survey's coverage of state legislation affecting social welfare, 1942-1946, is contained in Folders 1595-1596. Correspondence re developments in state departments of public welfare, 1948, is included in Folder 1597. The material in Folder 1598 pertains to an article by George Britt, managing editor of the Survey dealing with social welfare aspects of the 1950 Census.

Folder 1599 contains material on the Survey Midmonthly editorial advisory committee, and Folder 1600 includes suggestions made by staff members in 1948 on an editorial program for the Survey Graphic.

Folders 1601-1612 contain requests for permission to use or reprint Survey articles. These requests came from authors, church groups, radio programmers, and from such digest magazines as Negro Digest, the World Digest, Everybody's Digest, and the Digest Unit.

Correspondence re suspension of publication of the Survey (Folders 1613-1614) completes this section.

Because correspondence and memoranda in this section are frequently signed with initials only, prominent staff members are listed below:

      Beulah Amidon
      Paul L. Benjamin
      Ann Reed Brenner
      George Britt
      Robert W. Bruere
      Bradley Buell
      Kathryn Close

Mollie Condon
Thomas Devine
Hannah Gallagher
Arthur P. Kellogg
Florence Loeb Kellogg
Paul U. Kellogg
Bruno Lasker
Loula D. Lasker
Mary Ross
Janet Sabloff
Gertrude Seymour
S. Adele Shaw
Geddes Smith
Gertrude Springer
Victor Weybright

SECTION FIVE: OPERATIONAL RECORDS (Folders 1615-1721)

The operational files contain personnel material, promotional material, correspondence with companies engaged in publication of the magazines, and the papers of the production department.

The personnel section of the operational files contains letters of application (Folders 1615-1616), letters of recommendation (Folder 1617), material on the Survey's compensation insurance coverage (Folder 1618), and the employee retirement plans (Folder 1619). Folder 1620 comprises routine inter-office memos re vacation schedules, working conditions, etc.

Folders 1621-1650 contain material which can be broadly classified as promotional. Survey Associates frequently held dinner meetings when a special number was issued or to celebrate an anniversary; these dinners served public relations purposes. Folders 1621-1629 include material re such dinners and the 20th, 25th, 30th, 33rd, and 40th anniversaries.

Folders 1630-1635 include subscription and advertising records, 1919-1934; business office reports, 1925-1948; circulation figures, 1948-1952; and house lists. This section also contains material on Survey subscription campaigns (Folders 1636-1639). Folders 1640-1641 contain material on the education and church committees of the Survey. Folders 1642-1644 contain press releases, 1937-1947, and Folders 1645-1650 comprise "puffs", letters of commendation used in promotional work.

Copyright certificates are included in Folders 1651-1653. Folders 1654-1658 contain correspondence with U.S. post offices, with the U.S. Census of Manufactures, and with the World War II government censor. Folder 1659 contains correspondence with the War Production Board, 1942-1945.

Folders 1660-1672 comprise business correspondence with the *Survey* real estate agent, the printers, the paper suppliers, the binding company, etc. Material re agents and agencies selling *Survey* subscriptions is found in Folders 1673-1678. Additional subscription department correspondence as well as material re book and magazine orders handled by the *Survey* is contained in Folders 1679-1684.

The files of the production department (Folders 1685-1721) contain plans of the department (Folder 1685), material re photography in the issues (Folders 1686-1690), and routine correspondence of the department (Folders 1691-1693). Folders 1694-1718 contain photographs, cartoons, and charts kept on file by the production department; individuals prominent in this segment include Lauren Ford (Folder 1694), Marion Greenwood (Folder 1696), Lewis Hine (Folders 1697-1699), and Otto Neurath (Folder 1704). Folders 1719-1721 contain style books and loose papers of the department.

"FORGET-ME-NOT" FOLDER INVENTORY

The dates following the names indicate inclusive dates of correspondence. The inventory normally does not note the routine editorial correspondence which is contained in most folders.

Folder Title and Description of Contents	Folder
Abbott, Grace, 1916-1939. Correspondence arising from her work as head of the Children's Bureau. Exchange of the bitterness of the 1936 presidential campaign and the impatience of the *Survey* audience with open discussion of controversial issues.	326-327
Abbott, Lawrence, 1916-1940. Routine correspondence with Abbott, president of the *Outlook*.	328
Addams, Jane, 1915-1940. Correspondence arising from her work as head resident of Hull House and member of the *Survey* board of directors. Correspondence re World War I, pacifism, militarism, Americanization, and national self-righteousness. Kellogg told her (October 31, 1925) of the Survey's attack on conditions in the steel industry. Materials on her death and memorials to her.	329-338
Adie, David C., 1930-1942. Adie was head of the Buffalo Council of Social Agencies and commissioner of the New York Department of Social Welfare. Correspondence re the reading habits of social workers, the relation of public and private welfare agencies in Buffalo, and the effect of the defense boom on the relief load.	339
Adler, Felix, 1917-1929 Routine correspondence with Adler, the head of New York's Society for Ethical Culture.	340

Folder Title and Description of Contents	Folder
Allen, Ethel Richardson, 1925-1931. Material on adult education, especially work with immigrants, in California. In 1927 she won the Harmon-Survey award for her distinctive contributions to social work in the field of adult education.	341
Allen, Judge Florence E., 1922-1947. She was the first woman appointed to the U.S. Circuit Court of Appeals. In asking her to address the National Conference on Social Welfare, Kellogg discussed the conference and his presidency of it (December, 1938).	342-343
Almy, Frederic, 1916-1935. He was head of the Buffalo Charity Organization Society, 1894-1921. Correspondence re the needs of reformers in 1917, the problems which would confront Woodrow Wilson after World War I, the relation of the National Conference on Social Work to the national association of social workers, and unemployment.	344-345
Amidon, Beulah, 1925-1951. Correspondence arising from her work as an associate editor of the Survey in the fields of education and industry, 1925-1952. Correspondence re conservation, Major Jane E. Wrieden of the Salvation Army, and Social action.	346-350
Andrews, John B., 1917-1942. Correspondence arising from his work for the American Association for Labor Legislation. Material on health insurance, workmen's compensation, labor standards during World War I, and unemployment.	351-353
Armes, Ethel, 1916-1937. Correspondence re her public relations work for several organizations.	354
Arnstein, Leo, 1943-1944. He was commissioner of New York City's Department of Public Welfare.	355

SURVEY ASSOCIATES, INC.

Folder Title and Description of Contents | Folder

Atwater, Pierce, 1938-1944. | 356
Letter (November 3, 1943) asking him to serve on an editorial advisory committee discussed the work of the Midmonthly.

Austin, Mary, 1925-1950. | 357
She served as a Survey "contact" with the Southwest. Kellogg's memo (March 11, 1930) on the Survey's becoming obsessed with big-city problems.

Baker, Frank W., 1917. | 358
He criticized the Survey's coverage of the IWW trial in Washington.

Baker, Helen Cody, 1931-1945. | 359-362
She was publicity secretary for the Council of Social Agencies of Chicago. Material on the junior league and volunteers, unemployment, depression plans, relations among relief agencies, Mary Van Kleeck, discrimination and the National Conference of Social Work, problems of Negro social workers, and the changing nature of social welfare.

Baker, Newton D., 1916-1937. | 363
Correspondence arising from his work as Secretary of War. Material re labor standards during World War I, problems of the draft, the role of voluntary associations in a democracy, the presidential campaign of 1928, and labor unions.

Balch, Emily Greene, 1936-1948. | 364
She was the founder of the Women's International League for Peace and Freedom.

Baldwin, Roger N., 1929-1951. | 365-366
Correspondence arising from his work for the American Civil Liberties Union. Material on the Mooney-Billings cases, the origin of the ACLU, and civil liberties during World War II and the Korean War.

Folder Title and Description of Contents	Folder
Bamberger, Louis, 1936-1939. Correspondence re reprints of an article by Pearl Buck.	367
Barnes, Dora M., 1923-1927. Correspondence arising from her work as a field representative of the Survey.	368
Bates, Sanford, 1937-1950. Material on juvenile delinquency and correctional treatment for children.	369
Batten, Samuel Z., 1909-1922. Material on prohibition problems in Maine (1911).	370
Battle, George G., 1939-1942. He was co-chairman of the Council against Intolerance in America.	371
Benjamin, Edward B., 1943-1944. He was a southern industrialist who did an article on postwar planning.	372
Benjamin, Paul L., 1917-1950. He was an associate editor of the Survey and director of the Buffalo Council of Social Agencies. Material on labor problems in the North-west and on the coordination of social agencies and defense councils.	373-374
Berle, Adolph A., 1927-1951. He was an Assistant Secretary of State and a Brain Truster. Material on banking, foreign affairs, and the liberal point of view in the world situation.	375
Bernays, Murray C., 1945-1948. He was an attorney who played a key role in formulating the U.S. policy regarding Nazi war criminals. Material on the Nuremberg trials.	376

Folder Title and Description of Contents	Folder
Bicknell, Ernest P., 1917-1935. Correspondence arising from his work with the American Red Cross.	377
Billikopf, Jacob, 1918-1951. Correspondence arising from his work as a Survey board member, as an "Impartial Chairman" in the men's clothing industry in New York, and as director of the Federation of Jewish Charities of Philadelphia. Material on the depression, unemployment, labor relations, the Sacco-Vanzetti case, and the conditions of Jews in Germany in the 1930's.	378-383
Bing, Alexander M., 1917-1940. He was president of the City Housing Corporation of New York. Material re the controversy between the City Housing Corporation and its homeowners (1935-1936), and Bing's resignation from the Survey board of directors.	384-385
Blair, Lawrence, 1936-1938. He was a Michigan State professor whose substantive correspondence was returned to his family.	386
Bliss, C. N., 1918-1931. Correspondence re the American Red Cross and fund-raising plans.	387
Bliven, Bruce, 1927-1946. Bliven was an editor of the New Republic. Correspondence primarily re editors' problems.	388
Bondfield, Margaret, 1927-1942. She was a Member of Parliament and the Labor Party's Minister of Labor. Material on conditions in England, British trade unionism, and J. Ramsay MacDonald.	389
Bookman, C. M., 1930-1948. He was secretary of the Community Chest of Cincinnati. Material on social work, relief and reform, public and private welfare, and conditions in Cincinnati and Ohio.	390-391

SURVEY ASSOCIATES, INC.

Folder Title and Description of Contents | Folder

Bowen, Mrs. Joseph T., 1916-1943. | 392
    Correspondence arising from her work with the Juvenile Protective Association of Chicago. Material on the adverse reaction to the Survey's stand on World War I.

Brady, Mary B., 1923-1942. | 393-394
    Correspondence arising primarily from her work as director of the Harmon Foundation. Extensive material on the Harmon Awards, administered by Survey Associates, for distinctive contributions to fields of social welfare.

Brandeis, Louis D., 1916-1952. | 395-396
    Xeroxed material on the British labor movement, prohibition, unemployment, the settlements and social work, and Herbert Hoover and the depression. The original manuscripts are held by the Brandeis University Library.

Brenner, Ann Reed, 1929-1951. | 397
    She was for many years financial and membership secretary of Survey Associates and book review editor. Material on conditions in Germany (1932) and a controversy over a birth control advertisement.

Brennock, Rev. T. L., 1931-1933. | 398
    Correspondence arising from his work with the Catholic Charities of New York City. A statement by Kellogg on why the U.S. ought to recognize Russia.

Brisbane, Arthur, 1928-1936. | 399
    He was a columnist for the New York Journal.

Britt, George, 1947-1952. | 400-403
    Correspondence arising from his position as managing editor of the Survey Graphic.

Brooks, A. A., 1934-1940. | 404
    He indexed the Survey. Correspondence re his work indexing Lillian Wald's Windows on Henry Street.

Folder Title and Description of Contents	Folder
Broun, Heywood, 1928-1937. Broun, a columnist for the New York *World-Telegram*, wrote (June, 1932) criticizing both major parties and explaining why he intended to vote for the Socialist party.	405
Brown, Irving, 1941. He was an authority on gypsies.	406
Bruere, Robert W., 1917-1947. Both he and his wife were associate editors of the *Survey*. Material on industrial relations, World War I and civil liberties, IWW prisoners in the Leavenworth prison, the depression, and unemployment.	407-408
Bruno, Frank J., 1935-1951. Material on social work, especially the International Conference on Social Welfare.	409
Buell, Raymond L., 1929-1944. Correspondence arising from his work for the Foreign Policy Association. Material on U.S. neutrality, academic freedom, the relation of national policy to the democratic process, and the depression.	410
Burlingham, C. C., 1936-1949. Material on communism, civil liberties, and foreign affairs.	411
Burns, Allen T., 1918-1942. Correspondence arising from his work with immigrants and with community chests and councils. Material on Americanization, public and private welfare, and relief.	412-413
Burritt, Baily B., 1919-1947. Correspondence arising from his work as director of the Association for Improving the Condition of the Poor. Material on private and public welfare, the community chest and its techniques, and social work and its relation to nursing and to public health.	414

Folder Title and Description of Contents	Folder
Byington, Margaret F., 1935-1938. Correspondence arising from her work with the New York School of Social Work.	415
Cabot, Philip T., 1920-1939. Correspondence re the administration of the Cabot Fund and re his article on electric power.	416
Cabot, Richard C., 1911-1939. Cabot was a Harvard professor of social ethics and the founder of hospital social service at Massachusetts General Hospital. Frequent exchanges between Kellogg and Cabot on *Survey* policy and scope. Material on industrial espionage, the Cabot Fund, steel investigation, and social ethics and social work.	417-419
Calkins, Marion "Clinch", 1920-1946. She was a free lance writer who wrote *Some Folks Won't Work*. Correspondence is primarily personal.	420-421
Cardozo, Benjamin N., 1938. The Cardozo papers were probably removed from the *Survey* files; obituary material remains.	
Chamberlain, Joseph P., 1916-1949. Extensive correspondence arising from his position as president of Survey Associates. Correspondence re health insurance, foreign affairs, the international opium problem, German-Jewish refugees, unemployment, and civil liberties.	423-425
Chamberlain, Mary, 1920-1939. She was a *Survey* staff member, 1913-1920. Obituary material.	426
Chase, Stuart, 1931-1952. Correspondence soliciting articles from Chase and materials on housing and postwar planning.	427

SURVEY ASSOCIATES, INC.

Folder Title and Description of Contents | Folder

Chenery, William L., 1936-1950.   428
    Correspondence arising from his position as publisher of
    Collier's.

Claghorn, Kate H., 1934.   429
    She was a member of the staff of the New York School of
    Social Work.

Clapper, Raymond, 1938-1942.   430
    Material on social work and the press and on Clapper's
    column criticizing Eleanor Roosevelt's role in the Office
    of Civilian Defense.

Clark, Evans, 1926-1948.   431-433
    Correspondence arising primarily from his position with
    the 20th Century Fund to which Survey Associates applied
    for grants. Material on the Committee on the Cost of
    Medical Care, public housing and taxation, collective
    bargaining, and hospital social service.

Coffee, Rabbi Rudolph I., 1916-1942.   434
    Material on prohibition, the Mooney-Billings cases, civil
    liberties, and Jewish prison services.

Colcord, Joanna C., 1924-1951.   435
    She worked for the New York Charity Organization Society
    and the Russell Sage charity organization department.
    Material on social work, social reform, and the relation
    of social work to other professions (including the rela-
    tion of organized medicine to social work).

Collier, John, 1918-1947.   436-438
    Material arising from his work as U.S. Commissioner of
    Indian Affairs, 1937-1945.

Commons, John R., 1920-1940.   439
    Material on industrial relations, unemployment, working
    conditions in Wisconsin hotels, and unionism.

Folder Title and Description of Contents	Folder

Conant, Richard K., 1935-1940.   440
    He was commissioner of the Massachusetts Department of Public Welfare. Material on the Massachusetts Conference of Social Work.

Cooke, Morris L., 1918-1951.   441-445
    He was a consulting engineer and director of the Pennsylvania Giant Power Survey. Material on public utilities, national planning, unemployment, and engineers and public life.

Cooley, Rossa B., 1914-1948.   446-451
    She was principal of the Penn Normal, Industrial and Agricultural School, the oldest school for Negroes in the South. Material on rural education and rural life.

Coolidge, Calvin, 1929-1932.   452

Cooper, Charles C., 1917-1931.   453-455
    Correspondence arising from his work as head resident of Kingsley House in Pittsburgh. Material on settlements, social work, the National Conference on Social Welfare, the 1919 steel strike and conditions in the steel industry, and community chest fund-raising.

Cooper, Mrs. Charles C., 1930-1937.   456
    Correspondence primarily re her husband.

Costigan, Edward P., 1937-1939.   457
    Routine correspondence with Costigan, a senator from Colorado.

Couzens, James, 1923-1937.   458
    Correspondence primarily re his work as U.S. senator from Michigan. Material on unemployment and federal relief.

Folder Title and Description of Contents	Folder
Crowl, Donald B., 1950-1951. Correspondence re his article on airplane safety.	459
Curtis, Frances G., 1932-1952. She was a member of the Survey board of directors.	460
Curtis, Isabella, 1926-1943. Material on the Penn Normal School.	461
Cutting, Bronson, 1933-1935. He was a U.S. senator from New Mexico.	462
Daniels, Josephus, 1940. Correspondence re U.S. policy toward Mexico during the Wilson administration and re the Spanish Civil War.	463
Darrow, Clarence, 1933-1938. Routine items and obituary material.	464
Davis, Horace B., 1929-1934. He applied to the Cabot Fund for money to finance investigation of spy systems in steel corporations.	465
Davis, J. Lionberger, 1916-1949. He was a St. Louis banker and a member of the Survey's National Council. Correspondence re the 1924 presidential campaign and the Survey's problems (1948).	466-467
Davis, Katherine B., 1933. Correspondence re the publication of her biography.	468
Davis, Michael M., 1923-1949. These folders contain extensive material on the origin and development of the Committee on Research in Medical Economics of which Davis was director and Paul Kellogg a member. There is also material on hospital social services, medical costs, public health, social workers and medical care, and the AMA. Davis formerly was director of medical services for the Julius Rosenwald Fund.	469-478

Folder Title and Description of Contents	Folder
Deardorff, Neva, 1929-1945. Correspondence re unemployment insurance, social work, and youth work and child welfare.	479
de Forest, Robert W., 1891-1931. He was president of Survey Associates, of the Russell Sage Foundation, and of the New York Charity Organization Society. Material on editorial freedom and responsibility, the scope of the Survey, and the 1919 steel strike.	480-485
de Schweinitz, Karl, 1918-1952. Correspondence arising from his work for welfare organizations in New York and Philadelphia. Correspondence re social work, unemployment, the depression, emergency relief, and a Pennsylvania relief controversy (1937-1938).	486-487
Devine, Edward T., 1918-1946. He was an editor and staff member of the Survey for many years. Correspondence re his Red Cross work in France during World War I, the U.S. Coal Commission, the settlements (and unemployment), unemployment, work relief, and social work. Kellogg credited Devine (April 19, 1937) with throwing the emphasis of social work from relief to prevention.	488-492
Dickson, W. B., 1934-1942. Material on Dickson's efforts to better conditions in the steel industry. This folder contains minutes of meetings of U.S. Steel Corporation (of which Dickson was an officer).	493
Dinwiddie, Courtenay, 1934-1943. He was secretary of the National Child Labor Committee. Correspondence re the Internal Revenue Department ruling that donations to welfare organizations engaged in effecting legislation were not deductible.	494

SURVEY ASSOCIATES, INC.

Folder Title and Description of Contents	Folder
Douglas, Paul H., 1929-1949. Material on unemployment and unemployment insurance. Douglas advised Paul Kellogg on unemployment insurance matters.	495
Draper, Ernest G., 1933-1949. Routine correspondence with Draper, an Assistant Secretary of Commerce and member of the Federal Reserve Board.	496
Duggan, Stephen P., 1917-1946. Material on the Foreign Policy Association and its predecessor, the Committee on American Policy; and on the National Conference on the Foreign Relations of the U.S. (1917).	497
Dummer, Mrs. William F., 1919-1937. Correspondence re prostitution, illegitimacy, delinquent girls, and mental hygiene.	498
Eastman, Crystal, 1917-1928. Material on pacifism, World War I, health insurance and the British Women's Labor Conference of 1926; a discussion of the policy of the American Union against Militarism from which Paul Kellogg and Lillian Wald wished to resign.	499
Eastman, Lucius R., 1931-1941. Eastman succeeded Robert de Forest as president of Survey Associates. Material on the depression and relief and minutes of a meeting held re the Survey's economic planning issue.	500
Eliot, Charles W., 1917-1936. Eliot was president of Harvard. Correspondence re the British labor movement, socialism, and democracy.	501

Folder Title and Description of Contents	Folder

Eliot, Thomas D., 1917-1951. ... 502-503
  He was a sociology professor at Northwestern University.
  Correspondence re the American Legion, juvenile courts,
  and Eliot's criticism (1925) of the Survey for attempting
  too broad a scope.

Elliott, John L., 1931-1942. ... 504-505
  Correspondence arising from his work as founder of the
  Hudson Guild (New York City) and director of the Ethical
  Culture Society. Material on unemployment, social
  planning, refugees, and youth work.

Elmhurst, Mrs. Leonard K., 1920-1940. ... 506
  She made large contributions to Survey Associates.

Embree, Edwin R., ... 507
  Embree was president of the Julius Rosenwald Fund. Material on religion and academic freedom, and on the work
  of the Rosenwald Fund with Negroes and rural education.

Emerson, Dr. Haven, 1919-1951. ... 508-513
  Correspondence arising primarily from his positions as
  associate editor of the Survey and professor of public
  health administration at Columbia. Material on the
  National Quota Act (1924), prohibition, unemployment
  and health, and on the proposed reorganization of the
  Children's Bureau (1929-1930).

Epstein, Abraham, 1934-1940. ... 514
  Material on old age reserves. Correspondence with Mrs.
  Epstein re the Spanish refugee situation (1940).

Evans, Mrs. Glendower, 1917-1933. ... 515
  She was a Survey "contact" in Boston. Correspondence re
  civil liberties and the Sacco-Vanzetti case.

Farrand, Livingston, 1934-1939. ... 516
  Routine correspondence with Farrand, president of Cornell
  University.

Folder Title and Description of Contents	Folder
Feiler, Arthur, 1939-1942. He was a member of the staff of the New York New School for Social Research.	517
Feis, Herbert, 1922-1950. Material primarily on industrial relations in Kansas and Oklahoma (1922-1923).	518
Fels, Samuel S., 1919-1948. He was president of the Fels Naptha Company and a large contributor to Survey Associates. Material on unemployment, the David Lilienthal-Arthur Morgan controversy re TVA, and consumers and the American economy.	519-522
Feiser, James L., 1922-1952. Correspondence arising primarily from his work as vice-chairman of the American Red Cross, including reports of disaster relief work. The correspondence indicates the Red Cross' sensitivity to criticism.	523-524
Filene, A. Lincoln, 1925-1939. He was a Boston financier.	525
Filene, Edward A., 1918-1941. He was a Boston businessman and founder of the Twentieth Century Fund. Material on mass production and consumption, medical economics, credit unions, economic planning, unemployment, and the New Deal.	526-528
Finley, John H., 1930-1939. He was an editor of the New York Times.	529
Fitch, John A., 1917-1952. He was a member of the staff of the New York School of Social Work and a former editor of the Survey. These folders contain extensive material on industrial relations, particularly in steel; trade unionism, civil liberties, unemployment, social work, and the National Conference on Social Welfare.	530-537

SURVEY ASSOCIATES, INC.

Folder Title and Description of Contents	Folder
Flexner, Bernard, 1925-1944. Correspondence re the Sacco-Vanzetti case.	538
Folks, Homer, 1918-1948. Correspondence arising primarily from his work with the American Red Cross, the State Charities Aid Association (and their Welfare Legislation Information Bureau), and the National Child Labor Committee; Paul Kellogg gave his impressions of the 1940 White House Conference on Children in a Democracy.	539-540
Forbes, James, 1924-1935. Correspondence re efforts to obtain work and financial assistance for Forbes, a former employee of the New York Charity Organization Society and of the Association for Improving the Condition of the Poor.	541
Foreign Policy Association, 1918-1951. Kellogg was a founder and member of the board of directors of the FPA. The folders contain minutes of board meetings, reports, pamphlets; there is material on the organization and development of the FPA. Paul Kellogg discussed the scope and policy of the FPA in a letter to Christina Merriman (January 22, 1927).	542-556
Frankel, Lee K., 1916-1931. He was vice-president of the Metropolitan Life Insurance Company in charge of the welfare division and a member of the National Council of Survey Associates. Exchange re the Survey purchasing stock in the City Housing Corporation of New York.	557
Frankfurter, Felix, 1918-1946. Correspondence re the British labor situation (1918), industrial problems, the child labor amendment, civil liberties, the TVA, Louis Brandeis, economic recovery, and Frankfurter's nomination to the Supreme Court. Correspondence with John Haynes Holmes re the collapse of the liberal movement in America and a copy of Frankfurter's remarks to a meeting of the Survey board and staff on "What We Confront in American Life" (1932).	558-561

Folder Title and Description of Contents	Folder
Gannett, Lewis S., 1917-1951. Gannett was an American Red Cross Correspondent in France (1918) and covered the Paris Peace Conference. Material on World War I, international labor movements, the American Red Cross, and the French labor situation.	562-563
Garrison, Lloyd K., 1934-1948. He was dean of the University of Wisconsin Law School. Material on labor relations.	564
Gavit, John Palmer, 1917-1948. For many years Gavit was a contributor to and editor of the Survey, specializing in the field of foreign affairs. Material on immigration, the international opium problem, neutrality and isolation, and Survey policy and problems.	565-573
Geddes, Sir Patrick, 1929-1932. He was a British scholar. Obituary material.	574
Gleason, Arthur, 1918-1923. He served as a Survey "contact" in Europe. Material on World War I, the British labor situation, and American labor relations.	575-576
Gleason, Mrs. Arthur, 1923-1933. Correspondence arising primarily re her book on her husband.	577
Glenn, John M., 1916-1949. He was director of the Russell Sage Foundation and vice-president of Survey Associates. Material on post-World War I unrest, the proposed Association of Social Workers, the 1919 steel strike, prohibition, and James Forbes.	578-579
Glenn, Mrs. John M., 1919-1938. Material on the American Red Cross, the International Conference on Social Welfare Committee of the National Conference on Social Welfare, and refugee social workers.	580

Folder Title and Description of Contents	Folder
Goldman, Henry, 1929-1936. Correspondence re problems created by the depression.	581
Gompers, Samuel, 1918-1924. He was president of the American Federation of Labor. Material on the British Labor Party.	582
Greenwood, Arthur, 1932-1945. He was secretary of the British Labor Party research department.	583
Hackett, Francis, 1918-1948. Primarily correspondence re his articles for the Survey; a memo (June, 1923) explained the working scheme of the Survey.	584
Hall, George, 1939. He was secretary of the New York Child Labor Committee.	585
Hall, Helen (Mrs. Paul Kellogg), 1929-1952. She was head resident of the University House Settlement in Philadelphia and later of the Henry Street Settlement in New York. Material on social work ethics, settlements, consumers, criminal syndicalism, and unemployment.	586-588
Hallowell, Robert, 1919-1939. He was treasurer of the New Republic. He advised the Survey on financial matters and occasionally designed covers for the magazine.	589
Hamilton, Dr. Alice, 1917-1945. She was a professor of industrial hygiene at Harvard and an expert on industrial poisons. Material on the post-World War I situation in Europe, conditions in the felt hat industry, and conditions in Germany in 1933.	590-591

Folder Title and Description of Contents	Folder

Hanrahan, John, 1932-1947. 592
   He was a publisher's counsel. This folder contains a 34-page analysis of the Survey Graphic (June, 1932). Material on freedom and responsibility of the press.

Hapgood, Norman, 1918-1931. 593
   Material on civil liberties.

Hard, William, 1932-1944. 594
   He was a freelance writer and roving editor for the Reader's Digest. Material on the consumers movement and a proposed consumers department for the Survey.

Harmon Awards, 1926-1927. 595
   This folder contains nominations for the 1926 Harmon awards for a distinctive contribution to a field of social welfare.

Harmon, William E., 1917-1927. 596
   He was founder of the Harmon Foundation and a member of the Survey Associates' National Council. Material on student loans, the Harmon Awards program, and old age assistance and security.

Harris, Helen, 1934-1946. 597
   She was headworker at Union Settlement, New York City. Material on Spanish refugees (1939).

Harrison, Earl G., 1938-1948. 598-599
   He was a lawyer who held several government posts in immigration and naturalization. The folders contain two annual reports for the Department of Immigration and Naturalization.

Harrison, Shelby M., 1917-1952. 600-602
   He was director of the Russell Sage Foundation. Material on the Foundation's surveys and exhibits department, surveys, relief, unemployment, the National Conference on Social Welfare and race relations, and on Negro youths in cities.

Folder Title and Description of Contents	Folder

Hart, Hastings H., 1918-1932.
    He directed the Russell Sage Foundation's child-helping department and was a consultant on delinquency and penology. Material on child welfare, probation, and prison conditions.
    603

Hart, Hornell, 1918-1935.
    He was a professor of social economy at Bryn Mawr College. Material on religion and mental health.
    604

Hart, Joseph K., 1921-1949.
    Correspondence arising from his position as associate editor of the Survey in education.
    605

Hastings, George A., 1935-1942.
    He worked in public relations. Material on inheritance and gift taxes.
    606

Haynes, John R., 1920-1937.
    He organized a West Coast Survey Roundtable. Material on inheritance and gift taxes.
    607

Hays, Arthur Garfield, 1935-1951.
    He was a counsel for the American Civil Liberties Union and advised the Survey on libel matters.
    608

Hecht, George J., 1937-1947.
    Routine correspondence arising from his work as president of Parents Magazine.
    609

Henderson, Fred, 1933-1947.
    He was a British socialist who wrote a series of articles for the Survey based on his impressions of America.
    610

Henderson, Leon, 1934-1947.
    Correspondence arising from his work for the remedial loans department of the Russell Sage Foundation and from various posts he held as an economist during the New Deal.
    611

SURVEY ASSOCIATES, INC.

Folder Title and Description of Contents | Folder

Herring, Hubert C., 1935-1944. | 612
Correspondence arising from his work as director of the Committee on Cultural Relations with Latin America.

Hillman, Sidney, 1932-1946. | 613
He was president of the Amalgamated Clothing Workers of America and a member of the Survey board of directors. He advised the Survey on labor situations and problems.

Hine, Lewis W., 1918-1940. | 614-615
Correspondence primarily re Paul Kellogg's efforts to find work for Hine, an interpretive photographer.

Hodson, William, 1930-1942. | 616
Correspondence arising from his work as commissioner of New York City's Department of Public Welfare. Material on relief and public assistance and on James Forbes.

Hoehler, Fred K., 1931-1951. | 617-619
Correspondence arising from his work as director of the American Public Welfare Association and of the Illinois Department of Public Welfare and from various posts held with the government. Material on relief measures and unemployment in Cincinnati during the depression and on collaboration between the APWA and the Survey.

Holmes, Rev. John Haynes, 1922-1949. | 620-621
Material on pacifism and militarism, World War I and World War II, the New York City Affairs Committee, and the American Civil Liberties Union.

Hoover, Herbert, 1922-1940. | 622
Primarily attempts to solicit articles from Hoover. Correspondence re Russian famine and relief.

Hopkins, Harry L., 1931-1946. | 623
Correspondence arising primarily from his work as administrator of FERA and WPA.

Folder Title and Description of Contents	Folder
House, Grace B., 1925-1948. Correspondence arising from her work as assistant principal at the Penn Normal School.	624
Howe, Frederick C., 1925-1939. Material on the European situation (1926), the Progressive League for Al Smith, and the Consumers' Conference (c. 1933).	625
Hughes, Charles E., 1913-1947. Material on World War I and on the 1921 Conference on the Limitation of Arms.	626
Hunt, Edward Eyre, 1921-1931. Correspondence arising from his work for the Department of Commerce during the 1920's. Material on unemployment and on the business cycle.	627
Huyck, E. N., 1928-1939. Material on rural doctors.	628
Ickes, Harold L., 1932-1948. Material on the presidential election of 1932, on candidates for the position of commissioner of Indian Affairs, on housing, and on the salmon swindle in Alaska.	629
Ihlder, John, 1917-1948. Extensive material on housing during World War I, housing in the District of Columbia, and the National Housing Conferences.	630-631
Issler, Ann Roller, 1921-1952. She was a free lance writer and a West Coast correspondent and subscription field representative of the *Survey*.	632-636
Ittleson, Henry, 1933-1947. Correspondence re contributions to Survey Associates, the NRA, and education and democracy.	637

SURVEY ASSOCIATES, INC.

Folder Title and Description of Contents	Folder
Jacobs, Philip P., 1922-1938. Correspondence arising from his work as public relations director for the National Tuberculosis Association.	638
Japan Editors' Club, 1951. Material on a contest run by the Survey offering a prize for the best answer to the editors' question, "How can the editors' club aid democracy against totalitarianism?"	639
Johnson, Alexander, 1917-1941. Johnson was a pioneer in social work. Material on care of the feeble-minded, the aged, the origin and development of social work, the beginnings of public charities, and Sinclair Lewis' book, Ann Vickers.	640-641
Kane, Francis Fisher, 1920-1939. He was a Philadelphia attorney. Correspondence re the 1920 Espionage Act, prohibition, the Indian Rights Association, and public defender movements.	642-643
Kaufmann, Fritz, 1932-1947. Correspondence arising from his work in various capacities for the New York State Employment Service. Minutes, reports, memos, and statistics on problems of relief and unemployment during the depression.	644-647
Kelley, Florence, 1925-1939. Her papers were returned to her son, Nicholas Kelley; some routine material remains.	648
Kelley, Nicholas, 1933-1947. Correspondence arising from his work as counsel for Chrysler Motors. Material on company spies, labor relations, trade unionism, and his resignation from the Survey board of directors.	649

Folder Title and Description of Contents	Folder
Kellogg, Arthur P., 1916-1932. Arthur Kellogg was financial manager and managing editor of the Survey until his death in 1934. Correspondence re Survey staff matters and staff members.	650
Kellogg, Dr. John H., 1942-1943. He was superintendent of the Battle Creek Sanitarium, Michigan.	651
Kellogg, Paul U., 1907-1948. Kellogg was editor of the Survey from 1909-1952. Correspondence re Survey policy and scope, personnel, finances, and articles. Particularly significant are Kellogg's memo re the relation of the Charities Publication Committee to the Russell Sage Foundation (1907); an exchange between Kellogg and Bruno Lasker, an associate editor, on the nature of the Survey Graphic (1923); a report of a conference Robert Bruere, associate editor, held with Louis Brandeis re the business cycle; and Kellogg's letter to Social Work Today, an answer to the magazine's criticism of the position taken by social workers before World War I. Material on labor relations, occupational standards (1917), the Sacco-Vanzetti case, consumers, and unemployment.	652-662
Kenderdine, John D., 1921-1949. Correspondence arising from his work as associate editor and business manager of the Survey.	663
Keppel, Frederick P., 1936-1943. Paul Kellogg applied to the Carnegie Corporation, of which Keppel was president, for financial assistance.	664
Kingsbury, John A., 1918-1945. Correspondence arising from his work as secretary of the Milbank Memorial Fund and as a member of the Survey board of directors. Material on health demonstrations, public health, health insurance, and on Kingsbury's resignations from the Milbank Fund, the WPA, and the Association for Improving the Condition of the Poor.	665-667

SURVEY ASSOCIATES, INC.

Folder Title and Description of Contents	Folder
Knight, Howard R., 1925-1947. Correspondence arising from his work as secretary of the National Conference on Social Welfare. Material on the International Conference on Social Welfare.	668-672
Knowles, Morris, 1919-1932. He was a Pittsburgh engineer and a member of Survey Associates' National Council. Material on flood control.	673
Krehbiel, Edward, 1919-1942. Correspondence primarily arising from his work as Pacific Coast representative of the Survey. Material on social movements in England, immigration, syndicalism, and charges of bolshevism made against the Survey.	674-675
LaFollette, Robert M., 1919-1922. Material on a World War I peace treaty.	676
LaFollette, Robert M., Jr., 1925-1939. Material on unemployment, the Progressive National Committee, and the Supreme Court (1937).	677
Lamont, Thomas W., 1923-1946. He was a partner in the J. P. Morgan Company. Material on America's entry into World War I.	678
Lane, Winthrop D., 1914-1947. Correspondence arising from his work as a Survey staff member and contributor. Lane was the Survey's authority on prisons and prison reform. Material on military prisons, suffragette pickets, conditions in District of Columbia prisons (1920), and on a New York milk employees strike.	679-683
Lasker, Bruno, 1920-1952. Correspondence arising from his work as a Survey staff member and later from his work with the American Council, Institute of Pacific Relations. Material on the National Federation of Settlements' prohibition study, democracy in social work, consumers, education and democracy, and race relations.	684-687

SURVEY ASSOCIATES, INC.

Folder Title and Description of Contents	Folder
Lasker, Loula D., 1919-1952. She was a founder of the Survey Graphic and an associate editor of the Survey whose special field was housing.	688-689
Lathrop, Julia C., 1917-1932. Correspondence arising from her work as chief of the Children's Bureau. Paul Kellogg commented on a proposed national conference for social workers (March, 1919).	690
Leach, Henry Goddard, 1921-1951. Correspondence arising from Leach's position as editor of the Forum; exchange of advice, criticism, etc.	691
Leach, Mrs. Henry Goddard, 1922-1951. She contributed substantially to the Survey and was a member of the boards of the Survey and the Foreign Policy Association. Material on the Pittsburgh Survey, FPA policy, and the need for a militant peace organization in the 1930's.	692
Lee, Joseph, 1926-1937. Routine correspondence with Lee, a Boston philanthropist and playground movement leader.	693
Lee, Porter R., 1929-1939. Correspondence arising from his work as director of the New York School of Social Work. Material on unemployment, problems created by the depression, and the relations of casework to social action.	694
Leet, Dorothy, 1938-1946. Correspondence arising from her position as secretary of the Foreign Policy Association.	695
Lehman, Herbert H., 1928-1949. Material on legislation in New York State during his term as governor, unemployment, and the European food shortage (1946).	696-697

Folder Title and Description of Contents   Folder

Leiserson, William M., 1921-1946.   698-700
    Leiserson was an Antioch College professor who held govern-
    ment posts on the National Mediation Board and the National
    Labor Relations Board. Material on unemployment, the New
    York Employment Insurance Law, and labor relations.

Lenroot, Katharine F., 1933-1944.   701-702
    She succeeded Grace Abbott as chief of the Children's Bu-
    reau. Material on attacks on the Children's Bureau, the
    place of the Bureau in the federal government, and children
    in wartime.

Lewisohn, Adolph, 1915-1938.   703
    He was a founder of the Survey Graphic. Material on pri-
    sons and prison labor.

Lewisohn, Irene, 1927-1940.   704
    She was associated with the Neighborhood Playhouse of
    New York City.

Lewisohn, Sam A., 1924-1951.   705
    He was a founder of the Survey Graphic and chairman of the
    American Management Association. Material on unemployment
    and on the Wagner Public Employment Service Bill. Kellogg
    stated his conception of the Survey Graphic (October, 1935).

Lindeman, Eduard C., 1924-1934.   706
    Material on the Survey's special number (February, 1927) on
    democracy and fascism which he helped edit and an exchange
    between Lindeman and Kellogg on settlements.

Lindsay, Samuel McCune, 1925-1942.   707
    He was a professor at Columbia University and chairman of
    the National Child Labor Committee.

Lindsey, Judge Ben B., 1925-1935.   708-709
    Material on his fight with the Ku Klux Klan in Colorado
    (1925) and on family and domestic courts.

SURVEY ASSOCIATES, INC.

Folder Title and Description of Contents | Folder

Locke, Alain, 1924-1952. | 710-713
    He was a philosophy professor at Howard University and one of the Survey's authorities on aspects of the race problem in America. He edited the special number on Harlem (March, 1925). Material on Harlem in the depression.

Lovejoy, Owen R., 1921-1949. | 714-715
    Correspondence arising from his work as secretary of the National Child Labor Committee and as secretary of the Children's Aid Society.

Lowenstein, Solomon, 1932-1941. | 716
    He was director of the Federation for the Support of Jewish Philanthropic Societies of New York City.

McCready, Caroline P., 1922-1940. | 717
    She was a founder of the Survey Graphic. Material on medical conditions in rural areas.

MacDonald, J. Ramsay, 1923-1937. | 718
    He was a Member of Parliament, founder of the British Labor Party, and British Prime Minister. Exchange between Kellogg and MacDonald on the progressive movement in the 1920's.

McDonald, James G., 1925-1947. | 719
    Correspondence arising from his work as chairman of the Foreign Policy Association and of the High Commission for Refugees Coming from Germany.

McDowell, Mary E., 1931-1936. | 720
    She was a Chicago settlement worker.

Mack, Julian W., 1917-1943. | 721-723
    Mack was president of Survey Associates. Correspondence re Survey finances and unemployment; extensive correspondence re a libel suit filed against the Survey by the Associated Gas and Electric Company, New York.

SURVEY ASSOCIATES, INC.

Folder Title and Description of Contents							Folder

Macy, Noel, 1923-1940.									724
    He was a publisher and member of the Survey board of directors. He commented on the Survey Graphic (December, 1936).

Macy, V. Everit, 1919-1935.								725
    He was a founder of the Survey Graphic and member of the Survey board of directors.

Magrath, Charles, 1929-1941.								726
    Material on the Canadian-American International Joint Commission and on J. Ramsay MacDonald.

Mallon, J. J., 1924-1951.									727
    Correspondence arising from his work as warden of Toynbee Hall. Material on unemployment and on the Barnett Fellowship.

Marsh, Benjamin C., 1925-1946.								728
    He directed the Farmers' National Council and the Peoples' Lobby. Material on farmers and electric power and on Latin American relations.

Masaryk, Thomas, 1940.									729
    An obituary of Masaryk, a Czecho-Slovak leader.

Matthews, William H., 1920-1946.								730
    Correspondence arising from his position as director of the family welfare division of the Association for Improving the Condition of the Poor. Material on the depression, relief, and the "ways of organized charity."

Mayer, Albert, 1936-1952.									731-732
    He was an architect who edited a Survey special number on housing and city planning.

Merriman, Christina, 1919-1931.								733
    Correspondence arising from her work as secretary of the Foreign Policy Association. The folder contains some of her personal papers sent to the Survey office files after her death.

SURVEY ASSOCIATES, INC.

Folder Title and Description of Contents   Folder

Middleton, J. S., 1934-1945.   734
    He was secretary of the British Labor Party.

Moak, Harry L., 1922-1951.   735
    Correspondence arising from his position as owner of a
    printing company of which Paul and Arthur Kellogg were
    shareholders.

Morgan, Arthur E., 1932-1946.   736-738
    Morgan was president of Antioch College and a director of
    the TVA. Extensive correspondence re a libel suit arising
    from an article by Morgan.

Morgenthau, Rita W., 1933-1942.   739
    She was educational director of the Neighborhood Playhouse
    of New York City. Material on vocational guidance for Youth.

Morgue, 1929-1934.   740-744
    These folders contain book reviews, case stories, letters-
    to-the-editor, and manuscripts which were held by Arthur
    Kellogg for possible publication.

Morrow, Dwight W., 1925-1931.   745
    He was ambassador to Mexico and a founder of the Survey
    Graphic.

Moskowitz, Mrs. Henry, 1925-1932.   746
    She was Al Smith's assistant and worked with Paul Kellogg
    in attempting to persuade Smith to write articles for the
    Survey.

Murphy, Frank, 1933-1942.   747
    He was governor of Michigan and later a Supreme Court jus-
    tice. Material on industrial relations and the 1937
    Michigan labor situation.

SURVEY ASSOCIATES, INC.

Folder Title and Description of Contents	Folder
Murphy, J. Prentice, 1922-1936. Correspondence arising from his work as secretary of the Philadelphia Children's Bureau. Material on fund-raising methods, social work ethics, and Grace Abbott's appointment to the Children's Bureau.	748
Neuberger, Maurine, 1951-1952. Correspondence re her article on social workers as lobbyists.	749
Neuberger, Richard L., 1936-1952. He was the Survey's "contact" on the Pacific Coast. Material on conservation, the Columbia Valley Authority, the great salmon swindle, and tuberculosis in Alaska.	750-753
Neurath, Otto, 1931-1946. He was an Austrian museum curator who developed the isotype, a method of graphic portrayal of social and economic statistics. Correspondence re efforts made to utilize his method in America, technocracy, world planning, and unemployment.	754-756
Norton, Charles D., 1921-1937. He was vice-president of the New York Charity Organization Society. He critized the Survey for attempting to publish weekly issues.	757
Paddock, Bishop Robert L., 1934-1939. Correspondence arising from his position as chairman of the American Friends for Spanish Democracy.	758
Parran, Dr. Thomas, 1934-1946. Parron was Surgeon General of the U.S. Material on public health, Negro health, syphilis, and tuberculosis.	759-760
Peabody, George Foster, 1922-1938. Material on the 12-hour day in the steel industry, the Penn Normal School, race relations, the 1932 presidential campaign, and public control of railroads.	761

SURVEY ASSOCIATES, INC.

Folder Title and Description of Contents | Folder

Peixotto, Jessica B., 1921-1932. | 762
    She was a University of California professor of social economics and a Survey "contact" on the Pacific Coast. Material on the California welfare situation in 1924.

Perkins, Frances, 1930-1950. | 763-764
    She was Secretary of Labor under Franklin Roosevelt. Material on unemployment, health insurance, social security, and housing.

Persons, W. Frank, 1920-1942. | 765-766
    Correspondence re the American Red Cross, employment measures, and the U.S. and New York Public Employment Services.

Pettit, Walter, 1935-1951. | 767
    He was a New York School of Social Work staff member.

Pinchot, Amos, 1918-1940. | 768
    Material on the People's League for Economic Security, social planning, reconstruction, and the Banking Act of 1935; Kellogg's reply to Pinchot's open letter in which he had refused to support Roosevelt's candidacy in 1936.

Pinchot, Gifford, 1918-1946. | 769
    Material on the power monopoly, conservation, unemployment, utility regulation, and the American Red Cross' refusal to aid coalminers in Pennsylvania.

Pratt, George D., 1924-1929. | 770
    He was a founder of the Survey Graphic. Material on conservation.

Purdy, Lawson, 1921-1940. | 771
    Material on the law and social work and on unemployment.

Folder Title and Description of Contents	Folder

Ratcliffe, S. K., 1923-1952.   772-775
    He was a British correspondent for the Survey. Material on labor and industrial conditions in England, the British Labor Party, and Mohandas Ghandi.

Reader's Digest, 1931-1952.   776-784
    The Digest had a contract with the Survey which gave it exclusive right to reprint articles (among magazines of this type). These folders contain correspondence re questions of policy and procedure, criticisms of the Digest, articles and collaboration on articles. Material on industrial arbitration, rural welfare, prison reform, and the mentally ill.

Reeder, Dr. R. R., 1931-1934.   785
    Material re his work with orphans.

Renold, Charles, 1926-1945.   786
    He was a progressive British manufacturer. A reply by Paul Kellogg to Renold's criticism of America.

Richberg, Donald, 1926-1946.   787-789
    Material on the progressive movement, America in the 1920's, the law and social progress, the Progressive Conference of 1931, employment, the NRA, and railroads and railroad labor organizations.

Roche, Josephine, 1932-1947.   790
    She was president of the Rocky Mountain Fuel Company and Assistant Secretary of the Treasury. Material on the 1938 National Health Conference and the 1946 International Labor Organization Conference.

Roosevelt, Franklin D., 1928-1943.   791
    Correspondence re the appointment of Felix Frankfurter to the Supreme Court and re the Children's Bureau; primarily correspondence soliciting articles and advice.

Folder Title and Description of Contents	Folder
Roosevelt, Mrs. Franklin D., 1929-1952. Material re the British Labor Party, World War I, and her role in the Office of Civilian Defense.	792
Ross, Mary, 1918-1949. She was an associate editor of the *Survey* in the field of health and worked for the Social Security Board. Correspondence re the American Red Cross, the Sacco-Vanzetti case, and old age reserves.	793-794
Rounds, Ralph S., 1930-1948. He was director of the Keith Fund and chairman of the Foreign Policy Association.	795
Routzahn, Evart G., 1923-1938. Correspondence arising from his work with the Russell Sage Foundation's department of surveys and exhibits. Material on fund-raising and publicity methods in social work.	796
Routzahn, Mary Swain, 1924-1950. Material on social work publicity methods and interpretation.	797
Rowell, Chester, 1934-1945. He was a newspaper editor and columnist.	798
Rubinow, Isaac M., 1924-1940. Correspondence re social work and law enforcement, public welfare and private charity, unemployment insurance and social security.	799-800
Ruml, Beardsley, 1931-1945. He was a member of the *Survey* board of directors. Material on employment services.	801

Folder Title and Description of Contents	Folder

Ryerson, Edward L., 1932-1944.   802-803
    He was chairman of the Inland Steel Company and a member of the Survey board of directors. Material on social security, employment and relief, Michigan labor unrest (1937), and labor conditions in the steel industry.

Scandrett, Richard B., Jr., 1935-1948.   804-807
    He was president of Survey Associates. Material re arbitration and labor relations, neutrality and isolation, Scandrett's criticism of Anne Morrow Lindbergh, the 1940 presidential campaign, and foreign affairs.

Scattergood, Alfred G., 1920-1939.   808
    He was vice-president of the Philadelphia Provident Trust Company.

Scattergood, J. Henry, 1921-1937.   809
    Correspondence arising from his work as assistant commissioner in the Office of Indian Affairs.

Schaffner, Halle, 1927-1950.   810
    She was in charge of the Midmonthly book review department.

Schaffner, Joseph H., 1920-1938.   811
    Schaffner, a member of Hart, Schaffner & Marx company, advised Paul Kellogg on financial matters.

Schieffelin, William J., 1925-1943.   812
    He was chairman of the New York Citizens Union which lobbied for better municipal government.

Schiff, Jacob H., 1918-1925.   813
    He was a member of the Henry Street Settlement board of directors.

Seager, Henry R., 1918-1932.   814-815
    He was a political science professor at Columbia University, a member of the Survey board of directors, and a founder of the Survey Graphic. Material on the British Labor Party and on labor relations; extensive correspondence re the Survey Graphic.

SURVEY ASSOCIATES, INC.

Folder Title and Description of Contents	Folder
Seligman, Edwin R., 1931-1939. He was a professor of political economy at Columbia University. Material on his refusal to associate himself with the Carl Schurz Foundation.	816
Senior, Max, n.d. An obituary of Senior, a Cincinnati businessman.	817
Seymour, Gertrude, 1931-1940. She was formerly an associated editor of the *Survey*. The correspondence is primarily personal.	818
Shaw, S. Adele, 1917-1928. Correspondence arising from her work as managing editor of the *Survey*. Material on the 1919 steel strike and the 1922 coal strike in Pennsylvania.	819-821
Shillady, John H., n.d. An obituary of Shillady, secretary of the National Association for the Advancement of Colored People.	822
Simkhovitch, Mary K., 1933-1951. She was a New York settlement worker. Material on the settlements, public housing, and the United Nations.	823
Sinclair, Upton, 1922-1939. Correspondence re "oscilloclasts", Lincoln University, and Sinclair's campaign for governor in California.	824
Smillie, Robert, 1929-1940. He was a Member of Parliament and leader of British miners during World War I.	825
Smith, Alfred E., 1919-1940. Material on Smith's policies as governor of New York, education, the Palisades Interstate Park commission, and federal relief.	826

Folder Title and Description of Contents	Folder
Smith, Geddes, 1919-1943. Correspondence arising from his work as a <u>Survey</u> staff member and as publications director for the Commonwealth Fund's Child Health Demonstration Committee. Material on housing, regional planning, and public health nursing.	827-828
Springer, Gertrude, 1920-1952. She was managing editor of the <u>Midmonthly</u>. Material on social work, relief, the National Conference on Social Welfare, and the relation of the <u>Midmonthly</u> to the <u>Survey Graphic</u>.	829-830
Steffens, Lincoln, 1930-1940. Routine correspondence.	831
Stern, Alfred K., 1926-1940. Correspondence arising from his work as director of the Julius Rosenwald Fund. Material on the Fund's projects, particularly for Negroes, in housing and education.	832-833
Stern, Edith M., 1938-1952. She was a free lance writer. Material on education of the handicapped, mental hospitals, and nursing.	834-835
Stimson, Henry L., 1939-1942. Correspondence re foreign policy with Stimson, Secretary of War.	836
Street, Elwood, 1920-1951. Correspondence arising from his work as director of the St. Louis and (later) Washington, D. C. Community Chests. Material on the American Red Cross, social work and social action, social work ethics, social welfare administration, and the 1934 tax bill limiting deductibility of contributions.	837-840
Strong, Anna Louise, 1920-1937. She was a journalist and foreign correspondent. Material on Russia, China, and refugees from the Spanish Civil War.	841

Folder Title and Description of Contents	Folder

Strong, Rev. Sidney, 1922-1938.
    Primarily correspondence re his daughter's articles.
    See above.
	842

Stroock, Sol M., 1938-1940. He was a New York attorney. Correspondence re the "Calling America" series.	843
Swift, Harold H., 1930-1944. He was a member of the Survey board of directors and of the Swift Company. Material on industrial relations with meatpackers, the depression, social planning, and Chicago's Back-of-the-Yards Neighborhood Council.	844-845
Swing, Raymond Gram, 1937-1950. He was a radio commentator and editor of the first number of the Survey's "Calling America" series. Material on Nazi refugees and on atomic power.	846
Tannenbaum, Frank, 1921-1941. Material on plans for a special number on Mexico (May, 1924) and on Latin America.	847
Tarbell, Ida M., 1931-1940. Routine correspondence.	848
Taylor, Graham, 1923-1936. Routine correspondence with Taylor, founder of the Chicago Commons. Microfilms of the Taylor-Survey papers held by the Newberry Library at Chicago are available here.	849
Taylor, Graham Romeyn, 1920-1942. He was at one time the Survey's representative in Chicago. Material on the Chicago Commission on Race Relations, the League of Free Nations Association, the American Association of Social Workers, and mendicancy in Mexico.	850-851

Folder Title and Description of Contents	Folder
Tousley, Clare M., 1920-1948. Correspondence arising from her work as assistant director of the New York Charity Organization Society. Material on junior leagues and family casework.	852
Tucker, Frank, 1918-1940. He was vice-president of the New York Provident Loan Society.	853
Tyson, Francis, 1919-1937. Material on the Pittsburgh Survey, Simon Patten, the 12-hour day in steel, and relief in Pennsylvania in the 1930's.	854
United States Department of Labor, 1920-1940. A report on standards to be met by children seeking working permits (1920) and material on infant mortality.	855
United States Treasury Department, 1922. Material on the danger of the introduction of cholera and typhus into America from Eastern Europe.	856
Van Kleeck, Mary, 1918-1936. Correspondence arising from her position as head of the Division of Industrial Studies for the Russell Sage Foundation. Material on conditions in bituminous coal mines, the work of the Sage Foundation, employment, the National Conference on Social Welfare, the International Association for Study and Improvement of Human Relations and Conditions in Industry, settlements and casework, and economic and social planning.	857-860
Van Loon, Hendrik Willem, 1921-1944. Correspondence re cartoons, covers and articles he did for the Survey. Van Loon's comments on the midwest, democracy, and World War II.	861-863
Van Waters, Miriam, 1922-1927. Correspondence arising from her work as juvenile court referee in Los Angeles.	864

SURVEY ASSOCIATES, INC.

Folder Title and Description of Contents	Folder
Veiller, Lawrence, 1927-1933. He was director of the National Housing Association.	865
Villard, Oswald Garrison, 1918-1944. He was editor of the Nation. He did an article for the Survey on conditions in Harlem (1935), but objected to the Survey's checking procedure and eventually withdrew it.	866
Wagner, Robert F., 1928-1949. Correspondence with Wagner, a U.S. senator, re unemployment, the Kellogg Peace Pact, the Supreme Court, social security, and urban redevelopment and housing.	867-868
Wald, Lillian D., 1918-1940. She was founder of the Henry Street Settlement and a member of the Survey board of directors. Material on J. Ramsay MacDonald, prohibition, the 1928 presidential campaign, the Children's Bureau, social research and community progress, and American neutrality in the 1930's.	869-873
Walker, Charles R., 1932-1946. Correspondence re articles he wrote for the Survey on Minnesota (1936), the CIO, and on the Farm Security Homestead projects.	874-875
Wallace, De Witt, 1929-1952. Wallace was publisher of the Reader's Digest; correspondence re the arrangements between the Survey and the Digest, giving the Digest exclusive right to reprint material; financial arrangements, and memos on collaboration.	876-878
Walnut, T. Henry, 1918-1946. He was a Philadelphia attorney. Material on prohibition and his resignation as U.S. District Attorney for Eastern Pennsylvania, civil liberties, and the Nuremberg trials.	879-880
Walsh, Frank P., 1921-c.1940. He was an attorney and counsel for the Republic of Ireland. Material on the Mooney-Billings cases and the Progressive National Committee of 1936 (including the Committee's by-laws).	881

SURVEY ASSOCIATES, INC.

Folder Title and Description of Contents — Folder

Warburg, Felix, 1920-1939. — 882
    He was a founder of the Survey Graphic. Correspondence re the lack of recognition of Lillian Wald's work.

Warburg, Paul M., 1919-1940. — 883
    Significant material on the founding and evolution of the Survey Graphic; also correspondence re the Federal Reserve Board and the depression and unemployment.

Weigert, Dr. H. W., 1943-1946. — 884
    His papers were returned to his family; some routine correspondence remains.

Wembridge, Eleanor Rowland, 1923-1940. — 885-886
    Correspondence arising from her work with the Women's Protective Association of Cleveland and as a juvenile court referee. She frequently wrote articles for the Survey. Material on professional social workers and the psychiatric approach to social work.

Weybright, Victor, 1932-1952. — 887-888
    Correspondence arising from his position as managing editor of the Survey Graphic; correspondence with John Palmer Gavit re American neutrality and pacifism.

Whipple, Leon R., 1934-1949. — 889
    He was a professor of journalism, book review editor of the Survey, and an advisor to Paul Kellogg.

White, William Allen, 1931-1943. — 890
    Material on the 1936 presidential campaign, the nomination of Felix Frankfurter to the Supreme Court, and American neutrality in the 1930's.

Wile, Dr. Ira S., 1934-1943. — 891
    He reviewed books for the Survey.

Folder Title and Description of Contents	Folder
Williams, Pierce, 1934-1946. Material on the labor situation on the Pacific Coast (1935), the WPA, the 1937 steel strike, and unemployment and relief.	892
Williams, Whiting, 1932-1944. He was a counsel in employee and public relations. Material on prohibition and the "labor problem."	893
Wise, Rabbi Stephen S., 1919-1945. He was president of the American Jewish Congress. Material on the 1919 steel strike; the Passaic, New Jersey, textile strike; and the "Calling America" issue on minorities.	894-895
Woods, Robert A., 1919-1939. He was a settlement pioneer. Material on education and on his book, The Preparation of Calvin Coolidge. Correspondence with Mrs. Woods.	896
Young, Art, 1943. An obituary of Young, a cartoonist.	897
Young, Owen D., 1931-1950. He was chairman of General Electric's board of directors. Material on management's social attitudes and on the public's impression of businessmen.	898
Zimand, Gertrude Folks, 1929-1948. Correspondence arising from her position as publicity and research director of the National Child Labor Committee. Material on child labor at the state and local levels.	899
Zimand, Savel, 1921-1949. Correspondence arising from his work as a foreign correspondent and with several health organizations.	900-901
Zorbaugh, Harvey, 1942. He was a professor of education at New York University.	902

SUPPLEMENT ONE

INDEX TO THE MEMBERSHIP RECORDS (Folders 46-325)

SURVEY ASSOCIATES, INC.

MEMBERSHIP RECORDS

Abbott, Mrs. Donald Putnam
Abbott, Grace
Abrons, Mr. and Mrs. Louis W.
Adams, Emma F.
Adams, Jessie B.

Addams, Jane
Addis, Mrs. Luise
Adelsberg, Hyman
Adloff, Mrs. Richard, Jr.
Adult Council of the Henry Street Settlement

Affelder, Mr. and Mrs. Louis
Agoos, Solomon
Alcroft, Mrs. Clara
Alderton, Mrs. Cora
Alexander, A. V.

Alexander Home
Alexander, Miss Elizabeth
Alexander, John F.
Alexander, Mrs. Sadie
Alexandria Community Chest

Alger, Mr. and Mrs. George
Allen County Community Chest
Allen, Mrs. Ethel Richardson
Allenton, Ida
Allison, Alma S.

Alschuler, Mrs. Alfred (Rose)
Altmeyer, Arthur J.
Altoona Community Chest
Altschul, Frank
Amalgamated Clothing Workers of America

Amberg, Julius H.
Amberson, William R.
American Association of Social Workers (Iowa Chapter)
American City Bureau
American Council of Volunteer Agencies For Foreign Service, Inc.

American Friends Service Committee
American Jewish Committee
American Jewish Joint Distribution Committee
American Legion (Detroit)
American Legion National Child Welfare Division

American Public Welfare Association
American Red Cross (National Headquarters)
American Red Cross (Local Chapters)
Ames, Mrs. John O.
Amherst, H. Wilder Charity

Anderson, Mrs. D. L. (Miss Carol Young)
Anderson, H. T.
Anderson, Margaret B.
Anderson, Rachel
Anderson, Mr. and Mrs. T. J.

Andrews, Rev. and Mrs. Benjamin
Andrews, Elizabeth
Andrews, Mrs. D. E.
Anker, Frederick
Annenberg, Walter

Anonymous
Anthony, Elbert
Archbold, Mrs. Harry R.
Areson, Clinton
Aries, Leonard P.

Arkansas Chapter of American Association of Social Workers
Arkush, Reuben
Armes, Irene Headley
Armstrong, Mrs. E. J.
Arnstein, Leo

Ascher, Mr. and Mrs. Charles
Ascoli, Max (Fund Inc.)
Ascoli, Mrs. Max
Ash, Harold
Asher, Mr. and Mrs. L. E.

Ashley, Mabel Pierce
Associated Catholic Charities
Associated Hospital Service
Associated Jewish Philanthropies
Association of Junior Leagues of America

Athey, Mrs. C. N.
Atwater, Mr. and Mrs. Pierce
Ausley, Zora
Austen Riggs Foundation
Austin, Gertrude

Avery, Eunice Harriet

Babbitt, Ellen C.
Babcock, Mrs. F. H.
Babcock, Ruth
Babcock, Mr. and Mrs. Wayne
Babson, Mrs. Sidney

Bachman, Richard
Bachrach, Mrs. Alfred
Backer, George
Backers, Mrs. Dona
Bacon, George

Bader, Edith
Baerwald, Paul
Bailey, George D.
Bain, Read
Baker, Harold

Baker, Mrs. John
Baldwin, Rachel
Baldwin, Robert N.
Baldwin, Roger N.
Baldwin, William H.

Balke, Clarence W.
Ballard, Ernest S.
Ballard, J. C.
Ballard, Russell
Ballenger, A. G.

Baltzby, Mary
Bane, Frank
Bane, Lita
Banham, Dr. Katherine
Banner, Gilbert

Banning, Margaret Culkin
Barber, Dorothy
Barber, June
Barker, Ada
Barker, Mrs. L. B. R.

Barker Welfare Foundation
Barnand, Chester
Barnand, Ellsworth
Barnard, Margaret
Barneby, Ruth

Barnes, Rev. Rankin
Barnes, Mr. and Mrs. Hobart W.
Barnett, Eugune
Barnett, Lewis
Bartlett, Harriet

Barton, Miss Betty
Baruch, Bernard M.
Barus, Mr. and Mrs. Maxwell
Bascom, Lelia
Bascom, William

Bastine, A. R.
Bates, Sanford
Boy City Community Chest
Beardsley, Mrs. John
Beasley, Robert W.

Beasly, Dr. B. T.
Beaufort, Mrs. Inez
Beaven and Associates
Becken, Benjamin
Becker, John

Becker, W. H.
Beckett, Charles
Beckett, Cynthia
Beckwith, Minerva
Beebe, Mrs. Ward

Beggs, Mrs. Frederick
Beisser, Paul T.
Belanger, Mrs. Agnes F.
Bell, Courtney
Bell, Edgar D.

Bell, Lorne W.
Bell, T. S.
Belmont, Mrs. August
Benham, Carrie
Benjamin, Alfred

Benjamin, Edgar P.
Benjamin, Edward B.
Benjamin, Fannie
Benjamin, Juluis E.
Benjamin, Paul L.

Benner, Paul
Benz, Mrs. Luke
Berea College
Beresford, Charles
Berger, Joseph

Berglund, Gustaf
Berkeley Community and War Chest
Berle, Mr. A. A., Jr.
Berle, Mrs. A. A., Jr.
Bernabei, Warren

Bernard, Dr. Viola W.
Bernays, Murray C.
Bernhard, A. M.
Bernhard, Mrs. Richard
Bernheim, Mrs. Henry J.

Bernheim, Mrs. Leonard
Bernstein, Rabbi Philip
Bernstein, Robert M.
Berry, Mrs. A. C. U.
Berry, Madeline

Bersh, A. E.
Beth David Hospital
Bicknell, Ernest P.
Biddle, Eric
Biddle, Mrs. Francis

Biddle, Georgina
Bigelow, Alida
Biggar, Olive
Bigger, Frederick
Bijur, Caroline

Billikopf, Jacob
Billikopf, Mrs. Ruth Marshall ("In Memoriam")
Bing, Alexander M.
Bingham, Barry
Binghana, Joseph W.

Bird, Mrs. Clarence E.
Birkner, Ruth
Bishop, E. Beryl
Bishop, Ruth
Black, Algernon

Blackey, Eileen
Blain, Dr. Daniel
Blaine, Mrs. Emmons
Blanchard, Ralph
Blanding, Sarah Gibson

Bliss, Mrs. Robert Woods
Bloom, Dr. M. S.
Bloom, Max
Blumenthal, Sidney
Blumgart, Dr. Leonard

Boggs, Mary Edna
Bok, Nellie Lee (Mrs. Curtis)
Bolton, Mrs. Frances
Bonbright, Elizabeth M.
Bondy, Robert E.

Bonsal, Mrs. Stephen
Bookman, C. M.
Booth, Mrs. Samuel
Borg, John
Borg, Sidney

Borton, Mrs. A. Wallace
Boston Provident Association
Bostrom, Mrs. Karl
Bostwick, Prudence
Botsford, Laura

Bottje, Wayne
Bottom, Raymond
Bouslog, M. P.
Bowen, Ruth
Bowie, Mrs. W. Russell

Bowles, Chester
Bowman, Ruth
Bowman, Waldo
Boynton, Mrs. Charles T.
Boy Scouts of America

Boys' Clubs of America
Bradley, Edith
Bradley, Otto
Bradley, Phillips
Bradley, Richards

Bradway, John
Brady, John
Brand, Mrs. Catherine
Brandeis, Mrs. Alfred
Brandeis, Elizabeth

Braucher, Howard S.
Brav, Stanley R.
Brecher, Leo
Breckinridge, Mrs. Eleanor
Bremner, Robert H.

Brenner, Ann Reed
Breyfogle, Charles C., Jr.
Brickley, Mrs. Alice F.
Britt, George
Brode, Jack

Bromley, Esther
Bronson, Rev. Oliver Hart
Bronson, T. C.
Brookings, Mrs. Robert
Brooklyn Association for Improving the Condition of the Poor

Brooklyn Bureau of Charities
Brooks, Richard
Brown, Dr. Blanche
Brown, Chester R.
Brown, Mrs. John Wesley

Brown, Joseph R.
Brown, Josephine
Brown, Dr. Lawrence
Brown, Dr. Philip
Brown, William Adams

Browne, Mary K.
Bruce, Jessica
Brueckner, William
Bruere, Henry
Bruere, Robert W.

Brumm, Mrs. J. L.
Brumnitt, Mrs. Dan
Brunner, Edmund
Bruno, Frank J.
Bruno, Mrs. Frank J.   (Joanna C. Colcord)

SURVEY ASSOCIATES, INC.

Brush Foundation
Bryan, Ethel
Bryant, Mrs. Myra
Bryson, Lyman
Bubbett, V. L.

Buchanan, Etha
Buck, Dr. Carl E.
Buell, Mrs. Alice Standish
Buell, Bertha
Buell, Bradley

Buell, Flora
Buffalo Foundation
Bulkley, Mary
Bunce, Alexander
Bundy, Mrs. Harvey

Burdick, Rev. Earl
Bureau of Catholic Charities
Bureau of Child Hygiene
Burger, John
Burgess, Ernest W.

Burhoe, Mrs. B. D.
Burkhard, Hans
Burlingham, Charles C.
Burnett, H. A.
Burnham, E. Lewis

Burnham, Mrs. William
Burns, Allen T.
Burns, Josephine
Burr, Dr. Emily T.
Burritt, Bailey B.

Burton, Mrs. J. C.
Busch, Henry M.
Bushman, John
Butler, Mrs. Carol
Butler, Charles

Butler, Mrs. Mary
Buttenheim, Harold
Buttenwieser, Mrs. Benjamin
Butzel, Fred M.
Bulwada, Mrs. John P.

SURVEY ASSOCIATES, INC.

Byck, Lawrence

Cabot, Philip
Campbell, Elizabeth
Cannon, Mrs. Henry White
Cannon, Mary A.
Cardozo, Benjamin

Chadbourne, William M.
Chaffee, H. Almon
Chamberlain, Ellen
Chamberlain, Joseph P.
Chase, Stuart

Chicago Commons
Chicago Community Trust
Clapp, Raymond
Clark, Evans
Curtis, Frances

Davis, J. Lionberger
Davis, Michael M.
Deardorff, Dr. Niva R.
DeForest, Robert W.
Dennison, Henry

Devine, Edward T.
Douglas, Mrs. Dorothy
Duggan, Stephen A.
Dummer, Mrs. W. F.

Eastman, Lucius R.
Elmhirst, Mrs. Leonard K.

Falk, Mr. and Mrs. Myron
Fels, Samuel S.
Field Foundation
Filene, Edward A.
Filene, Lincoln

Finley, John H.
Flexner, Bernard
Folks, Homer
Frankfurter, Felix

Gannett, Lewis
Garrison, Lloyd K.
Gavit, John Palmer
Gavit, Walter Palmer
Goldmark, Josephine

Graham, Frank P.
Griffith, Alice
Guffey, Joseph

Harrison, Earl G.
Harrison, Shelby M.
Haynes, John
Hays, Arthur Garfield
Hillman, Sidney

Hillman Foundation (Sidney)
Hoehler, Fred K.
Hofheimer Foundation
Hughes, Charles Evans
Humphrey, Hubert H.

Hutchins, Robert

Ickes, Harold
Ide, Mrs. Francis
Ihlder, John
Illing, Hans
Illinois Society for Prevention of Blindness

Immer, Ester
Ingalls, Mrs. Abbott
Ingersoll, Mrs. Raymond
Inglis, Agnes
Ingram, Frances

Inman, Samuel Guy
International Business Machines
International Labor Organization
International Ladies' Garment Workers Union
Irene Kaufman Settlement

Isaac, Stanley
Isenberg, Mrs. R. A.
Israel, Mrs. Rachel
Issler, Anne Roller
Ittleson Foundation

Ittleson, Mr. and Mrs. Henry J.

Johnson, Alvin

SURVEY ASSOCIATES, INC.

Kaufman, Edgar
Kawin, Ethel
Keezer, Dexter M.
Keith Fund
Kelly, Nicholas

Kellogg, Arthur P.
Kellogg, Florence Loeb
Kellogg, Mrs. Marion
Kellogg, Mrs. Mary F.   ("In Memoriam")
Kellogg, Mercy P.

Kellogg, Paul
Kellogg, Richard P.
Kenderine, John D.
Kenyon, Dorothy
Keyserling, Mr. and Mrs. Leon

Kingsbury, John A.
Knight, Howard
Krehbiel, Edward
Kuhn, Ferdinand
Kyron Foundation

Lamont, Mr. and Mrs. Thomas W.
Lancaster, William W.
Landis, James M.
Lane, Robert P.
Lasker, Mr. and Mrs. Albert

Lasker, Bruno
Lasker, Florina
Lasker, Loula D.
Lathrop, Julia C.
Lattimer, Gardner

Lawrence, David
Leach, Mrs. Henry G.
Lee, Joseph
Leffingwell, Russell
Lehman, Herbert

Leiserson, William
Lenroot, Katharine F.
Levinson, Mrs. Salmon O.
Levy, Mrs. David
Lewisohn, Samuel

Lowenstein, Solomon

McAlpin, David
McConnell, Bishop Francis
McCorkle, Daniel
McDowell, Mary E.
Mack, Julian W.

Mack, Mrs. Julian W. (Mrs. Emanuel Brunswick)
Macy, J. Noel
Mason, Mary T.
Maurice and Laura Folk Foundation
Mayer, Albert

Millbank, Albert
Miller, Dr. James Alexander
Moors, John

Norton, William J.

Ogden, Esther

Paddock, Bishop Robert
Parker, Dr. Valeria
Parsons, Phillip A.
Pinchot, Gifford
Polier, Justine Wise

Pope, Mr. and Mrs. Willard
Pope, Mrs. Willard
Porter, Rev. Lucius C.
Pound, Roscoe
Pratt, George D.

Procter, William

Robins, Mrs. Raymond
Rockefeller Foundation
Rockefeller, Nelson A.
Rogers, Lindsay
Roosevelt, Mrs. Franklin

Rosenthal, Lessing
Rosenwald Family Association
Rosenwald Fund (Juluis)
Rosenwald, Lessing
Rosenwald, William

Rounds, Ralph S.
Routzahn, Mary Swain
Russell Sage Foundation
Ryan, Monsignor John A.
Ryerson, Edward L. Jr.

Sand, Rene
Sandburg, Carl
Sarnoff, David
Scandrett, Richard B.
Scattergood, Alfred G.

Scattergood, J. Henry
Schwartenbach, Robert
Selekman, Benjamin
Senior, Max
Shaw, Robert

Sherwin, Belle
Sibley, Florence
Simkhovitch, Mrs. Mary
Solenberger, Edwin D.
Smith, Alfred E.

Steep, Mrs. Miriam
Stevenson, Dr. George S.
Swift, Harold

Tarbell, Ida
Taylor, Graham Romeyn Jr.
Tead, Ordway
Teller, Sidney
Terpenning, Walter

Todd, A. J.
Tucker, Mr. and Mrs. Carll
Twentieth Century Fund

University of Chicago Settlement

Van Kleeck, Mary

Wanger, Walter
Warburg, Felix
Warburg, James P.
Warburg, Paul
Warburg, Mrs. Paul

Weybright, Victor
Whaley, Nell
Whipple, Mrs. Katherine Wells (Leon)
Wilbur, Walter
Wile, Dr. Ira S.

Williams, Whiting
Winslow, Dr. C. E. A.
Wise, Rabbi Stephen S.
Wood, Arthur Evans

Young, Owen

Zuber, Mrs. Lucy Lay

18

An Inventory of the Papers of Louis H. Towley

PREPARED BY
John M. Herrick

SWB
T659

Towley, Louis Heiberg 1904-1959

Papers, 1925-1966

114 folders

The papers of Louis Towley were deposited in the Social Welfare History Archives Center of the University of Minnesota Libraries by Mrs. Louis (Marie) Towley in 1965. This collection, comprising five linear feet, is composed of the personal and professional papers of Towley, late professor of social work at the George Warren Brown School of Social Work, Washington University, St. Louis, Missouri. Correspondence, both personal and professional, constitutes a large portion of the collection, yet there is also a large section of articles, speeches and notes on all facets of social work and social work education. One major section contains class materials, notes, outlines and examinations given by Towley at George Warren Brown in the fields of public welfare administration, interpretation of public welfare, social work philosophy, and professional ethics and standards.

Louis Towley's professional background includes undergraduate work at Gustavus Adolphus College, St. Peter, Minnesota, and graduate work at the University of Minnesota in comparative literature and 18th-century drama. After a period of teaching and later, newspaper work, Towley entered the field of public welfare during 1934 in Minnesota. He held various positions in the field, among them, publicity director of the Minnesota Civil Works Administration and Emergency Relief Administration in 1934, as well as complaint correspondent and supervisor of correspondence and referrals. During 1936-1937, he was special assistant to the Director of Coordinated Field Services for the Minnesota Board of Control. From 1937-1942 Towley served as assistant to the Director of Public Welfare Assistance, Minnesota Division of Social Welfare, and just prior to World War II, he was made head of the Bureau of Procedures and Systems for the Minnesota Division of Social Welfare.

The war years made it necessary for the remaining staff (those who did not go into military service) to shift from one job to another and to care for several functions as staff shortages required. From 1942 until the fall of 1946, he was at one time or another Acting Chief of Public Assistance, supervisor of the field staff, supervisor of the Bureau of Procedures and Systems, and special assistant to the Director of Social Welfare. Towley's work always centered primarily on policy and procedural development by the state agencies that administered and integrated a program of public welfare services, financial and non-financial.

From September, 1944, to June, 1945, he was visiting Professor of Social Work at George Warren Brown School of Social Work. In the spring quarter, 1944, he taught a seminar in the Graduate School at the University of Minnesota where he had previously lectured to various classes in social work. Towley was made a full-time member of the faculty at George Warren Brown in 1946, where he taught until his death in 1959.

On a number of occasions Towley spoke at social work conferences, state, regional and national, usually on topics in the areas of public relations, public welfare policy and administration, community relationships and board functions, professional responsibilities and social work ethics. Many of these speeches are included in the collection.

From 1936 until his death Towley wrote for professional journals; this writing was largely topical with occasional papers on social welfare principles and philosophy. The collection indicates Towley's long-time interest centering on the professional obligations to communities that authorize and sponsor social welfare services. Towley's divergent interests are reflected in the many non-professional, that is, non-public welfare oriented writings contained in the collection. They include two unpublished novels, several short stories, assorted poems, editorials and book reviews. Towley's famous "Gover'ment Cow", a satire on New Deal rural relief measures (Survey Graphic, December, 1936), and the laudatory correspondence at the time of its publication serve as indications of his wide interests. Correspondence with musicians Dimitri Mitropoulos, Ernst Krenek and others, as well as with historian Douglas Southall Freeman demonstrate Towley's breadth of interests.

The collection has been arranged in seven sections, largely following the personal and professional life of Towley. These sections are:

1. Correspondence: personal, family, general, 1925-1959 (Folders 2-10)

2. Correspondence: professional, 1935-1959 (Folders 11-30)

3. Conference speeches with surrounding correspondence, 1940-1959 (Folders 31-57)

4. Speeches and articles, 1935-1959 (Folders 58-66)

5. Unpublished writings: novels, plays, skits and short stories, (Folders 67-77)

6. George Warren Brown School of Social Work, Washington University, St. Louis, Missouri: Curriculum materials, 1944-1959 (Folders 78-113)

7. Towley, Mrs. Marie. Correspondence, 1960-1966 (Folder 114)

SECTION 1. CORRESPONDENCE - PERSONAL, FAMILY, GENERAL, 1925-1959
            (Folders 2-10)

(Folder 1 contains biographical material, bibliographies of Towley's writings, and a portrait photograph).

Folders 2-10 trace the life of Towley from his undergraduate days at Gustavus Adolphus College, St. Peter, Minnesota, to his last days as Professor of Social Work at Washington University, St. Louis, Missouri. Letters between Towley and Professors Oscar Firkins and Guy Stanton Ford of the University of Minnesota reflect his desire to study literature in the Graduate School (Folder 3).

In his later years, Towley corresponded with Paul U. Kellogg, editor of the Survey; Mrs. Gertrude Springer, associate editor of the Survey; and other famous figures in the field of social welfare. Indicative of his wide interests are correspondence with Dimitri Mitropoulos, prominent orchestra conductor; Ernst Krenek, contemporary composer; and Douglas Southall Freeman, civil war historian and biographer of Robert E. Lee (Folders 2-10).

The correspondence in this section is not directly related to Towley's career in social welfare. The letters reflect instead his warm family life and the numerous interests and friendships developed in a life-time.

SECTION 2. CORRESPONDENCE - PROFESSIONAL, 1935-1959 (Folders 11-30)

From 1934 until 1946, Towley held various positions with the Minnesota Department of Welfare. The professional correspondence up to 1946 shows the activities he performed in Minnesota as well as the struggles occurring within the Welfare Department. Towley participated in numerous conferences on social and public welfare in Minnesota and around the United States. As issues arose, Towley never hesitated to comment on them. His professional correspondence is therefore reflective of attitudes within the social welfare professions (Folders 11-16).

In 1946, Towley accepted a full-time teaching position at the George Warren Brown School of Social Work, Washington University, St. Louis, Missouri. Correspondence with Benjamin Youngdahl, Dean of George Warren Brown, records this venture and later, the development of Towley's social work courses. Until his death in 1959, Towley continued to be an active participant in numerous social welfare conferences. This section of correspondence shows the many conferences he attended and the discussion of topics his speeches always precipitated (Folders 17-30).

Folders 11-15	1935-1945. There is no correspondence for 1938-1939 in the collection. These folders contain laudatory "puffs" on the article "Gover'ment Cow", published in 1936, as well as materials on the various social work conferences attended by Towley. References to the impact of World War II are scattered throughout this section.
Folders 16-20	1946-1949. Material re: Towley's resignation from the Minnesota Department of Public Welfare and his teaching position at Washington University; social welfare conferences and public welfare topics.
Folders 21-23	1950-1959. Correspondence with officials of Washington University, Benjamin E. Youngdahl (Dean of the George Warren Brown School of Social Work), social work and social welfare organizations, and many leaders of the social welfare professions. Towley discussed such topics as social work education, welfare boards, professionalization of social workers, social action, case work, academic freedom and public welfare administration.
SECTION 3.	**CONFERENCE SPEECHES WITH SURROUNDING CORRESPONDENCE, 1940-1959 (Folders 31-57)**
Folder 31	1940-1941. Minnesota Welfare Conferences. Material re: social service, welfare boards.
Folder 32	May 28-June 2, 1941. National Conference of Social Work. Contains Towley's papers, "The Use of Case Material for the Interpretation of Case Work--by the Public Agency," "The Rural Worker: What Worker Do We Want?," and "Social Action and Professional Responsibility."
Folder 33	April 23-26, 1941. Missouri Field Staff. Concerning public relations and social work.
Folder 36	1946. National Conference of Social Work. Papers: among them materials by Jane M. Hoey, Elizabeth and Karl de Schweinitz.
Folder 37	1948-1951. Materials relating to the Red Cross Home Service and the development of the local chapter staff in referral service, including mat-

	erials on the role of the family in a youth's career plans.
Folder 40-41	1949-1953. Oklahoma Department of Public Welfare consultative materials. Towley served as consultant on public welfare administrative procedures.
Folder 42	July 11-13, 1950. Wisconsin Institute for Social Caseworkers. "Social Welfare in a Troubled World."
Folder 43	November 26-28, 1951. Wisconsin State Welfare Conference. Notes for "Public Relations--Everyone's Job."
Folder 45	January 29, 1952. Family Service of Philadelphia. "The Role of the Social Agency in Influencing Community Policy."
Folder 46	November 19-22, 1952. Illinois Welfare Conference. "What Do Board Members Want from Board Service?"
Folder 47	March 7, 1953--April 20, 1953. University of Pittsburgh School of Social Work, Alumni Gathering. "The Aesthetic Component of Social Work."
Folder 50	November 30, 1955. Michigan Welfare Conference. "Critic on the Hearth."
Folder 51	May, 1955. New England Regional Conference of the Child Welfare League of America. "Broad Applications of a Basic Concept" and notes for "The Role of the Social Worker in His Community."
Folder 52	March, 1956. Family Service of St. Paul. Re: role of the private family agency.
Folder 53	May, 1956. National Conference of Social Work. Contains Towley's speeches: "The Board Members' Obligation--Agency Standards" and "Religion and Social Work."
Folder 54	1957. Council on Social Work Education. Curriculum study project on ethics and materials on the components of the social work curriculum.
Folder 55	1958. Wisconsin Welfare Conference. Re: the relationship between the social work profession and the community.

Folder 56   May, 1959. Jewish Family and Community Service. Re: 100th anniversary of the Jewish Family and Community Service, with a speech, "A Mature Agency Looks at the Future."

Folder 57   March, 1959. Minnesota Welfare Conference. Notes for a speech concerning individual social worker's role in general problem solving.

SECTION 4. SPEECHES AND ARTICLES, 1935-1959 (Folders 58-66)

Folder 58   Speeches and Articles, 1939-1943. Re: role of the American Association of Social Workers, social work and public welfare, role of the public assistance agency in family security, with a speech, "Security is More than Bread."

Folder 59   Speeches and Articles, 1943-1945. Re: Church and public welfare, public welfare administration, case work supervision, recruitment of social workers and county welfare services.

Folder 60   Speeches and Articles, 1945-1949. Re: public welfare, social work and philanthropy, welfare boards, public relations and the social agency and society.

Folder 61   Speeches and Articles, (1950-1955?). All the materials in this folder were undated. There are speech notes and paper drafts on social welfare and the welfare state, social action, social casework, county welfare organization and agencies, the Council on Social Work Education, A.D.C., "Notes Towards a Definition of Social Work Method," "Offstage Some Board Members Speak," "An Open Letter to All Kinds of People" and "The Scapegoat as a Diversion."

Folder 62   Speeches and Articles, 1950-1953. Contents: "They Don't See Eye to Eye," "The Climate of Social Work," "The Lengthening Years," "Professional Responsibility in a Democracy," and "Social Work's Function," also contains materials re: criticism of social work and A.D.C. and treason and political campaigning.

Folder 63   Speeches and Articles, 1953-1958. Contents: Ralph A. Fuch's "Our Clients in Mid-Century--Welfare in the Modern State," and Towley's "Footings for the Code of Ethics?," "N.A.S.W.—A Professional Step" and "Professions as Senior Partners of the Citizenry."

Folder 64   Speeches and Articles, 1939-1943. Notes re: protest literature, social work, social action and public welfare.

Folder 66   "Ethics for Social Workers". This paper, presumably written by Towley, appears to be a condensed version of a textbook. It contains important statements on an ethical philosophy for social caseworkers. The materials are supplemented by cases illustrating certain ethical principles.

PARTIAL SUBJECT INVENTORY

The list of subjects cited in the collection is certainly not definitive or all-inclusive. It is intended to serve as a set of guiding signposts to some of the most significant topics and personalities found in the collection. While materials relevant to social work, social action, professionalization, agency activities and public relations are cited in particular folders, these subjects themselves are broad enough to be scattered throughout the entire collection in many more folders than are indicated.

Academic Freedom
    Folders 23-24

Aid to Dependent Children (A.D.C.)
    Folders 61-62, 114

American Association of Schools of Social Work
    Folder 20

American Association of Social Workers
    Folders 15-16, 24-25, 27, 39, 48, 58

American National Red Cross
    Folder 38

American Public Welfare Association
    Folder 29

Bruno, Frank John
    Folders 12, 25-28, 44, 111

Bruno, Joanna Carver Colcord
    Folder 12

Casework
    Folders 21, 32, 36, 42, 61, 65

Child Welfare
    Folders 14, 20

Child Welfare League of America
    Folders 26, 44, 51

Children
    Folders 26, 62

Community Chests
    Folders 14, 18, 26

Community Relations
    Folders 55, 99-101

Community Welfare Councils
    Folder 60

Council on Social Work Education
    Folders 23-25, 51, 61

County Welfare Directors
    Folders 61-62

De Schweinitz, Elizabeth (Mrs. Karl)
    Folder 36

De Schweinitz, Karl
    Folders 27, 36

Family Service Association of America
    Folder 56

Fenlason, Anne
    Folders 58-59, 110

Freeman, Douglas Southall
    Folders 3, 65

"Gover'ment Cow"
    Folders 11, 26

Gray, James
    Folder 14

Group Work
    Folder 28

Hiroshima
    Folder 15

Hoey, Jane
    Folders 24, 36

Hull House Settlement
    Folder 13

Insurance
    Folder 36

Jewish Community Centers Association
    Folder 24

Junior League of St. Louis
    Folder 14

Kellogg, Paul Underwood
    Folders 11-12

Krenek, Ernst
    Folders 3-7, 9

Kurtz, Russell
    Folders 24, 26

La Rochefoucauld
    Folders 24, 26

Literature
    Folder 10

Minnesota Division of Social Welfare
    Folders 15-16

Minnesota Welfare Association
    Folders 29, 34

Missouri Association for Social Welfare
    Folder 14

Mitropoulos, Dimitri
    Folder 8

Music
    Folders 5-9

National Association of Social Workers
    Folders 25-29, 62-63

National Conference on Social Welfare (formerly National Conference
  of Social Work)
    Folders 15, 24, 27-28

Old Age
    Folders 63, 65

Poetry
    Folder 72

Public Assistance: Policies and Procedures
    Folder 98

Public Relations
    Folders 23, 33, 43, 60, 99-101

Public Welfare
    Folders 36, 58-64, 84-96, 102, 112

Public Welfare Administration
    Folders 15, 40-41, 58

Public Welfare Boards
    Folders 36-37, 46, 60, 62

Public Welfare in Minnesota
    Folders 11-16

Public Welfare in St. Louis, Missouri
    Folders 17-30

Recruitment
    Folders 60-61

Red Cross
    Folder 38

Religion
    Folders 27, 53

Retirement
    Folders 63, 65

Richmond, Mary Ellen
    Folders 25-26

Roosevelt, Eleanor
    Folder 11

Roosevelt, Franklin Delano
    Folder 15

Russell Sage Foundation
    Folder 15

St. Louis Council for Parent Education
    Folders 21-22

Schweitzer, Albert
    Folder 10

Social Action
    Folders 32, 45, 61-62, 105-107

Social Group Work
    Folder 28

Social Planning
    Folder 19

Social Planning Council, St. Louis, Missouri
    Folders 19, 24

Social Reform
    Folders 36, 12

Social Welfare (Certain folders are cited here, but almost the entire
  collection contains scattered references to this broad topic.)
    Folders 11-30, 58-66

Social Work
    Folders 19, 33, 47, 55, 58-64, 97, 107-113
  Agencies: Folders 23, 27, 56, 58, 60, 62-63
  Clients: Folders 36, 60
  Education: Folders 23, 61
  Ethics: Folders 54, 63, 66, 110
  Professionalization: Folders 24, 26, 32, 62-63, 107-113
  Recruitment: Folders 60-61
  Rural: Folders 2, 32, 103-104

Springer, Gertrude Hill
    Folders 12-13

Survey (periodical)
    Folders 11-12

Survey Graphic (periodical)
    Folder 19

Towley, Mrs. Louis (Marie)
    Folder 114

University of Minnesota
    Folders 14-15, 58

Vaile, Gertrude
    Folders 16, 25-27

Wallace, Henry
    Folders 17, 25-27

Washington University
    Folders 14, 15, 22-23
  George Warren Brown School of Social Work: Folders 14-16,
    21-22, 24, 37, 61, 78-113

World War II--Social Work in
    Folder 13

Youngdahl, Benjamin Emanuel
    Folders 11-17, 24, 27, 29, 114

Youngdahl, Luther W.
    Folders 17-19

Zaki, Elinor
    Folder 26

FOLDER INVENTORY

Folder

1   Bibliographies, Biographic Materials and a Photograph of Towley.

2   Correspondence: Personal--Family, 1935-1956.

3   Correspondence: Personal, 1926-1947.

4   Correspondence: Personal, 1948-1958.

5   Correspondence: Personal, re: Music, n.d.

6   Correspondence: Personal, re: Music, 1947-1948.

7   Correspondence: Personal, re: Music, 1948-1959.

8   Correspondence: Personal, re: Music--with Dimitri Mitropoulos, Contains Letter Covers and Clippings, 1948-1956.

9   Music: Programs.

10   Newspaper Clippings: 1945-1947. Re: Music, Books, and Albert Schweitzer.

11   Correspondence: Professional, 1935-1941. There is no correspondence for 1938-1939.

12   Correspondence: Professional, 1942.

13   Correspondence: Professional, 1943.

14   Correspondence: Professional, 1944.

15   Correspondence: Professional, 1945.

16   Correspondence: Professional, January-July, 1946.

17   Correspondence: Professional, August-December, 1946.

18   Correspondence: Professional, 1947.

19   Correspondence: Professional, 1948.

20   Correspondence: Professional, 1949.

Folder

21	Correspondence: Professional, 1950.
22	Correspondence: Professional, 1951.
23	Correspondence: Professional, 1952.
24	Correspondence: Professional, 1953.
25	Correspondence: Professional, 1954.
26	Correspondence: Professional, 1955.
27	Correspondence: Professional, 1956.
28	Correspondence: Professional, 1957.
29	Correspondence: Professional, 1958.
30	Correspondence: Professional, 1959.
31	1940, Minnesota State Welfare Conference.
32	1940, National Conference of Social Work: Papers.
33	1940, Missouri Field Staff.
34	1943, National Conference of Social Work: Regional Meeting in St. Louis, Missouri.
35	April 29-30, 1946, Kansas Welfare Conference.
36	1946, National Conference of Social Work: Papers.
37	1948-1950, Notes for Board Members Institute, George Warren Brown School of Social Work.
38	1948-1951, St. Louis Red Cross Workshop.
39	1949-1953, American Association of Social Work: St. Louis Chapter Bulletins.
40	1949-1953, Oklahoma Department of Public Welfare: Consultative Materials.
41	1954, Oklahoma Department of Public Welfare: Consultative Materials.

Folder

42	July 11-13, 1950, Wisconsin Institute For Social Caseworkers.
43	November 26, 1951, Wisconsin Welfare Conference.
44	January 8, 1952, Midwest Regional Conference of the Child Welfare League of America.
45	January 29, 1952, Family Service of Philadelphia.
46	November 19-22, 1952, Illinois Welfare Conference.
47	March 7, 1953--April 20, 1953, University of Pittsburgh, Alumni Gathering--School of Social Work.
48	January 12, 1954--February 22, 1954, South East Texas Institute of the American Association of Social Work.
49	October 26, 1954--July, 1955, Minnesota Welfare Conference.
50	November 30, 1955, Michigan Welfare Conference.
51	May, 1955, New England Regional Conference of the Child Welfare League of America.
52	March, 1956, Family Service of St. Paul.
53	May, 1956, National Conference of Social Work.
54	1957, Council on Social Work Education: Curriculum Study Project.
55	1958, Wisconsin Welfare Conference.
56	May, 1959, Jewish Family and Community Services.
57	March, 1959, Minnesota Welfare Conference.
58	Articles and Speeches, 1939-1943.
59	Articles and Speeches, 1943-1945.
60	Articles and Speeches, 1945-1949.

Folder

61	Articles and Speeches, (1950-1955?).
62	Articles and Speeches, 1950-1953.
63	Articles and Speeches, 1953-1958.
64	Articles and Speeches, 1939-1943: Notes.
65	Book Reviews, 1940-1959.
66	"Ethics for Social Workers". Probably written by Louis Towley.
67	<u>Kort Ekern</u>--Novel by Louis Towley.
68	"Lillo"--Paper for Professor Firkins' Comparative Literature Class, University of Minnesota, Graduate School.
69	Notes for a Novel in Progress by Louis Towley.
70	Notes, Quotes, Quips and Aphorisms.
71	Plays and Skits, 1936-1937.
72	Poems and Jingles.
73	Short Stories, 1936-1937.
74	Stories and Sketches (I).
75	Stories and Sketches (II).
76	<u>Teacher Beware</u>, 1937: Unpublished Novel by Louis Towley, pp. 1-170.
77	<u>Teacher Beware</u>, 1937: Unpublished Novel by Louis Towley, pp. 171-350.
78	Bruno, Frank J., Speeches: 1940-1942.
79	George Warren Brown School of Social Work: Official Materials and Class Schedules.
80	George Warren Brown School of Social Work: Memorial Brochures and Recruitment Bulletins.

Folder

81 George Warren Brown School of Social Work: Comprehensive Examinations, 1947.

82 George Warren Brown School of Social Work: Projected Faculty Writing Project, 1949-1951.

83 George Warren Brown School of Social Work: Administration Papers, 1953-1955.

84 History of Social Welfare: Bibliographies.

85 History of Social Welfare: Notes.

86 History of Social Welfare: Notes Taken in a Class Taught by Frank J. Bruno, 1954-1956.

87 Introduction to Public Welfare: Notes--on History, to 1935.

88 Introduction to Public Welfare: Notes (I).

89 Introduction to Public Welfare: Notes (II).

90 Introduction to Public Welfare: Notes (III).

91 Introduction to Public Welfare: Notes (IV).

92 Introduction to Public Welfare: Notes--re: Grant-in-Aid.

93 Introduction to Public Welfare: Course Outlines and Bibliographies, 1944-1958.

94 Introduction to Public Welfare: Examinations, 1948-1952.

95 Introduction to Public Welfare: Examinations, 1952-1959.

96 Introduction to Public Welfare: Student Papers.

97 Philosophy of Social Work: University of Minnesota, 1944: Notes.

98 Policies and Procedures in Public Assistance: Notes and Materials.

Folder

99	Public Relations and Interpretation: Correspondence, Bibliography, Class Outlines and Examinations, 1946-1959.
100	Public Relations and Interpretation: Lecture Notes (I).
101	Public Relations and Interpretation: Lecture Notes (II).
102	Public Welfare Administration Seminar: Notes and Student Paper.
103	Rural Social Work: Bibliographies, Notes and Class Outlines, 1948-1956 (I).
104	Rural Social Work: Correspondence, Notes, Student Papers and Examinations, 1948-1956 (II).
105	Social Action: Bibliographies, Notes, and Examinations, 1948-1953 (I).
106	Social Action: Bibliographies, Notes, and Examinations, 1948-1953 (II).
107	Social Work as a Profession: Class Notes and Materials (I).
108	Social Work as a Profession: Class Notes and Materials (II).
109	Social Work as a Profession: Class Notes and Materials (III).
110	Social Work as a Profession: Re: Ethics.
111	Social Work as a Profession: Student Papers.
112	Social Work as a Profession: Bibliographies, Examinations, and Class Outlines, 1944-1959.
113	Standards of the Profession: Advanced Social Work Seminar, 1954-1955.
114	Towley, Marie, Correspondence, 1960-1966.

19

An Inventory of the Papers of United Neighborhood Houses, Inc.

PREPARED BY
John M. Herrick

TABLE OF CONTENTS

INTRODUCTION. 1

PARTIAL SUBJECT INVENTORY 3

DESCRIPTION OF THE COLLECTION 14
    1. Administrative -- Policy-Making Committees 14
    2. Subjects and Ad Hoc Committees 29
    3. Member Settlements 44
    4. Associated Organizations 57

TABLE OF CONTENTS TO THE SCRAPBOOKS 74

UNITED NEIGHBORHOOD HOUSES, INC.

SWD5	United Neighborhood Houses, Inc., New York

Papers, 1898-1961

648 folders   88 (ℓ) folders

30 scrapbooks (19 in (ℓ) folders)

The Board of Directors of the United Neighborhood Houses, Inc. of New York City deposited the organization's papers in the Social Welfare History Archives Center in July, 1964. The papers arrived at the Archives Center in two four-drawer filing cabinets and several packing cases. The collection, which contains papers from 1898 to 1961 with the most complete sections from 1919 to 1961, comprises 45 linear feet after cleaning and processing. The Archives staff processed the collection during 1967-1968.

HISTORY:

The United Neighborhood Houses was preceded by the New York Association of Neighborhood Workers. Organized by Mary Kingsbury Simkhovitch and John Lovejoy Elliott on December 11, 1900, the Association's purpose was to "effect cooperation among those neighborhood workers who are working for neighborhood and civic improvement and to promote movements for social progress." It represented one of America's earliest efforts to unite settlement workers in a city-wide federation. The Association was mainly composed of volunteers with its financial obligations met by individual donations and membership dues. In 1919, following a reorganization during the war period, the Association incorporated and became the United Neighborhood Houses. Its purpose was to bring the experience of individual settlement houses in the New York City area to the attention of other houses and persons involved in settlement work and to unite the houses in coordinated projects for improvement of conditions in the crowded tenement areas.

The organization fought for higher standards in housing, for reform of tenement laws and for passage of ordinances requiring recreational facilities and health services for slum dwellers. UNH also pioneered in the field of child labor legislation, and throughout the 1920's agitated for housing reforms, alleviation of unemployment and the special problems of poverty-stricken urban residents. It advocated workman's compensation and during the Depression and its aftermath, studied and advocated relief and work programs. Responding to the reforms enacted in the New Deal, the United Neighborhood Houses played an active role in implementing these programs and advising their planners.

In the World War II era, the United Neighborhood Houses saw new challenges and developed new techniques and programs to cope with the unique problems posed by a domestic society in wartime. In the post-war era, the organization faced the problems of returning servicemen, housing shortages, social readjustment and neighborhood transitions. By conducting studies and absorbing new social work techniques, the organization redefined its objectives and methods to meet the challenges of the expanding city and the changing neighborhoods. Today, the United Neighborhood Houses serves its member settlement houses by helping them expand programs to meet current problems with effective solutions. Some of the recent problems which have confronted United Neighborhood Houses are juvenile delinquency, Day Care Centers, racial discrimination, fair housing, minority problems, recreation and health facilities in slum neighborhoods and urban redevelopment.

UNITED NEIGHBORHOOD HOUSES, INC.

FUNCTION:

The United Neighborhood Houses, in its desire to confront the many problems which no single settlement could solve, established committees to deal with such pressing social problems as housing, unemployment and the need for remedial social welfare legislation. The UNH has followed the precept that the settlement house is a unique social agency whose methods are different from those of other social welfare agencies. First, each settlement must adjust its program to the needs of its particular community. Secondly, the settlement house works with the whole family from pre-school children to the very old. Thirdly, the settlement house works with groups rather than individuals. The settlement house seeks to take whatever groups are indigenous to a given neighborhood and to channel their activities for constructive ends. It becomes a "club house" for the tenement women and the juvenile gangs of the streets. In its early days the UNH encounter the problem of helping immigrants adjust to their new "American" environment. In more recent years, the focus has been on the evolving character of the neighborho in the constantly changing urban setting. Such problems as mental health, civic education, juvenile delinquency, housing, and the socio-economic environment of the urban dweller have all influenced the ecological approach advanced by UNH to meet current difficulties. As the major federation of New York City's settlement UNH has persistently continued its programs in the face of rising administrative and clerical costs. Through its many workshops and committees, both standing and temporary, it has enabled member houses to exchange information and benefit from one another's experiences. It continues to bring them information on settlements and settlement problems--local, national, and international. It has provided skilled staff guidance to member houses on program and administration. Through its financial programs, UNH has tried to help member houses meet their rising deficits.

The League of Mother's Clubs, as the only New York city-wide federation of woman's clubs affiliated with the settlements, has served thousands of mothers from low income neighborhoods. Through its committees and its many special meetings and activities, the League has endeavored to widen the social and educational horizon of its members and make available to them the most recent information on homemaking, child care and training, and civic and social affairs.

ORGANIZATION OF THE COLLECTION:

The processed papers have been arranged as follows: first, papers dealing with administration and policy-making (Board of Directors, Executive Committee, Annual Reports, etc.); second, standing committees; third, "ad hoc" committees and topical materials; fourth, twenty-four scrapbooks of UNH records with a table of contents and six scrapbooks of newspaper clippings.

One caveat must be inserted--any scholar using the collection must consult all sections of the collection in searching for evidence on any particular topic. The scrapbooks often contain basic documentary material not found in the other sections and newspaper clippings which provide a chronology and detail often lacking elsewhere.

UNITED NEIGHBORHOOD HOUSES, INC.

PARTIAL SUBJECT INVENTORY

The list of subjects cited in the collection is certainly not definitive or all-inclusive. It is intended only as an indication of some of the most significant topics and individuals found in the collection. Since information on such prominent people in the organization as Helen M. Harris and Stanley M. Isaacs is scattered throughout the entire collection, they have not been listed in the Partial Subject Inventory. Nor have important records scrapbooks of the United Neighborhood Houses been included because a table of contents has been prepared for them.

ADDAMS, JANE
    Folders 18, 178

ADULT EDUCATION
    Folders 281-282, 397, 407, 537

AGING
    Folders 6, 243, 483

AMERICAN ASSOCIATION OF GROUP WORKERS
    Folder 391

AMERICAN ASSOCIATION OF SOCIAL WORKERS
    Folders 181-183

AMERICAN MEDICAL ASSOCIATION
    Folder 578

AMERICAN NATIONAL RED CROSS
    Folder 190

AMERICAN SOCIAL HEALTH ASSOCIATION   SEE AMERICAN SOCIAL HYGIENE ASSOCIATION

AMERICAN SOCIAL HYGIENE ASSOCIATION
    Folder 191

AMERICANIZATION
    Folders 1-2, 6, 163, 307-311

AMERICANS FOR DEMOCRATIC ACTION
    Folder 188

UNITED NEIGHBORHOOD HOUSES, INC.

ANTI-SEMITISM
    Folders 379, 381

ARTS AND CRAFTS
    Folders 6, 11, 23, 27-29, 54-58, 90, 175, 235, 328

ASSOCIATION FOR IMPROVING THE CONDITIONS OF THE POOR, NEW YORK
    Folders 45, 123, 173

ASSOCIATION OF BROOKLYN SETTLEMENTS
    Folders 481-511

ATHLETIC PROGRAMS
    Folders 64, 298

BALDWIN, ROGER
    Folder 7

BIRTH CONTROL
    Folders 539, 633, 635

BROOKLYN NEIGHBORHOOD HOUSES FUND
    Folders 481-511

CAMPS, SUMMER
    Folder 510

CARE (COOPERATIVE FOR AMERICAN REMITTANCES TO EVERYWHERE, INC.)
    Folder 201

CATHOLIC CHARITIES
    Folder 203

CHARITY ORGANIZATION SOCIETY, NEW YORK
    Folders 97, 126, 202

CHICAGO FEDERATION OF SETTLEMENTS
    Folder 205

CHILD LABOR
    Folder 132

CHILD WELFARE
    Folders 208-219, 577, 637

CHINA (AMERICAN RELIEF PROGRAMS FOR:)
    Folders 184-187, 543

CITY PLANNING
    Folder 220

CIVILIAN CONSERVATION CORPS (CCC)
    Folder 22

CIVILIAN DEFENSE
    Folders 225-226

CIVIL LIBERTIES
    Folders 2, 7, 16, 132-133, 148, 156-157, 172, 216, 301, 316-317, 393
        403, 415, 464, 492, 505, 574, 576, 585-586, 589, 592

CIVIL WORKS ADMINISTRATION
    Folders 227

COMMON HUMAN NEEDS (AUTHOR, CHARLOTTE TOWLE)
    Folder 578

COMMUNISM
    Folders 415, 589

COMMUNITY CHESTS
    Folder 229

CONSUMER PROTECTION
    Folders 38, 65-68, 149, 315, 493-496, 532-535, 623

COUGHLIN, FATHER CHARLES E.
    Folder 403

DAY CARE
    Folders 38-39, 236-271, 412-414, 416, 423

DEPRESSION (CA. 1929)
    Folders 20-21, 45-46, 69, 273, 288, 457, 552

DEVINE, EDWARD THOMAS
    Folder 97

DISCRIMINATION (RACIAL)
    Folders 513, 570

DRAMA
    Folders 90, 327, 438

EARHART, AMELIA
    Folder 275

EDUCATION
    Folders 6, 59, 91, 150, 170-171, 280-287, 443-446, 454

ELLIOTT, JOHN LOVEJOY
    Folders 45, 358, 474

FAIR EMPLOYMENT PRACTISES
    Folder 274

FEDERAL HOUSING ADMINISTRATION
    Folders 103-104, 598, 600

FEDERAL SECURITY AGENCY
    Folder 247

FEDERAL THEATRE PROJECT
    Folder 512

FOREIGN AFFAIRS   SEE ALSO NEUTRALITY
    Folders 6, 11, 47, 91, 519, 581, 585

HALL, HELEN
    Folders 202, 298, 357

HEALTH INSURANCE
    Folders 305-306

HOFFER, JOE R.
    Folder 397

HOPKINS, HARRY LLOYD
    Folder 173, 474

HOUSING
    Folders 2, 6, 11, 21, 33, 39, 65, 86, 94-134, 151-153, 174-175, 221, 224
            393, 418-421, 428-433, 454, 458-459, 504, 512-513, 539, 546-547,
            557, 588-589, 604, 645

HUGHES, CHARLES EVANS
    Folder 460

HULL HOUSE, CHICAGO
    Folder 462

IMMIGRANTS
    Folders 1-2, 6, 163, 231-232, 307-311, 340, 528, 571, 592, 626

INDIANS (AMERICAN)
    Folder 391

INTERNATIONAL CONFERENCE OF SOCIAL WORK
    Folders 329-330, 397

INTERNATIONAL SERVICES AND PROGRAMS
    Folder 543

JUVENILE DELINQUENCY
    Folders 276-279, 325-326, 333-335, 604

KELLOGG, PAUL UNDERWOOD
    Folders 7, 100, 336

KENNEDY, ALBERT JOSEPH
    Folders 7, 55, 91, 384, 570, 588

KOREAN CONFLICT
    Folders 66, 383, 578, 586

LABOR MOVEMENT
    Folders 132, 154, 156, 169, 508, 430-431, 505

LA GUARDIA, FIORELLO
    Folders 95, 122, 126, 437

LEAGUE OF MOTHERS' CLUBS, NEW YORK CITY
    Folders 46, 512, 569

LEHMAN, HERBERT
    Folders 99-100, 112, 143, 156, 159, 325-326

LINDEMAN, EDUARD CHRISTIAN
    Folders 285, 467

McCARTHY, JOSEPH R.
    Folders 156-157, 325-326, 592

McDOWELL, JOHN
    Folders 11, 298, 570-571, 576

MENTAL HEALTH AND MENTAL ILLNESS
    Folders 160-161, 199

MOSES, ROBERT
    Folder 390

MUMFORD, LEWIS
    Folder 11

MURRAY, CLYDE
    Folder 313

MUSIC
    Folders 175, 298, 467

MUSTE, A. J.
    Folder 45

NARCOTIC ADDICTS
    Folder 469

NATIONAL ASSOCIATION OF SOCIAL WORKERS
    Folders 392-393

NATIONAL CONFERENCE OF SOCIAL WORK
    Folders 394-398

NATIONAL CONFERENCE ON SOCIAL WELFARE
    Folder 398

NATIONAL EDUCATION ASSOCIATION
    Folder 399

NATIONAL FEDERATION OF SETTLEMENTS AND NEIGHBORHOOD CENTERS
    Folders 125, 193, 310, 493, 570-604

NATIONAL JEWISH WELFARE BOARD
    Folder 400

NATIONAL INDUSTRIAL RECOVERY ACT
    Folder 7

NATIONAL RECREATION ASSOCIATION
    Folder 277

NATIONAL SOCIAL WELFARE ASSEMBLY
    Folder 401

NATIONAL URBAN LEAGUE
    Folders 127, 402

NATIONAL YOUTH ADMINISTRATION
    Folders 22, 62

NATURALIZATION
    Folder 528

NEGROES
    Folders 6, 376, 402, 570

NEUTRALITY
    Folder 19

NEW YORK CITY EMERGENCY RELIEF BUREAU
    Folder 538

NURSERY SCHOOLS
    Folders 289, 467

UNITED NEIGHBORHOOD HOUSES, INC.

NYE, GERALD P.
    Folder 19

PEACE ORGANIZATIONS
    Folders 464, 559

PECK, LILLIE
    Folder 313

PLANNED PARENTHOOD
    Folders 633, 635

PLAY SCHOOLS ASSOCIATION
    Folder 441

POLICE, TRAINING
    Folders 425-426

POVERTY
    Folders 45, 173-177

PSYCHIATRIC SOCIAL WORK   SEE SOCIAL WORK, PSYCHIATRIC

PUBLIC EDUCATION ASSOCIATION
    Folders 444-446

PUBLIC HEALTH
    Folders 155-156

PUERTO RICANS
    Folders 15, 337, 340

RECREATION
    Folders 12, 60, 62-63, 91-92, 116, 118, 128, 163, 199, 208-209, 290
        381, 402, 424, 442, 450-453, 467, 512, 548, 615-622, 636, 640-641,
        645

RED CROSS   SEE AMERICAN NATIONAL RED CROSS

REFUGEES
    Folder 563

RELIEF
    Folders 7, 20-21, 163, 172-177, 273, 415, 458, 604

ROOSEVELT, ELEANOR
    Folders 298, 386

SEX EDUCATION
    Folders 6, 454

SIMKHOVITCH, MARY K.
    Folders 1, 96, 100, 115, 173, 298, 313, 390, 474, 579, 593

SLUMS
    Folders 16, 95-97, 132, 512

SOCIAL ACTION
    Folders 7, 45, 70, 307, 394-398

SOCIAL EDUCATION
    Folders 464-465

SOCIAL HYGIENE
    Folder 191

SOCIAL SECURITY
    Folders 65, 158-160, 247

SOCIAL WELFARE, LAWS AND LEGISLATION, U.S.
    Folders 119, 132-159, 223-224, 272, 310-311, 505, 533-535, 555, 557, 574, 598

SOCIAL WORK
    Ethics
        Folder 6
    Professionalization
        Folders 91, 325-326, 646
    Psychiatric
        Folders 315, 384, 411

SOCIAL WORK AND THE CHURCH
    Folders 257-259

SOCIAL WORK TODAY (PERIODICAL)
    Folder 393

SURVEY (PERIODICAL)
    Folders 336, 579

SWOPE, GERARD P.
    Folder 7

THOMAS, NORMAN
    Folder 122

TOWLE, CHARLOTTE
    Folder 578

UNITED NEIGHBORHOOD HOUSES, INC.
    Administration
        Folders 1-2, 11, 30-53, 164-168, 449, 466, 550-553, 620
    Anniversaries
        Folders 291-298, 352, 356, 385
    Casework
        Folders 163, 168, 202, 312-326, 411, 467, 545, 580, 617
    Finances
        Folders 11-12, 15, 30-36, 69-89, 91, 93, 428, 497-501, 536, 539-540,
            604, 626, 638
    Group Work
        Folders 12, 60, 90, 163, 198-199, 303, 313, 367, 427, 480, 544, 615-
            622, 643, 645
    History
        Folders 1-2, 6-7, 8-17, 20-21, 48, 168-169, 206, 291-293, 303, 348,
            357, 373-374, 378, 385, 465, 482, 491, 508, 557, 566, 594
    Neighborhoods
        Folders 8-11, 61, 300, 325-326, 403-405, 449, 470, 491, 579, 588
        Ethnic Composition
            Folders 380, 529
    Personnel
        Folders 595, 632
    Philosophy of
        Folders 197, 205, 457-463, 467

UNEMPLOYMENT
    Folders 20-22, 45-46, 58, 91, 132-133, 173-177, 288, 437, 457, 464, 539

UNITED NATIONS
    Folders 601-603

VETERANS
    Folders 103, 476, 480

VOLUNTEERS
    Folders 111, 180, 190, 287, 303, 313, 477-478, 646

WAGNER, ROBERT FERDINAND
    Folder 459

WALD, LILLIAN D.
    Folders 70, 159, 173, 474

WALKER, JAMES J.
    Folder 122

WELFARE COUNCIL OF NEW YORK CITY
    Folders 44, 538, 587, 605-648

WELFARE AGENCIES, PUBLIC AND PRIVATE (DEBATE OVER OBJECTIVES)
    Folders 179, 202, 257

WHITE HOUSE CONFERENCE ON CHILDREN AND YOUTH, 1950
    Folder 208

WORLD WAR, 1914-1918, SETTLEMENTS
    Folder 91

WORLD WAR, 1939-1945, SETTLEMENTS
    Folders 26, 46-47, 102-103, 120 236, 251, 256, 285, 358, 367, 476, 568

WPA (WORKS PROGRESS ADMINISTRATION)
    Folders 22, 55, 58, 61, 91, 100, 173-177, 437, 474, 512, 526, 528,
        538-539, 564

YOUTH
    Folders 62-63, 219, 276-279, 333-335, 427, 434, 467, 480, 511, 629,
        647-648

UNITED NEIGHBORHOOD HOUSES, INC.

FOLDER TITLE AND DESCRIPTION OF CONTENTS	FOLDER

ADMINISTRATIVE -- POLICY-MAKING

Association of Neighborhood Workers, 1898-1919   1
    The Association of Neighborhood Workers was the predecessor organization of the United Neighborhood Houses. The folder contains a copy of Mary Simkhovitch's "A Settlement Catechism"; bulletins of the Association of Neighborhood Workers; analyses of the Association's yearly activities, committee work and special projects; a brief summary of United Neighborhood House work to 1930; minutes of the Association, 1913-1916; references to the Association from Hartley House News, Willoughby House annual reports, and Riis House; 1916 report on the theory and practice of girls' work.

Historical materials, 1919-1935   2
    An historical survey of the executive leadership of UNH; copies of important correspondence regarding housing; notes about important items retained in UNH files, e.g. original constitution, data surrounding the founding; Americanization of immigrants; clippings concerning UNH's response to the Lusk Committee's charges that the settlements were "breeding grounds of sedition and anarchy."

Certificate of Incorporation, 1920   3
    Statement of purpose.

Charter Revision Committee, 1923   4
    The UNH Executive Committee set up this committee to consider revision of UNH's charter.

Constitution and Bylaws, 1942-1947   5
    Bylaws and revisions adopted at UNH's annual meeting, 1947.

Annual Meetings, 1925-1929   6
    Correspondence, programs, reports of various committees, minutes; topics discussed are health, old age pensions for social workers, ethical standards in social work, social education of youth, Negroes in New York, American foreign policy, report of Arts and Festivals Committee, report of UNH on future problems in interracial harmony, functions of the settlement, summer camps, sex and social education, assimilation of the Southern Italian family; notes of a speech by Carleton J. H. Hayes on nationalism and imperialism and U.S. foreign policy; includes photographs used in annual report.

Annual Meetings, 1931-1934, 1937   7
    Correspondence, minutes of Boys' and Girls' Directors Round Table, press releases; topics include unemployment, inflation, effect of New Deal programs on capitalism, synopsis of UNH committee work during each year, relief and industry, group work, unionization, progressive education, social action and

FOLDER TITLE AND DESCRIPTION OF CONTENTS	FOLDER

the settlement, racketeering, the role of the settlement in a democracy. Speeches: A. J. Muste, chairman of the Conference for Progressive Labor Action, "Are We Moving Toward a Dictatorship?"; Gerard Swope, President of General Electric Company, on the National Industrial Recovery Act; "Adult Education in the Settlements"; Stanley M. Isaacs and Albert J. Kennedy, "The Influence of the UNH--What Has Been and Can Be Accomplished"; Goodwin B. Watson, "The New America"; Roger Baldwin, Director of the American Civil Liberties Union, "Patriots, Aliens and Reds"; Paul U. Kellogg, editor of the <u>Survey</u>, "Opportunities Before the Settlements."

Annual Meetings, <u>Proceedings</u>, 1939   8-10
    Copies of the complete <u>Proceedings</u>; settlement methods, administration and program, the concept of "neighborhood," public and private recreational programs, labor and the settlement, consumer interests.

Annual Meetings, 1940, 1942-1945   11
    Correspondence, annual reports; settlements' social action program, finances, the neighborhood as a social unit, the returning soldier, wartime domestic crises, consumer interests, unemployment, volunteers, dissolution of WPA's housing program, expansion of UNH and theory and practice of its committees, finances, functions of music in the settlement, relation of settlements to groups in neighborhoods, dramatics, festival arts projects, intersettlement works; telegram from Lewis Mumford on American foreign relations. Speeches: Stanley M. Isaacs on reorganization of UNH along "democratic" lines; John McDowell, of the National Federation of Settlements, "Current Trends in the Settlement Movement." Participants included Helen Hall, Stanley M. Isaacs, Mary Simkhovitch.

Annual Meetings, 1946-1947, 1949   12
    Correspondence, memoranda; housing, day care, finances, unemployment, fund-raising in New York City, fine arts, consumer interests. Speeches: Edward Corsi, the shift from the settlement's role in providing recreation to training of community leaders; outline of Grace Gosselin's speech on the shift in settlement objectives; address on "Why Are Public Assistance Costs Rising?"

Annual Meeting, 1950   13-14
    These folders contain correspondence, reports, memoranda dealing with annual meetings, the history of UNH and its predecessor organization. "Fifty Years of Service," a synopsis of UNH's activities is included.

Annual Meetings, 1951-1952   15
    Correspondence, annual reports, financial statements, publications, press releases, programs, committee materials;

FOLDER TITLE AND DESCRIPTION OF CONTENTS	FOLDER

    the Korean conflict, civil liberties, consumer interests, Puerto Rican migration into various neighborhoods, financing non-sectarian neighborhood work, housing, urban development, Association of Brooklyn Settlements. A copy of a speech by Ollie Randall, "Services for the Aging in a Neighborhood Setting" is included.

Annual Meetings, 1953-1954   16
    Correspondence, agenda, financial reports, committee lists, publicity releases; address of A. A. Berle, Jr. re New York City and the slum problem; papers about the 1954 Supreme Court desegregation decision.

Annual Meetings, 1955-1956   17
    Correspondence, agenda, guest lists, financial statements, press releases; analysis of UNH's projects and activities. Speeches: Helen M. Harris on changing objectives of UNH; Henry Epstein, Deputy Mayor of New York, "Blueprint for Youth"; speech notes of Helen M. Harris and Stanley M. Isaacs.

Annual Luncheons, 1925-1929   18
    Correspondence, reservations lists, programs; speakers included Jane Addams, Mary Simkhovitch, Governor Alfred E. Smith, John L. Elliott.

Annual Luncheons, 1935, 1937   19
    Correspondence, reservations lists, invitations, seating lists; speakers included Louis Fischer, Stanley M. Isaacs, Gerald P. Nye, Dorothy Detzer on such topics as "Preparedness for Peace."

Record of Work, 1929-1934   20
    Papers on the Depression, unemployment, relief, settlement financing.

Record of Work, 1935-1936   21
    Papers on housing, unemployment, relief.

Record of Work, 1937-1938   22
    Papers on the National Youth Administration, WPA, Social Service Employee's Union, CCC Camps.

Record of Work, 1938-1939   23
    Some topics are housing, music, dramatics, visual arts.

Record of Work, 1939-1940   24
    Committee reports; housing, arts and crafts, education.

Record of Work, 1940-1941   25
    Committee reports; housing, juvenile work, finances.

UNITED NEIGHBORHOOD HOUSES, INC.

FOLDER TITLE AND DESCRIPTION OF CONTENTS	FOLDER

Record of Work, 1943-1944   26
    Topics include wartime relief, problems of families with members in the armed forces.

Record of Work, 1947   27-29
    Topics include art, drama and music in the settlements.

Board of Directors, Agenda and Minutes, 1941-1946   30
    Includes financial statements, member house dues records, planning notes for special conferences.

Board of Directors, Agenda and Minutes, 1946-1948   31
    Bylaws, financial statements, papers on UNH's function, current programs and future needs of the settlements.

Board of Directors, Agenda and Minutes, 1948-1950   32
    Financial statements and regular Board papers.

Board of Directors, Agenda and Minutes, 1950-1951   33
    Press releases, financial statements, analyses of financial contributions; pamphlet: "Integration in Housing."

Board of Directors, Agenda and Minutes, 1951-1952   34
    Bylaws, annual reports, financial statements.

Board of Directors, Agenda and Minutes, 1952-1953   35
    Bylaws, annual reports, financial statements; housing, recent immigration to the settlement neighborhoods.

Board of Directors, Agenda and Minutes, 1953-1954   36
    Settlement administration, financing, current problems facing the settlements.

Board of Directors, Agenda and Minutes, 1954-1955   37
    Finances, day care, juvenile delinquency.

Board of Directors, Agenda and Minutes, 1955-1956   38
    Immigration, social action, milk prices, day care, financing, mental health.

Board of Directors, Agenda and Minutes, 1956-1957   39
    Committee reports, financial statements; day care, housing.

Board of Directors, Correspondence, 1933-1940   40
    The functions of the Board are discussed.

Board of Directors, Member House Directors, 1949-1953   41
    Lists of member house directors used by UNH.

Board of Directors, Nominating Committee, 1927-1947   42
    Lists of Board members, correspondence concerning nominations.

UNITED NEIGHBORHOOD HOUSES, INC.

FOLDER TITLE AND DESCRIPTION OF CONTENTS	FOLDER
Board of Directors, Nominating Committee, 1947-1948 Lists of Board members, correspondence concerning nominations.	43
Board of Directors, Tenative Plan for Affiliation with the Welfare Council of New York City, 1947-1948 Correspondence re proposed affiliation of UNH with the Council.	44
Executive Committee, 1927-1935 Correspondence, minutes, lists of committee members; relief and unemployment, social action, poverty. Correspondents include the Association for Improving the Conditions of the Poor, John L. Elliott, A. J. Muste.	45
Executive Committee, 1935-1939 Correspondence, minutes, reports from UNH's standing committees; German treatment of minority groups, relief administration controversy, financing, housing, plans of member houses for 1936, the Depression.	46
Executive Committee, 1940 Correspondence, minutes; foreign affairs, housing, finances, relations of UNH to member houses.	47
Executive Committee, Nominating Committee, 1940 History of the UNH, functions of the Committee on Structure.	48
Executive Committee, Officers, 1919-1929 Lists of Executive officers.	49
Executive Committee, Policy and Reorganization Committee, 1934-1947 Correspondence, minutes, papers of the committee established to redefine the goals and activities of UNH.	50
Executive Committee, Committee on Scope and Planning, 1928 Correspondence, minutes of the committee established to acquaint member settlements with the "plan" and "scope" of UNH activities.	51
Executive Committee, Committee on Structure, 1939 Papers reflecting the possibility of reorganizing UNH; reports of special meetings held by Stanley M. Isaacs.	52
Executive Committee, Settlement Board Liaison Representatives, 1940-1941 Correspondence, lists of representatives from member settlements who served as liaisons to UNH's executive board.	53
Arts and Festivals Committee, 1920-1937 Correspondence, minutes; publicity for settlement meetings; entertainment, art festivals.	54

UNITED NEIGHBORHOOD HOUSES, INC.

FOLDER TITLE AND DESCRIPTION OF CONTENTS	FOLDER
Arts, (Visual) Committee, 1932-1940 Correspondence, minutes, reports: "A Survey of Arts and Crafts in New York City for 1932-1933," WPA art projects, Albert J. Kennedy on the necessity for art in the settlements.	55
Art Committee, 1959 Correspondence about an exhibition of paintings produced in the settlements at the Guggenheim museum.	56
Dramatic Committee, 1939-1940 Correspondence, memoranda to settlement directors on the use of dramatics in the settlements.	57
Music Committee, 1939-1940 Papers dealing with the use of music in the settlements and the employment of "relief" musicians under WPA.	58
Boys' and Girls' Workers Committee, 1924-1936 Correspondence, minutes, bulletins; education, social objectives, group organization, past activities, therapeutic effects of dancing, opportunities for urban boys in rural areas.	59
Boys' and Girls' Workers Committee, 1939-1940 Correspondence, minutes; recreation and its philosophy, youth club leadership, group work methods. In December, 1940, the committee changed its name to the Committee on Group Work.	60
Boys' and Girls' Workers Committee, Sub-committee on Use of Neighborhood and Community Resources, 1934-1940 Correspondence, papers dealing with the removal of WPA personnel from settlements and the difficulty of developing a suitable method for analyzing the features of a neighborhood.	61
Boys' and Girls' Workers Committee, Sub-committee on Vocational Guidance Correspondence, minutes, agenda; Federal Security Agency, National Youth Administration, employment for youth.	62
Girls' Workers Committee, 1916-1928 Correspondence, minutes; scholarships, recreation. The Playground and Recreation Association is a prominent correspondent. A 1916 report on child development from 6 to 12 years of age is included.	63
Boys' Athletic League, 1932 Correspondence concerning the decision of the Athletic League to finance itself independently of UNH.	64
Consumer Committee, 1936-1951 Correspondence, papers; consumer protection, social security, community health services, food prices, housing.	65

UNITED NEIGHBORHOOD HOUSES, INC.

<u>FOLDER TITLE AND DESCRIPTION OF CONTENTS</u>   <u>FOLDER</u>

Consumer Committee, 1952-1953   66
    Correspondence, minutes; legislative proposals, price stabili-
    zation, domestic effects of the Korean conflict.

Consumer Committee, Consumer Council to the Governor, 1956   67
    Statement by Dr. Persia Campbell re consumer credit legislation.

Consumer Committee, New York City Milk Consumers' Protective   68
Committee, 1934-1938
    Correspondence, papers; milk consumption among the poor, milk
    prices, WPA and milk prices.

Finance Committee, 1925-1935   69
    Minutes; analysis of member house dues; dues receipts; finan-
    cial statements, 1926-1930; lists of individual contributors,
    1927-1931; appeals. The papers reflect the financial crisis
    of UNH during the Depression.

Finance, Appeals, 1925-1937   70
    Correspondence, appeal lists; social action program, settle-
    ment philosophy; statement of Lillian Wald on the importance
    of UNH; special appeal for victims of the Louisville flood.

Finance, Appeals, 1938-1945   71
    Correspondence of Stanley M. Isaacs regarding UNH contribu-
    tions.

Finance, Appeals, 1945-1948.   72

Finance, Appeals, 1948-1950.   73

Finance, Appeals, 1951-1952.   74

Finance, Appeals, 1952-1953.   75

Finance, Foundation Appeals, 1939-1945   76
    Brief description of the work of UNH; correspondence.

Finance, Member House Dues, 1927-1940   77
    Correspondence, dues receipts from other member houses; study
    showing number of people using various settlements, ca. 1927.

Finance, Prospective Member Houses, 1935-1937   78
    Correspondence and materials re organizations considering
    membership in UNH.

Financial Statements, 1923-1946   79
    UNH financial statements, monthly and yearly.*

Financial Statements, 1948-1952.   80

*Similar items filed in Legal Folder 1.

UNITED NEIGHBORHOOD HOUSES, INC.

FOLDER TITLE AND DESCRIPTION OF CONTENTS	FOLDER

Financial Statements, 1952-1954.* ... 81

Finances, Greater New York Fund, 1939-1947 ... 82
    Correspondence, itemized reports of expenditures, applications for admission, statement on the GNYF purpose, financial statements.

Finances, Greater New York Fund, 1948-1949. ... 83

Finances, Greater New York Fund, 1950-1952 ... 84
    Explanatory materials for fund applicants; contains a copy of UNH's application for 1952.

Finances, Re Brunie Committee, Greater New York Fund, 1951-1952 ... 85
    The Brunie Committee wanted to give the fund-gathering federations of New York City a free hand in raising funds from privately owned firms by getting the Greater New York Fund out of that field. The papers reflect UNH's role in this controversy.

Finances, Greater New York Fund - Discretionary Grants, Field Service Project, 1945-1948 ... 86
    Correspondence, applications of UNH to GNYF for discretionary grants stating purposes for the grants, indicating research projects of UNH; some topics are recreation, housing.

Finances, Prospective Contributors, 1947-1950 ... 87
    Lists of prospective contributors.

Finances, Retirement and Pension Plan, 1946-1949 ... 88
    UNH conducted a survey of its member houses re instituting a common retirement plan. Correspondence, reports, pension plan proposals, and article reprints are included.

Finances, Salary Questionnaire, 1949 ... 89
    Questionnaires sent out by UNH to member houses and returned by them with data on salaries paid to all personnel, including a final summary of salary statistics and recommendations.

Groupworkers and Dramatic Specialists, 1945 ... 90
    Minutes and announcements re role of dramatics in group work.

Headworkers Group, 1932-1945 ... 91
    Correspondence, minutes, agenda, reports, questionnaires sent to members to reassess objectives. Post-war construction, art exhibits, recreation, personnel recruitment, Albert J. Kennedy's report on settlements as socialization factors, financing, social education, declining sense of social responsibility of settlements post-World War I, Japan, professionalization, WPA, unemployment.

*Similar items filed in Legal Folder 1.

UNITED NEIGHBORHOOD HOUSES, INC.

FOLDER TITLE AND DESCRIPTION OF CONTENTS	FOLDER

Headworkers Group, 1946-1951 — 92
Correspondence, minutes, agenda, reports; some subjects are relation of UNH to member settlements, consumer interests, recreation, youth programs.

Headworkers Group, 1951-1952 — 93
Correspondence, minutes, agenda, reports, bylaws; financing, support for non-sectarian agencies, civil defense, Greater New York Fund, employment, housing, Puerto Rican immigrants.

Housing Committee, 1920-1927 — 94
Correspondence, minutes, publicity notice of Mrs. Samuel A. Barnett's lectures on housing; New York City Building Code and Tenement House Laws, low income housing, the Advisory Housing Conference of New York City, UNH's "committee of experts" to advise the settlements on housing and to formulate a suitable program for relief of tenement residents.

Housing Committee, 1927-1929 — 95
Correspondence, agenda; "Role of Private Initiative in Solving the Housing Problem," UNH's recommendations for tenement reform and slum eradication, history of slum problem in New York City, Mayor Fiorello La Guardia's answer to social program.

Housing Committee, 1930-1934 — 96
Correspondence, minutes, news releases, summaries of committee activities; Reconstruction Finance Corporation, old-law tenements. Stanley M. Isaacs and Mary Simkhovitch are prominent correspondents.

Housing Committee, 1936 — 97
Correspondence, minutes, agenda; New York City housing projects, tenement houses. Among organizations and correspondents are Mrs. Samuel I. Rosenman, Welfare Council of New York City, Edward T. Devine, Stanley M. Isaacs; also included are studies of New York City land rental and land usage by income group, and tenement houses.

Housing Committee, 1936-1937 — 98
Correspondence, minutes, reports; Wagner-Steagall Housing Bill and tenants' responses to the legislation, tenement housing inspectors. Also includes a statement of Harold Ickes on housing reform.

Housing Committee, 1937-1938 — 99
Correspondence, minutes; analyses of housing legislation, history of the housing committee. Among correspondents are Mrs. Samuel I. Rosenman, Herbert M. Lehman.

Housing Committee, 1939 — 100
Correspondence, minutes, agenda, reports; Paul Kellogg's committee for housing, Mary Simkhovitch's history of housing in New York City, WPA and housing.

UNITED NEIGHBORHOOD HOUSES, INC.

FOLDER TITLE AND DESCRIPTION OF CONTENTS | FOLDER

Housing Committee, 1939-1940 — 101
Correspondence, minutes, agenda, reports; housing legislation, low-rent housing, financing housing projects.

Housing Committee, 1941-1942 — 102
Correspondence, minutes, agenda, reports; incomes of tenement families, effect of war on rentals, housing legislation.

Housing Committee, 1943-1944 — 103
Correspondence, minutes; rats in New York City, unsanitary housing conditions, housing for veterans, war-time housing, Federal Housing Administration.

Housing Committee, 1944-1947 — 104
Correspondence, minutes, materials used to inform a committee on old law tenements from the Federal Public Housing Authority; reports on community facilities programs in New York City housing projects; "More than a Roof," a pamphlet on tenement housing.

Housing Committee, 1948-1952 — 105
Correspondence, memoranda, chiefly concerned with the decision of the New York City Housing Authority to build housing projects with insufficient space allotments for nursery schools and recreation, conflicts between the Housing Authority and agencies operating community facilities, rent control, housing codes.

Housing Committee, Demonstration Area Study, 1934-1937 — 106
Papers re the study of space use in New York City.

Housing Committee, Joint Advisory Committee on Community Activities in Housing Projects, 1940-1946 — 107
Correspondence, minutes. The committee was formed to analyze and plan community activities such as recreation. A UNH pamphlet, "Community Relations on Public Housing Projects Areas," is included.

Housing Committee, Housing Projects, 1951-1952 — 108
Pamphlets re housing projects both pending construction and already completed.

Housing Committee, Housing Voice, 1937 — 109
A paper issued to convey the status of housing legislation and to record the Housing Committee's activities.

Housing Committee, Legislation, 1932-1940 — 110
Correspondence, minutes, memoranda re housing legislation, recreational facilities, housing surveys.

UNITED NEIGHBORHOOD HOUSES, INC.

FOLDER TITLE AND DESCRIPTION OF CONTENTS	FOLDER

Housing Committee, Letter Writing Campaign, 1936 — 111
In 1936, New York proposed a moratorium on the Dwellings Law which went into effect on January 1, 1936. Correspondence, lists of volunteers, reflect UNH's response.

Housing Committee, Multiple Dwellings Law, 1936-1937 — 112
Correspondence, papers re the law. Pamphlet, "The Tenant's Rights and the Landlord's Duties." New York Governor Herbert Lehman is a prominent correspondent.

Housing Committee, National Public Housing Conference, 1937-1938 — 113
Correspondence, newsletters, papers.

Housing Committee, National Public Housing Conference, 1946-1957 — 114
Correspondence, newsletters, legislative reports.

Housing Committee, New York City Housing Authority, 1945-1951 — 115
Correspondence, papers; recreational facilities in housing projects, publicity over housing standards. An article by Mary Simkhovitch on housing is included.

Housing Committee, New York City Housing Authority, 1951-1952 — 116
Correspondence, papers; recreation centers, housing projects, minimum welfare standards.

Housing Committee, Queensbridge Houses, 1940-1946 — 117
Correspondence re housing in Queensbridge.

Housing Committee, Subcommittee on Recreation Facilities in Public Housing Projects, 1949-1955 — 118
Correspondence, reports re recommendations for recreational facilities.

Housing Committee, Rent Control, 1937-1938 — 119
Correspondence, pamphlets re rent control legislation.

Housing Committee, Resource Material, 1942-1946 — 120
Pamphlets and papers on war-time housing shortages, old law tenements, the French crisis over housing shortages.

Housing Committee, Resource Material, 1946-1950 — 121
Correspondence and papers, reports of the James Weldon Community Center on the age and ethnic background of its members.

Housing Committee, Stanley M. Isaacs, 1929-1942 — 122
Correspondence of Stanley M. Isaacs with New York City Mayor James J. Walker, Fiorello La Guardia, Norman Thomas and others concerning New York City's housing and social problems.

UNITED NEIGHBORHOOD HOUSES, INC.

FOLDER TITLE AND DESCRIPTION OF CONTENTS	FOLDER

Housing Committee, Studies, 1927-1928 — 123
    Wages in the U.S.A. during the Harding-Coolidge era of "prosperity," Carey Batchelor's study of tenement families. Reports: Brooklyn Bureau of Charities, Department of Service and Relief, Annual Report of the Association for Improving the Condition of the Poor (A.I.C.P.), A.I.C.P. report on housing.

Housing Committee, Studies, 1939-1945 — 124
    Correspondence, summaries of housing legislation. Studies: standards for war housing, architectural plans for housing projects, Federal Public Housing Authority studies of recreation, education and health activities in housing projects, Harlem housing.

Housing Committee, Studies, National Federation of Settlements, 1954-1955 — 125
    Copy of a National Federation of Settlements housing study.

Housing Committee, Tenement House Department of Charity Organization Society, 1936-1938 — 126
    Correspondence with Fiorello La Guardia and others about housing problems.

Housing Committee, Urban League, 1957 — 127
    Minutes, proposals, studies.

Housing Committee, Wagner Houses, 1954-1958 — 128
    Correspondence concerning the inclusion of recreation centers in Wagner Houses.

Housing Committee, Yorkville Housing Committee, 1956-1957 — 129
    Summaries of committee meetings; evictions, rental problems, income and housing.

Housing Committee, Civil Service Examinations, 1951 — 130
    Copies of the 1951 Civil Service examination with answers.

Housing Education Bureau, 1935-1937 — 131
    Correspondence, playscript about housing.

Legislative Committee, 1927-1934 — 132
    Correspondence, agenda, minutes, pamphlets; housing, sanitation, fire protection, child welfare, New York City's education system, reform of housing laws, child labor laws, unemployment, relief. Correspondents include New York Governor Herbert Lehman, Frances Perkins.

Legislative Committee, 1938-1948 — 133
    Correspondence, agenda, minutes, news releases, reports; public education, housing, child care, social security legislation, civil rights, public health, consumer protection, unemployment insurance, minimum wages.

UNITED NEIGHBORHOOD HOUSES, INC.

FOLDER TITLE AND DESCRIPTION OF CONTENTS | FOLDER

Legislative Committee, Automobile Accident Compensation Plan, 134
(AACP), 1936
    Correspondence, minutes, reports, proposed statute drafts,
newspaper clippings, speeches. UNH studied a new plan to
compensate auto accident victims.

Legislative Committee, Automobile Accident Compensation Plan, 135
1937-1938
    Correspondence, minutes, reports.

Legislative Committee, Automobile Accident Compensation Plan, 136
1938
    Correspondence, minutes, reports.

Legislative Committee, Automobile Accident Compensation Plan, 137
    Correspondence, minutes, reports.

Legislative Committee, Automobile Accident Compensation Plan, 138
Newspaper Clippings, 1935-1937.

Legislative Committee, Automobile Accident Compensation Plan, 139
Newspaper Clippings, 1938-1939.

Legislative Committee, Automobile Accident Compensation Plan, 140
Political, 1936-1937.

Legislative Committee, Automobile Accident Compensation Plan, 141
Publicity, 1936-1938.

Legislative Committee, Automobile Accident Compensation Plan, 142
Publicity, 1938.

Legislative Committee, Automobile Accident Compensation Plan, 143
Reference Material, 1934-1938.

Legislative Committee, Automobile Accident Compensation Plan, 144
Speeches, 1937-1938.

Legislative Committee, Automobile Accident Compensation Plan, 145
Sponsoring Organizations, 1936-1937.

Legislative Committee, Automobile Accident Compensation Plan, 146
Statute Drafts, 1936-1937.

Legislative Committee, City Council Election, 1939 147
    Correspondence re UNH's part in the election.

Legislative Committee, Subcommittee on Civil Rights, 1939-1940 148
    Bills, article "Lynching Goes Underground," discrimination
in labor unions, alien registration, arts and crafts.

UNITED NEIGHBORHOOD HOUSES, INC.

FOLDER TITLE AND DESCRIPTION OF CONTENTS	FOLDER
Legislative Committee, Consumer Protection, 1940 Correspondence, New York State bills re consumer interests.	149
Legislative Committee, Public Education, 1939-1940 Correspondence, bills, analyses of public education expenditures.	150
Legislative Committee, Housing, 1939 Correspondence, minutes, comparative analyses of various New York State housing bills.	151-152
Legislative Committee, Housing, Press Clippings, 1939 UNH's role in lobbying for housing legislation in New York is documented.	153
Legislative Committee, Labor Subcommittee, 1940 Correspondence re labor legislation.	154
Legislative Committee, Public Health, 1939-1940 Correspondence re UNH legislative proposals on local and national health legislation.	155
Legislative Committee, Research Material, 1945-1954 Copies of speeches, bills, memoranda; care of retarded children, education, public housing, mental health, public health, discrimination in housing, "red scare" legislation, union purges, social welfare laws re permanently placed children. <u>Congressional Record</u> reprints of New York Senator Herbert H. Lehman's speeches on Soviet Russia, the Taft-Hartley Act, Senator Joseph McCarthy and civil liberties.	156
Legislative Committee, Resource Material, 1954 Copies of bills, speeches, memoranda; discrimination in housing, civil liberties, Senator Joseph McCarthy, education, "red scare," social welfare.	157
Legislative Committee, Subcommittee on Social Security, 1940 Correspondence, bills.	158
Legislative Committee, 1932-1934 Correspondence, tentative drafts of bills, articles on unemployment, Lillian Wald's social insurance bill. Prominent correspondents are the American Association for Social Security, Herbert Lehman.	159
Mental Health Committee, 1951-1953 Correspondence, reports; Madison House's Guidance Center, "General Standard of a Mental Health Clinic," "Mental Health Clinics in Settlement Houses." The folder shows the role of UNH in clarifying concepts for mental health guidance centers by soliciting responses from member settlements.	160

UNITED NEIGHBORHOOD HOUSES, INC.

FOLDER TITLE AND DESCRIPTION OF CONTENTS	FOLDER
Mental Health Committee, Mental Health Project for Association of Brooklyn Settlements, 1956-1958 Correspondence and memoranda re requests for a grant to finance a mental health project.	161
New Areas Committee, 1943-1944 Correspondence concerning new areas of New York City in need of special welfare agencies.	162
Personal Service Workers' Committee, 1935-1947 Correspondence, minutes, reports; the role of the social service department of the neighborhood house, settlements and relief, studies of recipients of settlements' personal service programs, group work and recreation, housing, naturalization and its problems, education, unemployment, casework technique, relation of settlements to other public and private agencies, wartime consumer needs.	163
Personnel Committee, 1942-1945 Correspondence and applications for employment.	164
Personnel Committee, 1945-1952 Correspondence and records re employment.	165
Personnel Committee, 1952-1954 Correspondence and records re employment.	166
Personnel Standards, 1942-1945 Memorandum of agreement reached between the social service employees union and settlement houses, personnel studies for settlement houses.	167
Program Committee, 1924-1945 Correspondence, minutes, reports; the changing ethos of the "new" generation of social workers, finances, National Federation of Settlements, community hhests.	168
Publicity Committee, 1943-1948 Correspondence, newspaper clippings, press release; the history of settlement movement in the U.S.A., leading settlement work personalities, housing, urban life, child labor and the labor movement.	169
Schools and Education Committee, 1946-1950 Resource materials concerning government and data from groups interested in providing state and federal funds for education, the National Commission for the Public Schools, the New York City Board of Education.	170
Schools and Education Committee, 1950-1951 Papers, press releases from the Public Education Association.	171

UNITED NEIGHBORHOOD HOUSES, INC.

FOLDER TITLE AND DESCRIPTION OF CONTENTS	FOLDER

Social Welfare Committee, 1948-1951 172
   Correspondence, public assistance forms from the New York
   City Department of Welfare; Welfare Commissioner Raymond
   Hilliard's investigation of the "loyalty" of welfare
   recipients and Welfare Department personnel.

Unemployment and Relief Committee, 1931-1936 173
   Correspondence, minutes and an unemployment survey; poverty
   in New York City, proposed tax reforms to meet Depression
   emergencies, WPA and relief. Among correspondents are John L.
   Elliott, Lillian Wald, Mary Simkhovitch, Edward T. Devine,
   Harry Hopkins and the Association for Improving the Condition
   of the Poor.

Unemployment and Relief Committee, 1936-1940 174
   Correspondence, minutes, reports; WPA, food-order stamp
   plan, child welfare, housing.

Unemployment and Relief Committee, 1940-1943 175
   Correspondence, minutes, records; housing, relief legislation,
   social security, WPA recreation, war-time activities, art,
   drama, music projects during and pre-World War II.

Unemployment Committee, Study on Resources for the Unemployed, 176
1932-1933
   UNH conducted a study of projects of self-help and self-
   expression for the unemployed in the settlement, exclusive
   of relief projects; results included.

Unemployment Committee, Settlement Case Reports, 1932-1933 177
   Correspondence; Christodora House, a member settlement,
   sent case studies of relief recipients to UNH for use
   in formulating suggestions for reform of relief procedures.

SUBJECTS

Addams (Jane) Luncheon, 1927 178
   Correspondence and papers concerning a special luncheon
   held for Jane Addams.

Adie (David C.) Luncheon, 1932 179
   David C. Adie, Commissioner of Social Welfare in New York,
   spoke on "The Place of the State in a Program of Social
   Welfare." Some issues raised are the attitude of state
   welfare agencies toward social and public welfare, cooperation between public and private social work agencies, social
   planning.

Advertising Women of New York, Manhattan, 1950-1951 180
   A 1950 survey made by the Advertising Women concerning what
   Manhattanites think about voluntarily supported welfare organi-
   zations, the role of volunteers in welfare projects.

FOLDER TITLE AND DESCRIPTION OF CONTENTS	FOLDER

American Association of Social Workers, New York City   181
Chapter, 1937-1953
    Group Work Committee minutes; statement of chapter policies; article, "Social Work in the New York City Public School System"; legislative committee reports on housing and discrimination in housing.

American Association of Social Workers, <u>Social Policy</u>   182
<u>Bulletins</u>, 1953-1954
    <u>Bulletins</u> for members concerning general social welfare programs, social security, agricultural workers, the Old Age and Survivors' Insurance Program.

American Association of Social Workers, Temporary Inter-   183
Association Council, 1952-1955
    The Council was composed of those social welfare organizations which in October, 1955, formed the National Association of Social Workers. Plans for the merger, proposed bylaws, memoranda of understandings.

American Committee in Aid of Chinese Industrial Cooperatives   184
(Indusco), 1947-1948
    Helen M. Harris, then Executive Secretary of UNH, served on the Board of Directors of Indusco. Correspondence, reports; Indusco's aid for China, charges of American exploitation and imperialism in China, rise of Chinese communism and the revolution, problems of Chinese government and social conditions.

American Committee in Aid of Chinese Industrial Cooperatives   185
(Indusco), 1948-1949.

American Committee in Aid of Chinese Industrial Cooperatives   186
(Indusco), 1949.

American Committee in Aid of Chinese Industrial Cooperatives   187
(Indusco), 1950-1952.

Americans for Democratic Action, 1947-1953   188
    Stanley M. Isaacs of UNH was a board member of A.D.A. Correspondence, reports, memoranda; New York City government, housing, education, Governor Thomas E. Dewey and New York's financial condition.

American Jewish Committee, New York Chapter, 1946-1951   189
    Memorandum on the McCarran Law, police brutality in New York City.

American National Red Cross, New York Division, 1948-1953   190
    Correspondence, papers; civil defense, use of volunteers, the blood bank program.

UNITED NEIGHBORHOOD HOUSES, INC.

FOLDER TITLE AND DESCRIPTION OF CONTENTS	FOLDER

American Social Hygiene Association, 1939-1947 — 191
    Correspondence concerning social hygiene programs in the settlements, minutes of settlement house workers meeting on social hygiene education programs, minutes of the Institute on Human Relations for settlement workers dealing with social hygiene.

Amersterdam Community Center, New York City, 1956 — 192
    Minutes, group workers leader's manual; ethnic composition of the neighborhood, programs offered.

Arden House Conference, 1957-1959 — 193
    Invitations, papers concerning the action-research workshop of the National Federation of Settlements dealing with "Neighborhood Goals in a Rapidly Changing World."

Baden Street Settlement, Rochester, New York, 1949-1953 — 194
    Correspondence, agenda, annual reports. In 1949, Baden Street organized United Neighborhood Houses of Western New York State. Baden Street worked closely with UNH in formulating their programs.

Bell Park Gardens, Bayside, Long Island, New York, 1950 — 195
    Correspondence concerning a survey of 791 of the 800 families residing in Bell Park Gardens about neighborhood life.

Better Times, 1919-1920 — 196
    Papers regarding Better Times, a publication of UNH, later taken over by the Welfare Council of New York City.

Boston Settlement Council, 1955 — 197
    Booklet published by the Settlement Council of the United Community Services of metropolitan Boston, pictures and historical sketches of settlements in the greater Boston area, an essay on the "Settlement Idea," giving a succinct statement of settlement philosophy.

Bronx River Settlement, New York City, 1953-1958 — 198
    Correspondence, annual report, statement of the settlement's group work activities, 1956; housing evictions for having illegitimate children.

Brooklyn Council for Social Planning, 1948-1954 — 199
    Correspondence, publicity, speeches; "Planning for Group Work and Recreation," court procedures, physical and mental health.

Bulletins, 1940 — 200
    The Bulletins describe the committee work of UNH.

UNITED NEIGHBORHOOD HOUSES, INC.

FOLDER TITLE AND DESCRIPTION OF CONTENTS	FOLDER

CARE (Cooperative for American Remittances to Everywhere, Inc.)   201
Philippine Community Center Project, 1951-1952
    Newsletters, speeches: "Democratic Potentials in Southeast
    Asia: The Philippine Community Center Projects"; "Philippine
    Community Centers--Their Role in Developing Community and
    Social Relationships."

Case Workers and Family Visitors Committee, 1932-1934   202
    The Committee was formed to acquaint caseworkers with pro-
    fessional techniques. Correspondence, minutes of meetings
    for caseworkers and representatives of the Charity Organiza-
    tion Society and the Association for Improving the Condition
    of the Poor; casework techniques, social service workers in
    the settlements, emergency relief administration, unemployment,
    inter-agency cooperation. Some speakers were Helen Hall,
    Dorothy Baldwin.

Catholic Charities, 1922-1926   203
    Material re inclusion of Catholic Charities of New York in UNH.

"Cavalcade of Human Welfare," 1951-1952   204
    In 1951, the New York City Welfare Council announced plans for
    a "Cavalcade of Human Welfare" to be held in 1953. Stanley M.
    Isaacs and other members of the New York City Welfare Council
    objected to this program for reasons outlined in the correspondence.

Chicago Federation of Settlements, 1945-1958   205
    Correspondence, executive council minutes, annual reports,
    general meeting agenda and reports, news bulletins, speeches:
    Stanley M. Isaacs, "The Settlement in Civic Affairs," a 1954
    "Report to Jane Addams, Sixty Years Later," "Settlements and
    Neighborhood Centers--the Measure of Their Work," "Differentials
    In Service In a Settlement Neighborhood," "Public Relations
    In the Daily Life of Your Agency."

Children's Art Show, 1944-1945   206
    UNH sponsored an exhibition of children's art in the settle-
    ments and then presented the paintings to the children of the
    Soviet Union. Correspondence and photographs, a brief history
    of the settlement movement, its purposes and functions.

Christmas Drive, 1924-1925   207
    Correspondence. In 1924 UNH received permission from the
    New York City Department of Welfare to conduct a Christmas
    Fund Drive.

Citizens Committee of 100 for Children and Youth, New York, 1950   208
    Correspondence, reports; the White House Conference on
    Children and Youth, recreation programs, juvenile delin-
    quency, public housing, group work.

FOLDER TITLE AND DESCRIPTION OF CONTENTS	FOLDER
Citizens' Committee on Children of New York City, 1947-1948 Correspondence, reports; children's centers in public housing projects, settlement services for children and youth.	209
Citizens' Committee on Children of New York City, 1948-1950 Correspondence, minutes. Helen M. Harris of UNH was on the Board of Directors.	210
Citizens' Committee on Children of New York City, 1950 Some topics are juvenile courts, children's health center.	211
Citizens' Committee on Children of New York City, 1951-1953 Correspondence, reports, minutes, budgets; childrens' court procedures, financing welfare projects, social welfare reform legislation.	212
Citizens' Committee on Children of New York City, 1953 Correspondence, Board of Director's minutes; care of the mentally retarded, housing, day care, child abuse, mental health, financing child welfare programs, history of the New York City Department of Health. Helen M. Harris and Stanley M. Isaacs of UNH served on the Committee.	213
Citizens' Committee on Children of New York City, 1954 Correspondence, reports, minutes of Board of Directors, legislative section reports; placing children in foster homes, care of the mentally retarded, day care, juvenile probation and parole, financing of children's courts.	214
Citizens' Committee on Children of New York City, 1954 Correspondence, reports, agenda, Board of Directors' minutes, legislative section materials; juvenile delinquency, budgets, youthful offender statutes, mental health, school boards and communist teachers.	215
Citizens' Committee on Children of New York City, 1955 Correspondence, reports, minutes; foster care for children, juvenile courts, mental retardation, mental health.	216
Citizens' Committee on Children of New York City, 1955-1957 Correspondence, reports, memoranda; procurement of teachers, foster homes, counseling centers for mentally retarded, professional careers in social work, domestic relations courts, mental health, adoption agencies, development of moral ideals in public schools, the Welfare and Health Council and the Community Council of New York City, child care services.	217
Citizens' Committee on Children of New York City, 1957-1960 Correspondence, minutes, reports, memoranda; New York City Department of Health, child care, foster homes, effectiveness of New York City government in dealing with welfare problems, mental health, education.	218

UNITED NEIGHBORHOOD HOUSES, INC.

FOLDER TITLE AND DESCRIPTION OF CONTENTS	FOLDER
Citizens' Committee on Children of New York City, The Program of the New York City Youth Board, 1954 A report submitted to members of the Committee by Alfred J. Kahn.	219
Citizens' Conference on City Planning, 1948-1950 Correspondence, reports; UNH participated in the work of the Conference demonstrating its interest in the need for effective city government and planning.	220
Citizens' Housing and Planning Council of New York, Inc., 1953-1959 Minutes of Committee on Relocation Problems, reports, legislative information.	221
Citizens' Union of the City of New York, 1951-1959 Correspondence and reports re the legislative program of the Citizens Union, city political reforms, racketeering, candidates for city offices.	222
Civic Legislation League of New York State, 1949-1951 Helen M. Harris and Stanley M. Isaacs of the UNH served on the League's advisory committee. Child and family welfare, education, health, housing, juvenile corrections. The League attempted to provide social workers with the understanding necessary to secure effective social welfare legislation.	223
Civic Legislation League of New York State, 1951-1952 Correspondence; compulsory school attendance for non-resident migratory children, children's courts, family and child welfare, corrections, education, housing and health. A legislative history of several League-sponsored bills and an article on the publication of names of welfare recipients.	224
Civil Defense, Recruitment Training Session, 1951-1952 Correspondence concerning neighborhood houses, civil defense in neighborhoods, recreation programs, loyalty oaths.	225
Civil Defense, New York City, 1958 Bi-monthly publications.	226
Civil Works Administration, 1934 Correspondence concerning UNH's cooperation with the C.W.A. to plan cultural festivals.	227
Claremont House, New York City, 1943-1945 Correspondence, publicity, report concerning Negro-white relations.	228

UNITED NEIGHBORHOOD HOUSES, INC.

FOLDER TITLE AND DESCRIPTION OF CONTENTS	FOLDER

Community Chest Committee, 1942 — 229
   Correspondence, minutes; war "Chests" in New York City, settlements and the "Chests," social action and community planning.

Community Service Society, 1947-1949 — 230
   Correspondence, newspaper clippings concerning neighborhood development in New York City.

Correspondence, Miscellaneous, 1947-1949 — 231
   Immigrants, day care, delinquency.

Correspondence, Miscellaneous, 1952-1953 — 232
   Immigration, day care, personnel practices.

Corsi (Edward) Luncheon, 1931 — 233
   Correspondence, seating lists for a special luncheon for Edward Corsi, New York Commissioner of Education.

(The) Daily Compass, New York City newspaper, 1951 — 234
   Articles by Alexander Crosby, "How They Wrecked the Welfare Department," New York City.

Dance Committee, 1921-1940 — 235
   Correspondence, papers concerning dancing and its use in the settlements.

Day Care, 1944-1947 — 236
   Correspondence; debate over use of federal and state funds, settlements and social action, day care centers, wartime and peacetime transition in day care philosophy, history of day care in the settlement movement.

Day Care, 1948-1954. — 237-240

Day Care, Agency Financing, 1956 — 241
   Correspondence concerning allocation of state funds to private and public agency day care programs.

Day Care, Agency Membership in Day Care Council, 1947-1949 — 242
   Correspondence concerning policy and standards of the Day Care Council.

Day Care Centers for the Aging, 1951-1952 — 243
   Correspondence, memoranda, questionnaire re proposed project for settlement house day centers for the aging.

Day Care, Child Care Center, Parents' Association of New York 1945-1948 — 244
   Correspondence, clippings, newsletter re parents' eligibility for day care programs and the threat of the program's discontinuance.

UNITED NEIGHBORHOOD HOUSES, INC.

FOLDER TITLE AND DESCRIPTION OF CONTENTS	FOLDER
Day Care, Civil Service Classification, 1949-1958 Staff classification and salary schedules, recommendations to New York City Department of Welfare.	245
Day Care, Emmett R. Gauhn, Benjamin Fielding, Stanley M. Isaacs, Correspondence, 1947-1948 Correspondence, papers concerning the controversy over the decision of Emmett R. Gauhn, Chairman of the New York State Youth Commission, to discontinue state aid to child care centers. Stanley M. Isaacs of the UNH and Benjamin Fielding, New York City Welfare Commissioner corresponded with Emmett Gauhn re this decision.	246
Day Care, Federal Programs, 1949-1950 Day care programs, White House Conference on Children and Youth, Social Security Administration, Federal Security Agency, manpower and mobilization.	247
Day Care, Hearings, Statements, 1948-1951 Correspondence, statements of Helen M. Harris before the Joint Budget Hearing of the New York Senate Finance and Assembly Ways and Means Committee.	248
Day Care, Joint Committee of Welfare Department and Day Care Center, 1948-1951 Memoranda, minutes, agenda concerning the continuing debate over day care, its purpose and the administrative problems associated with the program.	249
Day Care, Legislation, 1945-1951 Copies of New York State bills relating to the establishment of Day Care Centers, legislative records indicating intent of the Legislature.	250
Day Care, Mayor's Committee on Wartime Day Care and History of Day Nurseries, 1940-1946 An historical sketch of day nursery care in the United States and memoranda from the Mayor's Committee on day care in wartime.	251
Day Care, Open House Tours, 1947-1948 Correspondence, memorandum. Various "open-house" tours were given by settlements to New York congressmen.	252
Day Care Program, Steering Committee, 1947 Papers concerning continuation of day care centers.	253
Day Care, Publicity, 1946-1949 Helen M. Harris, Executive Director of UNH, on the need of federal funds for continuation of day care centers.	254

FOLDER TITLE AND DESCRIPTION OF CONTENTS	FOLDER

Day Care, Publicity, 1952 — 255
 Correspondence, memoranda on publicity for the Day Care Council.

Day Care, Rochester, New York, Conference, 1947-1949 — 256
 Correspondence, minutes, memoranda; education, personnel, salaries, wartime and peacetime day care programs, budgets.

Day Care, Sectarianism, Problem of, 1952-1954 — 257
 Correspondence, papers concerned with the problem of financing private and sectarian day care centers with public funds. The New York City debate is detailed in these folders.

Day Care, Sectarianism, Problem of, 1954. — 258

Day Care, The Case for Day Care, 1947-1948 — 259
 Correspondence, memoranda, reports; the case for child day care centers in New York City. Some organizations and people represented are Dr. Harry Emerson Fosdick, Welfare Council of New York City, Day Care Council of New York City.

Day Care, Welfare Council of New York City, Project Committee on Day Care, 1947-1950 — 260
 Correspondence, minutes, memoranda; definition of day care, its purpose and methods, day care facilities.

Day Care, Welfare Council of New York City, Selected Group Day Care Committee, 1947-1949 — 261
 Correspondence, memoranda; day care program administration, pre-school and after school care.

Day Care Council, Executive Committee Meetings, 1948-1952 — 262
 Correspondence, notes, report from the Social Service Committee on the Day Care Council, lists of committee members.

Day Care Council, Finance, 1949-1951 — 263
 Dues receipts of various settlements to the Day Care Council.

Day Care Council, Minutes, 1949-1951 — 264
 Minutes; day care teacher salaries, fund allocations, personnel practices, agency relations.

Day Care Council, Nominating and Bylaws Committee, 1948-1953 — 265
 Correspondence and papers.

Day Care Council, Personnel Committee, 1947-1952 — 266
 Salaries of day care workers, personnel practices.

Day Care Council, Personnel Committee, 1952-1953 — 267
 Correspondence, Day Care Bulletins.

UNITED NEIGHBORHOOD HOUSES, INC.

FOLDER TITLE AND DESCRIPTION OF CONTENTS	FOLDER
Day Care Council, Requests for Day Care Information, 1953 Correspondence largely from people interested in obtaining free day care.	268
Day Care Council, Requests for Day Care Information, 1953-1954 Correspondence largely from people interested in obtaining free day care.	269
Day Care Week, 1951 Correspondence, memoranda, speeches during New York City's "Day Care Week," 1951.	270
Day Care Week, Publicity, 1951 Correspondence, press releases.	271
Democratic State Committee, 1949-1954 The Democratic Party asked UNH to suggest legislation for improving welfare conditions in New York City. These recommendations cover such fields as child day care programs, discrimination in housing, public assistance, milk and margarine taxes.	272
Depression Relief Measures, 1934 Results of a survey of member settlements studying participation in depression relief measures.	273
Discrimination in Employment, 1946-1948 Correspondence, articles, newspaper clippings concerning UNH's fight for fair employment in New York City.	274
Earhart, (Amelia), Reception, 1928 On July 8, 1928, UNH held a reception in honor of Miss Earhart. Press releases, routine materials are included.	275
East Harlem Youth Project, 1944 Correspondence, papers concerning UNH's grant to be used in a juvenile delinquency project in East Harlem.	276
East Harlem Youth Project, 1944-1945 Correspondence, evaluation of a UNH Youth Project. The National Recreation Association is a correspondent.	277
East Harlem Youth Project, 1945-1946 Correspondence; report on certain neighborhoods studied, aims of the project, recreational needs, post-war adjustment.	278
East Harlem Youth Project, Aguilar Lounge Project, 1944-1946 Papers concerning a Harlem Project in a local library, successful encouragement of reading and discussion among youth.	279

UNITED NEIGHBORHOOD HOUSES, INC.

FOLDER TITLE AND DESCRIPTION OF CONTENTS	FOLDER

Education, Board Members' Seminar, 1940 — 280
Correspondence, registration materials for a course taught by Eduard C. Lindeman for settlement board members. Papers on the settlements in wartime and the use of volunteers are included.

Education Committee, 1943-1946 — 281
Minutes, reports; adult education.

Education Committee of New York City, Board of Education, 1939-1952 — 282
Correspondence, reports, pamphlets; adult education, budgets, community education and settlements.

Education Committee of New York City, Board of Education, 1953-1954 — 283
Correspondence, papers concerning New York City fund allocations, statements of Helen M. Harris of UNH on budget estimates of the New York City Board of Education.

Education Committee of New York City, Board of Education, 1955-1956 — 284
Reports, pamphlets; budgets, community education.

Education Project, 1942-1943 — 285
Correspondence, minutes of a meeting called by settlement headworkers to discuss an experiment in group education; questionnaire used to study settlement workers' attitudes on war, peace, and the social effects of war; Eduard Lindeman's educational programs; review of education projects in New York settlements for post-war planning.

Educational Films, 1946-1952 — 286
Correspondence used to obtain educational films for settlements.

Education Program, 1933 — 287
Correspondence; UNH offered a course on "Giving Parties" for directors, club leaders, and volunteers.

Emergency Work Bureau Training Course, 1933 — 288
The Emergency Relief Bureau conducted a recreational training course at Christodora House. Cynthia Knowles and Grace Gosselin of UNH assisted in construction of the course. The materials reflect the desire of settlements to keep the unemployed "busy" during the Depression.

Federal Nursery Schools, 1939 — 289
Correspondence re Federal Nursery Schools.

Federation of Jewish Philanthropies, 1946-1954 — 290
Pamphlets on activities, employment services, student training at Community Centers, recreational facilities sponsored by Jewish Community of Greater New York.

UNITED NEIGHBORHOOD HOUSES, INC.

FOLDER TITLE AND DESCRIPTION OF CONTENTS	FOLDER

Fiftieth Anniversary of the Founding of University Settlement 291
and the Settlement Movement in the United States, 1936
    Program.

Fiftieth Anniversary, 1950-1951   292
    Correspondence, pamphlets, memoranda, press releases relating
to UNH's Fiftieth Anniversary celebration, publicity memoranda
on UNH's history and purpose, editorials, outline of 50 years
of UNH services, brief history of original 15 New York City
settlements.

Fiftieth Anniversary, 1951   293
    Correspondence; copies of speeches delivered; pamphlets
describing UNH, its history and function.

Fiftieth Anniversary, 1951   294
    Correspondence, Dinner Committee material.

Fiftieth Anniversary, 1951   295
    Correspondence, dinner reservations.

Fiftieth Anniversary, 1951   296
    Programs, seating lists.

Fiftieth Anniversary Dinner, 1951   297
    Publicity, formal arrangements.

Fiftieth Anniversary Dinner, 1951   298
    Speakers' correspondence, planning committee minutes, speeches;
music and the arts in the settlements, history of UNH, volunteers. Speakers included Eleanor Roosevelt; James J. Mallon,
Warden of Toynbee Hall; Mary Simkhovitch; Helen Hall; John
McDowell; Stanley M. Isaacs.

Foreign Students, Employment, 1948-1949   299
    Correspondence concerning Americans working with foreign
students.

"Good Neighbor" Committee, 1940-1941   300
    Bylaws, reports of work accomplished, annual report, descriptive pamphlet on the Committee which tried to promote social
and racial unity among neighbors of diverse origins.

Greater New York Emergency Conference on Inalienable Rights, 1939   301
    Correspondence.

Healthiest Mother Contest, 1926   302
    Correspondence, entrance forms.

UNITED NEIGHBORHOOD HOUSES, INC.

FOLDER TITLE AND DESCRIPTION OF CONTENTS	FOLDER
Helen M. Harris, Speech Notes, 1948-1954 Speech notes of Helen M. Harris, Executive Secretary to UNH, 1948-1954. Most of the notes are incomplete and undated. Social welfare, illegal narcotics use, volunteers, settlement houses and social action, group work and historical materials on the settlement movement.	303
Hospital Council of Greater New York, 1951-1953 Annual reports and bulletins of the Hospital Council of Greater New York.	304
Hospitalization Insurance Plan, 1948-1949 Correspondence, reports, materials related to United Neighborhood Houses' attempt to establish a hospitalization plan for New York settlement workers.	305
Hospitalization Insurance Plan, 1949-1953 Papers concerning United Neighborhood Houses' health plan.	306
Immigration, Adult Activities Committee, 1924-1935 Correspondence, minutes, lists of members; Americanization, immigration.	307
Immigration, Displaced Persons, 1948-1949 Materials from Citizens' Committee on Displaced Persons, UNH's correspondence with Congressmen on increasing quotas of displaced persons in U.S.A., legislative summaries and voting analyses of legislation on immigration.	308
Immigration, New York Committee on Naturalization and Immigration, 1947-1951 Correspondence, minutes, reports; UNH's role in naturalization programs in New York City.	309
Immigration, United Neighborhood Houses and National Federation of Settlements re Reformation of Immigration Statutes, 1941-1952 Alien registration forms, materials on settlement work in promoting naturalization programs for immigrants, pamphlets on need for immigrant law reform by various groups.	310
Immigration, United Neighborhood Houses and National Federation of Settlements re Reformation of Immigration Statutes, 1952 National Federation of Settlement's resolution on immigration, Congressional debates on the Immigration Act of 1952, paper by the American Jewish Committee on recent developments in American immigrant policy, Helen M. Harris' statement made before the President's Commission on Immigration and Naturalization.	311
In-Service Training Course for Settlement Staff and Board Members, 1939-1940 Correspondence, agenda, attendance records.	312

UNITED NEIGHBORHOOD HOUSES, INC.

<u>FOLDER TITLE AND DESCRIPTION OF CONTENTS</u>   <u>FOLDER</u>

In-Service Training Course for Settlement Staff and Board Members,   313
1943-1945
    Correspondence, reports, minutes of a special planning
    committee; discussion on the role of settlements, past
    and present, and their activities with Stanley M. Isaacs,
    President of UNH, Clyde Murray and Lillie Peck of National
    Federation of Settlements and Mary K. Simkhovitch. Training
    of settlement personnel, work with teenagers, group workers'
    methods, development of methods for appraising settlement
    programs, intercultural work, social work techniques, super-
    vision of staff and volunteers, impact of war on family life,
    music for social groups, dramatics, theory of voluntary social
    service.

In-Service Training Course for Settlement Staff and Board Members,   314
1946
    Correspondence, routine materials.

In-Service Training Course for Settlement Staff and Board Members,   315
1947
    Correspondence, agenda, reservations, planning committee
    minutes; consumer interests, psychiatric caseworker at Henry
    Street Settlement.

In-Service Training Course for Settlement Staff and Board Members,   316-317
1948
    Correspondence, reservations, agenda, speeches; government
    investigations of alleged subversion, civil rights.

In-Service Training Course for Settlement Staff and Board Members,   318-319
1949
    Correspondence, reservations, agenda, speeches; Point-Four
    Program, United Nations, Puerto Rican assimilation and settle-
    ment responsibility, American business and foreign policy.

In-Service Training Course for Settlement Staff and Board Members,   320
1950
    Correspondence, agenda, reservation lists.

In-Service Training Course for Settlement Staff and Board Members,   321
Speakers' Correspondence, 1950
    Correspondence, headworkers' meetings, minutes, newspaper
    clippings, agenda, report of staff workers' meetings. Walter
    Gellhorn was a speaker at the West-End Conference.

In-Service Training Course for Settlement Staff and Board Members,   322
1951
    Correspondence, minutes of session on the aging, planning
    committee materials, agenda; housing, juvenile problems.

In-Service Training Course for Settlement Staff and Board Members,   323
1951
    Correspondence, registration materials, completed registration
    forms.

UNITED NEIGHBORHOOD HOUSES, INC.

FOLDER TITLE AND DESCRIPTION OF CONTENTS | FOLDER

In-Service Training Course for Settlement Staff and Board Members, 1952 — 324
   Correspondence, minutes, agenda, reports. The theme of the course was the United Nations and the settlements' relationship to it.

In-Service Training Course for Settlement Staff and Board Members, 1953-1954 — 325-326
   Correspondence, minutes, agenda, reports; role of the settlement worker, Puerto Ricans, dislocated families, subversive activities, housing, social action, role of voluntary agency in city and state welfare programs, juvenile delinquency, professionalization, address by Senator Herbert Lehman on McCarthyism, changing concept of the "Neighborhood."

Intersettlement Senior Dramatic Committee, 1927-1928 — 327
   Correspondence, minutes, programs.

Intersettlement Dance Committee, 1933 — 328
   Minutes, memoranda, financial statement.

International Conference of Social Work, United States Committee, 1948-1953 — 329
   Correspondence; papers on social welfare in India, training for leadership in individualized areas, studies programs.

International Conference of Social Work, 1958-1959 — 330
   Correspondence, list of officers.

International Settlements, 1941-1956 — 331
   Correspondence and pamphlets on Italian and British social work.

Isaacs, (Stanley M.) Dinner, 1954 — 332
   Correspondence, publicity about UNH's sponsorship of a memorial dinner for Stanley M. Isaacs, President of UNH.

Juvenile Delinquency, 1954-1956 — 333
   Correspondence, reports, clippings; UNH's program for combating delinquency, mental health, schools, youth camps, social action, juvenile delinquency, gang wars.

Juvenile Delinquency, 1956-1958 — 334
   Correspondence, reports, clippings; Citizens' Committee on Children of New York City, youth camps, gang war, delinquency preventatives.

Juvenile Delinquency, 1958-1961 — 335
   Correspondence concerning prevention programs, articles on mental health, newspaper clippings; UNH worked with member houses in setting up programs for youth employment, special education, care of emotionally disturbed youth, collaboration with law enforcement agencies, study of parent-child relations in troubled homes. Study: correction facilities for youth.

UNITED NEIGHBORHOOD HOUSES, INC.

FOLDER TITLE AND DESCRIPTION OF CONTENTS	FOLDER

Kellogg, Paul and the _Survey_, 1952-1958 — 336
  Statement of the _Survey_ at its discontinuance, eulogy for Paul U. Kellogg, editor.

La Hermosa Project, Church and Community Center, 1957 — 337
  Report on a project designed for Puerto Ricans in New York City.

Leisure Time Questionnaire, 1927 — 338
  Sent to settlement workers before the UNH conference of February 8, 1927, to see how they spent their leisure time. Completed forms are included.

Lower East Side Program Directors, 1949-1952 — 339
  Correspondence, minutes, survey of memberships.

Melrose House, 1947-1950 — 340
  Correspondence, descriptive brochure of settlement purpose, programs for Puerto Rican immigrants.

MEMBER SETTLEMENTS: Materials from settlements that have been or are members of UNH.

Bronx House, New York City, 1943-1956 — 341
  Correspondence, reports, financial materials, committee minutes; recreation for older persons, finances.

Christodora House, New York City, 1940-1953 — 342
  Bylaws, reports, dues receipts to UNH; problems facing the settlement, aims and objectives, neighborhoods.

Church of All Nations and Neighborhood Houses, New York City, 1940-1953 — 343
  Routine material, annual reports; activities and purposes, group work and refugee problems.

Colony Houses, Inc., New York City, 1940-1953 — 344
  Dues receipts, letter from Helen M. Harris re UNH's relation to its member houses, purposes of Colony Houses, low-rent housing proposals.

East Side House, New York City, 1940-1953 — 345
  Bylaws and papers re the relation between UNH and neighborhood houses, summer camp, art classes.

Educational Alliance, New York City, 1941-1953 — 346
  Material re activities, music, art, youth services, union relations, history of the Alliance, sectarian patterns.

Five Towns Community House, Lawrence, Long Island, New York, 1944-1953 — 347
  Correspondence, statement of purpose and objectives; facilities and programs offered to the neighborhood, history of the center.

UNITED NEIGHBORHOOD HOUSES, INC.

FOLDER TITLE AND DESCRIPTION OF CONTENTS | FOLDER

Forest House, New York City, 1945-1953 — 348
    Community conference reports, historical sketch of Forest House; neighborhood activities, juvenile delinquency.

Goddard Neighborhood Center, New York City, 1939-1953 — 349
    Statement of purpose, annual reports, programs to prevent juvenile delinquency, statement of Goddard Center's relationships with other social welfare agencies.

Good Neighbor Federation, New York City, 1942-1951 — 350
    Correspondence, newspaper clippings, reports; New York City Youth Board activities, juvenile delinquency in Harlem, controversy over closing of the Federation.

Grand Street Settlement, New York City, 1942-1953 — 351
    Activities of Grand Street Settlement for 1951, discussion of the impact of television on society.

Greenwich House, New York City, 1934-1954 — 352
    Obituaries for Mary K. Simkhovitch and a copy of a speech she gave on the 50th anniversary of University Settlement in 1936, speech of 1946 about Mary K. Simkhovitch's retirement as Director of Greenwich House, clippings and articles on her work at Greenwich House, history of Greenwich House, relationship of Greenwich to UNH.

Grosvenor Neighborhood House, New York City, 1939-1953 — 353
    Statement of purpose under articles of incorporation, lists of Board of Directors.

Haarlem House, New York City, 1940-1953 — 354
    Annual reports, dues receipts from UNH, brief description of history of Haarlem House.

Hamilton House, New York City, 1945-1953 — 355
    Description of activities, statement of Hamilton House outlining its role in developing the social welfare of the neighborhood around the Governor Alfred E. Smith House.

Hartley House, New York City, 1946-1953 — 356
    Dues receipts from UNH, 50th anniversary material, lists of members of Board of Directors.

Henry Street Settlement, New York City, 1928-1953 — 357
    Financial statements, year end reports, newspaper clippings re Helen Hall, a <u>Survey</u> article by Helen Hall on "Communist Investigations," reports of visiting nurse service, 1928-1929.

UNITED NEIGHBORHOOD HOUSES, INC.

FOLDER TITLE AND DESCRIPTION OF CONTENTS	FOLDER

Hudson Guild, New York City, 1943-1954 — 358
   History of New York settlements, role of settlements in combating high prices, 50th anniversary of Hudson Guild, work with adults, neighborhood activities, articles reprinted from the Survey Midmonthly, "Welcome Sailor!" by Madeleine D. Ross, on the role of Hudson House in providing social activities for sailors, and the role of settlements in restoring servicemen and plant workers to peace time work. Mary Simkhovitch and John L. Elliott are prominent correspondents.

James Weldon Community Center, Inc., New York City, 1950-1953 — 359
   Correspondence pertaining to membership in UNH, finances, material on problem of interracial neighborhoods.

Jewish Association for Neighborhood Centers, New York City, 1943-1953 — 360
   Characteristics of various Jewish centers, social action, public-private welfare program in New York City, the layman in social welfare.

Jewish Association for Neighborhood Centers, New York City, 1954-1957. — 361

Jewish Settlement House of the East Side, New York City, 1943-1950 — 362
   Correspondence, board members' materials, personnel directory.

Juvenile House of Juvenile Service League, Inc., New York City, 1941-1950 — 363
   Correspondence, financial reports, materials reflecting Juvenile House's recreation programs.

Labor Temple, New York City, 1941-1956 — 364
   Correspondence, reports, study of programs offered, press releases.

Lavanburg Social Center, New York City, 1947-1956 — 365
   Correspondence, materials re recreation, social action, courses in institutional care of problem children.

Lenox Hill Neighborhood Association, New York City, 1939-1955 — 366
   Bylaws, background on Lenox Hill children's homes.

Madison House, New York City, 1941-1953 — 367
   Salaries, history of Madison House, effective settlement house work, community needs, adolescent problems, recreation, tenements, social action, group work, World War II activities, casework, health work, profile of members: residence, occupation, nationality, sex, age, religion.

Manhattanville Neighborhood Center, Inc., New York City, 1946-1953 — 368
   Annual reports, correspondence from Helen Harris to Harry Emerson Fosdick, Clyde Murray.

UNITED NEIGHBORHOOD HOUSES, INC.

FOLDER TITLE AND DESCRIPTION OF CONTENTS | FOLDER

Morningside Community Center, Inc., New York City, 1947-1953 — 369
    Purposes, dues receipts.

Music School Settlement, New York City, 1947-1952 — 370
    Membership lists, dues payments, materials re housing and activities.

Neighborhood House, New York City, 1938-1954 — 371
    Programs, material on housing problems and activities.

110th Street Neighborhood Club, New York City, 1948-1957 — 372
    Correspondence, newspaper clippings, description of Club, data on Maryal Knox.

Prescott House, New York City, 1943-1953 — 373
    Routine materials dealing with Prescott House's history and activities.

Recreation Rooms and Settlement, New York City, 1946-1953 — 374
    Materials on the settlement's history and on the beginnings of UNH.

Red Hook Community Association, Inc., New York City, 1946-1951 — 375
    Financial statements, statement of purpose, annual reports.

Jacob A. Riis Settlement, New York City, 1941-1953 — 376
    Neighborhood problems, health programs, venereal disease, housing, low-income families, Negro integration problems.

Riverdale Neighborhood and Library Association, New York City, 1950-1951 — 377
    Routine correspondence.

Riverside Community House and Ethical Society, New York City, 1938-1953 — 378
    Correspondence, annual reports; activities, budgets, history, purpose.

School Settlement, New York City, 1942-1953 — 379
    Membership lists, settlement purposes, ethnic values in the neighborhood, anti-Semitism.

South Brooklyn Neighborhood Houses, New York City, 1941-1953 — 380
    History, daily community problems, neighborhood difficulties, settlement purposes, ethnic tensions and interactions.

Stuyvesant Neighborhood House, New York City, 1934-1950 — 381
    Correspondence, program schedules, committee reports and minutes; milk prices, anti-Semitism, personnel standards, wartime recreation programs, termination of Stuyvesant Neighborhood House, August 31, 1950.

Stuyvesant Community Center, New York City, 1950-1953 — 382
    History of settlement, activities, summer programs, gang wars.

UNITED NEIGHBORHOOD HOUSES, INC.

FOLDER TITLE AND DESCRIPTION OF CONTENTS — FOLDER

Union Settlement Association, New York City, 1940-1953 — 383
Correspondence, financial statements; a union for social service workers, neighborhood activities, block organization projects, Korean Conflict and settlement's role in the neighborhood and community organization, an old age center in East Harlem.

University Settlement, New York City, 1940-1953 — 384
Albert J. Kennedy's letter of resignation after 60 years of service; statement on history and purpose of University Settlement; statement by Dr. George W. Henry, psychiatrist, concerning his work with homosexuals, largely conducted in space donated by University Settlement.

University Settlement, New York City, Seventieth Anniversary, 1954-1956 — 385
Correspondence, publicity material, photographs, speeches; the anniversary of the first settlement house in America. Speakers include Stanley M. Isaacs, Robert Moses, Agnes Meyer, Charles Cook. History of University Settlement, voluntary efforts in America, a brief synopsis of American settlement history.

Williamsburg Settlement, New York City, 1945-1953 — 386
Bylaws and constitution, dues receipts from UNH, publicity on humanitarianism medal given to Mrs. Eleanor Roosevelt.

Willoughby House Settlement, New York City, 1945-1954 — 387
Correspondence, dues receipts, general business data.

Member Settlement Salary Studies, 1918-1922 — 388
Expenditure reports from member settlements, materials used to construct UNH's annual study of member houses' wages.

Member Settlement Statistics, 1936-1948 — 389
Correspondence, various statistics compiled by UNH on nationalities in various settlements; agencies participating in Greater New York Fund for 1943.

Moses (Commissioner Robert) Controversy, 1949-1953 — 390
Correspondence, newspaper clippings, reports; land use for recreation, New York Housing Authority. Correspondents include Helen M. Harris, Mary K. Simkhovitch, Robert Moses.

National Agencies, 1945-1954 — 391
Materials received by UNH from various national organizations such as the NAACP, The American Indian Fund and American Association of Group Workers.

National Association of Social Workers, New York Chapter, 1956-1960 — 392
Correspondence, annual reports, bylaws; religious discrimination in hiring probation officers, Youth Court Act, social workers' salaries, New York State regulation of social work practice.

FOLDER TITLE AND DESCRIPTION OF CONTENTS	FOLDER

National Association of Social Workers, Social Policy and Action   393
Committee, Subcommittee on Housing, 1955-1958
> Correspondence, minutes; housing, delinquency, mental retardation, indigents' right to counsel and other civil liberties, Social Work Today controversy, loyalty investigation in New York City Department of Welfare, statement of purpose of National Association of Social Workers.

National Conference of Social Work, 1944-1954   394
> Paper by Helen M. Harris, "Social Agencies, Loyalty Oaths and Civil Defense"; National Conference Bulletins.

National Conference of Social Work, Committee on Methods of Social   395
Action, 1949-1954
> Helen M. Harris served as Chairman of this Committee. The papers reflect UNH's role in discussing broad issues of social action at the conference. Topics include civil liberties, loyalty oaths, citizen responsibility for social action, methods of social action, excerpts from an unpublished M.A. thesis, "Trends in Social Action, as Shown in Proceedings of the National Conference of Social Work, 1914-1952," and a paper on "Social Action as A Social Work Process."

National Conference of Social Work, Committee on Methods of Social   396
Action, 1954
> Correspondence, Bulletins; social action, social workers and loyalty oaths.

National Conference of Social Work, Program Committee, 1951-1955   397
> Helen M. Harris, Executive Director of UNH, served on the Program Committee. Correspondence, Bulletins, memoranda, a paper on "Purpose of Conference of Social Work" by Joe R. Hoffer, materials on adult education, International Conference of Social Work.

National Conference on Social Welfare, 1956-1960   398
> UNH participated in many committees and conferences of NCSW. The folder contains Conference Bulletins, Executive Committee minutes, a constitution of the NCSW, agenda and reports.

National Education Association, 1951-1953   399
> Legislative news letters, copies of "The Public and Education," papers on federal aid to education and school construction.

National Jewish Welfare Board, 1945-1952   400
> Correspondence, printed materials about recreation and cultural needs of New York City Jews.

National Social Welfare Assembly, 1952-1954   401
> Materials sent to UNH from the National Social Welfare Assembly concerning abuses in social welfare, housing.

UNITED NEIGHBORHOOD HOUSES, INC.

FOLDER TITLE AND DESCRIPTION OF CONTENTS | FOLDER

National Urban League, 1943-1954   402
Correspondence, press releases, reports; interracial social planning in war industry committees, court work, family counseling, recreation, technical vocations for Negroes.

Neighborhood Opinion Poll, 1939-1940   403
UNH conducted a poll on neighborhood opinions of civil liberties, war and politics. This was one of the first systematic attempts to analyze the opinion of settlement members. Some topics are civil rights, presidential elections and third term, Father Charles E. Coughlin, military service.

Neighborhood Planning Committee, 1936   404
UNH created this committee to plan for social services in New York City. Correspondence, statements of purpose and function.

Neighborhood Study, 1927-1928   405
UNH, under its research secretary, Carey Batchelor, conducted a survey in 1928 to determine what social and physical elements an "ideal" neighborhood should possess. Correspondence, reports, and studies.

New York City Affairs Committee, 1953   406
Correspondence, materials of a committee created to promote an efficient method of handling municipal government in New York City.

New York City, Board of Estimates, 1949-1953   407
Budgets for the day care program of the Department of Welfare, urban land use, adult education.

New York City Council, 1950-1952   408
Correspondence, reports; general welfare council, school districts, air polution, labor relations.

New York City, Civil Service, 1951-1953   409
Reform of Civil Service System in New York City.

New York City, Department of Health, 1947-1953   410
Programs for poor, venereal disease, "free" public clinics, nutritional food programs.

New York Kindergarten Association, 1947-1952   411
Correspondence, minutes of the Association's Advisory Committee; project to develop a unified service to children and parents utilizing a staff including teachers, caseworkers, psychiatrists, nurses, and pediatricians. The Association wanted to set up programs in schools to prevent personality deviations, through early recognition and guidance.

FOLDER TITLE AND DESCRIPTION OF CONTENTS	FOLDER

New York City, Department of Health, Day Care Division, 412
Sanitary Code #201, 1952-1954
    Correspondence re sanitary code and revisions.

New York City, Department of Health, Proposed Budget Cut, 413
Day Care Division, 1953-1955
    UNH's opposition and recommendations.

New York City, Department of Welfare, Day Care, 1947-1949 414
    Procedures to be followed in determining the cost of day care and the family's share in it, family eligibility.

New York City, Department of Welfare, General, 1945-1953 415
    Correspondence, clippings, articles; communists working in the New York City Department of Welfare, Welfare Commissioner Raymond Hilliard's "purge" of leftist social workers, circulation of "phony" stories about welfare recipients, eligibility requirements, relief; UNH's role in several hearings is traced.

New York City, Department of Welfare, Joint Committee, Day Care 416
Council and Department of Welfare, 1953-1957
    Minutes, announcements, salary scales, budgets; liability insurance, education programs, day care programs.

New York City, Department of Welfare, Medical Advisory Board, 417
1950
    Correspondence, minutes; minimum nutritional requirements, medical services, tuberculosis patients.

New York City, Mayor's Advisory Council, 1954-1956 418
    UNH's interest in city affairs and planning is reflected in the correspondence and reports. Housing, consumer interests, sanitation are discussed.

New York City, Mayor's Committee for Better Housing, 1954-1955 419
    Correspondence, papers; neighborhood facilities in a low rent housing project, slum clearance, recreational facilities in housing projects.

New York City, Mayor's Committee for Better Housing, Reports, 1955 420
    Studies and reports on low-rent housing, relocation, housing for the aged, discrimination and integration, middle income housing and tax concessions, private versus public sponsored housing projects, housing and city planning.

New York City, Mayor's Advisory Council, Subcommittee on Consumer 421
Interests, Housing and Neighborhood Improvement, 1954-1956
    Incomplete minutes of the subcommittee, official bulletins on consumer interests; housing, physically handicapped children.

UNITED NEIGHBORHOOD HOUSES, INC.

FOLDER TITLE AND DESCRIPTION OF CONTENTS | FOLDER

New York City, Mayor's Committee on Management Survey, 422
Yavner-Strayer Report, 1951-1952
    UNH supported the budget request of the Community Education
    Division of the Board of Education for 1952-1953. Recreation
    and the Board of Education's social welfare aims are included.

New York City, Mayor's Committee on Management Survey of the 423
City of New York, 1952-1953
    Correspondence, reports; pay of day care consultants, muni-
    cipal employee salary increases.

New York City, Mayor's Office, 1951-1956 424
    Correspondence, press releases and statements by UNH, the
    Mayor's Office and other organizations on urban improve-
    ment, juvenile delinquency, welfare program problems, housing
    reform, recreational needs.

New York City, Police Department, Bureau of Public Relations, 425
1952-1955
    Community relations, policy corruption, traffic enforcement,
    juvenile delinquency.

New York City, Police Department, Bureau of Public Relations, 1955 426
    Community relations, police activities.

New York City, Youth Board, 1947-1952 427
    Analysis of group work services, purposes of Youth programs,
    data on types and sizes of groups, role of group workers,
    Stanley M. Isaacs' statement on UNH and youth work, summer
    program activities, yearly plans of welfare board, services
    for youth in area of greatest need, reports on group work
    projects in private agencies, Youth Board programs carried
    on in settlement houses, "Survey of One Worker Operations."

New York Fund for Children, Finance, 1949-1951 428
    Correspondence and applications of UNH to the Fund for support,
    material re public housing, UNH and "Neighborhood Houses" Month
    and UNH's financial needs.

New York State Committee on Discrimination in Housing, 1948-1950 429
    Correspondence, minutes, memoranda on legislation to end
    discrimination in housing.

New York State Committee on Discrimination in Housing, 1951-1952 430-431
    Eviction of tenants for racial reasons, discrimination under
    FHA, American Civil Liberties Union and the Committee on
    Metropolitan Life Insurance Company's eviction of 21
    Stuyvesant Town families, social status of those complaining
    of discrimination, New York law against discrimination in housing,
    employment, religious and ethnic discrimination. Pamphlets
    on organized labor and the anti-discrimination law, democracy
    on the job.

UNITED NEIGHBORHOOD HOUSES, INC.   691

FOLDER TITLE AND DESCRIPTION OF CONTENTS   FOLDER

New York State Committee on Discrimination in Housing,   432
1952-1954
    Materials on slum clearance, effects of displacement on the
    family, relocation problems, laws forbidding discrimination
    and segregation, legislation for investigation of discrimina-
    tion in housing, enforcement and role of UNH and the Committee.

New York State Committee on Discrimination in Housing,   433
Re Metcalf-Jack Bill, 1952-1953
    UNH supported the bill to create a committee to investigate
    discrimination in housing projects.

New York State Department of Education, Youth Council Services,   434
1946-1949
    Lists of publications of and relating to Youth Council Services.

New York State Welfare Conference, 1958   435
    Agenda.

Noblemaire (Mme. Rene Margot) Gracie Mansion Reception,   436
1953-1954
    Visit of the honorary secretary of the International Federation
    of Settlements, Mme. Margot-Noblemaire, to UNH in January, 1954.
    Publicity, articles, photographs, brief biographical sketch of
    Mme. Noblemaire and her contributions to settlements and human
    welfare.

Non-Partisan Citizens' Committee to Keep Politics Out of Relief,   437
1937
    Correspondence, statements, minutes, notices to Mayor Fiorello
    H. La Guardia; layoff of WPA workers in settlement houses, the
    "investigation" of the New York City Emergency Relief Bureau,
    unemployment.

Open Air Theatre, 1928   438
    Correspondence, programs, materials used by UNH in promoting
    "open air" theatre projects among its member houses.

Outline for a Study of UNH, ca. 1931.   439

Pamphlets, ca. 1930   440
    UNH programs and pamphlets, undated, ca. 1930.

Play Schools Association, 1942-1953   441
    Correspondence and near-print materials on the importance
    of play school programs for children of working mothers in the
    war and post-war years, program philosophy, purposes and
    objectives.

Pomonok Community Center Day Camp, Flushing, New York, 1954-1955   442
    Correspondence, income statements, board of directors' minutes,
    bylaws; recreation, dramatics, finance.

UNITED NEIGHBORHOOD HOUSES, INC.

FOLDER TITLE AND DESCRIPTION OF CONTENTS	FOLDER

Public Education, 1940   443
Reports on school lunches in New York City.

Public Education Association, 1950-1953   444
Correspondence, reports, committee minutes, proposals and studies of P.E.A.; attempts to establish better school facilities, higher teachers' salaries and more progressive educational policies, taxes for schools, integration.

Public Education Association, 1953-1954.   445

Public Education Association, 1954-1955.   446

Puerto Rico, 1948-1951   447
Articles: the police and the community, population and progress in Puerto Rico, Puerto Rico's development of a welfare program.

Queensbridge Community Association, Long Island, New York, 1946-1949   448
Correspondence, reports on activities, staff questionnaires, dues receipts.

Radio Scripts, 1944   449
Radio scripts used in settlement publicity; philosophy of settlement work, settlement administration, volunteers, neighborhoods.

Recreation Facilities Committee, 1934   450
Correspondence, reports from settlements to UNH on efficient use of playground space and the importance of recreation facilities for youth.

Recreation Committee, 1952   451
Materials from the New York Housing Authority on costs of New York Community Programs. UNH was concerned with development and improvement of community recreation programs.

Recreation Project, 1936-1937   452
Fiscal report is included.

Recreation Reclassification Committee, 1954   453
The committee was formed to aid the New York Civil Service Commission in its job of reclassifying the network of recreation positions in the various city departments; salary qualifications for various positions as well as a definition of recreation are included.

Reports, 1945-1947   454
Miscellaneous committee reports: "How the School and Community Worked Together In the Lower West Side," housing, settlement councils, "The Responsibility of the Settlement House in Regard to Sex Education."

UNITED NEIGHBORHOOD HOUSES, INC.

FOLDER TITLE AND DESCRIPTION OF CONTENTS | FOLDER

Savings Bank Life Insurance, 1939-1940 — 455
  Correspondence concerning UNH's course on savings bank life insurance.

Scholarships, 1931-1940 — 456
  Correspondence, reports regarding UNH's scholarship awards, including a summary of UNH's scholarship program, 1924-1933.

Settlement Activities and Finances, 1932 — 457
  UNH's analysis of member settlements' activities during 1924-1932, noting especially those activities and workers "dropped" due to "hard times." Included are reports from individual settlements belonging to UNH describing financing and activities during the Depression.

Settlement and Home Relief Committee, 1934 — 458
  UNH established this committee as a liaison between the Home Relief Bureau and settlements. Stanley M. Isaacs of UNH was active in getting the settlements to help disseminate information about Home Relief Committee measures.

Settlement House Reports on Housing Violations and Children's Court Material, 1954 — 459
  Correspondence about complaints of illegal housing conditions and neighborhood houses' dealings with juvenile courts. Some of this material was used by Mayor Robert F. Wagner in his attempt to reform the New York City Housing Authority.

Settlement Summary, ca. 1919 — 460
  UNH's response to questions of organized charity, industry and Americanization; "An Appeal for Settlements," signed by Charles Evans Hughes and others after World War I.

Settlement Survey, 1927-1928 — 461
  The Welfare Council of New York City in cooperation with UNH made a special survey in 1927 of settlements in New York City to determine how they could best meet changing economic and social conditions. Correspondence, questionnaires, reports are included.

Settlements (Miscellaneous), 1940-1950 — 462
  Correspondence, reports from various settlements and city federations of settlements, a brochure from Hull House of Chicago on its purpose and history.

Settlements (Miscellaneous), 1952-1957 — 463
  Correspondence, reports from other settlement associations and individual settlement houses.

Social Education Committee, 1932-1933 — 464
  Correspondence, minutes, notices on certain concerns for child labor and minorities. Some issues are peace organizations, unemployed teachers, academic freedom.

UNITED NEIGHBORHOOD HOUSES, INC.   694

FOLDER TITLE AND DESCRIPTION OF CONTENTS	FOLDER

Social Education, 1927-1929   465
    UNH sponsored courses in social education to be taught at
    member settlements. Enclosed are summaries of social
    education discussions and selected bibliographies and an
    history of social education courses of UNH.

Staff Luncheons, 1921-1928   466
    Contains reports made by the Executive Secretary of UNH, after
    visiting headworkers' of member settlements which describe many
    problems of member houses; finances, housing, procurement of
    personnel.

Studies, 1936-1955   467
    Studies conducted by, participated in, or collected by UNH:
    "The Case Workers in the Settlement," "A Plan for an Inquiry
    on the Place of the Settlement House in the Social Service
    Structure of Today," "The Manhattanville Nursery Child Care
    Project," "Function of the Young Women's Hebrew Association
    in Providing Community Center Activities," "Report on Youth
    and Health Committee of the Lower West Side District Health
    Committee," "Report on the Recreational Need and Interests of
    Younger Teenage Girls in the Chelsea District of New York City"
    (wartime recreational needs), "How the School and Community
    Worked Together in the Lower West Side," "The State of Music
    in New York's Neighborhood Houses and Community Music Schools,"
    "Fuel Consumption Survey," study of personal service depart-
    ments of settlements, "Outline and Bibliography for Seminar
    for Board Members of New York Settlements" by Eduard C.
    Lindeman, "A Study of the Policies of Settlement Houses in
    New York City in Reference to the Care of Athletic Injuries
    and their Liability for such Injuries," "Songs for Victory
    Sing" (a collection of patriotic songs, 1943), "Camp Ellen
    Marvin--Creative Arts Project."

Studies, 1955-1956   468
    The relocation of Manhattanville Neighborhood Center, the
    Muscular Dystrophy Social Group and the Muscular Dystrophy
    Camp.

Studies, Narcotics, 1955   469
    Materials to be used by neighborhood houses in studying
    narcotics use, reports of studies, material assembled by UNH.

Studies, Outline of Neighborhood Services for Securing Community   470
Information, 1940
    Materials used to prepare community studies by neighborhood
    houses assembled by UNH.

Summer Camps, 1920-1923   471
    Publicity photographs, camp counselors' materials.

UNITED NEIGHBORHOOD HOUSES, INC.

<u>FOLDER TITLE AND DESCRIPTION OF CONTENTS</u>   <u>FOLDER</u>

Summer Camp Cost Project, 1948-1952   472
    Reports on the cost of operating camps.

Summer Programs, 1928-1948   473
    Correspondence and lists showing settlements and their summer
    activities, plans for programs in settlements.

Thirty-fifth Anniversary Dinner, 1936   474
    Correspondence, programs, transcript of talk by Harry L.
    Hopkins on WPA history, statements by Lillian D. Wald, John L.
    Elliott, Mary K. Simkhovitch on housing and relief.

Ticket Committee, 1934-1940   475
    Correspondence, writing contests, free concert and circus
    tickets.

Veterans, 1944-1946   476
    Correspondence, a selected bibliography on the World War II
    veteran, lists of veterans' services in New York City, materials
    for a discussion group of veterans and civilians formed to
    facilitate the re-entry of veterans into civilian life. Reports:
    "The Veteran and the Settlement," "The Problem of the Ages,"
    care of youth during war time.

Volunteers, 1925-1948   477
    Correspondence, volunteer forms, lists of volunteers, studies,
    memoranda re use of volunteers in the settlements.

Volunteers, 1950   478
    Correspondence, surveys made on need and use of volunteers in
    health, welfare, educational and recreational organizations of
    New York City, some settlement reports on use of volunteers.

Women's City Club of New York City, 1948-1952   479
    Correspondence, constitution and bylaws, committee papers;
    reform of New York State government, state finances.

Youth Subcommittee, 1942-1944   480
    Correspondence, papers on delinquency, recreation, attitudes
    of children in the settlements, use of volunteers, reintegration
    of veterans into the community, group work practices with young
    people.

ASSOCIATED ORGANIZATIONS

Association of Brooklyn Settlements and Brooklyn Neighborhood   481
Houses Fund, Constitution and Bylaws, 1946-1951
    Constitution and bylaws with revisions.

Brooklyn Neighborhood Houses Fund, Activities, 1943-1952   482*
    Descriptions of settlement's activities, history of BNHF.

*Similar items filed in Legal Folder 2.

UNITED NEIGHBORHOOD HOUSES, INC.

FOLDER TITLE AND DESCRIPTION OF CONTENTS — FOLDER

Brooklyn Neighborhood Houses Fund, Aging, 1946-1961 — 483
Correspondence, reports, newspaper clippings; programs for the aged inaugurated by the BNHF, special services for the ages.

Brooklyn Neighborhood Houses Fund, Baseball, 1953 — 484
Correspondence detailing BNHF's attempts to obtain passes to baseball games for children from the settlements.

Brooklyn Neighborhood Houses Fund, Board of Trustees, Minutes and Announcements, 1944-1948 — 485
These folders reflect the special problems of the BNHF, e.g., in 1948, the BNHF complained that the UNH cared too much for social action and not enough for settlement problems.

Brooklyn Neighborhood Houses Fund, Board of Trustees, 1948-1949 — 486
Minutes and announcements.

Brooklyn Neighborhood Houses Fund, Board of Trustees, 1949-1951 — 487
Minutes and announcements.

Brooklyn Neighborhood Houses Fund, Board of Trustees, 1952-1955 — 488
Minutes and announcements.

Brooklyn Neighborhood Houses Fund, Board of Trustees, 1955-1956 — 489
Minutes and announcements.

Brooklyn Neighborhood Houses Fund, Brooklyn College, 1947-1952 — 490
The folder details the relationship between BNHF and the Brooklyn College Settlement House Institute.

Brooklyn Neighborhood Houses Fund, "Brooklyn Neighborhoods," ca. 1947 — 491
The folder contains Herbert J. Ballon's history of the Brooklyn settlements with profiles of the various Brooklyn "Neighborhoods" and a bibliography.

Brooklyn Neighborhood Houses Fund, Civil Liberties, Loyalty Oath, 1950-1951 — 492 - 492A
UNH statement to member houses of the New York City Department of Welfare to have volunteers in the civilian defense program take a loyalty oath.

Brooklyn Neighborhood Houses Fund, Consumer Committee, 1948-1949 — 493
Bulletins of the National Association of Consumers, repeal of the Federal Anti-Margarine Law, statements by the National Federation of Settlements on consumer interests, gas rates and milk prices.

Brooklyn Neighborhood Houses Fund, Consumer Committee, Milk Prices, 1934-1950 — 494
Correspondence, a 1934 survey for study of milk prices in New York City conducted by UNH. Other topics are New York milk cooperatives, sanitary measures in milk production.

UNITED NEIGHBORHOOD HOUSES, INC.

FOLDER TITLE AND DESCRIPTION OF CONTENTS	FOLDER
Brooklyn Neighborhood Houses Fund, Consumer Committee, Price Control Project, 1951 Correspondence and reports. UNH conducted a campaign in 1951 to gain support for a price control plan.	495
Brooklyn Neighborhood Houses Fund, Consumer Committee, Resource Material, 1947-1952 Statement by Stanley M. Isaacs on "High Prices," studies of gas rates, anti-inflation proposals.	496
Brooklyn Neighborhood Houses Fund, Finances, 1946-1949 Correspondence, papers.	497
Brooklyn Neighborhood Houses Fund, Finances, 1949-1952 Correspondence, papers.	498
Brooklyn Neighborhood Houses Fund, Finances, Discretionary Fund Committee, 1951 Minutes, papers of the committee established to make recommendations concerning the disposition of current funds.	499
Brooklyn Neighborhood Houses Fund, Finances, Distribution Committee, 1946-1950 Correspondence, minutes; distribution of funds, a brief history of the BNHF.	500
Brooklyn Neighborhood Houses Fund, Finances, Joint Benefit, 1946 Minutes, discussion of a joint benefit between the BNHF and the UNH.	501
Brooklyn Neighborhood Houses Fund, UNH Ford Foundation Appeal, 1955 In 1955, the UNH applied to the Ford Foundation for a grant to study juvenile delinquency.	502
Brooklyn Neighborhood Houses Fund, Greater New York Fund, 1951-1952 UNH created a special "Pro Tem Committee in the Interest of the Independent Agencies" to present the views of the "independent social agencies in New York City" that would have suffered under a proposed reorganization of the Greater New York Fund. The folder reflects UNH views and activities.	503
Brooklyn Neighborhood Houses Fund, Housing Committee, 1927-1951 Correspondence, reports, typed excerpts from a UNH scrapbook on the UNH and housing from 1920-1934, public statements on the bill to reorganize the New York Housing Authority in 1947.	504
Brooklyn Neighborhood Houses Fund, Legislative Committee, 1945-1952 Correspondence re unemployment, public assistance, the Rankin Un-American Committee, purposes of the Legislative Committee, labor relations.	505

UNITED NEIGHBORHOOD HOUSES, INC.

FOLDER TITLE AND DESCRIPTION OF CONTENTS | FOLDER

Brooklyn Neighborhood Houses Fund, Publicity, 1951 | 506
    Minutes of meetings held by settlement headworkers to discuss publicity campaigns, tentative outline for a publicity campaign.

Brooklyn Neighborhood Houses Fund, Report, Annual, 1947 | 507
    Lists of officers and committee members; BNHF activities are discussed.

Brooklyn Neighborhood Houses Fund, Staff Workers' Council, 1949-1952 | 508
    Correspondence, minutes; history of the settlement movement, programs for staff workers' of settlements belonging to UNH.

Brooklyn Neighborhood Houses Fund, Structure Committee, 1949 | 509
    Correspondence, reports; structure and organization of BNHF.

Brooklyn Neighborhood Houses Fund, Summer Camps, 1942-1951 | 510
    Rules and regulations for camps and counselors, brochure on camp counselors' in wartime, Group Workers' Bulletin from the Social Hygiene Division.

Brooklyn Neighborhood Houses Fund, Youth United, 1952 | 511*
    Correspondence, materials on Youth United and its attempts to help the settlements with juvenile problems.

League of Mothers' Clubs, 1926-1936 | 512**
    Correspondence, minutes, a brief history of UNH; historical sketch of the League, its functions and purpose; WPA, Federal Theatre Project, finances, summer recreational activities, housing, slum clearance.

League of Mothers' Clubs, 1936-1939 | 513
    Correspondence, minutes, reports; housing, discrimination.

League of Mothers' Clubs, 1940-1941 | 514
    Correspondence, routine materials, lists of officers.

League of Mothers' Clubs, Annual Dinner, 1936 | 515
    Program.

League of Mothers' Clubs, Annual Dinner, 1937 | 516
    Correspondence, programs.

League of Mothers' Clubs, Annual Dinner, 1939 | 517
    Program.

League of Mothers' Clubs, Annual Dinner, 1940 | 518
    Correspondence, routine materials, speech by Mary K. Beard, "America Through Mother's Eyes."

*Similar items filed in Legal Folder 2.

**Similar items filed in Legal Folders 3-4.

FOLDER TITLE AND DESCRIPTION OF CONTENTS	FOLDER

League of Mothers' Clubs, Annual Dinner, 1941 519
    Speech notes on world situation and tasks of the League.

League of Mothers' Clubs, Annual Dinner, 1942 520-521
    Correspondence, reservations and guest lists.

League of Mothers' Clubs, Annual Reports, 1922-1923, 1928-1929. 522

League of Mothers' Clubs, 1938-1939 523
    Annual reports, membership materials, committee reports, incomplete monthly reports of League activities.

League of Mothers' Clubs, Annual Reports, 1940-1942. 524

League of Mothers' Clubs, Benefits, 1931-1935 525
    Brochures, programs, benefit dances and dinners.

League of Mothers' Clubs, Boat Trip, 1935-1936 526
    Correspondence re arrangements for UNH's Boat Trips for children and adults, noting cooperation of WPA.

League of Mothers' Clubs, Boat Trip, 1936-1940 527
    Correspondence, papers.

League of Mothers' Clubs, Citizenship Campaign, 1937-1938 528
    Correspondence and statement of objectives; WPA Adult Education Division, campaign to increase naturalization among neighborhood immigrants.

League of Mothers' Clubs, Citizenship Campaign Forms, 1936-1937 529
    League of Mothers' Clubs conducted a survey of its members to determine countries of origin and length of citizenship. The completed forms are included.

League of Mothers' Clubs, Club Dues, 1939-1943 530
    Routine correspondence.

League of Mothers' Clubs, Constitution and Bylaws, ca. 1942 531
    Constitution and bylaws of UNH.

League of Mothers' Clubs, Consumer Committee, Food Price Study, 1941-1942 532
    Materials sent to the League on food supplies, consumer food prices.

League of Mothers' Clubs, Consumer Protection Committee, Meat Grading Bill, 1941 533
    Correspondence, material re a meat grading bill the League was eager to have passed.

UNITED NEIGHBORHOOD HOUSES, INC.

FOLDER TITLE AND DESCRIPTION OF CONTENTS	FOLDER

League of Mothers' Clubs, Consumer Protection Committee, Milk 1937-1942 — 534
  Correspondence, clippings, material on New York City milk prices, analysis of "milk" bills.

League of Mothers' Clubs, Consumer Protection Committee, Report, 1941-1942 — 535
  Reports of year's work, material re meat grading bill and milk legislation.

League of Mothers' Clubs, Contributors, 1933-1937 — 536
  Diagram of executive structure and lists of contributors.

League of Mothers' Clubs, Adult Education Project, 1935 — 537
  Correspondence, newspaper clippings re the League's adult education activities.

League of Mother's Clubs, Emergency Relief Material, 1935 — 538
  Correspondence on New York City Emergency Relief Bureau, WPA, Welfare Council of New York City.

League of Mother's Clubs, Executive Committee, 1931-1936 — 539
  Minutes, reports, material re unemployment, housing, birth control, WPA, finances.

League of Mothers' Clubs, Financial Statements, 1935-1937. — 540

League of Mothers' Clubs, 1939-1940 — 541
  A brochure, "Fun on Foot," by Maxine E. Akens.

League of Mothers' Clubs, General Assemblies, 1936-1942 — 542
  Correspondence, programs, Mother's Day assembly, planning materials.

League of Mothers' Clubs, General Assembly Meetings, 1942 — 543
  Correspondence, minutes; China relief, international welfare.

League of Mothers' Clubs, Group Work Course, 1939-1940 — 544
  Resource materials for a class on group work activities.

League of Mothers' Clubs, Headworkers Committee, 1936 — 545
  Correspondence between the League and UNH Headworkers Committees.

League of Mothers' Clubs, Housing, Better Homes Exhibit, 1923-1926 — 546
  Correspondence, materials detailing the planning and purpose of the Better Home's Exhibit of November 22-27, 1926. Correspondents: The Tenement House Committee, Nurses Association of Henry Street Settlement, Child Study Association of America, United States Children's Bureau. Included is a Metropolitan Life Insurance Company "model budget" for low-income families.

UNITED NEIGHBORHOOD HOUSES, INC.

FOLDER TITLE AND DESCRIPTION OF CONTENTS | FOLDER

League of Mothers' Clubs, Housing Committee, Studies, 1928-1940 — 547
    Studies: "What the Tenement Family Has and What It Pays for It," "A Study of 1092 Tenement Families," "Vacancy and Housing Survey," "Tenements and Tenants," the neighborhood serviced by University Settlement, Harlem Housing survey, housing facilities in one eighteen-block area of New York City.

League of Mothers' Clubs, In-Service Training Course, 1940-1942 — 548
    The course was sponsored by UNH and the WPA Recreation Training School for Settlement workers. Correspondence, minutes, course materials; wartime services, practicing democracy in the settlements, recreation.

League of Mothers' Clubs, Interpretation of Work, 1943 — 549
    Interpretative statement of the League's function and purpose, analysis of contributions and campaigns; better housing, and milk prices.

League of Mothers' Clubs, Leaders of Mothers' Clubs, 1941-1942 — 550
    Correspondence and materials on planning for meetings and events, function of organizational meetings.

League of Mothers' Clubs, Leaders, Presidents and Delegates, 1936-1940 — 551
    Correspondence, minutes. The League had periodic meetings of the leaders and presidents of member settlement house mothers' clubs.

League of Mothers' Clubs, Leaders, Presidents and Delegates, 1941-1944 — 552
    Papers, function and purpose of Mothers' Clubs, 1943-1944 statement on the purpose of the League after the Depression and in wartime.

League of Mothers' Clubs, Leaders, Presidents and Delegates, Lists, 1936-1942 — 553
    Lists of members of settlement house mothers' clubs, leaders, and subcommittee members.

League of Mothers' Clubs, League of Women Voters, 1940-1941 — 554
    Correspondence, materials on voting and responsibility.

League of Mothers' Clubs, Legislative Committee, 1940-1941 — 555
    Correspondence, materials on government reform.

League of Mothers' Clubs, Memberships, 1937-1938 — 556
    Correspondence on memberships of settlement houses in the League.

League of Mothers' Clubs, "Mother's News," 1932-1936 — 557
    A League officer's manual, 1936 newsletters; housing, League history, social welfare legislation.

UNITED NEIGHBORHOOD HOUSES, INC.

FOLDER TITLE AND DESCRIPTION OF CONTENTS   FOLDER

League of Mothers' Clubs, Motion Picture Committee, 1936-1942   558
    Correspondence, materials. The Committee arranged for
    showings of educational films and tours of movie-making
    companies.

League of Mothers' Clubs, Peace Campaign, 1936-1940   559
    Correspondence, papers showing the League's stand against war
    and for peace. Some topics are Foreign Policy Association,
    Cordell Hull, wage fixing during wartime, conscription,
    participation of the League in peace demonstrations.

League of Mothers' Clubs, Public Speaking Class, 1939-1940   560
    Lists and notices.

League of Mothers' Clubs, Publicity, 1931-1945   561
    Correspondence, publicity materials on purpose and function
    of the League.

League of Mothers' Clubs, Questionnaire on Committee Preferences,   562
1936-1937
    Completed questionnaires re committee assignments.

League of Mothers' Clubs, Refugees Fund, 1938-1940   563
    Correspondence, papers on fund-raising to aid European refugees,
    including a detailed analysis of the European Jewish refugee
    problem.

League of Mothers' Clubs, Speakers Bureau, 1932-1941   564
    Correspondence, papers on WPA Public Educational Forum,
    parents' club meeting.

League of Mothers' Clubs, Spring Dances, 1936-1944   565
    Correspondence, financial statements, programs of UNH's
    annual spring costume dance and party.

League of Mothers' Clubs, Thirtieth Anniversary Meeting, 1943   566
    Routine correspondence, reservation materials, a dramatic
    sketch of the history and work of the League.

League of Mothers' Clubs, Travel Club, 1936-1941   567
    Correspondence, papers on the League's planning group for
    short trips and tours for members.

League of Mothers' Clubs, Victory Conference, 1942   568
    Consumer interests in wartime, post-war planning, inter-
    racial activities.

League of Mothers' Clubs, Women's Conference, 1941   569
    Papers on the conference held to discuss the League's purpose
    and function.

FOLDER TITLE AND DESCRIPTION OF CONTENTS	FOLDER

National Federation of Settlements, Board of Directors, 1948-1950   **570**

    Helen M. Harris served as vice president of the NFS. The folder consists largely of material relating to her work experience. Board reports cover all phases of NFS activities, rent control, child welfare, discrimination in housing, President Truman's Point-Four Program, social action, unemployment, budgets, study of settlements and cities. Prominent correspondents are John McDowell and Albert J. Kennedy.

National Federation of Settlements, Board of Directors, 1950-1952   **571**

    Papers on immigration, membership dues, the activities of John McDowell.

National Federation of Settlements, Board of Directors, 1952-1953   **572**

    Membership standards, day care programs.

National Federation of Settlements, Budget Committee, 1950-1952   **573**

    Helen M. Harris of UNH was a member of this committee. Lea D. Taylor, President of NFS, is represented.

National Federation of Settlements, Conference on Unfinished Business in Social Legislation, 1949   **574**

    Papers dealing with all the social welfare issues concerning NFS in 1949, anti-margarine laws, rent control, displaced persons, civil rights, housing, public health, social security, consumer interests, Displaced Persons Act of 1948. Reprints from the *Survey Graphic* and the *Survey Midmonthly*.

National Federation of Settlements, New York Conference, 1922   **575**

    Program.

National Federation of Settlements, Cleveland Conference, 1949   **576**

    Settlement House membership in the Detroit area, methods used to study member settlements, history of the settlement house movement, housing, rent control, discrimination in employment and housing, public welfare, farm prices and surplus produce, public health, civil rights. Speech: "The Settlement as a Vital Force in Social Welfare." Prominent personalities include John McDowell and Helen Hall.

National Federation of Settlements, Rochester Conference, 1950   **577**

    Personnel practices in the settlements, problems of agricultural workers, social security, child welfare, housing, settlements and social action, neighborhood representation on settlement boards, case studies of low-income families, displaced persons, immigration, education, casework field services.

UNITED NEIGHBORHOOD HOUSES, INC.

FOLDER TITLE AND DESCRIPTION OF CONTENTS	FOLDER

National Federation of Settlements, Atlantic City Conference, 1951 — 578
   The United Nations and war and peace, loyalty oaths, consumers and a wartime economy, the American Medical Association and their opposition to Charlotte Towle's Common Human Needs, social education and social action.

National Federation of Settlements, Milwaukee Conference, 1952 — 579
   International relations, United Community Defense services, NFS's "Neighborhood," narcotics, public assistance rolls, employment of school age youth, minority group tensions, narcotic addicts, termination of publication of the Survey. Mary K. Simkhovitch is discussed in the papers.

National Federation of Settlements, Cleveland Conference, 1953 — 580
   Agenda, committee reports, summary of resolutions passed by NFS from 1911-1952; urban and rural social workers, lobbying for social welfare measures, government and public housing. A Treasurer's report and statistical materials on population, dependency, mobility and employment are included.

National Federation of Settlements, New York Conference, 1954 — 581
   Cooperation of UNH and NFS to construct a social action program, group welfare programs, technical assistance programs, American policy in Indo-China.

National Federation of Settlements, Directories, Member House and City and Regional Settlement Federations, 1957 — 582
   Directory of all member houses.

National Federation of Settlements, Field Service, 1948. — 583

National Federation of Settlements, General, 1943-1947 — 584
   Correspondence, minutes, reports, settlement budgets; youth programs, transition programs between war and peace, the International Federation of Settlements, Negro relations.

National Federation of Settlements, General, 1948 — 585
   Correspondence, minutes, reports; Chinese-American relations, finances, foreign aid and European recovery, civil rights, housing, social education and action, consumer interests, international social work.

National Federation of Settlements, General, 1948-1950 — 586
   Criteria for agency membership in NFS, settlements in wartime, the work of the International Association of Settlements, methods for conducting case studies of low-income families, repeal of margarine taxes, the Fiftieth Anniversary of the National Consumers League, the McCarran Act, Korean Conflict. Studies: spatial aspects of local community planning and organization on six decades of settlement work. John McDowell is represented in the papers.

UNITED NEIGHBORHOOD HOUSES, INC.

FOLDER TITLE AND DESCRIPTION OF CONTENTS	FOLDER

National Federation of Settlements, General, 1950-1951 587
   Cooperative relationships between the Pittsburgh Housing
   Authority and Soho Community House, international social
   work, problems of the Welfare Council of New York City,
   structure and function of the settlements, social welfare
   legislation, housing.

National Federation of Settlements, General, 1951-1953 588
   Korean Conflict prisoners and their treatment, communist
   propaganda, juvenile delinquency and housing problems in
   New York City, the role of the settlements in fostering the
   concept of world citizenship, Aid to Dependent Children laws,
   the study of social education and action programs, the role
   of the federal government in housing programs. Albert J.
   Kennedy's definition of a neighborhood (ca. 1932) is included.

National Federation of Settlements, General, 1957 589
   Executive Committee minutes, agenda, report of the Dues
   Committee, material from the Social Education and Action
   Committee. Indian affairs, housing, and civil rights are
   among the topics discussed.

National Federation of Settlements, List of Members, 1940-1948 590
   Lists of member houses.

National Federation of Settlements, Membership Drive, 1948-1949. 591

National Federation of Settlements, President's Committee on 592
Immigration and Naturalization, 1952-1953
   Immigration and settlement work, Senator McCarthy and the
   "climate of fear," the McCarran-Walter Act and restrictive
   immigration legislation.

National Federation of Settlements, Publicity and Studies, 593
1931-1952
   Studies and papers by Mary K. Simkhovitch and Lillie Peck;
   training aspects of group work, social work agencies,
   consumer interests, the Survey, NFS bylaws, social work
   education.

National Federation of Settlements, Review of Officers and 594
Delegates' Lists, 1911-1931
   A description of each NFS conference held and the resolutions
   passed.

National Federation of Settlements, Salary Studies, 1947-1953 595
   Studies of job qualifications, education requirements,
   personnel practices.

National Federation of Settlements, Social Education and Action 596
Committee, 1949-1951
   Materials on displaced persons, social welfare legislation.

UNITED NEIGHBORHOOD HOUSES, INC.

FOLDER TITLE AND DESCRIPTION OF CONTENTS | FOLDER

National Federation of Settlements, Special Financial Campaign, 1949-1950   597
    Correspondence, papers dealing with NFS's special fund drive.

National Federation of Settlements, Steering Committee for Federal Lobbying, 1947-1948   598
    Statements made before government committee's representatives by NFS officers, analysis of social welfare legislation, housing, FHA, American economic situation.

National Federation of Settlements, <u>Summer Service Bulletins</u>, 1949-1952.   599

National Federation of Settlements, United Community Defense Service, Inc., Newsletters, 1951-1952   600
    FHA, field services, social welfare legislation.

National Federation of Settlements, United Nations Seminar, 1952   601
    The United Nations and the settlements, social action programs, refugee problems, international economic stability. Papers: "Settlements Role in Building World Minded Citizens," "Making the U.N. Live in Settlement Neighborhoods."

National Federation of Settlements, United Nations Seminar, Pamphlets, 1952   602
    Pamphlets, articles, editorials on the U.N.'s role in social welfare.

National Federation of Settlements, United Nations Seminar, Pamphlets, 1952   603
    Material on current social welfare issues before the U.N. General Assembly.

National Federation of Settlements, UNH Reports to NFS Board of Directors, 1948-1953   604
    UNH's reports to NFS on general problems facing New York City settlements. Discussion of housing shortages, the high cost of living, impact of post-war readjustment on child day care programs, settlement financing, public welfare and relief programs, Puerto Rican discrimination, violations of housing codes, juvenile delinquency, urban population changes and social mobility.

Welfare and Health Council of New York City, Board of Directors, 1953   605*
    Correspondence.

*Similar items filed in Legal Folder 5.

UNITED NEIGHBORHOOD HOUSES, INC.

FOLDER TITLE AND DESCRIPTION OF CONTENTS | FOLDER

Welfare and Health Council of New York City, Board of Directors, 606
1954-1955
    Correspondence, annual election, reports; Helen M. Harris of
    UNH served on the Board of Directors.

Welfare and Health Council of New York City, Contributions, 607
1948-1953
    List of personal contributions.

Welfare and Health Council of New York City, Affiliation Plan, 608
1947
    Affiliation plan between UNH and Welfare Council.

Welfare and Health Council of New York City, Advisory Committee, 609
1946-1949
    Advisory Committee proposals for improved welfare services in
    various fields.

Welfare and Health Council of New York City, Advisory Committee, 610
1949-1951
    Advisory Committee proposals.

Welfare and Health Council of New York City, 1951-1952 611
    Advisory Committee proposals.

Welfare and Health Council of New York City, Central Coordinating 612
Committee, 1949-1950
    Minutes dealing with current substantive issues.

Welfare and Health Council of New York City, Central Coordinating 613
Committee, 1950-1951
    Minutes.

Welfare and Health Council of New York City, Central Coordinating 614
Committee, 1951-1952
    Minutes.

Welfare and Health Council of New York City, Conference Group on 615
Group Work and Recreation Committee, 1948-1950
    Correspondence, materials, mostly steering committee items.
    Helen M. Harris of UNH served on this committee.

Welfare and Health Council of New York City, Conference Group on 616
Group Work and Recreation Committee, 1950-1951
    Correspondence, papers.

Welfare and Health Council of New York City, Conference Group on 617
Group Work and Recreation, Steering Committee, 1945-1947
    Correspondence, minutes; welfare agency standards, methods of
    group work, public relations and welfare agencies, immigration,
    in-service training courses for schools of social work, social

UNITED NEIGHBORHOOD HOUSES, INC.

FOLDER TITLE AND DESCRIPTION OF CONTENTS	FOLDER

action programs, recreation, cooperation with youth councils, coordination between the Welfare Council and welfare agencies, professional criteria for social workers in group work and recreation. Reports re housing, care for the handicapped.

Welfare and Health Council of New York City, Conference Group on Group Work and Recreation, 1947-1948   618
    Correspondence, minutes.

Welfare and Health Council of New York City, Conference Group on Group Work and Recreation, Steering Committee, 1949   619
    Correspondence, papers.

Welfare and Health Council of New York City, Conference Group on Group Work and Recreation, Steering Committee, 1952   620
    Correspondence, minutes, membership lists.

Welfare and Health Council of New York City, Conference Group on Group Work and Recreation, Steering Committee, 1952-1953   621
    Correspondence, minutes.

Welfare and Health Council of New York City, Conference Group on Group Work and Recreation, Subcommittee on Recreation in Public Housing, 1947-1949   622
    Correspondence, minutes.

Welfare and Health Council of New York City, Consumer Problems Committee, 1948   623
    Correspondence, recommendations.

Welfare and Health Council of New York City, Correspondence, 1947-1949   624
    Correspondence, newsletters; the function of the Welfare Council, relief programs, mental hygiene, social welfare research projects.

Welfare and Health Council of New York City, Correspondence, 1951-1953   625
    Correspondence, newsletters, annual reports, minutes of special committees, monthly bulletins; Catholic Charities and Planned Parenthood, day care, education, adoptions, rehabilitation of the handicapped, health, aged, chronically ill, care of alcoholics, drug use, administration of health and welfare service; Helen M. Harris of UNH served on several committees of this organization.

Welfare and Health Council of New York City, Correspondence, 1954   626
    Correspondence, minutes of the central planning board, various studies on such topics as transportation for the handicapped, voluntary agencies and fee schedules, integration of immigrants.

UNITED NEIGHBORHOOD HOUSES, INC.

FOLDER TITLE AND DESCRIPTION OF CONTENTS	FOLDER
Welfare and Health Council of New York City, Greater New York Fund, 1950 Correspondence, reports, studies to analyze the policies and procedures of the Greater New York Fund.	627
Welfare and Health Council of New York City, Interim Report of the Central Harlem Street Club's Project, 1948 An "historical account" of the development of the Project, which shows its objectives, plans, and hopes for the future.	628
Welfare and Health Council of New York City, Project Committee on Employment and Guidance of Youth, 1950-1951 Minutes, reports on selective service, and assorted projects.	629
Welfare and Health Council of New York City, Joint Committee, Board of Education, 1947-1949 Correspondence, reports, papers of Dorothy C. Kahn.	630
Welfare and Health Council of New York City, New York State Youth Commission, 1949-1950 Correspondence, minutes, reports.	631
Welfare and Health Council of New York City, Personnel Standards Study, 1943 "Summary of a Study of Personnel Standards in Group Work Agencies in New York City," by Henry J. Kellermann; "Suggestions for the Use of Personnel Study Materials," by the Research Bureau of the Welfare Council.	632
Welfare and Health Council of New York City, Planned Parenthood, 1952-1953 Correspondence, minutes, materials reflecting controversy over admission of Planned Parenthood Committee of Mothers' Health Council of New York City.	633
Welfare and Health Council of New York City, Planned Parenthood, 1953 Correspondence, statements of principles.	634
Welfare and Health Council of New York City, Planned Parenthood, 1953 Correspondence, newspaper clippings re conflict over admission of Birth Control Clinic to Welfare Council.	635
Welfare and Health Council of New York City, Publications and Studies, 1944-1946 Correspondence, studies on leadership and responsibility in planning for public and voluntary recreation service in New York City; functions, programs, purposes, bylaws and activities of UNH.	636

UNITED NEIGHBORHOOD HOUSES, INC.

FOLDER TITLE AND DESCRIPTION OF CONTENTS	FOLDER

Welfare and Health Council of New York City, Publications and Studies, 1946-1950 — 637
  Correspondence, welfare projects, summary of conference on child care, Welfare Council newsletters.

Welfare and Health Council of New York City, Rateable Share Plan, 1946-1947 — 638
  UNH's dues payments to Welfare Council.

Welfare and Health Council of New York City, Report on Puerto Rican Children, 1950 — 639
  The report discusses needs of Puerto Rican immigrant children.

Welfare and Health Council of New York City, Recreation Planning Committee, 1947-1948 — 640
  Correspondence, press releases, memoranda, summary of the history of recreation planning and coordination in New York City, 1911-1940.

Welfare and Health Council of New York City, Recreation Survey, 1944-1945 — 641
  The Welfare Council of New York City did a survey of the recreational facilities available in New York City settlements; raw data and finished statistical tables are included.

Welfare and Health Council of New York City, Reorganization, 1946 — 642
  Correspondence, minutes on proposed reorganization of Welfare Council and its financial difficulties.

Welfare and Health Council of New York City, Settlement Evaluation Outline of Membership Committee of the Section on Social Group Work and Recreation, 1939 — 643
  Statement of policy, philosophy and objectives; arts and crafts.

Welfare and Health Council of New York City, Settlement Survey, 1928 — 644
  Materials used in a survey of programs offered in city settlements.

Welfare and Health Council of New York City, Subcommittee on Membership Statistics, 1948 — 645
  Correspondence, committee materials; informal education and group work services, recreation in public housing projects. Several members of UNH staff served on this subcommittee.

Welfare and Health Council of New York City, Training Committee, 1949-1950 — 646
  Correspondence, minutes; professionalism, role of volunteers, educational standards.

UNITED NEIGHBORHOOD HOUSES, INC.

FOLDER TITLE AND DESCRIPTION OF CONTENTS	FOLDER
Welfare and Health Council of New York City, Youth Councils Committee, 1945-1950 Correspondence, materials re UNH's liaison with the Welfare Council of New York City on youth problems.	647
Welfare and Health Council of New York City, Youth Council Project Committee, 1948-1952 Correspondence, summaries of minutes.	648

LEGAL FOLDERS

Financial Statements, 1924-1928 Monthly financial statements.	1
Brooklyn Neighborhood Houses Fund, 1947-1952 Speech on the United Nations, list of charitable foundations, certificate of incorporation of Youth United, history of the Brooklyn Neighborhood Fund, and report on work with Youth United.	2
League of Mothers' Clubs, Monthly Bulletins, 1925-1930 The monthly bulletins informed members of the activities of the League. Some issues and personalities discussed are Mayor James J. Walker, housing, foreign policy, educational programs, sanitation.	3
League of Mothers' Clubs, Monthly Bulletins, 1930-1934 Foreign affairs, President Herbert Hoover, education, housing, birth control and tenement laws.	4
Welfare Council of New York City, Bylaws, 1950-1951 Copies of bylaws.	5

UNITED NEIGHBORHOOD HOUSES OF NEW YORK, INC. - SCRAPBOOKS

Some of the scrapbooks were titled and these titles have been retained. However, as in Scrapbook #4, 1919-1924, Public Health Committee, materials other than Public Health Committee data are included.

# 1	1919-1924	#18	1935-1937
# 2	1919-1923, Bulletins	#19	1937-1938
# 3	1919-1922	#20	1938-1939
# 4	1919-1924, Public Health Committee	#21	1939-1940
# 5	1920-1924, Arts and Festivals, Drama Committee	#22	1940-1941
		#23	1941-1942
# 6	1924-1925	#24	1942-1943
# 7	1925-1926	#25	Newspaper clippings, 1920-1928
# 8	1926-1927		
# 9	1927-1928	#26	Newspaper clippings, 1928-1935
#10	1929-1930		
#11	1928-1933, League of Mothers' Clubs	#27	Newspaper clippings, 1935-1939
#12	1930-1931	#28	Newspaper clippings, 1939-1946
#13	1932-1933	#29	Newspaper clippings, 1947-1952
#14	1933-1934		
#15	1934-1935	#30	Newspaper clippings, 1958
#16	1935-1936		
#17	1935-1937, League of Mothers' Clubs		

UNITED NEIGHBORHOOD HOUSES, INC.   713

TABLE OF CONTENTS TO SERIES OF UNITED NEIGHBORHOOD HOUSES SCRAPBOOKS

In attempting to describe the contents of the scrapbooks, "A" has been used to indicate the verso of the page. Scrapbooks 25-30, which are composed of newspaper clippings only, should be used as a supplement to the narrative.

Scrapbook 1, 1919-1924, (filed in legal folders 6-11)

Folder I
legal f. 6   1-1:   UNH meetings, minutes; Executive Committee, minutes and reports on Americanization and other topics.
                1-1A: Salary studies.
                1-2:   Executive Committee, minutes.
                1-3:   Executive Committee: Lusk Committee investigation, wartime services, Bolshevism.
                1-3A: Executive Committee, minutes.
                1-4A: Executive Committee: volunteers, etc.

Folder II
legal f. 7   1-5:   Executive Committee: incorporation of UNH.
                1-5A: Executive Committee, minutes: UNH constitution, publicity.
                1-6:   Executive Committee, monthly meeting of UNH Association: volunteers.
                1-6A: Executive Committee, minutes: Lusk Committee.
                1-7:   Association, minutes.
                1-8:   Executive Committee, minutes: volunteers; Legal Committee.
                1-9:   Meetings: Americanization, Lusk Committee.
                1-10:   Executive Committee, minutes: boys' work, settlement movement in Russia.

Folder III
legal f. 8   1-11:   Association of Neighborhood Workers, UNH Committees, minutes.
                1-11A: Meetings, minutes.
                1-12:   Meetings.
                1-12A: Executive Committee, minutes.
                1-13:   Annual meetings: activities of UNH; report of Executive Secretary.
                1-14-
                  18A: Executive Committee, minutes.

Folder IV
legal f. 9   1-19:   Joint Meeting of Advisory and Executive Committee.
                1-19A: Meetings, minutes.
                1-20:   Executive Committee, minutes: immigrant work, housing.

	1-21:	Executive Committee, minutes; Headworkers' and Presidents' Meetings; Boards of Directors.
	1-21A:	Executive Committee, minutes; Legislative Committee.
	1-22:	Meetings, minutes.
	1-23:	Executive Committee, minutes.
	1-24:	Meetings, minutes.
	1-24A:	Executive Committee, minutes.
	1-25:	Executive Committee, annual meeting, 1921; reports.
	1-25A-26A	Executive Committee, minutes.
	1-27:	Meeting, minutes.
	1-28:	Meeting, minutes.
	1-29-31:	Executive Committee, minutes.
	1-32:	Meeting, minutes: housing, child welfare.
Folder V legal f. 10	1-33:	Executive Committee, minutes.
	1-34:	Meetings, minutes.
	1-35:	Meetings, minutes.
	1-36:	Executive Committee, minutes.
	1-37:	UNH meetings, minutes: activities.
	1-38:	Season of 1922-1923.
	1-39:	Executive Committee of UNH.
	1-40:	Meeting, minutes: music, settlement financing, etc
	1-41:	Agenda.
	1-42:	Executive Committee, minutes: "Social Welfare--How Shall We Vote?"
	1-43:	Meetings, minutes: function of play and recreation in the settlements.
	1-44:	Executive Committee, minutes.
	1-45:	Meetings, minutes.
	1-46:	Agenda.
	1-47:	Meetings, minutes: Toynbee Hall, British settlements.
	1-48:	Meetings, minutes: immigration.
	1-49:	Executive Committee, minutes.
	1-50-51:	Housing resolution.
	1-52:	Executive Committee, minutes.
	1-53-55:	Meetings, minutes.
	1-56:	Agenda.
	1-57:	Meetings, minutes.
	1-58:	Agenda.
	1-59:	Executive Committee.
	1-60:	Meetings, minutes.
	1-61:	Meetings, minutes.
	1-62-63:	Executive Committee, minutes.
	1-64:	Meetings, minutes.
Folder VI legal f. 11	1-65:	Executive Committee, minutes.
	1-66:	Executive Committee, minutes.
	1-67:	Agenda.

1-68:	Executive Committee, minutes.
1-69-70:	Meetings, minutes.
1-71:	Executive Committee, minutes.
1-72:	Resolution: immigration; Executive Committee papers.

Scrapbook 2, 1919-1923, <u>Bulletins</u>, (filed in legal folder 12)

Folder I
legal f. 12

2-1-2:	Announcements and agenda.
2-3-4:	Health Committee, announcements and agenda.
2-5-8:	Agenda, activities, social settlements after 25 years; prohibition, European settlements, unemployment.
2-9-11:	Activities and agenda.
2-12-14:	Activities and agenda.
2-15-20:	Activities and agenda: Lusk education act, volunteers, unemployment.
2-21-26:	Activities and agenda: League of Mothers' Clubs, Arts and Festivals Committee, dramatics, etc.
2-27-29:	<u>Bulletins</u>, season of 1922-1923: recreation, housing.

Scrapbook 3, 1919-1922, (filed in legal folders 13-14)

Folder I
legal f. 13

3-1:	Index.
3-2:	Committee on Cooperation (between settlements).
3-3-4:	Lusk Committee on Immigration and Naturalization.
3-5-6:	Finance Committee: Lusk Committee.
3-7-13:	Lusk Committee, Senior Girls' Association.
3-14:	Americanization.
3-15-16:	Wartime services; "What the Settlements Stand For."
3-17:	Unemployment.
3-18:	Girls' Workers, finances.
3-19-27:	Girls' Work, athletics.
3-28:	Cooperative Purchasing Plan.

Folder II
legal f. 14

3-29-30:	Cooperative Purchasing Plan.
3-31-35:	Boys' Workers, etc.
3-36:	Settlement Conference.
3-37-38:	Unemployment Committee.
3-39-44:	Program Committee.
3-45-49:	League of Mothers' Clubs, summer recreation, camping, etc.
3-51-52:	Armistice Day celebrations.
3-53-54:	Finances, Russian settlements.
3-55-58:	Activities: anti-litter campaign, special meetings, etc.

Scrapbook 4, 1919-1924, Public Health Committee and other materials, (filed in legal folders 15-17)

    Folder I
    legal f. 15
- 4-1: Minutes: social hygiene in the settlements.
- 4-2-3: Public Health Committee, minutes.
- 4-4: Infant mortality.
- 4-5-13: Public Health Committee.
- 4-14-23: Boys' Workers, Athletic League, Cooperative Purchasing Plan.
- 4-24-30: Boys' and Girls' Workers Association.

    Folder II
    legal f. 16
- 4-31-36: Intersettlement Girls' Association.
- 4-37-40: League of Mothers' Clubs.
- 4-41: Constitution of League of Mothers' Clubs.
- 4-42-46: Tenement House Committee of the Charity Organization Society.
- 4-47-52: Girls' Club; recreation.

    Folder III
    legal f. 17
- 4-53-61: Girls' Work Association.
- 4-62: Americanization; "Melting Pot"; League of Nations.
- 4-63-83: Girls' Work Association.
- 4-84: Financial Statements.
- 4-85-86: Board of Directors.
- 4-87: Amendment to UNH Constitution.
- 4-88-91: Routine material.
- 4-92-93: Talk by Henry M. Bush, "Underlying Principles of Settlement Club Work."
- 4-94-95: Girls' Work Association.
- 4-96-97: League of Mothers' Club and Girls Athletic Association
- 4-98: League of Mothers' Club, Bulletins.

Scrapbook 5, 1920-1924, Arts and Festivals, Dramatics Committee and other materials, (filed in legal folders 18-20)

    Folder I
    legal f. 18
- 5-1-30: Minutes, agenda, programs, reports.

    Folder II
    legal f. 19
- 5-31-52: Ibid.

    Folder III
    legal f. 20
- 5-53-57: Ibid.

Scrapbook 6, 1924-1925, (filed in legal folders 21-23)

    Folder I
    legal f. 21
- 6-1-2: Administration Committee, minutes.
- 6-5-7: Administration Committee, Arts and Festivals Committee.

UNITED NEIGHBORHOOD HOUSES, INC.

	6-8-10:	Arts and Festivals Bulletins, minutes.
	6-11-14:	Flower booths and Arts and Festivals Committee.
	6-15-16:	May Day Festival.
	6-17-19:	Flower booths.
	6-20-22:	List of Board Members, regular meeting agenda, reports; finances.
	6-23-29:	UNH regular meetings, minutes.
	6-30-31:	Debating League, resolved: the U.S. should adopt a child labor amendment.
	6-32-33:	Athletics.
Folder II legal f. 22	6-34-35:	Athletics.
	6-36-37:	Older Boys' Association, minutes.
	6-38-40:	Notices re athletics.
	6-41-42:	Older Boys' Association, minutes; Constitution of Older Boys' Association.
	6-43-44:	Boys' Work
	6-45-46:	Headworkers and Legal Committee: organization of UNH.
	6-47-48:	Executive Committee, minutes: finances and organization, etc.
	6-49:	Executive Committee, minutes.
	6-50-51:	Executive Committee, minutes.
	6-52-53:	Girls' Workers data.
	6-54-55:	Girls' Association.
	6-56-64:	Girls' Workers, meetings, minutes.
Folder III legal f. 23	6-65-86:	League of Mothers' Clubs.
	6-87:	Legal Committee, notices, minutes.
	6-88:	Legal program of UNH: censorship of motion pictures, out-of-wedlock birth, etc.
	6-89-92:	Luncheon Committee, programs, etc.

Scrapbook 7, 1925-1926, (filed in legal folders 24-26)

Folder I legal f. 24	7-1-2:	Administration Committee.
	7-3:	Administration Committee, minutes.
	7-5-10:	Arts and Festivals Committee, minutes.
	7-11-13:	UNH meetings, minutes.
	7-14-15:	UNH Association, meetings and minutes: housing, Board of Trustees, Jane Addams on "Patriotism and Internationalism," Mrs. J. C. Bernheim and beginnings of psychiatry.
	7-16-17:	Annual meeting, minutes; Mary Simkhovitch on the function of settlements; John L. Elliott and Graham Romeyn Taylor on delinquency, 1925; Treasurer's report; program committee, minutes.
	7-18-23:	Boys' and Girls' Athletic Committee.

Folder II
legal f. 25

7-24:	Athletic programs.
7-25-26:	Headworkers' meeting: education.
7-27-28:	Executive Committee, minutes: volunteers, birth control, housing.
7-29-30:	Executive Committee, minutes: finances, housing.
7-31:	Executive Committee, minutes: housing.
7-32-32A:	Senior Girls' Association; Executive Committee: housing.
7-33-36:	Girls' Work, Girls' Association: athletics.
7-37:	Intersettlement Senior Girls' Association.
7-38-40:	Girls' Workers: scholarships.
7-41:	Senior Boys' and Girls' Association.
7-42:	League of Mothers' Clubs: Executive Committee of UNH, re Governor Smith's Housing Plan.
7-43:	Legal and Legislation Committee: motion picture censorship, housing.
7-44:	League of Mothers' Clubs.

Folder III
legal f. 26

7-45-52:	League of Mothers' Clubs, Bulletins.
7-53-54:	League of Mothers' Clubs, Executive Committee re education and child welfare.
7-55-56:	League of Mothers' Clubs re dances.
7-57-58:	League of Mothers' Clubs.
7-59-61:	UNH Executive Committee, second Annual Luncheon: Jane Addams.
7-62-65:	Conference to Clean Up The Parks, minutes, etc.

Scrapbook 8, 1926-1927, (filed in legal folders 27-31)

Folder I
legal f. 27

8-1-2:	Arts and Festivals Committee; Drama Committee, minutes.
8-3-7:	Drama Committee, statement of purpose, etc.
8-8:	May Day; Annual Meeting programs.
8-9:	Ethical standards for wages in social work.
8-10:	Conference on Health; Negroes in New York; music in the settlements.
8-11:	James T. Shotwell on internationalism, UNH Annual Meeting, minutes: social education.
8-12:	Annual Report of Executive Secretary of UNH, Administration Committee.
8-13:	List of Committees of UNH; UNH Association meetings, minutes.
8-14:	Employment Bureau materials.
8-15:	Employment survey; UNH meetings; music, graphic arts.
8-16:	UNH Association meetings, minutes.

Folder II
legal f. 28

8-17:	UNH Association meetings, minutes.
8-18:	UNH Association meetings: housing.
8-19:	UNH Association meetings, Program Committee.
8-20:	Board meeting; Program Committee.
8-21:	Board of Directors, meetings.
8-22:	Boys' and Girls' Conference.
8-23-24:	Conference on Social Education; Social Education Committee.
8-25-26:	Social Education.
8-27-30:	Social Education Course.
8-31:	Social Education Course re ethics, Annual Meeting reports.
8-32-33:	Executive Committee.

Folder III
legal f. 29

8-34:	Executive Committee.
8-35:	Board of Directors; Executive Committee.
8-36:	Executive Committee.
8-37-39:	UNH accountant's report.
8-40-41:	Headworkers'; Board notices.
8-42-43:	Girls' Workers, notices.
8-44-45:	Girls' Workers, Intersettlement Girls' Athletic Association.
8-46-47:	Girls' Workers.
8-48:	Legal Committee on housing, wages.

Folder IV
legal f. 30

8-49:	1927, legislative program: housing, child welfare, motor vehicles.
8-50:	League of Mothers' Clubs, mass housing meeting.
8-51:	Letter of Alfred E. Smith to UNH on housing.
8-52:	Legal Committee; Advisory Housing Committee.
8-53-54:	Advisory Housing Committee: tenement houses.
8-55:	UNH Nominating Committee, list of Executive Committee officers.
8-56-57:	Executive Committee; annual luncheon.
8-58:	Annual luncheon.
8-59-66:	League of Mothers' Clubs: housing, letter to Mayor Walker, property taxation.
8-67-68:	Questionnaires, budgets: day camps, summer work.
8-69:	Summer projects.
8-70:	Association of Volunteers in Social Service.
8-71:	League of Mothers' Clubs, list of officers.

Folder V
legal f. 31

8-72-73:	League of Mothers' Clubs, Executive Committee, minutes: commercial action of the U.S. in Mexico, vice in Harlem, decision to integrate Mothers' Clubs.
8-74:	League of Mothers' Clubs, Executive Committee.
8-75-76:	League of Mothers' Clubs: homemaking, housing; Committee on Health.
8-77-78:	League of Mothers' Clubs: housing.

	8-79-80:	League of Mothers' Clubs: housing, mass housing march, letter to Governor Al Smith.
	8-81:	"Mother Power," statement of purpose of the League.
	8-82:	League of Mothers' Clubs, statement of purpose.
	8-83-84:	League of Mothers' Clubs: Bulletins, luncheon programs.
	8-85-87:	League of Mothers' Clubs: Bulletins, housing, an end to war, philosophy of League work, housing tours.

Scrapbook 9, 1927-1928, (filed in legal folders 32-36)

Folder I
legal f. 32

9-1-11:	Arts and Festivals Committee, minutes: dramatics.
9-12:	Lists of artists.
9-13:	Headworkers material.
9-14:	Annual Meeting, pamphlet.
9-15-16:	Ninth Annual Conference, minutes: housing, boys' and girls' work.
9-17:	Annual Meeting, minutes: camps, child care.

Folder II
legal f. 33

9-18:	Association and Board Meeting, minutes.
9-19:	Fourth Annual Luncheon, Dr. Henry Sloane Coffin, speaker.
9-20-22:	Program Committee, minutes, speakers' material.
9-23-24:	UNH Annual Conference.
9-25-26:	Social Education Committee, minutes, lists of members.
9-27:	Social Education Committee, discussion on alternatives to marriage and sex.
9-28:	Social Education Committee, discussion on mental development, with contributions from James Harvey Robinson: religion, ethics, eugenics, intermarriage, birth control, sex education, racial and religious discrimination, Negroes in Mississippi Negro deportation, NAACP.
9-29:	Reports on member houses: pressing problems, activities.
9-30:	Social Education Committee, results of a questionnaire on pertinent problems.

Folder III
legal f. 34

9-31:	Social Education Committee, topics for discussion.
9-32:	Social Education Committee: sex education.
9-33:	Executive Committee, minutes, reports of activities.
9-34-35:	Executive Committee, minutes.
9-36:	Committee on Plan and Scope, Executive Committee.
9-37:	Committee on Plan and Scope, minutes; statements on function and history of UNH.
9-38:	Committee on Plan and Scope, Budget and Finance Committees.
9-39:	Monthly statements; list of members of UNH, 1927-1928.
9-40:	Financial appeal results, lists of settlements that were not members of UNH.

	9-41:	Girls' Association.
	9-42-44:	Girls' Workers Committee.
Folder IV		
legal f. 35	9-45-46:	Girls' Workers scholarships.
	9-47:	Girls' Association scholarships; Legislative Committee, minutes: housing, crime prevention.
	9-48:	Legislative Committee.
	9-49:	1928, tentative legislative program: child welfare, housing.
	9-50:	Legislative Committee: salaries of immigration inspectors, birth control.
	9-51:	Legislative Committee: housing, slum clearance.
	9-52A:	Legislative Committee: budgets, housing, sanitation.
	9-53:	Legislative Committee, lists of members of advisory housing committee; Tenement Housing Committee of the Charity Organization Society and housing reform.
	9-54:	Legislative Committee, advisory housing committee.
	9-55:	Ninth Annual Meeting, Annual Luncheon.
	9-56:	Legislative Committee: housing.
Folder V		
legal f. 36	9-57:	Headworkers and Board members, Luncheon Committee.
	9-58:	List of improvements and construction in the settlements.
	9-59:	Survey of employment work done by individual settlements.
	9-60:	Residence questionnaires.
	9-61:	City neighborhoods, requirements for religious facilities.
	9-62:	Summer camp materials.
	9-63:	Use of volunteers, staff questionnaires.

Scrapbook 10, 1929-1930, (filed in legal folders 37-43)

Folder I		
legal f. 37	10-1-2:	Index to scrapbook.
	10-3:	Arts and Festivals Committee.
	10-4:	Arts and Festivals Committee: social service through the arts.
	10-5:	Arts and Festivals Committee.
	10-6:	May Day festivals.
	10-7:	Children's theatre.
	10-8:	Intersettlement Dramatic Committee, minutes and announcements.
	10-9:	United Players' Guild, Bulletin.
	10-10:	Entertainment Committee.
	10-12-13:	Board of Directors, minutes.
	10-14:	Annual Conference, minutes: juvenile delinquency, Negro assimilation.
	10-15:	Annual Conference, reports: housing, education, immigration, health.

	10-16:	Annual Conference, financial statement, Albert J. Kennedy on "Settlement Education for Esthetic Appreciation."
	10-17-18:	Program Committee, minutes.
	10-19:	UNH Association meeting, agenda and minutes.
	10-20:	Association Meeting, minutes and agenda: discussion of European folk schools, Reinhold Niebuhr was a speaker.
Folder II legal f. 38	10-21:	Association meeting: progressives with liberal power.
	10-22:	UNH Association meeting, minutes: Negro-white relations.
	10-23:	Boys' Workers Association.
	10-24:	Seminar Project: "Working with the Southern Italian Family."
	10-24A:	Social Education Committee: Southern Italian family in New York.
	10-25:	A History of the Development of Social Education in UNH.
	10-26:	Social Education Committee, "Modern thought as expressed in Modern Art."
	10-27:	Social Education Course, minutes: modern art, philosophy of art.
	10-28-32:	Executive Committee, minutes.
Folder III legal f. 39	10-33:	Executive Committee and Board of Directors, minutes.
	10-34:	Housing.
	10-35:	Contribution lists.
	10-36-37:	Financial statements, 1928.
	10-38:	Athletic Association, minutes.
	10-39-40:	Girls' Athletic Association and intersettlement athletic materials.
	10-41:	Girls' Work Committee: social education, personality studies, progressive legislation, Frances Perkins.
	10-42:	Girls' Work Committee: education.
	10-43:	Housing Committee: objectives.
	10-44:	Housing Committee, minutes.
	10-45:	Housing Committee, minutes; tenement occupation survey.
Folder IV legal f. 40	10-46:	Letter to Governor Franklin D. Roosevelt of New York re housing.
	10-47:	Press releases re housing.
	10-48:	Multiple Dwellings Laws.
	10-49:	Annual Luncheon, Legislation Committee, Legal Committee.
	10-50:	Publicity statement, program, tickets, papers: old law tenements, John Lovejoy Elliott, Mary K. Simkhovitch.
	10-51:	Governor Franklin D. Roosevelt on housing.

Folder V		
legal f. 41	10-52:	Finances, headworkers' reports: functions and activity of UNH.
	10-53:	Residence questionnaire.
	10-54:	Recreation, play schools.
	10-55:	Open-air theatre.
	10-56:	Open-air theatre.
	10-57:	Visual arts section of Arts and Festivals Committee.
	10-58-60:	Arts and Festivals Committee: May Day Festival.
	10-61-66:	Play Bulletins (dramatic).
Folder VI		
legal f. 42	10-67:	Arts and Festivals Committee, concert ticket lists.
	10-68:	1930 Annual Conference, minutes: social work adventures, Clare Tousley; UNH Association meeting, minutes of Program Committee; Board Meetings, minutes.
	10-69:	Social Education Meeting, minutes: Association meeting, minutes.
	10-70:	Executive Committee, minutes: housing, Norman Thomas; list of Board of Directors.
	10-71:	Executive Committee, minutes: housing, art exhibit, etc.
	10-72:	Planning Committee: restatement of settlement point of view.
	10-73:	Financial statement.
	10-74:	Budget Committee, financial statement.
	10-75:	Girls' Workers.
	10-76:	Girls' Athletic Association.
	10-77:	Girls' Workers Association.
Folder VII		
legal f. 43	10-78:	Boys' and Girls' Workers: social education, music appreciation, play and recreation; Girls' Workers, minutes.
	10-79:	Housing, recreation; Housing Committee materials.
	10-80:	Study of old law tenement rentals, Housing Committee materials, Legislative Committee material.
	10-81:	Settlement staff: music, number of old law tenements.
	10-82:	Bibliography on social welfare, summer camp expenditures.
	10-83-84:	Report of information given out by UNH.

Scrapbook 11, 1928-1933, (filed in legal folders 44-49)
The entire scrapbook documents the activities of the League of Mothers' Clubs.

Folder I		
legal f. 44	11-1:	Resume of activity.
	11-2-4:	Routine materials.
	11-5:	Annual meeting, minutes, etc.
	11-6:	Child welfare.
	11-7:	Better homes, housing, minimum standards for a neighborhood.

	11-8-9:	Dance in honor of John L. Elliott, founder of the League.
	11-10:	Executive Committee.
	11-11:	Leadership course.
	11-12:	Health Committee.
	11-13:	Homemaking.
	11-14:	Homemaking.
	11-15:	Housing, interesting fragment on "inside rooms" and health hazards.
	11-16:	Housing, tenement houses.
	11-17-21:	Routine activities.
Folder II legal f. 45	11-22:	Housing Committee.
	11-23:	Bulletins, activities.
	11-24:	Activities.
	11-25:	Nominating Committee.
	11-26:	Child study.
	11-27:	Mid-winter carnival.
	11-28:	Executive Committee.
	11-29:	Finances.
	11-30:	Health and homemaking.
	11-31:	Health and homemaking.
	11-32:	Leaders' forums: recreation, family relationships, housing.
	11-33:	Bibliography on health education.
	11-34-35:	Routine activities.
	11-36:	Speakers' Bureau materials.
	11-37-38:	Summer activities.
	11-39:	Child study, travel clubs.
	11-40:	Brooklyn branch of the League.
	11-41:	Activities.
Folder III legal f. 46	11-42-44:	Executive Committee, routine activities.
	11-45:	Executive Committee: child welfare, health.
	11-46:	Financial materials.
	11-47:	Executive Committee, Health Committee.
	11-48:	Housing, etc.
	11-49:	Recreation.
	11-50:	Activities.
	11-51:	Officers' Manual.
	11-52-54:	Routine activities.
Folder IV legal f. 47	11-55:	Work done in non-profit organizations.
	11-56:	Speakers' Bureau.
	11-57:	Travel Club.
	11-58:	Membership lists.
	11-59:	Summer boat trips.
	11-60:	Summer activities.
	11-61:	Constitution, record of UNH activities.
	11-62:	Brooklyn Branch of the League.
	11-63-64:	Annual Dance.
	11-65:	Executive Board materials.
	11-66:	Executive Board: health, finances, child welfare.

UNITED NEIGHBORHOOD HOUSES, INC.

Folder V
legal f. 48
	11-67:	Finances.
	11-68:	Finances.
	11-69:	Annual Benefit.
	11-70:	Benefit dance; health, depression.
	11-71:	Routine material.
	11-72:	Housing.
	11-73:	Paper, "Mental Health in the Depression."
	11-74:	Anniversary materials.
	11-75:	Songs.
	11-76:	Songs.
	11-77:	Peace parade.
	11-78:	Leaders and Officers Conference.
	11-79:	Picnic and sewing classes.
	11-80:	Summer activities.
	11-81:	Activities.
	11-82:	Brooklyn Branch of the League.
	11-83:	Annual dance materials.

Folder VI
legal f. 49
	11-84:	Executive Board: housing, peace, health, recreation, music, legislation.
	11-85:	Routine activities.
	11-86:	Dinner.
	11-87:	Dinner.
	11-88:	Dinner, health, legality of birth control.
	11-89:	Housing, rental survey.
	11-90:	Legislative and civil work; leaders material.
	11-91:	Peace, legislation.
	11-92:	Folk Dance and Music Festival.
	11-93:	Folk Dance and Music Festival; homemaking, speakers' bureau.
	11-94:	Summer activities, Travel Club.
	11-95:	Travel Club.

Scrapbook 12, 1930-1931, (filed in legal folders 50-57)

Folder I
legal f. 50
	12-1:	Index to scrapbook.
	12-2:	Arts and Festivals Committee on aim of social music.
	12-3:	Arts and Festivals Committee.
	12-4:	Arts and Festivals Committee, Visual Arts Committee.
	12-5:	Arts and Festivals Committee, Play Bulletin.
	12-6:	Dramatic Play Bulletins, Arts and Crafts Committee.
	12-7:	Third Annual Arts and Crafts Exhibit; philosophy of recreation.
	12-8:	Arts and Crafts, an art exhibition.
	12-9:	List of members of the League.
	12-10:	Seventh Annual Luncheon.

UNITED NEIGHBORHOOD HOUSES, INC.

                    12-11:   Meeting re social workers and the attack on social and industrial evils, (recapitulation of social legislation of UNH and the work of Jane Addams, Lillian Wald, etc.); plans for the Depression: unions, strikes, historical examples of what could be done, political action, e.g. Jane Addams turning down money from capitalists; speech by Charles C. Webber of Union Theological Seminary.

Folder II
legal f. 51   12-12:   Association meetings, minutes.
                    12-13:   Association, minutes: Mark McCloskey speaking on the changing standards of practice in the settlements; program for an investigation of all New York City politics.
                    12-14:   Annual Conference; Roger Baldwin of the American Civil Liberties Union on patriots, aliens, and "Reds"; progressive education; housing; new settlement challenges; Paul Kellogg on opportunities for the settlements.
                    12-15:   Legislation.
                    12-16:   Statement on labor: A.F. of L., communism, the Progressive Movement.
                    12-17:   Minutes of lectures given by A. J. Muste on labor and unemployment; Hoover Commission; the relative position of income groups in the United States; compulsory unemployment insurance.
                    12-18:   Personal Service and Health Workers, minutes.
                    12-19:   Boys' Workers Conference.
                    12-20-24:   Girls' Workers materials.

Folder III
legal f. 52   12-25:   Girls' Work.
                    12-26:   Girls' Work.
                    12-27:   Executive Committee: unemployment.
                    12-28:   Executive Committee: music, birth control.
                    12-29:   Executive Committee, minutes: statement of the settlement point of view.
                    12-30:   Program Committee.
                    12-31:   Financial statements, 1926-1930.
                    12-32:   Legislative Committee, program.
                    12-33-34:   Housing Committee.
                    12-35:   Arts and Crafts Committee, Legislative Committee, Visual Arts Committee.
                    12-36:   Camping, legislation.

Folder IV
legal f. 53   12-37-39:   Unemployment Committee.
                    12-40:   Girls' Work Committee.
                    12-41:   Brochure on recreation, headworkers' information requests, study of users of UNH services.
                    12-42:   Bibliography on social welfare, nature of UNH information requests.

UNITED NEIGHBORHOOD HOUSES, INC.

Folder V
legal f. 54
- 12-43: Dances.
- 12-44: List of new activities in New York settlements, 1929-1931: birth control clinics and psychiatric workers, headworkers and services on settlement boards; list of five settlements and their methods of financing, list of settlements and year they were established.
- 12-45: Visual Arts; Arts and Crafts Committee, Albert J. Kennedy chaired this Committee.
- 12-46: Arts and Crafts Committee, financial statements.
- 12-47: Arts and Crafts Committee.
- 12-48: Visual Arts Committee.
- 12-49: <u>Play Bulletin</u> (dramatic), January-May, 1932.
- 12-50: <u>Play Bulletin</u> (dramatic), November-December, 1931.
- 12-51: Annual Spring Conference, financial statement.
- 12-52: Annual Conference, minutes, reports: unemployment, relief. Helen Hall, John L. Elliott are mentioned. Headworkers' on standardization of work of the settlements; Program Committee materials.
- 12-53: Program Committee.
- 12-54: Mayor James J. Walker's estimate of available relief funds in New York City; analysis of unemployment and relief, also UNH's programs.
- 12-55: Statement of social workers re relief, closing of Home Relief Bureaus.

Folder VI
legal f. 55
- 12-56: Camp life, anti-war parade.
- 12-57: Association meeting, minutes: headworkers, education, relief.
- 12-58: Association meeting, minutes: depression, relief, employment insurance, immigration and Americanization.
- 12-59: Luncheon in honor of Edward Corsi, Commissioner of Immigration.
- 12-60: Executive Committee; Board of Directors, lists of members, minutes and announcements.
- 12-61: Executive Committee, minutes: housing.
- 12-62: Executive Committee, minutes: unemployment, housing, etc.
- 12-63: A special inter-settlement conference group on the depression; Executive Committee, minutes: home relief and unemployment, housing, visual arts.
- 12-64: Inter-settlement study group: marriage, etc.
- 12-65: Unemployment.
- 12-66: UNH work and member houses.
- 12-67: Papers re entertainment.

Folder VII
legal f. 56
- 12-68: Theatre Benefit.
- 12-69: Financial statement, girls' athletics.
- 12-70: Girls' athletics.
- 12-71: Girls' athletics.
- 12-72: Association meeting, minutes.

	12-73:	Directors of Boys' and Girls' Work Course: progressive education, children's clubs.
	12-74:	Directors of Boys' and Girls' Work Course: progressive education, children's clubs.
	12-75:	Recreation Workers and Boys' and Girls' Workers: 1919 and 1932 children's work program comparisons.
	12-76:	Scholarships.
	12-77:	Legislation Committee program, 1932: housing, letter to Governor Franklin D. Roosevelt; Executive Committee notices.
	12-78:	Housing and Headworkers' Committee.
	12-79:	Housing Committee: tenements, etc.
Folder VIII		
legal f. 57	12-80:	Executive Board: housing, legislation for unemployment; "News and Notes" of UNH's activities, November, 1931-March, 1932.
	12-81:	Legislative Committee.
	12-82:	Housing and relief.
	12-83:	Headworkers' Committee.
	12-84:	Camp.
	12-85:	Settlement camps, facilities of member houses.
	12-86:	Personal requests and their disposition.

Scrapbook 13, 1932-1933, (filed in legal folders 58-61)

Folder I		
legal f. 58	13-1:	Concert ticket lists.
	13-2:	Visual Arts Committee, ticket lists.
	13-3-4:	Visual Arts Committee, minutes.
	13-5:	Arts and Crafts exhibit in New York City settlements.
	13-6:	Annual Conference, minutes.
	13-7:	Annual Conference, minutes: report of A. J. Muste, Chairman of the Conference for Progressive Labor Action, "Are We Moving Toward a Dictatorship?" on the National Industrial Recovery Act.
	13-8:	Headworkers Committee: settlement work.
	13-9:	Headworkers meeting: social education.
	13-10:	Luncheon: the state in a program of social welfare.
	13-11:	Special Committee on Relief, minutes; resolution of UNH on relief; meeting of Case Workers: relief versus cash payment programs.
	13-12:	Case Workers meeting, minutes.
	13-13:	Case Workers Committee and Special Relief Committee: unemployment project.
	13-14:	Case Workers Committee and Social Education Committee.
Folder II		
legal f. 59	13-15:	Social Education Committee.
	13-16:	Executive Committee and Board of Directors re members; Social Education Committee.

UNITED NEIGHBORHOOD HOUSES, INC.

	13-17:	Executive Committee, minutes; some topics are relief, housing, legislation, etc.
	13-18:	Executive Committee, minutes.
	13-19-21:	Executive Committee, minutes: housing, treatment of Jews in Germany.
	13-22:	Walter Lippmann editorial re private charity and public money in relief.
	13-23:	Girls' Athletic Association.
	13-24-25:	Girls' Athletic Association.
	13-26-27:	Athletics.
	13-28:	Club work and social aims.
	13-29:	Boys' and Girls' Workers Committee: unemployment and progressive education.
	13-30:	Boys' and Girls' Work, Executive Committee papers.
	13-31:	Boys' and Girls' Work Committee: civic education.
Folder III legal f. 60	13-32:	Boys' and Girls' Work, summary of scholarship program; Unemployment Committee.
	13-33:	Intersettlement dances.
	13-34:	Intersettlement dances.
	13-35:	Legislative Committee, 1933 program; telegram sent to President Franklin D. Roosevelt on legislative programs.
	13-36:	Legislative Committee.
	13-37:	Legislative Committee: unemployment, Lillian Wald Unemployment Insurance Bill.
	13-38:	Legislative Committee: social legislation.
	13-39:	Housing Committee.
	13-40:	Housing Committee; Legislative Committee.
	13-41-43:	Legislative Committee papers.
Folder IV legal f. 61	13-44:	League of Mothers' Clubs, rent survey, "Tenements and Tenants--A Study of Tenement Families."
	13-45:	Publicity meetings, press releases.
	13-46:	Intersettlement newspaper.

Scrapbook 14, 1933-1934, (filed in legal folders 62-65)

Folder I legal f. 62	14-1:	Index to scrapbook.
	14-2:	Arts and Crafts Committee; Visual Arts Committee.
	14-3:	Art exhibit, Annual Dinner.
	14-4:	Program and standards for the visual arts in tenement neighborhoods, 1934.
	14-5:	Dramatic consultant service.
	14-6:	Ticket Committee.
	14-7:	Fifteenth Annual Conference, financial statement, conference reports on the influence of UNH past and future, peace parade, dissent.
	14-8:	Adult education, aims of personal service workers.
	14-9:	Anti-war parade, unemployment relief activities.

	14-10:	Unemployment relief.
	14-11:	Research Committee; Unemployment Relief Committee.
	14-12:	Committee on Unemployment Relief, Emergency Committee on Unemployment.
	14-13:	Civil Works Service Bureau, Personal Service Workers.
	14-14:	"Duties of a Social Service Worker in a Settlement House"; Case Workers and Personal Service Workers, minutes.

Folder II
legal f. 63

	14-15:	Association meeting, minutes; Housing Committee; history of New York City housing.
	14-16:	Camping meeting.
	14-17:	Education; Program Committee.
	14-18:	Social Education Committee; Executive Committee, list of members.
	14-19:	Executive Committee, minutes: housing, relief, unemployment insurance, visual arts.
	14-20-22:	Executive Committee, minutes.
	14-23:	Executive Committee and Nominating Committee, minutes; Publicity and Finance Committee.
	14-24:	Finance appeals.
	14-25:	Financial statements.
	14-26-30:	Girls' Work Athletics.

Folder III
legal f. 64

	14-31-33:	Girls' Athletic Committee: play day.
	14-34:	Boys' and Girls' Work Committee, Program Committee.
	14-35:	Boys' and Girls' Work Committee, minutes.
	14-36:	Boys' and Girls' Work Committee, Program Committee, Play Ground Leadership and Facility Committee.
	14-37:	Boys' and Girls' Workers: recreation facilities.
	14-38:	Intersettlement Dance Committee.
	14-39:	Intersettlement Dance Committee, Legislative Committee: child labor, unemployment insurance.
	14-40:	Legislative Program, 1940.
	14-41:	Child labor legislation.
	14-42:	Legislative Committee re unemployment insurance.
	14-43:	Unemployment insurance, UNH discussion of National Recovery Act.
	14-44:	Publicity, Intersettlement Newspaper, 1934: common needs of settlements.
	14-45:	Eighth Annual Luncheon, Intersettlement Committee.

Folder IV
legal f. 65

	14-46:	Eighth Annual Luncheon, Program Committee: social rebuilding of New York.
	14-47:	Eighth Annual Luncheon, an open letter from UNH to New York City's mayor on social progress and housing.
	14-48:	Press releases, Emergency Committee on Unemployment: housing.
	14-49:	Housing Committee.

UNITED NEIGHBORHOOD HOUSES, INC.

14-50:	Press releases; obtaining federal funds for housing and social reform.
14-50A:	Housing Committee.
14-51:	Musical opportunities in New York City settlements, consumer milk survey.
14-52:	Milk survey papers.

Scrapbook 15, 1934-1935, (filed in legal folders 66-70)

Folder I
legal f. 66

15-1:	Speech notes on housing.
15-2:	Index to scrapbook.
15-3:	Arts and Crafts Committee re dramatics.
15-4:	Dramatic project.
15-5:	Arts and Crafts Committee, Visual Arts Committee, New York City Mayor's Art Committee.
15-6-8:	Arts and Crafts Committee.
15-9:	Visual Arts Committee, minutes.
15-10:	Arts and Crafts Committee.
15-11:	Arts and Crafts Committee: National Federation of Settlements' poetry division.
15-12-13:	Ticket Committee: complimentary tickets.
15-14:	Association meetings: relief, special UNH luncheon program.
15-15:	Headworkers' meetings.
15-16:	Headworkers' Committee.
15-17:	Headworkers' symposium, presided over by Paul U. Kellogg: "Where Are the Settlements Going," with Mary K. Simkhovitch, Helen Hall and others.
15-18:	Headworkers' meeting: relief, development of neighborhood associations.
15-19:	Annual Conference, routine material.

Folder II
legal f. 67

15-20:	Jane Addams "Memorial" meeting, May 23, 1935.
15-21:	Annual Conference: "Cementing the Relationship Between the Settlement and the Workers' Unemployed Union," dramatics in the settlements, relief, unemployment, government censors.
15-22:	Education; Boys' and Girls' Work Committees.
15-23:	Executive Committee, minutes.
15-24:	Executive Committee, minutes.
15-25:	Executive Committee, agenda and minutes.
15-26:	Policy and Reorganization Committee, Executive Committee: relief.
15-27:	Executive Committee: allocation of federal funds, peace parades, finances.
15-28:	Finances, dues of member houses to UNH and the National Federation of Settlements, contributions.
15-29:	Financial statements, 1934-1935.
15-30:	Financial statements, theatre benefit.
15-31:	Theatre benefit.
15-32:	Theatre benefit, list of patrons.
15-33:	Intersettlement Play Day, athletics.

UNITED NEIGHBORHOOD HOUSES, INC.

Folder III
legal f. 68
- 15-34-37: Athletics: girls.
- 15-38: Boys' and Girls' Work, Executive Committee materials.
- 15-39: Boys' and Girls' Work.
- 15-40: Boys' and Girls' Workers meeting, minutes: peace groups.
- 15-41: Boys' and Girls' Work: facilities of certain settlements for children of varying ages.
- 15-42: Boys' and Girls' Work, Committee on Organization and Standards, reports of child study groups.
- 15-43: Boys' and Girls' Work, nominating committee; UNH legislative program, 1935.
- 15-44: Legislative Committee, statements and minutes: unemployment insurance.
- 15-45: Housing Committee, Legislative Committee.

Folder IV
legal f. 69
- 15-46: Housing Committee, minutes: statement of Harold Ickes, Secretary of Interior, on housing, housing legislation.
- 15-47: Legislative Committee, housing newspaper clippings, statements of UNH on minimum housing requirements.
- 15-48: Headworkers Committee, topics for housing and study groups; Housing Committee, minutes.
- 15-49: Housing Committee, Legislative Committee.
- 15-50: Ninth Annual Luncheon, publicity.
- 15-51: Ninth Annual Luncheon, program and newspaper clippings: list of health activities, clinics scheduled in member houses.
- 15-52: Personal Service Workers, guide for interviewing clients, guide for referring clients to Home Relief Bureau.
- 15-53: Personal Service Workers, minutes and reports: casework technique, relief unemployment, casework information service of UNH, intake policies.
- 15-54: Personal Service Workers: intake policies and special services of the family agencies of New York
- 15-55: Personal Service Workers: casework technique; Unemployment Committee.

Folder V
legal f. 70
- 15-56: Personal Service Workers.
- 15-57: Personal Service Workers: relief, rent surveys, Workers' Unemployed Union.
- 15-58: Citizens Conference on Unemployment, statistics concerning relief bonds.
- 15-59: Relief, municipal lottery.
- 15-60: Executive Committee: relief, newspaper clippings.
- 15-61: List of settlements receiving relief benefits.

Scrapbook 16, 1935-1936, (filed in legal folders 71-74)

Folder I
legal f. 71
- 16-1-2: Arts and Crafts Committee: WPA and visual arts.

	16-3:	Statement by Albert J. Kennedy on "The Settlement and the Federal Art Project."
	16-4:	Dramatics Committee, minutes and materials.
	16-5:	Ticket Committee.
	16-6:	Tickets and athletics.
	16-7:	Recreation and boys' work.
	16-8:	National Conference of Social Work: group work.
	16-9:	Boys' and Girls' Workers: group work.
	16-10:	American Association of Social Workers: professional social work requirements; Headworkers Committee.
	16-11:	Summer activities, Headworkers Committee.
	16-12:	Headworkers Committee.
	16-13:	Association meetings, minutes: destruction of National Recovery Act, Headworkers luncheon.
	16-14:	Association meetings.
	16-15:	Conference.
	16-16:	Annual Conference, financial statement.
	16-17:	Headworkers Committee.
	16-18:	Executive Committee.
Folder II legal f. 72	16-19:	Executive Committee, minutes.
	16-20-22:	Executive Committee, minutes.
	16-23:	Contributors, finances.
	16-24-29:	Theatre benefit.
	16-30-33:	Financial statements.
	16-34:	Girls' athletics.
	16-35:	Athletics.
Folder III legal f. 73	16-36-42:	Athletics.
	16-43:	Girls' Athletic Committee, minutes.
	16-44-45:	Boys' and Girls' Work, study group.
	16-46:	Legislative Committee.
	16-47:	Boys' and Girls' Work.
	16-48:	Boys' and Girls' Work.
	16-49-50:	Peace Committee.
	16-51-55:	Boys' and Girls' Workers, Scholarship Committee, Bulletins, UNH activities.
Folder IV legal f. 74	16-56-57:	Boys' and Girls' Workers.
	16-58-61:	National Youth Administration Advisory Committee, settlement activities.
	16-62:	UNH conference re WPA and NYA training of workers and volunteers.
	16-63:	NYA and Headworkers Committee.
	16-64-65:	Personal Service Workers Committee on medical care for WPA families, camping, casework technique.
	16-66:	Personal Service Workers Committee.
	16-67:	Personal Service Workers: health.
	16-68:	Thirty-fifth Anniversary luncheon, publicity.
	16-69-70:	Annual luncheon, news releases; Harry Hopkins, WPA chief, guest speaker.

UNITED NEIGHBORHOOD HOUSES, INC.

Folder V
legal f. 74A
- 16+71: Description of UNH, history, committees and their work; Executive Committee reports.
- 16-72: Housing Committee, draft of resolution to Mayor La Guardia.
- 16-73: Housing Committee: legislation.
- 16-74: Housing Committee: appeal to President Roosevelt for federal housing program, housing reports.
- 16-75: Housing Committee.
- 16-76: Housing Committee, statement of Edward T. Devine on the Charity Organization Society and housing.
- 16-77: Housing Committee.
- 16-78: Unemployment and Relief Committee.
- 16-79: Unemployment and Relief Committee on Works Progress Administration.
- 16-80: WPA, meeting protesting dropping people from relief rolls; Legislative Committee, minutes: housing, child labor.
- 16-81: Legislative Committee.

Scrapbook 17, 1935-1947, (filed in legal folders 75-78)
The entire scrapbook documents the activities of the League of Mothers' Clubs.

Folder I
legal f. 75
- 17-1: Summer activities.
- 17-2-7: Boat trips.
- 17-8: Annual Dinner.
- 17-9: Constitution.
- 17-10-11: Annual Dinner.
- 17-12: Adult Education and Leaders' Council.

Folder II
legal f. 76
- 17-13-14: Annual Dance.
- 17-15: Routine material.
- 17-16-17: Housing.
- 17-18: Annual Dinner, budget.
- 17-19: Routine material.
- 17-20: Housing, <u>Bulletins</u>.
- 17-21: Adult education and Works Progress Administration.
- 17-22: "Mothers News," League <u>Bulletins</u>.
- 17-23: Dance Committee.
- 17-24: Executive Board, minutes.
- 17-25: Housing petition.
- 17-26: Housing materials.
- 17-27: "Mothers News."
- 17-28: Routine material.
- 17-29: Routine material.
- 17-30: Elections, program of UNH's Executive Committee.
- 17-31: Summary of Activities, 1935-1936.
- 17-32: Routine material.
- 17-33: Summer program; medical and recreational material.

Folder III
legal f. 77
- 17-34: Spring Festival.
- 17-35-38: Summer activities.

	17-39:	Photographs of boat trips.
	17-40:	Boat trips.
	17-41-42:	Annual dinner and dance.
	17-43:	Steering Committee: citizenship, peace, housing, schools.
	17-44:	Committee on Citizenship, Presidents' and Leaders Luncheon.
	17-45:	Summary of events, 1937.
	17-46:	Peace Committee.
	17-47:	Routine activities.
Folder IV legal f. 78	17-48:	Motion Picture Committee, minutes and material.
	17-49-51:	Routine activities.
	17-52:	Motion Picture Committee.
	17-53:	Financial Committee.
	17-54:	Steering Committee, routine activities.
	17-55:	Peace Committee.
	17-56:	Housing Committee, includes "A Study of 1092 Tenement Families," 1937.
	17-57:	Steering Committee, Peace Committee.
	17-58:	Housing Committee.

Scrapbook 18, 1935-1937, (filed in legal folders 79-84)

Folder I legal f. 79	18-1:	Arts and Crafts Committee, Visual Arts Committee.
	18-2:	Arts and Crafts Committee.
	18-3:	Arts and Crafts Committee, includes a booklet describing 1937 Art Exhibit with statements by Albert J. Kennedy and art teachers in the settlements.
	18-4:	Arts and Crafts Committee.
	18-5:	Summer activities: boat trips.
	18-6:	Summer activities: boat trips, free tickets to cultural events.
	18-7:	Annual Conference papers.
	18-8-9:	Headworkers Committee, meetings.
	18-10:	Summer activities: Works Progress Administration camps.
	18-11:	Summer activities: camping.
	18-12:	Executive Committee, members, minutes, agenda.
Folder II legal f. 80	18-13:	Executive Committee, minutes: WPA, unemployment, home versus work relief.
	18-14:	Executive Committee, minutes: WPA, relief.
	18-15:	Executive Committee, minutes: housing, Non-Partisan Citizens' Committee to Keep Politics Out of Relief, visual arts, etc.
	18-16:	Executive Committee, routine activities.
	18-17:	Finance Committee, theatre benefit.

	18-18:	Theatre benefit.
	18-19:	Financial statements, 1936-1937.
	18-20-21:	Boys' and Girls' Work, athletics.
	18-22:	Girls' Athletic Association, Executive Committee, minutes.
	18-23:	Questionnaire on girls' athletic activities in the settlements.

Folder III
legal f. 81

	18-24:	Camp training course.
	18-25:	Minutes of training course.
	18-26:	Camp counselors.
	18-27-28:	Boys' and Girls' Workers, Executive Committee, bulletins: volunteers, also includes a bibliography on volunteers.
	18-29:	Boys' and Girls' Workers; Executive Committee: National Youth Administration, relief, WPA.
	18-30-31:	Peace Committee.
	18-32-33:	National Youth Administration.
	18-34:	Summer programs for youth.
	18-35:	Survey on ownership of old law tenements for Housing and Legal Committees.

Folder IV
legal f. 82

	18-36:	Housing Survey, Housing Committee.
	18-37:	Housing Committee, minutes.
	18-38:	Housing Committee, minutes: Housing Legislation and Housing Education.
	18-39:	Housing Committee: federal and state legislation.
	18-40:	Housing Committee.
	18-41:	Legislative Committee re housing, etc.
	18-42:	Legislative Committee, reports of legislation favored.
	18-43-45:	Legislative Committee, resolutions and minutes.

Folder V
legal f. 83

	18-46:	Housing Education Bureau.
	18-47-49:	Personal Service Workers: relief, WPA, casework.
	18-50:	Advisory Committee on Nursing; WPA, veterans.
	18-51:	Publicity.
	18-52:	Luncheons, reservations list.
	18-53:	U.S. Foreign Policy, and War and Peace Committee.
	18-54:	Peace Committee.
	18-55-56:	Settlement workers, salary study.
	18-57:	Unemployment Committee.

Folder VI
legal f. 84

	18-58-62:	Unemployment Committee: WPA, art projects, relief.
	18-63:	WPA and recreation.
	18-64:	Non-partisan Citizens' Committee to Keep Politics Out of Relief.
	18-65:	Unemployment Committee.

Scrapbook 19, 1937-1938, (filed in legal folders 85-88)

Folder I
legal f. 85
- 19-1-3: Annual meeting, minutes: report on committee activities, progressive education.
- 19-4: Luncheon; Headworkers' meeting.
- 19-5-6: Headworkers' meetings.
- 19-7-8: Arts and Crafts Committee.
- 19-9: Arts and Crafts, Visual Arts Committees.
- 19-10: Complimentary tickets.
- 19-11: Legislative Committee, chairmen of various committees meeting.
- 19-12: Housing Committee; legislation.
- 19-13: Legislative Committee.
- 19-14-17: Boys' and Girls' Work Committee.

Folder II
legal f. 86
- 19-18: Intersettlement recreation.
- 19-19-20: Boys' and Girls' work.
- 19-21-23: Intersettlement activities.
- 19-24-25: Intersettlement Group on Public Affairs.
- 19-26-28: Boys' and Girls' Work, scholarships.
- 19-29-30: Boys' and Girls' Work, girls athletics.
- 19-31-34: Girls' Athletic Association.

Folder III
legal f. 87
- 19-35: Basketball tournament.
- 19-36-38: Executive Committee.
- 19-39: Financial statement.
- 19-40: Personal Service Workers.
- 19-41-42: Salary questionnaire.
- 19-43: Unemployment Committee.
- 19-44: WPA activities.

Folder IV
legal f. 88
- 19-45-47: Unemployment Committee.
- 19-48: Theatre Benefit Party.
- 19-49-52: Housing Committee.
- 19-53: League of Mothers' Clubs, Annual Report, 1937-1938.
- 19-54: Boat trips, Legislative Committee.
- 19-55: Legislative Committee.
- 19-56-58: Legislative Committee.

Scrapbooks 20 through 24 have been maintained in scrapbook form in portfolios as received from UNH. No attempt has been made to put these in folders. The indexes of these scrapbooks are copied from the indexes found in each scrapbook.

Scrapbook 20, 1938-1939

- 20-1: Arts and Festivals Committee, complimentary tickets.
- 20-4: Visual Arts exhibit.
- 20-12: UNH Association General, suggested board meetings and projects.

UNITED NEIGHBORHOOD HOUSES, INC.

20-13:	Savings Bank Life Insurance.
20-15:	Annual Luncheon reports re unemployment, relief, housing legislation.
20-17:	Annual Conference re volunteer work, city administration.
20-24:	Summer work in settlements.
20-25:	President's Tea.
20-26:	Headworkers' meetings.
20-29:	Spring Conference of UNH re the settlements' main task for 1939-1940.
20-30:	Education: Adult Education Committee.
20-32:	Executive Committee, minutes and announcements.
20-38:	Committee procedure.
20-39:	Finance Committee.
20-40:	Lists of contributions, theatre benefit.
20-45:	Financial statements from October, 1938-September, 1939.
20-47:	Boys' and Girls' Work, Intersettlement Senior Association.
20-55:	Work scholarships.
20-56:	Study Groups.
20-60:	Minutes and announcements.
20-62:	Settlement party.
20-64:	Camera clubs.
20-66:	Camera clubs.
20-67:	National Youth Administration Committee.
20-68:	Cellar Club Survey.
20-71:	Personal Service Workers.
20-72:	Health Committee.
20-76:	Unemployment Committee.
20-73:	Curtailment of WPA.
20-75:	Nursery School and Kindergarten.
20-80:	Legislative Committee, minutes and announcements.
20-85:	League of Mothers' Clubs.
20-87:	League Dinner.
20-88:	Leaders' meetings.
20-89:	Delegates meetings.
20-90:	Dance.

Scrapbook 21, 1939-1940

21-1:	Arts and Festivals Committee.
21-3:	Drama and Dance.
21-11:	Music Committee.
21-16:	Visual Arts Exhibit.
21-18:	Complimentary tickets.
21-22:	UNH Association Board, Liaison Board members.
21-24:	UNH Association General.
21-28:	Savings Bank Life Insurance.
21-31:	In-service training course.
21-35:	Executive Committee, minutes and announcements.
21-38:	Special resolutions re World Situation.
21-40:	Committee on Structure.
21-41:	Nominating Committee.

UNITED NEIGHBORHOOD HOUSES, INC.

21-42:	Finances, theatre, printed matter.
21-46:	Theatre.
21-50:	Special appeal.
21-54:	Statements, October 1939-September, 1940.
21-57:	Executive Committee.
21-58:	Committee on Supervision of Group Work.
21-59:	Committee on Vocational Guidance.
21-60:	Committee on Neighborhood Resources.
21-61:	Committee on Physical Education.
21-63:	Work scholarships.
21-64:	Inter-settlement Senior Federation.

Headworkers Committee.

| 21-70: | General correspondence. |

Housing Committee.

21-73:	Minutes and announcements.
21-75:	General correspondence.
21-77:	Survey of recreational facilities in housing developments.

Legislative Committee.

21-78:	Minutes and announcements.
21-79:	General correspondence.
21-82-83:	Civil rights, public education.
21-84:	Legal general, milk.
21-85:	Personal Service Workers.
21-88:	Health Workers.

Publicity.

| 21-90: | UNH Bulletins. |

Unemployment Committee.

21-92:	Minutes and announcements.
21-96:	Fuel survey.
21-99:	Committee on Immediate Needs.

League of Mothers' Clubs.

21-106:	General.
21-110:	Dinner.
21-113:	Assemblies.
21-115:	Delegates meeting.
21-117:	Leaders' Chapter Group.

Dance Journal.

21-122:	Nominating Committee.
21-124:	Motion Picture.
21-125:	Milk subcommittee.

Scrapbook 22, 1940-1941

Arts and Festivals Committee.

22-1:	Music Committee.
22-4:	Music Course.
22-9:	Art Committee.
22-10:	Tickets.
22-11:	Summer Boat Trips.

Association Board of UNH.

| 22-12: | Liaison Board members. |
| 22-30: | Board member seminar. |

UNITED NEIGHBORHOOD HOUSES, INC.

	Association General.
22-13:	Association and Headworkers meetings.
22-15:	Alien Registration.
22-18:	Annual Conference.
22-23:	Committee on Urgent Planning.
22-24:	Civil Service Investigation.
22-25:	Civil Rights Committee.
22-26:	Consumer Protection Committee.
22-29:	Penny Milk.
	Executive Board.
22-35:	Minutes and announcements, Lillian Wald.
	Boys' and Girls' Work.
22-39:	Minutes.
22-42:	Executive Committee (Boys' and Girls' Work becomes Committee on Group Work)
22-45:	Settlement and the Present Emergency.
22-45:	Vocational Guidance and Social Hygiene Study Group, Bibliography on Social Service in wartime.
22-46:	Senior activities.
	Hints on Job Procurement.
22-47:	Social Group Work report re supervision.
	Finance-Monthly statements.
22-49:	Appeals.
22-50:	Theatre Benefit.
	Headworkers Committee.
22-53:	Correspondence and regional meetings.
	Housing Committee.
22-54:	Minutes and announcements.
22-55:	Joint Advisory Committee on Activities in Housing Projects.
22-56:	Annual Report.
	Health Committee.
22-57:	Minutes and materials.
	Legislative Committee.
22-59:	Program for the year.
22-60:	Minutes and announcements.
	Personal Service Workers' Committee.
22-64:	Health Committee.
22-67:	Volunteer survey.
22-68:	WPA Clothing.
	Unemployment and Relief Committee.
22-69:	General correspondence, minutes.
22-71:	Food Stamp Plan.
22-72:	City wide organization.
22-76:	Fuel survey.

Scrapbook 23, 1941-1942

23-1:	Index.
23-4:	Board of Directors, minutes and announcements.
23-11:	Members of the Executive Board and Board of Directors.
23-13:	Financial material, statements and reports.

23-16:	Report of English settlements in wartime.
23-17:	UNH Annual Conference.
23-21:	Bylaws.

Headworkers Committee.

23-22:	Minutes.
23-26:	Boys' and Girls' Workers.
23-28:	New York meetings.

Drama Committee.

23-30:	Bulletins, minutes, reports.

Personal Service and Health Workers Committee.

23-33:	Minutes and reports.

Visual Arts Committee.

23-36:	Art exhibits.
23-38:	Poster contest.

Legislative Committee.

23-42:	Minutes.
23-43:	List of members.
23-44:	Price control materials.
23-45:	Farm work for young people program.
23-46:	Special recommendations.

Public Education Committee.

23-48:	Minutes.
23-49:	Legislative recommendations, lists of members.

Civil Rights Committee.

23-50:	Minutes.

Housing Committee.

23-51:	Minutes.
23-54:	Old Law Tenement Study.
23-58:	Maximum income study for recipients of public housing.
23-59:	Study of tenant-management relations.
23-60:	Public housing.

Consumer Protection Committee.

23-62:	List of members, surplus food commodities.
23-63:	Food price study.

Unemployment and Relief Committee.

23-68:	Clothing questionnaire study.
23-69:	List of members.
23-70:	Minutes.
23-71:	Appropriation for Department of Welfare.
23-72:	WPA.

Air Raid Protection.

23-73:	Study and recommendations.
23-74:	Local legislation re fire fighting equipment.

UNH Association Meetings.

23-75:	Minutes.

Joint Committee on Excise Taxation of Charitable, Religious and Educational Organizations.

23-76:	Materials re theatre benefit.
23-78:	Correspondence.
23-84:	Publicity releases re theatre benefit.

                League of Mothers' Clubs.
- 23-98: Service training course.
- 23-104: Presidents' and delegates' meetings.
- 23-102: Annual Dinner.
- 23-111: Victory Conference.
- 23-112: Publicity brochure.
- 23-113: LMC and League of Women Voters.

Scrapbook 24, 1942-1943

- 24-1: Board of Directors.
- 24-2: Lists of members and minutes.
- 24-6: Annual meeting materials, financial statements, nominating committee for Board of Directors.
- 24-8: Annual report.
- 24-9: Finances, contributions.
- 24-10: Resolution on the dissolution of the WPA.
- 24-11: UNH re delinquency.
- 24-11A: UNH re Community Chest Committee.
- 24-13: Headworkers Committee.
- 24-15: National Federation of Settlements and UNH, Joint Committee Report.
- 24-16: NFS Conference and Stanley M. Isaacs' address.
- 24-17: Reprint article from the *Survey* by M. K. Simkhovitch, "Neighborhood Planning and the Settlements."
- 24-18: Group Workers' Committee.
- 24-19: Personal Service and Health Workers Committee.
- 24-21: Drama Committee.
- 24-22: Personnel Standards in New York City Group Work Agencies.
- 24-23: Committee on Personnel Standards and Practices.
- 24-25: Use of Volunteers.
- 24-26: Group Work and the War.
- 24-27: UNH's report on Volunteers and their placement in the settlements.
- 24-27A: Mayor's Committee on Wartime Care of Children.
- 24-28: UNH Music Committee.
- 24-29: Civil Defense training course for volunteers, Music Committee.

                League of Mothers' Clubs.
- 24-31: Materials, agendas, miscellaneous.
- 24-32: Committee of Leaders.
- 24-34: Club activities.
- 24-35: "Songs for Victory Sing," published by the League of Mothers' Clubs, 1943.

The following scrapbooks which are composed only of newspaper clippings give a chronological history of the United Neighborhood Houses.

Scrapbook 25, 1920-1928.

Scrapbook 26, 1928-1935.

Scrapbook 27, 1935-1939.

Scrapbook 28, 1939-1946.

Scrapbook 29, 1947-1952.

Scrapbook 30, 1958.

20

An Inventory of the Papers of the United States Committee of the International Conference of Social Work

PREPARED BY
Nancy M. Wiggins

SWD7   United States Committee of the International Conference of Social Work

Papers, 1928-1965

40 folders

At the 50th National Conference of Social Work in Washington, D.C., 1923, Dr. Rene Sand, a guest from Belgium, suggested that similar conferences be organized on an international basis. His proposal was favorably received by the National Conference of Social Work (NCSW), the American Association of Social Workers, and a number of American foundations which agreed to contribute financial support for the first International Conference of Social Work (ICSW) held in Paris in 1928.

The NCSW, as the organization promoting the ICSW in the United States, appointed a Committee on the International Conference of Social Work which made arrangements for the U. S. delegation to the Paris Conference and issued credentials to delegates. Arrangements for succeeding International Conferences in 1932 and 1936 were similarly handled in the United States by the Committee on the 2nd International Conference and the Committee on the 3rd International Conference which were appointed by the executive committee of the NCSW. A Committee on the 4th International Conference, which had been planned for Brussels in 1940, met until 1939 when political tensions interrupted the work of the ICSW.

Following the war, the executive committee of the NCSW appointed a new Committee on International Conference, and by 1949, the U. S. Committee of the ICSW existed as an autonomous Associate Group of the NCSW and consisted of thirty-three members appointed by the president of the National Conference.

In November, 1950, the U. S. Committee of the International Conference came to the conclusion that its form of organization was inadequate and voted to ask the National Conference of Social Work to reconstitute the Committee as a semiautonomous group within the NCSW. The executive committee decided that it would be desirable to reorganize the U.S. Committee with representation from various organizations in the country having an interest in international social work.

In 1951 the NCSW initiated the formation of a Joint Negotiating Committee to consider and make recommendations on the future structure of the U. S. Committee. The Committee consisted of representatives of the following organizations: the American Association of Schools of Social Work, the American Association of Social Workers, the American Public Welfare Association, the National Conference of Social Work, and the National Social Welfare Assembly. Seeking to increase ICSW membership and participation in the United States, the Joint Negotiating Committee adopted a resolution on reorganization of the U. S. Committee which included the following provisions: 1) The U. S. Committee would be based on individual membership with the cooperation of those organizations which chose to affiliate for membership promotion, finance, and program planning; 2) the U. S. Committee would be an Associate Group of the National Social Welfare Assembly (NSWA) and relate closely to the activities of the Assembly Committee on International Social Welfare. Following approval of the resolution by the NCSW, the NSWA, and the existing U. S. Committee, a cooperative agreement between the reorganized U. S. Committee and the Assembly was negotiated under which the Assembly agreed to serve as the secretariat for the U. S. Committee.

The U. S. Committee for the International Conference of Social Work is presently a semiautonomous unit within the NCSW. It represents the interests of the Conference in this country by promoting memberships, selecting official U. S. representation for International Conferences, sponsoring meetings on international social welfare subjects, fund raising, and formulating program recommendations.

U. S. Committee papers, as received at the Social Welfare History Archives Center from the National Conference on Social Welfare in April, 1967, appear to be fragmented records when compared to the file classification schedule which was also received from NCSW. Before shipment to the Archives Center, much of the material was sent from New York to Columbus, Ohio, and in some cases, the original file folders were not retained nor were the contents of packages of documents labeled. When possible, original filing units have been retained; in other instances an attempt has been made to retrieve scattered documents and arrange them chronologically by topic.

Because of the dual functions performed by some U. S. Committee members within both the Committee and the International Conference, and due to the location of the ICSW secretariat in the United States, the papers of both organizations, as received at the Archives Center from the NCSW, were sometimes mixed. An attempt has been made to separate the correspondence of individuals which reflects their functions in the U. S. Committee from that reflecting their responsibilities within the ICSW. Material supplementing this collection may be found in the papers of the International Conference of Social Work which are also held by the University of Minnesota Social Welfare History Archives Center.

PARTIAL SUBJECT INVENTORY

ASIA FOUNDATION
    Folder 18

CHILD WELFARE
    Folders 26, 35

FINANCIAL SUPPORT FOR ICSW
    Folders 4-5, 37

FOREIGN VISITORS AND SPEAKERS IN U.S.
    Folder 11

FRIEDLANDER, WALTER
    Folder 33

INDUSTRIALIZATION
    Folders 18-25, 36

INTERNATIONAL CONFERENCE OF SOCIAL WORK, CONFERENCES

    HAGUE CONFERENCE, 1947
        Folder 2

    ATLANTIC CITY CONFERENCE, 1948
        Folder 2

    PARIS CONFERENCE, 1950
        Folder 16

    TORONTO CONFERENCE, 1954
        Folders 17, 39

    MUNICH CONFERENCE, 1956
        Folders 18-25

    TOKYO CONFERENCE, 1958
        Folders 26-29

KRAUS, HERTHA
    Folder 30

LOCAL COMMITTEES OF ICSW IN UNITED STATES
    Folders 32-36

MINNESOTA CHILD WELFARE CONFERENCE, 1956
    Folder 35

NATIONAL SOCIAL WELFARE ASSEMBLY
    Folders 13, 31, 38

REORGANIZATION OF U. S. COMMITTEE, 1951-1952
    Folder 13

TERMINOLOGY STUDY
    Folder 40

URBANIZATION
    See folders re Munich Conference: 18-25

WORLD WAR II. POSTWAR PROBLEMS IN EUROPE
    Folder 2

FOLDER TITLE AND DESCRIPTION OF CONTENTS	FOLDER
Constitution and Certificate of Incorporation, 1952 Includes correspondence re alternate proposals for constitution revision.	1
Historical Material, 1928-1948 Minutes, reports of pre-war activities, and correspondence re postwar problems in Europe.	2
Executive Committee, 1955 Correspondence and minutes.	3
Evaluation Committee, 1956 Correspondence and minutes. Committee examined questions of financial support for the ICSW, U. S. Committee membership and role in the ICSW, and changes in leadership and staff services.	4
Membership and Finance Committee, 1952-1959 Correspondence, minutes, and membership lists. Committee secured support from foundations, community chests, and corporations and promoted memberships in campaigns for ICSW in the United States.	5
Nominating Committee, 1948-1955 Correspondence and minutes. Committee prepared lists of names to be voted upon by ICSW members in United States for election to U. S. Committee.	6
Nominating Committee, 1956 Correspondence, minutes, and ballot tallies.	7
Nominating Committee, 1957 Correspondence, minutes, and membership lists.	8
Program Committee, 1952-1955 Correspondence, minutes, and membership lists.	9
Program Committee, 1956-1957 Memoranda and minutes.	10
Program Committee - Subcommittee on Speakers for State Conferences, 1953 Correspondence and papers. As part of the Department of State's exchange of persons program, foreign visitors were made available for participation at state conferences of social work.	11
Committee on Relationship - U. S. Committee and ICSW Secretariat, 1949-1950 Correspondence and summaries of discussions.	12

FOLDER TITLE AND DESCRIPTION OF CONTENTS	FOLDER
Joint Negotiating Committee on Reorganization of the U. S. Committee, 1951-1952 Meeting notices, minutes, reports, and resolutions. Committee passed resolution to reconstitute the U. S. Committee of the ICSW as an associate group of the National Social Welfare Assembly.	13
Financial and Administrative Status Reports, 1953-1957 Reports to U. S. Committee membership from the Executive Secretary.	14
Correspondence and Papers, General, 1945-1965 Includes Statement of Understanding, 1957, with National Association of Social Workers.	15
International Conference - Paris, 1950 Correspondence and lists of U. S. delegates' assignments at Conference.	16
International Conference - Toronto, 1954, 1953-1954 Correspondence and papers surrounding U. S. Committee participation. Includes papers of the subcommittee on exhibits and the editorial subcommittee which prepared the U. S. Report to the Conference.	17
International Conference - Munich, 1956 - Papers, General, 1955-1956 Miscellaneous correspondence includes material re Asia Foundation grants for delegates' travel expenses.	18
International Conference - Munich, 1956 - Exhibit, 1955-1957 Correspondence, papers, and reports of the subcommittee for the U. S. Exhibit. Using Pittsburgh, Pennsylvania as a prototype, the exhibit dealt with problems of industrialization and urbanization.	19
International Conference - Munich, 1956 - Promotion and Orientation, 1955-1956 Minutes, correspondence, and promotional mailings.	20
International Conference - Munich, 1956 - Publicity, 1954-1957 Correspondence, press releases, news clippings, and drafts of articles used to publicize the conference. Includes report on health aspects of industrialization by Dr. Jerome Peterson.	21
International Conference - Munich, 1956 - U. S. Participation, 1955-1956 Correspondence re assignments of U. S. members to commissions and study groups. Contains lists of U. S. registrants for conference.	22

U.S. COMMITTEE OF THE ICSW

FOLDER TITLE AND DESCRIPTION OF CONTENTS	FOLDER
International Conference - Munich, 1956 - U. S. Report (Preparations), 1954-1956 Correspondence, minutes of editorial committee, and local community reports used in preparing preliminary drafts.	23
International Conference - Munich, 1956 - U. S. Report, 1956 Final report as presented at Conference.	24
International Conference - Munich, 1956 - Post-Conference Summary and Reports, 1956-1957 Correspondence and U. S. Committee summary.	25
International Conference - Tokyo, 1958 - Exhibit, 1956-1957 Correspondence and minutes of subcommittee. U. S. Committee was assisted by the U. S. Information Service in preparation of exhibit which emphasized the mutuality of Japanese and American interest in field of child welfare.	26
International Conference - Tokyo, 1958 - Publicity and Promotion, 1957 Correspondence and news clippings.	27
International Conference - Tokyo, 1958 - Study Group, 1957 Correspondence and papers of the subcommittee charged with responsibility for formulating and outlining a study guide on the conference theme, "Mobilizing Resources for Social Needs"; includes the U. N. Social Commission document, <u>Maintenance of Family Levels of Living</u>.	28
International Conference - Tokyo, 1958 - U. S. Participation, 1957-1958 Correspondence re U. S. delegation to Conference and minutes of subcommittee which prepared the U. S. Report.	29
Affiliated Schools and Seminars for International Study and Training (ASSIST), 1950-1954 Bylaws, minutes, correspondence, and papers. ASSIST organized and managed study tours and seminars for its own members and for university and other membership organizations with international educational aims.	30
Joint Agreement Between the U. S. Committee and the National Social Welfare Assembly, 1952-1953 Correspondence and papers re negotiation of the details of a working relationship between the NSWA and the U. S. Committee following the decision to reorganize the national committee of the ICSW.	31
Local Committee Organization, 1953 Correspondence, minutes, and papers.	32

U.S. COMMITTEE OF THE ICSW

FOLDER TITLE AND DESCRIPTION OF CONTENTS	FOLDER

Local Committees - California, 1950-1958 — 33
Correspondence, minutes, and papers. Most correspondence is with Walter A. Friedlander, School of Social Welfare at University of California, Berkeley.

Local Committees - Detroit, Michigan, 1957 — 34
Correspondence.

Local Committees - Minnesota, 1955-1957 — 35
Correspondence. Includes report of the Minnesota Welfare Conference in St. Paul in April, 1956.

Local Committees - New England, 1953-1957 — 36
Correspondence. Includes reports of study group examining area problems related to industrialization, 1956.

Form Letters and Memos to Members, 1949-1957 — 37
Financial support of ICSW is emphasized.

National Committee on International Organization for Social Welfare, 1945-1948 — 38
Correspondence and minutes. This committee, a permanent body under the aegis of the National Social Welfare Assembly, was an outgrowth of the December 18, 1945 Conference of National Voluntary Agencies in New York, and it submitted statements and proposals to the U. N. Economic and Social Council.

Publicity and Exhibits, 1954-1956 — 39
Correspondence and material re U. S. Committee exhibits at state and national conferences. Includes material related to International Conference exhibit at Toronto, 1954.

Terminology Study, 1955-1957 — 40
Correspondence with local committees which formulated tentative definitions of social work terms. National committees of the ICSW in English-speaking countries participated in this study to formulate mutually acceptable definitions of 19 social work terms.

21

An Inventory of the Papers of the United States Veterans Administration, Social Work Service

PREPARED BY
Pamela J. Matson

SWD2   United States Veterans Administration. Social Work Service

          Papers, 1921-1963

          136 folders   2 (𝓛) folders

    After World War I, the readjustment problems of servicemen returning to civilian life, especially those with neuropsychiatric disabilities, were turned over to the American National Red Cross workers who were stationed by the Red Cross in government offices of the War Risk Insurance Bureau, the United States Public Health Service, and the Federal Board of Rehabilitation. In 1921, Congress established the Veterans Bureau by consolidating the administration and functions of those three agencies. The World War Veterans Act of June, 1924, authorized the furnishing of hospitalization so far as existing government facilities permitted to ". . . veterans of any war, military occupation, or military expedition since 1897 not dishonorably discharged and without regard to nature or origin of their disabilities."

    A medical council advisory to the Director and Medical Director of the Bureau was established in 1924. Members of this Council included a number of prominent physicians such as Dr. Allen K. Krause, Dr. H.A. Pattison, Dr. William A. White, and Dr. Ray Lyman Wilbur. In 1924, the Council recommended that social workers be placed in the Veterans Bureau regional offices and hospitals. As a result, Frances A. Foster was brought in as Chief Social Worker to develop a program of social work for the Veterans Bureau. In 1926, the Red Cross withdrew its social workers from the Veterans Bureau neuropsychiatric hospitals and casework positions in the regional offices. However, many former Red Cross psychiatric social workers remained in their jobs as government civil service staff. By 1927, the Red Cross had withdrawn all its social workers from the general medical and tuberculosis hospitals as well.

    In 1931, the Veterans Bureau, Pension Bureau, and National Homes for Disabled Volunteer Soldiers were combined to form the Veterans Administration. Cutbacks resulting in a greatly reduced social work staff were ordered as necessary for government economy during the depression years. Despite economic problems, the Social Work Service continued to grow in the late 1930's, and the United States' entrance into World War II necessitated even greater increases in the social work staff. Meanwhile, the educational requirements for social workers gradually increased. In the early 1940's, the Veterans Administration began its cooperation with certain schools of social work through agreements which provided for the placement of students for field work at various Veterans Administration facilities. The use of volunteers in Veterans Administration social work was initiated in the 1940's.

    Reorganization of the Veterans Administration was effected by Public Law 293 in 1946 which ". . . abolished the Medical Services as then constituted and authorized a Department of Medicine and Surgery under a Chief Medical Director; appointments of doctors, dentists, and nurses were to be made in accordance with regulations prescribed by the Administrator without regard to civil service requirements. . . ." Public Law 293 also established the Special Medical Advisory Group to advise the Administrator and Chief Medical Director on medical problems. The Social Work Advisory Council, established in 1946, acted in a similar capacity to the Social Work Service in developing a sound program of social services in the Veterans Administration. Many institutes were held at various Veterans Administration facilities to inform social workers about new ideas and trends in Veterans Administration social work and the profession of social work itself.

During the twenty years after World War II, services to veterans were expanded to include out-patient care, foster home care, trial visits, and increased work with the blind. Patients with chronic illnesses and tuberculosis patients who had not been properly discharged caused particular concern. Recruiting social workers from schools of social work and increasing the educational standards and salaries of social workers are continuing concerns to the Veterans Administration Social Work Service. The Social Work Service also works with the community to which a veteran returns following hospitalization. It attempts, through education and counseling of the patient and his family, to make the physical and personal home environment as favorable to the patient as possible.

Some landmark dates concerning the Veterans Administration Social Work Service are:

1921	Veterans Bureau established.
1924	World War I Veterans Act furnished hospitalization to veterans.
1926-27	Withdrawal of American National Red Cross social workers from Veterans Bureau hospitals.
1931	Veterans Administration formed combining Veterans Bureau, Pension Bureau, and National Homes for Disabled Volunteer Soldiers.
1940's	Work with schools of social work in placing students at Veterans Administration facilities for field work. Beginnings of Veterans Administration Voluntary Service.
1943	Public Law 16 provided rehabilitation for disabled veterans.
1946	Public Law 293 reorganized Veterans Administration and established Special Medical Advisory Group. Social Work Advisory Council established.
1950's	Institutes held at various Veterans Administration facilities.
1953	Reorganization of Veterans Administration.

VETERANS ADMINISTRATION SOCIAL WORK SERVICE

In February of 1966, the Social Work Service, Department of Medicine and Surgery of the Veterans Administration, placed on permanent deposit at the Social Welfare History Archives Center ". . . those historical records identified by Mr. Delwin M. Anderson, Director of Social Work Service, as inactive and therefore no longer of general use by members of the staff." The papers were deposited following conversations and correspondence between Mr. Anderson, Dr. Joseph McNinch, Chief Medical Director of the Veterans Administration, and Mr. Clarke A. Chambers, Director of the Social Welfare History Archives Center. Previous to shipment of the files, the Veterans Administration obliterated names of veterans to preserve the confidentiality of the records.

The papers may be used by

> all qualified scholars with the special permission of the Director of the Center. All scholars using these papers will sign an agreement, before they are permitted to use them, by which they will agree:
> 1. to maintain the confidentiality of all illustrative case records of a given veteran by omission of all names and other identifying information;
> 2. to present to the Archives Center a copy of their research report, article, or manuscript for forwarding to the Director, Social Work Service.

The following statement appears on the outer front flap of each folder of the Veterans Administration material:

Caution

> This file may contain information entitled to confidential treatment, and its use is not authorized without special permission of the Social Welfare History Archives Center.

The collection covers the years from 1921 to 1963 and comprises 136 regular and 2 legal size folders in a basically chronological arrangement with some subject files.

The papers are arranged in four general divisions: administrative papers, general correspondence and papers, subject files, and publications.

The administrative papers (folders 1-15) consist of annual reports and working papers, minutes of the Medical Council Conferences, reports to the Medical Council, medical supervisors' reports, and minutes and papers of the Special Medical Advisory Group, the Social Work Advisory Council, and minutes of the area chief social workers meetings.

The general correspondence and papers (folders 16-96) cover the years from 1921 to 1963 and are arranged chronologically. In the original Veterans Administration files, these folders were labeled "Social Work Service. History." Because the entire collection is considered to be history by the Social Welfare History Archives Center, the folders were re-labeled "Correspondence and Papers, General." These folders include routine administrative correspondence and papers, as well as quarterly narrative reports, technical bulletins, and all-station letters. Some subjects which frequently recur are: civil service, educational standards and salaries for social workers, recruitment of social workers, psychiatric and neuropsychiatric social workers, evaluation of Veterans Administration social work, statistics on social workers and veterans under Veterans Administration care, foster homes, trial visits, and out-patient care. From 1938 on, an annual or biennial bibliography of recommended readings was compiled for Veterans Administration social workers. The response of the Veterans Administration to inquiries of congressmen concerning individual cases and general policies can be seen in folders 25, 26, and 31. Highlights of each year are listed in the folder inventory.

The alphabetical subject files (folders 97-128) contain the papers held by subject in the original collection e.g. aging, vocational rehabilitation, and military social work. Letters from Tuskegee, Alabama; Seattle, Washington; and Outwood, Kentucky had previously been pulled from the general correspondence folders so they, too, have been placed in the alphabetical subject file. The original arrangement of the case study folders has been retained.

Publications of the Veterans Administration (folders 129-136) include Information Bulletins and Program Guides, leaflets, pamphlets, and reprints. Because most of the Guides and Bulletins were already pulled from the general correspondence, those remaining were pulled also, so they could be filed together.

A listing of top administrative personnel of the Veterans Administration, 1921-1964, is appended to this inventory.

PARTIAL SUBJECT INVENTORY

ADJUDICATION PROCESS (Determines eligibility for hospital and other benefits)
Folders 24, 44-51, 107-108

AGED VETERAN
Folders 52-64, 77-79, 83-87, 97

AMERICAN LEGION
Folders 9, 25

AMERICAN NATIONAL RED CROSS
Folders 16-21, 28, 44-47, 52-55

BLINDNESS
Folders 11, 38-40, 48-64, 70-73, 80-82, 93-96, 107-108, 119-121

BECKLEY, HELEN (Executive Secretary of the American Association of Hospital Social Workers)
Correspondence with Irene Grant, Chief of the Social Work Service.
Folder 23

CANCER
Folders 25, 85-87

CHRONIC ILLNESS
Folders 48-51, 56-73, 80-82, 85-87, 93-96

CIVILIAN LIFE - RE-ENTRY
Folders 31, 44-47, 56-60, 65-73, 77-79, 85-87

COMMUNITY RELATIONS (Community relationships with returning veterans and with the Veterans Administration facilities in the vicinity)
Folders 24, 33-34, 41-43, 70-73, 85-96

DE SCHWEINITZ (KARL) ARTICLE ("Social Work in the Public Social Services," Social Work Journal, July, 1955)
Folders 100-102

DIABETES
Folder 25

DOMICILIARY CARE (Convalescent care)
Folders 12-14, 41-43, 48-55, 65-69, 80-82, 107-108, 110-115

FAMILY CARE PROGRAM
Folders 41-47, 56-60

FEDERAL LEGISLATION
Public Law 16, 1943 (Provided rehabilitation for disabled veterans)
Folders 35-37
Public Law 293, 1946 ("Medical Corps Bill")
Folders 33-34, 52-55

FEDERAL LEGISLATION, continued
    Public Law 85, Title 38, 1958 (Consolidated all laws administered
        by Veterans Administration)
        Folders 77-79

FOSTER HOME PROGRAM
    Folders 12-14, 35-37, 44-47, 56-64, 70-76, 80-96, 129

GUARDIANSHIP
    Folders 18-20, 25

HOSPITAL SOCIAL WORK
    Folders 10, 22, 38-40, 52-55, 107-108

IDA S. LATZ FOUNDATION (Incorporated in 1950 in Los Angeles to aid the
    disabled veteran "over and above government benefits")
    Folders 52-55, 61-64, 74-76

INTERNATIONAL SOCIAL SERVICE
    Folders 70-73, 93-96

NEUROPSYCHIATRIC AND PSYCHIATRIC SOCIAL WORK
    Folders 5-8, 11-14, 16-17, 21-27, 31-32, 35-37, 41-43, 56-60,
    65-76, 83-92, 107-108, 129

OUT-PATIENT CARE
    Folders 32-34, 61-64, 74-82, 88-92

PROSTHETIC DEVICES
    Folders 89-92, 103-104

PSYCHIATRIC SOCIAL WORK see NEUROPSYCHIATRIC AND PSYCHIATRIC SOCIAL WORK

PUBLIC LAWS see FEDERAL LEGISLATION

PUBLIC WELFARE AGENCIES, COOPERATION WITH
    Folders 24-28, 31, 48-51

RECORDS, CONFIDENTIALITY OF
    Folders 24, 27-32, 35-37, 88-92

SOCIAL WORKERS - RECRUITMENT
    Folders 12-14, 17, 29-30, 52-55, 65-76, 80-84, 88-96

SOCIAL WORKERS - TRAINING PROGRAM
    Folders 12-14, 23, 33-40, 44-47, 52-60, 70-76, 80-82, 98, 107-108, 117

TRIAL VISIT PROGRAM
    Folders 11, 27, 29-30, 48-60, 65-79, 83-92, 129
    See also CIVILIAN LIFE - RE-ENTRY

TUBERCULOSIS
    Folders 5-8, 11, 22-27, 29-31, 33-47, 56-60, 74-79, 107-108, 110-115,
    119-121, 125

VENEREAL DISEASE
    Folders 24-26, 28-30, 70-73, 107-108, 119-121

VOCATIONAL REHABILITATION
    Folders 28-34, 65-76, 119-121

VOLUNTARY SERVICE (Volunteer workers in the Veterans Administration)
    Folders 12-14, 38-40, 44-55, 70-76

Folder Inventory

Folder Title and Description of Contents | Folder

Annual Reports, 1926-1959, 1963. — 1-2
For 1958, there are two semi-annual reports; for 1959, an annual report of improvements; and for 1963, a paper entitled A Year in Review.

Annual Reports, Working Papers, 1926-1957. — 3-4
Arranged chronologically.

Conferences of the Medical Council, Minutes, 1924-1931, 1939. — 5-8
Excerpts from the minutes of the first two conferences including the address to the first council by the Administrator. The third through the twelfth conferences are covered by a Program which contains the agenda and supporting papers as well as progress reports on the recommendations of the previous conference and a Report which includes speeches to the council as well as committee reports. The Program of the twelfth conference (folder 8) contains a report of progress on the recommendations of all the conferences to 1931. No Report is available for the thirteenth conference (1939).

Reports to the Medical Council, 1924-1943. — 9
Constitution of the Medical Council, correspondence and papers surrounding the meetings of the Council, Program for the Executive Committee and various committee reports. The emphasis is on the period between 1939 and 1943.

Medical Supervisors' Reports, 1927-1952. — 10
Suggested procedures, guides for area consultants, policy and regulation statements, evaluation of Social Work Service, and hospital social work.

Special Medical Advisory Group, 1945, 1951-1956. — 11
Modernization of medical services.

Social Work Advisory Council, 1946-1963. — 12-14
Casework, recruitment of social workers, professional education, and in-service training.

Folder Title and Description of Contents	Folder
Area Chief Social Workers Meetings, Minutes and Papers, 1946-1955. Policies regarding administration and programs such as appointments, promotions, responsibility, procedures, and casework.	15
Correspondence and Papers, General, 1921-1924. Early beginnings of the Veterans Bureau and the establishment of the Social Work Service; duties of social workers and psychiatric social workers; American National Red Cross workers; initial procedures in establishing Veterans Bureau facilities.	16
Correspondence and Papers, General, 1925. Setting up the Social Work Service in the Veterans Bureau central office and out-lying facilities; psychiatric social work; follow-up nursing; and hiring procedures.	17
Correspondence and Papers, General, 1926.	18-20
Correspondence and Papers, General, 1927. Extension of Veterans Bureau responsibilities.	21
Correspondence and Papers, General, 1928-1929. Tuberculosis patients, hospital social work, clinical records, social problems of illness, classification of social workers as professionals, and transfer of case files.	22
Correspondence and Papers, General, 1930-1933. Initial effects of the depression on the social work program, student field work, junior social workers, social histories, correspondence between Irene Grant and Helen Beckley.	23
Correspondence and Papers, General, 1934-1936. Evaluation of social work at individual stations, further effects of depression on program, social aspects of the adjudication process, release of data to public welfare agencies, laws and regulations relating to venereal disease, and excerpts from minutes of Regional Conference of Veterans Administration Psychiatric Social Workers.	24

Folder Title and Description of Contents	Folder
Correspondence and Papers, General, 1937-1938. Interpretation of social work to the community, social factors in diabetes, cooperation with state boards, and "The Allergy Patient" by Esther C. Hachtel presented to the National Conference of Social Work.	25
Correspondence and Papers, General, 1939. Medical and social aspects of cases, summary of social work in the Veterans Administration, central clearance indexing on public assistance in West Virginia, and social service exchange.	26
Correspondence and Papers, General, 1940-1941. Social service exchange; disability ratings; social aspects in the treatment of general medical, tuberculosis, and neuropsychiatric patients; and "Training Interns in the Social Aspects of Illness" by Ethel Cohen.	27
Correspondence and Papers, General, 1942. Social Security Act of 1936, syphilis case study, social data in army and navy records, vocational training, and survey of Social Work Service activities.	28
Correspondence and Papers, General, 1943. Conservation of manpower in government agencies, correspondence between the Secretaries of War and Navy and Administrator, and placement of students of social work in Veterans Administration facilities for field work.	29-30
Correspondence and Papers, General, 1944. Furnishing information on veteran's condition to veteran, relatives, and employers; and Travelers Aid.	31
Correspondence and Papers, General, 1945. Release of information in connection with National Service Life Insurance, in-service training and scholarship program, and practices of Social Work Service during World War II.	32
Correspondence and Papers, General, 1946. Training of student social workers, relationship of Veterans Administration and medical schools, reactions to Public Law 293, letter from President Harry Truman on provision of out-patient care.	33-34

VETERANS ADMINISTRATION SOCIAL WORK SERVICE

Folder Title and Description of Contents | Folder

Correspondence and Papers, General, 1947. | 35-37
    Recommended changes in personnel ceilings, reactions to Newsweek and Readers Digest articles, reorganization of Department of Medicine, and correspondence with Charlotte Towle on area chief standards and with Sue Spencer on training of veterans as social workers.

Correspondence and Papers, General, 1948. | 38-40
    Social Work Advisory Council, hospital social service, volunteer workers, and student social workers and loyalty examinations.

Correspondence and Papers, General, 1949. | 41-43
    Family care history at Tuskegee, Alabama; neuropsychiatric research unit; social service exchange; statement for Hoover Commission; tuberculosis research program; and staff development program.

Correspondence and Papers, General, 1950. | 44-47
    Staff development program, bibliography on history of Veterans Administration, veterans on enforced furlough, cutbacks in Social Work Service, training programs for hospital aides, planning for psychotic patients at home, clinical training for occupational therapy, and army social service program.

Correspondence and Papers, General, 1951. | 48-51
    Medical schools and social work rounds; volunteer agencies; relationship of Veterans Administration and American Medical Association; post-war activities of Veterans Administration; a study of length of patients' stay in hospitals; parapelegics; employment of blind social workers; early standards for social workers in Veterans Administration; and social security program for the permanently and totally disabled.

Correspondence and Papers, General, 1952. | 52-55
    Participation in group activity, clinical training for physical therapists, Public Law 293, brief history of the care of veterans in the United States, reference list of Veterans Administration publications, Special Medical Advisory Group, and reorganization of Veterans Administration.

VETERANS ADMINISTRATION SOCIAL WORK SERVICE

Folder Title and Description of Contents	Folder
Correspondence and Papers, General, 1953. Planning for patient's discharge, training of residents, bibliography on the aged, nursing program in Veterans Administration, evaluation of social service program, Council on Social Work Education, lobotomized patients, social rehabilitation, and correspondence between the Administrator and the Chairman of Senate Committee on Appropriations.	56-60
Correspondence and Papers, General, 1954. Economy in the Veterans Administration, decentralization of Veterans Administration, field work placements, and social research in a Veterans Administration hospital setting.	61-64
Correspondence and Papers, General, 1955. Evaluation of social work program, management improvement, nursing program, summary of Veterans Administration policies and programs, standards for hospitals, and United Nations' request for study of training for welfare personnel.	65-69
Correspondence and Papers, General, 1956. Social work as a community mobilizer; International Social Service; correspondence with Bernard Baruch on veterans with chronic illness; hiring handicapped veterans; management development program; and research and education in Veterans Administration social service.	70-73
Correspondence and Papers, General, 1957. Recruitment of social workers, physical therapists, and occupational therapists; management development program; and National Association of Veterans Employment Councils.	74-76
Correspondence and Papers, General, 1958. Consultants in social work, Special Medical Advisory Group, planning for the patient's discharge, Public Law 85, Title 38, and research in Veterans Administration social work.	77-79
Correspondence and Papers, General, 1959. Veterans Administration contributions to social work education; management development program; peacetime veterans - eligibility for medical treatment; and Council on Social Work Education.	80-82

Folder Title and Description of Contents	Folder
Correspondence and Papers, General, 1960. Evaluation of Social Work Service, summer employment of students, United Nations' study of national developments in family, youth, and child welfare, and half-way houses.	83-84
Correspondence and Papers, General, 1961. Extra-Veterans Administration educational duty, social work and community development, cancer cases, half-way houses, social work research in Veterans Administration, analysis of patients in VA and non-VA hospitals, and organization of Veterans Administration.	85-87
Correspondence and Papers, General, 1962. Social work in community development, extra-Veterans Administration educational duty, research on suicides, coordination of legal and social work services in Veterans Administration, analysis of patients in Veterans Administration and non-VA hospitals, research activities in Veterans Administration, quarter-way houses, civil defense, prosthetic devices, organization of Veterans Administration, and restoration center for veterans who have reached maximum hospital benefits and who have a potential to return to community living within one year.	88-92
Correspondence and Papers, General, 1963. Multiple sclerosis, community placement for other than psychiatric patients, relation of clinical social work to comprehensive medical care, International Social Service, National Service Corps, and community home-maker services.	93-96
Aging, Care of, 1956, 1963. Summary of the care of the aging veteran by Veterans Administration to 1956; and _The Older American_, report of the President's Council on Aging.	97
Atlanta University, School of Social Work, Correspondence, 1942-1944. Placement of students at the Atlanta University School of Social Work at Tuskegee, Alabama, Veterans Administration facility for field work experience.	98

Folder Title and Description of Contents	Folder
Histories of Veterans Administration Social Work Service, 1926, 1948-1950. Some of the histories were written by persons outside the Veterans Administration.	99
Information for Karl de Schweinitz article, c. 1955. These folders include most of the information which was sent to Mr. de Schweinitz for his article, "Social Work in the Public Social Services," which appeared in the Social Work Journal, Vol. XXXVI, no. 3, July, 1955.	100-102
Institute for the Crippled and Disabled, 1942-1954. Cerebral palsy, services of the Institute, vocational rehabilitation, and prosthetic devices.	103-104
Military Social Work, 1944-1950. Clinical social service in Army hospitals, military experience and civilian employment in social work, and military psychiatric social work.	105
North Atlantic Group of Social Workers, 1944-1947. This group, founded to improve ". . . standards of personnel practices in the Administration and to raise standards of personnel performance in the agency's social work program," included social workers from the Bronx, Northport, Lyons, Castle Point, Coatesville, and Newington. It was discontinued in 1947 because of ". . . increased pressure of work."	106
Orientation to the Social Service Program, 1946-1952. Materials for new Veterans Administration employees to acquaint them with various aspects of the Social Work Service program.	107-108
Outwood, Kentucky, Correspondence, 1926-1946. Routine correspondence between this veterans facility and the central office which had been pulled from the general correspondence and papers.	109
Program Planning and Statements, 1946-1957. Explanations and information about various Social Work Service policies and programs during these years, e.g. legislation, cooperation with public welfare agencies, evaluation of Social Work Service, and summaries of the programs.	110-115
Seattle, Washington, Correspondence, 1925-1942. Routine correspondence between this veterans facility and the central office which had been pulled from the general correspondence and papers.	116

VETERANS ADMINISTRATION SOCIAL WORK SERVICE

Folder Title and Description of Contents | Folder

Training Program for Social Workers, 1945-1946. | 117
    This program was recommended by the Special Medical Advisory Group and involved the training of professional social workers at schools and colleges, with field work at some Veterans Administration facilities.

Tuskegee, Alabama, Correspondence, 1926-1936. | 118
    Routine correspondence between this veterans facility and the central office which had been pulled from the general correspondence and papers.

Vocational Rehabilitation, 1925-1944. | 119-121
    Although the years from 1940 to 1944 receive the most emphasis, some earlier pamphlets and papers are included. Vocational rehabilitation dealt with prospective employers and home service as well as with the veteran and potential employee himself.

West Roxbury Veterans Facility (MA Thesis), 1945. | 122
    This thesis was done at Simmons College by Hazel E. Brown.

Early Case Studies, 1926-1935. | 123-124

Case Studies re TB (fictitious), 1932, 1938. | 125
    Leo Dixon case and another case study involving tuberculosis.

Case Studies for General Hines, c. 1942. | 126
    These materials were collected for the Administrator as examples of Social Work Service casework.

Illustrations of VA Casework, 1945-1946. | 127-128

Information Bulletins and Program Guides. Psychiatry and Neurology Division, 1952-1961. | 129
    Papers on various aspects of the Veterans Administration program; e.g. trial visits, foster homes, community nursing, psychiatric care, and clinical psychology.

Information Bulletins and Program Guides. Social Work Service, 1957-1962. | 130
    These contain ". . . all aspects of program development . . . new methods . . . medical care contributing to diagnosis, . . . veterans benefits, . . . and development of community resources."

Folder Title and Description of Contents	Folder

Veterans Administration. Bulletins and Leaflets.
    VA Benefits in Brief, 1958-59, 1961-62, 4 Vols.
    Disaster Relief Handbook, April 19, 1957.
	131

Veterans Administration. Bulletins and Leaflets.   132

    Veterans Administration Information Service. VA Fact Sheet. IS - 10.
        Functions and Purposes of Veterans Administration. March, 1957.

    Veterans Administration Information Service. VA Fact Sheet. IS - 1.
        Federal Benefits Available to Veterans and Their Dependents. December, 1957.

    Veterans Administration Information Service. VA Fact Sheet. IS - 1.
        Federal Benefits for Veterans and Dependents. January, 1959.

    Veterans Administration Information Service. VA Fact Sheet. IS - 1.
        Federal Benefits for Veterans and Dependents. January, 1960.

    Veterans Administration Information Service. VA Fact Sheet. IS - 1.
        Federal Benefits for Veterans and Dependents. January, 1961.

    Veterans Administration Information Service. VA Fact Sheet. IS - 10.
        Functions and Purposes of Veterans Administration. May, 1961.

Veterans Administration. Bulletins and Leaflets, et cetera.   133

    Office of the Assistant Administrator for Personnel
        Evaluation Summary. Veterans Administration Personnel Program. February, 1961.

    Office of Personnel. Program Guide 5-4.
        The Role of the Personnel Officer in a Veterans Administration Field Station. September, 1958.

    Office of Personnel. Program Guide 5-6.
        Employee Training. For Whom and What Kind? March, 1960.

Folder Title and Description of Contents	Folder
Veterans Administration. Bulletins and Leaflets, et cetera, continued.	133

    VA Pamphlet 03-1. <u>The 4 - S Program</u> . . . <u>an Evaluation</u>. April, 1960.

    VA Pamphlet 5-19, <u>Veterans Administration Management Development Program</u>. <u>Questions and Answers</u>. September, 1956.

    VA Pamphlet 5-26. <u>Handicapped</u>? <u>Not on the Job</u>! March, 1959.

    VA Pamphlet 5-27. These are Yours! <u>Employment Benefits for Veterans Administration Employees</u>. April, 1959.

    VA Pamphlet 5-29. <u>Common Sense about Evaluating and Recognizing Performance</u>. March, 1960.

    VA Pamphlet 7-10. <u>Occupations of Totally Blinded Veterans of World War II and Korea</u>. January, 1956.

    VA Pamphlet 10-27. <u>Irregular Discharge</u>. <u>The Problem of Hospitalization of the Tuberculous</u>. October, 1948.

    VA Pamphlet 10-46. <u>You as a Volunteer</u>. <u>A Handbook for Volunteer Hospital Workers</u>. May, 1957.

<u>Reprints</u>   134

    Breckinridge, Sophisba, and Stanton, Mary. "The Law of Guardian and Ward With Special Reference to the Children of Veterans." <u>The Social Service Review</u>. Vol. XVII, No. 3, September, 1943.

    Hanlon, Julian G., M.S.W., "The Role of the Mental Health Service in the Local Health Department." <u>Public Health Reports</u>. Vol. 72, No. 12, December, 1957.

    Littauer, David, M.D., and Flance, I. Jerome, M.D., "Home Care Has Made a Place for Itself, Report on Three-Year Program Indicates." <u>The Modern Hospital</u>. August, 1957.

    Middleton, William S., M.D., "The Patient-Physician Relationship." <u>The Wisconsin Medical Journal</u>. June, 1955.

    Nagler, Benedict, M.D., "Emotional Significance of Severe Trauma," <u>Virginia Medical Monthly</u>. Vol. 81, Pages 152-155, April, 1954.

VETERANS ADMINISTRATION SOCIAL WORK SERVICE   773

Folder Title and Description of Contents   Folder

Reprints, continued.   134

    Nagler, Benedict, M.D., "Modern Concepts in the Treatment
        of Psychiatric Patients." American Journal of
        Occupational Therapy. Vol. IX, No. 5, Part II,
        September-October, 1955.

    Nunemaker, John C., M.D., "Postgraduate Training Problems
        in the Veterans Administration." New York State
        Journal of Medicine. Vol. 55, No. 4, February 15, 1955.

    Stipe, Jack H., "Social Service in the Veterans
        Administration." Journal of Social Casework.
        February, 1948.

    Ullman, Leonard P., and Berkman, Virginia Conner,
        "Efficacy of Placement of Neuropsychiatric Patients
        in Family Care." American Medical Association Archives
        of General Psychiatry. Vol. 1, pp. 273-274, September, 1959.

    Veterans Administration Multiple Sclerosis Study Group.
        "Isoniazid in Treatment of Multiple Sclerosis." The
        Journal of the American Medical Association. Vol. 163,
        January 19, 1957.

Vanguard (Central Office Newsletter) 1956-1959.   135
    The Newsletter was published bi-weekly by the
    Veterans Administration Central Office Personnel
    Service. In June, 1958, the name was changed to the
    Vanguard. The file is not complete.

United States Government Publications, 1955-1959.   136
    Publications of various departments of the United
    States Government.

    United States Civil Service Commission. Classification
        in a Nutshell. October, 1955. Originally published
        by the United States Department of Agriculture. Office
        of Personnel.

    United States Congress. House Committee on Veterans Affairs.
        85th Congress. Second Session. Veterans Administration
        Hospital Program. June 26, 1958.

    United States Congress. House Committee on Veterans Affairs.
        86th Congress. First Session. Hearings before the
        Committee on Veterans Affairs. Veterans Administration
        Hospital Policy. March 4, 1959.

Folder Title and Description of Contents　　　　　　　　Folder

United States Government Publications, 1955-1959, continued.　　136

    United States Department of Health, Education, and Welfare. <u>Aging</u>. May, 1959.

    United States Department of Health, Education, and Welfare. Social Security Administration. <u>Social Security Amendments of 1958</u>. August 29, 1958.

    United States Department of Health, Education, and Welfare. Social Security Administration. <u>Social Security Amendments of 1958</u>. <u>What They Mean to You</u>. September, 1958.

Reorganization of the Veterans Administration, 1953.　　　　Legal Folder 1

Legal Size Material, 1939-1963.　　　　　　　　　　　　　　　Legal Folder 2
    Social aspects of medical care, vocational rehabilitation, statistical summary of Veterans Administration patients, and National Service Corps.

APPENDIX

Veterans Administration Administrative Personnel 1921-1964

Director or Administrator of the Veterans (Bureau) Administration

C.R. Forbes	c. 1921 - 1923
General Frank T. Hines	c. 1923 - 1945
General Omar N. Bradley	1945 - c. 1948
General Carl Gray, Jr.	c. 1948 - c. 1953
Harvey V. Higley	c. 1954 - 1958
Sumner G. Whittier	1958 - 1961
John S. Gleason, Jr.	1961 -

Chief Medical Director

Dr. E. O. Crossman	c. 1924 - c. 1926; c. 1928 - c. 1930
Dr. B. W. Black	c. 1926 - c. 1928
Dr. Charles M. Griffith	1931 - c. 1945
Major General Paul R. Hawley	c. 1945 - c. 1948
Dr. Paul B. Magnuson	c. 1949 - 1951
Admiral J. T. Boone	1951 - 1955
Dr. William S. Middleton	1955 - 1963
Major General Joseph H. McNinch	1963 -

Chief or Director, Social Work Service

Frances A. Foster	1926
Irene Grant	1926 - c. 1946
Jack Stipe	c. 1946 - c. 1949
Roger J. Cumming	c. 1949 - 1964
Delwin M. Anderson	1964 -

An Inventory of the Papers of Benjamin E. Youngdahl

PREPARED BY
Jane S. Davis

TABLE OF CONTENTS

INTRODUCTION AND DESCRIPTION OF THE COLLECTION 1
    1. Correspondence - personal, family, general (Folders 3-12) 2
    2. Poems (Folder 13) 3
    3. Minnesota Correspondence and Papers (Folders 14-21) 3
    4. Washington University (Folders 22-70) 4
    5. Organizations (Folders 71-109) 5
    6. Speeches, Notes, Publications (Folders 110-121) 7

PARTIAL SUBJECT INVENTORY 8

FOLDER INVENTORY 12

SWB Youngdahl, Benjamin Emanuel 1897-
Y88
        Papers, 1920-1966

        121 folders 2 (ℒ) folders

    This collection comprises the personal and professional papers of
Benjamin E. Youngdahl, noted public welfare administrator and social work
educator who was Dean of the George Warren Brown School of Social Work,
Washington University, 1945-1962. Most of the collection is correspondence, but there is also a large section of his speeches, speech drafts,
and notes, which reveal his concern with social work education, social
action, and the nature of social work. The collection essentially be-
gins with his work in Minnesota public welfare, but the bulk of the
papers are from his years at Washington University.

    A native of Minnesota, Youngdahl is a member of a prominent Swedish
Lutheran family and was educated at Gustavus Adolphus College, St. Peter,
Minnesota and at Columbia University, New York. During the years 1923-
1933, he was a Professor of Sociology and Economics at Gustavus Adolphus
College. In 1933 Youngdahl became Director of Social Service for the
Minnesota State Emergency Relief Administration and then, in 1937, Director of Public Assistance under the Minnesota State Board of Control.
This was a period of controversy surrounding the new public welfare programs, culminating in the resignation of Youngdahl in 1939; the papers
reflect this controversy and form one of the richest parts of the collection. Following his resignation he became Associate Professor of Social
Work at Washington University, St. Louis, where he has spent the remainder
of his career in social work education. In 1943 he became a Professor of
Social Work, and following a year spent with UNRRA, he was appointed Dean
of the George Warren Brown School of Social Work in 1945. He retired as
Dean in 1962, but continued to teach and has remained active in social
work.

    Throughout his career, Youngdahl has been an active leader in many
social work organizations, thus exercising a decisive influence on the
profession of social work, especially social work education. In 1947-
1948 he was President of the American Association of Schools of Social
Work. Three years later he became President of the American Association
of Social Workers, 1951-1953, and in 1955 he was elected President of the
National Conference of Social Work, now the National Conference on Social
Welfare.

    Youngdahl has published many speeches and articles on social work, a
portion of which are in this collection. His honors are many, including
an LL.D. from Gustavus Adolphus College in 1954 and citations from Gustavus
Adolphus and Washington University in 1960 and 1961, respectively. He was

the recipient of the Florina Lasker Award in Social Work for 1963, an award citing his concern for civil liberties.

Youngdahl gathered together the material for this collection from his papers in his office at Washington University and at his home. When the papers arrived at the Minnesota Social Welfare History Archives, they filled eight Paige boxes and were arranged both in subject folders and miscellaneous folders. The ephemera included in the collection is being held separately; the bulk of the periodicals are Minnesota state welfare publications. Also being held separately is the scrapbook kept by Mrs. Youngdahl during the depression; the scrapbook provides background material for the papers of that period. As Youngdahl said: "It includes the most valuable material and it seems to me the most useful from the standpoint of an historian." The collection has been arranged in six sections, which follow both the course of Youngdahl's career and his own subject arrangement of the papers. The sections are

1. Correspondence - personal, family, general, 1921-1966 (Folders 3-12).
2. Poems, 1920-1929 (Folder 13).
3. Minnesota Correspondence and Papers, 1933-1939 (Folders 14-21).
4. Washington University, 1939-1966 (Folders 22-70).
5. Organizations, 1939-1966 (Folders 71-109).
6. Speeches, notes, publications, 1939-1966 (Folders 110-121).

SECTION 1. CORRESPONDENCE - PERSONAL, FAMILY, GENERAL, 1921-1966 (Folders 3-12)

(Folders 1-2 contain biographical material, photographs, and newspaper clippings.)

Prominent in the personal correspondence are Anne W. Oren, Professor of Social Work, Edna Gellhorn, St. Louis citizen and social work pioneer, and Louis Towley, colleague in Minnesota and at Washington University. Letters and memoranda from Towley and his wife, Marie, occur throughout the collection. (See also the Louis Towley collection.)

Letters to Youngdahl's sons, Mark, Kent, and James, form the bulk of the family correspondence (Folders 4-5). There is also correspondence with his brothers, Reuben Youngdahl, prominent Lutheran pastor, and Luther Youngdahl, former Minnesota governor and Federal judge, as well as with his sister, Ruth Youngdahl Nelson.

The general correspondence section contains correspondence not directly related either to his roles as public welfare administrator or Dean, or to an organization. Included are letters of appreciation, letters to public officials, and letters concerning invitations, awards, honors, and retirement. (Folders 6-12) Folder 6 contains correspondence on his year with UNRRA and also a letter to Harry Truman. Correspondence with Adlai Stevenson occurs in folders 6-7, 9-10, and 12. There is material on the Newburgh, New York, public welfare controversy in folder 8.

SECTION 2. POEMS (Folder 13)

Personal poems, mostly undated, written by Youngdahl during the 1920's.

SECTION 3. MINNESOTA CORRESPONDENCE AND PAPERS (Folders 14-21)

Youngdahl was Director of Social Service, Minnesota State Emergency Relief Administration (1933-1937) and Director of Public Assistance, Minnesota State Board of Control (1937-1939). The papers for the period 1933-1939 form a self-contained unit, giving an excellent picture of Minnesota during the depression, particularly the controversies surrounding the public welfare programs. Included in folders 14-17 is Youngdahl's "Home File" which, he said, "includes copies of letters, correspondence, etc., that had the potential of legal action, that had political overtones, and that related to the constant struggle between the Social Service Division and other divisions (some politically motivated)." A set of the Minnesota state welfare publications (1935-1961) is being held separately from the Youngdahl collection, as is the scrapbook kept by Mrs. Youngdahl, 1932-1946.

Folders 14-17   1933-1939. Folder 17 contains material re Youngdahl's resignation and appointment at Washington University (July 1939).

Folders 18-19   1933-1939. Speeches and notes re social work, social welfare, social security, rural welfare, transients, old age.

Folder 20   1939. Contains a draft of a History of Public Welfare in
                 Minnesota. This draft was apparently never finished or
                 published, but it is a valuable source for the controversy
                 surrounding the public welfare programs, 1933-1939. Young-
                 dahl traces the activities of the various public welfare
                 administrations during that period.

SECTION 4.   WASHINGTON UNIVERSITY (Folders 22-70)

   The bulk of the material in this section is concerned with Youngdahl's
position as Dean of the George Warren Brown School of Social Work at Washington University, 1945-1962. His activities as Dean can be traced in
these papers, both in the School of Social Work and in the University as a
whole.

   Of particular interest are the following folders:

Folders 23-24   1963-1965. Material re the first Benjamin E. Youngdahl
                 Lecture, at Washington University, given by Vice-President
                 Hubert Humphrey on October 28, 1965.

Folders 25-27   Contains correspondence with Frank Bruno, who preceeded
                 Youngdahl as Dean; their relationship remained close after
                 Bruno's retirement until his death. In Youngdahl's letters
                 to Bruno and his wife, the former Joanna Colcord, one can
                 find his opinions on current events, public officials, and
                 social work in general. There is material re President
                 Dwight D. Eisenhower, Senator Joseph McCarthy, Oveta Culp
                 Hobby, Jane Hoey, the American Association of Social Workers,
                 and Luther Youngdahl.

Folders 29-34   1945-1965. Correspondence with the Chancellor, Vice-Chan-
                 cellor and Deans re School of Social Work and issues
                 affecting the University. There is material re admission
                 of Negroes to the University, American Red Cross, American
                 Civil Liberties Union, honorary degrees, and academic
                 freedom.

Folders 37-44   1950-1966. Material relating directly to the George Warren Brown School of Social Work and Youngdahl's activities as Dean, with some material after his retirement. Many of the papers deal with the daily business of running a professional school, but there is also material on the curriculum and admissions, issues in social work, and social work as a profession. Also, folder 42 contains material on the issue of privacy in social work and an article by Louis Towley on Aid to Dependent Children.

Folders 57-58   1945-1958. Contain material on the admission of Negroes to the George Warren Brown School of Social Work for the first time in 1947. Youngdahl was instrumental in changing the admissions policy.

Folder 63   This folder contains material for a study of the Department of Psychiatry at the Washington University Medical School. It is closed until 1971.

Folder 65   1939-1957. Material for class lectures, mostly on public welfare and the economics of welfare.

Folder 67   1945-1962. Correspondence with Louis Towley, containing material on public welfare and the American Red Cross. Memorial services for Towley.

SECTION 5. ORGANIZATIONS (Folders 71-109)

Folders 71-72   1946-1952. American Association of Schools of Social Work. Youngdahl was President of AASSW in 1947-1948, although not many of the presidential papers are included here. Materials re curriculum, admissions, faculty work loads and salaries. AASSW resolution re Charlotte Towle and <u>Common Human Needs</u>.

Folders 73-76   1950-1955. American Association of Social Workers. Youngdahl was President of AASW in 1951-1953. Minutes of National Board Meetings, 1951-1952. Materials re Charlotte Towle and *Common Human Needs*, Temporary Inter-Association Council (TIAC), segregation.

Folder 79   1949-1965. American Civil Liberties Union. Youngdahl became a member of the National Committee of ACLU in 1953. Material re J.B. Matthews' article in *American Mercury*, "Communism and the Colleges" (May, 1953).

Folders 86-87   1953-1966. Council on Social Work Education. Material re curriculum policy, libraries of social work, recruitment.

Folders 91-92   1949-1965. Health and Welfare Council, St. Louis. Material on medical social work, government vs. voluntary agencies, public housing, and a training program for community welfare research. Prior to 1958 the agency was called the Social Planning Council.

Folders 99-100 1954-1963. National Association of Social Workers. Includes some material of Temporary Inter-Association Council and Provisional Officers on formation of NASW. Papers and correspondence of NASW Committee on Ethics, especially re principle of privacy in welfare cases. Material re welfare training.

Folders 102-104 1943-1964. National Conference on Social Welfare. Youngdahl was President of NCSW, 1955-1956. Material re election of Youngdahl as President. Youngdahl's response to speech by Linus Pauling on disarmament (May 13, 1958). Papers and correspondence of NCSW Committee on Conferencing. Some material on Temporary Inter-Association Council and common services in social welfare.

SECTION 6. SPEECHES, NOTES, PUBLICATIONS (Folders 110-121)

The speeches, speech drafts, and notes included in this section present the growth and expression of Youngdahl's ideas throughout his career. His major concerns are trends in social work, social work education, and public welfare; these concerns centered on his conception of what a social worker should be.

A list of the printed speeches will be found at the beginning of folder 115 and also in any folder relevant to a particular speech. Also included in this section are book reviews and <u>Stones for Bread</u>, a 1940 study of poverty in rural Missouri.

PARTIAL SUBJECT INVENTORY

The Partial Subject Inventory is a guide, not an index, to prominent topics and personalities in the collection. Included in this list are subjects scattered through different folders and sections. Material on Youngdahl's main concerns, especially social work education, social work as a profession, and social action are indicated here but are to be found throughout the collection.

Academic Freedom
    Folder 34

Addams, Jane
    Folders 114, 116

American Civil Liberties Union
    Folders 29, 79

American Red Cross
    Folders 29, 67

Bruno, Frank
    Folders 25-27

Child Welfare
    Folders 42, 83, 108, 110, 112, 114-116

Civil Rights and Civil Liberties
    Folders 11, 25, 57, 58, 105, 111, 114

Colcord, Joanna C.
    Folders 25-27

Depression, 1933-1939
    Folders 14-21, 117

Disarmament
    Folder 102

Elections in U. S., Presidential
    1952 Folders 6, 25, 74
    1956 Folder 7
    1960 Folder 99

Gellhorn, Edna
    Folders 3, 32

Hobby, Oveta Culp
    Folders 25, 76

Hoey, Jane
    Folders 25, 34

Humphrey, Hubert
    Folders 4, 9, 23, 24

Kennedy, John F.
    Folders 9, 10, 11, 80, 99

Negroes, Admission of
    Folders 29, 57, 58, 114

Old Age
    Folders 19, 65, 90, 116

Poverty
    Folders 14-21, 110, 118

Public Welfare
    Folders 6, 8, 14-21, 25, 65, 67, 85, 99, 100, 111, 115, 117
  History of, in Minnesota
    Folder 20

Relief
Folders 14-21

Rural Life and Welfare
Folders 18, 110, 115, 118

Social Action
Folders 96, 102, 111, 115-117

Social Welfare
and Law
Folders 12, 44, 100
and Common Service Needs
Folder 104

Social Work
Education
Folders 29, 37-44, 71, 72, 86, 87, 99, 111, 115 (see 22-70)
Ethics of
Folders 44, 99, 100
Leadership in
Folders 25, 29, 117
Nature and Development of
Folders 86, 110, 111, 113-116

Stevenson, Adlai
Folders 6, 7, 10, 12

Temporary Inter-Association Council
Folders 76, 99, 102

Towle, Charlotte
Folders 72, 73

Towley, Louis
Folders 3, 17, 42, 67, 113 (see also Folders 14-70)

Truman, Harry
Folder 6

White House Conference on Children and Youth
  1950
    Folders 108, 112, 115
  1960
    Folder 108

World War II
    Folders 110, 111

FOLDER INVENTORY

Folder

1. Biography and Photographs

2. Clippings
    November 5, 1942 - December, 1963

3. Correspondence, personal
    August 15, 1929 - February 18, 1966

4. Correspondence, personal - family
    December, 1930 - September 29, 1964

5. Correspondence, personal - family
    October 2, 1964 - February 18, 1966

6. Correspondence, general
    March 30, 1921 - November 24, 1952

7. Correspondence, general
    January 30, 1953 - February 18, 1960

8. Correspondence, general
    June 2, 1960 - February 3, 1962

9. Correspondence, general
    February 4, 1962 - May 17, 1962

10. Correspondence, general
    May 18, 1962 - May 5, 1963

11. Correspondence, general
    May 6, 1963 - March 5, 1964

12. Correspondence, general
    June 2, 1964 - January 10, 1966

Folder

13. Poems
    1920-1929

14. Minnesota Correspondence and Papers
    December 12, 1933 - October 31, 1934

15. Minnesota Correspondence and Papers
    November 10, 1934 - December 29, 1934

16. Minnesota Correspondence and Papers
    January 15, 1935 - May 25, 1936

17. Minnesota Correspondence and Papers
    June 24, 1936 - November 10, 1939

18. Minnesota Correspondence and Papers
    Speeches and Notes
    1933 - October 21, 1936

19. Minnesota Correspondence and Papers
    Speeches and Notes
    1937 - June 29, 1939

20. Minnesota Correspondence and Papers
    History of Public Welfare in Minnesota draft
    1939

21. Minnesota Correspondence and Papers
    Minnesota State Board of Control Field Supervisor's
    Manual   April 15, 1939

22. Washington University
    Alumni, George Warren Brown School of Social Work

23. Washington University
    Benjamin E. Youngdahl Lectures
    December, 1963 - December 2, 1965

Folder

24.   Washington University
               Benjamin E. Youngdahl Lectures
               Winter, 1966

25.   Washington University
               Bruno, Frank
               June 13, 1946 - December 29, 1954

26.   Washington University
               Bruno, Frank
               January 6, 1955 - October 12, 1955

27.   Washington University
               Bruno, Frank
               October 13, 1955 - December 15, 1964

28.   Washington University
               Burke, William
               August 2, 1943 - March 20, 1958

29.   Washington University
               Correspondence, University Officers
               September 24, 1945 - December 18, 1950

30.   Washington University
               Correspondence, University Officers
               January 5, 1951 - February 23, 1953

31.   Washington University
               Correspondence, University Officers
               March 7, 1953 - November 24, 1954

32.   Washington University
               Correspondence, University Officers
               January 20, 1955 - December 20, 1957

33.   Washington University
               Correspondence, University Officers
               January 2, 1958 - March 24, 1960

Folder

34. Washington University
    Correspondence, University Officers
    April 11, 1960 - October 18, 1965

35. Washington University
    Cresap, McCormick and Paget Report
    September 28, 1959 - December 28, 1959

36. Washington University
    Emery, E. Van Norman
    October 12, 1946 - March 8, 1954

37. Washington University
    George Warren Brown School of Social Work
    February 6, 1940 - March 31, 1950

38. Washington University
    George Warren Brown School of Social Work
    April 1, 1950 - February 27, 1952

39. Washington University
    George Warren Brown School of Social Work
    March, 1952 - December 15, 1953

40. Washington University
    George Warren Brown School of Social Work
    Jan. 27, 1954 - September 21, 1956

41. Washington University
    George Warren Brown School of Social Work
    October, 1956 - December 11, 1959

42. Washington University
    George Warren Brown School of Social Work
    January, 1960 - November 14, 1961

43. Washington University
    George Warren Brown School of Social Work
    1962 - January 30, 1963

Folder

44. Washington University
     George Warren Brown School of Social Work
     March 13, 1963 - February 7, 1966

45. Washington University
     Hayden, Helen
     September 27, 1945 - March 10, 1956

46. Washington University
     Hayden, Helen
     March 12, 1956 - October 26, 1956

47. Washington University
     Hayden, Helen
     November 16, 1956 - May 5, 1958

48. Washington University
     Health, Education and Welfare Department (U.S.)
     February 23, 1950 - November 20, 1962

49. Washington University
     Health Service
     July 19, 1946 - November 15, 1961

50. Washington University
     Illinois Departments of Public Welfare, Mental Health
     February 18, 1946 - April 21, 1965

51. Washington University
     Information, Office of
     March 23, 1949 - February 3, 1962

52. Washington University
     Institutes
     March 18, 1947 - October 11, 1957

53. Washington University
     Jewish History Committee
     November 1, 1963 - March 25, 1964

Folder

54. Washington University
     Lewis, Ruth
     July 16, 1953 - January 22, 1957

55. Washington University
     Library, Social Work
     1949 - May 23, 1962

56. Washington University
     Missouri Public Welfare agencies
     October 28, 1941 - October 23, 1962

57. Washington University
     Negroes, Admission of
     1945 - December 31, 1947

58. Washington University
     Negroes, Admission of
     January 2, 1948 - 1958

59. Washington University
     Public Relations, office of
     October 9, 1949 - November 6, 1951

60. Washington University
     St. Louis City Welfare Offices
     April 10, 1950 - January 22, 1962

61. Washington University
     "Show Me Social Work"
     October 19, 1952 - March 18, 1954

62. Washington University
     Student Records, Office of
     1949 - June 13, 1961

63. Washington University
     Study of Department of Psychiatry
     December 7, 1964 - February 18, 1965
     Closed until 1971

Folder

64. Washington University
    Summer Sessions
    June 21, 1944 - November 29, 1960

65. Washington University
    Teaching Materials
    1939 - September, 1957

66. Washington University
    Tenure
    February 3, 1964 - February 13, 1964

67. Washington University
    Towley, Louis
    September 24, 1945 - May 21, 1962

68. Washington University
    Tuition
    September 7, 1945 - May 6, 1960

69. Washington University
    Vasey, Wayne
    October 4, 1962 - November 12, 1965

70. Washington University
    Veterans
    October 22, 1945 - February 17, 1955

71. American Association of Schools of Social Work
    February 1, 1946 - November 30, 1950

72. American Association of Schools of Social Work
    January 12, 1951 - June 10, 1952

73. American Association of Social Workers
    January 10, 1950 - October 20, 1951

74. American Association of Social Workers
    June 11, 1952 - September 30, 1952

75. American Association of Social Workers
    October 9, 1952 - October 11, 1952

Folder

76. American Association of Social Workers
December 18, 1952 – October 3, 1955

77. American Association of Social Workers
November 12, 1946 – November 26, 1951

78. American Bar Association
April 22, 1953 – September 15, 1953

79. American Civil Liberties Union
June 28, 1949 – October 15, 1965

80. Americans for Democratic Action
March 28, 1963 – April 5, 1963

81. American Foundation for the Blind, Inc.
December 28, 1962 – June 3, 1963

82. Associated Research Councils
December 20, 1949 – August 9, 1950

83. Child Welfare League of America
April 29, 1948 – November 17, 1965

84. Columbia University Bi-Centennial
August 5, 1953 – June 7, 1954

85. Connecticut University, Institute on Public Welfare
August 5, 1953 – February 5, 1954

86. Council on Social Work Education
January 30, 1953 – October 31, 1961

87. Council on Social Work Education
November 2, 1961 – February 7, 1966

Folder

88. Family and Children's Service, St. Louis
April 22, 1940 - October 9, 1962

89. Family Service Association of America
November 21, 1947 - December 9, 1963

90. Gustavus Adolphus College, Institute on Aging
August 31, 1959 - September 8, 1959

91. Health and Welfare Council, St. Louis
June 1, 1949 - December 3, 1956

92. Health and Welfare Council, St. Louis
January 28, 1957 - November 22, 1965

93. Iowa Welfare Association
August 21, 1951 - November 8, 1951

94. Metropolitan Church Federation
June 30, 1961 - December 7, 1965

95. Minnesota University, General Extension Division
November 24, 1964 - May 10, 1965

96. Minnesota Welfare Association
May 14, 1951 - March 31, 1964

97. Missouri Association for Mental Health
February, 1959 - August 16, 1960

98. Missouri Association for Social Welfare
April 25, 1940 - April 20, 1962

99. National Association of Social Workers
November 15, 1954 - June 27, 1963

100. National Association of Social Workers
September, 1963 - May 19, 1965

Folder

101. National Association of Social Workers, St. Louis
     May 27, 1965 - November 15, 1965

102. National Conference on Social Welfare
     April 29, 1943 - May 13, 1958

103. National Conference on Social Welfare
     July 24, 1963 - January 31, 1964

104. National Conference on Social Welfare
     February 3, 1964 - August 18, 1964

105. National Federation for Constitutional Liberties
     July 21, 1942 - January 1943

106. National Lutheran Council
     March 11, 1964 - April 20, 1965

107. St. Louis Social Welfare organizations
     April 24, 1951 - February 18, 1966

108. White House Conference on Children and Youth
     December 13, 1949 - December 9, 1959

109. Wisner Lecture
     February, 1963 - April 24, 1963

110. Speech Drafts and Notes
     1940 - May 8, 1944

111. Speech Drafts and Notes
     September 9, 1945 - November 14, 1950

112. Speech Drafts and Notes
     December 15, 1950 - September 29, 1951

113. Speech Drafts and Notes
     November 9, 1951 - June 19, 1953

Folder

114. Speech Drafts and Notes
     September 23, 1953 - January 21, 1965

115. Speeches and Articles
     April 11, 1940 - November 14, 1950

116. Speeches and Articles
     1951 - January, 1960

117. Speeches and Articles
     January 20, 1962 - April 21, 1965

118. <u>Stones for Bread</u>   September, 1940

119. Book Reviews   1940-1959

120. Programs and Announcements
     December, 1939 - May 26, 1949

121. Programs and Announcements
     July, 1951 - January 11, 1965

23

An Inventory
of the Papers
# of Gertrude Folks Zimand

PREPARED BY
Loren W. Crabtree

SWB Zimand, Gertrude Folks, 1894 (?)-1966
Z65
     Papers, 1915-1966

     34 folders

     The papers of Gertrude Folks Zimand were deposited in the Social Welfare Archives Center of the University of Minnesota Libraries on May 1, 1967. Comprising 2 linear feet, the papers were processed in July, 1967, in the Archives Center. The inclusive dates of the papers are 1915-1966, with the bulk of the materials covering the years 1925-1955.

     Born in 1894 (?) in New York City, Gertrude Folks Zimand was the daughter of the noted social worker and reformer, Homer Folks. After graduation from Vassar College in 1916, Mrs. Zimand entered the work of the National Child Labor Committee (NCLC) which had been founded by her father in 1904 and of which he was chairman, 1935-1944. She worked as a field investigator, edited the agency's magazine, American Child, was research director and associate general secretary until 1943, after which she was general secretary until her retirement in 1955. Thereafter she was briefly temporary general secretary following the resignation of Sol Markoff; a member of the NCLC board of trustees; and a founder of the National Committee on Employment of Youth.

     Her professional life was devoted to the activities of the NCLC, which included campaigns for state laws to keep children in school until age 14, 8-hour work days for children 14 and 15, a federal child labor amendment, and other related welfare reforms. The New Deal of Franklin D. Roosevelt brought many of the NCLC's programs to fruition and led the National Committee on Employment of Youth, which devotes its attention to the employment problems of teen-agers and young adults, especially those in poverty and minority groups. A prolific writer, Mrs. Zimand wrote many articles and books, including Young Workers in the United States (1953), Young Workers and Their Vocational Needs (1955) and Children in the Theater (1941). That she was a significant worker in child welfare is attested to by former Secretary of Labor James P. Mitchell, who, in 1955 upon Mrs. Zimand's retirement, praised "the impact of her work, directly on the lives of children throughout the United States."

     Married in 1926 to Savel Zimand, a journalist and health educator, Mrs. Zimand had two children, Harvey Folks Zimand, a lawyer, and Rhoda Folks Zimand (Mrs. Rhoda Bernstein,) registrar of Harpur College, in Binghamton, New York. Mrs. Zimand died May 10, 1966, at age 71.

The collection is divided into 3 major categories: (1) Mrs. Zimand's personal papers, folders 1-5, (2) papers related to the work of the National Child Labor Committee, folders 6-26, and (3) ephemeral publications related to the NCLC, folders 27-34.

PARTIAL SUBJECT INVENTORY

This list is intended to be only a guide to some of the prominent individuals and topics found scattered throughout this collection. Certain topics, such as child labor, appear in virtually every folder and thus have not been indexed.

CHARITABLE GIVING
    Folder 17

DILLON, HAROLD J.
    Folder 18

EDUCATION OF CHILDREN
    Folders 18-21

EMPLOYMENT AND UNEMPLOYMENT (ESPECIALLY OF CHILDREN)
    Folders 17, 22, 26, 34

FEDERAL CHILD LABOR AMENDMENT
    Folders 1-2, 24-25

FOLKS, HOMER
    Folders 4, 13-16

FRIENDS SEMINARY
    Folder 5

JOHNSON, F. ERNEST
    Folders 1-2

KELLOGG, PAUL
    Folders 1-2

MARKOFF, SOL
    Folders 1-2

MIGRANT LABOR
    Folders 19-21

NATIONAL CHILD LABOR COMMITTEE
    Anniversary: folder 16
    Annual corporate meetings: folder 12
    Annual reports: folders 13-15
    Board of trustees: folders 7-10
    Budget: folders 7-10
    Constitution and By-laws: folder 6
    Executive Committee: folder 11
    National Committee on Employment of Youth: folder 26
    Publications: folders 27-34

PARENT-TEACHERS ASSOCIATION
    Folder 5

PROBATION
    Folder 17

UNIVERSITY OF CINCINNATI
    Folder 4

WALD, LILLIAN
    Folders 1-2

WORLD WAR II
    Folder 23

FOLDER INVENTORY

<u>Folder Title</u> and <u>Description</u> <u>of</u> <u>Contents</u>   Folder

Correspondence: 1915-1966   1-2
  With Paul Kellogg, Lillian Wald, et al, concerning various
  anniversaries and dinners. The bulk of the material deals
  with lobbying for the federal child labor amendment in the
  1930's. Documents from Mrs. Zimand's Vassar days and a
  record of a 1919 conference with French government officials.
  Correspondence re: her retirement in 1955 as NCLC executive secretary. Correspondence with Sol Markoff and
  F. Ernest Johnson concerning Markoff's resignation and Mrs.
  Zimand's taking over as temporary executive secretary of
  NCLC. Some later, more personal correspondence.

Articles and Speeches: 1927-1965   3
  These were prepared for a variety of journals and occasions,
  but all deal in some way with Mrs. Zimand's interest in
  child welfare.

"Academic" Papers: 1924-1926   4
  Outline and notes for course taught by Mrs. Zimand at the
  University of Cincinnati. One letter commending her work
  and one news clipping about it.

Friends Seminary: 1943-1946   5
  Correspondence and mimeographed announcements re: Mrs.
  Zimand's work as President of the PTA of Friends Seminary.

National Child Labor Committee - Constitution and By-laws: 1937-   6
  1963
  One copy of the 1937 By-laws, and 3 copies of 1963 revisions.

National Child Labor Committee - Board of Trustees: 1953-1966   7-10
  Incomplete run of the minutes of the Board meetings, legal
  documents re: the operations of the NCLC, budget data,
  occasional eulogies and miscellaneous policy statements.

National Child Labor Committee - Executive Committee: 1960-1965   11
  Minutes of the Committee's meetings, financial and budget
  statements, memoranda concerning financial details.

National Child Labor Committee - Annual Corporate Meetings: 1955-   12
  1964
  Incomplete run of the mimeographed minutes.

National Child Labor Committee - Annual Reports: 1928-1963   13-15
  Printed and mimeographed. Incomplete series, with some
  related reports. The reports are more complete after 1944
  than before.

Folder Title and Description of Contents	Folder
National Child Labor Committee - 50th Anniversary: 1955 Correspondence re: Mrs. Zimand's role in the NCLC and the work of the Committee itself.	16
Articles and Studies: 1924-1965 These are on a great variety of subjects; e.g., giving to charitable organizations, probation of children, employment surveys, and a businessman's view of Franklin D. Roosevelt's administration.	17
Child Labor and Formal Education: 1942-1955 Papers and pamphlets on this by Zimand and Harold J. Dillon.	18
Child Labor in Agriculture (including Migrant Labor): 1932-1965 1932 study on this subject, with most data coming from the 1920's. Press clippings and published brochures, 1950-1951 study of migrant farm labor in Colorado. Materials re: the education of migrant children, 1960-1965.	19-21
Child Labor in Various Work Situations - Miscellaneous Publications on: 1924-1953 Publications dealing with child labor in mines, the theater, bowling alleys, etc.	22
Child Labor in Wartime: 1942-1944 Pamphlets, and a 1944 copy of the Annals on "Adolescents in Wartime."	23
Federal Child Labor Legislation and Amendment: 1927-1954 Articles on the amendment, brochures recommending its passage, senate hearings on legislation. Clippings re: legislation in 1950's.	24-25
National Committee on Employment of Youth: 1959-1965 Information concerning the organization and work of the Committee; minutes of the executive committee, news releases, summary of the NCEY's status in 1965.	26
The American Child: 1926-1966 Incomplete run of this official publication of the National Child Labor Committee, which was edited for many years by Mrs. Zimand.	27-32
Child Labor Facts: 1927-1940 Incomplete run of these annual pamphlets prepared by Mrs. Zimand to depict the conditions existing in child labor.	33

Folder Title and Description of Contents   Folder

Youth and Work: 1955-1965   34
    Incomplete run of this quarterly newsletter of the NCLC
    on projects, programs and publications for youth employ-
    ment.

24

An Inventory of the Papers of Savel Zimand

PREPARED BY
Carol E. Jenson

SWB   Savel Zimand, 1891-
Z651
         Papers, 1917-1959, 1967

         31 folders

On May 1, 1967, some of the papers of Savel Zimand, journalist and health educator, were deposited in the Social Welfare History Archives Center of the University of Minnesota Libraries. The inclusive dates of the collection are 1917-1967 with the bulk of the materials covering the years 1917-1945. A photostat of a letter of February 22, 1955, from Ira Hiscock, Chairman of the Department of Public Health at Yale University, indicates that Zimand made a "generous contribution of books and original illustrations of materials" to that institution.

Zimand was born in Iassy, Romania, on May 14, 1891. After studying at the University of Berlin's Seminar of Oriental Languages and the Hohere Webeschule from 1909 until 1912, he emigrated to the United States in 1913 and became a naturalized citizen in 1919. After working as a mechanic and teaching languages for three years, Zimand worked for the Department of Economics of the New York Public Library from 1917 to 1919. He also was a research assistant for the War Labor Policies Board from 1918 to 1919. He served on the Board of Directors of the Bureau of Industrial Research from 1919 to 1920. While at the Bureau he compiled an extensive bibliography of the labor movement which was published in 1921 as Modern Social Movements. In 1921, the Bureau also published a fifty-five page pamphlet by Zimand opposing The Open Shop Drive.

Zimand was also very interested in the problems of the reconstruction of Germany following World War I. He was a close friend of postwar German political leader Karl Liebknecht and wrote the introduction to Liebknecht's Militarism and translated the work into English in 1917. Zimand also edited and translated Liebknecht's The Future Belongs to the People.

From 1920 to 1924, Zimand traveled in Europe and Asia as a special correspondent from the New York Times, the New York Evening Post, the Survey, and the Globe and Commercial Advertiser. He made a trip to the U.S.S.R. in 1922 and returned to do a series of articles on the New Economic Policy. Later, in 1926, under sponsorship of the Foreign Policy Association, he wrote State Capitalism in Russia, an economic analysis based largely on official Russian sources. In 1924, he traveled to India and wrote numerous articles on Gandhi, the Indian nationalist movement, and the tragedy of the Jaito Massacre in which large numbers of Sikhs were killed when fired upon by Indian Government troops. In 1928, his writings on India were incorporated into a book published as Living India. Zimand's journalistic work in all of these areas is reflected in the clippings included in this collection.

During the late 1920s, the subject-matter in Zimand's articles began to change as he moved into the health education field. In 1927, he wrote a New York Times article on the lowering of the death rate in New York City. However, for a time his chief interests remained international, and he worked for the Economic Division of the Carnegie Endowment for International Peace from 1927-1929.

From 1929 to 1934, Zimand served as an administrative assistant and then as administrative director of the Bellevue-Yorkville Health Demonstration which was carried out in cooperation with the Department of Health, City of New York. The Demonstration was financed by the Milbank Memorial Fund to experiment with methods for the prevention of disease. In 1934, Zimand joined the Department of Health and served in several positions before he became Director, Bureau of Health Education in 1943. In 1936, he did a number of articles for several New York newspapers on the need for additional public health nurses. He edited the annual reports of the Department which were published under various titles: <u>Health for 7,500,000 People</u>, 1937; <u>Health for New York City's Millions</u>, 1938; <u>Advances in New York City's Health</u>, 1939; and <u>Twelve Months of Health Defense</u>, 1940. While at the Department, Zimand also edited several periodicals including <u>Our Nurses</u>, and <u>Neighborhood Health</u>. A good many of the clippings included in the collection are reviews of the annual reports edited by Zimand.

In 1946, Zimand became Director, Health Education, for the New York City Cancer Committee of the American Cancer Society. He held that position until his retirment in 1954 when he became a consultant on public health education for the Committee.

Zimand was married on March 8, 1926, to Gertrude Folks who died in 1966. They were the parents of two children: Harvey Folks, a lawyer, and Rhoda Folks (Bernstein), the Registrar of Harpur College, Binghamton, New York. Gertrude Folks Zimand's papers are on file at the University of Minnesota Social Welfare History Archives Center.

The collection falls into four main categories. The correspondence section is very small, less than one inch, and is by no means the full extent of Zimand's correspondence. Materials relating to the New York City Cancer Committee of the American Cancer Society include the educational activities of which Zimand was the director. Pamphlets, periodical publications, and other materials relating to the Department of Health, City of New York, and its Bellevue-Yorkville Health Demonstration have been removed from the collection and have been filed in the Ephemera Collection at the Social Welfare History Archives under New York City Department of Health. The section of the Zimand Papers entitled "Articles and Reports" is primarily clippings of articles written by Zimand and of reviews of Zimand's books. These nine folders have been filed separately in portfolios because of the size of the large scrapbook pages.

The collection also contains one folder of materials donated by Mr. Zimand which relate to the Gertrude Folks Zimand Memorial Lecture at Vassar College and to the Gertrude Folks Zimand Memorial Award, the first of which was awarded to Dr. Kenneth Clark in 1967. Mr. Zimand also gave a number of his books to the University of Minnesota Social Welfare History Archives Center. Because of their pertinence to the collection, the following volumes have been retained with the collection:

Liebknecht, Karl. <u>Militarism</u>. New York, 1917.

Zimand, Savel. <u>Modern Social Movements</u>. New York, 1921.

———, ———. The Open Shop Drive. New York, 1921.

———, ———. State Capitalism in Russia. New York, 1926.

The remaining books have been deposited in the Ephemera Collection:

New York City Department of Health. Selected Radio Talks, 1944-1945. New York, 1945.

Zimand, Savel. Bellevue-Yorkville Health Demonstration, Annual Reports, 1930-1932. New York, 1930-1932.

———, ———, ed. Advance in New York City's Health. New York, 1940.

———, ———, ——. Health for New York City's Millions. New York, 1939.

———, ———, ——. Health for 7,500,000 People. New York, 1938.

———, ———, ——. Twelve Months of Health Defense. New York, 1941.

PARTIAL SUBJECT INVENTORY

BEARD, CHARLES A.
    Folder 2

FOLKS, HOMER
    Folder 31

FOREIGN POLICY ASSOCIATION
    Folder 12

GERMANY
    Folders 23-24, 27

GUILD SOCIALISM
    Folder 24

HEALTH EDUCATION
    Folders 3-4, 9, 12-21, 27, 31

HOLMES, JOHN HAYNES
    Folder 5

INDIA
    Folders 6, 26-28

IRELAND
    Folder 24

JAITO MASSACRE
    Folder 26

KELLOGG, PAUL U.
    Folder 7

LABOR RELATIONS
    Folders 24-25

LIEBKNECHT, KARL
    Folder 23

LUXEMBURG, ROSA
    Folder 23

MAYO, KATHERINE
    Folder 27

MILITARISM
    Folder 23

NATIONAL BROADCASTING COMPANY
    Folder 8

NEW ECONOMIC POLICY
    Folder 25

NEW YORK CITY CANCER COMMITTEE
    Folders 12-21

OPEN SHOP MOVEMENT
    Folder 24

SMILLIE, ROBERT
    Folder 24

UNION OF SOVIET SOCIALIST REPUBLICS
    Folders 10, 25

WORLD WAR I
    Folders 23, 27

ZIMAND, GERTRUDE FOLKS
    Folder 22

FOLDER TITLE AND DESCRIPTION OF CONTENTS | FOLDER

Correspondence: General, 1917-1929.   1

Correspondence: Beard, Charles A., 1917, 1928 (?).   2

Correspondence: Board of Education, City of New York, 1952.   3

Correspondence: Health Education, 1930-1940.   4

Correspondence: Holmes, John Haynes, 1926-1964.   5

Correspondence: 1922 Trip to India, 1923-1930.   6

Correspondence: Kellogg, Paul U., 1921-1941.   7

Correspondence: National Broadcasting Company, 1929.   8

Correspondence: Yale University, Department of Public Health,   9
1948-1959.

Correspondence: Union of Soviet Socialist Republics.   10

Correspondent Credentials: 1920-1927.   11

New York City Cancer Committee - General: 1948-1953.   12

New York City Cancer Committee - Conferences: 1948.   13

New York City Cancer Committee - Exhibits: 1946-1948.   14

New York City Cancer Committee - Film and Lecture Programs: 15
1947-1948.

New York City Cancer Committee - Pamphlets: undated.   16

New York City Cancer Committee - Poster Contest: 1946-1953.   17

FOLDER TITLE AND DESCRIPTION OF CONTENTS	FOLDER
New York City Cancer Committee - Posters: undated (late 1940s).	18
New York City Cancer Committee - Program for Organized Labor: 1949.	19
New York City Cancer Committee - Radio Spot Announcements: 1946-1947.	20
New York City Cancer Committee - Surveys: 1948-1949, 1951.	21
Gertrude Folks Zimand Memorial Award and Lecture: 1967.	22

The following are filed in portfolios.

Articles: 1917-1919 Liebknecht, the reconstruction of Germany.	23
Articles: 1920-1921 Labor relations, reviews of <u>Modern Social Movements</u>.	24
Articles: 1922-1923 Coal miners in the U.S., New Economic Policy (N.E.P.) in the U.S.S.R.	25
Articles: 1924-1925 India, Jaito Massacre.	26
Articles: 1926-1929 India, health in New York, reviews of <u>Living India</u>.	27
Articles and Reports: 1930-1934 India, health in New York.	28
Articles and Reports: 1935-1937 Public health campaigns, public health nurses, comments on 1937 annual report of Department of Health, City of New York.	29
Articles and Reports: 1938 Comments on 1938, 1939 annual reports of Department of Health, City of New York.	30
Articles and Reports: 1940-1959.	31

Index

INDEX TO COLLECTIONS

Page numbers following the entries refer to the first page of the collection in which the entry appears

ACTION. See American Council to Improve Our Neighborhoods
ADA. See Americans for Democratic Action
Abbott, Edith, 173
Abbott, Grace, 173, 203, 533
Abbott, Lawrence, 533
Academic Freedom, 111, 503, 533, 615, 777
Academy of Certified Social Workers, 203
Accreditation of Schools of Social Work, 203
Acheson, Dean Gooderham, 111
Adams, Margaret E, 203
Addams, Jane, 111, 173, 203, 403, 533, 637, 777
Adie, David Craig, 533, 637
Adler, Felix, 111, 533
Adler, Herman Morris, 111
Adoption, 91, 481
Adult Education, 41, 111, 167, 203, 403, 637
Adult Education Association, Council of National Organizations, 203
Aged. See Old Age
Aid to Families with Dependent Children, 615
Airplane Safety. See Safety Measures, Airplanes
Albany Home for Children, New York, 85
Aliens, 403

Allen, Ethel Richardson, 111, 533
Allen, Florence Ellinwood, 533
Allen, Kathleen, 203
Allen, Loma M, 1
Almy, Frederic, 111, 533
Alt, Edith, 203
Alt, Herschel, 13, 203
American Association for Health Physical Education and Recreation, 203
American Association for Labor Legislation, 111
American Association for Organizing Family Social Work, 203, 503. See also Family Service Association of America; Family Welfare Association of America
American Association for Social Security, 637
American Association of Group Workers, 203, 637. See also National Association of Social Workers
American Association of Hospital Social Workers, 203; Section on Psychiatric Social Work. See American Association of Psychiatric Social Workers. See also American Association of Medical Social Workers; National Association of Social Workers, Medical Social Work Section

American Association of Leisure
Time Educators, 203
American Association of Medical
Social Workers, 203, 755
See also American Association
of Hospital Social Workers;
National Association of Social
Workers, Medical Social Work
Section
American Association of Psy-
chiatric Social Workers, 203.
See also National Association
of Social Workers, Psychiat-
ric Social Work Section
American Association of School
Social Workers. See Nation-
al Association of School
Social Workers
American Association of Schools
of Social Work, 193, 203,
777. See also Council on
Social Work Education; Na-
tional Association of Schools
of Social Administration;
National Council on Social
Work Education
American Association of Social
Workers, 111, 173, 203, 615,
637, 777. See also National
Association of Social Workers
American Association of Visit-
ing Teachers. See National
Association of School Social
Workers
American Cancer Society. See
American Society for the Con-
trol of Cancer;
New York City Cancer Commit-
tee, 809
American Civil Liberties Union,
777
American Committee in Aid of
Chinese Industrial Coopera-
tives, 637

American Council to Improve
Our Neighborhoods, 403
American Dietetic Association,
203
American Farm School, Salonika,
Greece, 111
American Field Service, 41
American Foundation for the
Blind, 777
American Friends Service Com-
mittee, 41
American Heart Association,
203
American Hospital Association,
111, 203
American Jewish Committee, 637
American Labor Party, 173
American Legion, 533, 755
American Medical Association,
637
American National Red Cross,
111, 203, 533, 615, 637, 755,
777
American Orthopsychiatric Asso-
ciation, 203
American Psychiatric Association
203
American Public Health Asso-
ciation, 203
American Public Welfare Associa-
tion, 193, 203, 615
American Recreation Society, 203
American Red Cross. See Ameri-
can National Red Cross
American Social Hygiene Associa-
tion, 637
American Society for the Control
of Cancer, 203
American Union Against Militar-
ism, 111, 533
American War Community Ser-
vices, 503
Americanization, 637. See also
Immigrants; Naturalization

INDEX

Americans for Democratic Action, 637, 777
Amidon, Beulah, 111, 533
Anderson, Delwin M, 755
Anderson, Joseph Paul, 193, 203
Andress, Bart, 173
Andrews, John Bartram, 111, 533
Anti-Semitism, 111, 173, 637. See also Minority Groups; Race Problems
Arkansas Conference of Social Work, 193
Arkansas, University, Dept. of Social Welfare, 193
Armed Forces, 203
Armes, Ethel Marie, 533
Arneson, Kathleen Elaine Caroon, 173
Arnstein, Leo, 533
Arts and Crafts, 41, 637
Asia Foundation, 745
Assembly of Youth. See U.S. Assembly of Youth
Associated Jewish Philanthropies, Boston, Massachusetts, 173
Associated Youth Serving Organization, 203, 503
Association for Improving the Condition of the Poor, New York. .See New York (City) Association for Improving the Condition of the Poor
Association for the Study of Community Organization, 203
Association of American Medical Colleges, 203
Association of Brooklyn Settlements, 637
Association of Community Chests and Councils, 503
Association of Neighborhood Workers, New York. See United Neighborhood Houses, New York
Association of Teachers of Preventive Medicine, 203
Association of Training Schools, 203
Athletic Programs, 203, 637
Atlanta University, School of Social Work, 755
Atwater, Pierce, 533
Austin, Mary C, 111, 533
Automobile Insurance. See Insurance, Automobile
Ayer, W C, 13

Baden Street Settlement, Rochester, New York, 1, 637
Baird-Wingefield Foundation, 41
Baker, Edith M, 203
Baker, Frank W, 533
Baker, Helen Cody, 533
Baker, Newton Diehl, 533
Balch, Emily Greene, 111, 533
Baldwin, Roger Nash, 111, 533, 637
Bamberger, Louis, 533
Barnes, Dora M, 533
Barnett, Eleanor, 203
Barnett, Henrietta Octavia (Rowland), 403
Barnett, Samuel Augustus, 403
Barnett Memorial Fellowship, 40
Barrett, John P B, 481
Barrett, Kate Waller, 481
Barrett, Robert South, 481
Bartelme, Mary Margaret, 111
Bartlett, Harriett M, 203
Bates, Sanford, 533
Batten, Samuel Zane, 533
Battle, George Gordon, 533
Bayes, William, 481
Beard, Charles Austin, 809
Bech, Elizabeth Brockett, 203
Beck, Bertram Maurice, 203

INDEX

Beck, Francis, 203
Beckley, Helen, 203, 755
Bellsmith, Ethel, 203
Benjamin, Edward Bernard, 533
Benjamin, Paul Lyman, 203, 533
Benner, Paul V, 203
Berkman, Tessie, 203
Berkowitz, Louis, 41
Berle, Adolph Augustus, 533
Bernays, Murray C, 533
Bernstein, Saul, 203
Berwind, Charles, 13
<u>Better</u> Times, 637
Bicknell, Ernest Percy, 533
Big Brother and Big Sister Federation, 13
Big Brothers of America, 13
Billikopf, Jacob, 173, 533
Billings, Warren K, 533
Bing, Alexander Max, 533
Birth Control, 111, 173, 637
Birth Control Federation of America, 111
Blaine, Anita McCormick, 111
Blair, Lawrence, 533
Blenkner, Margaret, 203
Blind, 755;
  Institutional Care, 755
Bliss, Cornelius Newton, 533
Bliven, Bruce, 533
Boardman, Rhea, 203
Boehm, Werner William, 203
Bondfield, Margaret Grace, 111, 533
Bondy, Robert Earl, 173
Bonus Army, 1932, 203
Bookman, Clarence Monroe, 503, 533
Booth, Charles Brandon, 13
Borah, William T, 111
Bowen, Louise (deKoven), 533
Bowker, Horace, 41
Boy Scouts of America, 41, 503
Boyd, Neva Leona, 403
Boys and Girls. See Children

Boys' Athletic League, New York. See New York (City) Boys' Athletic League
Brady, Mary B, 533
Brandeis, Alice Goldmark, 111
Brandeis, Louis Dembitz, 111, 533
Brandt, Lilian, 111, 173
Braucher, Howard S, 173, 503
Breckinridge, Sophonisba Preston, 203
Brenner, Ann (Reed), 111, 533
Brennock, T L, 533
Brisbane, Arthur, 533
British Labour Party. See Labour Party (Great Britain)
Britt, George, 111, 533
Brooklyn Neighborhood Houses Fund, 637
Brooks, A A, 533
Broun, Heywood, 533
Brown, Hester, 481
Brown, Irving Henry, 533
Bruere, Martha S Bensley, 111
Bruere, Robert Walter, 111, 533
Bruno, Frank John, 203, 533, 615, 777
Bruno, Joanna Carver Colcord. See Colcord, Joanna Carver
Buben, Zdenka, 203
Buell, Bradley, 111
Buell, Raymond Leslie, 533
Bulsara, Jal Feerose, 91
Burke, William Willard, 777
Burlingham, Charles Culp, 533
Burns, Allen Tibbals, 111, 533
Burpee, Lawrence Johnson, 111
Burritt, Bailey Barton, 533
Butler, Evelyn, 203
Byington, Margaret Frances, 503, 533

CARE. See Cooperative for American Remittances to Everywhere

CCC. See U.S. Civilian Conservation Corps
Cabot, Charles M, 111
Cabot, Philip T, 111, 533
Cabot, Richard Clarke, 111, 203, 533
Cabot Fund, 533
Cairns, Thomas, 13
Calkins, Marion "Clinch," 111, 533
"Calling America," 533
Camps, Day, 41
Camps, Summer, 13, 41, 637
Canada, 91
Canadian Association of Social Workers, 203
Canadian National Committee of the International Conference of Social Work, 91
Canadian Welfare Council, 91
Cancer, 755, 809
Cannon, Ida Maud, 203
Cannon, Mary Antoinette, 203
Cape, T Wilson, 193
Capital Punishment, 111
Cardozo, Benjamin Nathan, 533
Carnegie Corporation of New York, 503
Carpenter, Herschel Daniel, 403
Carpenter, Niles, 203
Carstens, Christian Carl, 85, 503
Carter, Genevieve W, 203
Casework, 1, 41, 91, 173, 203, 393, 403, 503, 615, 637. See also Psychiatric Social Work
Casey, George, 13
Catholic Big Brothers of New York City, 13
Catholic Church, Charities, 637
Chamberlain, Helen, 111
Chamberlain, Joseph Perkins, 111, 503, 533
Chamberlain, Mary, 111, 533
Chandler, Jane, 193

Chapin, Francis Stuart, 503
Charitable Giving. See Donations to Charities
Charities, 111
Charities and the Commons, 111
Charity Organization Society of the City of New York, 111, 637. See also New York (City) Association for Improving the Condition of the Poor
Chase, Stuart, 533
Checklist, 203
Chenery, William Ludlow, 533
Cheyney, Alice S, 111
Chicago Federation of Settlements. See Federation of Settlements, Chicago, Illinois
Chicago Peace Society, 111
Child Care Centers, 41
Child Labor, 111, 173, 203, 533, 637, 801;
Laws and Legislation, 111, 203, 801
Child Placing. See Adoption; Foster Home Care, Children
Child Welfare, 85, 173, 203, 503, 533, 637, 745, 777, 801. See also Children
Child Welfare League of America, 85, 111, 481, 615, 777
Children, 1, 85, 91, 111, 203, 403, 533, 615, 637, 777, 801;
Education, 801;
Institutional Care, 85;
Negro. See Negro Children.
See also Child Welfare
Children's Bureau. See U.S. Children's Bureau
Chronic Illness Newsletter, 203
Chronically Ill, 755
Church and Social Work, 85, 111, 173, 481, 503, 637
Citizens' Committee of 100 for Children and Youth, New York. See New York (City) Citizens'

Committee of 100 for Children and Youth, New York
Citizens' Committee on Children of New York City, 637
City Planning. See Regional and Municipal Planning
Civil Defense. See Civilian Defense
Civil Rights and Civil Liberties, 173, 203, 403, 533, 637, 777
Civil Service, 111, 203
Civil Works Administration. See U.S. Federal Civil Works Administration
Civilian Conservation Corps. See U.S. Civilian Conservation Corps
Civilian Defense, 41, 203, 403, 637
Claghorn, Kate Holladay, 533
Clapper, Raymond, 533
Clark, Evans, 533
Clark, Thomas Campbell, 13
Clinics, Psychiatric, 203
Cockerill, Eleanor, 203
Coffee, Rudolph Issac, 533
Cohen, Ethel, 203, 755
Cohen, George Lion, 403
Cohen, Nathan Edward, 203
Cohn, Fannia M, 111
Coit, Stanton, 403
Colburn, Fern M, 403
Colcord, Joanna Carver, 203, 533, 615, 777
Cole, Jean, 481
Collier, Elizabeth, 481
Collier, John, 111, 533
Colorado Coal Strike, 111
Columbia University, 111
Committee for Extension of Labor Education, Washington, D.C., 111
Committee on Cultural Relations with Latin America, Seminar in Mexico, 111

Committee on Discrimination in Housing, New York. See New York (State) Committee on Discrimination in Housing
Committee on Industrial Relations to Secure a Federal Commission on Industrial Relations, New York, 111
Committee on Research in Medical Economics, New York, 111
Common Council for American Unity. See Foreign Language Information Service
Common Human Needs, 203, 637, 777
Commons, John Rogers, 533
Commonwealth Fund, 203, 503
Communism, 637
Community Chests. See Community Funds and Chests
Community Chests and Councils of America. See United Community Funds and Councils of America
Community Council of Greater New York, 41
Community Council of St. Louis, Missouri, 111
Community Development, 91
Community Funds and Chests, 1, 13, 41, 173, 203, 481, 503, 533, 615, 637
Community Organization, 203
Community Organization, 173, 203, 503
Community Welfare Councils, 533, 615
The Compass, 203
Conant, Richard K, 533
Condon, Mollie, 111
Conference Board of the Associated Research Councils, Committee on International Exchange of Persons, 777

Conference on Education for Psychiatric Social Work, Dartmouth, 203
Conference on Education for Social Work, 193
Conferences in Social Welfare, 503
Conrad, Irene, 203
Conscientious Objectors, 203, 403
Conservation of Natural Resources. See Natural Resources
Consumers, 403, 503, 533, 637
Convalescent Care, 755
Cook, Waldo Lincoln, 111
Cooke, Morris Llewellyn, 111, 533
Cooley, Rossa Belle, 111, 533
Coolidge, Calvin, 533
Coolidge, Ellen Wayles, 403
Cooper, Charles C, 403, 533
Cooper, Ruth, 203
Cooper, Sarah Brown (Ingersoll), 533
Cooperative for American Remittances to Everywhere, 637
Cost and Standard of Living 403
Costigan, Edward Prentiss, 203, 533
Cottage Mothers, 85
Coughlin, Charles Edward, 637
Coulter, Ernest Kent, 13
Council for Rheumatic Fever, 203
Council of National Organizations of the Adult Education Association of the United States. See Adult Education Association, Council of National Organizations
Council on Social Work Education, 193, 203, 403, 615, 777. See also American Association of Schools of Social Work; National Association of Schools of Social Administration; National Council on Social Work Education
Couzens, James, 533
Creel, George, 111
Crime Prevention, 91
Crippled Children, 203
Crittenton, Charles Nelson, 481
Crosby, Helen, 173
Crowl, Donald B, 533
Cummings, Roger J, 755
Currency Reform, 111
Curtis, Frances Greely, 533
Curtis, Isabella, 533
Cutting, Bronson Murray, 533

Daniels, Josephus, 533
Darrow, Clarence Seward, 533
Dartmouth Conference on Education for Psychiatric Social Work. See Conference on Education for Psychiatric Social Work, Dartmouth
Davis, Stanley Powell, 173, 203
Davis, Horace Bancroft, 533
Davis, J Lionberger, 111, 533
Davis, Katherine Bement, 533
Davis, Michael Marks, 111, 203, 533
Davis, Ozora Stearns, 111
Dawley, Almena, 203
Dawson, John B, 203
Day Camps. See Camps, Day
Day Care, 1, 41, 637;
  Laws and Regulations, 1
Deardorff, Neva Ruth, 203, 533
Death Penalty. See Capital Punishment
De Forest, Robert Weeks, 111, 533

Delinquent Girls, 481. See also Juvenile Delinquency
Demobilization
 Industrial, 503;
 Military, 203
Democracy, 111
Depressions, 1, 41, 85, 167, 173, 203, 403, 481, 503, 533, 637, 755, 777
De Schweinitz, Elizabeth McCord, 203
De Schweinitz, Karl, 193, 203, 503, 533, 615, 755
Deutsch, Albert, 13
Devine, Edward Thomas, 111, 533, 637
Devine, Thomas, 111
Diabetes, 755
Dickson, W B, 533
Dilliard, Irving, 111
Dillon, Harold J, 801
Dinwiddie, Courtenay, 503, 533
Directory of Social and Health Agencies of New York City. See Community Council of Greater New York
Disarmament, 777
Discrimination
 Racial and Ethnic, 91, 111;
 in Employment. See Fair Employment Practices
Displaced Persons, 111, 203
D'Issertelle, Edna, 203
Dock, Lavinia Lloyd, 111
Donations to Charities, 801
Douglas, Paul Howard, 533
Draft, Military, 41, 203
Drama, 403, 637
Draper, Ernest Gallaudet, 533
Drew, Julia K, 203
Drown, Edward Staples, 111
Duggan, Stephen Pierce Hayden, 533
Dummer, Ethel (Sturges), 533

Dunham, Arthur H, 173, 203

Earhart, Amelia, 403, 637
Eastman, Crystal, 533
Eastman, Lucius R, 533
Economics, 533
Edison, Thomas Alva, 111
Education, 1, 481, 533, 637, 801
Eisenhower, Dwight David, 481, 777
Eldridge, Seba, 173
Elections in U.S., Presidential, 111, 533, 777
Eliot, Charles William, 503, 533
Eliot, Thomas Dawes, 533
Elledge, Caroline H, 203
Elliot, John Lovejoy, 111, 403, 533, 637
Elliott, Lula Jean, 203
Elmhurst, Dorothy Sillard, 533
Embree, Edwin Rogers, 533
Emergency Relief Bureau Supervisors Seminar, New York City. See New York (City) Emergency Relief Bureau Supervisors Seminar
Emerson, Haven, 111, 533
Emerson, Kendall, 173
Emerson, Ralph Waldo, 167
Emerson, Ruth, 203
Emery, E Van Norman, 777
Employment and Unemployment, 1, 111, 173, 403, 533, 637, 801;
 Laws and Legislation, 203.
 See also Fair Employment Practices
Epstein, Abraham, 533
Epstein, Benjamin Robert, 173
Ernst, Morris Leopold, 111
European War, 1914-1918. See World War, 1914-1918
Evans, Elizabeth Gardiner, 533

Ewing, Oscar Ross, 203

FHA. See U.S. Federal Housing Administration
Fair Employment Practices, 637. See also Employment and Unemployment
Falk, Leon, 173
Family and Children's Service, St. Louis, Missouri, 777
Family Life, 1, 173
Family Service Association of America, 503, 615, 777. See also American Association for Organizing Family Social Work
Family Service Society of St. Louis, Missouri, 203
Family Welfare Association of America, 173, 203. See also American Association for Organizing Family Social Work
Farm Tenancy, 111
Farquharson, Alexander Charles, 91
Farrand, Livingston, 533
Fascism, 173, 533
Federal Civil Defense Administration. See U.S. Federal Civil Defense Administration
Federal Conservation Program. See Natural Resources
Federal Emergency Relief Administration. See U.S. Federal Emergency Relief Administration
Federal Housing Administration. See U.S. Federal Housing Administration
Federal Security Agency. See U.S. Federal Security Agency
Federal Theatre Project. See U.S. Federal Theatre Project
Federation of Settlements, Chicago, Illinois, 637

Feiler, Arthur, 533
Feis, Herbert, 533
Feiser, James L, 533
Fels, Samuel Simeon, 111, 533
Fenlason, Anne (Ferguson), 615
Ferguson, Virginia S, 203
Field, Erlund, 403
Field Work, 41, 203, 503
Fierman, Frank, 203
Filene, A Lincoln. See Filene, Lincoln
Filene, Edward Albert, 533
Filene, Lincoln, 533
Finch, Norman B, 203
Finley, John Houston, 533
Fisher, Jacob, 173
Fisher, Raymond, 203
Fitch, John Andrews, 111, 173, 203, 533
Five Towns Community Chest, Nassau County, New York, 41
Five Towns Community Council, Nassau County, New York, 41
Five Towns Community House, Lawrence, Long Island, New York, 41. See also Margaret Sage Industrial School, Inwood, Long Island, New York; Nassau Industrial School, Inwood, Long Island, New York
Flanner House, Indianapolis, Indiana, 111
Flexner, Bernard, 533
Florence Crittenton Association of America, 481
Florence Crittenton Homes Association, 481
Folks, Gertrude. See Zimand, Gertrude Folks
Folks, Homer, 533, 801, 809
Forbes, James, 111, 533
Ford, Henry, 111
Foreign Affairs, 533, 637
Foreign Language Information Service, 111

Foreign Policy, U.S. See U.S. Foreign Policy
Foreign Policy Association, 111, 533, 809. See also League of Free Nations Association, New York
Forest Products Laboratory, Madison, Wisconsin. See U.S. Forest Products Laboratory, Madison, Wisconsin
Fosdick, Harry Emerson, 111
Foster, Francis A, 755
Foster Home Care
  Adults, 481, 755;
  Children, 85, 203, 481
Frankel, Lee Kaufer, 533
Frankfurter, Felix, 111, 533
Freedom of Speech, 111
Freedom of the Press, 111, 533
Freeman, Douglas Southall, 615
French, David, 203
French, Lois Meredith, 203
Friedlander, Walter Ferdinand, 91, 745
Friends Seminary, New York, 801
Furuseth, Andrew, 111

Gandhi, Kasturbai, 111
Gandhi, Mohandas Karamchand, 111, 533
Gannett, Lewis Stiles, 533
Garrison, Lloyd Kirkham, 533
Garson, Fannie Adler, 1
Gavit, John Palmer, 111, 533
Geddes, Sir Patrick, 111, 533
Gellhorn, Edna, 777
Gendall, Gilbert, 13
Genocide, 91
Gentile, Felix, 13
George Warren Brown School of Social Work, Washington University. See Washington University, George Warren Brown School of Social Work

Germany, 809
Gertrude Folks Zimand Memorial Award and Lecture, 809
Gibbs, Howard, 203
Giddings, Franklin Henry, 111
Gild Socialism. See Guild Socialism
Gillmore, Daniel S, 111
Ginsburg, Ethel, 203
Girls, Delinquent. See Delinquent Girls
Girls and Boys. See Children
Glasser, Melvin Allan, 203
Gleason, Arthur Huntingdon, 111, 533
Gleason, Helen (Hayes), 111, 533
Glenn, John Mark, 111, 503, 533
Glenn, Mary Willcox, 503, 533
Goddard, Agnes Brown Leach. See Leach, Agnes Brown
Golden Age Clubs, 403
Golden Anniversary White House Conference on Children and Youth, Washington, D.C., 1960. See White House Conference on Children and Youth, Washington, D.C., 1960
Goldman, Henry, 533
Goldman, Jane A, 1
Goldmark, Josephine Clara, 111
Goldmark, Pauline Dorothea, 111
Goldstein, Samuel A, 173
Goldstein, Sidney Emanuel, 173
Goldstine, Dora, 203
Gompers, Samuel, 533
Gooden, Opal, 203
Gordon, Eckka, 203
Gordon, William E, 203
"Gover'ment Cow," 615
Government and Social Welfare. See Social Welfare, Laws and Legislation

Graham, Frank Porter, 111
Granger, Lester B, 111, 203
Grant, Irene, 203, 755
Gray, James, 615
Green, Elizabeth, 173
Green, William, 111
Greenwood, Arthur, 533
Grosselin, Grace, 637
Grossman, George, 13
The Group, 203
Group Work, 1, 41, 203, 393, 403, 615;
  Canada, 203;
  Ethics, 203
Grueninger, Walter F, 111
Guardianship and Custody, 85, 755
Guild Socialism, 809
Guyler, Cathryn, 203

Hachtel, Esther C, 755
Hackett, Francis, 111, 533
Hagan, Margaret Wood, 203
Half-Way Houses, 755
Hall, Frederick Smith, 173
Hall, George A, 533
Hall, Helen, 111, 173, 403, 533, 637
Hallowell, Robert, 533
Hambrecht, Leona, 203
Hamilton, Alice, 111, 533
Hamilton, Gordon, 173, 203
Handicapped, 203;
  Rehabilitation, 91
Handicrafts. See Arts and Crafts
Hanrahan, John Keith, 111, 533
Hapgood, Norman, 533
Hard, William, 533
Hardwicke, Sarah, 203
Harmon, William E, 111, 533
Harmon Foundation, Inc., 533
Harper, Ernest Bouldin, 193, 203

Harris, Helen M, 533, 637
Harris, Nancy B, 1
Harrison, Earl Grant, 533
Harrison, Shelby Millard, 111, 503, 533
Hart, Hastings Hornell, 533
Hart, Hornell Norris, 533
Hart, Joseph Kinmont, 111, 533
Hastings, George Aubrey, 533
Hayden, Helen Elsa, 777
Hayes, Roland, 111
Haynes, George Edmund, 91, 203
Haynes, John R, 533
Hays, Arthur Garfield, 533
Hays, Margaret C, 1
Health, 1, 111, 403, 503, 533, 809
Health Agencies, Voluntary.
  See Voluntary Health Agencies
Health and Welfare Council, St. Louis, Missouri, 615, 777
Health Education, 809
Health Insurance, 111, 203, 403, 533, 637;
  Czechoslovakia, 91
Hecht, George Joseph, 533
Hedges, Benjamin Van Doren, 13
Hemmy, Mary, 203
Henderson, Fred, 533
Henderson, Leon, 533
Hendry, Charles E, 203
Henry, Edna G, 203
Henry Ford Peace Expedition, 111
Here's to Youth (Radio Program), 403
Herring, Hubert Clinton, 533
Hersey, Evelyn Weeks, 91
Higgins, Frances, 13
Hillman, Sidney, 111, 533
Hine, Lewis Wickes, 533
Hobby, Oveta Culp, 777
Hodges, Barbara, 203
Hodson, William W, 173, 203, 503, 533

Hoehler, Fred Kenneth, 91, 111, 203, 533
Hoey, Jane Margueretta, 91, 203, 615, 777
Hoffer, Joe Ralph, 203
Hoffman, Isaac, 203
Holbrook, David H, 203, 503
Hollis, Ernest Victor, 193
Holmes, John Haynes, 111, 533, 809
Holsinger, Mary B, 173
Hoover, Herbert Clark, 533
Hopkins, Harry Lloyd, 111, 173, 203, 533, 637
Hopkirk, Howard W, 85
Hopkirk, Ruth Hathaway, 85
Hospital Social Work. See Medical Social Work
Hospitals
  Outpatient Services, 755;
  Psychiatric, 203;
  Social Service, 111, 203;
  Veteran, Social Service, 203
House, Grace B, 111, 533
Housing, 1, 41, 91, 111, 203, 403, 533, 637;
  Laws and Legislation, 203, 637
Howard, Donald Stevenson, 203
Howe, Frederick Clemson, 111, 533
Howells, William Dean, 111
Hughes, Charles Evans, 533, 637
Hull House, Chicago, Illinois, 615, 637
Humphrey, Hubert Horatio, 777
Hunt, Edward Eyre, 533
Huyck, E N, 533
Hygiene, Social. See Social Hygiene

IWW. See Industrial Workers of the World

Ickes, Harold LeClaire, 533, 637
Ida S. Latz Foundation, 755
Ihlder, John, 111, 533
Illinois, Dept. of Mental Health, 777
Illinois, Dept. of Public Welfare, 777
Immigrants, 1, 41, 111, 403, 503, 533, 637. See also Americanization; Naturalization
Income Tax, 533
India, 111, 809
Indians of North America, 533, 637
INDUSCO. See American Committee in Aid of Chinese Industrial Cooperatives
Industrial Demobilization. See Demobilization, Industrial
Industrial Relations, 111, 533, 745
Industrial Workers of the World, 533
Industrialization, 91
Industry, Working Conditions, 111
Infant Welfare. See Maternal and Infant Welfare
Ingram, Frances, 403
Institute of International Education, 111
Insurance
  Automobile, 637;
  Health. See Health Insurance;
  Old Age. See Old Age Insurance;
  Social. See Social Insurance;
  Unemployment. See Unemployment Insurance
Intercollegiate Bureau of Occupations, Dept. of Social Workers. See American Association of Social Workers

INDEX

International Association of
Pupil Personnel Workers, 203
International Committee of
Schools of Social Work, 91
International Conference of
Social Work, 91, 193, 203,
503, 637;
1st, Paris, 1928, 91;
2nd, Frankfurt, 1932, 91;
3rd, London, 1936, 91;
4th, Atlantic City, New Jersey,
1948, 91;
5th, Paris, 1950, 91;
6th, Madras, 1952, 91;
7th, Toronto, 1954, 91;
8th, Munich, 1956, 91;
9th, Tokoyo, 1958, 91;
10th, Rome, 1961, 91;
11th, Petropolis, Brazil,
1962, 91;
12th, Athens, 1964, 91;
13th, Washington, D.C., 1966,
91;
Canadian National Committee.
See Canadian National Committee of the International
Conference of Social Work;
United States Committee. See
United States Committee of the
International Conference of
Social Work
International Conference on
Social Welfare, 533, 745
International Congress of Mental Hygiene, 203
International Congress of
Women, 111
International Federation of
Social Workers, 91
International Industrial Relations Institute, 111
International Joint Commission
(U.S. and Canada), 111
International Migration Service,
503

International Relations, 111
International Seamen's Union
of America, 111
International Services and
Programs, 203, 403, 503, 637,
755
Ireland, 809
Isaacs, Stanley Myer, 637
Issler, Ann (Roller), 533
Ittleson, Henry, 533

Jackson, Roxanna, 481
Jacobs, Elizabeth R, 203
Jacobs, Phillip Peter, 533
Japan Editors' Club, 533
Japanese-Americans, 503
Jarrett, Mary Cromwell, 203
Jenks, Donald, 13
Jerdone, Gertrude M, 1
Jeter, Helen Rankin, 173, 203
Jewish Association for Neighborhood Centers, New York.
See New York (City) Jewish
Association for Neighborhood
Centers
Jewish Big Brothers of New York
City, 13
Jewish Social Welfare, 173
Jewish Welfare Board. See
National Jewish Welfare
Board
Johnson, Alexander, 111, 533
Johnson, Alvin Saunders, 111
Johnson, Frederick Ernest, 801
Johnson, M Asenath, 41
Joint Commission on Accreditation of Hospitals, 203
Joint Vocational Service, 203.
See also Social Work Vocational Bureau
Junior League of St. Louis,
Missouri, 615
Juvenile Courts, 533
Juvenile Delinquency, 13, 41,
85, 173, 203, 403, 481, 533

637. See also Delinquent Girls

Kahn, Dorothy Caroline, 173, 203
Kane, Francis Fisher, 533
Kate Waller Barrett Training School, Akron, Ohio, 481
Kaufman, Edgar J, 173
Kaufmann, Fritz, 533
Kawin, Ethel, 111
Keegan, Robert F, 173
Kelley, Florence, 111, 173, 533
Kelley, Jerry L, 203
Kelley, Nicholas, 533
Kellogg, Arthur Piper, 111, 203, 533
Kellogg, Florence Loeb, 111
Kellogg, Helen (Hall). See Hall, Helen
Kellogg, John Harvey, 533
Kellogg, Marion Pearce Sherwood, 111
Kellogg, Mercy Pearce, 111
Kellogg, Paul Underwood, 111, 173, 203, 403, 533, 615, 637, 801, 809
Kellogg, Richard Patrick, 111
Kendall, Katherine A, 91
Kenderdine, John D, 111, 203, 533
Kennedy, Albert Joseph, 111, 403, 637
Kennedy, John Fitzgerald, 777
Kenworthy, Marion Edwena, 203
Keppel, Frederick Paul, 533
Kidneigh, John Christopher, 203
Kingsbury, John Adams, 533
Kingsley House Settlement, Pittsburgh, Pennsylvania, 111
Kirchwey, George Washington, 111
Klein, Philip, 173, 203
Knight, Howard Roscoe, 203, 503, 533
Knights of Columbus, 111

Knowles, Morris, 533
Knox, William J, 1
Konopka, Gisela Peiper, 203
Korean War, 1950-1953, 91, 637
Korpela, Janet W, 203
Kraft, Louis, 203
Kraus, Hertha, 91, 745
Krehbiel, Edward Benjamin, 533
Krenek, Ernst, 615
Kriegsfeld, Irving M, 1, 403
Krughoff, Merrill F, 203
Ku-Klux Klan, 111
Kuolt, Oscar W, 173
Kurtz, Russell Harold, 203, 615
Kyron Foundation, 111

Labor, 111, 173, 403, 503, 533, 637, 809;
  Laws and Legislation, 173
Labor Party (Great Britain), 533
Labor Party (U.S.), 173
Labour Party (Great Britain), 111
LaFollette, Robert Marion (1855-1925), 533
LaFollette, Robert Marion (1895-1953), 533
La Guardia, Fiorello Henry, 637
Lamont, Thomas William, 533
Lane, Robert Porter, 203
Lane, Winthrop David, 533
Lansdale, Robert Tucker, 203
La Rochefoucauld, Francois, Duc De, 615
Lasker, Bruno, 111, 533
Lasker, Loula Davis, 111, 533
Lathrop, Julia Clifford, 533
Latz Foundation. See Ida S. Latz Foundation
Lay, Madeleine, 203
Leach, Agnes Brown, 533
Leach, Henry Goddard, 533
League of Free Nations Association, New York, 111. See

also Foreign Policy Association
League of Mothers' Clubs, New York. See New York (City) League of Mothers' Club
League to Enforce Peace, 111
Leahy, Agnes Berkeley, 203
Lee, Joseph, 111, 503, 533
Lee, Porter Raymond, 203, 533
Leet, Dorothy, 533
Lehman, Herbert Henry, 173, 533, 637
Leiserson, William Morris, 111, 533
Lenroot, Katharine Frederica, 91, 203, 503, 533
Levinrew, George, 203
Levy, David Mordecai, 203
Lewis, Ruth Endicott, 203, 777
Lewisohn, Adolph, 111, 533
Lewisohn, Irene, 533
Lewisohn, Sam Adolph, 533
Liebknecht, Karl Paul August Friedrich, 111, 809
Lincoln, Arleigh Leon, 193
Lindeman, Eduard Christian, 13, 167, 533, 637
Lindenberg, Sidney C, 1
Lindsay, Ben B, 533
Lindsay, Samuel McCune, 111, 533
Liquor Problem, 533
Literature, 403
Liveright, Alice F, 173
Lobbying, 1, 393, 403
Lochner, Louis Paul, 111
Locke, Alain LeRoy, 533
Lockouts. See Strikes and Lockouts
Louard, V Benjamin, 41
Lovejoy, Owen Reed, 203, 533
Low Income. See Poverty
Lowell, Josephine Shaw, 111
Lowenfeld, Henry, 111
Lowenstein, Solomon, 533

Lund, Harald H, 173
Lurie, Harry Lawrence, 173, 203, 503
Luxemburg, Rosa, 809

McBee, Marion, 203
McCall, Bertha, 503
McCarthy, Joseph Raymond, 637, 777
McClary, Howard C, 1, 41
McCloy, John Jay, 203
McCoy, Joseph, 13
McCready, Caroline P, 533
McDonald, James Grover, 533
MacDonald, James Ramsay, 111, 533
McDowell, John, 203, 403, 637
McDowell, Mary Eliza, 533
McFarland, Frances, 403
McGuinn, Walter, 203
Mack, Julian William, 111, 533
MacKaye, Percy, 111
McLean, Francis Herbert, 111, 503
McMahon, Kate, 203
McMain, Eleanor, 403
McMillen, Wayne, 203
McNeil, Clarid F, 203
Macy, Noel, 533
Macy, V Everit, 533
Maetzgold, Audrey J, 203
Magrath, Charles Alexander, 111, 533
Mallach, Aubrey, 203
Mallon, James Joseph, 403, 533, 637
Marcus, Grace, 203
Margaret Sage Industrial School, Inwood, Long Island, New York, 41. See also Five Towns Community House, Lawrence, Long Island, New York; Nassau Industrial School, Inwood, Long Island, New York
Markoff, Sol, 801

Marsh, Benjamin Clarke, 533
Masaryk, Thomas Garrigue, 533
Maternal and Infant Welfare, 481
Maternity Homes, Community Relationships, 481
Matthews, William Henry, 111, 533
Maxted, Mattie Cal, 193
Maxwell, Mary, 203
Mayer, Albert, 111, 533
Mayo, Katherine, 809
Mayo, Leonard W, 203
Mazel, Karl, 111
Mc. See Mac
Medical Care, 1, 393, 403; Cost of, 533
Medical Social Work, 203
Medical Social Work, 91, 203, 755; Education, 203; Practice, 203; Recruitment, 203
Menninger, William Claire, 13
Mental Clinics. See Clinics, Psychiatric
Mental Health and Mental Illness, 1, 173, 203, 533, 637
Mental Hospitals. See Hospitals, Psychiatric
Mental Retardation, 637
Merrell, Constance, 41
Merriman, Christina, 533
Metropolitan New York Conference of Social Work, 4th, 1936, 173
Mexico, 111, 533
Michaels, Ellen, 203
Mid-Century White House Conference on Children and Youth, Washington, D.C., 1950. See White House Conference on Children and Youth, Washington, D.C., 1950

Middleton, James S, 533
Migrant Labor, 203, 801
Migrants, 91, 203
Milbank Memorial Fund, 503
Milford Conference, 203, 503,
Militarism, 111, 533, 809. See also Pacifism
Military Demobolization. See Demobilization, Military
Military Draft. See Draft, Military
Military SocialWork, 203
Mills, Elisabeth, 203
Minimum Wage Laws. See Labor, Laws and Legislation
Minkoff, Isaiah, 173
Minnesota, Board of Control, Division of Public Assistance, 777
Minnesota Child Welfare Conference, 1956, 745
Minnesota, Dept. of Social Security, Division of Social Welfare, 615
Minnesota State Emergency Relief Administration, 777
Minnesota Welfare Association, 615, 777
Minority Groups, 403, 481, 503. See also Anti-Semitism; Negroes; Puerto Ricans; Race Problems
Missouri Association for Mental Health, 777
Missouri Association for Social Welfare, 615, 777
Mitropoulos, Dimitri, 615
Moak, Harry L, 533
Monfort, Gertrude, 1
Montreal, Canada, 111
Mooney, Thomas J, 111, 533
Mooney-Billings Case. See Mooney, Thomas J; Billings, Warren K

Moore, Coyle E, 193
Moore, John, 203
Moore, Madeleine, 203
Moors, John Farwell, 111
Morgan, Arthur Ernest, 533
Morganthau, Rita (Wallach), 533
Morrow, Dwight Whitney, 533
Morton, Helen, 403
Moses, Robert, 637
Moskowitz, Belle (Lindner) Israels, 533
Moss, Celia R, 203
Moss, Mary Blanche, 203
Mudgett, Margaret, 203
Mumford, Lewis, 111, 637
Mumm, Louise, 173
Municipal Planning. See Regional and Municipal Planning
Murphy, Frank, 533
Murphy, John Prentice, 533
Murray, Clyde E, 203, 403, 637
Music, 41, 403, 637
Muste, Abraham John, 637
Myrdal, Gunnar Karl, 91
Myrick, Helen, 203

NAHRO. See National Association of Housing and Redevelopment Officials
NASW News, 203
NBC. See National Broadcasting Company
NEA. See National Education Association of the United States
Narcotic Addicts, 533, 637
Narcotics, 41, 533
Nasmyth, George William, 111
Nassau Industrial School, Inwood, Long Island, New York, 41. See also Five Towns Community House, Lawrence, Long Island, New York; Margaret Sage Industrial School, Inwood, Long Island, New York
National Association for the Study of Group Work. See American Association of Group Workers
National Association of Housing and Redevelopment Officials, 403
National Association of Jewish Center Workers, 41
National Association of Legal Aid Organizations, 203
National Association of School Social Workers, 203. See also National Association of Social Workers, School Social Work Section
National Association of Schools of Social Administration, 193. See also American Association of Schools of Social Work; Council on Social Work Education; National Council on Social Work Education
National Association of Social Workers, 203, 615, 637, 777; Medical Social Work Section, 203. See also American Association of Hospital Social Workers; American Association of Medical Social Workers; Psychiatric Social Work Section, 203. See also American Association of Psychiatric Social Workers; School Social Work Section, 203. See also National Association of School Social Workers; Social Work Research Section, 203. See also Social Work Research Group; Metropolitan Washington Chap-

ter, Washington, D.C., 393; Southern Minnesota Chapter, 203. See also American Association of Social Workers
National Association of Travelers Aid Societies. See National Travelers Aid Association, New York
National Association of Visiting Teachers and Home Visitors. See National Association of School Social Workers
National Broadcasting Company, 809
National Child Labor Committee, New York, 801
National Civic Federation, 111
National Committee for Mental Hygiene, 203
National Committee for Planned Parenthood, 111
National Committee on Employment of Youth, 801
National Committee on Personnel in the Social Services, 203
National Committee on Social Work in Defense Mobilization, 203
National Committee on Visiting Teachers, 203
National Conference of Catholic Charities, 203, 503
National Conference of Charities and Correction, 111. See also National Conference of Social Work; National Conference on Social Welfare
National Conference of Christians and Jews, 41
National Conference of Jewish Social Service, 173
National Conference of Social Work, 111, 193, 203, 481, 503, 637. See also National Conference of Charities and Correction; National Conference on Social Welfare
National Conference on Facilities for Athletics, Recreation, Physical and Health Education, 1st, Jackson's Mill, West Virginia, 1946, 203
National Conference on Labor Legislation, 111
National Conference on Prevention and Control of Juvenile Delinquency, 203
National Conference on Professional Preparation in Health Education, Physical Education and Recreation, 203
National Conference on Social Welfare, 41, 203, 533, 615, 637. See also National Conference of Charities and Correction; National Conference of Social Work
National Convention of Rank and File Groups in Social Work, 1st, Pittsburgh, 1935, 37
National Coordinating Committee on Social Service Employee Groups, 37
National Council of Jewish Women, 41
National Council of Rehabilitation, 203
National Council on Social Work Education, 193, 203. See also American Association of Schools of Social Work; Council on Social Work Education; National Association of Schools of Social Administration
National Defense, 203
National Education Association of the United States, 203, 637;

American Association for Health, Physical Education and Recreation. See American Association for Health, Physical Education and Recreation
National Federation for Constitutional Liberties, 777
National Federation of Settlements and Neighborhood Centers, New York, 41, 403, 637
National Florence Crittenton Mission, 481
National Foundation for Infantile Paralysis, 203
National Health and Welfare Retirement Association, 41
National Health Council, 91, 203
National Housing Agency. See U.S. National Housing Agency
National Industrial Recovery Act, 1933, 637
National Information Bureau, New York, 403, 503
National Jewish Welfare Board, 637
National Legal Aid and Defense Organizations. See National Association of Legal Aid Organizations
National Organization for Public Health Nursing, 203
National Psychiatric Social Workers' Club. See American Association of Psychiatric Social Workers
National Recovery Administration. See U.S. National Recovery Administration
National Recreation Association, 203, 637
National Resources Planning Board. See U.S. National Resources Planning Board

National Retail Dry Goods Association, 173
National Social Welfare Assembly, 173, 193, 203, 403, 503, 637, 745
National Social Work Council, 173, 203, 503
National Social Workers Exchange, 203
National Travelers Aid Association, New York, 755
National Urban League, 637
National Vocational Service, 203
National Youth Administration. See U.S. National Youth Administration
Natural Resources, 111, 173, 533
Naturalization, 637. See also Americanization; Immigrants
Neely, Ann Elizabeth, 203
Negro Children, 85
Negro Youth, 13
Negroes, 1, 41, 193, 481, 503, 637;
Children. See Negro Children;
Education, 1, 85, 777;
in Medical Social Work, 203.
See also Anti-Semitism; Minority Groups; Race Problems
Neighborhood: A Settlement Quarterly, 403
Neighborhood Houses Fund, Brooklyn, New York. See Brooklyn Neighborhood Houses Fund
Nelson, Ruth Youngdahl, 777
Neuberger, Maurine (Brown), 533
Neuberger, Richard Lewis, 111, 533
Neurath, Otto, 533
Neuropsychiatric Social Work. See Psychiatric Social Work

Neutrality, 533, 637. See also Pacifism
Nevins, Allan, 111
New Deal, 111, 167
New York Association of Neighborhood Workers. See United Neighborhood Houses, New York
New York (City) Association for Improving the Condition of the Poor, 637. See also Charity Organization Society of the City of New York
New York (City) Board of Education, 809
New York (City) Boys' Athletic League, 637
New York City Cancer Committee. See American Cancer Society, New York City Cancer Committee
New York (City) Charity Organization Society. See Charity Organization Society of the City of New York
New York (City) Citizens' Committee of 100 for Children and Youth, 637
New York (City) Citizens' Committee on Children. See Citizens' Committee on Children of New York City
New York (City) Dept. of Health, 809
New York (City) Emergency Relief Bureau, 637; Supervisors Seminar, 173
New York (City) Jewish Association for Neighborhood Centers, 637
New York (City) League of Mothers' Clubs, 637
New York (City) Playground and Recreation Association, 637
New York (City) Public Education Association, 637

New York (City) Welfare Council, 41, 173, 637
New York Metropolitan Conference of Social Work, 4th, 1936. See Metropolitan New York Conference of Social Work, 4th, 1936
New York, People's Institute, 111
New York School of Social Work, 173
New York (State) Civil Service, 173
New York State Commission Against Discrimination, 111
New York (State) Committee on Discrimination in Housing, 637
New York State Conference on Social Work, 173
New York State Employment Service, 111
Newstetter, Wilber Irwin, 203
Nicholson, Charles T, 481
Nordly, Carl Leonard, 203
Norman Sarett Memorial Foundation, 41
North Atlantic Group of Social Workers, 755
Norton, Charles D, 533
Nottingham, Ruth D, 481
Nursery Schools, 41, 637
Nye, Gerald Prentice, 637

Odencrantz, Louise, 203
Office of Defense Mobilization, 111
O'Grady, John, 203
Old Age, 41, 173, 203, 393, 403, 615, 637, 755, 777
Old Age Insurance, 111
Open and Closed Shop, 809
Opium, 533
Oren, Anne Winslow, 777
Orphanages, 85
Orphans, 85

Outpatient Care. See Hospitals, Outpatient Services

Pacifism, 111, 403, 533. See also Militarism; Neutrality
Paddock, Robert L, 533
Pan American Union, 91
Parents, 85
Parran, Thomas, 533
Patriotic Fund of Canada, 111
Payne, Elizabeth E, 203
Payne, Virgil, 481
Peabody, George Foster, 111, 533
Peace, 403, 637
Pearl Harbor, Attack On, 1941, 203
Peck, Lillie M, 111, 403, 637
Peixotto, Jessica Blanche, 533
Pelton, Garnet I, 203
Penn Normal, Agricultural, and Industrial School, St. Helena Island, South Carolina, 111, 533
Pennsylvania, 111
People's Institute, New York. See New York, People's Institute
Perkins, Frances, 111, 503, 533, 637
Perkins, Wilma Lord, 1
Persons, William Frank, 173, 533
Pettit, Walter William, 533
Philanthropy, 111
Phillipson, Elma, 203
Physical Education, 1
Pinchot, Amos Richards Eno, 111, 533
Pinchot, Gifford, 533
Pittsburgh Survey, 111
Planned Parenthood. See Birth Control
Planned Parenthood Federation of America. See Birth Control Federation of America

Play Schools Association, 41, 637
Playground and Recreation Association, New York. See New York (City) Playground and Recreation Association
Playgrounds, 111
Poetry, 403
Police, Training, 637
Poole, Mary L, 203
Porterfield, Austin Larimore, 193
Poverty, 403, 637, 777
Pratt, George Dwight, 533
Pray, Kenneth Louis Moffatt, 173, 203
Preston, Clarence R, 481
Primo, Quintin, 1
Prisons, 111, 533
Private Practice of Social Work, 393
Probation, 801
Progressive Party, 111
Progressivism, 533
Prohibition, 111, 403, 533
Prosthesis, 755
Prostitution, 91, 173. See also Sex Education; Social Hygiene; Venereal Disease
Psychiatric Clinics. See Clinics, Psychiatric
Psychiatric Hospitals. See Hospitals, Psychiatric
Psychiatric Social Work, 203, 393, 637, 755. See also Casework
Public Assistance. See Public Welfare
Public Education Association of New York City. See New York (City) Public Education Association
Public Health, 91, 203, 533, 637, 809

Public Health Nursing, 91
Public Health Service. See
  U.S. Public Health Service
Public Relations, 1, 111, 481,
  615, 637
Public Utilities, 533
Public Welfare, 111, 203, 393,
  481, 503, 533, 615, 637, 755,
  777;
  Finance, 37, 173;
  in Minnesota, 615, 777;
  in Missouri, 777;
  in Nassau County, New York, 41;
  in St. Louis, Missouri, 615,
  777.
  See also Social Welfare
Puerto Ricans, 637
Pulsifer, Doris U, 1
Purcell, Catharine, 203
Purdy, Lawson, 533
Putnam, Amelia (Earhart). See
  Earhart, Amelia

Rabinoff, George W, 173
Race Problems, 41, 111, 173,
  203, 393, 533, 637, 777;
  in the Military, 111.
  See also Anti-Semitism; Minority Groups; Negroes
Ratcliffe, Samuel Kerkham, 533
Ray, Florence, 203
The Reader's Digest, 533
Rebmann, G Ruhland, 13
Recreation, 1, 41, 111, 203,
  403, 637
Red Cross. See American National Red Cross
Reeder, Rudolph Rex, 533
Refugees, 91, 403, 533, 637
Regional and Municipal Planning,
  1, 111, 203, 533, 637. See
  also Urban Renewal
Registration of Social Workers
  in California, 393

Rehabilitation, 91;
  of the Handicapped. See
  Handicapped, Rehabilitation
Relief. See Public Relief
Religious Emphasis and Training,
  481
Renold, Sir Charles Garonne, 533
Revelle, Gladys, 481
Rheumatic Fever, Council for.
  See Council for Rheumatic
  Fever
Rhyne, Jennings Jefferson, 193
Rice, Elizabeth P, 203
Richberg, Donald Randall, 533
Richmond, Mary Ellen, 615
Robbins, Jane, 403
Robins, Margaret Drier, 111
Roche, Josephine Aspinwall, 533
Rochester, New York, Social
  Problems, 1
Rockefeller Foundation, 111,
  503
Rogers, Kenneth H, 13
Roosevelt, Eleanor (Roosevelt),
  533, 615, 637
Roosevelt, Franklin Delano, 111,
  481, 533, 615
Rosenman, Dorothy Reuben, 637
Rosenwald, Julius, 111
Rosner, Joseph, 203
Ross, Elizabeth Healy, 203
Ross, Mary, 111, 533
Round Table, 403
Rounds, Ralph Stonwell, 533
Routzahn, Evart Grant, 533
Routzahn, Mary Brayton, 533
Rowe, Helen, 203
Rowell, Chester Harvey, 533
Rubinow, Isaac Max, 111, 173,
  533
Rudwin, Maximillian Josef, 173
Rune, Beardsley, 533
Rural Service And Programs,
  91, 111, 193, 503

Rural Sociology, 111, 615, 777
Russell, Marian E, 203
Russell Sage Foundation, New York, 111, 203, 503, 615
Russia, 111, 173, 533, 809
Ryan, Phillip Elwood, 203
Ryerson, Edward Larned, 533
Ryman, Pauline, 203

Sabloff, Janet, 111
Sacco-Vanzetti Case, 111, 533
Safety Measures, Airplanes, 533
Sage, Margaret Olivia Slocum, 41
St. Louis, Missouri Community Council. See Community Council of St. Louis, Missouri
St. Louis Council for Parent Education, 615
St. Louis Social Planning Council. See Health and Welfare Council, St. Louis, Missouri
Saloshin, H Etta, 203
Salavation Army, 91, 481, 533
Sand, Rene, 91, 203
Sanitation, 637
Sanville, Florence, 111
Sark, H M L H, 91
Scandrett, Richard Brown, 533
Scattergood, Alfred Garrett, 533
Scattergood, Joseph Henry, 533
Schaffner, Halle, 111, 533
Schaffner, Joseph H, 533
Schieffelin, William Jay, 533
Schiff, Jacob Henry, 533
School Social Work, 203
Schools of Social Work. See Social Work, Education
Schroeder, Agnes H, 203
Schwartz, Edward Edgar, 203
Schwimmer, Rosika, 111
Scoville, Mildred, 203
Seager, Henry Rogers, 533
Seamen, 111
Selective Service. See Draft, Military
Selective Service System. See U.S. Selective Service System
Selekman, Benjamin Morris, 173
Seligman, Edwin Robert Anderson, 533
Senior, Max, 533
Senior Citizens. See Old Age
Settlements, 1, 111, 403, 533, 637;
Anniversaries, 403
Sex Education, 637. See also Prostitution; Social Hygiene; Venereal Disease
Seymour, Gertrude, 533
Shapiro, Harry Lionel, 173
Shaw, S Adele, 533
Sheldon, Rowland, 13
Shilladay, John H, 533
Shimp, Everett, 203
Shortly, Michael Joseph, 203
Shotwell, James Thomson, 111
Shutz, Margaret, 203
Shyne, Ann, 203
"Sickness" Insurance. See Health Insurance
Sikkema, Mildred, 203
Silver, Harold, 203
Simkhovitch, Mary Melinda (Kingsbury), 403, 533, 637
Simons, Savilla Millis, 91
Sinclair, Upton Beall, 533
Slawson, John S, 173
Slums, 637
Smalley, Ruth Elizabeth, 203
Smillie, Robert, 111, 533, 809
Smith, Alfred Emanuel, 533, 637
Smith, Frank Fremont, 203
Smith, Geddes, 111, 533
Smith, Hilda Worthington, 403
Smith, R Templeton, 173
Smith, Reba Barrett, 481
Social Action, 1, 173, 203, 615, 637, 777
Social Casework. See Casework
Social Change, 167

Social Education, 637
Social Group Work. See Group Work
Social Hygiene, 637. See also Prostitution; Sex Education Venereal Disease
Social Insurance, 111, 533, See also Social Security
Social Planning. See Social Change
Social Planning Council, St. Louis, Missouri. See Health and Welfare Council, St. Louis, Missouri
Social Policy, 91, 167, 203
Social Reform, 533, 615
Social Security, 111, 173, 203, 503, 533;
Czechoslovakia, 91.
See also Social Insurance
Social Service, Medical. See Medical Social Work
Social Service Review, 173
Social Settlement of Rochester. See Baden Street Settlement, Rochester, New York
Social Settlements. See Settlements
Social Welfare, 85, 533, 615, 637, 777;
Laws and Legislation, U.S., 173, 203, 637.
See also Public Welfare
Social Welfare Assembly, National. See National Social Welfare Assembly
Social Work, 13, 111, 203, 393, 533, 615, 777;
Canada, 203;
Certification, 203;
Education, 41, 91, 193, 203, 393, 615, 755;
England, 503;
Ethics, 203, 393, 615, 637;
Europe, 91;
Field Work. See Field Work;
Finance, 503;
Germany, 503;
Minnesota, 203;
Personnel, 91, 203, 481, 503;
Placement, 203;
Practice, 203;
Recruitment, 1, 203, 393, 503, 615, 755;
Research, 203;
Salaries, Pensions, Etc., 37;
Working Conditions, 37, 111, 203;
and the Church. See Church Social Work
Social Work Journal, 203
Social Work Research Group, 203. See also National Association of Social Work, Social Work Research Section
Social Work Today, 37, 637
Social Work Vocational Bureau, 203. See also Joint Vocational Service
Social Work Year Book, 173
Social Workers Discussion Club, New York, 37
Solender, Sanford, 203
Sollins, I V, 173
Solomon, Maida, 203
Soule, Theodate, 203
Spain, Civil War, 1936-1939, 111, 533
Spanish Refugee Relief Campaign, New York, 111
Spellman, D D, 481
Spencer, Anna Garlin, 111
Spencer, Sue, 193, 203, 755
Springer, Gertrude (Hill), 203, 533, 615
Stamm, Joseph, 481
Stanton, Katherine A, 393
Steel Industry, 533;
Working Conditions, 111

Steel Strike, 1919, 533
Steffens, Lincoln, 533
Stella, Joseph, 111
Step-Parents. See Parents
Stern, Alfred K, 533
Stern, Edith (Mendel), 533
Stevenson, Adlai Ewing, 777
Stevenson, George Salvadore, 203
Stewart, Jane, 203
Stewart, Sara Vance, 1
Stimson, Henry Lewis, 533
Stipe, Jack, 755
Street, Elwood, 533
Strikes and Lockouts, 111
Strong, Anna Louise, 533
Strong, Sidney, 533
Stroock, Sol M, 533
Summer Camps. See Camps, Summer
Survey, 111, 403, 533, 615, 637
Survey Associates, New York, 111, 403, 533
Survey Graphic, 111, 533, 615
Survey Midmonthly, 111, 533
Suskind, Harry H, 1
Svendsen, Margaret, 203
Swanson, Mayme, 481
Sweat, Lili G, 203
Swift, Arthur L, 203
Swift, Harold Higgins, 111, 533
Swift, Linton B, 173, 203
Swing, Raymond Gram, 533
Swope, Gerald P, 637

TIAC. See Temporary Inter-Association Council of Social Work Membership Organizations
TVA. See Tennessee Valley Authority
Tandy, W Lou, 173
Tannenbaum, Frank, 111, 533
Tarail, Theodore T, 203
Tarbell, Ida Minerva, 533
Taxation, 503
Taylor, Graham, 403, 533

Taylor, Graham Romeyn, 111, 203, 533, 637
Taylor, Lea Demarest, 403, 637
Taylor, Maurice, 173
Technical Assistance, 91
Temporary Inter-Association Council of Social Work Membership Organizations, 203, 777
Tenant Farming. See Farm Tenancy
Tennessee Valley Authority, 503, 533
Theater, 637
Thomas, Addie, 203
Thomas, Julia, 481
Thomas, Norman Mattoon, 637
Thompson, Christine Robb, 203
Thorpe, Ruth, 481
Tolan Committee, 503
Tousley, Clare M, 503, 533
Towle, Charlotte, 755;
   Common Human Needs, 203, 637, 777
Towley, Louis Heiberg, 615, 777
Towley, Marie, 615
Trade Unions, 403
Transients, 173, 503
Travelers Aid Association. See National Travelers Aid Association, New York
Trecker, Harleigh Bradley, 203
Trial Visit Program, 755
Tuberculosis, 203, 755
Tucker, Frank, 533
Tyson, Francis Doughton, 533

UNESCO. See United Nations Educational, Scientific and Cultural Organization
UNICEF. See United Nations, Children's Fund
Unemployment. See Employment and Unemployment
Unemployment Insurance, 111, 203, 533

Unions. See Trade Unions
United Community Defense Services, New York, 203, 403
United Community Funds and Councils of America, 203
United Defense Fund, 203
United Fruit Company, 111
United Nations, 91, 203, 637;
Children's Fund, 91;
Educational, Scientific and Cultural Organization, 91;
General Assembly, Universal Declaration of Human Rights, 91;
Relief and Rehabilitation Administration, 203
United Neighborhood Houses, New York, 41, 637
USO. See United Service Organization for National Defense
United Educational Program, Committee on Interpretation of Unemployment Relief, 173
United Service Organization for National Defense, 503
U.S. Armed Forces, Racial Discrimination. See Race Problems in the Military
U.S. Army, 203
United States Assembly of Youth, 503
U.S. Children's Bureau, 193, 203, 403, 503, 533
U.S. Civilian Conservation Corps, 111, 637
U.S. Commission on Industrial Relations, 111
United States Committee of the International Conference of Social Work, 745
U.S. Dept. of Defense, 203
U.S. Dept. of Health, Education and Welfare, 203
U.S. Dept. of Labor, 173, 203, 503, 533

U.S. Dept. of State, 91
U.S. Employment Service, 393, 403
U.S. Farm Security Administration, 403
U.S. Federal Civil Defense Administration, 203
U.S. Federal Civil Works Administration, 173, 203, 637
U.S. Federal Emergency Relief Administration, 173, 203
U.S. Federal Housing Administration, 637
U.S. Federal Security Agency, 203, 637;
Family Security Committee, 173
U.S. Federal Theatre Project, 637
U.S. Foreign Policy, 111
U.S. Forest Products Laboratory, Madison, Wisconsin, 111
U.S. Government and Social Welfare. See Social Welfare, Laws and Legislation, U.S.
U.S. Industrial Relations Commission. See U.S. Commission on Industrial Relations
U.S. National Housing Agency, 203
U.S. National Recovery Administration, 203, 503
U.S. National Resources Planning Board, 203
U.S. National Youth Administration, 173, 637
U.S. Navy, 203
U.S. Office of Civilian Defense. See Civilian Defense
U.S. Office of Defense, Health, and Welfare Services, Advisory Committee on Social Welfare, 173
U.S. Office of Economic Opportunity, 1
U.S. Office of Vocational Rehabilitation, 203

U.S. Office of War Information, 203
U.S. President's Committee on Economic Security, 111, 173
U.S. President's War Relief Control Board, 503
U.S. Public Health Service, 203
U.S. Selective Service System, 203
U.S. Supreme Court, 111
U.S. Treasury Dept., 533
U.S. Veterans Administration, 203, 755
U.S. War Manpower Commission, 403
U.S. War Production Board, 403, 533
U.S. Works Progress Administration, 41, 403, 637
U.S. Young Adult Council, 403, 503
Universal Declaration of Human Rights. See United Nations, General Assembly, Universal Declaration of Human Rights
Unwed Mothers, 481;
  Community Relationships, 481
Urban Renewal, 1, 41, 403. See also Regional and Municipal Planning
Urbanization, 745

Vaile, Gertrude, 203, 615
Van Arx, Hugo, 111
Van Hyning, Conrad Klein, 203
Van Kleeck, Mary, 91, 111, 173, 203, 503, 533
Van Loon, Hendrik Willem, 111, 533
Van Vliet, Lenore Gottfried, 203
Van Waters, Miriam, 111, 533
Vasey, Wayne, 203, 777
Veiller, Lawrence Tunure, 533
Venereal Diseases, 203, 481, 637, 755. See also Prostitution; Sex Education; Social Hygiene

Vergara, Laura, 91
Veteran Students, 777
Veterans, 503, 637, 755;
  Community Relations, 755;
  Disabled, 203, 755;
  Laws and Legislation, 755;
  Medical Care, 203, 755
Veterans Administration. See U.S. Veterans Administration
Vetereans' Hospitals. See Hospitals, Veteran
Villard, Oswald Garrison, 111, 533
Vocational Education, 403
Vocational Rehabilitation, 203, 481, 755;
  Office of Vocational Rehabilitation. See U.S. Office of Vocational Rehabilitation
Voluntary Health Agencies, 91
Volunteers, 1, 13, 41, 203, 503, 637, 755

WPA. See U.S. Works Progress Administration
Wadley, Mary E, 203
Wadman, Ruth, 203
Wagner, Margaret, 203
Wagner, Robert Ferdinand, 111, 203, 533, 637
Wald, Lillian D, 111, 403, 533, 637, 801
Walker, Charles Rumford, 533
Walker, James John, 637
Wallace, DeWitt, 533
Wallace, Henry Agard, 615
Walnut, Thomas Henry, 111, 533
Walsh, Francis Patrick, 111, 533
War Office of Psychiatric Social Work, 203
War Production Board. See U.S. War Production Board
War Relief Control Board. See U.S. President's War Relief Control Board

INDEX

Warburg, Felix Moritz, 533
Warburg, Paul Moritz, 533
Ward, Harry Frederick, 111
Washington, Forrester Blanchard, 173
Washington, D.C., Social Conditions, 111
Washington University, 615, 777;
George Warren Brown School of Social Work, 615, 777
Waters, Lena R, 203
Webbink, Paul, 173, 203
Weigert, Hans Werner, 533
Welfare Council of New York City. See New York (City) Welfare Council
Wells, Amy, 203
Wembridge, Eleanor Harris (Rowland), 533
West, Walter Mott, 203
Wetzel, Harold Edwin, 193
Weybright, Victor, 111, 533
Weyker, Grace, 203
Whipple, Leonidas Rutledge, 111, 533
White, Gaylord Starin, 403
White, Grace, 203
White, Virginia K, 203
White, William Allen, 111, 533
White House Conference on Aging, Washington, D.C., 1961, 393
White House Conference on Children and Youth
Washington, D.C., 1951, 403, 637, 777;
Washington, D.C., 1960, 777
White House Conference on Children in a Democracy, Washington, D.C., 1939-1940, 173
Wickenden, Elizabeth, 203
Wickman, Katherine Moore, 203
Wile, Ira Solomon, 533
Williams, Frankwood Earle, 173
Williams, Ichabod T, 41
Williams, Mornay, 111

Williams, Pierce, 111, 533
Williams, Whiting, 533
Winnett, Nolan S, 13
Wise, Stephen Samuel, 111, 533
Witherspoon, Ruth M, 1
Witte, Edwin Emil, 111
Witte, Ernest Frederic, 203
Women in the Armed Forces, 203
Women's Christian Temperence Union, 481
Women's Peace Party, Chicago, Illinois, 111
Women's Trade Union League, 111
Woods, Eleanor Howard (Bush), 403
Woods, Helen E, 203
Woods, Robert Archey, 403, 533
Woodward, Ellen S, 91
Woodward, Luther Ellis, 203
Work Camps, 403
Workmen's Compensation, 111
Workmen's Compensation Publicity Bureau, New York, 111
Workmen's Compensation Service Bureau, 111
Works Progress Administration, See U.S. Works Progress Administration
World Assembly of Youth, 91, 403, 503
World Citizens Association, 111
World Council of Churches, 91
World Health Organization, 91
World Peace Foundation, Boston, Massachusetts, 111
World War, 1914-1918, 111, 533, 809;
Settlements, 637;
Social Work, 111
World War, 1939-1945, 111, 167, 173, 403, 503, 745, 777, 801;
Japanese Resettlement, 203;
Psychiatric Social Work, 203;
Settlements, 1, 41, 85, 403, 637;

Social Work, 41, 91, 173, 203, 403, 481, 615, 755
Wright, Josephine, 481
Wynn, Robert, 13

YWCA. See Young Women's Christian Association of the United States of America
Yale, University, Dept. of Public Health, 809
Young, Arthur Raymond, 533
Young, Helen, 203
Young, Owen D, 533
Young Adult Council. See U.S. Young Adult Council
Young Women's Christian Association of the United States of America, 111, 173
Youngdahl, Benjamin, 203, 615, 777

Youngdahl, Luther William, 615, 777
Youngdahl, Reuben Kenneth Nathaniel, 777
Youngdahl, Ruth. See Nelson, Ruth Youngdahl
Youngdahl Family, 777
Youth
    Employment, 41;
    Negro. See Negro Youth
Youth Services and Programs, 41, 203, 403, 503, 533, 637, 801

Zaki, Elinor, 615
Zimand, Gertrude Folks, 533, 801, 809
Zimand, Savel, 533, 809
Zorbaugh, Harvey Warren, 533
Zucker, Henry L, 203

Z
7164
C4
M55